Lecture Notes in Computer Science 14698

Founding Editors

Gerhard Goos
Juris Hartmanis

Editorial Board Members

Elisa Bertino, *Purdue University, West Lafayette, IN, USA*
Wen Gao, *Peking University, Beijing, China*
Bernhard Steffen , *TU Dortmund University, Dortmund, Germany*
Moti Yung , *Columbia University, New York, NY, USA*

The series Lecture Notes in Computer Science (LNCS), including its subseries Lecture Notes in Artificial Intelligence (LNAI) and Lecture Notes in Bioinformatics (LNBI), has established itself as a medium for the publication of new developments in computer science and information technology research, teaching, and education.

LNCS enjoys close cooperation with the computer science R & D community, the series counts many renowned academics among its volume editors and paper authors, and collaborates with prestigious societies. Its mission is to serve this international community by providing an invaluable service, mainly focused on the publication of conference and workshop proceedings and postproceedings. LNCS commenced publication in 1973.

Margherita Antona · Constantine Stephanidis
Editors

Universal Access in Human-Computer Interaction

18th International Conference, UAHCI 2024
Held as Part of the 26th HCI International Conference, HCII 2024
Washington, DC, USA, June 29 – July 4, 2024
Proceedings, Part III

 Springer

Editors
Margherita Antona
Foundation for Research and Technology -
Hellas (FORTH)
Heraklion, Crete, Greece

Constantine Stephanidis
University of Crete, and Foundation for
Research and Technology - Hellas (FORTH)
Heraklion, Crete, Greece

ISSN 0302-9743   ISSN 1611-3349 (electronic)
Lecture Notes in Computer Science
ISBN 978-3-031-60883-4   ISBN 978-3-031-60884-1 (eBook)
https://doi.org/10.1007/978-3-031-60884-1

Foreword

This year we celebrate 40 years since the establishment of the HCI International (HCII) Conference, which has been a hub for presenting groundbreaking research and novel ideas and collaboration for people from all over the world.

The HCII conference was founded in 1984 by Prof. Gavriel Salvendy (Purdue University, USA, Tsinghua University, P.R. China, and University of Central Florida, USA) and the first event of the series, "1st USA-Japan Conference on Human-Computer Interaction", was held in Honolulu, Hawaii, USA, 18–20 August. Since then, HCI International is held jointly with several Thematic Areas and Affiliated Conferences, with each one under the auspices of a distinguished international Program Board and under one management and one registration. Twenty-six HCI International Conferences have been organized so far (every two years until 2013, and annually thereafter).

Over the years, this conference has served as a platform for scholars, researchers, industry experts and students to exchange ideas, connect, and address challenges in the ever-evolving HCI field. Throughout these 40 years, the conference has evolved itself, adapting to new technologies and emerging trends, while staying committed to its core mission of advancing knowledge and driving change.

As we celebrate this milestone anniversary, we reflect on the contributions of its founding members and appreciate the commitment of its current and past Affiliated Conference Program Board Chairs and members. We are also thankful to all past conference attendees who have shaped this community into what it is today.

The 26th International Conference on Human-Computer Interaction, HCI International 2024 (HCII 2024), was held as a 'hybrid' event at the Washington Hilton Hotel, Washington, DC, USA, during 29 June – 4 July 2024. It incorporated the 21 thematic areas and affiliated conferences listed below.

A total of 5108 individuals from academia, research institutes, industry, and government agencies from 85 countries submitted contributions, and 1271 papers and 309 posters were included in the volumes of the proceedings that were published just before the start of the conference, these are listed below. The contributions thoroughly cover the entire field of human-computer interaction, addressing major advances in knowledge and effective use of computers in a variety of application areas. These papers provide academics, researchers, engineers, scientists, practitioners and students with state-of-the-art information on the most recent advances in HCI.

The HCI International (HCII) conference also offers the option of presenting 'Late Breaking Work', and this applies both for papers and posters, with corresponding volumes of proceedings that will be published after the conference. Full papers will be included in the 'HCII 2024 - Late Breaking Papers' volumes of the proceedings to be published in the Springer LNCS series, while 'Poster Extended Abstracts' will be included as short research papers in the 'HCII 2024 - Late Breaking Posters' volumes to be published in the Springer CCIS series.

I would like to thank the Program Board Chairs and the members of the Program Boards of all thematic areas and affiliated conferences for their contribution towards the high scientific quality and overall success of the HCI International 2024 conference. Their manifold support in terms of paper reviewing (single-blind review process, with a minimum of two reviews per submission), session organization and their willingness to act as goodwill ambassadors for the conference is most highly appreciated.

This conference would not have been possible without the continuous and unwavering support and advice of Gavriel Salvendy, founder, General Chair Emeritus, and Scientific Advisor. For his outstanding efforts, I would like to express my sincere appreciation to Abbas Moallem, Communications Chair and Editor of HCI International News.

July 2024   Constantine Stephanidis

HCI International 2024 Thematic Areas and Affiliated Conferences

- HCI: Human-Computer Interaction Thematic Area
- HIMI: Human Interface and the Management of Information Thematic Area
- EPCE: 21st International Conference on Engineering Psychology and Cognitive Ergonomics
- AC: 18th International Conference on Augmented Cognition
- UAHCI: 18th International Conference on Universal Access in Human-Computer Interaction
- CCD: 16th International Conference on Cross-Cultural Design
- SCSM: 16th International Conference on Social Computing and Social Media
- VAMR: 16th International Conference on Virtual, Augmented and Mixed Reality
- DHM: 15th International Conference on Digital Human Modeling & Applications in Health, Safety, Ergonomics & Risk Management
- DUXU: 13th International Conference on Design, User Experience and Usability
- C&C: 12th International Conference on Culture and Computing
- DAPI: 12th International Conference on Distributed, Ambient and Pervasive Interactions
- HCIBGO: 11th International Conference on HCI in Business, Government and Organizations
- LCT: 11th International Conference on Learning and Collaboration Technologies
- ITAP: 10th International Conference on Human Aspects of IT for the Aged Population
- AIS: 6th International Conference on Adaptive Instructional Systems
- HCI-CPT: 6th International Conference on HCI for Cybersecurity, Privacy and Trust
- HCI-Games: 6th International Conference on HCI in Games
- MobiTAS: 6th International Conference on HCI in Mobility, Transport and Automotive Systems
- AI-HCI: 5th International Conference on Artificial Intelligence in HCI
- MOBILE: 5th International Conference on Human-Centered Design, Operation and Evaluation of Mobile Communications

List of Conference Proceedings Volumes Appearing Before the Conference

1. LNCS 14684, Human-Computer Interaction: Part I, edited by Masaaki Kurosu and Ayako Hashizume
2. LNCS 14685, Human-Computer Interaction: Part II, edited by Masaaki Kurosu and Ayako Hashizume
3. LNCS 14686, Human-Computer Interaction: Part III, edited by Masaaki Kurosu and Ayako Hashizume
4. LNCS 14687, Human-Computer Interaction: Part IV, edited by Masaaki Kurosu and Ayako Hashizume
5. LNCS 14688, Human-Computer Interaction: Part V, edited by Masaaki Kurosu and Ayako Hashizume
6. LNCS 14689, Human Interface and the Management of Information: Part I, edited by Hirohiko Mori and Yumi Asahi
7. LNCS 14690, Human Interface and the Management of Information: Part II, edited by Hirohiko Mori and Yumi Asahi
8. LNCS 14691, Human Interface and the Management of Information: Part III, edited by Hirohiko Mori and Yumi Asahi
9. LNAI 14692, Engineering Psychology and Cognitive Ergonomics: Part I, edited by Don Harris and Wen-Chin Li
10. LNAI 14693, Engineering Psychology and Cognitive Ergonomics: Part II, edited by Don Harris and Wen-Chin Li
11. LNAI 14694, Augmented Cognition, Part I, edited by Dylan D. Schmorrow and Cali M. Fidopiastis
12. LNAI 14695, Augmented Cognition, Part II, edited by Dylan D. Schmorrow and Cali M. Fidopiastis
13. LNCS 14696, Universal Access in Human-Computer Interaction: Part I, edited by Margherita Antona and Constantine Stephanidis
14. LNCS 14697, Universal Access in Human-Computer Interaction: Part II, edited by Margherita Antona and Constantine Stephanidis
15. LNCS 14698, Universal Access in Human-Computer Interaction: Part III, edited by Margherita Antona and Constantine Stephanidis
16. LNCS 14699, Cross-Cultural Design: Part I, edited by Pei-Luen Patrick Rau
17. LNCS 14700, Cross-Cultural Design: Part II, edited by Pei-Luen Patrick Rau
18. LNCS 14701, Cross-Cultural Design: Part III, edited by Pei-Luen Patrick Rau
19. LNCS 14702, Cross-Cultural Design: Part IV, edited by Pei-Luen Patrick Rau
20. LNCS 14703, Social Computing and Social Media: Part I, edited by Adela Coman and Simona Vasilache
21. LNCS 14704, Social Computing and Social Media: Part II, edited by Adela Coman and Simona Vasilache
22. LNCS 14705, Social Computing and Social Media: Part III, edited by Adela Coman and Simona Vasilache

47. LNCS 14730, HCI in Games: Part I, edited by Xiaowen Fang
48. LNCS 14731, HCI in Games: Part II, edited by Xiaowen Fang
49. LNCS 14732, HCI in Mobility, Transport and Automotive Systems: Part I, edited by Heidi Krömker
50. LNCS 14733, HCI in Mobility, Transport and Automotive Systems: Part II, edited by Heidi Krömker
51. LNAI 14734, Artificial Intelligence in HCI: Part I, edited by Helmut Degen and Stavroula Ntoa
52. LNAI 14735, Artificial Intelligence in HCI: Part II, edited by Helmut Degen and Stavroula Ntoa
53. LNAI 14736, Artificial Intelligence in HCI: Part III, edited by Helmut Degen and Stavroula Ntoa
54. LNCS 14737, Design, Operation and Evaluation of Mobile Communications: Part I, edited by June Wei and George Margetis
55. LNCS 14738, Design, Operation and Evaluation of Mobile Communications: Part II, edited by June Wei and George Margetis
56. CCIS 2114, HCI International 2024 Posters - Part I, edited by Constantine Stephanidis, Margherita Antona, Stavroula Ntoa and Gavriel Salvendy
57. CCIS 2115, HCI International 2024 Posters - Part II, edited by Constantine Stephanidis, Margherita Antona, Stavroula Ntoa and Gavriel Salvendy
58. CCIS 2116, HCI International 2024 Posters - Part III, edited by Constantine Stephanidis, Margherita Antona, Stavroula Ntoa and Gavriel Salvendy
59. CCIS 2117, HCI International 2024 Posters - Part IV, edited by Constantine Stephanidis, Margherita Antona, Stavroula Ntoa and Gavriel Salvendy
60. CCIS 2118, HCI International 2024 Posters - Part V, edited by Constantine Stephanidis, Margherita Antona, Stavroula Ntoa and Gavriel Salvendy
61. CCIS 2119, HCI International 2024 Posters - Part VI, edited by Constantine Stephanidis, Margherita Antona, Stavroula Ntoa and Gavriel Salvendy
62. CCIS 2120, HCI International 2024 Posters - Part VII, edited by Constantine Stephanidis, Margherita Antona, Stavroula Ntoa and Gavriel Salvendy

https://2024.hci.international/proceedings

Preface

The 18th International Conference on Universal Access in Human-Computer Interaction (UAHCI 2024), an affiliated conference of the HCI International (HCII) conference, provided an established international forum for the exchange and dissemination of scientific information on theoretical, methodological, and empirical research that addresses all issues related to the attainment of universal access in the development of interactive software. It comprehensively addressed accessibility and quality of interaction in the user interface development life-cycle from a multidisciplinary perspective, taking into account dimensions of diversity, such as functional limitations, age, culture, background knowledge, etc., in the target user population, as well as various dimensions of diversity which affect the context of use and the technological platform and arise from the emergence of mobile, wearable, ubiquitous, and intelligent devices and technologies.

UAHCI 2024 aimed to help, promote, and encourage research by providing a forum for interaction and exchanges among researchers, academics, and practitioners in the field. The conference welcomed papers on the design, development, evaluation, use, and impact of user interfaces, as well as standardization, policy, and other non-technological issues that facilitate and promote universal access.

Universal access is not a new topic in the field of human-computer interaction and information technology. Yet, in the new interaction environment shaped by current technological advancements, it becomes of prominent importance to ensure that individuals have access to interactive products and services that span a wide variety of everyday life domains and are used in fundamental human activities. The papers accepted to this year's UAHCI conference present research, methods, and practices addressing universal access issues related to user experience and interaction, and approaches targeted to provide appropriate interaction means to individuals with specific disabilities, but also issues related to extended reality – a prominent technological medium presenting novel accessibility challenges, as well as advancements in learning and education.

Three volumes of the HCII 2024 proceedings are dedicated to this year's edition of the UAHCI conference. The first focuses on topics related to User Experience Design and Evaluation for Universal Access, and AI for Universal Access. The second focuses on topics related to Universal Access to Digital Services, Design for Cognitive Disabilities, and Universal Access to Virtual and Augmented Reality, while the third focuses on topics related to Universal Access to Learning and Education, Universal Access to Health and Wellbeing, and Universal Access to Information and Media.

Papers of these volumes were accepted for publication after a minimum of two single-blind reviews from the members of the UAHCI Program Board or, in some cases, from members of the Program Boards of other affiliated conferences. We would like to thank all of them for their invaluable contribution, support and efforts.

July 2024

Margherita Antona
Constantine Stephanidis

18th International Conference on Universal Access in Human-Computer Interaction (UAHCI 2024)

Program Board Chairs: **Margherita Antona**, *Foundation for Research and Technology - Hellas (FORTH), Greece*, and **Constantine Stephanidis**, *University of Crete and Foundation for Research and Technology - Hellas (FORTH), Greece*

- Basel Barakat, *University of Sunderland, UK*
- Joao Barroso, *INESC TEC and UTAD, Portugal*
- Ingo Bosse, *University of Teacher Education in Special Needs, Switzerland*
- Laura Burzagli, *National Research Council of Italy (CNR), Italy*
- Pedro J.S. Cardoso, *Universidade do Algarve, Portugal*
- Silvia Ceccacci, *University of Macerata, Italy*
- Nicole Darmawaskita, *Arizona State University, USA*
- Carlos Duarte, *Universidade de Lisboa, Portugal*
- Pier Luigi Emiliani, *National Research Council of Italy (CNR), Italy*
- Andrina Granic, *University of Split, Croatia*
- Gian Maria Greco, *Università di Macerata, Italy*
- Francesco Ermanno Guida, *Politecnico di Milano, Italy*
- Simeon Keates, *University of Chichester, UK*
- Georgios Kouroupetroglou, *National and Kapodistrian University of Athens, Greece*
- Monica Landoni, *Università della Svizzera Italiana, Switzerland*
- Barbara Leporini, *CNR-ISTI, Italy*
- John Magee, *Clark University, USA*
- Daniela Marghitu, *Auburn University, USA*
- Jorge Martin-Gutierrez, *Universidad de La Laguna, Spain*
- Maura Mengoni, *Università Politecnica delle Marche, Italy*
- Silvia Mirri, *University of Bologna, Italy*
- Federica Pallavicini, *Università degli Studi di Milano-Bicocca, Italy*
- João M. F. Rodrigues, *University of the Algarve, Portugal*
- Frode Eika Sandnes, *Oslo Metropolitan University, Norway*
- J. Andres Sandoval-Bringas, *Universidad Autónoma de Baja California Sur, Mexico*
- Muhammad Shoaib, *University College Cork, Ireland*
- Hiroki Takada, *University of Fukui, Japan*
- Philippe Truillet, *Université de Toulouse, France*
- Kevin C. Tseng, *National Taipei University of Technology, Taiwan*
- Gerhard Weber, *TU Dresden, Germany*

The full list with the Program Board Chairs and the members of the Program Boards of all thematic areas and affiliated conferences of HCII 2024 is available online at:

http://www.hci.international/board-members-2024.php

HCI International 2025 Conference

The 27th International Conference on Human-Computer Interaction, HCI International 2025, will be held jointly with the affiliated conferences at the Swedish Exhibition & Congress Centre and Gothia Towers Hotel, Gothenburg, Sweden, June 22–27, 2025. It will cover a broad spectrum of themes related to Human-Computer Interaction, including theoretical issues, methods, tools, processes, and case studies in HCI design, as well as novel interaction techniques, interfaces, and applications. The proceedings will be published by Springer. More information will become available on the conference website: https://2025.hci.international/.

General Chair
Prof. Constantine Stephanidis
University of Crete and ICS-FORTH
Heraklion, Crete, Greece
Email: general_chair@2025.hci.international

https://2025.hci.international/

Contents – Part III

Universal Access to Health and Wellbeing

Universal Access to Information and Media

Universal Access to Learning and Education

"Mismatched Aid" - Tasks for Counselling, Development, and Implementation

Marcel Feichtinger[1]([⊠]) [iD], Liane Bächler[2] [iD], and Tobias Bernasconi[3] [iD]

[1] Technische Universität Dortmund, Emil-Figge-Str. 50, 44227 Dortmund, Germany
`Marcel.Feichtinger@tu-dortmund.de`
[2] University of Cologne, Habsburgerring 1, 50674 Cologne, Germany
`Liane.Baechler@uni-koeln.de`
[3] University of Cologne, Klosterstr. 79b, 50931 Cologne, Germany
`Tobias.Bernasconi@uni-koeln.de`

Abstract. The social participation of individuals with disabilities is significantly influenced by barrier-free design and the appropriate use of assistive technologies. The collaboration among various qualified stakeholders plays a pivotal role in facilitating the provision of aids and promoting the effective use of assistive technologies. This article delves into the subjects of access and barriers within the context of specialized schools catering to physical, motor, and intellectual disabilities in North Rhine-Westphalia, the most populous federal state in Germany. Through a questionnaire survey, responses were obtained from teachers concerning 4,027 pupils who utilized assistive technologies, predominantly aids from the field of Augmentative and Alternative Communication. The findings highlight a deficiency in resources and an identified need for enhanced qualifications. Additionally, teachers report challenges related to compatibility issues between assistive technologies and users at various proficiency levels. The complexities of impairments often impede the seamless integration of assistive technologies, as they may be deemed "ill-suited" due to their complexity or impracticality in everyday use. Criticism is also directed towards the intricate and time-consuming process of aid provision. The gathered data serves as the foundation for drawing conclusions aimed at advising, developing of devices, and supporting pupils leveraging assistive technologies. Consequently, this article directly addresses central socio-political and scientific challenges in the ongoing pursuit of comprehensive participation for individuals with disabilities.

Keywords: Assistive Technology · Intellectual, Physical, and Motor Disability · Special School

1 Introduction

The attainment of comprehensive social participation hinges on the principles of barrier-free design and accessibility across pivotal domains of social activity. Within the framework of diverse societies, particularly those emphasizing the inclusion of individuals with disabilities, the concepts of access and accessibility assume paramount importance.

M. Antona and C. Stephanidis (Eds.): HCII 2024, LNCS 14698, pp. 3–15, 2024.
https://doi.org/10.1007/978-3-031-60884-1_1

Despite normative socio-political imperatives, the effective implementation of assistive technology for users remains an elusive goal. The twin pillars of accessibility and the provision of essential aids are consequently recognized as central challenges for the future, crucial for fostering genuine participation among individuals with disabilities.

Heumann underscores the significance of incorporating assistive technologies within the disability realm, stating, "For most of us, technology makes things easier. For a person with a disability, it makes things possible" [quoted from Edyburn, 2020, p. 11]. In order to foster empowerment processes, active involvement of assistive technology users in the development and selection processes is essential, with the goal of achieving self-determined and comprehensive participation across all facets of society. It is posited that both analogue and digital interfaces, along with accessibility design, occupy a crucial space for negotiating global relations within an increasingly individualized and digitalized culture.

Nevertheless, the successful provision of assistive technologies for individuals with disabilities necessitates an effective interplay between development, guidance, and utilization. This is especially pertinent in contexts where achieving universal access proves challenging [refer to Bühler, 2016; Stephanidis et al., 2019]. Such interaction unfolds within a continuum of solutions, encompassing assistive technology (AT), design for all, accessibility, and reasonable accommodation [Bühler, 2016, p. 162f]. Achieving this requires a transdisciplinary integration of rehabilitation science research with computer science, medical technology, engineering, and (curative) education.

The right to accessibility, enshrined in German legislation and the UN Convention on the Rights of Persons with Disabilities (Art. 3), presents a fundamental socio-political and scientific challenge that demands transdisciplinary approaches, such as human-computer interaction. While accessibility remains an abstract and general concept, specific curative measures are directed towards individuals, particularly addressing the interplay among impairments, activities, environmental factors, and participation [refer to Bosse & Feichtinger, 2022]. Selecting suitable assistive technologies in schools also entails a complex interplay, involving various stakeholders. Not only does this call for collaboration among teachers, but also funding bodies, assistive technology companies, independent consultants, parents/guardians, therapeutic staff, the users themselves, and, if necessary, personal assistants. This cooperation is essential for aligning the care process with user skills, needs, and requirements and ensuring the sustainable implementation of assistive technologies in the school environment [cf. Bosse & Feichtinger, 2022]. The selection and subsequent implementation of assistive technology may not always work.

In the federal state of North Rhine-Westphalia (NRW), a questionnaire survey was conducted to assess the current situation and delve into the challenges schools face [see Bernasconi, Bächler & Feichtinger, 2023]. This survey targeted teachers and gathered data from a total of 4,027 pupils utilizing assistive technology at special schools with a particular educational emphasis on intellectual disability (ID) physical, and motor disability (PMD). Among other questions, teachers were asked to identify difficulties encountered in everyday school life and the implementation of assistive technology support. The study specifically targeted users of Augmentative and Alternative Communication (AAC), ensuring a comprehensive dataset in this regard.

The findings revealed significant challenges, including a pronounced shortage of personnel and spatial resources, coupled with diverse qualification requirements. Furthermore, some teachers reported that the provided aids were deemed unsuitable or that pupils showed disinterest. Issues were also raised regarding the complexity of user software requirements and the time-consuming nature of aid provision and maintenance. Additionally, the specific nature of impairments directly influenced the furnishing of assistive devices. The subsequent analysis of the collected data will focus on potential fitting problems, allowing for informed conclusions to be drawn for assistive technology guidance, development, and support.

2 Empirical Investigation

Two distinct questionnaires were developed for the study, targeting 1) school managers and 2) teachers of pupils using assistive technology. The school management questionnaire sought general information regarding the percentage of pupils with AT needs and structural aspects related to the entire school. In contrast, the teacher questionnaire focused on specific research questions and was categorized into the following areas:

- General questions about AT requirements
- Questions about AT support
- Questions about cooperation and structures
- Final open-ended questions about challenges, barriers and wishes

Teachers were instructed to complete an individual questionnaire for each pupil in their class requiring AT. The questionnaire included both open and closed questions covering the assessment of individual abilities and needs, as well as the structural integration and design of support. Given their familiarity with the pupils from daily interactions, teachers were well-positioned to provide information about needs, necessities, and barrier. Both questionnaires underwent a pre-test to ensure comprehensibility and technical accuracy. Participation in the survey was voluntary, and the student questionnaire ensured maximum anonymity by excluding personal data, even if the individual school was identifiable.

At the start of the 2022/2023 school year, 162 schools (121 focusing on intellectual disability, 41 on physical and motor disability) were contacted. By the end of October 2022, 121 schools participated in the survey, resulting in a response rate of 74.6%. The evaluation considered 114 fully completed school management questionnaires and 4,027 teacher questionnaires. This response rate represents the most extensive current dataset on pupils with AT needs in North Rhine-Westphalia (NRW). Descriptive analysis was employed for quantitative data, while qualitative data underwent computer-assisted analysis using inductive category formation.

2.1 Evaluation of the School Management Questionnaire

The 114 returned forms are categorized into 69.7% for intellectual disability, 22.8% for physical and motor disability, and 7.9% for both (special educational focuses). According to official school statistics for the state of North Rhine-Westphalia, the number of pupils with special educational needs in intellectual disability for the 2022/23 school year was 25,831, with 21,435 being educated at special schools for intellectual disability. Of 11,443 pupils with physical and motor disabilities, 7,556 attended special schools for physical and motor disability (excluding special school vocational colleges [cf. MSB 2023a, p. 88]). The school management questionnaires cover 21,039 pupils, representing 72.57% of the total. Among these, 36.3% are female, and 63.7% are male, roughly corresponding to the official school statistics reporting proportions of 34.8% and 65.2%, respectively [MSB, 2023b]. School principals report 6,636 pupils as severely disabled according to the NRW School Act, accounting for 31.5%, thus aligning with previous surveys for NRW [Bernasconi, 2017].

Regarding the use of Augmentative and Alternative Communication aids, special schools providing data on this question reported a total proportion of 31.6% for ID and 32.9% for PMD.

2.2 Quantitative Analysis of the Teacher Questionnaires

The teachers' questionnaires, each corresponding to one pupil in need of assistive technology, encompassed 4,027 individual surveys, covering 19.1% of the 21,039 pupils identified by the school principals. The following results pertain to the 4,027 identified pupils with specific AT needs, revealing that 59.8% of them receive individual assistance. See Fig. 1 for the overall landscape comprising the aids used.

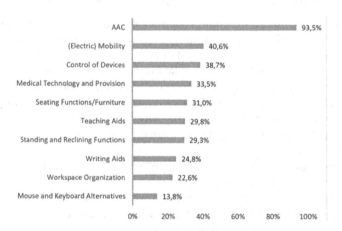

Fig. 1. Categories of aids used (n = 4,027)

The documented assistance reveals a diverse spectrum of needs, delineated by the application areas of Assistive Technology as outlined by Wendt & Lloyd (2011) and Feichtinger (2020). It is essential to consider, in interpreting these findings, that the questionnaires were expressly directed towards Augmentative and Alternative Communication users. Within German special schools, there is often a distinct categorization between AT and AAC. The notable prevalence of aids within the AAC domain can be attributed to the prominence of AAC in school settings, with specific AAC aids beyond this scope being less familiar during the survey period. While assistive devices from the AAC field and primary teaching aids exhibit a higher prevalence in the ID category compared to the PMD category, the proportion of assistive devices facilitating (physical) functions, essential for mobility and care, takes precedence in the PMD domain. This suggests a specialization in the types of assistive devices employed, aligned with the specific requirements associated with the nature of the disability.

3 Results from the Open-Ended Question

Results from the open-ended question are presented below, gathered through the query, "Where do you see difficulties with regard to AT support in everyday school life?". To minimize cognitive distortions, the challenges and barriers mentioned were independently coded by multiple individuals, followed by systematic sorting and analysis. A total of 3,714 codes were assigned, with 1,387 pertaining to the PMD domain and 2,327 to the ID domain. It's crucial to note that the number of codes should not be confused with the number of respondents.

The overarching findings reveal that 42% of respondents identified a lack of material, personnel, and time resources as the primary challenges in AT support in everyday school life (Fig. 2).

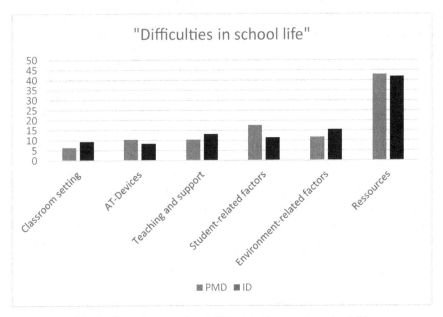

Fig. 2. General categories of difficulties in everyday school life

These issues were intricately connected to challenges in both the preparation and execution of lessons and support. For instance, highlighted were difficulties in offering AAC groups due to staff shortages, and the compromised effectiveness of modeling because of poor staffing levels. Simultaneously, teachers grappled with a substantial workload, exemplified by statements such as "very time-consuming to familiarize oneself with complex communication aids," "constant support required when working with the Talker," and "complicated purchasing structures" concerning device provisioning. As revealed in the assessment of the resource problem, there was not enough time for communication and consultation.

In both PMD and ID special schools, challenges also arose from heterogeneous class compositions, varying group sizes, and insufficient space. Despite these difficulties, a mere 1.08% of the teachers' codes included statements criticizing the attitude or commitment of the staff.

3.1 Results Related to "Non-fit"

The feedback from respondents indicates instances of misalignment between the assistive device and the user, manifested in various categories. These discrepancies are explicitly captured under the rubric of "the aid does not fit" and implicitly under that of "student-related factors," specifically in the subcategories of "impairment prevents use" and "pupils not interested." The majority of statements explicitly reference AAC, while some mention assistive devices, and a few statements cannot be definitively assigned to either one. The coding process was intricate, particularly when dealing with similar statements that differed in the interviewees' subjectively significant perspectives [cf. Kuckartz & Rädiker, 2022, p. 56]. An example of this is the statement "the device is hardly used/not accepted/refusal → excessive demands?". During coding, it was imperative to adhere strictly to the presumed intention of the interviewees and to categorize the material accordingly [cf. Kuckartz & Rädiker, 2022, p. 99f]. For instance, the statement "hardly used/not accepted/refusal" could potentially be sorted under "pupils not interested." However, the addition "refusal → excessive demands" implies active engagement with the tool, indicating a factor beyond a mere lack of pupil interest. Consequently, it was appropriately assigned to the category "the aid does not fit." As already noted, this approach had to be followed to ensure the statement's thematic alignment accurately reflected the respondents' intended meaning.

This approach also applies to statements like "The student only plays with the device," which could be identified as a didactic problem. Therefore, in thematic sorting, this statement is appropriately assigned to the category "The tool does not fit." The central consideration here is that the tool is evidently not being used in the manner respondents believe it should be, even though a lack of interest ("Pupils not interested" category) is not explicitly mentioned in this specific example. The evaluated statements from the *open question* were primarily taken from the subcategories shown in bold in Table 1 and Table 2.

If the statements related to other categories, we tried to also take these into account. For this reason, the care and provision of devices and the students' lack of interest in particular were included in the evaluation. Combining the codes from PMD and ID shifts the percentage values towards the ID values, due to more participants from the ID area than from the PMD area having taken part in the survey.

Table 1. Upper category "devices"

Topmost category "devices"	PMD	ID
"Aid does not fit"	**58.33%**	**52.88%**
"Assistive device care"	11.11%	22.51%
"The process of providing devices is problematic"	30.56%	24.61%

Table 2. Topmost category "student-related factors"

Topmost "student-related factors"	PMD	ID
"Impairment prevents use"	**40.33%**	**45.83%**
"Pupils not interested"	**34.16%**	**35.61%**
"Other native language"	5.35%	10.23%
"Corona. absences and distance learning"	11.93%	3.03%
"Skills unclear"	8.23%	2.65%

"The Aid Does Not Fit" (PMD). When questioned about difficulties in AT support, teachers from special schools focused on PMD made statements related to devices, forming the top category at 10.38%, which aligns with the size of the other leading category, "teaching and support." Within the category "assistive technology," we derived three distinct subcategories from the data: "The aid does not fit" (58.33%), "Assistive device care" (11.11%), and "Process of providing assistive technology is problematic" (30.56%). In the "the aid does not fit" category, 21.43% of responses stemmed from fittings that were overly complex or, in a few cases, not complex enough, justifying a "non-fit." 17.86% of statements indicated design weaknesses, such as poorly functioning voice output, lack of protection against salivation, or inadequate battery power.

Another portion of teachers' statements suggested that the aid failed to achieve the intended goal (16.67%). In the context of communication devices, this indicated a preference for other forms of communication or viewing the aid exclusively as a teaching or learning tool rather than a communication aid. Responses also highlighted issues related to the lack of mobility of aids for use during breaks (15.48%), during transportation between school and home, or due to fixed installations as table-only devices. 14.29% of respondents mentioned control problems, primarily relating to eye controls and challenges in attaching the device to wheelchairs.

In the "Assistive device care" category cited were devices that were faulty and "often defective." Additionally, challenges in the process of providing assistive devices were identified, such as long waiting times for applications and extended repair times without access to replacement devices. Overall, the supply channels were perceived as complicated, and diagnostics were characterized as lengthy and complex.

"The Aid Does Not Fit" (ID). Regarding pupils at schools with a focus on ID the allocation of statements to the category "assistive devices" came in slightly below the PMD value (10.38%) at 8.25%. Within this category, the subcategories were distributed as follows: "the assistive device does not fit" accounted for 52.88%, "assistive device care" for 22.51%, and "process of providing devices is problematic" for 24.61% of the assigned statements. Analysis of the category "the aid does not fit" reveals that 46.53% of the responses related to the aspect of the aid not supporting the desired target activity. The most frequent statements in this connection included a preference for other forms of communication, the use of the device as a "toy," and instances of the aid being thrown.

Challenges and barriers accounting for 30.69% were attributed to intellectual overload, primarily due to the complexity of the communication aid. 11.88% of the challenges were linked to the lack of mobility of devices, including issues such as "interfering with walking." Design weaknesses mentioned in this context (7.92%) included the use of ambiguous symbols, high effort required to create pages/slides, and "difficult switching" between apps. Control and attachment problems of the aid played a minor role in the ID focus, accounting for a combined 2.97%. Within the broader category of "devices" (22.51%), almost every second statement was related to the problem of uncharged batteries. Difficulties in the process of providing assistive devices at special schools with a focus on ID (24.61%) included long waiting times for applications, extended repair times without access to replacement devices, and the challenges of dealing with rejections by funding agencies.

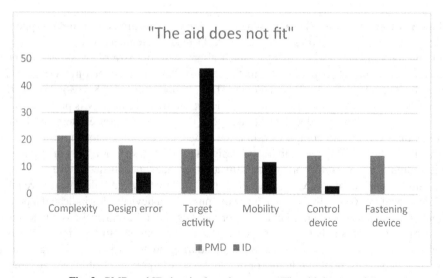

Fig. 3. PMD and ID data in the subcategory "The aid does not fit"

"Impairment Prevents Use" (PMD). Within the category "student-related factors," the subcategory "Impairment prevents use" accounted for 40.33% of the provided information. Other subcategories included "Corona, absences, and distance learning" (11.93%), "unclear skills" (8.23%), and "other native language" (5.35%). The subcategory "students not interested," directly related to "non-fit," was attributed to 34.16% of the statements. Examples of this include statements such as "the child still shows little motivation to use their communication aid and does not want to work differently from the other children" and "shows no interest in using their aid."

The subcategory "impairment prevents use" is further segmented into distinct factors: "basic needs and health problems" (7.82%), "behavior, restlessness, concentration" (7%), "motor skills" (14%), "vision" (7.82%), and "autism spectrum" (3.7%). Factors hindering assistive technology (AT) support included a focus on ensuring basic needs and the unpredictability of using eye control ("basic needs and health problems"). In the realm of "motor skills," references were made to progressive illnesses, among other things, which complicated the use of devices. In the areas of "hearing" and "vision," a total of five pupils were described as deaf-blind, leading to challenges in controlling assistive devices, among other difficulties.

"Impairment Prevents Use" (ID). Among the statements recorded by teachers at the special school for intellectual disability, 45.83% were associated with the subcategory "impairment prevents use" within the broader category of "student-related factors." Other subcategories included "Corona, absences, and distance learning" (3.03%), "unclear skills" (2.65%), and "other native language" (12.88%). The sub-category "pupils not interested," directly related to "non-fit," accounted for 35.61% of the statements. Illustrative statements within the ID focus area include "rejection of all work that seems like school, little to no initiative" and "the pupil understands the device but seems to have no desire to communicate with it."

Within the subcategory "Impairment prevents use," 5.3% of the responses were categorized under "basic needs and health problems." Further sub-subcategories included "hearing" (0.76%), "vision" (3.03%), "behavior, restlessness, concentration" (21.21%), "motor skills" (5.3%), and "autism spectrum" (10.23%). While the content of the statements differs in terms of frequency compared to those of the PMD special schools, the subject matter remains consistent (Fig. 4).

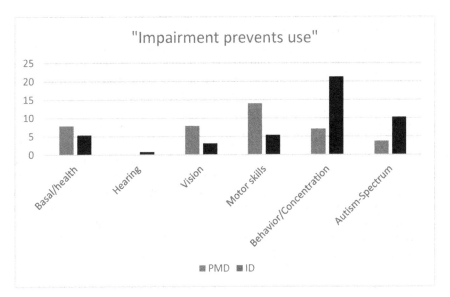

Fig. 4. PMD and ID data in the subcategory "impairment prevents use"

3.2 Comparison of PMD and ID Results

The overall results of the open questions did not reveal major differences between the PMD and ID special schools in the main categories. Concerning the categories presented here, the covered topics are comparable in content, but they significantly differ in the frequency of mentions, indicating distinct support needs in school practice. In the PMD sector, we found a broad distribution of responses in the category "the aid does not fit," ranging from 14.29% to 21.43% (see Fig. 3). When control and fastening problems are combined, they constitute the largest proportion of responses at 28.58%.

In contrast to the PMD sector results, in the ID sector challenges in the control and attachment of aids are scarcely mentioned. Instead, conflicting care goals are recorded most frequently at 46.53%: for instance, users of AAC preferring other forms of communication or using the devices mainly as toys. 30.65% of the responses highlight users being overwhelmed by complex application problems, with no mentions of sub-optimal fittings as significant challenges or barriers. While motor, visual, and basal or health challenges pose difficulties for AT support in the PMD area, the ID area primarily faces challenges related to behavior, concentration, or restlessness, as well as challenges arising in the autism spectrum.

4 Interpretation of the Data

The data derived from the questionnaire survey, particularly within the categories "the aid does not fit," "pupils not interested," and "impairment prevents use," encapsulates two distinct thought patterns that provide insights from different perspectives into the non-fit between aids and users.

In the categories "the aid does not fit" and "pupil not interested," respondents describe situations where an aid has already been provided but is subjectively deemed unsuitable for various reasons. This perspective centers on the inadequacies of the assistive devices. On the other hand, the category "Impairment prevents use" encompasses situations focusing on functional impairments that antedate the provision of an assistive device.

The results highlight a direct connection between specific needs arising from physical and intellectual impairments and the ensuing requirements for assistive devices. It remains uncertain to what extent fitting difficulties related to user motivation stem from a lack of didactic competence on the part of teachers or time and personnel constraints.

A holistic examination of the quantitative and qualitative results underscores that, despite the myriad tasks and high demands of everyday work, that implementing AT support at various school levels takes significant effort. This suggests a notable level of commitment and motivation on the part of teachers [cf. Bernasconi, Bächler & Feichtinger, 2023]. In any case, the data on challenges and barriers contain crucial information for the counselling, development, and implementation of AT in special schools that cater to both physical and intellectual development.

5 Conclusions

We conclude the following from the results presented and their interpretation.

Counselling. The data material underscores the significance of diagnostics in the assistive technology consultation process, extending beyond device provision to encompass process-related support diagnostics. A comprehensive diagnosis should consider not only the user's skills but also the environment and existing framework conditions to identify potential challenges and barriers. Clear and achievable objectives should be defined to manage expectations effectively. Simultaneously, attention must be given to the scope for development, incorporating flexible options for aid use and expansion. The selection of user programs should avoid both too-complex and too-simple fittings, with trial periods recommending themselves as beneficial. During consultations, explicit agreements should be concluded, covering aspects such as the form of further exchanges and for ensuring full battery charges.

Development. Challenges for developers emerge in the realms of hardware, software, and assistive technology services. Hardware needs to strike a balance between being robust to withstand falls and salivation yet being lightweight and mobile enough to let pupils access aids at any time. Modular solutions adaptable to various purposes, such as student workstations and breaks, are conceivable. Standardized and user-friendly mounting systems should be available. Desired features for rechargeable batteries include quick-charging functionality or easy swapping.

Software, as part of user programs, should cater to different developmental levels, facilitating smooth transitions between systems. Users should have the opportunity for trial use to gain experience with user programs at a low threshold.

Implementation. Transitioning from consultation to support requires aligning expectations between counselors and those implementing aid use in daily life. Differing assessments and perspectives must be discussed, distinguishing whether "playing with the aid" is seen as unproductive or if the pupil is in an explorative phase, gaining experience with the user program through playful interaction. Understanding whether pupils are genuinely disinterested or if the environment hasn't effectively conveyed the advantages of the aid is crucial. User involvement in advising and supporting aid selection and use is essential for successful accompaniment, systematically organized within support plans and professionally supervised by qualified staff.

The presented conclusions were derived from data collected at special schools for PMD and ID. However, differences in focus stem not from support locations but from interactions between health problems, physical functions, environmental factors (e.g., assistive technology), and personal factors (e.g., motivational starting position). Adequately supporting desired activities and enabling participation is crucial (cf. Bio-psycho-social Model of Functioning, Disability and Health, ICF). Therefore, the above conclusions should apply irrespective of the supporting school.

6 Summary Conclusion

On one hand, it is surprising that, despite the presence of well-established assistive technology competencies at the special PMD and ID schools, a partial result of the present study points up a mismatch between aids and users. Combining the categories "pupils not interested" and "impairment prevents use" yields an overall share of 15.69% of the total challenges and barriers. On the other hand, this result is not surprising given the lack of resources critiqued by the respondents. This deficiency directly impacts everyday school life, as well as the realms of advice, development, and support related to aid provision.

Information exchange among caregivers and counselor qualifications emerge in this study as crucial factors for successful AT provision. Given the complexity of the impairments and their effects on teaching and daily school life, accompanying individuals must possess extensive knowledge and professional counseling skills. Developers of assistive devices are tasked with making individual adaptations to hardware and software feasible and verifying the fit of equipment after a certain period of use in everyday life. Users are also reliant on short repair times or the prompt provision of replacement devices.

It is clear that counselling, development and implementation of AT cannot be encompassed within the general knowledge of teachers across all types of schools. Therefore, establishing specialized advisory structures that are equipped with appropriate resources is a *conditio sine qua non* for facilitating genuine participation by users and further minimizing fitting problems in the future.

Disclosure of Interests. The authors have no competing interests to declare that are relevant to the content of this article.

References

Bernasconi, T.: Anteil und schulische Situation von Schülerinnen und Schülern mit schwerer und mehrfacher Behinderung an Förderschulen in Nordrhein-Westfalen. Ergebnisse einer empirischen Untersuchung in den Förderschwerpunkten körperliche und motorische Entwicklung und geistige Entwicklung. Vierteljahresschrift für Heilpädagogik und ihre Nachbargebiete **86**(4), 309–324 (2017)

Bernasconi, T., Bächler, L., Feichtinger, M.: Bedarf und Einsatz von Assistiver Technologie und Unterstützter Kommunikation in den Förderschulen mit den Förderschwerpunkten Geistige Entwicklung und Körperliche und motorische Entwicklung in Nordrhein-Westfalen. UK Forschung **13**(1), 4–15 (2023)

Bosse, I., Feichtinger, M.: Menschen mit körperlichen und motorischen Beeinträchtigungen. In: Luthe, E.-W., Müller S.V., Schiering I. (eds.) Assistive Technologien im Sozial- und Gesundheitssektor, pp. 177–202. Springer, Wiesbaden (2022). https://doi.org/10.1007/978-3-658-34027-8_10

Bühler, C.: Barrierefreiheit und Assistive Technologie als Voraussetzung und Hilfe zur Inklusion. In: Bernasconi, T., Böing, U. (eds.) Schwere Behinderung & Inklusion. Facetten einer nicht ausgrenzenden Pädagogik (Impulse: Schwere und mehrfache Behinderung, vol. 2, pp. 155–169. Athena, Oberhausen (2016)

Edyburn, D.L.: Rapid literature review on assistive technology in education - Research report, University of Wisconsin-Milwaukee (2020)

Feichtinger, M.: Unterstützte Kommunikation, Assistive Technologien und Teilhabe. In: Boenisch, J., Sachse, S.K. (eds.) Kompendium Unterstützte Kommunikation, pp. 287–295). W. Kohlhammer, Stuttgart (2020)

Kuckartz, U., Rädiker, S.: Qualitative Inhaltsanalyse. Methoden, Praxis, Computerunterstützung, 5th edn. Juventa Verlag, Weinheim (2022)

Ministerium für Schule und Bildung des Landes NRW [MSB]: Statistik-TELEGRAMM 2022/23 (2023a). https://www.schulministerium.nrw/system/files/media/document/file/statistiktelegramm-2022.pdf. Accessed 02 Feb 2024

Ministerium für Schule und Bildung des Landes NRW [MSB]: Das Schulwesen in Nordrhein-Westfalen aus quantitativer Sicht 2022/23 (2023b). https://www.schulministerium.nrw/system/files/media/document/file/quantita_2022.pdf. Accessed 02 Feb 2024

Stephanidis, C., Salvendy, G., Antona, M., Chen, J.Y.C., Dong, J., Duffy, V.G.: Seven HCI grand challenges. Int. J. Hum.-Comput. Interact. **35**(14), 1229–1269 (2019)

Wendt, O., Lloyd, L.L.: Definitions, history, and legal aspects of assistive technology. In: Lloyd, L.L., Wendt, O., Quist, R.W. (eds.) Assistive Technology. Principles and Applications for Communication Disorders and Special Education (Augmentative and Alternative Communication Perspectives, vol. 4, pp. 1–22). Howard House, Bingley (2011)

Towards Inclusion in Higher Education: The Case of the Skills for a Next Generation Project

Bruno Giesteira[1] , Viviane Peçaibes[2]([✉]) , Pedro Cardoso[3] ,
Guilherme Vila-Maior[4], and Isabel Quaresma[1]

[1] Faculty of Fine Arts, University of Porto, Porto, Portugal
bgiesteira@fba.up.pt
[2] Faculty of Fine Arts, University of Porto, ID+, Porto, Portugal
up201707850@edu.fba.up.pt
[3] University of Aveiro, DigiMedia, Aveiro, Portugal
[4] Faculty of Engineering, University of Porto, Porto, Portugal

Abstract. Inclusion is founded on principles grounded on accepting individual differences and valuing human diversity, where all citizens have equal rights. The lack of inclusion has unfortunately been prevalent throughout the history of humanity. Poverty, unemployment, and other situations in which people are deprived of their rights as citizens are demonstrations of social exclusion. This is today a societal concern, and universities are also attentive to how this affects their students, aiming to grant their fundamental rights to learn regardless of individual characteristics, such as Gender, Sexuality, Language, Neurotypicality and Perceptual Accessibility. In short, fostering an inclusive and quality education. In this context, the project Skills for a Next Generation (S4NG), a European Funded Project, aims to promote academic inclusion and diversity at the University of Porto. Its Axis 4.2 aims to create a digital platform for sharing experiences and pedagogical content, some of it gamified as tools to be used to manage and monitor the inclusion. Methods: We developed a methodology based on Human Centred Design (HCD), co-creating with stakeholders and potential users. This helped us better understand how to reconcile their diverse needs and expectations, and to gather knowledge about their contexts. The S4NG Axis 4.2 methodology is composed of 7 steps: User Research, Platform Information Architecture, Monitoring and Registration of Contents, Gamification Strategies, Co-Design of Gamified Content, Platform's User Interface and Functional prototype of the platform and games. As results we created a range of 40 games /physical, digital and hybrid) for teachers, students and staff. These games were divided into 3 categories: Informative Games, Sensitisation Games and Interventive Games.

Keywords: Inclusivity · Universal Design · Positive Play · Games

1 Introduction

Inclusion relates to social stability through social citizenship, where all citizens have equal rights in society (Sheppard 2006, 22). It is based on principles such as accepting individual differences and valuing human diversity (Heidrich 2020). The lack of

M. Antona and C. Stephanidis (Eds.): HCII 2024, LNCS 14698, pp. 16–31, 2024.
https://doi.org/10.1007/978-3-031-60884-1_2

recognition of the values of diversity has become prevalent throughout human history (Hughes 2016). The resulting exclusion refers to social groups that may be in a situation of poverty, unemployment, and other shortages in which they are deprived of their rights as citizens (Sheppard 2006, 10). Social exclusion is a concern of contemporary society and, often, policies have not been sufficient to mitigate circumstances that affect populations (Marcos, Toledo, and Escobar 2022).

Today, universities are concerned with inclusion and exclusion in their academic contexts, as they are determinants at personal, social, and cultural levels (Marcos, Toledo, and Escobar 2022). The European Network of Inclusive Universities[1] (EUni4All-Network), financed by the ERASMUS + European Programme, aims to build a network of universities working for inclusion to serve as a reference for students with disabilities and improve their decision-making in terms of their mobility options and University studies. The University of Porto currently participates in this network assuming the project Skills for a Next Generation (S4NG), a project financed by the European Found, which aims to promote actions focused on recognising and valuing differences and promoting justice and equity in access to knowledge, learning and research. The Axis 4.2 of this project aimed to create a digital platform for sharing experiences and pedagogical content, some of it gamified and monitoring the inclusion. It had a methodology based on Human Centred Design (HCD) through a set of steps that involved a human perspective throughout the process. This methodology aimed to co-creating with stakeholders throughout the design process, focusing on inclusion, and helping us better understand how to reconcile the different needs and expectations of the actors involved in the process and the complexity of the context – in the same way as Holmes (2018) mentions: that with this involvement of people, opportunities for visibility open up through society for those who were once invisible.

This paper is distributed into six major sections: 1) this Introduction; 2) an overview of the adopted methodology; 3) user research; 4) the developed games; 5) the implemented platform; and finally, 6) where we summarise our final considerations and indicate future work.

2 Overview of S4NG's Methodology

We developed a methodology based on Human Centred Design (HCD), co-creating with stakeholders and potential users, to develop games and a platform to support them centred on the user. Meaningful involvement with users facilitates the identification of problems and results in learning experiences and the discovery of functional aspects, and, in this sense, we created a methodology that has its starting point in an in-depth information-gathering process with the target audiences, in order to guide the rest of the project's steps. The S4NG Axis 4.2's methodology is then composed of 7 steps (Fig. 1).

1. User Research consisted of in-depth interviews (Dicicco-Bloom and Crabtree 2006) with members of the university's Inclusion Support Centre and members of the other axes of the project; Focus Group sessions (Wilkinson 1998) with a voluntary sample of Professors; Monitoring of Professors' classes according to the Shadowing observation

---

[1] URL: https://www.euni4all-network.com - access 2023/04/03.

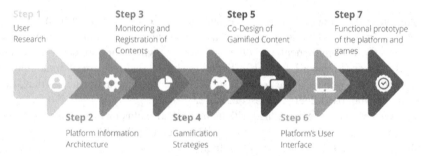

Fig. 1. S4NG Axis 4.2 methodology

method (Hammond e Wellington 2021); and Online Surveys and Cultural Probes (Hammond e Wellington 2021) with students. All of these qualitative and quantitative data were organised and underwent content analysis.

2. Platform Information Architecture was based on the analysis from Step 1. We created User Personas (Goodwin 2009); Context Scenarios (Cooper, Reimann, Cronin and Noessel 2014); defined Functional, Informational, Environmental and User Requirements (Goodwin 2009), and the design of Wireflows (Szabo 2017).

3. Monitoring and Registration of Contents consisted of a survey of different types of information visualisation. With it, we were able to create different templates for visualising data on inclusion in higher education, which later became available on the platform's homepage.

4. Gamification Strategies consisted of a survey of inclusive and serious games (in the context of education and inclusion) and a survey of inclusive platforms. This survey helped us understand the different mechanics, dynamics, and aesthetics of games for inclusion. This step was very important for devising game concepts able to meet the needs of our target audiences and of the complexity of the context.

5. Co-Design of Gamified Content was a stage in which we conducted a 3-h Co-Design Session (Burkett 2012; Dekker e Willians 2017; McKercher 2020) attended by members of the academic community (students, teachers, researchers, and staff) to gather their (the players) points of view about the games under development. All participants had the opportunity to experience any of the game prototypes.

6. Platform's User Interface was the stage in which we developed low and high-fidelity prototypes for the web and mobile, planned and conducted usability tests (Dumas and Redish 1999), analysed the results, and iterated the prototype.

7. Functional prototype of the platform and games was the final development and implementation of the platform, and of the analogue and digital games.

3   User Research

The User Research phase was fundamental for us to understand the complexity of the context of inclusion in the academic environment. We employed different methods in order to gather as much information as possible from various users – students, teachers, and staff with and without special educational needs.

3.1 In-Depth Interviews and Survey

We conducted in-depth interviews with 2 persons from the University's Inclusion Support Centre and 2 colleagues from Axis 4.1 (University of Porto's Observatory for Inclusion and Innovation). To get the point of view of students from the various faculties of the University of Porto complex, we carried out an Online Survey with 15 students aged between 17 and 55. Although the sample was small (its purpose was not of a statistical nature, quite the opposite), it was very diverse and covered practically all the faculties. According to the responses, as target audiences and main needs, we identified that:

- Students, researchers, and student-workers: their main challenge is time management, trying to find strategies to reconcile the demands of their professional, academic, and personal lives.
- Teachers: need support and strategies to deal with inclusion in the classroom. For teachers of advanced age, need support to enhance intergenerational dialogue and help with mobility and functional diversity.
- Non-teaching Staff need support and strategies to deal with inclusion at all levels of care for students, but also for teachers, as they are one of the first points of contact with the university for outsiders.

  From the respondents' answers, we identified the following set of minorities:

- International students (with different cultures, regions, nationalities, ethnicities, religions).
- Gender (female, non-binary – gender identity) and LGBTQIA +.
- Maternity and paternity status (who are often working).
- First generation students – the only ones in their family to reach higher education (they may have difficulty managing relationships, degree of difficulty, level of performance, poorer socio-economic backgrounds, maladjustment, extra effort).
- Vulnerable groups (often imposed by financial and social inequalities).
- Physical disability: visual and motor.
- Mental health disabilities: autism, psychiatric and psychological disorders, obsessive-compulsive disorder, depression, and anxiety, among others.

3.2 Focus Groups with Teachers

Focus groups with teachers from different faculties in remote and face-to-face sessions were elemental to gathering a deeper understanding of their needs in the classroom. With it we were able to see how teachers identify students from different minorities:

- Some of the students are signposted via the student file in the university portal, but this signpost is in a difficult-to-access place that teachers often can't find.
- There is a fringe of students who are not signposted by the service because they don't identify with any need due to stigma.
- Some students show isolating behaviour and difficulties integrating with other students and teachers, while others show excessive participation or disruption.
- Teachers share important information about students to foster mutual support.
- Teachers are often unable to perceive the manifestations or recognise many of the needs.

The strategies used by teachers include:

- The use of distance orientation meetings so that students with autism feel more at ease with the teacher.
- Asking questions and trying to figure out how to interact with different students.
- Promoting interaction and presentation dynamics to foster closeness between students and between student and teacher.

3.3 Shadowing with Teachers During Classes

We applied the shadowing method with 3 teachers from 3 faculties in 4 different face-to-face classes (Fig. 2). The main behaviours of the teachers were that, regardless of the course or faculty, we noticed that the students were well received and that the teachers were willing to share content, engage in dialogue, listen, and give the students freedom. The classes we observed had different formats (workshop, lecture, project presentation). However, we observed that the teachers were sympathetic to the students (especially minority students) and showed an egalitarian and inclusive attitude. The students' behaviour was different in each observed class. This is due to the profile of each course and the format of the lessons. Some of the behaviour of non-signposted students was in line with an identified minority, but their colleague's showed naturalness and apparent acceptance of differences. We realised that students can be grouped by minorities because they feel more comfortable and secure.

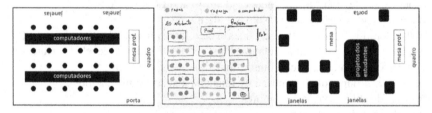

Fig. 2. Shadowing: Classes mapping

3.4 Cultural Probes with Students

We developed a cultural probe to accompany the student for a week, to help us better understand the challenges and barriers to inclusion that arise in the academic context throughout the participant's day. As a way of being close to the students, we used mobile phones and the WhatsApp social network[2]. The profiles of the 4 participants were LGBTQIA+, International Student, Neurodivergent (Schizophrenia, Depression and Delusional Disorder), Special Educational Needs (dyslexia and twice-exceptional), and Student-Worker and Student-Maternity. We had a daily flow of conversation and quick feedback on the answers. From their testimonies, we see there are a number of daily difficulties they faced:

---

[2] URL: https://www.whatsapp.com/.

- Issues of acceptance of difference on the part of some students inside and outside the classroom.
- Lack of information sharing about different types of minorities and the legislation/ rights they have in the academic environment.
- Too many tasks/ classes that demand and tire out students who need to work and/ or are in a maternity or paternity situation.
- Emotional imbalances that can be personal or triggered by colleagues.
- Difficulties socialising and feeling safe in interpersonal relationships.
- Resistance or low awareness among other people in the academic community.

4   Games for Inclusion

Our User Research's contributions were conclusive for the team to deliberate on the gamified content to be developed, accounting for users' behaviours, needs and expectations, with particular emphasis on:

- *Identification of minorities to be addressed with the games*: autism, ADHD, dyslexia, anxiety, depression, deafness, blindness, LGBTQIA +, international student, student-worker, and maternity/paternity.
- *Teachers are not yet comfortable using games in class*, but they see it as a good strategy to complement and reinforce the content given in class.
- *Teachers are willing to play games to learn about good inclusion practices* in a more dynamic way compared to having access to reports and other reading materials.
- *Students are willing to play games on their own and with other people about issues related to inclusion* and see the game as a way of getting closer to different people and as a way to integrate.
- *Students think it is important for games to help inform and sensitise people about aspects of everyday life* that occur within the academic environment when it comes to inclusion.
- *Students think it is important to raise awareness among teachers and staff* about issues related to gender identity, LGBTQIA + and other minorities, in order to impact teachers' behaviour and socialisation with students inside and outside the classroom.

Based on these conclusions, we began ideating game concepts. We created a total of 37 games (analogue and digital), 4 of which were created with the collaboration of groups of students from the University of Porto in a co-creation regime during classes, in two master courses and in a post-graduate course[3]. We co-created game concepts and produced paper and downloadable prototypes (Fig. 3), which were used to check for obstacles or difficulties in player interactions and to evaluate concepts, albeit informally, with potential target audiences. The content we produced for all games was reviewed by experts in inclusion.

---

[3] Specialisation Course in Interaction Design, Web, and Games (FBAUP, FEUP, UPTEC).URL: https://sigarra.up.pt/fbaup/en/CUR_GERAL.CUR_VIEW?pv_ano_lectivo=2023&pv_ori gem=CUR&pv_tipo_cur_sigla=E&pv_curso_id=17441.

Fig. 3. Games: Paper Prototype (left) and Low-Fi Prototype (right).

In the end, we have implemented a total of 28 games (analogue and digital) to cater for the different identified minorities[4]. We classified them into three groups: *Informative Games, Sensibilisation Games, and Interventive Games.*

4.1 Informative Games

Informative games we developed are instruments to support the learning of good inclusion practices in the classroom and in other academic contexts (Fig. 4). This set of games aims to meet the needs of teachers that were pointed out, especially, during the Focus Groups:

- User Research (UR) participants mentioned they needed to learn strategies and to have more information about different minorities, but they didn't have time to digest content that required a lot of reading time, or that they had to spend a lot of time on training or life-long education courses.
- The strategies and information on inclusion are directly related to teachers' activities in the classroom, as well as to staff activities in care and service provision. This inclusion content aligned with the daily activities of teachers and staff allows players to learn from the games and feel able to quickly apply the strategies.
- Finally, as we saw in the UR, teachers and staff are willing to play as long as it is not too time-consuming.

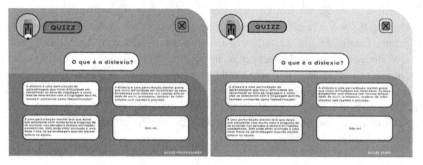

Fig. 4. Informative Games: Quiz to learn about dyslexia for teachers (left) and for staff (right).

---

[4] At the time of writing, a video featuring the games can be found at:URL: https://www.gieste ira.pt/_SKILLS/Games.mp4.

Considering these three issues, we opted to implement quizzes because they feature very simple gameplay with a heavy focus on conveying information to players. The 20 quizzes we developed feature content validated by inclusion experts and can be played directly on the online platform we describe in Sect. 5.

4.2 Sensitisation Games

Sensitisation games work as tools to promote players' empathy and awareness of issues related to autism, ADHD, LGBTQIA+, international students, working students and those in a maternity/paternity situation (Fig. 5).

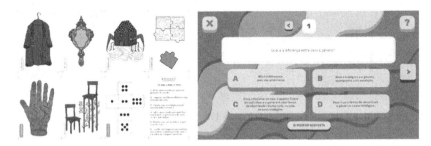

Fig. 5. Sensibilization Games: *LifeStories*, pages to print (left), and *Taboo* (right).

The games we developed aim to promote positive debate and invite people to integrate into an inclusive and diverse community. Their game mechanics' aim is for players to have a shared space where they feel safe and at ease to talk about their challenges in the field of inclusion, exchange life stories, get closer, support, and learn from each other.

UR showed that students (LGBTQIA+) have a need for greater closeness. PArticipantes from UR mentioned tend to isolate themselves. For this reason, we developed a physical game in which students sit and play together: *LifeStories*. It has the form of 30 illustrated cards, 1 action card, and a dice, in which all the elements can be printed on a home printer. The game's mechanics provide a safe environment for sharing experiences and promote empathy between players. By means of UR, we also realised that students can often have doubts about themselves and their behaviour in relation to gender and gender identity issues. As such, the *Lifestories* invites players to share stories inspired by its illustrations for talking, listening, and learning together about gender issues.

During the UR, students mentioned the need for teachers to be open to debate on issues related to LGBTQIA+, to promote the breaking down of stigmas and taboos around the subject. Taboo is a game we created that focuses on LGBTQIA+ groups and invites players (students and teachers) to learn together about gender issues, gender identity and sexuality in the classroom. The game has 5 levels, and each level has 6 questions that the teacher chooses and projects on the screen in the classroom so that the students can together read the questions and answer possibilities. The game promotes a debate dynamic so that the players come up with a single answer together. This convergence enhances learning, strengthens the connection between players and teachers and makes it easier to break down taboos and stigmas linked to the theme.

4.3 Interventive Games

Interventive games are instruments that can be a resource in times of crisis (anxiety, obsessive-compulsive disorder, or panic); and as learning and retention resources and content for students with autism, dyslexia, attention deficit and blindness. Their game space promotes playfulness that makes it easier to bring people together and empowers them to the point where they feel safe and willing to act (Fig. 6).

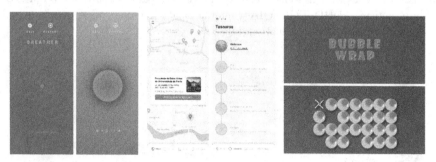

Fig. 6. Interventive Games: Breather (left) and UP Treasure Hunt (middle), and Bubble Wrap (right).

While in contact with people suffering from anxiety during UR, we were told about the crises that can happen during class, exams, presentations, etc., and that they needed a tool to help them have self-control. Some students mentioned the effectiveness of breath control but also that doing it without support was difficult, especially during a moment of crisis. *Breather* is a game for mobile phones intended for such a purpose: to be an interventional resource for controlling anxiety crisis situations, obsessive-compulsive disorder or panic attacks. In this playful experience, the player receives support from the game to control their own breathing in order to offer a calming effect. Players can play as often and for as long as they wish, enabling self-control.

During the UR, we listened to international students mentioning the need to better understand the venues and services offered by the university. We also realised that the university's campus camp has many stories that are linked to the history of the city of Porto, as well as curiosities that often only students from a particular faculty know about. A treasure hunt dynamic piques the players' curiosity by engaging them and motivating them to tour the faculties while learning more about the context and the city they live in. With this in mind, we developed *UP Treasure Hunt*, which invites international students to explore the city of Porto and the different buildings in the university complex to search for treasures. In this digital game for smartphones, the player can take a selfie in a certain spot, find a *QRcode* that unlocks a curiosity and find a certain place from half of a photograph. In each of these interactions, the player learns a little about the history and importance of each faculty and is also shown the basic services offered, such as the canteen and library, among others.

One of the strategies participants mentioned during UR was popping bubble wrap. They reported this action produced a great calming effect on them, but because it makes noise when it pops, they can't have the plastic in class without disturbing others. They also mentioned that the plastic runs out and that they usually have to go out and buy new ones. We then realised that this could be turned into a game. *Bubble Wrap* is a game that serves as an interventional resource for managing anxiety crises, obsessive-compulsive disorder, or panic attacks. In this ludic experience, the player needs to blow the bubbles on the screen to offer a calming effect). The game has 2 different modes: the simple mode, in which the player can randomly blow each plastic bubble on the screen until they finish the bubbles and then choose a new plastic bubble to blow, and the "Simon" mode, in which the player needs to blow the bubbles according to the game's instructions. The player determines when the game ends.

5   Games for Inclusion

Axis 4.2 aims to create a digital platform for sharing experiences and pedagogical content, some of them gamified and for monitoring inclusion levels, serving as an autonomous tool for the university and also as a working tool for the Observatory for Inclusion. On this platform, we offer support to the academy's activities through gamified tools created by axis 4.2 to be used inside and outside the classroom.

We created 4 personas – 2 (two) students, 1 (one) teacher and 1 (one) staff (Fig. 7). These personas reflect UR's findings, as one persona is a student with a special need (blind) and the other persona is an international LGBTQIA+ student. These specificities represent the group of identified minorities. The teacher persona portrays a person who needs help learning about inclusion and who wants to make their classes more accessible. The Staff persona is an elderly person who has mobility difficulties. Through this set of Personas, we were able to serve the main groups identified in our UR.

Fig. 7. Examples of personas: Carla (Staff - left) and Flora (Blind Student - right).

With these personas in mind, we developed the following general structure for the platform:

- *Mainpage*: users can access information such as Programmes, Campaigns, Contacts, and Courses to deepen the learning environment on Inclusion and Accessibility.

- *Teaching & Learning*: a section that brings together the greatest user needs, documents, tools, methods, and guides on how to deal with students' specific needs, how to make your classes and teaching more accessible and how to be more inclusive with your students. All this content is divided into three subtopics: Policies and Guidelines, Support Resources, and Pedagogical Methods.
- *Literature*: users can find content such as Online Articles, Studies, and Dissertations, among others.
- *Testimonies*: users can interact with the platform by sharing stories with the community. With the possibility of creating a publication, selecting the categories in which it fits and giving it a title and message, users can also add multimedia content (such as images, videos, and audio) with the possibility of publishing anonymously.
- *Games*: where users can find physical and digital games (developed by the axis 4.2 team). In each game, the user can find the necessary information to know how to play and referrals to similar games present in the platform.

This structure aims to deliver:

- A section aimed at University of Porto community, namely Professors and students to know more about a more inclusive and accessible teaching environment, considering facilities, services, digital information, legislation, and timely dissemination in turn the Inclusivity subjects.
- A gamified content categories deem to help a better understanding of various topics related to inclusity, accessibility and awareness-raising approaches for the academic community, such as sexual, gender, linguistic, motor, and cognitive incapacities and divergences, mental well-being.
- A section in which the academic community can report and share their experiences of inclusion in the context of academic environment access to a literary section for academic and personal enjoyment around the themes of Inclusion and Accessibility.
- A general search feature on the platform, the possibility of changing the platform's font size, and accessing profile data and other user account settings.

We understand that the structure defined for the platform meets the needs of the aforementioned personas and is aligned with the specificities of a large part of the target audience we had access to during the UR. The web platform, in the data of the publication, is being currently in used at University of Porto in the following web address: http://www.up.pt/inclusao.

Afterwards, we created a low-fi prototype to help us better understand the visual organisation of the navigation and contents, aiming for accessibility for people who are blind or have low vision and then developed a hi-fi prototype (desktop and mobile). Throughout its design stages, we aimed to include the largest possible number of people by making information available in the most possible number of people and various ways and modalities. Since visually impaired users may be unable to see or interpret visual content, the platform provides text or audio that accurately describes all visible content. Similarly, users with hearing or cognitive impairments may not be able to hear or have difficulty interpreting audio, so the platform has other layers of information, such as subtitled text, images, or videos, to ensure greater accessibility and diversity in access to content (Fig. 8).

Fig. 8. Low-fi prototype (on the left), hi-fi prototype desktop (middle): main page and menu and hi-fi mobile version (on the right).

We designed a menu made up of different coloured tabs located at the top of the platform that users can navigate with the mouse and the Tab key, making it easier for blind users to access content and navigate. Each menu tab corresponds to a section we identified in the information architecture: Teaching and Learning (green), Games (orange), Testimonies (blue) and Literature (yellow). As a requirement of Inclusive Design, we dedicated contrasting colours to the tabs and added the option of increasing or decreasing the font size at the top of the platform.

Within the tabs, users can use different filters that are always available on the left-hand side of the platform (Fig. 9). In these filters, the user can select content by groups of identified minorities. So, if the user only wants to access information on that tab related to anxiety, clicking on the filter will only show content related to the chosen topic.

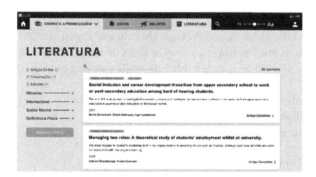

Fig. 9. Hi-fi prototype: Filters.

We also created different templates for visualising data regarding inclusion at the university (Fig. 10). All the templates feature image description resources that screen readers can read to make it easier for blind users to understand.

In the Games section (Fig. 11), the user can view all the available games, choose between physical or digital games, and filter them by type of minority. By clicking on the game they want, users are taken to a dedicated page where they can see the game's objective, rules, how to play, and a ranking of ratings (made by other players). For physical games, users are also given access to instructions on downloading and printing the PDF file.

Fig. 10. Hi-fi prototype: Templates.

Fig. 11. Hi-fi prototype: Games section (left) and dedicated game page (right).

User Tests & Findings. The prototype was tested with 8 participants (3 teachers and 5 students). We used the Think Aloud Protocol (Martin and Hanington 2012) as a method in which participants must perform a group of tasks on the platform. The participant is encouraged to say everything they are thinking while carrying out the following tasks:

- Access the platform login.
- Find a publication.
- Choose a physical and a digital game.
- Use search filters.
- Create a new testimony.

As some highlights of the tests, we highlight that:

- We must place the user profile and login in the top corner of the platform so that
- it is always visible, as, during the tests, it was within the platform settings, which made it difficult for students to find it.
- The search using the bar was quickly understood, making searching for specific files easier.
- The terminology and choice of titles for the categories and subcategories in the filters section should be revised because it was misleading users, especially as they didn't know the names and acronyms of minorities (e.g. ADHD, LGBTQIA +). This made it difficult to use the filters and find games for a particular typology, which significantly impacted navigation through the platform.

- The majority of testers carried out the creation of a new testimonial; we identified that the format of the form made it easier to understand how to complete it but that it is necessary to add to this form the possibility of publishing an anonymous testimonial.

Results showed that the structure of the platform is easy to understand and navigate and features the kind of essential content users turn to for academic purposes, or simply due to the inclusivity and accessibility features of such content.

6 Conclusion

6.1 Summary and Contributions

In this paper, we presented the work of Axis 4.2 of the Skills for a Next Generation project: the results from our User Research, the Platform that features 28 of the 37 games we designed, and the typology of the Games we developed with some examples.
As contributions, we can highlight:

- **Data collected**: we realised the complexity of the context of inclusion in higher education. We understood the diverse needs of teachers, students and staff and engaged the academic community with the objectives of axis 4.2. The entire design process helped us to identify the minority groups we were focussing on to fulfil their different expectations.
- **Platform**: the development process helped us make decisions about accessibility and navigation, considering the different needs of the various target audiences. Based on the contributions of User Research, we developed a tool that will support Axis 4.1 (University of Porto's Observatory for Inclusion and Innovation) and will be a way of learning and sharing testimonies about good inclusion practices.
- **Games**: we have created a set of games that fulfil the users' needs and are capable of transmitting knowledge about strategies and good practices for inclusion inside and outside the classroom in a simple, easy and engaging way, raising awareness among the academic community and encouraging the sharing of life stories with a focus on fostering empathy; and being interventional tools to support crisis situations.

We believe that this project demonstrates that there is a great need for tools to support inclusion in higher education, but that design has the capacity to respond to this demand in a creative and ludic way. We know that gamified content in this context calls users to action and provides the conditions for the academic community to be more inclusive and better prepared to understand and embrace diversity.

6.2 Future Work

As mentioned above, we had to split the project into two phases. With this in mind, we indicate the following as future work:

- **Regarding the Platform** - we intend to make the necessary adjustments that will be perceived with increased use, make content updates, and we intend to add a list of free-access external games (not created by the Axis 4.2 team) that will serve as an additional resource to augment the existing gamified content set.

- **Regarding the Games** - continuing the development of the remaining 9 games, in which we will employ machine learning and artificial intelligence to help people learn basic sign language gestures and help people understand how a person with autism spectrum disorder with hypersensitivity feels in environments; help teachers, students and staff practise good inclusion practice strategies, as well as providing people with more informative content.

Acknowledgments. This   research   was   supported   by:

Without them, there wouldn't be the possibility to go forward with this project, meaning that each day, there is a need to support, care and focus on the domains that unite the project: Health, Engineering and Design.

Furthermore, the researcher had the pleasure of collaborating with Inclusion Support Centre at the University of Porto. Without them the researchers wouldn't have had the opportunity to support the project in such a rich qualitative approach.

The authors also worked with Estefania Graciett de Almeida Larez an Occupational Therapist, whose path in the domains of health, interaction design and user experience, was fundamental to conceptualising game dynamics, as well as to contribute not only in all project phases but also for a better understanding of players, tasks, contexts and caregivers, who have a decisive weight in the user's care.

At last, the authors appreciate the collaboration with Students from the University of Porto, namely the Bachelor's in Communication Design, and the students from the Post-Graduation in Interaction Design and Games. Without them, the speculation of ideas would have been left by a linear development. All the hypotheses that these students developed are possible to apply, so many considerations of their projects and criticisms of them were essential to have a distance and understand how it can become more mature.

References

Burkett, Ingrid. An introduction to Co-Design. Australia: Knode (2012). https://www.yacwa.org.au/wp-content/uploads/2016/09/An-Introduction-to-Co-Design-by-Ingrid-Burkett.pdf

Cooper, C., Reimann, R., Cronin, D., Noessel, C.: About Face: The Essentials of Interaction Design, 4th edn. Wiley Publishing (2014)

Dekker, M.R., Williams, A.D.: The use of user-centered participatory design in serious games for anxiety and depression. Games Health J. **6**(6), 327–333 (2017). https://doi.org/10.1089/g4h.2017.0058

DiCicco-Bloom, B., Crabtree, B.F.: The qualitative research interview. Med. Educ. **40**(4), 314–321 (2006). https://doi.org/10.1111/j.1365-2929.2006.02418.x

Dumas, J.S., Redish, J.C.: A Practical Guide to Usability Testing, 1st edn. Intellect Books, GBR (1999)

Hammond, M., Wellington, J.: Research Methods: The Key Concepts, 2nd edn. Routledge Key Guides. Taylor & Francis, New York (2021)

Heidrich, R.O.: Desafios para a inclusão no Brasil. In: Sanfelice, G.R., Bassani, P.S. (ed.) Diversidade cultural e inclusão social, pp. 73–82. Universidade Feevale (2020)

Holmes, K., Maeda, J.T.A.: Mismatch: How Inclusion Shapes Design. The MIT Press (2018)

Hughes, C.: Diversity Intelligence. Palgrave Macmillan US (2016). https://doi.org/10.1057/978-1-137-52683-0

Dumas, J.F., Redish, J.C.: A Practical Guide to Usability Testing. Greenwood Publishing Group Inc., USA (1993)

Goodwin, K.: Designing for the Digital Age: How to Create Human-Centered Products and Services. Wiley (2009)

Ku, B., Lupton, E.: Health Design Thinking - Creating Products and Services for Better Health. MIT Press (2020)

Marcos, M.G., Toledo, M.R., Escobar, C.R.: Towards inclusive higher education: a multivariate analysis of social and gender inequalities. Societies **12**(6), 184 (2022). https://doi.org/10.3390/soc12060184

Martin, B., Hanington, B.: Universal methods of design: 100 ways to research complex problems, develop innovative ideas and design effective solutions. Rockport (2012)

McGonigal, J.: A Realidade em Jogo: por que os games nos tornam melhores e como eles podem mudar o mundo. Brasil: Best Seller (2012)

McKercher, K.A.: Beyond Sticky Notes. Cammeraygal Country, Australia: Inscope Books 2020

Sheppard, C.: Inclusive Equality: The Relational Dimensions of Systemic Discrimination in Canada. McGill-Queen's University Press (2010)

Szabo, P.W.: User Experience Mapping. Packt Publishing, UK (2017)

Wilkinson, P.: A brief history of serious games. In: Dörner, R., Göbel, S., Kickmeier-Rust, M., Masuch, M., Zweig, K. (eds.) Entertainment Computing and Serious Games. LNCS, vol. 9970, pp. 17–41. Springer, Cham (2016). https://doi.org/10.1007/978-3-319-46152-6_2

Unlocking Opportunities: Empowering Autistic Adults in Vocational Training and Employment Through Assistive Technologies

David Gollasch[(✉)] [ID], Christin Engel[ID], Meinhardt Branig[ID],
Jan Schmalfuß-Schwarz, and Gerhard Weber[ID]

Department of Computer Science, Chair of Human-Computer Interaction,
TUD Dresden University of Technology, 01062 Dresden, Germany
{david.gollasch,christin.engel,meinhardt.branig,
jan.schmalfuss-schwarz,gerhard.weber}@tu-dresden.de

Abstract. This paper explores the challenges faced by autistic individuals in vocational training and their transition to the general labor market in Germany. It focuses on how assistive technologies (AT) can enhance their employment prospects. The research employs observations and interviews at a Vocational Training Center (VTC) to understand the specific needs of autistic people in workplace settings, particularly office-based environments. The study identifies key challenges, support measures, and factors influencing dropout rates in vocational training. It also highlights the potential benefits of AT in fostering a more inclusive work environment and aiding autistic individuals in overcoming employment barriers. The findings emphasize the need for AT that is adaptable to individual needs and compatible with various work settings, ultimately promoting inclusion and better employment outcomes for people with autism.

Keywords: neurodivergence · autism · ASD · assistive technology · vocational training · general labour market · context analysis

1 Introduction

This paper examines the challenges and potential of assistive technology (AT) in supporting autistic individuals in vocational training and their transition to the labor market, particularly in office-based environments. Despite possessing valuable skills, autistic individuals face significant employment barriers, with unemployment rates for those without intellectual disabilities as high as 50% [20]. The difficulties in social communication and sensory processing contribute to underutilization of their potential, leading to adverse effects such as social isolation and stress [20, 22]. Furthermore, misconceptions and lack of awareness about autism often hinder their employment prospects [17]. Addressing these

M. Antona and C. Stephanidis (Eds.): HCII 2024, LNCS 14698, pp. 32–46, 2024.
https://doi.org/10.1007/978-3-031-60884-1_3

challenges requires a multi-faceted approach, including improved access to vocational services [6] and workplace adaptations [14].

This paper aims to identify and categorize factors influencing the employment of autistic individuals, analyze vocational training environments, and explore how AT can be effectively used to overcome these barriers and enhance their integration into the general labor market.

Research Question: What are the major high-level requirements of AT for autistic persons to support a successful vocational training as well as transition into the first labor market focusing on office-based work environments?

We comprehensively analyze vocational training and workplace integration for autistic individuals in Germany. Following this motivation, the study delves into the specific challenges within work environments and vocational training for those with Autism Spectrum Disorder (ASD). Our methodology encompasses mixed methods of observations and interviews at a Vocational Training Center (VTC). The results section provides a synthesis of the work shadowing and thematic analysis of interviews. Subsequent sections discuss the role of AT and propose recommendations for policymakers, VTCs, and technology developers. The paper concludes with a summary of findings and suggests directions for future research.

2 Autistic People in Work Environments and Vocational Training

A recent German study [7] reveals that adults with Autism-Spectrum Disorder (ASD) without intellectual disabilities, despite higher education levels, face a higher unemployment rate (25.2%) compared to the general population (5.2%). This unemployment significantly impacts their lives, leading to issues like social isolation and depression [20]. Research focuses on both negative workplace factors and predictors of successful employment for those with ASD. Factors such as parental and employer support, job characteristics, and personal attributes like social skills, communication ability, and intelligence are crucial for employment success [12,23]. Intelligence often emerges as a significant predictor [12,21]. Despite the deficit-focused diagnostic criteria for ASD, a resource-oriented perspective [3] highlights their potential in the labor market. However, ASD is associated with various social and psychological challenges, making vocational training essential for professional success.

2.1 Autism and Vocational Training

Individuals with ASD face significant challenges in vocational training due to inconsistent access to services [6]. The necessity of an initial assessment to access vocational services is crucial [1]. In the US, for instance, legislation like IDEA supports transition services for disabilities, including ASD [6]. However, autistic individuals are less likely to develop vocational qualifications [7]. Studies by Alverson et al. [1] show the benefits of vocational rehabilitation, with employed individuals with ASD more likely to have accessed such services. Existing support services often do not meet the specific needs of those with ASD. Chen et al. and Vogeley et al. [6,20] highlight the inadequacy of current vocational services in terms of quality and preparation for autistic individuals, especially those with high intelligence. Their support framework includes assessment, job coaching, and peer instruction. Figure 1 illustrates the transition from education over to work in Germany and the corresponding institutions that make up the support system for autistic persons. However, current research on the effectiveness of these programs remains limited and often non-representative, leaving many without necessary support [6,20].

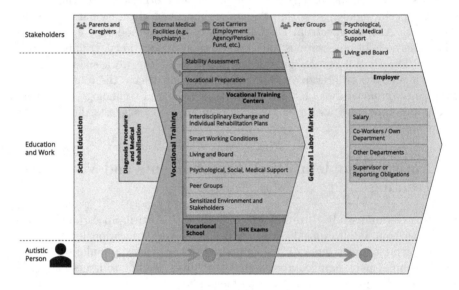

Fig. 1. Schematic representation of components of vocational rehabilitation training and transition to the general labor market

2.2   Autism in Work Environments

Education is foundational for employment, yet people with ASD face additional challenges in the workplace, including interpersonal difficulties leading to unemployment [7]. The job search and career development are particularly challenging for those with ASD, requiring jobs that cater to their specific needs and strengths [2]. While ASD is often defined by deficits, many characteristics, like focused attention and routine enjoyment, are advantageous in work settings [23]. However, time management and social interactions present significant hurdles [17]. The heterogeneity in ASD symptoms and skills necessitates tools like the Autism Work Skills Questionnaire (AWSQ) for optimal job matching [8]. Work environment factors, especially sensory processing issues, greatly influence job satisfaction for individuals with ASD [14]. These individuals often face misalignment between their intellectual capabilities and job responsibilities, leading to dissatisfaction and a lack of motivators [20]. The specific work environment needs for people with ASD are under-researched, requiring more focus on environmental adaptations for better job outcomes [14,20]. Additionally, social challenges and employer misconceptions often limit job opportunities, highlighting the importance of supported employment programs and the need for more research in this area [17,20].

2.3   Assistive Technology in Workplace Environments

Work environment adaptation is crucial for people with ASD. Research highlights the potential of Assistive Technologys (ATs) in supporting autistic individuals at work [21,22,24]. Wali and Sanfilippo discuss AT tailored to sensory needs, categorizing them into personal digital assistants and environmental adaptations [21]. However, challenges like limited interaction due to use of devices like headphones are noted. Walsh et al. focus on technologies improving specific job skills and overall employment outcomes for people with ASD, underscoring the need for more evidence-based research [22]. Syriopoulou-Delli and Stefani review mobile devices and software applications, including Virtual Reality (VR) and Augmented Reality (AR), targeting communicative and vocational skills. They highlight the effectiveness of tablets and the necessity for more research in diverse work activities [18]. Current reviews call for further research to better support people with ASD in workplace environments, emphasizing technology's role in reducing work-related challenges and enhancing skill development.

Sensory, Communication, and Task Support Technologies. AT offers significant benefits in workplace environments for individuals with ASD, addressing sensory overload, communication challenges, and task management. Sanfilippo et al. [15] and Gedam and Paul [9] discuss multi-sensor systems and wearables for managing sensory inputs and stress levels. In communication, technologies like AR are used for training of prosody in speech and understanding [4,5]. However, challenges in verbal communication and the need for more direct communication support are noted [16,19]. For task management, iPads, and iPod Touches have been effectively used for structuring tasks and reducing the need for personal assistance, enhancing independence [10,11]. Studies show these technologies improve work performance and behavioral training [6,13]. However, there is a need for more research, especially in designing AT tailored to the diverse work skills and communication needs of people with ASD. Most studies are limited in participant numbers and conducted under laboratory conditions, indicating a need for context-specific evaluations and standardized methods [24].

3   Methodology

This paper employs a mixed-methods approach to explore the use of assistive technologies in vocational training for autistic individuals in Germany.

The methodology combines qualitative observations (work-shadowing) and semi-structured interviews, providing a comprehensive view of the experiences and challenges faced by these individuals.

Observations or Work Shadowing: Conducted in one selected Vocational Training Center (VTC), these observations focus on the day-to-day experiences of autistic trainees. They aim to capture the real-world application of training techniques and the integration (or lack thereof) of assistive technologies in these settings.

The observational study was meticulously structured to examine various vocational training groups, focusing on their typical work sessions. The groups included:

– First-year Information Technology (IT) trainees, comprising 8 individuals.
– Second-year IT trainees, also consisting of 8 individuals.
– A mixed group in Tax Clerk training, from the first and third years, with 5 trainees.
– Participants in a Preparatory Vocational Year, totaling 8 individuals.
– First-year Commercial Professions training group, consisting of 8 trainees.

The observation approach involved silently accompanying the trainees during their morning activities. We meticulously documented observations using a catalog of 32 work-context-related questions. These questions covered aspects such as the social context, service-oriented context, and physical context of their work environment.

The results were methodically categorized into distinct areas: the workers, work tools, work environment, work tasks, and workspace, following the context analysis framework of ISO 6385:2016. The goal of this structured observation was to provide a detailed description of varied office work environments, assess their suitability for autistic trainees, and aid in further research efforts.

Interviews: Semi-structured interviews with six trainers, and VTC-related experts provide more in-depth insights. These interviews are designed to understand the perceived effectiveness of current training methods and AT, as well as to identify unmet needs and potential areas for improvement. We performed these interviews alongside our work-shadowing sessions if possible, else separately, and based on our 32 work-context-related questions.

Participant Selection and VTCs: In our study, we focused on multiple groups of trainees from various vocational fields within a specific Vocational Training Center (VTC). These groups represented different years of training, either taught individually or in combined classes, each comprising approximately 8 participants. A key aspect of our participant selection was the inclusion of autistic trainees within these groups, as they were a primary focus of our research. The selection of vocational fields was guided by our interest in office-based occupations. Consequently, we examined groups in information technology training, tax clerk training, commercial professions, and a group engaged in a preparatory year for vocational education. The chosen VTC was specifically selected for its ongoing transition towards autism-friendly vocational training. This center has seen an increase in autistic trainees and offers a wide range of relevant vocational fields. This convergence of an increasing need for supportive measures and existing expertise in accommodating autistic individuals made this VTC an ideal setting for our study. Insights gained from this environment were particularly valuable, as they included both the challenges faced by autistic trainees and the strategies employed by the VTC to support them, as reflected in our interviews.

4   Results

4.1   Work Shadowing Summary

The work shadowing at the Vocational Training Center (VTC) encompassed a comprehensive analysis of the training environment, considering social, physical, and service-oriented contexts. This section briefly summarizes major observations and commonalities of all work-shadowing sessions.

Training and Environment. Trainees were grouped by year and specialization, focusing on tasks like programming and network protocols, with an emphasis on independent work and group collaboration. Regular training schedules included structured breaks and accommodations for sensory needs. Classrooms for IT trainees were standard in layout based on an office-like environment, with facilities for group work and individual focus. For the commercial professions, we observed a layout more common in schools, ideal for frontal lessons. Other classrooms offered a grouped layout.

Physical Context. The physical environment featured standard classrooms similar to open-plan offices with 10 to 12 workspaces, with sensory considerations like controlled lighting and noise levels. The rooms were equipped with typical office furniture and technology, without special adaptations beyond standard workstations. Each trainee has a fixed workspace within the room.

Social Dynamics. Interaction among trainees, including those with ASD, was collaborative and supportive, with minimal disruption from the work environment. The trainers were aware of individual challenges and adapted their approaches accordingly. The Preparatory Vocational Year serves as a critical period for participants, offering them the opportunity to acquaint themselves with one another. This initial phase of mutual acquaintance fosters the development of a trusting environment, laying a foundational atmosphere of camaraderie and support that benefits all trainees throughout their subsequent years of vocational training. This early establishment of trust and familiarity among participants is instrumental in creating a cohesive and supportive learning community, essential for their overall development and success in the program.

Service-Oriented Context. Throughout the observational study across five distinct vocational training sessions, tasks consistently emphasized practical application, ranging from project work and online research to specialized tasks like financial documentation with specialized software, maintenance of records, tax assessments for various business forms, and development and delivery of presentations. The trainees also engaged in diverse clerical duties, including telephone service, design of posters and catalogs, and preparation of business correspondence such as letters, emails, offers, delivery notes, invoices, and payment reminders. In commercial training, activities extended to document management, accounting, inventory, and form creation. This comprehensive approach across various disciplines fostered both independent problem-solving and collaborative learning, leveraging standard digital tools to enhance vocational skills and workplace readiness.

In summary, the vocational training program provided a structured, supportive environment, balancing the need for independent work with group collaboration, in a standard educational setting tailored to accommodate diverse learning needs.

4.2   Key Challenges in Vocational Settings and Analysis of Dropout-Influencing Factors

The research based on our trainer and expert interviews reveals several key challenges faced by autistic individuals in vocational settings. A primary issue is the difficulty in *social communication* and *sensory processing*, which often leads to feelings of being overwhelmed in traditional work environments. Additionally, the study uncovers a notable dropout rate from traditional vocational training programs among autistic trainees, attributed to factors such as *lack of tailored support*, *inflexible training methods*, and an *unsupportive social environment*. Analysis of these dropout rates indicates a need for more individualized approaches in training and a more profound understanding of the unique needs of autistic individuals. The research also sheds light on the existing support measures in Vocational Training Centers (VTCs).

The thematic analysis of expert interviews identified several challenges in vocational rehabilitation for individuals with disabilities, particularly focusing on autistic trainees in computer science, commercial professions, tax clerk training as well as participants of a Preparatory Vocational Year at a VTC.

Vocational Rehabilitation Context. Germany's legal framework for rehabilitation and inclusion is outlined (cf. Fig. 1), emphasizing the role of VTC in providing practical training and vocational qualifications. Trainees, predominantly financed by the German Federal Employment Agency (GFEA), undergo a rigorous assessment process and are offered various training formats, including part-time options.

Clientele and Training Characteristics. The client profile at VTC has shifted towards cognitive and mental impairments, with an increasing number of autistic trainees. Training prerequisites include a weekly work capacity, clinical diagnosis, completed medical rehabilitation, and funding approval. A preparatory year is essential before starting the training, with stringent selection criteria.

Training Adaptation and Support. Autistic trainees often settle in quickly, with specialized support systems in place. The VTC aims for the "Autism-friendly Vocational Training Center" certificate, focusing on structural and process quality criteria. Interdisciplinary support and tailored training formats, such as theory-reduced programs, are provided to accommodate diverse learning needs.

Challenges and Transition to Labor Market. Access to vocational training is contingent on medical diagnosis and treatment availability. Mobility and social acceptance, especially in external vocational schools, pose significant challenges. Time management issues and the structured environment of VTC contrast with the diverse conditions of the general labor market. The transition requires adaptation to different working conditions and independent management of health and social aspects.

Summary of Identified Challenges. The thematic analysis of expert interviews identified several key challenges faced by autistic trainees in VTCs, impacting their successful training and transition to the labor market. These challenges include navigating the legal and organizational framework of vocational rehabilitation in Germany, which often involves complex interactions with public bodies and adherence to specific legal rights and provisions. Autistic trainees, who now form a significant portion of the VTC clientele, mostly deal with cognitive and mental impairments and receive less family support. Meeting the requirements for training entry, such as work capability and medical diagnoses, poses additional barriers. The VTCs' response to these challenges includes specialized support and adaptations, like theory-reduced training formats and internships, aimed at easing the training process and enhancing job market integration. However, the transition to work remains fraught with challenges related to social skills, time management, and adapting to conventional work environments, underscoring the need for targeted support and accommodations.

In summary, while VTCs offer supportive and adapted training environments, the transition to the general labor market presents multiple challenges for autistic individuals, necessitating a comprehensive approach to address these barriers effectively.

4.3 Support Measures Currently in Place

The examined VTC provides a support system at different levels to overcome factors that negatively affect the work ability of people with ASD or mental disorder. In Table 1, we summarize the specific measures to support trainees at the studied VTC regarding the addressed factors.

Table 1. Summary of Support Measures at VTCs

ASD-Related Factors

– Diagnostics and medical care: medical and psychological care on site, close cooperation with the autism ambulance of the local university hospital
– Consultations or psychological counseling possible during working hours
– Individual support to acquire coping strategies with curative educators
– Repetition of the training year possible in case of longer absences due to illness
– Sensitizing and continuing education of all stakeholders involved at the VTC
– Reduction of working hours and individual breaks possible
– Part-time training possible in the future
– Theory-reduced training possible

External Factors

– Parent-independent financing by the GFEA, utilities, and housing secured
– Individual support with social concerns from social education workers
– Support in the search for an internship company
– Up to six months of further support beyond the apprenticeship

Personal Factors

– Social skill courses, e.g., communication course
– Support in dealing with personal challenges (e.g., by psychologist, co-trainee)
– High acceptance of queer people (e.g., transgender person)
– Vocational preparation before the training to find a suitable training area of interest
– Easy change of specializations within the training profession in the first 18 months
– Interdisciplinary rehabilitation plan meeting every half year about every participant and creation of an individual rehabilitation plan
– Working together in peer groups with other autistic people or people with mental disorder
– Encourage for being able to work independently and for giving presentations

Workplace-Related Factors

– Wearing headphones with noise cancellation while working
– Partition walls in some rooms
– Roller blinds for glare protection
– Height adjustable tables
– Small work groups
– Fixed working rooms and workplaces
– Individual aids, e.g., communication cards

5   Overcoming Challenges by Means of Assistive Technology

Overall, the findings highlight a significant gap in the current vocational training framework for autistic individuals beyond intervention by educators. There is a potential of assistive technologies in addressing these challenges and supporting more successful training outcomes.

In the following, we derive requirements for AT supporting people with ASD in different contexts. We refer to ATs as devices, tools, or software solutions designed to enhance the quality of life, accessibility, and inclusion of people with various limitations, including those with ASD. AT should be used not only for skill acquisition, but also to assist with work-related tasks, such as time management, task prioritization, and task completion. This approach ensures that individuals can continue to benefit from AT even after they have acquired the necessary skills, thus more effectively addressing these skills. Furthermore, it allows maintaining support without depending on the specific context and available support system.

Early Introduction. ATs should be introduced as early as possible in the vocational training process, as it requires systematic training to be effectively utilized [18]. This allows individuals to become familiar with the tools and incorporate them into their daily routines, thus preparing them for the demands of the workplace. The devices have to be financed by cost givers. In addition, vocational training should include the use of AT to help individuals explore which tools best match their abilities, learning profiles, and needs [18]. This exploration can be facilitated by trainers or teachers, who can provide guidance and support during the selection process. A standardized person-technology matching protocol would be helpful.

Keep AT When Transitioning to Labor Market. When individuals move into the labor market, they should be able to take their chosen AT with them and adapt it to their new work context. Therefore, high-level tasks and workplace integration as well as relating stakeholders of different contexts should be considered when designing AT for autistic people. This includes making AT it portable and adaptable to different work environments and tasks, and ensuring that it can be used for both skills training and workplace support.

Further Requirements. The context of use should meet certain requirements to ensure its effectiveness. These include

- providing adequate support for individuals during the training and implementation phases,
- ensuring compatibility with the work environment (e.g., common software, hardware, ambient light, noise level, stakeholders, etc.), and
- considering the specific needs of the individual when selecting and adapting AT solutions.

AT can also support stakeholders in the understanding of people on the autistic spectrum and vice versa.

Adaptivity. The degree of heterogeneity of people with ASD is high. Therefore, there is no one-size-fits-all approach and generalization is rarely possible. Consequently, ATs should specifically address the factors we described earlier, rather than focusing on the whole spectrum of autism, and must be adaptable to address individual needs.

External factors cannot be addressed by AT, depending on legal or cost specific factors.

Coping with Overstimulating Contexts. Challenges with overstimulating contexts could be addressed by active noise-canceling headphones, for example. Solutions were required that allow reduction of ambient noise while enabling interaction with colleagues.

Availability to and Benefits of AT for Co-Workers. New forms of communication could also improve work condition for all co-workers, as all people need non-distracting times while working, for example. This improves the suitability of such in diverse contexts. In contrast, several challenges relating to personal factors can be supported with AT. Especially tasks that require time scheduling or structured work can be supported by wearables, tangibles, and software without distracting co-workers. AT can also be beneficially applied to increase the understanding in direct or indirect forms of conversation for all participating parties. Here, ATs could support both - neurotypical and neurodivergent communication partners.

Provide AT for Workplace Situations, Not Only for Training. Additionally, other factors like the improvement of social skills have traditionally been addressed through training. It would be worthwhile to investigate whether ATs, such as augmentation AT, can support people with ASD at the workplace within social interactions (e.g., helping with small talk). By focusing on adaptability and targeting specific factors, assistive technologies can better be tailored to the diverse needs of individuals with ASD, the individual tasks and contexts to promote a more inclusive work environment for all people.

6   Discussion

This study provides insights into the challenges faced by individuals with ASD in vocational training and employment in Germany. Despite limitations such as sample size and potential bias, the findings have implications for vocational training centers and employers.

Access to Vocational Training. The study highlights barriers in accessing rehabilitation for autistic individuals, underscoring a significant gap in support systems. The dependence on parental commitment for successful outcomes is critical, emphasizing the need for more inclusive access to vocational training and employment opportunities.

Systemic Challenges. German health and social care systems are not optimally designed to support autistic individuals, particularly in vocational training and employment. This gap contributes to high unemployment and underemployment rates among this demographic. The study suggests the necessity for holistic consideration of personal, external, and workplace-related factors in supporting autistic individuals.

Role of Assistive Technology. While AT is useful in skill acquisition, there is a need for its application in workplace support, emphasizing adaptability to individual needs and the context. The study highlights the importance of introducing AT early in vocational training and ensuring its compatibility with various work environments.

Supporting Transition to Labor Market. The transition from vocational training to employment is marked by challenges such as mobility, time management, and adapting to different work environments. AT can play a crucial role in this transition, aiding in task management and adapting to new workplace contexts.

Limitations and Further Research. The study primarily reflects the perspectives of VTC trainers, suggesting the need for further research involving in-depth interviews with autistic trainees. Such research could provide a more comprehensive understanding of their experiences and needs, particularly regarding the effectiveness of AT in the workplace.

In summary, while vocational training centers in Germany are beginning to adapt to the needs of autistic trainees, there is a significant need for systemic improvements and individualized support, including the effective use of AT, to better facilitate their transition into the general labor market.

7   Implications and Recommendations

This study's findings have significant implications for policymakers, Vocational Training Centers (VTCs), and technology developers in Germany, particularly in the context of supporting individuals with Autism Spectrum Disorder (ASD).

For Policy Makers. Policymakers should consider revising current health and social care systems to better accommodate the unique needs of individuals with ASD, particularly in vocational training and employment sectors. There is a need for policies that ensure more inclusive access to vocational training and rehabilitation, beyond the current reliance on family support. Additionally, funding mechanisms for assistive technologies (AT) should be expanded to make these tools more accessible, considering their vital role in the workplace for individuals with ASD.

For Vocational Training Centers. VTCs need to adopt a more individualized approach to training, recognizing the diverse needs of autistic trainees. This includes integrating AT into training programs early and systematically, ensuring trainees are familiar with these tools by the time they enter the workforce. VTCs should also focus on developing partnerships with employers to facilitate smoother transitions for trainees into the general labor market, providing ongoing support during this critical phase.

For Technology Developers. Developers of AT should prioritize creating adaptable, context-sensitive technologies that cater to the varying needs of individuals with ASD. This includes designing AT that can be tailored to different work environments and tasks, ensuring its utility beyond just skill acquisition. There is also a need for research and development in AT that supports both skill training and workplace integration, particularly in direct and indirect forms of communication.

In summary, the broader implications of this study call for a collaborative effort among policymakers, VTCs, and technology developers to create a more inclusive and supportive environment for individuals with ASD in vocational training and the workplace. This includes policy reforms, individualized training approaches, and the development of versatile AT solutions.

8   Conclusion

This study provides a comprehensive analysis of vocational training and rehabilitation for autistic individuals in Germany, focusing on office-based work environments. We conducted context observations at a VTC and expert interviews to identify challenges and effective practices in vocational training and transition to the labor market. Our findings underscore the importance of enhancing access to rehabilitation services, supporting systems, and the potential role of assistive technology (AT) in facilitating successful vocational training and workplace integration.

The research highlights a crucial need for increased rehabilitation access and supportive systems for autistic individuals, facilitating proper diagnosis, treatment, and improved work outcomes. The study also reveals various measures implemented at the VTC to address challenges faced by autistic trainees. Significantly, it illuminates the role of AT in transitioning from vocational training to the labor market. While current AT focuses on skill acquisition, there's a pressing need to explore its application in specific workplace tasks for autistic individuals.

Looking forward, the study advocates a more holistic while individualized approach in vocational training and employment for autistic individuals. This encompasses broader access to support systems, heightened awareness and understanding among employers, and development of new AT tailored for workplace support.

Future research should delve deeper into the experiences of autistic trainees, incorporating their perspectives on training programs and support systems. Additionally, a thorough context analysis in real workplaces is necessary to grasp the challenges faced by autistic individuals in employment settings. Identifying suitable contexts for AT application and customizing these technologies to individual needs will be pivotal in bridging the gap between vocational training and employment. Respecting the diversity within the autistic population and providing equal employment opportunities is vital, along with involving all stakeholders in the design process and enhancing collaboration between neurotypical and neurodivergent individuals.

Acknowledgments. The project is funded by the German Federal Ministry of Labor and Social Affairs (BMAS) under the grant number FT 1 - 58330.

References

1. Alverson, C.Y., Yamamoto, S.H.: Employment outcomes of vocational rehabilitation clients with autism spectrum disorders. Career Dev. Transit. Except. Individ. **40**(3), 144–155 (2017)
2. Ara, Z., Hong, S.R.: Exploring design space of collaborative career-seeking experience for people on autism spectrum (2023)
3. Attwood, T., Gray, C.: The discovery of "aspie" criteria. Morning News **11**(3), 18–28 (1999)
4. Benssassi, E.M., Gomez, J.C., Boyd, L.E., Hayes, G.R., Ye, J.: Wearable assistive technologies for autism: opportunities and challenges **17**(2), 11–21. https://doi.org/10.1109/MPRV.2018.022511239
5. Boyd, L.E., et al.: SayWAT: augmenting face-to-face conversations for adults with autism. In: Proceedings of the 2016 CHI Conference on Human Factors in Computing Systems, pp. 4872–4883. ACM. https://doi.org/10.1145/2858036.2858215
6. Chen, J.L., Leader, G., Sung, C., Leahy, M.: Trends in employment for individuals with autism spectrum disorder: a review of the research literature. Rev. J. Autism Dev. Disord. **2**, 115–127 (2015)
7. Espelöer, J., Proft, J., Falter-Wagner, C.M., Vogeley, K.: Alarmingly large unemployment gap despite of above-average education in adults with ASD without intellectual disability in Germany: a cross-sectional study. https://doi.org/10.1007/s00406-022-01424-6
8. Gal, E., Ben Meir, A., Katz, N.: Development and reliability of the autism work skills questionnaire (AWSQ). Am. J. Occup. Ther. **67**(1), e1–e5 (2013)
9. Gedam, S., Paul, S.: A review on mental stress detection using wearable sensors and machine learning techniques. IEEE Access **9**, 84045–84066 (2021). https://doi.org/10.1109/ACCESS.2021.3085502
10. Gentry, T., Kriner, R., Sima, A., McDonough, J., Wehman, P.: Reducing the need for personal supports among workers with autism using an iPod touch as an assistive technology: delayed randomized control trial **45**(3), 669–68. https://doi.org/10.1007/s10803-014-2221-8
11. Hill, D.A., Belcher, L., Brigman, H.E., Renner, S., Stephens, B.: The apple ipad^{TM} as an innovative employment support for young adults with autism spectrum disorder and other developmental disabilities. J. Appl. Rehabil. Couns. **44**(1), 28–37 (2013)
12. Holwerda, A., Van Der Klink, J.J., Groothoff, J.W., Brouwer, S.: Predictors for work participation in individuals with an autism spectrum disorder: a systematic review. J. Occup. Rehabil. **22**, 333–352 (2012)
13. Mechling, L.C., Gast, D.L., Seid, N.H.: Using a personal digital assistant to increase independent task completion by students with autism spectrum disorder **39**(10), 1420–1434. https://doi.org/10.1007/s10803-009-0761-0
14. Pfeiffer, B., Brusilovskiy, E., Davidson, A., Persch, A.: Impact of person-environment fit on job satisfaction for working adults with autism spectrum disorders **48**(1), 49–5. https://doi.org/10.3233/JVR-170915. https://content.iospress.com/articles/journal-of-vocational-rehabilitation/jvr915

15. Sanfilippo, F., Raja, K.B.: A multi-sensor system for enhancing situational awareness and stress management for people with ASD in the workplace and in everyday life. In: Proceedings of the 52nd Hawaii International Conference on System Sciences, pp. 4079–408. https://doi.org/10.125/59845

16. Schelinski, S., Roswandowitz, C., von Kriegstein, K.: Voice identity processing in autism spectrum disorder **10**(1), 155–16. https://doi.org/10.1002/aur.1639

17. Solomon, C.: Autism and employment: implications for employers and adults with ASD. J. Autism Dev. Disord. **50**(11), 4209–4217 (2020). https://doi.org/10.1007/s10803-020-04537-w

18. Syriopoulou-Delli, C.K., Stefani, A.: Applications of assistive technology in skills development for people with autism spectrum disorder: a systematic review. Res. Soc. Dev. **10**(11), e163101119690 (2021)

19. Tomczak, M.T.: Employees with autism spectrum disorders in the digitized work environment: perspectives for the future. J. Disabil. Policy Stud. **31**(4), 195–205 (2021)

20. Vogeley, K., Kirchner, J.C., Gawronski, A., van Elst, L.T., Dziobek, I.: Toward the development of a supported employment program for individuals with high-functioning autism in Germany. Eur. Arch. Psychiatry Clin. Neurosci. **263**, 197–203 (2013)

21. Wali, L.J., Sanfilippo, F.: A review of the state-of-the-art of assistive technology for people with ASD in the workplace and in everyday life. In: Pappas, I.O., Mikalef, P., Dwivedi, Y.K., Jaccheri, L., Krogstie, J., Mäntymäki, M. (eds.) I3E 2019. LNCS, vol. 11701, pp. 520–532. Springer, Cham (2019). https://doi.org/10.1007/978-3-030-29374-1_42

22. Walsh, E., Holloway, J., McCoy, A., Lydon, H.: Technology-aided interventions for employment skills in adults with autism spectrum disorder: a systematic review. Rev. J. Autism Dev. Disord. **4**, 12–25 (2017)

23. Walsh, L., Lydon, S., Healy, O.: Employment and vocational skills among individuals with autism spectrum disorder: predictors, impact, and interventions **1**(4), 266–275. https://doi.org/10.1007/s40489-014-0024-7

24. Wang, M., Jeon, M.: Assistive technology for adults on the autism spectrum: a systematic survey. Int. J. Hum. Comput. Interact., 1–20 (2023)

Deaf in STEM: A New Approach to Measuring Problem Solving, Deductive Reasoning, Creativity, and Ability

Shireen Hafeez[✉]

Deaf Kids Code, West Lafayette, IN 47906, USA
shireen@deafkidscode.org

Abstract. Deaf Kids Code (DKC), founded in 2015 by Shireen Hafeez, is a national organization aimed at equipping Deaf, deaf, and hard of hearing students with computer science, technology, and design thinking skills to enhance their societal and economic participation. Utilizing Deaf role models from diverse professional backgrounds, DKC has reached over 15,000 participants across 50 locations nationally, extending its impact internationally as well. The organization adopts a kinesthetic learning model, emphasizing experiential learning and fostering a growth mindset among students, positioning them as creators, not just consumers, of technology. DKC's objectives include expanding STEM/CS learning opportunities, inspiring students towards STEM careers, and advocating for integrating such education into deaf education curricula. Collaborations with industry giants like Scratch Foundation, Microsoft, Google, AWS, and Dell Tech Crew bolster DKC's efforts, while interventions like ASL-accessible digital tools and partnerships with educational institutions and corporations further bridge the digital divide for the Deaf community. Through internships, shadowing opportunities, and specialized workshops, DKC facilitates hands-on learning experiences and career pathways in technology for Deaf individuals, paving the way for greater inclusivity and empowerment in the tech industry.

Keywords: Deaf Education · Disability and Computer Science · Workforce Development · Inclusive Education · Vocational Rehab · Disability Services · Disability Career Training

1 Introduction

1.1 Organization

Deaf Kids Code (DKC) is a national outreach organization established in 2015 by Shireen Hafeez. The mission of the organization is to promote computer science, technology, and design thinking skills to students who are Deaf, deaf, and hard of hearing (HOH) as a tool to increase their ability to participate in society socially and economically. The organization has facilitators who serve as Deaf role models and come from professional backgrounds like engineering, graphic design, and education. We have served more

M. Antona and C. Stephanidis (Eds.): HCII 2024, LNCS 14698, pp. 47–57, 2024.
https://doi.org/10.1007/978-3-031-60884-1_4

than 15,000 participants in over 50 locations nationwide through our programming. We have also supported learning opportunities for international partners in Indonesia, Vietnam, Mexico, Puerto Rico, Panama, Guatemala, Pakistan, Kenya, and China. The organization uses a kinesthetic learning approach (Tranquillo, 2008), emphasizing an experiential process for each student.

Purpose. To promote a growth mindset to change Deaf students' attitudes towards how they interact with technology. To help students understand they can be both consumers and creators of technology. The organization's first principle is that 'the digital age is the great equalizer'. The barriers to participating in society faced by previous generations can be largely overcome because of the digital age.

Terminology. Deaf and deaf will be interchangeably used throughout the course of this paper. The capital D in Deaf refers to a cultural and linguistic identity that includes American Sign Language (ASL) terms. The lower case usage of the word refers to the spectrum of deaf identities and is meant to be inclusive of Deaf and Hard of Hearing communities.

Objectives. a) To increase the number of Deaf participants in STEM/CS by expanding our curriculum to include machine learning modules. b) To inspire more students to pursue employment in STEM. c) To inspire more Deaf Education and to embed this education into the day-to-day curriculum in an interdisciplinary manner. All objectives are backed by a deaf-culturally-centered foundation with role models with STEM backgrounds. DKC also emphasizes developing students' agency in the learning process. Teachers learning alongside the students is encouraged. This provides informal training without the pressure and demands on the limited bandwidth of the educator. The project building experience supports demonstrated problem solving, applied deductive reasoning, and logic.

1.2 Impact

We have trained outreach teams with the National Technical Institute for the Deaf (NTID) on our curriculum. NTID's North Regional STEM Center (based in Alabama) has spread the DKC curriculum to over 14 states in the southeast. The schools we work with are provided our programming at no cost, and, in exchange, faculty are required to learn alongside students, providing them with informal training.

Partnerships with Scratch Foundation, Microsoft MakeCode, Google Pixel (live captioning technology), AWS certifications, and Dell Tech Crew are a few examples of industry collaborations.

1.3 Interventions

Building more digital access tools that support Deaf students who depend on American Sign Language (ASL). The lack of ASL content in the computer science and technology curriculum has long been a barrier to access for this part of the population. Creating this type of content increases access to learning for communities that are generally deprived of these opportunities. ASL is an entirely different language from spoken

English. For native ASL users, embedded captions alone do not bridge the information gap. Universal design principles are still not widely utilized in online courses or virtual learning platforms.

Scratch Foundation is the world's largest free creative coding platform and community for young people. Most Deaf students have inequitable access to these types of online computer science learning experiences, and lack of inclusionary elements widen the digital divide. DKC created the "ASL Getting Started with Scratch" online tutorial to help fill that gap and reach a disenfranchised community of students.

CourseBolt, a DKC project facilitated by Deaf in the Cloud founder Rob Koch, is an online teaching platform featuring courses taught in ASL by a Deaf role model and technologist. Topics like Data Science and SQL are featured and offer real world applications. CourseBolt helps adults looking to "skill up" and increase their competitiveness in the workforce.

Deaf Powerhouses in Tech is a series of pre-recorded presentations by Deaf/deaf/HOH technologists facilitated by DKC. All featured technologists have had similar experiences in terms of their personal journey, identities, struggles, and positions in the tech workforce. The technologists provide practical advice, serve as a roadmap, and teach best practices in self-advocacy to deaf communities at large.

Microsoft MakeCode Arcade is an online integrated development environment (IDE) for developing retro arcade games using drag-and-drop block programming and JavaScript. The IDE allows students to write, edit, run, test, and debug code in a browser. In order to increase its reach in deaf communities, DKC created an ASL tutorial on how to navigate the platform. This instructional video is embedded on the Microsoft MakeCode Arcade website.

We also collaborated with NTID by giving them our launch project with Khan Academy, which, after years of partnership, allowed us to create our own tutorials in ASL. They also agreed that once a certain number of videos are completed in a subject, they will eventually allow ASL to become an official language on their open source learning platform. This monumental effort requires a national coalition in order for the community at large to eventually become beneficiaries. NTID was successful in winning additional funding through their arm organization DeafTEC. The leads of the effort agreed that the initial videos should be on Basic Algebra.

1.4 Outreach

Several internship/shadowing opportunities have been created in partnership with Cook BioTech. A number of CompTIA A + certifications were obtained by deaf participants through a bootcamp we initiated in partnership with the National Technical Institute for the Deaf (NTID). AWS hosted a "Teen in Tech Day" in partnership with Detroit Public Schools and the Michigan Department of Education-Low Incidence Outreach. UIPath hosted a "Teen in Tech Day" in partnership with the Lexington School for the Deaf. Salesforce hosted a "Teen in Tech Day" in partnership with Indiana School for the Deaf. P&G offered an IT training internship and apprenticeship program, which successfully trained almost a dozen students transitioning out of high school.

2 Discussion

The digital age has enabled a new generation of people on all spectrums of deafness to participate in society in ways that would have been unthinkable decades ago. This level of potential contribution to the world has accelerated a rise in conversations in the arena of accessibility, as well as diversity, equity, and inclusion. Those discussions have not been exclusive to the confines of educational institutions. They have also expanded into for-profit spaces. Companies are beginning to recognize the valuable contributions from these high potential untapped communities. Thus far, Deaf Kids Code (DKC) has been able to expand its reach at the scale it has because of the creation of opportunities, the increase in accessible learning tools, culturally-centered instruction, and the incorporation of universal design. All these advances have democratized the promotion of computer science and technology skills. While the national CS education community has reached out to more under-represented groups, students with disabilities have generally been excluded from outreach efforts in the mainstream. According to Katherine Schaeffer of the Pew Research Institute (2023), approximately 15% of all students attending public school K-12 have a disability so they are bypassing a significant portion of the student population.

Though these expansion efforts have led to more research and data collection, the employment outcome has largely not been affected. In other words, the alignment of skilled talent and employer demand is still a work in progress. Vocational rehabilitation, career counselors, and transition service agencies often miss that online learning, certificate programs, apprenticeships, and other training opportunities are also a pathway to acquire high-demand job market skills. In today's tech landscape, employers do not need to rely solely on prior job titles and degrees to assess a candidate's abilities. STEM skill acquisition can be a game changer for disenfranchised students. According to the U.S. Bureau of Labor (2023), "information technology occupations are projected to grow much faster than the average for all occupations from 2022 to 2032. About 377,500 openings are projected each year, on average… The median annual wage for this group was $100,530 in May 2022, which was higher than the median annual wage for all occupations of $46,310." These projections are significant for stakeholders: the essential dynamics needed to increase opportunities lack a meaningful ecosystem. The transition of people from school to vocation training and career is largely broken.

According to the National Deaf Center (2019), unemployment still remains mostly stagnant: only 53.3% of deaf people aged 25–64 were employed in 2017, compared to 75.8% of hearing people, an employment gap of 22.5%. This percentage does not include the additional breakdown of the severely underemployed and low wage earners, often overlooked in these statistics. Another report showed that less than 2% of deaf people work in Information Technology sectors. A larger push can be made towards these career pathways. Not only does messaging need to be more inclusive on a national level, more funds and time should be spent building capacity.

Traditionally schools are not designed to cultivate talent of individuals or equipped to explore alternative pathways. This is especially true when it comes to disability and deaf education programs. John Rosales (2021) and his colleague claim that standardized tests only determine which students are good at taking tests, offer no meaningful measure of progress, and have not improved student performance. In addition, they claim that foundationally the tests are racist, classist, and sexist, and that scores are not predictors of an individual's future success. Elaine Smolen wrote, "The world of Deaf/Hard of Hearing education has changed dramatically since our program's founding in 1906. For much of the 20th century, Deaf/Hard of Hearing students attended residential schools for the deaf where they learned American Sign Language (ASL) or other forms of visual communication. Today, approximately 85% of those children attend mainstream schools with their typically hearing peers" (Columbia News). This is a significant point because the vast majority of this student population are often not beneficiaries of STEM programs, if they exist in their schools.

The World Health Organization (WHO) estimates that there are approximately 466 million people worldwide with disabling hearing loss, about 6.1% of the world's population. Of these individuals, 34 million are children, and most live in low- and middle-income countries. As of 2021, according to the Hearing Loss Association of America, there are an estimated 48 million Americans living with some degree of hearing loss. An estimated 6.6 million Americans aged 12 and older have severe to profound hearing loss in one or both ears.

A white paper I co-published through Microsoft Research (Hafeez, 2021) laid out the disparity in detail. We wrote, "Currently, computer science is not integrated as a standard part of the K-12 general education curriculum in many schools. Some schools do not include computer science courses due to a lack of resources, training, and expertise. Within K-12 Special Education programs, there are multiple challenges. It is difficult to imagine when students can learn computer science, given the time spent on remediating reading, writing and mathematics for students with dyslexia, other learning disabilities, and attention deficits (Ferrell, Bruce, & Luckner, 2014) and engaging in speech therapy, physical therapy, and occupational therapy. Students' needs for this facilitation support often require them to be out of the classroom during these learning opportunities. Consequently, the lack of participation in these learning experiences contributes to these students' inability to compete with their peers who can leverage a much wider variety of learning opportunities."

DKC facilitators use a kinesthetic method when teaching. Sessions are primarily lead by Deaf role models with STEM backgrounds. Our 'secret sauce': we emphasize freedom of creativity and students' agency in the learning process. Students figure out how to problem solve on their own and apply their own deductive reasoning and logic.

The organization has successfully orchestrated several collaborative partnerships, including with the National Technical Institute for the Deaf (NTID) in Rochester, New York. Shortly after NTID established its North Regional Stem Center (NRSC) in Alabama, Deaf Kids Code provided training to the team there and taught them some of our curriculum. The team also shadowed DKC in several states, which helped them develop their own methodology to evangelize CS, technology, and design thinking skills.

To date, the most significant pilot we facilitated was launching a CompTIA A + certification boot camp for the deaf in partnership with NTID. CompTIA is a recognized leader in professional technical certifications. Obtaining an A + certification indicates the job seeker knows the basics of hardware, networks, and computer systems. Consequently, someone with an A + certification can qualify for such roles as entry-level IT person, field service technician, IT support manager, and data support technician.

The partnership between the DeafTEC Resource Center and CompTIA to establish the 'DeafTEC Ready' program provided a full-time 10-week hands-on training course (bootcamp) in person on May 25 - August 5, 2022 on the Rochester Institute of Technology campus for 12 non-matriculated Deaf/HOH individuals. The bootcamp was taught in ASL by NTID professor James Mallory. Bootcamp participants from around the country learned technical skills such as repairing and maintaining computer equipment, networks, and operating systems as well as key workplace skills like professional communication and problem-solving. After completing their training, participants sat for the CompTIA A + (Core 1 and Core 2) certification exams.

Upon successful certification, participants received direct job placement assistance from CompTIA's career services staff. Certified participants also received credit for three 3-credit courses from NTID's Applied Computer Technology associate degree program that can be used to pursue an associate degree at NTID or another college that accepts the credit. The report also states, "This professional development, referred to as the DeafTEC Ready program, will be offered in a direct communication environment in which all instructors and learners know ASL, allowing everyone to communicate freely. By participating in the DeafTEC Ready program, learners who are deaf/HOH will learn technical skills such as repairing and maintaining computer equipment, networks, and operating systems, as well as key workplace skills such as professional communication and problem solving. After completing their training, the learners will sit for CompTIA A + certification exams, the industry standard for launching a career in IT. Upon successful certification, these individuals will receive direct job placement assistance from CompTIA's career services staff. Certified individuals will also receive credit for three courses in NTID Applied Computer Technology associate degree programs. These courses can be used toward an associate degree at NTID or at other colleges across the country that accept the credit. The project will help meet industry's need for computer support technicians and for a more diverse workforce by increasing participation of deaf/HOH individuals in highly skilled technician careers. This increased participation can also increase acceptance of deaf/HOH individuals within these workplaces and beyond. The project will increase access to CompTIA training materials and exams by reducing language barriers that will not only help deaf/HOH test-takers but other English language learners. Thus, the project can help people from different communities obtain CompTIA A + certification and enter the IT workforce. The DeafTEC Ready program will also help employers develop the sensitivity and skills to create an inclusive workplace where not only deaf/HOH employees but all employees can succeed. This project is funded by the Advanced Technological Education program that focuses on the education of technicians for the advanced-technology fields that drive the nation's economy."

This initiative was intended to have underemployed/unemployed deaf adults from around the country interested in skilling up in a fully accessible learning environment. Those individuals had to commit to staying in the program for its entirety and residing on the Rochester campus. The program included 12 deaf participants, of which 10 passed the Core 1 and Core 2 exams. Five found employment, four of which were in tech positions. Two are enrolled in RIT/NTID's Applied Computer Technology associate degree program. Donna Lange (one of the co-PIs of the program) shared some quotes from the students who participated in this historic program. One student who participated in the pilot said, "This bootcamp made a major difference for my life. It pivoted my career trajectory. Despite the hard parts, I would absolutely do this bootcamp again. I am really grateful to everyone. Thank you to everybody who made this possible. You changed my life and created opportunities for me." Another participant stated, "In a few years, I'm going to know eleven other deaf people in the technology industry." This feedback must be considered a significant marker in measuring the confidence gap that feeds into the disparity of participation in the larger overall field of tech and the deaf. More transition programs should use this as a model in their workforce development initiatives.

According to the NSF report, Pearson VUE, which hosted the exam, shut down the tests of a few of the Deaf participants. Some of the issues test takers faced were "noise in the background." Apparently they weren't aware that there was no set standard to providing accommodations and that flexibility in supporting each individual may be unique from one another. NTID needed to write a letter to Pearson VUE explaining that some test takers are Deaf and request extended time. The attached letter stated, "As has been our experience in the past with our AAS students, the boot camp participants had a difficult time taking online exams with online proctors." Co-PI Mallory spent a considerable amount of time scheduling online exams and confirming that the Deaf test takers would have extended time for the test, and ensuring they were provided approved standard accommodation. Lange stated, "Communication barriers were prevalent during the testing process. When the proctor comes on the screen before the exam starts, they give instructions and need to approve the testing area. We developed a plan for our participants, who do not use their voice, to hold up a paper sign indicating that they are Deaf, needed to use the chat feature for communication, and would immediately discard the paper outside of the room. This worked a few times. However, when one participant was four questions into the test, the proctor shut down the test, stating that having a paper was not allowed."

Other issues mentioned in the NSF report claimed that when they contacted Pearson VUE to see if proctors could be informed ahead of time that a test taker was Deaf, they were told that this could not be done since they have hundreds of proctors located all over the world. Proctors are assigned to their tests right before the exam starts, and they simply did not have a system in place that could alert proctors to the situation. As a result of these findings, they are working with CompTIA and Pearson VUE to find a solution to ensure a more inclusive experience for future participants. Lange also said, "This is just one more example of the challenges Deaf individuals face in earning industry-recognized certifications and underlines the need for accessible test centers."

As part of our early quest to build out more equitable access to STEM education in American Sign Language, we forged a partnership with Khan Academy. Khan Academy was one of the first and most globally used open source educational platforms. Along with their thousands of video tutorials that span dozens of different subjects, they also have different language options embedded in numerous tutorials via subtitles. We were able to achieve an agreement with the company that ASL access to the tutorials should be available. We built 36 videos that provide ASL interpreters within the computer science video library. After getting feedback from the community, we decided that the optimal results and benefits from this initiative will be best served if we had the topics actually taught or led by native ASL users. Luckily, the Khan Academy team gave us full reign to do so, and also agreed that if we created a full topic, ASL would be added as a language option on their site. We then approached our partners at NTID and requested that their institute take charge of the project. They were successful in getting a budget added into their NSF DeafTEC Resource Center award #1902474. After feedback from the Deaf community, it was decided that the most urgent topic was Basic Algebra. We flew in a half dozen math teachers from Deaf schools to convene on standard signs and the overall goals of the project. Since then over 270 videos are being piloted by teachers from the California School for the Deaf, Fremont, Colorado School for the Deaf and Blind, Rocky Mountain Deaf School, and the Texas School for the Deaf, and the Utah Schools for the Deaf and Blind. More data on the impact of that has not been released for this paper.

We have had involvement with two more open source learning platforms. These partnerships allowed us the liberty to create tutorials on their platforms in ASL by using a culturally centered approach in which the tutorial is facilitated by a culturally Deaf person whose native language is ASL. Our collaborations with Scratch Foundation and Makecode Arcade are both open source free block based creative learning segways into entry level CS. Scratch originally came out of the MIT Media Lab; Makecode Arcade was created by researchers at Microsoft.

Founded in 2007, Scratch is the world's largest free coding community for kids. In 2022, they reached more than 100 million registered users. It is a web-based block-based platform that allows for collaboration and encourages individual creativity. Its premise of "learning to code" is not simply about gaining a set of technical skills, it's about developing a voice and learning how to organize, express, and share ideas. Children who make projects with Scratch use coding to bring their ideas to life through the animation capabilities. Deaf Kids Code partnership led to creating a "Getting Started with Scratch" tutorial in American Sign Language that was embedded in their website video library.

The instructional video we created on the MakeCode Arcade was launched in January 2020, and describes itself as "a retro 2D online game development environment. With a few blocks or lines of code, you can create your own custom games for others to play." All of these projects fall under our first principle: 'the digital age is the great equalizer'. These companies enthusiastically appreciate our ability to increase inclusion to Deaf students. The feedback from educators regarding access to these language-centered learning tools was that it supported them as an additional resource, especially during CS ed Week and hour of code.

Digital inclusion and access are vital aspects to the infrastructure of a CS/tech education pathway, but workforce development is yet another layer. We had launched a new program called Teen in Tech where we would offer a day of shadowing and career exploration in a live in person experience. We had provided several of these immersive shadowing field trips with UIPath in New York City, Amazon Web Services (AWS) in Detroit, and Salesforce in Indianapolis.

An example of AWS experience involved all vital stakeholders like the Michigan Department of Education - Low Incidence Outreach (MDE-LIO), Detroit Public Schools Community District, and the Michigan Department of Civil Rights (MDCR) Division on Deaf, DeafBlind, and Hard of Hearing (DODDBHH). We included a presentation from Brenden Gramer, a Deaf software engineer from Amazon, followed by a career showcase highlighting different professional job titles and duties, and then offered the students a hands-on learning experience, which included an introduction to AWS cloud computing software. The feedback from students was that they never understood what cloud computing was, even though they used Google Drive and other technologies regularly. Their perspective on where they can see themselves in the future was altered in a positive way.

The superintendent Celeste Johnson of Detroit Public Schools was astonished at the response and enthusiasm of her students. She said, "students with disabilities are bypassed entirely from these types of opportunities. This was life changing for them and to me as I've been in education for 30 years and have never seen something so modern and forward in terms of workforce development for our kids."

Another example of the impact from Teen in Tech we hosted at UIPath in NYC. We supported two days of programming for eight high school students from the Lexington School for the Deaf, of which none had any previous coding experience. The day before our trip to UIPath was to first introduce them to the basics of coding, building algorithms, deductive reasoning to solve some of the challenges we gave them. By the time they were being instructed to use UIPath automated software, the students were able to write code and created their own digital automated bot. If they hadn't attended our session the day before, they would not have understood concepts like "run the code."

The guidance counselor from the school was impressed with her students and how quickly they could grasp concepts that otherwise were perceived as out of reach. We also lead a family-based program out of LaunchCode in St. Louis, MO, where students learned front-end programming, and we had a panel of leading employers from the area discuss inclusion hiring and skills they are looking for. In that showcase were Deaf representatives from Boeing, Geospatial Association, Nestle, and more. The families that participated were inspired and felt that this changed their plans about how to navigate post-graduation skill development. Vocational rehabilitation in all these cases have done little in modernizing their knowledge and partnerships within the states they support.

Recently we have launched machine learning modules into our curriculum. With the high demand of artificial intelligence and machine learning skills, the increase of employment gaps could be exacerbated if education does not catch up to integrating these concepts. Even in the mainstream tech industry, technologists are constantly having to continue their education to keep us with the rapidly ever-changing landscape. We have hosted programming sessions to 200 students using visual recognition training on their laptops and the students were able to grasp the concepts within the first set of trying. Many of them would use ASL signs to train the computer to recognize and correctly identify. Some students wanted to experiment with other objects to train the computer to differentiate colors, shapes, etc. They were able to understand the logic and come up with their own experiments when programming.

We learned early on that the deprivation of exposure to successful role models, learning opportunities, and practical universal design approaches were the essential foundations to supporting this population. Educators lacked the understanding that alternative pathways in acquiring digital skills existed. Most in these arenas of education and workforce develop an understanding of the disparity in meaningful pathways that bridge the vocation and employment skills gap. This is especially profound in special education, deaf programs, vocational rehab, transition services, and schools for the deaf.

Our methodology also demands that educators learn alongside our students as a form of informal training. We have found this to be successful and encouraging to otherwise intimidated educators. Examples of the ripple effect post-DKC programming are Indiana School for the Deaf set up a makerspace, Rhode Island School for the Deaf created a robotics club, and some teachers who became champions for CS in their schools. This generation of digital natives have so much talent and ability to apply their unique perspectives into the ecosystem of innovation. Luckily there are deaf founders that are setting a precedent.

Wavio was created in 2015 by an all-Deaf founding team based on their own lived experiences. They wanted to be able to access the world that was not reliant on hearing people. They used AI and Machine Learning technology to recognize and classify millions of sounds. They created a unit that connects to a home Wi-Fi system that can transmit alerts to one's device like a smartphone, iPad, or laptop. Their technology can also be programmed to recognize any sound from the doorbell to a crying baby. While there are mainstream user cases for this technology, the foundation conception of this was from the deaf experience. InnoCaption founder is also deaf and founded this mobile app-based provider of real-time captioning of phone calls for the deaf and hard of hearing. Imanyco, founded by a deaf woman, was created to help people identify in the live captions who the individual speakers are. Her app, Koda, transcribes the words of each individual speaker so that you know exactly who is speaking. "Since it's a web-based application, you can start using it immediately on any device that is connected to the internet, without needing to download anything beforehand."

There are many more innovations that have and are being deaf lead not mentioned here, but these examples cited are meant to exemplify the possibilities of cultivating more deaf people into the ecosystem. These high potential untapped communities of students are the future leaders and innovators who will better our world.

Disclosure of Interests.   The author has no competing interests to declare that are relevant to the content of this article.

References

Bat-Chava, Y.: Diversity of deaf identities. Am. Ann. Deaf **145**(5), 420–428 (2000)

Columbia News. https://news.columbia.edu/news/evolution-deaf-and-hard-hearing-education-tea chers-college. Accessed 10 Jan 2024

Computer and Information Technology Occupations. https://www.bls.gov/ooh/computer-and-inf ormation-technology/home.htm#:~:text=About%20377%2C500%20openings%20are%20p rojected,for%20all%20occupations%20of%20%2446%2C310. Accessed 02 Feb 2024

DellTechnologies: Thought leadership perspectives. https://www.dell.com/wp-uploads/2021/12/ deafkidscode-440x440.jpeg. Accessed 15 Jan 2024

Education for employment pathways. https://www.microsoft.com/en-us/research/uploads/prod/ 2021/02/Report-Education-for-Employment-Pathways.pdf. Accessed 17 Jan 2024

Google Blog. https://blog.google/outreach-initiatives/grow-with-google/computer-science-stu dents-disabilities. Accessed 31 Jan 2024

Hear Me Out. https://hearmeoutcc.com/capital-d-small-d-deaf. Accessed 20 Dec 2023

Khan Academy instructional mathematics videos in ASL. https://www.rit.edu/ntid/sites/rit.edu.ntid/files/deaftec/math-conference/McAnlis%20et%20al%20Khan%20Academy%20Instructional%20Videos%202022.pdf. Accessed 30 Jan 2024

LinkedIn article. https://www.linkedin.com/pulse/introducing-launch-coursebolt-free-online-course-library-/?trk=organization-update-content_share-article. Accessed 15 Jan 2024

Napier, J.: The D/deaf–H/hearing debate. Sign Lang. Stud. **2**(2), 141–149 (2002)

National Council on Aging. https://www.ncoa.org/adviser/hearing-aids/hearing-loss-statistics. Accessed 15 Jan 2024

National Deaf Center. https://nationaldeafcenter.org/wp-content/uploads/2019/10/Deaf-People-and-Employment-in-the-United-States_-2019-7.26.19ENGLISHWEB.pdf. Accessed 13 Jan 2024

Pilot program to prepare adults who are deaf or hard-of-hearing for skilled technical positions in information technology. https://www.nsf.gov/awardsearch/showAward?AWD_ID=2100330. Accessed 20 Dec 2023

Rosales, J., Walker, T.: The racist beginnings of standardized testing: from grade school to college, students of color have suffered from the effects of biased testing. ASEE Peer (2021)

Schaeffer, K.: What federal education data shows about students with disabilities in the U.S. Pew Research Center (2023)

Scratch Team Blog. https://medium.com/scratchteam-blog/tagged/deaf-kids-code. Accessed 25 Jan 2024

Supporting deaf people: Closing the employment gap. https://nationaldeafcenter.org/news-items/supporting-deaf-people-closing-the-employment-gap. Accessed 05 Jan 2024

Tranquillo, J.: ASEE PEER: Kinesthetic learning in the classroom. ASEE PEER (2008)

Where to Start: Backward Design. https://tll.mit.edu/teaching-resources/course-design/backward-design/#:~:text=Backward%20design%20prioritizes%20the%20intended. Accessed 31 Dec 2023

World Health Organization. https://www.who.int/news-room/fact-sheets/detail/deafness-and-hearing-loss. Accessed 14 Jan 2024

USA Today. https://www.usatoday.com/story/news/2017/04/02/fundraising-efforts-help-deaf-children-learn-coding/99959284. Accessed 20 Jan 2024

YouTube. https://youtu.be/DEaw9IZjuqo?si=SD6yGDfv9dGoe8yu. Accessed 20 Jan 2024

Helping Individuals with Blindness or Severe Low Vision Perform Middle School Mathematics

Joshua Howell$^{(\boxtimes)}$ ⓘ, Francis Quek ⓘ, Angela Chan ⓘ, and Glen Hordemann ⓘ

Texas A&M University, College Station, TX 77843, USA
`howjosh@tamu.edu`

Abstract. This paper addresses the performance of mathematics by Individuals with Blindness or Severe Low Vision (IBSLV) at the middle school level. At these levels, students can no longer rely on counting strategies and tangibles to perform mathematics but must instead rely on processes that are accomplished procedurally. These strategies, however, often prove difficult for IBSLV, as they depend on students having vision in order to read, insert, and manipulate mathematical text at precise locations on the page. In this research, we investigate how two computer systems can help IBSLV perform multidigit arithmetic in the same manner as their sighted peers—i.e., by reading, inserting, and manipulating mathematical text in a spatially oriented way. The first system is Math Melodies, an iOS application which uses Apple's VoiceOver and an onscreen keyboard to help IBSLV perform multidigit arithmetic. The second system is MathSTAAR, a device developed by the authors of this research, which affixes an embossed, tactile grid to an iPhone screen and has IBSLV insert and manipulate mathematical text using speech. We found that while both systems allowed participants to solve more than 90% of problems correctly, MathSTAAR's approach helped participants do so more quickly and with less frustration. Additionally, 12 of the 14 participants preferred MathSTAAR to Math Melodies, specifically noting that the former's use of a tactile grid and speech commands helped them keep track of their onscreen location.

Keywords: Accessibility · Visual Impairment · Mathematics

1 Introduction

This paper begins from the proposition that the way we read, perform, and share mathematics is not an invariant, objective ideal but is instead, like natural language [1], a social construct which makes use of our embodied nature. This can most clearly be seen in the way mathematics notations work hand-in-glove with our visual-spatial working memory [2], the way we offload our cognition to the environment (e.g., the page), and the way mathematics, in both its spoken and written forms, helps us communicate with other mathematicians at all levels. The interplay between our embodiment and these social constructs provides an instructive framework for understanding why mathematics notation in particular—e.g., the way it is read, the way it is written, the way it is manipulated, and the way it is shared—so often remains inaccessible to Individuals with

© The Author(s), under exclusive license to Springer Nature Switzerland AG 2024
M. Antona and C. Stephanidis (Eds.): HCII 2024, LNCS 14698, pp. 58–77, 2024.
https://doi.org/10.1007/978-3-031-60884-1_5

Blindness or Severe Low Vision (IBSLV), a population differently embodied than their sighted counterparts. In essence, we argue that the difficulties IBSLV face in mathematics do not come from an inability to *reason* mathematically but instead comes from mathematics notation being designed by the sighted, for the sighted.

Existing computer tools often do not provide sufficient affordances for IBSLV to utilize their visual-spatial working memory or offload their cognition to the environment (e.g., the device) in a spatially oriented way. Furthermore, what tools do exist often use specialized notation, thereby separating IBSLV from the larger community of mathematics by teaching them, in effect, a separate language.

1.1 Research Questions

Given these premises, this paper investigates the following research questions.

1. How can embodied cognition—with its implications for visual-spatial cognition and the offloading of cognition to the environment—be effectively leveraged in designing systems which help IBSLV perform mathematics in a manner similar to their sighted peers?
2. How can tangibility assist in this design given that IBSLV will (a) need to offload cognitive work to the environment but (b) will have more difficulty navigating that environment due to their diminished vision?

We address these questions by comparing two systems meant to assist IBSLV in solving multidigit addition and subtraction problems. The first is Math Melodies, an iOS application recommended by the Texas School for the Blind and Visually Impaired [3], the Perkins School for the Blind [4], and AppleVis [5]. The second is MathSTAAR, a system we have developed to help IBSLV read, perform, and share mathematics.

This research focusses on the performance of multidigit addition and subtraction at the middle school level. Work such as that done by Blackorby [6, 7] has found that the difficulties IBSLV face in mathematics begin here, the grade levels at which students can no longer rely on counting strategies and tangibles [8] to perform mathematics. Instead, they must rely on procedural processes [9] that make use of pencil and paper. As such, Steinbach has argued that "the best time to start tackling this propensity [for IBSLV to] lag behind in mathematics is in middle school." [10].

2 Related Works

In this section, we describe related works that fall into one of two categories: (1) research which has some bearing on answering our research questions and (2) tools that IBSLV use to solve mathematics problems. We note that to be included in this section work must have either (a) received a scientific evaluation with at least one IBSLV participant (excluding any who participated in the design of the tool) or (b) a well-documented tradition of use in the IBSLV community.

2.1 Nemeth Braille

Created in 1946 by Abraham Nemeth, a blind mathematician, Nemeth Braille is still used today to read and perform mathematics [11]. A number of factors suggest why this may be the case. First, Nemeth Braille is "complete," meaning that all mathematical expressions can be written unambiguously [12]. Second, because Nemeth Braille is written, IBSLV do not have to keep the entirety of an expression in short term memory. Instead, they can distribute aspects of their cognition (such as memory) to the page. Third, though individual expressions in Nemeth Braille are linearized, there remains a spatial component to Nemeth. This can most clearly be seen in Fig. 1 [13], in which the layout of the Braille mimics the layout of a traditional mathematics problem. This approach has been recommended by the National Federation of the Blind [14].

Fig. 1. A simple addition problem in Nemeth Braille

However, Nemeth also has drawbacks. First, Nemeth Braille inherently limits accessibility to the underlying mathematics contents, since Nemeth cells can only be accessed one at a time using the fingertips. Second, because it is a Braille system, it is not immediately sharable with those who cannot read it. This group includes those with sight as well as many IBSLV. Only between 10% to 28% of IBSLV know *literary* Braille [15]. And while it is unclear how many IBSLV know Nemeth, it is likely that the percentage of IBSLV who know this specialty form of Braille is lower.

2.2 Vanderheiden's Touch-and-Speak Model

In 1989, Vanderheiden introduced the "touch-and-speak" model as a way to make screen text more accessible to IBSLV. An alternative to screen readers, this model allows IBSLV to access both the content of information and its spatial location on the screen through touch (in essence, information is spoken aloud when touched) [16].

This model becomes more important as information becomes more complex. Vanderheiden notes that, "[i]n early computer systems, the spatial relationships between different items of text were usually quite simple" but that newer technologies "provide considerably greater flexibility in the display of information, and this has been taken advantage of by programmers." Using this technique, Vanderheiden argues, programmers can "provide the user with a highly intelligible voice under continuous control by the user." [16].

The Touch-and-Speak Model in Action. The touch-and-speak model has received attention since 1989. For the purposes of this study, two pieces of research are relevant.

The first is the Situated Touch Audio Annotator Reader (STAAR). Sold as an eReader for the blind, the system gives IBSLV access to the spatial layout of literary text by speaking text aloud as it is touched [17]. With this system, an iPad is augmented with an embossed tactile overlay which assists IBSLV in spatially situating themselves while they are reading. Additionally, the system reads the words to the IBSLV user at the pace at which the user glides their fingers over the words. In sum, STAAR is consistent with Vanderheiden's recommendations, as it provides "a highly intelligible voice under continuous control by the user." [18].

The second is the Talking Tactile Tablet (TTT). Developed by Hansen and Shute in conjunction with Touch Graphics, Inc., the TTT functions as a tablet with a tactile overlay on top. When a user touches the tablet, the system registers the location of the touch and reads some predefined script. TTT, however, follows fewer of Vanderheiden's specifications than STAAR does. It does not allow a user to control for speed of reading, for example. And while STAAR has a general-purpose tactile overlay, TTT's tactile overlays are specific to the expression being read. Despite this, Hansen and Shute found that IBSLV were able to solve geometric sequences using the system [19].

2.3 Performing Mathematics

In this section, we review two pieces of related work that help IBSLV perform mathematics. We note that, in order to be included in this section, a system needed to meet an additional criterion: The system could not merely perform mathematics for a participant (e.g., a calculator) but must instead provide affordances for IBSLV to solve problems themselves.

A Framework for Helping the Visually Impaired Learn and Practice Math. Elkabani and Zantout introduced a six-step framework for helping IBSLV students read, perform, and share mathematics. For our purposes, the relevant step is *Step 5: Rendering & Manipulating Math Content*. In this step, students use a desktop computer to perform algebra in different virtual "workspaces." This is primarily done using what the researchers refer to as "transformations" in which IBSLV students apply "manipulation functions" to different "sub-parts" of an expression. The outcome of these transformations is a new expression to which students can apply new transformations. By applying subsequent transformations, students can ultimately find a solution. Each "new" expression is saved in a hierarchy so that students and their teachers can check their work. Using a "separate temporary workspace," IBSLV can perform the four basic arithmetic operations [20].

We note that this system, in which participants access the expression using a keyboard, has participants navigate the parsing tree of an expression instead of its spatial layout. This limits participants ability to use their embodied cognition—most specifically their visual-spatial working memory. We also note, however, that this system does not require participants to learn a new type of mathematics notation, thereby affording them the ability to read, perform, and share mathematics with their sighted peers with ease. Additionally, the ability to save transformations in every step of the process allows participants to distribute their cognition in two ways. First, it allows them to distribute their memory to the system, so that they needn't remember every transformation they have performed. Second, it allows them to more easily share mathematics with others, as teachers can review student's work in order assess their performance [20] (Fig. 2).

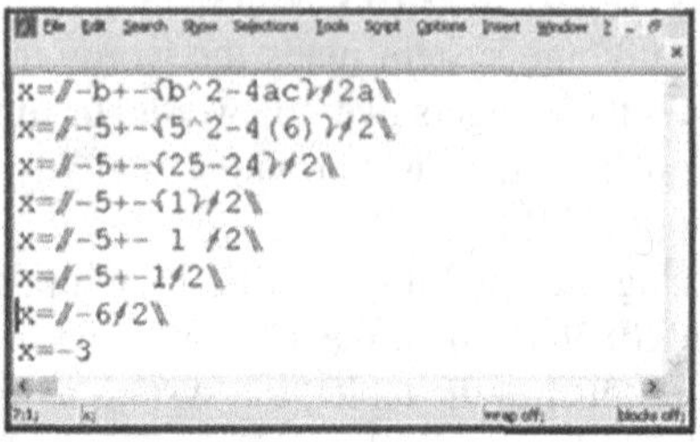

Fig. 2. A picture of the Lambda system [30]

The Lambda Editor. The Lambda Editor functions similarly to the Rendering and Manipulation Phase of Elkabani's and Zantout's framework. In this system, IBSLV are presented with a text editor which "treats the screen like a sheet of paper, in that text can be placed anywhere on it." Additionally, transformations result in new expressions so that participants can trace through their prior work if need be [21].

While the ability to place text anywhere on the screen has implications for the use of one's embodied cognition—and while the repeated display of transformed expressions allows one to distribute their cognition to the screen—participants need to learn a specialized notation called the Lambda Code. This means that sharing mathematics with someone who does not know the Lambda Code may be difficult. Finally, we note that The Lambda Editor is equipped with a calculator function, meaning the answer to some problems are "given" to IBSLV.

3 System Designs

3.1 Mathstaar

MathSTAAR is an application researcher have built for the iPhone 7 Plus [22, 23]. The system has been augmented with a tangible grid overlay (see Fig. 3). This tactile grid is distinct from other tactile overlays [19, 24, 25] in that the present grid is a general purpose—i.e., it is meant to help IBSLV navigate the otherwise smooth surface of the screen and is not meant to provide a tactile representation of the data the screen presents (e.g., the shape of the expression).

MathSTAAR primarily uses Vanderheiden's "touch-and-speak" model. Please note that given the inclusion criteria for participation in the study (see Sect. 4.2: *Study Design*), no participant could read the text on the screen, though some participants could see incomprehensible blurs.

Fig. 3. A participant uses MathSTAAR.

The application functions as follows.

1. When a participant touches a Math Element (e.g., a digit or operator), the system speaks the Math Element aloud.
2. When a participant touches the screen with two fingers simultaneously, the system reads the entire expression aloud.
3. When a participant is touching a portion of the screen that does not contain a Math Element, they hear soft, static feedback.
4. When a participant presses and holds the screen for two seconds, the system enters SPEECH INPUT MODE. Participants are notified they have entered this mode via a READY BEEP. In this mode, participants may issue a command using speech input. If the command is recognized by the system and accomplished successfully, the system emits a SUCCESS BEEP. If the command is not recognized or the command cannot be accomplished, the system emits a FAILURE BEEP.

These commands are as follows:

- INSERT: When a participant speaks a digit (e.g., "zero"), the digit is placed at the location of their touch.
- ERASE: When a participant speaks the word "erase," the Math Element they are touching is erased.
- RESET: When a participant speaks the word "reset," the screen clears all changes and is reset to its original state.
- BORROW: When a participant speaks the word "borrow," a slash is put through the number they have touched. When touching the number in the future, they hear the original number followed by the words "borrowed from."
- REMOVE: When a participant speaks the word "remove," a number which has been borrowed from is reset to its original state.

3.2 Math Melodies

Math Melodies is an application developed for iOS by Retina Italia Onlus [26]. Implemented using Apple's VoiceOver feature, the app uses a variation of Vanderheiden's touch-and-speak model. Additionally, Math Melodies also has purchase in the IBSLV community, having been recommended by the Texas School for the Blind and Visually Impaired [3], the Perkins School for the Blind [4], and AppleVis [5]. Extant research has shown that participants "found [Math Melodies] accessible and entertaining" [27] and were able to solve exercises correctly "most of the time" [28]. However, more specific findings—e.g., the percentage of problems solved correctly, how long it took participants to do so, and how difficult participants found the tasks—are not presently available. Choosing Math Melodies as a system to which to compare our system of MathSTAAR therefore serves two purposes. First, it allows us to compare our system to an industry standard. Second, it allows us to quantify the strengths and weaknesses of Math Melodies with scientific rigor.

As with MathSTAAR, the expression is displayed on the screen. While Math Melodies does not make use of a tangible grid overlay, the screen is divided into squares into which one Math Element may be placed (see Fig. 4). Like MathSTAAR, no participant could read the Math Elements on the screen, though some participants could see incomprehensible blurs.

The application functions as follows.

1. When a participant touches a Math Element, the system reads the Math Element aloud.
2. When a participant touches the text at the top of the screen, the system reads the entire expression aloud.
3. When a participant touches an empty square on the screen, the system emits a soft clicking noise.
1. Participants could only place numbers on the screen in predefined squares (see Fig. 4). When a participant touches one of these squares, they hear one of three prompts: "Equals. Press to insert an answer'" (to place an answer digit); "Carry; Press to insert an answer" (to place a carry digit); or "Regroup; Press to insert an answer" (to replace an old digit from which they have borrowed).
2. To insert or delete a digit in one of the squares described in Step 4, participants were instructed to perform the following four steps:

Fig. 4. A participant uses Math Melodies

- Participants double tapped the square.
- Action (a) caused a small, onscreen keyboard to appear at the bottom of the screen. This keyboard contained the digits 0–9 as well an "erase" button (see Fig. 4).

- To insert a digit into the selected space, the participant double tapped the digit on the onscreen keyboard.
- To erase a digit in a selected space, the participant double tapped the erase button.

4 Experimental Design

Prior to their trials, participants were asked to sign a consent form outlining details of the study such as its procedures, goals, and compensation. After signing the consent form, participants were asked to fill out a short questionnaire. This questionnaire allowed researchers to document important information such as the participant's gender, the nature of their visual impairment, and their mathematical knowledge. Those who participated in the study were given a $25 Amazon gift card. All materials and protocols were approved by our university's Internal Review Board.

4.1 Participants

Participant Qualifications. To qualify for this study, participants were required to have severe low vision. For our purposes, this is defined as having 20/200 vision or worse without corrective lenses. Participants were also required to have, at minimum, a middle school understanding of mathematics. This was so that any difficulties participants had while using the systems would be attributable to how well the system did or did not function and not a lack of mathematical knowledge. Finally, because both Math Melodies and MathSTAAR implemented Vanderheiden's touch-and-speak model, participants with severe hearing impairments were excluded from this study.

Recruitment. We used two strategies to recruit participants. First, researchers sent a mass email to students, teachers, and administrators at their university detailing the inclusion criteria mentioned in the previous subsection. Those interested in participating, as well as those who had questions about whether they qualified, contacted the lead researcher over email. Second, researchers contacted disability resource and service centers in their home state to forward recruitment emails to those who might qualify for our study. Those who were interested contacted the lead researcher on the project.

Fifteen participants were recruited for this study, 14 of whom had taken mathematics courses in college. However, it was later discovered that Participant 14 did not have the required math skills (the ability to perform addition and subtraction at the middle school level) and therefore should not have participated. Their data are not included in our analysis.

Please see Table 1 for the complete list of participants.

Table 1. A complete list of participants* Participant did not quality for study

Sex	Nature of Visual Impairment
Male	20/250
Female	20/400
Male	20/400
Female	20/200
Female	20/300
Male	20/400
Male	20/400
Female	20/400
Male	20/300
Female	20/400
Male	No vision
Male	No vision
Male	20/400
X	X
Male	No vision

4.2 Study Design

Familiarization Phase. To account for the possibility of learning curves, participants performed a "familiarization trial" with each system. In these trials, participants were given one addition problem and one subtraction problem with a maximum of three minutes to solve each. Neither system was evaluated during its familiarization trial. As one purpose of this research was to ascertain how these devices helped IBSLV offload their cognition (e.g., their memory) to the environment, participants were allowed to use the systems as they read their answers back to the researchers.

Finally, though participants needed to interact with the systems to read the expression, they were not required to interact with the system in order to solve for an answer. Given the variety of ways participants could come to an answer, participants were required to verbally communicate the answer to the researcher when they had finished.

Evaluation Phase. In the Evaluation Phase, participants performed 16 expressions— eight expressions with Math Melodies and eight with MathSTAAR. The study was within-subjects and counterbalanced with respect to which system the participant received first. Finally, the order of the eight expressions were randomized so that participants could not gain insight into the types of problems they received (e.g., increasing difficulty).

For an example list of expressions, as well as their descriptions, please see Table 2.

Problems at these levels of difficulty were chosen in consultation with a mathematics professor, who confirmed these were sufficient to demonstrate an ability perform multi-digit addition and subtraction at all levels. Lastly, many of the problems were sufficiently difficult that participants of average mathematical ability would be unable to solve them mentally.

Table 2. Examples of addition and subtraction problems as generated by Math Melodies

Difficulty (Increasing)	Addition	Subtraction
Level 1: *Addition.* Two two-digit numbers, one carry digit; *Subtraction.* Two two-digit numbers, no borrowing	26 + 93 ====	45 - 32 ===
Level 2: *Addition.* Three two-digit numbers, one carry digit; *Subtraction.* Two two-digit numbers, one borrow	92 70 + 47 ====	75 - 67 ====
Level 3: *Addition.* Three two-digit numbers, two carry digits; *Subtraction.* Two-digit number subtracted from three-digit number; no borrow	46 23 + 38 ====	356 - 35 ====
Level 4: *Addition.* Three four-digit numbers, four carry digits; *Subtraction.* Three-digit number subtracted from four-digit number;	5557 5795 + 6634 ======	6837 - 550 =====

As with the familiarization phase, participants had a maximum of three minutes per expression to solve for an answer. For consistency, expressions were generated by Math Melodies and were programmed into MathSTAAR to allow for a more direct comparison between the two systems.

During this phase, researchers recorded two categories of information: whether the expression was solved correctly and how long the participant worked on the problem. Participants were also given two NASA Task Load Index surveys (NASA-TLX) [29] to record their subjective workload—one after using each system. This data was used for the quantitative analysis. Additionally, researchers recorded participants' interaction with the system using a document camera. This data was used for the qualitative analysis. Research also asked questions about comments participants had made during the trials. Lastly, participants were asked which system they preferred.

5   Quantitative Results

To evaluate the effectiveness of MathSTAAR and Math Melodies, we measured three sets of statistics: correctness, the amount of time it took to solve each problem, and subjective workload as defined by the NASA-TLX. Normality of the Effort, Frustration, and Mental Demand data was verified using the Shapiro-Wilk Test [30]. A paired samples t-test was used to calculate p-values. The time-for-completion data and the NASA-TLX data for Performance and Temporal Demand were not normally distributed, so a nonparametric test, the Wilcoxon Signed Rank Test for Paired Samples [31], was used to find p-values. Finally, due to the increased risk of Type I errors when performing multiple tests (12 in total), we used Benjamini-Hochberg False Discovery Rate (BH-FDR) correction [32] to reduce alphas for statistical significance.

5.1   Correctness

Correctness was measured solely to ensure that MathSTAAR did not reduce the ability of subjects to perform mathematics. No statistical analysis was done on this data. Correctness was defined by the participant speaking the correct answer to the researcher. MathSTAAR had the same high correctness rate (94%) as Math Melodies (92%).

5.2   Completion Time

The time taken to complete each problem was measured as the difference between the point in time when the participant began a math problem and the point in time when they finished saying their answer back to the researcher. This metric was analyzed in three ways: (1) Overall completion time was used to broadly compare how long it took participants to complete eight problems with MathSTAAR vs. eight problems with Math Melodies. (2) The time taken by level was used to measure how the systems performed as complexity increased. (3) The time taken during addition and subtraction problems was used to compare how well the systems performed in these categories.

Overall completion time was significantly lower with MathSTAAR than with Math Melodies. Additionally, MathSTAAR outperformed Math Melodies with Level 2, Level 3, and Level 4 problems (see Table 2 for definitions). No statistical significance was detected for Level 1 problems. Finally, MathSTAAR had lower completion times for both addition and subtraction problems. For data from our statistically significant findings, please see Table 3 on the following page.

5.3   Nasa-Tlx

After BH-FDR correction, researchers found MathSTAAR reduced participants' Frustration to a statistically significant degree. There were no other statistically significant findings from our NASA-TLX data. For data from our statistically significant findings, please see Table 3 on the following page.

Table 3. Statistically Significant Time Findings

Metric	Statistics	MathSTAAR	Math Melodies
Overall Completion Time	Mean	65.73 s	89.67 s
	Standard Deviation	51.20 s	72.36 s
	Statistical Significance	$t(108) = 4.77$, $p < .0001$, $\alpha = 0.0042$	
Level 2 Time	Mean	41.70 s	68.07 s
	Standard Deviation	24.95 s	61.64 s
	Statistical Significance	$t(26) = 2.32$, $p = 0.008$, $\alpha = 0.025$	
Level 3 Time	Mean	51.96 s	84.26 s
	Standard Deviation	28.76 s	58.85 s
	Statistical Significance	$t(26) = 3.07$, $p < 0.001$, $\alpha = 0.0125$	
Level 4 Time	Mean	116.96 s	152.11 s
	Standard Deviation	68.91 s	85.66 s
	Statistical Significance	$t(26) = 3.09$, $p = 0.0016$, $\alpha = 0.017$	
Addition Time	Mean	76.59 s	105.02 s
	Standard Deviation	54.99 s	80.30 s
	Statistical Significance	$t(55) = 4.03$, $p < 0.001$, $\alpha = 0.008$	
Subtraction Time	Mean	54.26 s	73.45 s
	Standard Deviation	44.57 s	59.43 s
	Statistical Significance	$t(52) = 2.68$, $p = 0.002$, $\alpha = 0.02$	

6 Qualitative Results

The video recordings of the sessions yielded 317 min of video data which were ana-lyzed using a two-round open coding methodology [33]. In the first round, researchers segmented the videos into touch patterns—i.e., the path of a touch. Researchers indepen-dently labeled each touch pattern for directional movements (e.g., forward horizontal touch) and second order movements (e.g., "reading one's column"). A coding dictionary was created based on labeling agreements, with either a consensus label or new label being created for any disagreements.

In the second round of coding, researchers discussed any coding disagreements to reach a consensus label. Consensus was determined by reviewing the video segment together and referring back to the coding dictionary to discuss the most suitable label. Most disagreements were due to human error. Small modifications to the coding dic-tionary were made if a new, unexpected touch pattern was encountered. We calculated an inter-rater reliability Kappa score of 0.69, which was substantial enough to proceed with the coding process. Please see the coding dictionary below.

Table 4. Statistically Significant NASA-TLX Findings: Frustration

Statistics	MathSTAAR	Math Melodies
Mean	4.14	7.79
Standard Deviation	3.53	5.81
Statistical Significance	t (13) = 2.66, p = 0.027, α = 0.029	

6.1 Coding Dictionary

- **Keyboard on Screen**: *Math Melodies keyboard is visible on the screen*

Commands

- **Inserting [Carry I Answer I Digit]**: Participant is inserting either a carry digit, an answer digit, or a digit somewhere else on the screen.
- **Borrowing**: Participant is borrowing from the selected digit.
- **Erasing**: Participant is erasing the selected digit.
- **Speech: [Insert Carry I Insert Answer I Insert Digit I Borrow I Erase I Reset]**: SPEECH INPUT MODE has begun; a participant is either inserting a carry digit, inserting an answer digit, inserting a digit somewhere else on the screen, borrowing, erasing, or resetting the screen.

Navigation

- **Navigate to [First I Second I Third] Row**: *Participant navigates to a specific row. Navigate to [Ones I Tens I Hundreds I Thousands I Ten Thousands] Column: Participant Navigates to a Column.*

Reading

- **Touch While Answering**: Participant touches the answer while reading the answer back to the researcher.
- **Touching [Answer I Carry I Borrow]**: Participant is either touching an answer, carry or "borrow" digit.
- **Touching Operator**: Participant is touching the operator.
- **Check Work**: Participant returns to a solved part of the expression to check their work.

Directional Reads

- **Upward Diagonal Glide**: Participant glides their finger across the screen in an upward diagonal direction.
- **Upward Vertical [Glide I Glide w/ Pause I Tapping]**: In an upward vertical direction, the participant either glides their finger across the screen, glides their finger across the screen but pauses at each Math Element, or taps each Math Element.

- **Downward Vertical [Glide | Glide w/ Pause | Tapping]**: In a downward vertical direction, the participant either glides their finger across the screen, glides their finger but pauses at each Math Element, or taps each Math Element.
- **Upward Vertical [Glide | Glide w/ Pause | Tapping]**: In an upward vertical direction, the participant either glides their finger across the screen, glides their finger but pauses at each Math Element, or taps each Math Element.
- **Forward Horizontal [Glide | Glide w/ Pause | Tapping]**: In a forward horizontal direction, the participant either glides their finger across the screen, glides their finger but pauses at each Math Element, or taps each Math Element.
- **Backward Horizontal [Glide | Glide w/ Pause | Tapping]**: In a backward horizontal vertical direction, the participant either glides their finger across the screen, glides their finger but pauses at each Math Element, or taps each Math Element.

Non-Directional Reads

- **Swipe:** The participant makes a short swipe across the screen to move to the next Math Element. This is a feature of iOS's VoiceOver and was only available in Math Melodies.
- **Single Tap**: Participant touches a Math Element and instantly removes their finger.
- **Pause:** Participant touches a Math Element but does not instantly remove their finger.

6.2 Participant Strategies

In this section, we present our qualitative findings from observations of participants using MathSTAAR and Math Melodies. For the remainder of this section, we focus on the strategies participants most commonly used.

Math Melodies. *Reading Expressions.* Participants predominately approached reading the expression in two ways: (1) reading the operator and then immediately moving to the ones column to begin solving (without first reading the digits as numbers using a horizontal touch); (2) reading the operator as well as either some or all of the numbers.

Five participants read the entire expression by tapping the text at the top of the screen (see Fig. 4) for all of the expressions. Three participants read the expressions row-by-row using Forward Horizontal Glide w/ Pause and Forward Horizontal Tapping for six of the eight expressions. One participant read the operator before reading the digits in column-by-column fashion for six of the eight expressions. The remaining participants read the digits column-by-column first, read the operator second, and then began solving the expression using either the Downward Vertical Tapping or Downward Vertical Glide w/ Pause strategies.

Solving Expressions. In total, 13 participants read the expressions column-by-column when solving, while Participant 15 read both columns and rows. Swipes were utilized by those who were familiar with the VoiceOver feature on the iPhone (e.g., participants 4, 11, and 15) as it allowed the system to read elements of the screen aloud.

Only four participants consistently used carry digits for all addition problems. Similarly, only three participants who used borrowing in subtraction problems consistently used it in a majority of the expressions.

Participant 2 used mental math to solve all problems, while Participants 5, 7, and 9 used mental math in only some of the expressions. We also observed that a majority of participants touched the answer either immediately before or while reciting the answer to the researcher. We refer to this strategy as "Touch While Answering."

MathSTAAR. *Reading.* Like Math Melodies, participants using MathSTAAR mainly approached the expressions in two ways: (1) reading the operator and then immediately moving to the ones column to begin solving (without first reading the digits as numbers using a horizontal touch); (2) reading the operator and either some or all of the numbers.

Four participants read the entire expression (by touching the screen with two fingers) for seven of the eight expressions. Four participants read the expressions row-by-row using Forward Horizontal Glide w/ Pause touches and Forward Horizontal Tapping for four expressions. Three participants read the operator before reading the digits column-by-column for all expressions. The remaining participants read the digits column-by-column first, read the operator second, then began solving the expressions using either the Downward Vertical Tapping or Downward Vertical Glide w/ Pause strategies.

Solving expressions. Similar to Math Melodies, five of the participants who used carry digits (a majority of such participants) used them for all the addition expressions when required. For subtraction expressions, borrowing was less common (three participants). As with Math Melodies, Participant 2 used mental math to solve all expressions. Mental math was performed in half of the total expressions by Participant 5 and only one expression by Participant 7. Additionally, nine participants touched the answer either immediately before or while reciting their answer.

6.3 Preferences

When asked, 12 of 14 participants said they preferred MathSTAAR. The primary causes of this were (1) MathSTAAR's use of speech input and (2) its tangible grid overlay, which participants said helped them navigate the otherwise smooth surface of the screen.

7 Discussion

While the high correctness rate of both systems validates the way each implements Vanderheiden's touch-and-speak model, MathSTAAR did so while being less time consuming and less frustrating, both to a statistically significant degree (see Tables 3 and 4). Additionally, when asked which system they preferred and why, 12 of 14 participants said they preferred MathSTAAR and that the primary reason for this was MathSTAAR's use of speech input and a tangible grid overlay.

The importance of tools which allow IBSLV to both read and perform arithmetic more quickly cannot be overstated, as prior research has shown that IBSLV require, on average, between 1.5-times and twice the amount of time as their sighted counterparts to perform tasks [34]. Additionally, research has shown that ease-of-use (of which low frustration is a crucial component) is predictive of whether a tool will be used by IBSLV [35–37]. This finding is especially important with respect to mathematics, as IBSLV frequently do not progress past middle school mathematics [6, 7]. As such, we observe that IBSLV will be more likely to continue their journey to more complex mathematics if the process is both less time consuming and less frustrating.

These findings are further underscored by the relative low-level of difficulty of these problems. As was described in Sect. 1.1: *Research Questions*, these problems were chosen because middle school-level mathematics is where IBSVL begin to fall behind their peers [6, 7] and, as such, is where other researchers have argued interventions should first be made [10]. However, we note that even at these relatively low-levels, the techniques employed by MathSTAAR—most specifically, the speech input and the tangible grid overlay—allowed IBSLV to solve these problems more quickly and with less frustration to a statistically significant degree.

7.1 Research Questions

How can embodied cognition—with its implications for visual-spatial cognition and the offloading of cognition to the environment—be effectively leveraged in designing systems which help IBSLV perform mathematics in a manner similar to their sighted peers? With respect to spatial cognition, we observe that both MathSTAAR and Math Melodies employed Vanderheiden's touch-and-speak model, thereby giving participants access to the spatial arrangement of mathematical expressions. This served two purposes.

First, the use of a spatial arrangement allowed participants to bring their visual-spatial cognition to bear on the performance of multidigit arithmetic. We note that the findings presented in Sect. 6: *Qualitative Results* demonstrate that, with the exception of Participant 2 (who solved all problems mentally), the manner in which participants solved problems in both systems was a profoundly spatial one—e.g., participants used horizontal movements to read numbers and successive vertical movements to either add or subtract digits in columnar space. In Sect. 6.1: *Coding Dictionary*, these strategies are referred to as "Directional Reads." Additionally, participants were able to read, insert, and manipulate mathematical text at precise locations on the screen.

Second, because this spatial arrangement was the conventional way mathematics is expressed, participants performed multidigit addition and subtraction in the same manner as their sighted peers. Unlike the work cited in Sect. 2: *Related Work*, the ability to perform mathematics in this way can help IBSLV read, perform, and share mathematics with their sighted peers instead of separately.

With respect to distributed cognition, we observe that solving problems typically involved offloading one's cognition to the environment (e.g., the devices). The importance of this ability can be seen with respect to two strategies: the Touch While Answering strategy (in which participants reread their answers either before or while speaking it aloud to the researcher) and the Check Work strategy (in which participants revisited their past work to confirm its accuracy). Furthermore, the prevalence of the Touch While Answering strategy is consistent with how multidigit addition and subtraction is performed. This is so in two respects: (1) we observe that in the performance of addition and subtraction using pencil and paper, answers are not created all at once but in a series of step-by-step actions. Indeed, the final answer is only "discovered" when all steps have been completed. (2) This process is one in which an answer is written "backwards"—i.e., answers are written from right-to-left but are read from left-to-right. As such, the Touch

While Answering strategy would be impossible without the ability to offload memory to the screen in a spatially oriented way.

Finally, we note that one reason that MathSTAAR's speech input was preferred to Math Melodies' onscreen keyboard was that speech input, as used here, works better with spatial cognition. For example, to insert a digit at a specific place on the screen, participants touched that part of the screen and spoke the digit they wanted to insert. This process helped them keep their physical location. By contrast, an onscreen keyboard meant that participants needed to locate a position on the screen and then navigate to another location (the onscreen keyboard) to insert a number in the original space.

How can tangibility assist in this design given that IBSLV will (a) need to offload cognitive work to the environment but (b) will have more difficulty navigating that environment due to their diminished vision? We observe that, as was described in Sect. 6.3: *Preferences*, 12 of 14 participants preferred MathSTAAR to Math Melodies and that a key reason for this preference was MathSTAAR's use of a tangible grid overlay. According to the participants, this overlay helped them situate themselves on the otherwise smooth surface of the screen. This preference was most clearly articulated by Participant 13, who received the Math Melodies condition before the MathSTAAR condition. After the Math Melodies condition, this participant said they would have liked if the system had spoken aloud the column in which he was reading (e.g., the "ones column"). However, the participant said the extra verbal feedback was unnecessary in MathSTAAR due to the tangible grid overlay.

We also observe that these results further underscore the importance of tangibility in user interface design for IBSLV. The results presented here show that, for IBSLV in particular, tangibility plays an especially important role in assisting them in the navigation of an environment they would otherwise struggle to access.

8 Conclusion

In this paper we contribute an understanding of how embodiment can be used to convey the rich, spatial information encoded in mathematical notation, information important to both its reading and performance. We show that Vanderheiden's touch-and-speak model is particularly powerful for conveying this information. We also show that using a tangible grid overlay can lead to both quicker solving times and lower levels of frustration. These findings have implications for the way that speech input can be used to allow IBSLV to offload their cognition to the environment in a spatially oriented way as well as the importance of tangibility for helping IBSLV navigate an environment most would navigate via sight.

9 Future Work

Future work in this space exists on three fronts. First, this work can be expanded to different types of math problems, such as multiplication, division, and algebra. Second, as discussed in Sect. 8: *Conclusion*, systems such MathSTAAR may facilitate IBSLV and the sighted sharing mathematics. This should be studied with respect to multidigit addition, subtraction, division, and multiplication as well as more complicated mathematics, such as algebra and calculus. Third, it may be observed that math problems rarely exist by themselves. Instead, they are often embedded in surrounding text and graphics (e.g., textbooks), all of which are spatially arranged. Understanding how to support this more "real world" scenario is important for both the IBSLV community as well as research into HCI techniques involving embodiment and tangibility.

Acknowledgements. This project was supported by NSF Grant, CHS Program IIS-1910622.

References

1. Newen, A., De Bruin, L., Gallagher, S., Johnson, M.: The embodiment of language. In: Newen, A., De Bruin, L., Gallagher, S., Johnson, M. (eds.) The Oxford Handbook of 4E Cognition, pp. 622–640. Oxford University Press (2018). https://doi.org/10.1093/oxfordhb/978019873 5410.013.33
2. Hegarty, M., Kozhevnikov, M.: Types of visual-spatial representations and mathematical problem solving. J. Educ. Psychol. **91**(4), 684–689 (1999)
3. Texas School for the Blind and Visually Impaired, "Math Melodies," (2014). https://www.tsbvi.edu/tx-senseabilities/issues/spring-summer-2014-issue/math-melodies
4. Perkins School for the Blind, "Math Melodies App: Young Students," https://www.perkins.org/resource/math-melodies-app-young-students/
5. Apple Vis, "Math Melodies | AppleVis," (2017). https://www.applevis.com/apps/ios/education/math-melodies
6. Blackorby, J., Chorost, M., Garza, N., Guzman, A.: The academic performance of secondary school students with disabilities (2003)
7. Blackorby, J., Cameto, R.: Changes in school engagement and academic performance of students with disabilities. Wave 1 Wave 2 Overview 1–8 (2004)
8. Amato, S., Hong, S., Rosenblum, L.: The abacus: instruction by teachers of students with visual impairments. J. Visual Impairment Blindness **107**, 262–272 (2013). https://doi.org/10.1177/0145482X1310700403
9. Anderson, C.R., Hoffmeister, A.M.: Knowing and teaching middle school mathematics: a professional development course for in-service teachers. School Sci. Math. **107**(5), 193–203 (2007). https://doi.org/10.1111/j.1949-8594.2007.tb17783.x
10. Steinbach, S.: Looking beyond vision: supports for students who are blind or visually impaired in mathematics. In: NWEA (2022)
11. Navy, C.: The History of the Nemeth Code: An Interview with Dr. Abraham Nemeth. Raised Dot Computing Newsletter, (1993)
12. Nemeth, A.: The Nemeth Braille code for mathematics and science notation: 1972 revision. National Library Service for the Blind and Physically Handicapped by the American Printing House for the Blind (1972)
13. Denault, M.: Nemeth Spatial Arrangements. In: California Transcribers and Educators for the Blind and Visually Impaired (2012)
14. Castellano, C., Kosman, D.: Doing Math in Braille (2009). https://nfb.org/sites/default/files/images/nfb/publications/fr/fr28/fr280119.htm
15. Sheffield, R., Andrea, F., Morash, V., Chatfield, S.: How many Braille readers? Policy, politics, and perception. J. Vis. Impairment Blindness **116**, 14–25 (2022)

16. Vanderheiden, G.: Nonvisual alternative display techniques for output from graphics-based computers. J. Vis. Impairment Blindness **83**, 383–390 (1989)
17. El-glaly, Y.: Spatial Reading System for Individuals with Blindness. Virginia Polytechnic Institute and State University, Diss (2013)
18. Vanderheiden, G.: Nonvisual alternative display techniques for output from graphics-based computers. J. Vis. Impairment Blindness **83**(8), 393–390 (1989)
19. Hansen, E., Shute, V., Landau, S.: An assessment-for-learning system in mathematics for individuals with visual impairments. J. Vis. Impairment Blindness **104**(5), 275–286 (2010)
20. Elkabani, I., Zantout, R.: A framework for helping the visually impaired learn and practice math. In: 5th International Conference on Information & Communication Technology and Accessibility (2015)
21. Edwards, A., McCartney, H., Fogarolo, F.: Lambda: a multimodal approach to making mathematics accessible to blind students. In: Proceedings of the 8th International ACM SIGACCESS Conference on Computers and Accessibility (2006)
22. Howell, J., Chan, A., Hordemann, G., Quek, F.: Helping those with visiaual impairments read mathematics: a spatial approach. In: Proceedings of the 15th International Conference on PErvasive Technologies Related to Assistive Environments, Corfu (2022)
23. Howell, J., Chan, A., Hordemann, G., Quek, F.: Mathematics as interactive multimedia. In: 25th IEEE International Symposium on Multimedia, Laguna Hills (2023)
24. Landau, S., Wells, L.: Merging tactile sensory input and audio data by means of the talking tactile tablet. In: Proceedings of EuroHaptics (2003)
25. Kane, S., Morris, M.W.J.: Touchplates: low-cost tactile overlays for visually impaired touch screen users. In: Proceedings of the 15th International ACM SIGACCESS Conference on Computers and Accessibility, 2013
26. Retina Italia Onlus: "Math Melodies," Retina Italia Onlus. https://apps.apple.com/us/app/math-melodies/id713705958. Accessed 1 Feb 2023
27. Ahmetovic, D., Alampi, V., Bernareggi, C., Gerino, A., Mascetti, S.: Math melodies: supporting visually impaired primary school students in learning math. In: Proceedings of the 14th International Web for All Conference (2017)
28. Jafri, R.: Computers Helping People with Special Needs. In: Klaus, M., Deborah, F., Dominique, A., Petr, P., Wolfgang, Z. (eds.) 14th International Conference, ICCHP 2014, Paris, France, July 9-11, 2014, Proceedings, Part I, pp. 551–558 (2014). Springer, Cham https://doi.org/10.1007/978-3-319-08596-8
29. Hart, S.G., Staveland, L.E.: Development of NASA-TLX (task load index): results of empirical and theoretical research. In: Human Mental Workload, pp. 139–183. Elsevier (1988). https://doi.org/10.1016/S0166-4115(08)62386-9
30. Shapiro, S.S., WILK, M.B.: An analysis of variance test for normality (complete samples). Biometrika **52**(3–4), 591–611 (1965). https://doi.org/10.1093/biomet/52.3-4.591
31. Lee, J.C.: The Power of the Wilcoxon Signed Rank Test (1985)
32. Benjamini, Y., Hochberg, Y.: Controlling the false discovery rate: a practical and powerful approach to multiple testing. J. Roy. Stat. Soc. Ser. B Stat. Methodol. **57**(1), 289–300 (1995). https://doi.org/10.1111/j.2517-6161.1995.tb02031.x
33. Bryant, A., Charmaz, K.: The SAGE Handbook of Grounded Theory. SAGE Publications Ltd, 1 Oliver's Yard, 55 City Road, London England EC1Y 1SP United Kingdom (2007). https://doi.org/10.4135/9781848607941
34. Gompel, M., van Bon, W., Schreuder, R.: Reading by children with low vision. J. Vis. Impairment Blindness **98**, 77–89 (2004)
35. Santos, A., Ferrari, A., Medola, F., Sandnes, F.: Aesthetics and the perceived stigma of assistive technology for visual impairment. Disabil. Rehabil. Assistive Technol. **17**, 152–158 (2022)

36. Shinohara, K., Tenenberg, J.: A blind person's interactions with technology. Commun. ACM **52**(8), 58–66 (2009). https://doi.org/10.1145/1536616.1536636
37. Shinohara, K., Wobbrock, J.: SHARE ON in the shadow of misperception: assistive technology use and social interactions. In: CHI 2011: Proceedings of the SIGCHI Conference on Human Factors in Computing Systems, pp. 705–714 (2011)

Accessibility Barriers Faced When Interacting with Digital Teaching Materials: A Case of High School Students with Visual Impairment in Norway

Stephen Simei Kimogol[1]([envelope]) [ORCID] and Norun Christine Sanderson[2]

[1] Kjeller, Norway
skimogol@gmail.com
[2] Oslo Metropolitan University, Oslo, Norway
nsand@oslomet.no

Abstract. Access to education is a key element in promoting equality in Norway. Moreover, the inclusion of the ICT regulations in the education sector mandates universal design for all digital learning materials. Despite this requirement, recent studies conducted in Norway reveal that digital teaching materials lack accessibility and fail to meet current legal requirements. The objective of this study is to identify the barriers faced by high school students with visual impairments in accessing digital teaching materials. Using qualitative methods and thematic analysis, various accessibility challenges, including navigation difficulties, usability issues, incompatibility with assistive technologies, inaccessible multimedia, and a lack in digital skills, were identified. These findings indicate that existing digital teaching materials are not accessible, potentially impacting students' motivation and learning processes. The insights gained contribute to a better understanding of the needs of students with visual impairments, promoting the development of accessible digital teaching materials.

Keywords: Digital learning materials · Visual impairment · High school students · Accessibility · Universal design

1 Introduction

Inclusive education is vital for the achievement of equality and rights of education for people with disability, as enshrined in the United Nations UN Convention on the Rights of Persons with Disabilities (CRPD) [47]. The UN Sustainable Development Goal number four aims to "ensure inclusive and equitable quality education", and outcome target 4.5 aims to ensure equal access to education for vulnerable groups, including persons with disability [33]. Digital inclusion strengthens equality by ensuring everyone gets the digital literacy needed for education and employment [41]. The use of Information and Communications

Technology (ICT) in all aspects of education has tremendously increased recently [35]. Research has shown that technology can contribute to inclusion and provides new opportunities for participation for everyone [14, 48]. However, technology can also lead to exclusion if the solutions used are not universally designed [42].

Various initiatives have been undertaken globally to uphold the rights of people with disabilities. In the United States, Section 504 of the Rehabilitation Act and the Americans with Disability Act are some of the human rights laws that have a significant impact on the rights of people with disability. At the European level, the Web Accessibility Directive (WAD) [13] is a European Union initiative to build an inclusive society where all can participate in the digital economy and society. The EN 301 549 standard is another EU effort that is aimed at harmonizing accessibility standards [12]. The European Accessibility Act (EAA) is another initiative that is aimed at reducing barriers caused by different rules among the member states and thus facilitating trading and better accessible products and services across the region [8].

Norway has taken steps to ensure digital inclusion. The Web Content Accessibility Guidelines (WCAG) 2.1 standard was incorporated into Norwegian law in February 2023. The Anti Discrimination and Accessibility Act[1] prohibits any form of discrimination in Norway. Further, there is a persistent political view that the universal design of ICT will facilitate inclusive Norway [3] as indicated by the government's action plan: Sustainability and equal opportunities - a universally designed Norway (2021–2025) [24].

The Norwegian Education Act [11], Section 2-14 ensures the right to have necessary training in braille and technical aids for students with VI in primary and secondary education in Norway. The Act further states, Section 2-15, the right to free public primary and lower secondary education, including teaching materials. Section 13-3 of the Act, states that the responsible authority for public upper secondary education and training is the county authority. Statped[2] - a directorate under the Norwegian Ministry of Education offers special education services, develops, adapts, and produces teaching materials for sign language, blind children, and children with low vision (from here on called Statped books). Thus, their services are targeted at students at primary and secondary levels of education. The Norwegian Library of Talking Books and Braille (NLB) produces adapted learning materials for higher education. Persons with disabilities are provided with necessary assistive aids by municipal technical aids centers under the Norwegian Labour and Welfare Administration (NAV). The technical aids center also provides training on how to use the assistive aids.

According to the Norwegian government's action plan 2021–2025, universal design is viewed as an innovative strategy to plan and shape society and increase equality and inclusion [24]. The action plan states also that the education act committee has proposed a change from adapted learning to universal education and individually tailored education. This requires that Digital Teaching Mate-

---

[1] https://lovdata.no/dokument/NLE/lov/2017-06-16-51.

[2] https://www.statped.no.

rials (DTM) are universally designed. Despite the importance of accessibility, recent reports indicate that most DTMs in Norway do not meet the current legal requirements [37] and have shortcomings that could create barriers for students with disabilities, particularly those using assistive technologies [16]. To ensure accessible DTMs, it is necessary to identify the barriers experienced by students. This paper presents a study that aims to identify the possible barriers that high school students with visual impairments (VI) encounter when interacting with DTMs. Furthermore, the study seeks to understand these barriers from the perspectives of the students with VI and teachers of students with visual impairments.

2   Background

The ongoing digital transformation within the education sector has increased the use of technology in facilitating teaching and learning [14] as well as altered the use of teaching materials [18]. This transition was further accelerated by the COVID-19 pandemic [29,35].

In the literature, the terms digital teaching materials, digital learning materials, and digital learning aids seem to be used interchangeably. [38] argues that DTMs are generally viewed either as tools or as didactic learning programs. In relation to this, [18] presents a model consisting of four categories of teaching materials: primary text, secondary text, primary tools and secondary tools as shown in Fig. 1. [21] defined digital teaching materials (DTMs) as "a combination of digital tools, services and content specifically developed for use in schools and subjects. Typical examples include publishers' textbooks in digital format, websites associated with textbooks, animation, films, and learning games created for educational purposes" [21].

In their study on digital inclusion and accessibility barriers during the COVID-19 pandemic, [30] identified three distinct categories of digital content that differ in how they were produced. These are 1) digital content that is professionally developed by educational companies, 2) digital resources developed by teachers, and 3) digital content collected by teachers online and then refined to meet the needs of their students. All three categories present challenges and advantages, for example, the professionally developed digital content is often of high quality but usually requires the purchase of a license, while the teacher-developed digital resources can be of varying quality but does not require any license, and the digital resources collected online can save teachers' time. The authors argue that accessibility of the materials in all these three tiers varies.

2.1   How VI Users Access Digital Material

Assistive Technology (AT) is an umbrella term that describes all software and hardware that help people with disabilities accomplish tasks they otherwise could not do and foster independent living [34]. ATs currently used for non-visual web browsing include screen readers, speech recognition, alternative keyboards,

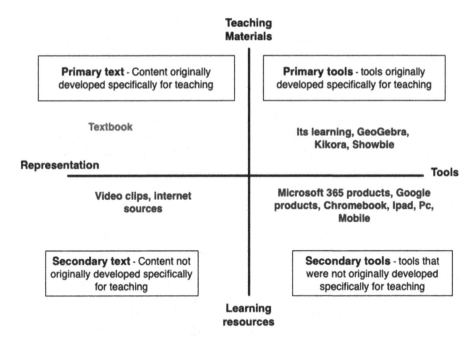

Fig. 1. Digital teaching materials model. (Adapted from [17,18])

braille displays, and refreshable braille [25]. People with VI navigate through the content of the user interface, primarily using the keyboard and screen reader in a serialized manner. This serialized navigation creates several challenges for people with VI according to [7]: the serialization of content creates an overload of vocal information, the user has no overview of the whole interface, screen readers can mix content and structure as well as announce content incorrectly depending on how the HTML is coded. Additionally, screen readers only read text content, which requires all visual elements to be coded correctly [2]. Regarding braille displays, some limitations identified in the literature are that the displays have limited character, usually a single line of 20 to 40 characters [27]. For individuals with low vision impairment, techniques used to help them interact with the interface are generally related to the magnification of graphical elements [2], which reduces the possibility of seeing the whole interface. Thus, the user has to interact with elements on the screen sequentially, increasing the cognitive load [2].

Some of the major challenges people with VI experience are registration and authentication and technical challenges, such as software updates affecting AT [15]. Further, authors suggested that there is a need for training on several levels, including the use of AT - which adds additional cognitive load, the use of AT in combination with other software, and how best to optimize the settings such that these two work seamlessly.

Students with VI typically use AT to access DTMs. In their study on AT use in the secondary level classroom, [46], found that the students used their AT devices to access a range of learning resources, including assignments, texts, emails, and learning platforms. They further found that AT use among the students during class hours varied considerably, and that students typically need more than one AT device to do their tasks [45, 46]. Similar findings were reported in [9], who also noted that students had clear preferences regarding the use of technology and braille. For students with VI, studying via eBook may require much interaction with the AT due to gestures and steps involved, which can be strenuous and time consuming [28].

2.2 Related Research

Several authors, e.g. [6, 23, 30, 39, 49] have emphasized the importance of keeping the cognitive load, i.e., the amount of working memory needed to process information, at a minimum in digital materials or resources used for learning so that the learner can focus their efforts on the content important for learning. With regards to DTMs, which may contain elements such as images, sounds, navigation, and text [30], this is highly applicable due to the high information density and complexity in the representation [23]. Thus, it becomes imperative that designers of DTMs reduce irrelevant content and elements that cause extraneous cognitive load such that learners can use their mental resources on the content that is truly essential for their learning [23, 49]. This becomes particularly relevant for people with VI, as they must split their cognitive energy between using the screen reader software and the browser and interacting with the content [44]. For example, blind users may have to listen to content before they establish whether it is essential or decide if the content is what they are looking for, thus "blind users typically go through reams of irrelevant content before they find what they need, thereby suffering from information overload" [39]. This is also supported in [6], where it is emphasized that DTMs should reduce unnecessary cognitive and bodily processes and foster students' cognitive and collaborative processes. Features that can cause unnecessary cognitive load include content that is inaccessible to students, e.g., due to poor contrast or not supporting the AT used, or content that is irrelevant to teaching aims. Examples of the latter include redundant details and images that draw the student's attention but do not yield any learning benefits. In a learning context, where students have to follow lectures and navigate through a page, it becomes important to establish the needs of different students to ensure optimal learning materials can be developed [30]. According to [19], accessibility in e-learning is viewed from two perspectives: Technical accessibility, which entails access to e-learning platforms (signing in and navigation), and pedagogical accessibility, which focuses on access to contents, tools for interactions and collaboration, and learning activities. [40] argues that "digital instructional materials are accessible when they adhere to applicable legal standards, and users can open, view, and interact with digital material".

[4] developed a framework based on the notion of affordances offered by DTMs and how the affordances are integrated into learning designs. As a point of reference, this study analyzed digital learning materials used in six courses in Danish lower secondary schools (7th-10th grade). The process of accessing content has several steps that the authors argue are time-consuming, with no apparent learning potential limiting time for other activities. The study identified several affordances: physical affordances, e.g., actions like typing, clicking, and mouse use, and a virtual affordance that includes navigating between web pages through hyperlinks, within-page navigation by scrolling, and view of media such as videos. The study found that only a few virtual affordances are made available within the DTMs, which do not fully utilize the affordances available in contemporary digital technologies. The authors therefore argue that the current digitalization of learning materials copies the traditional learning designs. Thus, the process is not capitalizing on the inherent affordances offered by digital technologies. They further argue that digitalization of learning materials is a challenging task and should take a user-oriented and pedagogical approach.

In a study that evaluated the accessibility of educational software [10], the authors state that computers offer potential for inclusion, but as most of them are based on visual communication which may lead to accessibility barriers for students with visual impairments, the need to focus on usability and accessibility still remains. The study further identified that the student must have been trained to use a keyboard and mouse alternative shortcuts to use DTMs effectively. [43] identified several challenges that make it difficult for students to access digital content. These include a lack of awareness among the teachers and designers, inadequate training, and limited access to tools that make the creation of accessible content. [20], discussing accessibility and multimodal interaction of DTMs, identified three vital elements for the accessibility of digital learning materials. These include typography, layout, and navigation. The authors pointed out that the lack of clear order might limit the readers' understanding of content, as the reader needs "to work cognitively to find a meaningful reading path" [20]. Since navigation structure helps users move within the content and know where they are and easily identify where they would like to go, it is important that the content is well organized and easily navigable with keyboard shortcuts.

3 Methodology

In this study, we used a qualitative research method. The selection of suitable research participants is crucial, requiring representation not only in demographics but also in the specific task domain, as highlighted in [26]. For instance, in this study, the emphasis was on high school students with visual impairment, which introduces specific characteristics necessary for participation. However, these criteria pose challenges in recruitment due to the need for participants to meet specific age and educational levels, coupled with the requirement of having experience in using DTMs. The combination of these constraints adds complexity to the recruitment process. Recruiting students with a representative sample of students with different visual impairment (VI) variations poses a challenge. It is therefore generally considered acceptable to have 5–10 participants for studies that consider specific disabilities [26].

3.1 Participants

The study was approved by the Norwegian Agency for Shared Services in Education and Research (SIKT). Four students with visual impairments and two teachers, one of whom also had a visual impairment, were recruited. All participants, including both students and teachers, were from the same ordinary public school. The four students were blind and they used AT such as screen readers. Participants were explicitly informed about the voluntary nature of their involvement and the option to withdraw consent at any time. The school implemented measures to safeguard participants' rights, ensuring that students were heard, and their rights were not violated. Consequently, a teacher was present during all student interviews to oversee the process.

3.2 Data Collection

We collected data through semi-structured interviews and interviewees were asked open-ended questions. We developed open-ended questions and follow-up probes based on literature studies. Open-ended questions allowed interviewees to express their experiences and barriers they experienced when using the DTMs. The interviews were conducted in March 2023 with each interview lasting about 45 min. The interviewees were given the option to select the most convenient venue for the interviews, either through an online (Teams) meeting or a physical setting. Three interviews were conducted in person at students' schools, while one took place online. Additionally, two interviews with teachers were conducted, one was done in person and the other via telephone. Five of the six interviews were recorded, while notes were taken during the unrecorded interview. The audio recordings were stored at Oslomet University's OneDrive with two-factor authentication and were only accessed by the authors and later deleted after transcription.

3.3 Data Analysis

Thematic analysis was used to get insights from the data, an approach used to identify and analyze patterns in data [5]. In brief, thematic analysis has six phases which include familiarizing with data, generating initial codes, searching for themes, reviewing themes, defining, and naming themes, and report production. We familiarized ourselves with the data by transcribing and later verified transcribed text accuracy and clarity while listening to the audio. The interviews were conducted in the Norwegian language, and the analysis focused on the transcribed text. The relevant excerpts used in the results section were translated into English. The identification of themes was done using Taguette[3], an open-source qualitative research tool. It has features such as highlighting, tagging, and tag-merging. With Taguette, the text underwent processes such as highlighting, chunk grouping, and tagging with codes. This tool streamlined the sorting of statements and the identification of potential excerpts. The analysis involved four iterations, resulting in the creation of numerous codes and sub-codes during the early thematic analysis stages. Concepts that appeared multiple times were highlighted, tagged, and grouped into sub-themes and later similar sub-themes were grouped into a main theme. For instance, aspects related to the accessibility of videos, images, and links from teachers were initially grouped into a single category. Similarly, issues concerning the use of DTMs in various contexts formed another category, later refined into a theme centered on navigation as the analysis progressed.

4   Results

The study focused on identifying the challenges and barriers students with visual impairment face while using DTMs. From the thematic analysis of the interviews, five major categories of barriers were identified: navigational barriers; usability and task completion; barriers related to images, videos, and secondary resources; compatibility barriers; and digital skills. Each of these is elaborated below. In the discussion below, P1, P2, P3, and P4 refer to students, while SP1 and SP2-VI refer to teachers.

4.1   Theme 1: Navigation

The students expressed that navigating DTMs was a significant challenge, requiring intense concentration. Because of the sequential nature of screen reader interaction, the absence of navigation features such as unlabeled buttons and unclear links, indicating uncertain destinations hinders effective interaction with the content. Consequently, the students find it challenging to perceive their location on the page (orientation) and locate the desired resource or content. Navigating content sequentially throughout a lesson proved to be both frustrating and time-consuming as expressed by one the students:

> It is such a messy set-up for me who uses tab and scrolls through everything, then it kind of gets so messy, so it requires a lot of concentration to get it done. It is the way you go through unnecessary buttons on websites, and it takes you a very long time to navigate past things you didn't necessarily need. It takes a lot more, and I have to scroll through everything when I return, while the others can press with the pointer and skip over. So, therefore, it takes much longer P4.

---

[3] https://www.taguette.org.

The participant went on to describe the challenges of navigating during lessons, emphasizing that at times, they refrain from using the resource altogether due to its perceived futility. The extended time it takes means that others in the class have typically finished reading by the time they get to it. Consequently, there are instances when they decide not to engage with the material, recognizing the impracticality of attempting it (P4). Lack of consistency in the layout and the presentation of content was found to be disorienting and it difficult to make a mental map of the content. A student expressed that "things aren't somehow consistent." They pointed out an example where one book features headings for each page, while another lacks such a structure, resulting in different formats and a lack of clear organization of document's hierarchy (P3).

While students expressed a desire to utilize the same resources as their sighted peers, they opted to use materials that had been adapted by Statped. In collaborative settings where tasks such as answering questions or making presentations based on readings are involved, the participant highlighted a preference for using Statped books. Despite the availability of other DTMs options used by their sighted peers, the participant emphasized the importance of having sufficient time to finish reading before discussions and to think through the content. Choosing the simplest solution, in this case, referred to opting for adapted books from Statped (P3). Students further expressed that the navigation process can be cumbersome during class, as it takes time to log in and locate the necessary information. As such students requested or teachers sent them resources in advance primarily to acquaint themselves with the structure rather than reading the content. In addition to the existing challenges in the DTMs, navigation barriers in secondary tools compound the difficulties for students with VI, as asserted by SP1. One instance of such a tool is OneNote, a component of Microsoft Package, employed by the school for organizing teaching materials and assignments. Unfortunately, this tool proves inaccessible to students with visual impairments (VI). Teachers argued that OneNote's confusing structure, challenging navigation, and poor compatibility with students' ATs contribute to the problem. Consequently, the school has adopted a shared folder system on OneDrive, allowing students with VI to access DTMs, assignments and adapted DTMs from Statped.

4.2   Theme 2: Usability

An additional concern related to usability, specifically in terms of effectiveness and efficiency on completing tasks such as locating content. One of the teachers expressed that the issue centers around the extended time it takes for these students to move through digital interfaces and locate the necessary information. In some cases, students requested help from their peers or teachers with navigation and finding content. Students expressed that they could have probably managed to find the content on their own, but considering the time constraints during the lessons, they would rather ask for help than waste their time. Due to these frustrations and reduced productivity, students preferred to use digital resources that have been adapted by Statped.

4.3   Theme 3: Multimedia Accessibility

Students with visual impairments encounter difficulties when resources contain only images without alternative text. One student expressed frustration with such content, emphasizing the importance of plain text over pictures for better accessibility (P3). Quote:

> Some teachers may only have pictures, which is a bit difficult for me. Then I'm like..You really should not have sent it ... Is it plain text? Thumbs up. Is it just pictures? No thanks.

When it comes to videos, visually impaired students face higher demands, potentially affecting their grades. A teacher highlighted the challenges, citing examples of videos in English with Norwegian subtitles. While sighted students benefit from translation and subtitles, visually impaired students miss out on these opportunities, placing greater pressure on them to master English (SP-VI). The teacher argued that this discrepancy could lead to discrimination, impacting grades in subjects where video content is integral to the curriculum (as above).

4.4   Theme 4: Compatibility Barriers

Interviewees highlighted the significant concern surrounding the lack of compatibility or absence of accessibility support for assistive technologies used by the visually impaired students. Difficulties arise when elements are incorrectly coded, making navigation through the keyboard and screen reader challenging. One participant illustrated this issue, stating that using the tab key only resulted in the tabs symbol without actual navigation within the window (P1). A teacher also shared an instance where the screen reader failed to reflect the visual change in focus when jumping to page numbers. Although visually the correct page was reached, the screen reader did not adjust the focus accordingly, causing difficulties for users relying on screen readers (SP2-VI). Consequently, students are compelled to resort to alternative resources. For instance, a student mentioned turning to Google Translate or searching the web for Spanish words instead of using the intended tool due to accessibility issues (P2). Additionally, another student pointed out challenges with drag-and-drop elements, which are often inaccessible to their assistive technologies, necessitating assistance from teachers or peers. The compatibility of DTMs with phones and tablets was also raised as an issue. While some applications like Teams are considered more accessible on phones, digital books from sources like Statped pose navigation challenges on mobile devices. A participant expressed frustration, stating, "I can't quite manage to search the page from mobile, so it's a bit boring to scroll to page 140 when you're on page one" (P1).

4.5   Theme 5: Digital Skills

A barrier identified during conversations with teachers was the lack of adequate digital skills. While most students had access to computers, phones, and iPads/tablets, not all were proficient in customizing their setup, especially those who had primarily used iPads/tablets before. Since students are required to use different software and perform specific tasks, teachers considered it necessary for them to have the skills to use computers and screen readers. SP1 emphasized that, "It is important to address this quickly when students come to us because if they are not proficient, it can become an obstacle in their subjects, and we don't want that." As such, the school offered training programs for students before they joined and provided additional assistance and follow-up after they started their studies. One teacher explained that students receive one-to-one training on using ATs with DTMs and the specific platforms used in the school to maximize the benefits of ATs, such as screen readers. They pointed out the diverse needs of students; some require assistance with keyboard shortcuts in both Windows and programs, while others need ongoing support to gain confidence in the programs and ATs they use.

5   Discussion

The study identified five barriers faced by students with VI in using DTMs. Navigational barriers, including inconsistent content layout and headings, ambiguous link text, and unnecessary buttons, were recurrently mentioned by participants. Previous research highlights the impact of missing information on users' navigation orientation, leading to increased cognitive load [32]. Findings further indicate that content is not presented consistently thus making the users uncomfortable from using the DTMs as this makes it difficult to predict where to find content or what will come next when navigating it. These results reflect those of [22], who explained that cluttered web pages and inconsistent design between pages confuse the users. The impact of this is that the students end up choosing resources that have been adapted by Statped as they are familiar with them. However, this discriminates against them in a way as it is expected that DTMs should at least be universally designed for all students to use them. As such the students are denied the opportunity to experience similar interaction experiences as their sighted peers.

A technical evaluation conducted by [16] on DTMs in Norway revealed accessibility issues such as navigation that can be related to the findings from this study. Today's educators have a broad range of resources at their disposal, providing them with the flexibility to tailor materials to the needs of students and curriculum objectives. Therefore, as highlighted by [18], teachers utilize tools such as OneNote to organize digital teaching materials from various sources. Findings indicate that students with VI not only struggle with the navigational issues in the DTMs but also with the inaccessibility of such tools. An implication of this finding is the possibility that even when DTMs have been made accessible if they are placed in inaccessible tools and unreachable for students with disability the academic effectiveness of the materials becomes inconsequential. Other studies such as [36] corroborate this argument. Compatibility problems between DTMs and ATs, such as screen readers and refreshable braille, present substantial challenges. Tasks that involve dragging and dropping components that demand mouse use, pose difficulties for VI students. Such issues and lack of keyboard access prevent students with VI from utilizing the AT at their disposal. A recent study in Norway emphasized the critical role of ATs in education. It argued that without AT technologies, many students with visual impairments would possibly not have participated in school and potentially students would not have completed school without AT [31]. This underscores the importance of ensuring that DTMs are compatible with ATs.

Previous research highlights the pivotal role of technical and pedagogical usability criteria in digital learning materials, emphasizing the necessity for learners to maintain a sense of control over their learning experiences [36]. In this study, the findings reveal the significant impact of usability concerns, specifically prolonged content navigational times. The lack of rich cues for navigation, and quick identification of essential sections leads to prolonged content exploration. The need for timely content access in a classroom setting becomes evident, with students with VI facing challenges in utilizing DTMs effectively for tasks like group work or in-class activities. Overall, the emphasis on ease of use proves critical, impacting students' work processes and productivity, with VI students sometimes relying on sighted peers or teachers for assistance in delivering assignments or navigating through DTMs, compromising their independence and active participation in group activities.

A recent report by [16] supports these findings, indicating that a majority of audio and video files in digital learning resources in Norway are presented without accompanying text, further emphasizing the prevalent issue of accessibility gaps in educational materials. The full affordance of DTMs cannot be realized if the formats in which content is presented lack accessibility. Examining teachers' perspectives and students' experiences, this study reveals that images, videos, and graphics remain inaccessible to students with VI, despite their widespread use. One significant challenge identified is the inaccessibility of images, particularly when lacking alternative text. Students with VI find it difficult to perceive information conveyed through images, a prevalent issue in DTMs created by teachers, such as PowerPoint slides and lecture notes. There is substantial diversity in the accessibility of these resources, mainly due to teachers lacking the skills, time, or resources to create accessible documents [30].

Digital skills emerge as an important factor, with students' lack of proficiency hindering effective interaction with DTMs and AT. Despite being digital natives, students may lack technical skills, reinforcing the importance of early training to enhance confidence and usage efficiency. Digital skills were also identified by [15] as a barrier faced by people with VI. The author argues further that AT creates an extra layer, i.e., additional cognitive and learning demands that require additional effort from the people with VI in using ICT solutions. The teachers remarked that the lack of digital skills is a barrier that limits students' interaction with DTMs and other secondary tools that the students use at the school. Lack of skills in keyboard shortcuts makes interacting and performing computing tasks challenging and generally results in them not getting the most value from AT at their disposal. Further, this limits their ability to interact, engage in learning, and demonstrate their knowledge independently. For students with VI, teachers argue that early training is vital, a perspective supported by [1], who argue that early introductions improve confidence, speed, and accuracy of usage.

This study has limitations, primarily related to the number of participants interviewed. Recruiting participants with diverse visual impairments posed difficulties. Additionally, the challenges and barriers outlined here are based on the subjective experiences of students and teachers. Consequently, these limitations hinder the generalizability of the results.

6   Conclusion

Digital learning materials offer the potential for fostering inclusive education; however, this potential faces hindrances from accessibility barriers for students with VI as highlighted in this study. The identified barriers include navigational issues, usability challenges, inaccessible multimedia elements, and compatibility issues with ATs. Factors such as inconsistent content layouts and a lack of keyboard support contribute to heightened cognitive load, impeding effective learning. The absence of alternative text, audio descriptions, and transcription in videos further compounds challenges. This study provides insights into the barriers faced by Norwegian high-school students with visual impairments, offering information to designers, developers, and producers to prioritize accessibility throughout the development process. Additionally, these insights will prove beneficial in the procurement of DTMs. Future studies can explore not only the technical accessibility but also the pedagogical usability of DTMs.

Acknowledgments. The authors would like to thank the participants in this study.

Disclosure of Interests. The authors declare that they have no conflict of interest.

References

1. Arslantas, T.K., Gul, A.: Digital literacy skills of university students with visual impairment: a mixed-methods analysis. Educ. Inf. Technol. **27**(4), 5605–5625 (2022)
2. Barreto, A., Hollier, S.: Visual disabilities. Web accessibility: A foundation for research, pp. 3–17 (2019)
3. Begnum, M.E.N.: Views on universal design and disabilities among Norwegian experts on universal design of ICT. In: Norsk konferanse for organisasjoners bruk av IT (NOKOBIT). Open Journal Systems, Bergen, Norway (2016)
4. Berthelsen, U.D., Tannert, M.: Utilizing the affordances of digital learning materials. L1-Educational Studies in Language and Literature, pp. 1–23 (2020)
5. Braun, V., Clarke, V.: Using thematic analysis in psychology. Qual. Res. Psychol. **3**(2), 77–101 (2006)

6. Bundsgaard, J., Hansen, T.: Kvaliteter ved digitale læremidler og ved pæda-
gogiske praksisser med digitale læremidler. forskningsbaseret bidrag til anbe-
falinger, pejlemærker og kriterier i forbindelse med udmøntning af midler til indkøb
af digitale læremidler [in Norwegian] [qualities of digital teaching aids and pedagogical practices with digital teaching aids. research-based contribution to recommendations, benchmarks and criteria in connection with the disbursement of
funds for the purchase of digital teaching aids.]. København. Undervisningsminis-
teriet (2013)

7. Buzzi, M.C., Buzzi, M., Leporini, B., Mori, G.: Designing e-learning collaborative
tools for blind people. In: E-Learning-Long-Distance and Lifelong Perspectives, pp.
125–144 (2012)

8. CRD, V.: Directive (EU) 2019/878 of the European parliament and of the council of
20 may 2019 amending directive 2013/36. EU as regards exempted entities, financial holding companies, mixed financial holding companies, remuneration, super-
visory measures and powers and capital conservation measures (2019)

9. D'Andrea, F.M.: Preferences and practices among students who read braille and
use assistive technology. J. Vis. Impair. Blind. **106**(10), 585–596 (2012)

10. Dini, S., Ferlino, L., Gettani, A., Martinoli, C., Ott, M.: Educational software and
low vision students: evaluating accessibility factors. Univ. Access Inf. Soc. **6**(1),
15–29 (2007)

11. Education Act: Act relating to primary and secondary education and training.
lov-1998-07-17-61. https://lovdata.no/dokument/NLE/lov/1998-07-17-61

12. ETSI, CENELEC, CEN: CENELEC: EN 301 549 V3. 1.1-accessibility requirements
for ICT products and services. European Telecommunications Standards Institute
(2019)

13. EU Commission: Directive (EU) 2016/2102 of the European parliament and of the
council (2016). https://eur-lex.europa.eu/legal-content/GA/TXT/?uri=CELEX:
32016L2102

14. Foley, A., Ferri, B.A.: Technology for people, not disabilities: ensuring access and
inclusion. J. Res. Spec. Educ. Needs **12**(4), 192–200 (2012)

15. Fuglerud, K.S.: The barriers to and benefits of use of ICT for people with visual
impairment. In: Stephanidis, C. (ed.) UAHCI 2011, Part I. LNCS, vol. 6765, pp.
452–462. Springer, Heidelberg (2011). https://doi.org/10.1007/978-3-642-21672-
5_49

16. Funka: Universell utforming i digitale læringsressurser [in Norwegian] [uni-
versal design in digital learning resources] (2021). https://www.funka.com/
no/forskning-og-innovasjon/arkiv---forskningsoppdrag/universell-utforming-i-
digitale-l\OT1\aeringsressurser/

17. Gilje, Ø., et al.: Bruk av læremidler og ressurser for læring på tvers av arbeidsformer
[in Norwegian] [the use of teaching tools and resources for learning across teaching
methods] ark&app report (2016)

18. Gilje, Ø.: På nye veier: læremidler og digitale verktøy fra kunnskapsløftet til fag-
fornyelsen [in Norwegian] [new perspectives on teaching material and digital tools in
the periode between two curriculum reforms]. Norsk pedagogisk tidsskrift **105**(2),
227–241 (2021)

19. Guglielman, E.: E-learning and disability: accessibility as a contribute to inclusion.
In: EC-TEL Doctoral Consortium, pp. 31–36 (2010)

20. Jensen, B.W., Moe, S.: Accessibility in multimodal digital learning materials. In:
Stephanidis, C., Antona, M. (eds.) UAHCI 2014, Part II. LNCS, vol. 8514, pp.
337–348. Springer, Cham (2014). https://doi.org/10.1007/978-3-319-07440-5_31

21. Kelentrić, M., Helland, K., Arstorp, A.T.: Professional digital competence framework for teachers. Norwegian Centre ICT Educ. **134**(1), 1–74 (2017)

22. Kharade, K., Peese, H.: Learning by e-learning for visually impaired students: opportunities or again marginalisation? E-learning Digit. Media **9**(4), 439–448 (2012)

23. Kieserling, M., Melle, I.: An experimental digital learning environment with universal accessibility. Chem. Teacher Int. **1**(2), 20180024 (2019)

24. Kulturdepartementet: Bærekraft og like muligheter - et universelt utformet norge [in norwegina] [sustainability and equal opportunities - a universally designed Norway] (2021). https://www.regjeringen.no/no/dokumenter/barekraft-og-like-muligheter-et-universelt-utformet-norge/id2867676/

25. Lazar, J., Allen, A., Kleinman, J., Malarkey, C.: What frustrates screen reader users on the web: a study of 100 blind users. Int. J. Hum.-Comput. Interact. **22**(3), 247–269 (2007)

26. Lazar, J., Feng, J.H., Hochheiser, H.: Research Methods in Human-Computer Interaction. Morgan Kaufmann, Cambridge (2017)

27. Leonardis, D., Claudio, L., Frisoli, A.: A survey on innovative refreshable braille display technologies. In: Di Bucchianico, G., Kercher, P.F. (eds.) AHFE 2017. AISC, vol. 587, pp. 488–498. Springer, Cham (2018). https://doi.org/10.1007/978-3-319-60597-5_46

28. Leporini, B., Buzzi, M.: Visually-impaired people studying via ebook: investigating current use and potential for improvement. In: Proceedings of the 2022 6th International Conference on Education and E-Learning, pp. 288–295 (2022)

29. Maatuk, A.M., Elberkawi, E.K., Aljawarneh, S., Rashaideh, H., Alharbi, H.: The Covid-19 pandemic and e-learning: challenges and opportunities from the perspective of students and instructors. J. Comput. High. Educ. **34**(1), 21–38 (2022)

30. Marcus-Quinn, A., Hourigan, T.: Digital inclusion and accessibility considerations in digital teaching and learning materials for the second-level classroom. Irish Educ. Stud. **41**(1), 161–169 (2022)

31. Mordal, S., Buland, T., Midtgård, T.M., Wendelborg, C., Wik, S.E., Tøssebro, J.: Betydningen av hjelpemidler og tilrettelegging for funksjonshemmede barn og unges mestring og deltakelse i skolen [in Norwegian] [the importance of assistive technologies and adaptation for disabled children and young people's coping and participation in school]. SINTEF-rapport **647** (2020). https://www.nav.no/no/nav-og-samfunn/kunnskap/forskningsrapporter-og-evalueringer-finansiert-av-nav/rapporter-navs-tiltak-og-virkemidler/betydningen-av-hjelpemidler-og-tilrettelegging-for-funksjonshemmede-barn-og-unges-mestring-og-deltakelse-i-skolen

32. do Nascimento, M.D., Brandão, A.A., de Oliveira Brandão, L., de MB Oliveira, F.C.: Overcoming accessibility barriers for people with severe vision impairment in web-based learning environments: a literature review. In: 2019 IEEE Frontiers in Education Conference (FIE), pp. 1–8. IEEE (2019)

33. United Nations: Transforming our world: the 2030 agenda for sustainable development, 21 october 2015, a/res/70/1 (2015). https://www.refworld.org/docid/57b6e3e44.html

34. Nicolau, H., Montague, K.: Assistive technologies. Web Accessibility: A Foundation for Research, pp. 317–335 (2019)

35. Nīmante, D., Kalniņa, D., Baranova, S.: Towards an inclusive digital learning environment in higher education: opportunities and limitations gleaned from working

students' remote learning experiences during Covid-19. In: Daniela, L. (ed.) Inclusive Digital Education, pp. 213–226. Springer, Cham (2022). https://doi.org/10.1007/978-3-031-14775-3_14

36. Nokelainen, P.: Conceptual definition of the technical and pedagogical usability criteria for digital learning material. In: EdMedia+ Innovate Learning, pp. 4249–4254. Association for the Advancement of Computing in Education (AACE) (2004)

37. Oslo Economics: Universell utforming av digitale læremidler – en analyse av status og relevante tiltak. rapport utarbeidet til barne-, ungdoms- og fam- iliedirektoratet [in norwegian] [universal design of digital teaching aids – an analysis of status and relevant measures. report prepared for the di- rectorate for children, youth and families] (2022). https://osloeconomics.no/wp-content/uploads/2022/01/OE-rapport-2021-69-Universell-utforming-av-digitale-laeremidler-i-grunnskolen.pdf

38. Petersen, M.A., Ulk, R.: Digitale læremidler, antropologi og et kvalitativt udgangspunkt i brugerne [in Danish] [digital teaching aids, anthropology and a qualitative starting point in the users]. Læremiddeldidaktik **3**(2), 4–9 (2010)

39. Ramakrishnan, I.V., Ashok, V., Billah, S.M.: Non-visual web browsing: beyond web accessibility. In: Antona, M., Stephanidis, C. (eds.) UAHCI 2017, Part II. LNCS, vol. 10278, pp. 322–334. Springer, Cham (2017). https://doi.org/10.1007/978-3-319-58703-5_24

40. Rice, M.F., Ortiz, K.R.: Evaluating digital instructional materials for k-12 online and blended learning. TechTrends **65**(6), 977–992 (2021)

41. Rohatgi, A., Bundsgaard, J., Hatlevik, O.E.: Digital inclusion in Norwegian and Danish schools-analysing variation in teachers' collaboration, attitudes, ICT use and students' ICT literacy. In: Equity, Equality and Diversity in the Nordic Model of Education, pp. 139–172 (2020)

42. Seifert, A., Cotten, S.R., Xie, B.: A double burden of exclusion? Digital and social exclusion of older adults in times of Covid-19. J. Gerontol. B **76**(3), e99–e103 (2021)

43. Ştefan, I.A., Hauge, J.B., Sallinen, N., Ştefan, A., Gheorghe, A.F.: Accessibility and education: are we fulfilling state of the art requirements? In: The International Scientific Conference eLearning and Software for Education, vol. 1, pp. 579–587. Carol I National Defence University (2021)

44. Theofanos, M.F., Redish, J.: Bridging the gap: between accessibility and usability. Interactions **10**(6), 36–51 (2003)

45. Tuttle, M., Carter, E.W.: Examining high-tech assistive technology use of students with visual impairments. J. Vis. Impair. Blind. **116**(4), 473–484 (2022). https://doi.org/10.1177/0145482x221120265

46. Tuttle, M., Carter, E.W.: Assistive technology use among students with visual impairments in academic classes. J. Spec. Educ. Technol. (2023) https://doi.org/10.1177/01626434231217050. 01626434231217050

47. United Nations: Convention on the rights of persons with disabilities (2008). https://www.un.org/development/desa/disabilities/convention-on-the-rights-of-persons-with-disabilities/optional-protocol-to-the-convention-on-the-rights-of-persons-with-disabilities.html

48. Warschauer, M.: Technology and Social Inclusion: Rethinking the Digital Divide. MIT Press, Cambridge (2004)

49. Whitenton, K.: Minimize cognitive load to maximize usability. Nielsen Norman Group **22** (2013)

Supporting Employee Engagement and Knowledge Transfer via Gamification in the Context of Sheltered Workplaces: A Literature Review and Interview Study

Frieder Loch[✉] and Esther Federspiel

Ostschweizer Fachhochschule, Rapperswil, Switzerland
frieder.loch@ost.ch

Abstract. Gamification describes the use of game design elements in non-game contexts. It is used in various domains to motivate users to exhibit a desired behavior. Gamification is applied in industrial settings, to motivate employees and improve quality. However, gamification with the aim of fostering knowledge sharing and in user groups with disabilities is underexplored and limited to case studies in specific use cases. This paper investigates the applications of gamification in sheltered workplaces for people with disabilities and identifies research directions. It reports a literature review and a qualitative interview study to identify motivations of employees and suggest matching gamification mechanics. Our findings indicate that gamification mechanics for these environments should avoid performance pressure and focus on motivations such as social relatedness and emphasize the achievement of teams. The paper presents and motivates prototypes of these mechanics.

Keywords: Gamification · Sheltered Workplaces · Production · Knowledge Sharing · Universal Design

1 Introduction

Gamification describes the use of game design elements in non-game contexts [6]. Gamification is often associated with the mechanics of points, badges, and leaderboards (PBL). Players earn points and badges for meaningful achievements and are then ranked on a leaderboard to compare their performance with that of their peers. PBL is the prevalent gamification mechanic in various domains [11]. There are many other gamification mechanics that address different motivations, such as avatar development, quest pursuit, or social connectedness. Various frameworks (e.g., the Octalysis framework [3]) structure these gamification mechanics.

Several studies point to the positive effects of gamification in different domains. Examples include manual work processes in production [19] and education [1]. Existing applications focus on improving performance and quality, while other outcomes of gamification remain underexplored. For example, using gamification to promote knowledge

© The Author(s), under exclusive license to Springer Nature Switzerland AG 2024
M. Antona and C. Stephanidis (Eds.): HCII 2024, LNCS 14698, pp. 94–111, 2024.
https://doi.org/10.1007/978-3-031-60884-1_7

sharing can increase job satisfaction and thereby positively impact the quality of work. Furthermore, most existing gamification projects do not address the needs of people with disabilities. By including the needs of people with disabilities in the design process, we can develop a solution that can be used by a wide range of people with different skills and abilities without the need for adaptation, and realize the principles of the universal design movement [2].

This paper contributes a research outline for the development of gamification mechanics for knowledge transfer in sheltered workplaces. The gamification mechanics address the needs of people with disabilities and should motivate knowledge transfer and enhance job satisfaction.

- It reports a qualitative literature review on the research area of gamification in industrial environments. It summarizes the research work and derives implications for gamifying additional work tasks, such as knowledge transfer.
- It reports an interview study in a sheltered workplace. The interviews address the motivations of employees to share their knowledge. It proposes gamification mechanics to support knowledge transfer.

2 Theory of Gamification

Gamification, the use of game elements in non-game contexts, has been established in several domains. The first part of this section provides an understanding of a game and its elements. The second part summarizes theoretical frameworks. Applications of gamification are summarized in the third section. A detailed discussion of gamification in industrial applications is provided in the following section.

2.1 Elements of Games

Gamification refers to the concept of game rather than play. While play is characterized by a broader and more open-ended interpretation, the definition of a game has elicited considerable scholarly debate. Suits (1978) describes a game as an effort to achieve a specific objective within a framework of established rules [25]. Jane McGonigal summarized the elements of games in her publication, "Reality is Broken: Why Games Make Us Better and How They Can Change the World." [23]. These elements include the objective, rules, a feedback system, and voluntary participation. The elements of games constitute a formal system that operates beyond the realm of ordinary life [4].

2.2 Theoretical Foundations

Different frameworks provide a structure to develop a gamified application: the game elements hierarchy by Werbach and Hunter (2012) [36], the Self-Determination Theory, along with the concept of intrinsic motivation by Deci & Ryan (1985) [5], and the Octalysis framework by Chou (2016) [3].

Game Hierarchy. Werbach and Hunter's Game Hierarchy describes the use of game elements in non-gaming contexts to increase engagement, motivation, and goal attainment [36]. The framework consists of:

- **Dynamics:** These dynamics represent the deeper emotional and psychological effects generated through the utilization of gamification mechanics, which influence the motivation and engagement of users.
- **Mechanics:** Actions and processes that maintain game activity and direct player interaction, such as point systems and challenges.
- **Components:** Visible elements like points and badges, directly perceptible to players and often the primary focus in gamification.

This hierarchy aims to deepen the understanding of how game elements at various levels can enhance engagement and motivation, influencing real-world behavior change and learning.

Self-Determination Theory (SDT). The SDT by Deci and Ryan (1985) [5], is a psychological theory of human motivation, emphasizing the influence of intrinsic and extrinsic motivations on behavior. SDT posits that optimal functioning and realization of potential are contingent upon satisfying three basic psychological needs:

- **Autonomy:** The need for self-direction and personal approval of one's actions.
- **Competence:** The need to effectively meet challenges and develop skills.
- **Relatedness:** The need for connection and interaction in a social context.

SDT suggests that meeting these needs enhances intrinsic motivation, leading to outcomes such as increased engagement, satisfaction, and overall well-being.

Octalysis. Yu-kai Chou's Octalysis Framework (2016) is a gamification model centered around eight core drives of human behavior [3]. These drives include:

- **Epic Meaning & Calling:** Engaging in something greater.
- **Development & Accomplishment:** Pursuit of progress and achievements.
- **Empowerment of Creativity & Feedback:** Creative expression and immediate feedback.
- **Ownership & Possession:** Desire for control and accumulation.
- **Social Influence & Relatedness:** Social elements like competition and collaboration.
- **Scarcity & Impatience:** Yearning for rare or exclusive items.
- **Unpredictability & Curiosity:** Need to discover upcoming events.
- **Loss & Avoidance:** Motivation to avoid loss or negative outcomes.

This framework is applied in product gamification, education, and marketing to enhance user experiences and influence behaviors. Chou emphasizes a balanced application of these drives for effective gamification design.

Discussion. The Game Hierarchy highlights the importance of structured mechanics and visible components in shaping the user experience, while SDT emphasizes the fulfillment of intrinsic psychological needs – autonomy, competence, and relatedness – for optimal motivation. Octalysis extends this understanding by mapping eight core drives that influence human behavior, offering a comprehensive view of motivational factors in gamification. These frameworks provide a robust theoretical foundation for designing gamified applications that engage and motivate users by balancing external rewards with intrinsic motivational elements.

3 Sheltered Workplaces

Sheltered workplaces are special environments that provide employment opportunities for people with cognitive or psychological disabilities. They provide structured workplaces that are specifically adapted to the needs of people with disabilities and support their skills development and independence. Sheltered workplaces are funded by the government and by providing services to the market. They sell their own products and provide services to other companies. Typical services include manual tasks such as commissioning, manual assembly, packaging, sorting, or printing.

Each team has a team lead who serves as the first point of contact for the employees and organizes the team's work processes. Work processes are adapted to the abilities of the employees. We chose a sheltered workplace as the application environment for the following reasons.

- Considering the needs and abilities of people with impairments, helps to develop a universal solution that benefits a diverse group of people, in the sense of universal design [2].
- Sheltered workplaces provide usage scenarios at the edges of the application context. This fosters the understanding of the robustness, flexibility, and overall performance of the gamification system.

These environments are open towards assistive technology. The introduction of technological assistance systems allows their employees to be more independent and participate in more complex processes.

4 Applications of Gamification

Gamification is applied in various domains. Question-and-answer platforms often allow to earn badges. Stack Overflow awards badges to reward helpful interactions, such as providing helpful answers. Badges grant new permissions, such as the ability to edit other answers. A meta-study confirms the potential of gamification, for instance in education [1]. One aspect that was associated with positive changes is social interaction. This is promoted by competitive and collaborative elements [29]. Pakinee and Puritat evaluate gamification elements, such as a ranking system that groups students based on their participation to enhance participation over time [26]. Another frequent application is in industry. This application is discussed in the following section.

4.1 Gamification in Industrial Environments

Gamification has been introduced in industrial environments and is expected to make workers more productive and reduce their error rate. Gamification can make manual tasks more engaging and increase job satisfaction. However, gamification in industry is still underexplored and the adoption is low [15]. Studies focus on case studies and are reported without quantitative evaluations [34]. A recent review concluded that research on the potential of specific gamification elements in industrial environments is needed [15]. Only few studies have been conducted in sheltered workplaces and have addressed the needs of people with disabilities, such as the study by Korn et al. [19].

In Industry 5.0, assistive systems aim to train users in acquiring new skills tailored to their individual needs and motivations [14]. Personalized gamification aligns with this objective. In addition to addressing sensory, cognitive, and motor aspects [24], it considers psychological differences, such as motivations, when determining the suitability of game elements [16]. The application of personalized gamification in production environments, especially in sheltered workplaces, is underexplored.

This literature review investigates gamification mechanics and their impact on psychological outcomes. In sheltered workplaces, the quantitative performance is often less important than the psychological outcomes. Therefore, we focus, in line with the "three primary elements of gamification" as described by Huotari and Hamari [13], on the psychological outcomes rather than performance.

4.2 Literature Review

Search Strategy. The articles were collected by searching scientific databases including "Science Direct", "IEEE Xplore", "Springer Link" using the search terms [Motivation, Gamification, Incentives]: for the application area, the search terms "Continuous Improvement Programs (CIP), Production, Industry 4.0, Manufacturing, Shop Floor Management". Articles that describe the application of gamification in industrial environments were included based on a screening of the abstract. We excluded articles that were not in English or not accessible completely.

Since the field is interdisciplinary and the area of application "improvement processes in production" has diverse names in different domains, the literature research was conducted in a snowball system. The review is not exhaustive and aims at providing an overview of the current approaches in gamification and evaluations.

Classification of the Articles. The literature included in the review was analyzed using the following classification schema: industrial context, described gamification mechanisms and elements, methodology, and identified psychological outcomes. While comprehending the gamified content aids in contextualizing gamification strategies, the methodology provides insights into the quality of the conducted studies.

4.3 Results of the Literature Review

The complete results of the review are given in the appendix (see Table 1).

Applied Gamification Elements, Mechanics and Dynamics. The literature review confirmed existing meta studies on gamification in other domains. Common gamification elements such as badges (6 occurrences) [7, 8, 15, 21, 33, 34] points (8 occurrences) [15, 20, 21, 30, 32–35] leaderboards (5 occurences) [15, 21, 30, 32, 34] and rewards [7, 34] were present in the surveyed literature.

Table 1. Results of the Literature Review

Article	Industrial context	Gamification mechanics/dynamics	Gamification elements	Method	Psychological output
Dolly et al., 2024	Assembly task in manufacturing and production	Progress bars, goals, strategy, time constraints, increasing complexity, loss aversion, achievements, and awards	Displaying performance, badges, rewards	Experiment, between group design, N = 20 university students	Significant effect on the perceived workload, an increase in mental demand, physical demand, temporal demand, effort, and frustration
Dvorak et al., 2023	Learning factory during an assembly step		Levels, badges, pop-ups, statements	Experiment between group design, N = 22 people from university environment	Higher motivation to work faster in the gamified rounds, due to the higher level of competition that the participants perceived (accompanied by more fun and identification with the execution of the task; pressure also)
Keepers, Nesbit et al., 2022	Manufacturing operations in industrial settings	Feedback, levels, progress bars	Leaderboards, points, badges,	Literature review	motivation
Tayal, et al., 2022	Supply chain management	Progress	Points, leaderboards	Literature review	Employee motivation in tedious work

(continued)

Table 1. (*continued*)

Article	Industrial context	Gamification mechanics/dynamics	Gamification elements	Method	Psychological output
Sochor, Schenk et al., 2021	Production and logistics	Production and logistics	Levelling system, trophy shelves, countdown timers, daily quests, performance graphs, fictional scenario, customizable avatars, open-world narrative; Epic Meaning and Calling; development and accomplishment; empowerment of creativity, ownership and possession, social influence, scarcity and impatience, unpredictability and curiosity, loss and avoidance	Experience Points, anonym leaderboards, employee of the week, traffic light smiley, pick-by-light system	Conceptual development of a gamification configurator for production and logistics
Ulmer et al., 2020	Validation in longboard production	Feedback, competition, cooperation, win state, rewards, achievements, quests, levels,	Points, teams, leaderboards, badges, skills, challenge	Conceptual development of a gamification framework for manual work combined with a case study for validation	

(*continued*)

Table 1. (*continued*)

Article	Industrial context	Gamification mechanics/dynamics	Gamification elements	Method	Psychological output
Warmelink et al., 2020	Logistic, production	Objectives & goals, multimedial feedback, metaphorical or fictional representations, levels, achievements, progress	Points,	Literature review	Anticipated outcome: Increased motivation
Korn et al., 2019	Student Experiment with simple redundant assembly task (10 colored Lego house assembling)	Feedback, progress and score	Time	Exploratory experimental research N = 23 (19 students & 4 trainees)	Significant higher joy in gamified group; gamified group stays in constant arousal while the other group drifts toward boredom; shows also more anger
Stadnicka & Deif, 2019	Acquisition of knowledge concerning lean manufacturing concept implementation		Lean games characteristics: subject lean manufacturing, incorporate lean tools, require teamwork, different complexity, require similar number of participants	N = 114 (students and workers from Poland and USA) Game play with surveys concerning motivational processing, cognitive and social processing knowledge test t0/t1	The game play increased attention, relevance and satisfaction as measured motivational outcomes in t1

(*continued*)

Table 1. (*continued*)

Article	Industrial context	Gamification mechanics/dynamics	Gamification elements	Method	Psychological output
Tsourma et al., 2019	Factory shopfloor	Rules, actions, levels, awards, achievements	Points, icon (badges)	Conceptual work for industry 4.0	Expected Impact: Increasing user motivation and participation in knowledge sharing and training
Liu, Huang et al., 2018	CNC machine operations in manufacturing	Competition, feedback, achievements,	Points, badges, leaderboards, challenge	Experiment with between group design (N = 60)	Increased job motivation and satisfaction through smartphone-based gamified job design
Lee et al., 2016	Automotive assembly line	Concrete goal and purpose; direct feedback of task performance & current progress; Empty cookie fill, set lottery number based on task performance (points exchange), exploration tour in exchange for task performance; virtual Pinata, balls to throw in exchange with task performance; match against selected opponent		Conceptual work with prototype testing (storyboard presentation)	Gamified interfaces provide higher motivation and a playful experience

(*continued*)

Table 1. (*continued*)

Article	Industrial context	Gamification mechanics/dynamics	Gamification elements	Method	Psychological output
Roh et al., 2016	Bolt tightening experimental condition	Gradual goal setting and feedback design; epic meaning through badges; Reactive audio-visual feedback, progress bar feedback, overall score through badges (trophy, medals, or stars); short/medium and long-term gamification		Explorative experimental setting N = 5 (age 25–27)	Excitement level and worthful emotion increased
Korn et al. (2015)	Assembly processes in sheltered workplaces	Goals & objectives, multimedial feedback, metaphorical or fictional representation, levels; Color of a pyramid step as progress, as error-indication; Pyramid board as qualitative feedback place		Literature review and prototype testing, N = 24 impaired people in a sheltered workplace	Task satisfaction, motivation and positive emotional state increased with the game

The following mechanics were most frequently utilized: progress bars (8 occurrences) [7, 15, 17, 18, 20, 28, 32, 35]; feedback [15, 17, 18, 20, 21, 28, 34, 35], levels (7 occurences) [8, 15, 18, 30, 33–35], leaderboards (5 occurences) [15, 21, 30, 32, 34] and displaying performance (4 occurrences) [7, 20, 30].

Time-related elements such as countdown timers [30] and daily quests [30] were also prevalent. Finally, goals were also frequently mentioned as employed gamification mechanisms (as mentioned in [7, 18, 35]). While the mechanics are partially absent, the connection between mechanics and dynamics, such as the overall narrative and the intended emotions, is also scarcely elucidated.

Psychological Outcomes. The literature review indicates that gamification enhances motivation for tasks, such as performing repetitive activities [18, 20, 21, 32, 33]. It also increases attention and perceived task relevance [31]. Furthermore, significant positive emotions are reported [17], including specific enjoyment of the task [17] and 'worthful emotion' [28]. Satisfaction is also heightened in gamified simple tasks within an industrial context [18, 21]. However, it is noted that gamification generally elevates emotional arousal [28], which may include negative emotions such as anger [17] and stress [7, 8]. These findings indicate that the implementation of gamification in sheltered workplaces must be approached with sensitivity, and negative emotional effects such as stress and anger should be anticipated during the design.

Discussion. Notwithstanding the documented presence of psychological outcomes, the predominant focus of most papers within our literature review lies in the enhancement of work task efficiency, thereby primarily targeting performance motivation. It is crucial to note, however, that in sheltered workplaces, performance motivation is not the primary concern, and the potential adverse psychological repercussions stemming from performance-oriented gamification necessitate consideration, as underscored by initial indications found in studies conducted by Korn et al. in 2019 and 2015 [17, 18].

The broader motivational constructs to be delineated through the incorporation of gamification mechanisms and elements are inadequately expounded upon in the majority of reviewed papers. Furthermore, only Dolly et al. in 2024 [7]delve into potential idiosyncratic variations in incentive structures (also observed by [9]). To comprehensively address these motivational factors, an in-depth understanding of what motivates individuals in sheltered workplaces is indispensable. This research gap is effectively filled by the following interview study.

5 Interview Study to Identify Gamification Mechanics

Designing successful gamification mechanics requires exploring the characteristics of the prospective users and of the environment. This requires being present on-site to study real work situations and discuss these observations with the prospective users.

The aim of the interviews was to understand what motivates people in sheltered workplaces to contribute to the improvement of their work processes. We inquired about their abilities to use technical devices and whether they would like to use them at work. We used a qualitative approach to reflect the diversity of skills and cognitive abilities of the employees.

5.1 Method

This section explains the interview method, the questionnaire, and the characteristics of the participants.

Semi-structured Interview. We developed a questionnaire to investigate the work environment and motivational factors. The interviews started with a warm-up consisting of a casual conversation about general work tasks. The main part of the interviews was conducted in line with specific types of work motivation, such as work environment, work characteristics, (social) support and trust. The interviews additionally encompassed questions concerning feedback processes and questions about the persons (e.g., experience with technology and technology acceptance).

Laddering. We used the laddering technique to derive the motives related to work engagement [10, 12, 27]. The laddering technique is used to understand customer motivations. It is a sequential method in which the interviewer poses a series of questions to the respondent, aiming to identify overarching meanings that influence the participant's perceptions [27]. Initially, interviewees were prompted to articulate their overall work motivation. They were then asked to explain the reasons for their specific motivation. Using this "probing" methodology, respondents ascend the "ladder of abstraction," reaching higher levels of complex constructs. In addition, participants were asked to list incentives that could motivate their respective feedback behaviors.

Participants. Participants were recruited from a large provider of sheltered workplaces. The participants embody a diverse spectrum of employees in terms of age, skill, and cognitive or physical ability. While one individual had recently completed their training, another was already of retirement age but continued to work. Among the respondents, two individuals were cognitively impaired, one psychologically, and one physically. All had been employed at the workplace for several years.

Analysis. The interviews were audio-recorded, transcribed, and analyzed. Each interview lasted between 20 and 30 min. Statements of the participants were assigned to different motivational factors (e.g., achievement, affiliation, or power motivation compare, for example, McClelland's motivation structure [22]). Incentives for motivation to contribute to knowledge transfer were assessed as well.

5.2 Results

The main motivational factors in sheltered workplaces are intrinsic. People take pride in their contribution. Furthermore, the social relation to their peers and superiors is important. The following section discusses the results of the interviews.

Work Environment and Characteristics. Work processes in sheltered workplaces are standardized to maintain quality and respect the specifications by the customers. The diverse abilities of employees require a degree of standardization. This limits the space for employee feedback.

Processes are Mostly Performed in Isolation. Only few workstations are directly connected to each other in a production line. This is necessary to reduce performance pressure. The work environment is also not very digitized. Displays or tablets are only present when it is required by the machinery that is being used.

Some employees are also deployed externally and work within other companies. Employees are especially proud of such tasks, as this demonstrates their ability. All respondents indicate a preference for engaging in more complex work processes.

Employees

Motivation. The interviews displayed a wide range of work motivations. While one individual exhibited high achievement motivation, performance pressure was a deterrent factor for others. Nevertheless, all participants take pride in their work, and they are motivated to come to work. It gives them meaning and a purpose. This was despite the high diversity in age, experience, and cognitive ability.

Social Relatedness. All participants expressed that the social factor is critical to their job satisfaction. Being surrounded by colleagues and having opportunities for social interaction is critical. Social interactions do not necessarily involve work-related topics but are also related to casual interactions. However, the desire of the people for social interaction varies greatly. The relationship with their team leaders is also critical.

Technological Acceptance. Most participants expressed that they would accept technological assistance within their work processes. *Degrees of independence.* People have various degrees of independence. Some commute to work over longer distances. Monitoring during work is not very close after people have learned a task.

Goals and Supervisor-Feedback. Depending on cognitive capacity people set and pursue their own goals ("Today I want to complete xxx pieces."). Interviewees adapt the goals to their level of performance on a given day and time. All respondents reported feeling proud when they achieve goals set by their superiors or goals, they have set for themselves.

A significant motivational factor is feedback from supervisors. Participants enjoy being trusted to do their work correctly and rely on the regular feedback from their team leads to judge whether they have done a good job.

Knowledge-Transfer-Processes. Despite the standardized work processes, employees, depending on their cognitive abilities, are motivated to share their ideas for improvement. Some aim to enhance efficiency, while others wish to demonstrate their competence. Explaining the processes and how they are related with each other is critical to help people understand why some processes "are the way they are".

Interview Method. The laddering method was only partially applicable to individuals with cognitive impairments. This was due to the limited abstraction ability of the participants of the interviews. Therefore, a more individualized approached to the interview will be evaluated.

Studies in Further Environments. We also wanted to see if we could find similar motivations among employees in sheltered and non-sheltered workplaces. The more intrinsic motivations found in this study, such as social relatedness or the recognition from peers and the team leader, may be less present in non-sheltered workplaces. The role of extrinsic motivations, such as pay, may be greater in such environments.

6 Gamification Mechanics

The gamification mechanics focus on social relatedness and individual development. These motivations were identified as key motivations in the interview. Competitive mechanics, such as points, badges, and leaderboards, would be inappropriate since a sheltered environment should be characterized by the absence of performance requirements and competition. Furthermore, the abilities of employees of sheltered workplace are diverse and their motivation may vary significantly throughout the day. Therefore, achieving goals and competing with peers would create performance stress, which is not desirable.

6.1 Positive Leaderboards

In some games, the goal is to "be the best," "keep up," or simply "win," which refers to being at the top of the leaderboard. In sheltered environments, such comparisons are inappropriate, as competition among non-competitive people leads to frustration and disappointment. Instead of a leaderboard that compares and displays individual performance, a dashboard could positively quantify a team's performance. The aim is to show how the performance of a team contributed to a larger aim. Some examples are presented below (Fig. 1).

- Team A has provided blinds to 52 houses this month.
- Team B has packaged beans to brew 20k cups of coffee today.
- Team C has renovated the interior of 50 train wagons interior this month and over XYZ passengers will appreciate your work

The results may also be supplemented by videos. Such videos could show how, for instance, blinds are used in buildings or homes. Explaining how small steps fit together and in what products they are used can motivate employees and make small and simple work processes more meaningful.

6.2 Avatar Editor

Avatars allow to have a personal presence in the virtual world of the application. Being able to customize their avatar to their liking makes players feel more connected to the application.

It is important to consider the diversity and inclusion when designing avatars in gamified applications. If avatars represent only a limited range of genders, ethnicities, or abilities, many users may feel excluded or unrepresented. An easy way to provide diverse avatars without creating a complex editor would be to abstract users to colorful shapes with faces (see Fig. 2).

Fig. 1. Possible implementation of the positive leaderboard.

Fig. 2. Possible implementation of the avatar editor.

All users start with the same set of shapes and faces. Additional shapes and faces may be offered as a reward for something (e.g., personal progress or for Christmas). These additional shapes may be seasonal (e.g., fir tree, ice cream cone, or leaf).

Avatars also provide a mechanism for users to display or visualize their current situation and emotional state. Making the avatar available to team leaders could help them support their team members and organize work processes accordingly. Avatars can also be displayed to colleagues based on the preferences of the individual employee, for instance to indicate a desire for social interaction.

7 Conclusions and Further Work

The study presented in this paper provided gamification mechanisms for application in continuous improvement processes. The development of the mechanism was based on an exploratory literature review and a qualitative interview study. The motivations are mainly based on intrinsic factors such as social relatedness and less on extrinsic factors. These insights are crucial in designing gamified interfaces that resonate with users' psychological motivations, thereby enhancing their engagement and satisfaction.

A workshop to evaluate a first set of prototypes with people with cognitive impairment is planned. We expect that working with concrete prototypes will better address the limited capacity for abstraction of people with impairments. Further interviews in non-sheltered workplaces are planned to evaluate whether similar gamification can be applied to such environments.

Extending our research to non-sheltered workplace environments allows to examine the scalability and adaptability of our gamification approach in more diverse settings. This expansion is critical to understanding the universal applicability of our findings and to tailoring gamification strategies to various work environments.

This paper not only contributes to the theoretical framework of gamification in human-computer interaction but also paves the way for practical applications that are inclusive and engaging. Future work will continue to implement the gamification mechanics identified in this paper.

Acknowledgments. This study was funded by the Swiss Innovation Agency through the project "Smart-KVP: Intuitive und motivierende Unterstützung für den kontinuierlichen Verbesserungsprozess in der Produktion" (grant number 108.093.1).

References

1. Backlund, P., Hendrix, M.: Educational games - are they worth the effort? A literature survey of the effectiveness of serious games. In: 2013 5th International Conference on Games and Virtual Worlds for Serious Applications (VS-GAMES), pp. 1–8. IEEE (2013)
2. Center for Universal Design: The Principles of Universal Design (1997). https://design.ncsu.edu/research/center-for-universal-design/. Accessed 26 Nov 2023
3. Chou, Y.-K.: Actionable gamification. Beyond points badges leaderboards. Octalysis Media (2014)
4. Crawford, C.: The art of computer game design. Reflections of a master game designer. Osborne/McGraw-Hill, Berkeley (1984)
5. Deci, E.L., Ryan, R.M.: Intrinsic motivation and self-determination in human behavior. Perspectives in social psychology. Plenum Press, New York (1985)
6. Deterding, S., Dixon, D., Khaled, R., et al.: From game design elements to gamefulness. In: Lugmayr, A., Franssila, H., Safran, C., et al. (eds.) Proceedings of the 15th International Academic MindTrek Conference: Envisioning Future Media Environments, pp. 9–15. ACM, New York (2011)
7. Dolly, M., Nimbarte, A., Wuest, T.: The effects of gamification for manufacturing (GfM) on workers and production in industrial assembly. Robot. Comput.-Integr. Manuf. **88**, 102722 (2024). https://doi.org/10.1016/j.rcim.2024.102722

8. Dvorak, J., Merforth, M., Kandler, M., et al.: Assessment of the potential of gamification in manual assembly. SSRN J. (2023). https://doi.org/10.2139/ssrn.4471436

9. Federspiel, E., Schaffner, D., Mohr, S.: Customer engagement in online communities: a new conceptual framework integrating motives, incentives and motivation. In: BLED 2014 Proceedings, vol. 21 (2014)

10. Gutman, J., Reynolds, T.J.: Laddering theory-analysis and interpretation. J. Advertising Res. **28**, 11 (1988)

11. Hallifax, S., Altmeyer, M., Kölln, K., et al.: From points to progression: a scoping review of game elements in gamification research with a content analysis of 280 research papers. Proc. ACM Hum.-Comput. Interact. **7**, 748–768 (2023). https://doi.org/10.1145/3611048

12. Herrmann, A., Schaffner, D.: Planung der Produkteigenschaften. In: Gassmann, O., Albers, S. (eds.) Handbuch Technologie- und Innovationsmanagement. Strategie — Umsetzung — Controlling. Gabler Verlag, Wiesbaden, s.l., pp. 379–396 (2005)

13. Huotari, K., Hamari, J.: A definition for gamification: anchoring gamification in the service marketing literature. Electron Markets **27**, 21–31 (2017). https://doi.org/10.1007/s12525-015-0212-z

14. Kaasinen, E., Schmalfuß, F., Özturk, C., et al.: Empowering and engaging industrial workers with Operator 4.0 solutions. Comput. Ind. Eng. **139**, 105678 (2020). https://doi.org/10.1016/j.cie.2019.01.052

15. Keepers, M., Nesbit, I., Romero, D., et al.: Current state of research & outlook of gamification for manufacturing. J. Manuf. Syst. **64**, 303–315 (2022). https://doi.org/10.1016/j.jmsy.2022.07.001

16. Klock, A.C.T., Gasparini, I., Pimenta, M.S., et al.: Tailored gamification: a review of literature. Int. J. Hum.-Comput. Stud. **144**, 102495 (2020). https://doi.org/10.1016/j.ijhcs.2020.102495

17. Korn, O., Rees, A.: Affective effects of gamification. In: Makedon, F. (ed.) Proceedings of the 12th ACM International Conference on PErvasive Technologies Related to Assistive Environments, pp. 1–10. ACM, New York (2019)

18. Korn, O., Funk, M., Schmidt, A.: Design approaches for the gamification of production environments. In: Proceedings of the 8th ACM International Conference on PErvasive Technologies Related to Assistive Environments. ACM, New York (2015)

19. Korn, O., Lang, J., Korge, A., et al.: Gamification of a Workday. In: Kaye, J., Druin, A., Lampe, C., et al. (eds.) Proceedings of the 2016 CHI Conference Extended Abstracts on Human Factors in Computing Systems, pp. 3114–3121. ACM, New York (2016)

20. Lee, J., Kim, J., Seo, K., et al.: A case study in an automotive assembly line: exploring the design framework for manufacturing gamification. In: Schlick, C., Trzcieliński, S. (eds.) Advances in Ergonomics of Manufacturing: Managing the Enterprise of the Future, vol. 490, pp. 305–317. Springer, Cham (2016). https://doi.org/10.1007/978-3-319-41697-7_27

21. Liu, M., Huang, Y., Zhang, D.: Gamification's impact on manufacturing: enhancing job motivation, satisfaction and operational performance with smartphone-based gamified job design. Hum. Ftrs. Erg. Mfg. Svc. **28**, 38–51 (2018). https://doi.org/10.1002/hfm.20723

22. McClelland, D.C.: Motives, personality, and society: Selected papers. Praeger Publishers (1984)

23. McGonigal, J.: Reality is broken. Why games make us better and how they can change the world. The Penguin Press, New York (2011)

24. Neumann, W.P., Winkelhaus, S., Grosse, E.H., et al.: Industry 4.0 and the human factor – a systems framework and analysis methodology for successful development. Int. J. Prod. Econ. **233**, 107992 (2021). https://doi.org/10.1016/j.ijpe.2020.107992

25. Paddick, R.J.: The grasshopper: games, life and utopia. By Bernard suits. Toronto, University of Toronto Press 1978. J. Philos. Sport **6**, 73–78 (1979). https://doi.org/10.1080/00948705.1979.10654153

26. Pakinee, A., Puritat, K.: Designing a gamified e-learning environment for teaching undergraduate ERP course based on big five personality traits. Educ. Inf. Technol. **26**, 4049–4067 (2021). https://doi.org/10.1007/s10639-021-10456-9

27. Reynolds, T.J., Phillips, J.M.: A review and comparative analysis of laddering research methods. In: Malhotra, N.K. (ed.) Review of Marketing Research, 5, vol. 5, pp. 130–174. Emerald Group Publishing Limited, Armonk (2008)

28. Roh, S., Seo, K., Lee, J., et al.: Goal-based manufacturing gamification: bolt tightening work redesign in the automotive assembly line. In: Schlick, C., Trzcieliński, S. (eds.) Advances in Ergonomics of Manufacturing: Managing the Enterprise of the Future, vol. 490, pp. 293–304. Springer, Cham (2016). https://doi.org/10.1007/978-3-319-41697-7_26

29. Sailer, M., Homner, L.: The gamification of learning: a meta-analysis. Educ. Psychol. Rev. **32**, 77–112 (2020). https://doi.org/10.1007/s10648-019-09498-w

30. Sochor, R., Schenk, J., Fink, K., et al.: Gamification in industrial shopfloor – development of a method for classification and selection of suitable game elements in diverse production and logistics environments. Procedia CIRP **100**, 157–162 (2021). https://doi.org/10.1016/j.procir.2021.05.024

31. Stadnicka, D., Deif, A.: A gamification approach application to facilitate lean manufacturing knowledge acquisition. Manag. Prod. Eng. Rev. (2019). https://doi.org/10.24425/mper.2019.131451

32. Tayal, S., Rajagopal, K., Mahajan, V.: Modernization with gamification on industry 4.0 in supply chain management 4.0. In: 2022 6th International Conference on Electronics, Communication and Aerospace Technology. IEEE (2022)

33. Tsourma, M., Zikos, S., Albanis, G., et al.: Gamification concepts for leveraging knowledge sharing in industry 4.0. IJSG **6**, 75–87 (2019). https://doi.org/10.17083/ijsg.v6i2.273

34. Ulmer, J., Braun, S., Cheng, C.T., Dowey, S., Wollert, J.: Human-centered gamification framework for manufacturing systems. Procedia CIRP **93**, 670–675 (2020)

35. Warmelink, H., Koivisto, J., Mayer, I., et al.: Gamification of production and logistics operations: status quo and future directions. J. Bus. Res. **106**, 331–340 (2020). https://doi.org/10.1016/j.jbusres.2018.09.011

36. Werbach, K., Hunter, D.: For the win. How game thinking can revolutionize your business. EBL-Schweitzer. Wharton Digital Press, Philadelphia (2012)

NSF Eddie Bernice Johnson INCLUDES Initiative: TAPDINTO-STEM National Alliance for Students with Disabilities in STEM, An Innovative Intersectional Approach of Diversity, Equity, and Inclusion for Students with Disabilities

Brittany McCullough[1(✉)], Scott Bellman[2], Andrew Buck[3], Overtoun Jenda[1],
Ronda Jenson[4], Daniela Marghitu[1], Tamara Massey-Garrett[1], Alexis Petri[5],
Carl Pettis[6], David Shannon[1], Kiriko Takahashi[7], and Jeff Traiger[5]

[1] Auburn University, Auburn, AL 36849, USA
bnw0005@auburn.edu
[2] University of Washington, Seattle, WA 98195, USA
[3] The Ohio State University, Columbus, OH 43210, USA
[4] Northern Arizona University, Flagstaff, AZ 86011, USA
[5] University of Missouri-Kansas City, Kansas City, MO 64108, USA
[6] Alabama State University, Montgomery, AL 36104, USA
[7] University of Hawaii at Manoa, Honolulu, HI 96822, USA

Abstract. Persons with disabilities are one of the most significantly underrepresented groups in STEM education and employment, comprising a disproportionately smaller percentage of STEM degrees and jobs compared to their percentages in the U.S. population [1]. TAPDINTO-STEM employs a collective impact approach with dozens of partnering institutions to increase the number of students with disabilities (SWDs) who complete associate, baccalaureate and graduate STEM degrees and enter the STEM workforce.

Keywords: Students with Disabilities · STEM Education · Mentoring

1 Introduction

The Alliance for Students with Disabilities for Inclusion, Networking, and Transition Opportunities in STEM (TAPDINTO-STEM) employs a collective impact approach with dozens of partnering organizations nationally to increase the number of students with disabilities (SWDs) who complete associate, baccalaureate and graduate STEM degrees and enter the STEM workforce. The Alliance is made up of 38 colleges and universities and 14 non-academic partners across the country, and has the following purpose, goals, and objectives:

- Purpose: Through the collective impact of the NSF INCLUDES TAPDINTO-STEM Alliance, post-secondary students with disabilities nationwide will increase the rate of persistence and graduation in STEM degree programs and increase their rate of transition to the STEM workforce.
- Goal: The project goal is to increase the quantity of persons with disabilities who complete associate, baccalaureate, and graduate degrees in STEM and enter the STEM workforce.
- Objectives: 1) Increase the quantity of students with disabilities (SWDs) completing associate, undergraduate, and graduate degrees in STEM. 2) Facilitate the transition of SWD from STEM degree completion into the STEM workforce. 3) Enhance communication and collaboration among institutions of higher education (IHEs), industry, government, national labs, and local communities in addressing the education needs of SWD in STEM disciplines.

2 Background and Related Work

Auburn University is leading this national alliance, which includes six regional hubs across the country. Auburn leads the Southeast Hub, and other hub lead institutions include Northern Arizona University (Mountain Hub), The Ohio State University (Northeast Hub), the University of Hawaii-Manoa (Islands Hub), the University of Missouri-Kansas City (Midwest Hub) and the University of Washington (West Coast Hub). The University of Missouri-Kansas City also serves as the backbone organization for the alliance, providing support in communications, data collection, dissemination, and organization.

This Alliance was created following the successful implementation of the Alabama Alliance for Students with Disabilities in STEM (AASD-STEM) [2], funded by NSF under the Research in Disabilities Education (RDE) program in 2009, and the Southeast Alliance for Persons with Disabilities in STEM (SEAPD-STEM) [3] under the NSF INCLUDES program in 2016. The TAPDINTO-STEM Alliance brings together leaders and researchers from several former NSF RDE Alliances, using their experience and expertise to expand this important work from regional efforts to a national scale.

The infrastructure created by the alliance allows for more partners to continue joining the movement, more connections to be made, and the opportunity for collaborative change to lead to expansion, sustainability, and scaling up of the Alliance and its activities (Fig. 1).

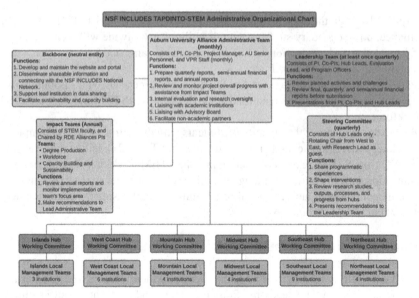

Fig. 1. TAPDINTO-STEM Organizational Chart

3 Research and Implementation

The primary intervention for the Alliance is mentoring and e-mentoring of SWD by peers and STEM faculty and professionals. This mentoring model is built on work that was done in previous NSF-funded projects for persons with disabilities and other NSF-supported programs for women, underrepresented minorities, and low-income and first-generation students. Other Alliance interventions for students include:

- Recruitment
- Faculty and peer mentor support
- Internship opportunities
- Conferences and graduate school/career fairs
- Social science research
- Capacity building institutes for students, faculty, and staff
- Creation of campus student organizations for SWD
- Webinars
- Networking opportunities

In addition to these activities, each hub is conducting its own research project as described below, focusing on topics that include (Fig. 2):

- Institutional factors and student persistence
- Impact of student support services on academic, social and employment outcomes
- Bias, discrimination, stigma and intersectionality
- Mentoring model through the lens of the Loss/ Momentum Framework
- Research in disabilities in a multicultural setting
- Longitudinal transition study of NSF-funded students with disabilities

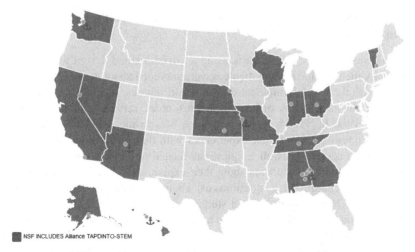

NSF INCLUDES Alliance TAPDINTO-STEM

Fig. 2. TAPDINTO-STEM Alliance Map (anchors represent hub lead institutions).

- **Islands:** This study focuses on students with disabilities (SWD) and the unique issues of culturally and linguistically diverse (CLD) SWD (i.e., Native Hawaiian, Pacific Island, and Asian American students) as there is a continued issue of access for these subset of students [15, 16]. The study will be conducted in stages. Stage 1 is designed to investigate factors (e.g., historical, social, cultural, disability, and other personal factors) that facilitate or impede students' attitude toward and access to postsecondary education and STEM, identity development in STEM, and persistence towards and graduation with a STEM degree to understand the students' needs, conditions, and circumstances. Then, in considering those factors and different educational stages students are in, we will identify effective strategies to develop a tailored bridge and mentoring activities (e.g., e-mentoring, internship, course guidance, research support, student-family activities) appropriate to individual students' needs, conditions, and circumstances. Subsequently, stage 2 will provide a personalized menu of mentoring activities tailored to specific SWD to support their retention and graduation.

- **Midwest:** Academic student success from college choice toward graduation is often dependent on how well students can navigate institutional policies and procedures. While some of the supports that institutions create generate helpful momentum for students, far too many rules create pain points. Consequently, many students prematurely leave without knowing if they have what it takes to succeed in college [4]. This scenario is magnified for students with disabilities [5], especially in difficult degree programs like STEM [6]. Therefore, the Midwest Hub is investigating to what extent and how TAPDINTO-STEM students experience their institutions' requirements and support for matriculation toward graduation as assisting or delaying their academic success [7]. More specifically, this examination uses the Completion by Design loss/momentum framework [4] that defines five phases where students experience their campus as providing loss or momentum through: access, entry, progress, completion, and transition. The overarching objective is to identify patterns in momentum or loss points across the institution in hopes of enhancing supportive factors and mitigating adverse ones for students with disabilities in STEM degree programs.

The Midwest Hub research team is using a mixed-method design where Alliance STEM faculty mentors and student mentees were surveyed about their experiences corresponding with the five loss/momentum framework phases. Alliance faculty mentors were surveyed about adequacy of institutional resources, services, and responsiveness in supporting SWD in STEM degree programs. Meanwhile, Alliance students were asked general questions about their experiences with their institutions' academic and disability support services as well as questions related to the loss/momentum phases. The "access" questions ask students about their experiences with the institution while they were in high school; "entry" questions ask about their experiences transitioning to college; "progress" questions ask about students' current semester; and "completion" and "transition" questions ask students who have advanced to their final year about completing their degree and their confidence in transitioning to the STEM workforce. This research project will continue with two additional survey administrations and follow-up qualitative interviews with Alliance faculty mentors and student mentees.

Another aspect of this study is to include a control group of students with disabilities in STEM degree programs and staff who support those students from non-Alliance institutions. The Midwest hub research team selected 33 comparison institutions using propensity-score matching, a procedure in which logistic regression predicts the probability that a case will belong to one of two groups. In our case, we used it to predict whether any institutions in the IPEDS database would belong to the same group as our target sample of the original 27 Alliance institutions. Institutions having the closest probability to each of the target institutions were selected as matches. More matches were selected than target institutions because some schools had the same predicted probabilities. The advantage of using logistic regression for matching is that logistic regression models can easily incorporate many different variables, whereas it is difficult to conduct matching by eye using more than a few variables. Currently, the Midwest hub research team is contacting target institutions for their participation in the comparison group.

- **Mountain:** The Mountain Hub is conducting research focused on bias, discrimination, and stigma experienced by college students with disabilities pursuing STEM degrees. The overarching research question is "Using an intersectionality lens, what are the disconnections and gaps between (a) the experiences of post-secondary STEM students with disabilities related to bias, discrimination, and stigma, (b) information and messaging available to IHE faculty and staff pertaining to inclusion and recognizing intersectionality, and (c) IHE faculty and staff perceptions that perpetuate bias, discrimination, and stigma?" To address this question, a mixed methods approach including PhotoVoice and surveys is being used.

To date, a pilot of the PhotoVoice approach has been completed. PhotoVoice was introduced as a qualitative approach in the mid-1990's [8]. In the social sciences, PhotoVoice has been an effective approach for collecting data about lived experiences and personal perceptions [9]. As a pilot, six students took photos of the college environment representing situations in which they feel included, excluded, or empowered. Students were then interviewed about their photos, the situations depicted, and their perceptions.

The pilot results showed examples of inaccessible spaces and interactions with faculty and instructors that assumed that disability equates to incompetence.

- **Northeast:** This study aligns with the Alliance goal of increasing STEM degree completion for students with ASD by examining students' use and perceptions of support services provided by either the STEM department or disability services. College SWD who use a variety of support services are significantly more successful in completing college [17]. This research study examines the use and value of support services aimed at improving SWD academic and employment outcomes. Services focused on academic outcomes include tutoring services provided by STEM departments and private tutors, disability support accommodations (extended time, distraction free environment for testing, notetakers, etc.) and assistive technology (speech-to-text; text-to-speech; electronic notetaker pens; etc.). Support related to social outcomes include peer mentoring and mentoring by teacher/faculty member, social skills instruction, and life coaching with a trained facilitator. Employment focused support services include career services (career fairs, stipends, job placement services, job coaching services etc.) and services provided by disability services/organizations (campus disability office, VR – job placement services, job coaching services). All support services are examined to identify those most valued by SWD and the extent to which such services should be tailored to students with different types of disability. Finally, use of these services is examined in relation to academic, social and employment outcomes.
- **Southeast:** The purpose of the Southeast Hub research is to examine key constructs in relation to students with disabilities (SWD) institutional commitment, persistence, and retention. This research study is focused on SWD persistence and is based on decades of research on student persistence [10] and research using social cognitive career theory (SCCT) to examine persistence among students with disabilities [11].

Thus far, data have been gathered from TAPDINTO-STEM students over three semesters (Fall 2022 to Fall 2023). Researchers have drawn from several survey scales they have used as part of a prior RDE project and current INCLUDES project [3, 12]. These surveys include measurement scales constructed to represent the constructs of interest in STEM careers, issues and challenges faced in college, self-advocacy knowledge and behaviors, academic efficacy, and intention to persist in their degree program with all scale reliability estimates exceeding .70. Finally, the researchers are further examining more specific aspects of persistence using the College Persistence Questionnaire [13, 14].

Initial findings include descriptions of sample characteristics, disability conditions, accommodations and services used by SWD, these findings also include a summary of variables in relation to persistence. More specifically, students who have reported greater persistence have also reported being more confident in facing academic, social and time management issues and challenges, more confidence to face issues related to their disability and be self-advocates, greater academic focus and academic efficacy and a greater sense of belongingness associated with TAPDINTO-STEM and their university.

- **West Coast:** The West Coast Hub has worked with Alliance students to solicit formative input and pilot a campus accessibility tool called "Equal Access: A Checklist for Making Science Labs Accessible." These activities took place in April 2023 at the TAPDINTO-STEM Alliance Convening which was held on the University of Missouri Kansas City campus. The West Coast Hub has refined the tool, originally developed with NSF funding as part of an Alliance called AccessSTEM (NSF# #HRD-0833504) and will develop a process for TAPDINTO-STEM students across the country to work in small teams with a faculty mentor's support to evaluate a science lab or science building on their campus. Students will participate in the development of a summary report for their campus that suggests different ways accessibility can be increased. West Coast Hub staff will follow up with each campus and faculty member at 3- and 6-month intervals to determine which, if any, recommendations were implemented. The study seeks to demonstrate that:

- students with disabilities, through their lived experiences and guidance from the accessibility checklist tool, can improve skills at identifying access barriers on their campus,
- improve skills at collaborating with and communicating with campus faculty and administrators about access barriers, and
- directly influence institutional change on their campus.

The study will also explore and share reasons why certain recommendations were not implemented.

4 Conclusions and Future Work

Over 200 scholars have participated to date in Alliance mentoring activities to date, and students have reported improvements in persistence in college, behaviors/skills, academic efficacy, research interests, and satisfaction with mentoring. The evaluation plan for the Alliance includes internal and external components and encompasses both formative/ongoing evaluation and summative/impact evaluation. Common metrics collected from all participating institutions include student participation and progress data, institutional data related to capacity to support SWD and project engagement, and measures related to the Collective Impact framework.

At the conclusion of the project's second year, findings show that the Alliance has made significant progress in several areas and has had a positive impact on students and alliance members. Students reported being positively impacted by their participation in a TAPDINTO-STEM convening held at the University of Missouri-Kansas City in March 2023 and in the Alliance mentoring program. Positive impacts include increased sense of belonging, intent to persist, and academic efficacy, and key findings are described below. All items mentioned used a five-point response scale.

4.1 Key Findings: Students' Perceptions of Impact

Overall Bridge Model Perceptions and Perceived Outcomes. Sixty (60) students responded to items in relation to their involvement in and perceived benefits of TAPDINTO-STEM bridge and cluster meetings. Students reported the greatest benefits related to commitment and confidence to complete their degree (M = 3.77), learning about valuable resources at their institution (M = 3.5), being better prepared for internships (M = 3.47) and developing closer relationships with faculty (M = 3.42). Students described having great confidence in their ability to succeed academically, having a goal to learn as much as they could (M = 4.55), being important learn a lot of new things (M = 4.53) and believing they could do all the work in the classes if they didn't give up (M = 4.27).

Mentoring Perceptions and Satisfaction. Students also reported being satisfied with the mentoring experience, with the highest levels of satisfaction related to the length of the session (M = 3.23), their mentor's ability to help them (M = 3.21), their relationship with their mentor (M = 3.20) and the overall experiences (M = 3.20). In addition, students strongly agreed that they were able to talk about career and life goals (M = 3.57), they felt respected and supported (M = 3.55), were encouraged to share their feelings (M = 3.48), felt comfortable approaching their mentor with questions (M = 3.46), and were satisfied with the mentoring experience (M = 3.45). Finally, in response to open-ended questions, students described the mentoring process as helping them build knowledge and skills (and their vita), prepare for internships, jobs, graduate school and other career opportunities.

Persistence and Career Preparation. Students expressed a strong intention to persist. They most strongly agreed that they intended to get their degree in their current major (M = 4.65), would continue their education in the same field (M = 4.62), get a job in the field (M = 4.60) and could see themselves working in the field for quite a while (M = 4.49). TAPDINTO-STEM students also had confidence in their skills as they prepared for internships and careers. They expressed the most confidence in their abilities to receive and give feedback (M = 3.91), learn about sources for potential internships (M = 3.70), talk with faculty and others about potential internship opportunities (M = 3.65), meet and engage with professionals in the field (M = 3.63), and apply for internship or job opportunities (M = 3.61).

Self-advocacy and Belongingness. At the Convening in March, TAPDINTO-STEM students (and others) described a sense of belongingness on their campus and the importance of self-advocacy. In spring 2023, students were asked about the sense of belonging and self-advocacy.

University Belongingness. Based on the initial examination in spring 2023, TAPDINTO-STEM students do perceive a sense of belongingness. They feel a strong affiliation with their university in that they have found it easy to establish relationships at my university (M = 3.81), they were proud to be a student at their university (M = 3.7) and feel a sense of pride when they meet someone from my university off campus (M = 3.67). They also indicate that there were supportive resources available to them on campus (M = 3.86), the university environment provides an opportunity to grow (M = 3.81), and their cultural customs are accepted (M = 3.81). Finally, TAPDINTO-STEM students held positive perceptions of faculty and staff, believing strongly that faculty/staff members care about them (M = 3.86), faculty/staff appreciate them (M = 3.77), and they feel like faculty value their contributions in class (M = 3.60).

Self-advocacy Behaviors. Our initial examination of self-advocacy reveals that TAPDINTO-STEM students are engaged in many effective behaviors, but there is room for improvement. That is, students indicated that they can explain their disability to their teachers (M = 3.91), they meet with teachers at the beginning of the semester to discuss accommodations (M = 3.80), they talk with someone when frustrated about problems related to my disability (M = 3.64), they ask the appropriate office to assist them in resolving problems (M = 3.57) and they let teachers know immediately about the specific accommodations they need (M = 3.52). On the other hand, other behaviors have more room for improvement. These pertain to apologizing when requesting approved accommodations, telling teachers over and over how to meet my needs and just accept it and do their best if a teacher forgets or refuses accommodations.

4.2 SOAR Data Portal

A data portal has also been developed for the uploading of data and allows for continuous feedback for project improvement. The SOAR Portal (Surmounting Obstacles for Academic Resilience) [18] was developed by a team of computer science faculty and doctoral students at UMKC as the Shared Measurement System for the alliance. The portal serves as the data collection system and repository for student, mentor, and leadership contact information, agreements, and data. In collaboration with the evaluation team, data collection measures were developed and include surveys and questionnaires which are presented to participants as forms for answering questions related to alliance objectives and reporting activities at established time intervals throughout the academic year. In addition, a data visualization dashboard has been initiated which generates dynamic charts based on data in the warehouse. Both Android and iOS mobile apps have been deployed for the SOAR portal.

Upcoming developments and significant improvements for SOAR include further developing the data visualization dashboard to comprise static, manually generated, and AI generated charts; the ability to upload externally collected data, including institutional data and the internal evaluation; and improved chatbot functionality. There is also anticipation of American Sign Language integration as a sign-to-text function, similar to talk-to-text. Additionally, we will add short instructional videos to help all users understand that the AI is used only for automatically aggregating the data into dynamic visualization and generating interpretations based on the dynamic visualization. This will enable individual users to see progress, momentum, and areas where additional uplift is required.

4.3 Hub-Level Research

The **Islands Hub** study on the unique issues of culturally and linguistically diverse students with disability has been pilot-tested among students with disabilities to examine the usability, accessibility, and content of the research instrument. Data collection will continue on a larger scale across all Islands Hub institutions, and once students have provided information, work will begin on developing a personalized menu of mentoring activities tailored to specific students to assist them in their STEM studies and help keep them on track for graduation.

The **Midwest Hub** research team is investigating the extent to which momentum or loss points within five phases of entry into college toward graduation impact Alliance students' academic journey from their first institutional contact through graduation. Currently, the researchers have secured IRB exemption and completed the first round of survey data collection from with the Alliance STEM faculty mentors and STEM SWD mentees. These groups will be surveyed twice more and be invited to participate in semi-structured interviews. Additionally, this project seeks to include comparison groups of SWD in STEM degree programs and staff who work with SWD in STEM degree programs from non-Alliance institutions through an analytical matching process that has yielded several similar institutions that will be contacted to participate. Prior to the final administration of the Alliance mentor and mentee surveys, provisional results will be disseminated to Alliance campuses so they can consider implementing any measures they believe may help their students move through the Completion by Design milestones.

The **Mountain Hub** will scale-up the PhotoVoice portion of the research by recruiting student participants across the Alliance and across undergraduate and graduate students. The resulting data will be used to inform the development of a survey to be districted across TAPDINTO STEM and nationally.

The **Northeast Hub** is currently recruiting and conducting structured interviews with Autistic STEM undergraduates at partner institutions to learn more about academic, employment, and social supports and services that are valued by individuals in this community and promote their success in higher education. Preliminary findings were presented by the research team and two TAPDINTO-STEM scholars from The Ohio State University (OSU) at the 25th International Conference on Autism, Intellectual Disability & Developmental Disabilities in January 2024. The concurrent breakout session, entitled Cultivating Neurodiverse STEM Cultures on Campus, described how the project's mentorship model led to the development of a funded student organization at the school, which aims to build community and advance sustainable, systemic change by empowering students and promoting accessible and inclusive STEM programs. Facilitators include: (i) connecting students to support staff and programs; (ii) leveraging technology to promote access and engagement; (iii) building community and peer networks; (iv) promoting friendly and flexible pedagogy; and (v) utilizing academic accommodations. Barriers include: (i) rigid and strict approaches to teaching and learning; (ii) difficulty accessing accommodations; (iii) inaccessible course materials; (iv) exclusionary assessments and expectations; and (v) time and resources required to address complex needs. The research team will expand the pool of study participants to additional partner schools across the Alliance and disseminate findings to inform faculty and empower students with key strategies that support the inclusion, persistence, and transition of neurodivergent STEM students.

In the **Southeast Hub**, data collection is ongoing and will continue each semester throughout the duration of the TAPDINTO-STEM alliance. Data collection is also expanding beyond the southeast region to include students throughout the national TAPDINTO-STEM alliance. Findings from this research will identify key variables related to persistence and be shared with campus leads to help students persist and earn degrees in STEM fields.

Project staff at the **West Coast Hub** have observed that students appreciate learning about best practices to increase access to postsecondary STEM programs. Students involved in piloting and refining the new science labs checklist tool were enthusiastic about advocating for change and learning new skills in this area. Activities to scale up the pilot project to include campuses at each Hub of the Alliance are currently underway. Completion of the study will inform the direction of future work. Such work could include broadening the scope of tools for students interested in accessibility auditing, further assessment of changes in student skills and confidence in impacting postsecondary campus accessibility and exploring the perceptions of postsecondary administrators who interface with students conducting such activities (Fig. 3).

Fig. 3. Group photo from Spring 2023 TAPDINTO-STEM convening held in Kansas City, MO

Acknowledgments. The Eddie Bernice Johnson INCLUDES Initiative: The Alliance of Students with Disabilities for Inclusion, Networking, and Transition Opportunities in Science, Technology, Engineering, and Mathematics (TAPDINTO-STEM) is supported by the National Science Foundation under NSF Award #2119902. Any opinions, findings, and conclusions or recommendations expressed in this material are those of the authors and do not necessarily reflect those of the National Science Foundation.

References

1. National Science Foundation, National Center for Science and Engineering Statistics. Women, Minorities, and Persons with Disabilities in Science and Engineering: 2015. Special Report NSF 15–311. Arlington, VA (2015). http://www.nsf.gov/statistics/wmpd/

2. Jenda, O., et al.: Effective strategies to attract gifted and talented students with disabilities in higher education STEM fields: alabama alliance for students with disabilities in STEM case study. In: Proceedings of the 18th International Conference on Transformative Science and Engineering, Business and Social Innovation, pp. 147–152 (2013)

3. Dunn, C., Shannon, D., McCullough, B., Overtoun, J., Qazi, M.: An innovative postsecondary education program for students with disabilities in STEM (Practice Brief). J. Postsecond. Educ. Disabil. **31**(1), 91–101 (2018)

4. Rassen, D., Chaplot,P., Jenkins, D., Johnstone, R.: Understanding the student experience through the loss/momentum framework: clearing the path to completion. The RPgroup and CCRC (2013). https://ccrc.tc.columbia.edu/publications/understanding-student-experience-cbd.html

5. Coghill, E.M.H.: An introduction to neurodiversity. In: Coghill, E.M.H., Coghill, J. (eds.) Supporting Neurodiverse College Student Success: A Guide for Librarians, Student Support Services, and Academic Learning Environments. Rowman & Littlefield (2021)

6. Zilvinskis, J.: Measuring quality in high-impact practices. Int. J. High. Educ. Res. **78**(4), 687–709 (2019)

7. York, T.T., Gibson, C., Rankin, S.: Defining and measuring academic success. Pract. Assess. Res. Eval. **20**(1), 5 (2019). https://doi.org/10.7275/hz5x-tx03

8. Wang, C., Burris, M.A.: Photovoice: concept, methodology, and use for participatory needs assessment. Health Educ. Behav. **24**(3), 369–387 (1997)

9. Bates, E.A., McCann, J.J., Kaye, L.K., Taylor, J.C.: "Beyond words": a researcher's guide to using photo elicitation in psychology. Qual. Res. Psychol. **14**(4), 459–481 (2017)

10. Reason, R.D.: An examination of persistence research through the lens of a comprehensive conceptual framework. J. Coll. Stud. Dev. **50**(6), 659–682 (2009)

11. Cardoso, E., Dutta, A., Chiu, C., Johnson, E., Kundu, M., Chan, F.: Social-cognitive predictors of STEM career interests and goal persistence in college students with disabilities from racial and ethnic minority backgrounds. Rehabil. Res. Policy Educ. **27**(4), 1–14 (2013)

12. Dunn, C., Shannon, D., McCullough, B., Jenda, O., Qazi, M., Pettis, C.: A mentoring bridge model for students with disabilities in science, technology, engineering, and mathematics. J. Postsecond. Educ. Disabil. **34**(2), 163–177 (2021)

13. Davidson, W.B., Beck, H.P., Milligan, M.: The college persistence questionnaire: development and validation of an instrument that predicts student attrition. J. Coll. Stud. Dev. **50**(4), 373–390 (2009)

14. Davidson, W.B., Beck, H.P., Grisaffe, D.B.: Increasing the institutional commitment of college students" enhanced measurement and test of a nomological model. J. Coll. Stud. Retent. Res. Theory Pract. **17**(2), 162–185 (2015)

15. King, K.A.: A review of programs that promote higher education access for underrepresented students. J. Diver. High. Educ. **2**(1), 1–15 (2009). https://doi.org/10.1037/a0014327

16. National Academies of Sciences, Engineering, and Medicine. Barriers and Opportunities for 2-Year and 4-Year STEM Degrees: Systemic Change to Support Diverse Student Pathways. Committee on Barriers and Opportunities in Completing 2-Year and 4-Year STEM Degrees. In: Malcom, S., Feder, M. (eds.) Board on Science Education, Division of Behavioral and Social Sciences and Education. Board on Higher Education and the Workforce, Policy and Global Affairs. The National Academies Press, Washington, DC (2016). https://doi.org/10.17226/21739

17. Newman, L.A., Madaus, J.W., Lalor, A.R., Javitz, H.S.: Support receipt: effect on postsecondary success of students with learning disabilities. Career Dev. Transit. Except. Individ. **42**(1), 6–16 (2019)
18. Petri, A.N., Ho, D.H., Wang, Y., Lee, Y.: Surmounting obstacles for academic resilience: a dynamic portal for supporting an alliance of students with disabilities. In: Antona, M., Stephanidis, C. (eds.) Universal Access in Human-Computer Interaction: 17th International Conference, UAHCI 2023, Held as Part of the 25th HCI International Conference, HCII 2023, Copenhagen, Denmark, July 23–28, 2023, Proceedings, Part II, pp. 356–376. Springer, Cham (2023). https://doi.org/10.1007/978-3-031-35897-5_26

"ICT for Inclusion" for Educational Leaders: Inclusive and Digital Distributed Leadership

Claudia Mertens(✉) [iD], Franziska Schaper[iD], and Anna-Maria Kamin[iD]

Universität Bielefeld, Universitätsstraße 25, 33615 Bielefeld, Germany
claudia.mertens@uni-bielefeld.de

Abstract. In today's rapidly evolving educational landscape "Information & Communication Technology" (ICT) has gained a pivotal role for inclusion. ICT is transforming the way we teach and learn, but also the way we administer educational institutions. Yet up to now, there are hardly any concepts for inclusive digital leadership in schools – even less so for distributed inclusive digital leadership. As school principals grapple with the complexities of managing their educational institutions in the digital age, the leadership dimensions "design of teaching concepts", "strategic development of their organization", "fostering cooperation", "developing ICT concepts", and "human resources development" (adapted by Eickelmann & Gerick, 2017 from Holtappels & Rolff, 2010) have become integral components of responsibility. In the era of digital transformation, the effective integration of ICT is essential for fostering inclusion: Heads of schools play a crucial role in leveraging the potential of ICT for inclusion, making it imperative for them to adapt to technological changes. Therefore, the above-mentioned tasks of digital leadership must be strategically combined with the idea of inclusion in a concept of inclusive digital leadership. And these inclusive digital leadership tasks should be shared among multiple stakeholders in the faculty staff in a concept of distributed inclusive digital leadership.

Keywords: design of teaching concepts · organizational development · fostering cooperation · ICT development · human resources development

1 Introduction: Distributed Leadership Concepts in a Digital World

The innovative potential of digital media for inclusive teaching practices can only be fully be unfold, if the use of ICT is accompanied by strategic school development measures (Waffner, 2021). Otherwise, changes will be confined to isolated spots of modernization. The leadership actions of school principals play an important role in driving this transformative process towards digitization of schools (Waffner, 2021) – and even more so in the transformative process[1] towards inclusive digitization.

---

[1] "The leadership actions of heads of schools are of high importance for the school change process" (Waffner, 2021) [translated by the authors].

© The Author(s) 2024
M. Antona and C. Stephanidis (Eds.): HCII 2024, LNCS 14698, pp. 125–143, 2024.
https://doi.org/10.1007/978-3-031-60884-1_9

To strengthen the role of heads of school in this context the German Ministry funded a project called LeadCom (see below), in which the digital leadership competencies shall be strengthened by concepts of further education. Yet, before elaborating concepts for further education the starting condition from which further actions can be derived is the analysis of the actual leadership tasks that school principals are confronted with. The project LeadCom, which stands for "Digital Leadership & Development of communication and cooperation", is situated in the context of a series of projects called "learning:digital". In the context of the project LeadCom 11 German universities work on "Distributed Digital Leadership" (for the definition see below). This paper stems from one of the sub-projects of LeadCom at the University of Bielefeld – focusing on the interlink between inclusion and digitization. The unique selling proposition of the sub-project at hand is the combination of three crucial topics, namely inclusion, digitization and leadership. The aim is to develop a concept for networking and further education – in order to make the most out of "digital inclusion" and to share good practice. In this context a sound elaboration of the status quo of the state of research is the basis for developing concepts of further education and networking activities.

The term "distributed leadership" is to be explained first, as it is the basis for the further conceptual elaborations: Let us, first of all, clarify the difference between leadership and administration: According to Kotter (1998) leadership can be defined as one of the most important function of a leader and leadership is linked to visions that shall inspire the members of staff. Management, on the contrary, in this view is linked to administration. School leaders face multiple leadership and administrative tasks. Therefore, it makes sense for them not to try to fulfill the leadership demands of an inclusive digital culture as a one-person project but it can be recommended to involve motivated stakeholders with expertise from the faculty to share the responsibility in the sense of distributed leadership. Waffner (2021) says: "Principals, school leadership teams, individuals responsible for pedagogical-didactic management, or those with specific tasks such as social workers, as well as media coordinators, can assume leadership positions[2]" (Waffner, 2021). In this way a media coordinator can also be a "leader of systemic change" (Ungar & Shamir-Inbal, 2016) and thus take a relevant role (Waffner, 2021).

Bolden (2004) defines the approach of distributed leadership as a "systemic perspective, whereby leadership responsibility is dissociated from formal organizational roles, and people at all levels are given the opportunity to influence the overall direction" (Bolden, 2004). Applied to the topic digital inclusion this means that it is not only the head of school but also the "expanded school leadership team" who have to integrate inclusive media concepts in the daily school routines. The idea behind is that the faculty may have in-depth expertise that goes beyond the isolated expertise of the head of school and that these members of staff may help to fulfill leadership tasks – sometimes even if the competence is not formally ascribed to them. For example, in German schools, so-called media representatives are chosen to take responsibility for writing media concepts, purchasing media equipment, maintaining it etc. It is very likely that these people will acquire a high expertise by fulfilling their job and that these jobs will prepare them

---

[2] "Principals, school leadership teams or any other member of staff responsible for pedagogical-didactic leadership or having other specific roles, such as social workers or media coordinators, can assume leadership positions" [translated by the authors].

to meet the challenges of similar media-oriented leadership tasks in the future - like e.g. introducing a digital platform. The advantages for the heads of school are that they are relieved from at least some of their digital leadership tasks – which gives them more time for other urgent leadership jobs such as communication or teambuilding or developing a vision. For the members of staff, the advantages are that they can bring in their expertise, deepen it and that they get recognition from their colleagues, the head of school and perhaps even from their pupils and their parents – which will probably, in turn, strengthen intrinsic motivation, self-determination and identification with the inclusive media concept of the school: a classical win-win situation of delegating responsibility.

To make the concept of "distributed leadership" usable for inclusive-media school development, the topic shall be dealt with starting out from the perspective of digitization, notably, the model by Eickelmann & Gerick (2018, respectively 2017), the Framework for North Rhine-Westphalia (Eickelmann, 2020) and the systematic review by Waffner (2021) – who analyzed school development in the digitally shaped world. For these three approaches, implications for inclusion will be elaborated by the authors. At the end of the respective section each dimension shall be scanned for success factors regarding inclusive school development (Drossel et al., 2023a, 2023b) and success conditions for equitable digitization-related school development processes will be derived based on the insights. In the second part of this subsection on inclusive digital leadership, the digitization perspective will be crosschecked against papers starting from the perspective of inclusion, like the index for inclusion (Booth & Ainscow, 2002). The perspective of inclusion shall be widened and be further developed by integrating reference points from the perspective of digitization. At the end of the paper the approaches will be synthesized. A tentative suggestion for a preliminary model with regard to dimensions for inclusive-digital leadership shall be proposed. Although the paper is primarily based on German concepts of Educational Sciences and is, therefore, based on the settings of the German education system, it also offers points of reference for inclusive digital school development in the international context, respectively for distributed leadership. It can be assumed that - despite the exemplary character of the model – the findings will not only be of relevance to the German context but also for other countries of the world.

2   Leadership Tasks - Starting from the Perspective of Digitization

The synopsis shall be opened with the findings of Waffner's systematic review: She synthesized the findings of 56 German and English studies published between 2016 and 2020 and presented empirical research findings on supportive aspects, areas of tension, and potentials of school development processes. Interestingly she identified the following recurring aspects that were dealt with in one third of the school development studies: (1)

vision & culture[3], (2) school organization and structure[4], (3) pedagogics and learning processes[5] and (4) professionalization by cooperation and networking[6] (Waffner, 2021).

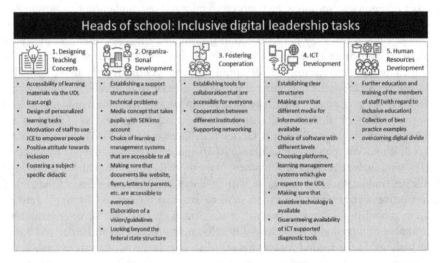

Fig. 1. Inclusive digital leadership tasks adapted from Eickelmann and Gerick (2017).

In accordance with Waffner's findings, the model of the five dimensions of digitization-related leadership by Eickelmann and Gerick (2017) offers several points of connection for inclusive digital leadership. The dimensions are **"design of teaching concepts"**, **"strategic development of their organization"**, **"fostering cooperation"**, **"developing ICT concepts"**, and **"human resources development"** (adapted by Eickelmann & Gerick, 2017 from Holtappels & Rolff, 2010). The outline for discussing the above-mentioned five subsections follows the same sequence. As a first step the dimension will be transferred and adapted to the aim of equitable and inclusion-sensitive leadership by the authors. As a second step, additional insights come from the study by Drossel et al. (2023a; 2023b), who diagnosed schools that were unexpectedly successful within the cross-national ICILS study. They identified schools whose students showed a comparatively high level of competence in terms of ICT skills, even though conditions such as the composition of the student body were challenging (e.g. economically less privileged families). The aim of the study was to get a good overview of the tasks, challenges and success factors for inclusive digital leaders – in order to provide a sound basis for further education concepts later on, as the integration of media can only unfold

---

[3] Ilomäki & Lakkala, 2018; Armistead, 2016; Cho et al., 2016; Gilmore & Deos, 2020, quoted from Waffner (2021).

[4] Razak et al., 2018; Hakansson et al., 2019; Sheninger, 2019; Cho et al., 2016 quoted from Waffner (2021).

[5] Blau & Shamir-Inbal, 2017, quoted from Waffner (2021).

[6] Ilomäki & Lakkala, 2018; Schiefner-Rohs, 2019; Agelii et al., 2019; Hakansson et al., 2019; Toh, 2016, quoted from Waffner (2021).

its innovative character when accompanied by strategically planned school development measures.

1. "Designing teaching concepts"

One of the dimensions that Eickelmann & Gerick (2017) consider is the design of teaching concepts. Let us now widen this dimension from the level of digital leadership to the level of inclusive leadership (in the sense of inclusive digital leadership), as digital media have big potentials for inclusive teaching concepts: With the integration of modern technologies, educators can create personalized learning experiences. They can make use of modern pedagogical methods (like media project work) that integrate technology to engage and motivate students while providing equal opportunities for all - including those with Special Educational Needs (SEN). In this context it is important to develop – as common sense within the staff – multidisciplinary standards for teaching (Wagner, 2021), which give respect to the UDL in the way teaching and learning is organized and in all teaching materials. The UDL is based on the concept of Universal Design (UD). The UD in turn is a concept that stems from the field of architecture aiming at designing products, tools, systems and buildings in a way that as many people as possible can use these without any or minor further adaption. The UDL again transfers this idea to concepts for learning. Learning arrangements and learning materials as well as physical and virtual learning environments/spaces should be free of barriers and accessible to all learners without any assistive technology. ICT can be a game-changer in this aspect because it makes it easier to apply the principles of the UDL. Yet, according to Lorenz et al. (2021) the percentage of teachers integrating digital media in teaching in Germany is only about 50% (rising to 73,3% in 2021 – possibly due to the COVID 19 crisis).

Digital-inclusive leaders do not necessarily have the chance to adopt the UDL-guidelines (www.cast.org) for teaching themselves – but they should take the role of a disseminator. Leaders should spread the idea of respecting the UDL, namely: providing "multiple means of engagement" (see www.cast.org) (by providing options for individual choice and autonomy, by varying demands, and by providing options for self-regulation, self-assessment and reflection, etc.), "multiple means of representation" (see www.cast.org) (by providing options for perception, by promoting understanding across languages and by activating background knowledge, etc.) and "multiple means of action and expression" (by providing options for physical action, by using multiple media etc.) (see www.cast.org). In the sense of a didactic double decker (Geissler, 1985, Wahl, 2013) heads of schools should not only apply these UDL guidelines themselves when disseminating the content to the members of staff but they should motivate the latter to do it likewise with their students. In summary: one of the leadership tasks is motivating members of staff for the use of ICT to empower pupils. The aim is to raise awareness for the accessibility of learning materials and learning spaces via giving respect to the UDL.

Looking at the success factors for inclusion-oriented & digitalization-related schooling as elaborated by Drossel et al. (2023a; 2023b) the following factors can be derived: Schools that were unexpectedly successful in the section "Designing teaching concepts" fostered methodological-didactical competencies of the staff regarding individualized schooling and differentiation options (Drossel et al., 2023a; 2023b), a systematic integration of prior knowledge and an open attitude towards the everyday life world of students (Drossel et al., 2023a; 2023b). Another success factor was offering voluntary learning opportunities and extracurricular activities (Drossel et al., 2023a; 2023b). As a consequence, the support of staff whilst designing inclusive digital teaching materials can be recommended (Drossel et al., 2023a; 2023b). Finally, a recommendation for action is integrating the existing knowledge of pupils and an openness for the digital everyday life of the pupils into school life. Extracurricular classes and activities should be offered on a voluntary basis to all students (Drossel et al., 2023a; 2023b).

2. Strategic development of the organization/Organizational development

As the next step, the second level that Eickelmann & Gerick (2017) identified for leadership in a digitized world shall be presented and applied to inclusion, namely "strategic organizational school development". The implementation of ICT within a school necessitates a well-structured organizational master plan taking all players and stakeholders into account (Schulte, 2021) - including a well-working media concept that gives respect to the needs of pupils with SEN. Yet, in their representative survey of a total of 1,512 secondary level I teachers Lorenz et al. (2021) report that just 67,7% of their interviewees say that a media concept was available at their institutions, which means that at the time 1/3 of the schools didn't have any media concept at all – not to speak of a digital-inclusive concept.

Initiating such a process of designing an inclusive media concept is of course complex and it is directly linked to other leadership tasks like creating an inclusive vision statement for the school. In the context of inclusion, it is not only important for the heads of schools to give a model for living inclusion but it is also important to motivate members of staff to adopt an open attitude towards pupils with SEN. At this point it can help to initiate reflection on the index on inclusion (Booth & Ainscow, 2002) because a positive attitude towards inclusion and towards digitization are crucial before starting to work on a strategic vision statement and/or before starting to work on an inclusive media concept (see below). If a media concept is already available, this should, in view of the authors, be re-designed by checking all aspects according to whether inclusion is fostered. The specific challenges of digitization for a particular school should regularly be reflected on and adapted to up-to-date standards. Success should be monitored (Eickelmann, 2023) and good practice should be used for refining the media concept. Endberg (2021) asks for an overall organizational philosophy.

With reference to Drossel et al. (2023a; 2023b), again some success factors for inclusion-oriented & digitalization-related organizational development can be identified. Successful schools in this category had developed media-oriented strategies & visions and pointed out their relevance (Drossel et al., 2023a; 2023b). They had interdisciplinary as well as subject-specific agreements on the inclusion-oriented implementation of ICT (Drossel et al., 2023a; 2023b). They integrated digital media in concepts, school programs, school regulations, mission statements, pedagogical concepts and school curricula while giving a special focus on/to a heterogeneous student body (ibid.). Furthermore, they established clear structures and binding tasks for inclusion-oriented & digitalization-related organizational development and they offered regular opportunities for exchange and networking (Drossel et al., 2023a; 2023b). As a consequence, it is recommended that ICT-and inclusion-oriented strategies and mission statements should be developed as a signpost for the staff. Interdisciplinary as well as subject specific agreements should be taken on the inclusion-oriented use of ICT (Drossel et al., 2023a; 2023b). Clear structures as well as opportunities for networking should be established (Drossel et al., 2023a; 2023b).

3. Fostering cooperation

Another dimension suggested by Eickelmann & Gerick (2017) is "fostering collaboration". Again, this idea shall be transferred to the context of inclusion: Collaboration is a cornerstone of effective education and plays a pivotal role for fostering inclusive and individualized education (Kuhl, 2021)[7]. ICT can be a benefit in this context as it can facilitate cooperative processes among teachers, parents and institutions. The use of online collaboration tools and platforms to foster cooperation is, therefore, an urgent leadership task. Collaboration is linked to sharing teaching materials/concepts as Open Educational Resources, for which knowledge about licenses and platforms are a prerequisite. Ideally, cooperation fosters the motivation of teachers and their self-efficacy in the context of inclusive media use. These aspects go far beyond the technical media equipment of infrastructure level: Offers and platforms are of little help if there is no culture of sharing in the faculty. In consequence, it is a leadership task to remunerate sharing and collaborating and to give rewards for doing so.

Yet, it is not only necessary to cooperate within the school itself; it is also important to cooperate with external institutions to leverage synergies (Eickelmann, 2023), such as other schools or universities but also publishing houses, media counseling centers, public community centers, private companies (Wagner, 2021). Decisions and results must be in accordance with the institutions of school supervision like the district government, education offices and school authorities (Eickelmann, 2023). To enable fruitful cooperation with other stakeholders it is important to have platforms for data transfer and other infrastructure, which are in compliance with data protection regulations and data privacy requirements. Again, this is especially true in the context of pupils with SEN, since information on the educational support needs of pupils are sensitive data, which should be accessible only to those people who are concerned with these.

Nevertheless, the technical prerequisites for collaboration are one aspect only. With the aim of establishing collaboration structures for the sake of digital inclusion heads of school need elaborated communication skills and team skills. Empathy is needed on behalf of the leaders to support networking and to motivate members of staff to share knowledge. The above-mentioned competencies all presuppose an inclusion-friendly and digitization-friendly attitude of the people involved. These skills belong to the so-called soft skills or future skills. Cooperation assumes a reflective and empathic leader but also a motivated faculty – where everybody is aware of his/her own strengths and weaknesses. The best teamwork is supposed to be happening when there is a lot of shared expertise. The results of a group of people with similar strengths can be supposed to be superior to the results of solo work, but a group of people with shared expertise can be

---

[7] https://www.pedocs.de/volltexte/2021/23413/pdf/Mueller_Kuhl_2021_1_QfI_Kooperation.pdf.

expected to get even more elaborated results. An example may help to demonstrate this: If there are five coordinators in a team, no decision will be taken because the time will be spent on discussing the decision. If there are five networkers only, this is also less than ideal because the working process might not be as effective as possible. If there are five expert specialists but no coordinator – the leadership task will not be filled and so on. So, it is the leader's responsibility to invite those people to collaborate who complement one another.

Likewise, the above-mentioned soft skills are not only leadership competencies but they are also the educational goal and learning objective of inclusion itself: Every pupil should have equal participation rights and should feel at ease. This also includes friendly interaction, as well as respect and tolerance. - On a higher administrative level, the district government should remunerate collaboration among different schools.

According to Drossel et al. (2023a; 2023b) success factors for fostering cooperation in the context of inclusive media education were supporting a respectful way of communication amongst all stakeholders and the development of school-crossing cooperation (e.g. with providers of IT services, school authorities, municipal partners etc.) to improve inclusion-oriented media education. Apart from this, inclusion-oriented ICT-supported learning should be developed in a joint process. Access to an efficient digital communication system should be established for heads of schools, teachers, students, parents and other stakeholders (Drossel et al., 2023a; 2023b). As a consequence, a transparent, barrier-free and accessible way of digital communication should be guaranteed for all stakeholders in school; networking opportunities across the school boundaries should be offered (with a focus on digital inclusion), learning processes should be conceived jointly (Drossel et al., 2023a; 2023b).

4. ICT Development

The fourth level by Eickelmann & Gerick (2017) is called ICT development. The relevance of this dimension shall be briefly outlined - sticking to the digitization level initially - before this dimension will be scanned again from the perspective of inclusion. Heads of schools must stay updated with the cutting-edge technologies, tools, and applications relevant to education. ICT development in the sense of technical infrastructure is therefore a central theme for school leaders (Eickelmann, 2023), as the effective integration of technology requires a well-designed infrastructure with adequate hardware, software and IT support (Wagner, 2021). On condition that the infrastructure is available, "standards for problem solving" can be developed (Wagner, 2021) and digital tools can be used for administrational purposes as well (Eickelmann, 2020) and also for remote and flexible work (Eickelmann 2023: 23). Yet, according to Mußmann et al. (2021) only 70% of teachers have adequate access to WIFI for all teachers, whereas in half of the schools there is no access to WIFI for pupils.

Now, this level shall be applied to inclusion again: Heads of schools need to understand how to make informed decisions about the selection, implementation, and maintenance of ICT tools and platforms that are accessible and beneficial for ALL students, including those with SEN. They have to convince local authorities of investing in accessible ICT-tools. Technical development also implies investing in assistive technology, such as screen readers, text to speech software, braille displays, screen magnifiers, speech recognition software, adaptive mice, subtitling programs, picture boards, electronic magnifiers, etc. So, knowledge about assistive technologies – introduced with the aim to enhance accessibility and independence for people with disabilities or other barriers - is an important task for digital-inclusive leadership. As a recent challenge, the school leaders' awareness for the utilization of artificial intelligence and big data in education - and how these innovations can be used for improved learning outcomes of ALL pupils - must be raised.

The section on ICT development shall be completed by the success factors for inclusion-oriented media-related ICT development as elaborated by Drossel et al. (2023a; 2023b) again. Success factors are a good and running technical infrastructure, a clear allocation of tasks among the staff, a strong leadership position of school leaders whilst planning the pedagogically-driven inclusion-oriented acquisition of IT, the systematic access to digital media and ICT infrastructure for ALL students and a consistent organization of the inclusion-oriented IT infrastructure development (Drossel et al., 2023a; 2023b). As a consequence, it can be recommended to allocate ICT-related tasks to the different stakeholders in a transparent way and to empower heads of school to plan a didactic-oriented acquisition of ICT tools – for the purpose of inclusion. Access to digital media should be developed and improved systematically and a modern infrastructure should be created (Drossel et al., 2023a; 2023b).

5. Human Resources Development

The last dimension elaborated by Eickelmann & Gerick (2017) is HR development. Even without having the perspective of inclusion in mind, the successful integration of ICT within a school requires a well-trained staff. Ideally, the faculty should be invited to participate in the media-education decision processes (Wagner, 2021) – and this is particularly relevant to inclusive media education. The latter implies a shift of mind and likewise an attitude of openness for new technical developments (Eickelmann, 2023). Heads of schools need to invest in the professional development of their staff to ensure that educators are proficient in using ICT for the benefit of ALL pupils effectively and this also implies that freedom for the design to ICT-based teaching concepts is provided (Wagner, 2021). This asks for strategies for HR-development focusing on further education, mentorship programs and the creation of a culture that values technological proficiency in inclusive school settings. Yet, these modules of further education do not necessarily need a costly "big" program of further education but it can also mean small elements of internal microlearning (Eickelmann, 2023). Transparency about areas of responsibilities and further education programs is indispensable (Eickelmann, 2023).

Like in the section above, where it was argued that the implementation of platforms will not guarantee a culture of sharing, it must be stated that the investment in ICT and in assistive technology will not guarantee the use of it. Equipment initiatives launched in Germany, like the so-called "DigitalPakt" provided schools – on condition that they had developed a media concept – with money to improve the media-technical infrastructure of the school. Yet, the "DigitalPakt" in Germany has led to the paradoxon that for example a lot of money has been spent on smartboards, which have hardly been used by the moment when they get technologically obsolete. Further education on hardware and software is again a sine qua non. Members of staff also have to be trained as far as digital inclusion (Eickelmann, 2023) is concerned. They have to know about the UDL, about didactic concepts for inclusive media projects, they need knowledge about how to profit from the technology which is available at the respective school, etc. By bridging the gap between technology and education, the aim is to empower heads of schools to create learning environments that are truly inclusive and capable of leveraging the potential of every student.

Finally, it is worth taking another look at the success factors elaborated by Drossel et al. (2023a; 2023b). Success factors for inclusion-oriented media-related HR development are internal and external modules for further education, which are offered on a regular basis that take heterogeneity into account (Drossel et al., 2023a; 2023b). Assessing training needs in the area of inclusive media education is a continuous task. Awareness for digital divide must be raised amongst the heads of schools (Drossel et al., 2023a; 2023b). As a consequence, programs of further education on digital inclusion should be announced regularly (Drossel et al., 2023a; 2023b). Training needs should be diagnosed and special modules for overcoming digital divide should be offered (Drossel et al., 2023a; 2023b).

To sum up the points elaborated up to now: Even from the perspective of digitization the leadership tasks for heads of school are multifaceted. School leaders have to take the consequences that the digital age has for society into account, namely new forms of communication, new forms of handling and sharing information, new ethic dimensions in the mission statement, new risks of digital exclusion and new dimensions in teacher education. The recent progress in the technological development of ICT, such as artificial intelligence, has to be considered in further education of the school staff and in a new attitude towards ICT. School leaders, quite often having taken their degree in the pre-digital age, are not always adequately prepared to face these new challenges. And if they do not have a private interest in technology (or an intrinsic interest in further education in ICT matters for themselves) it is possible that they will lack the expertise to take well-founded decisions for their schools and staff.

The model by Eickelmann & Gerick (2017) is a brilliant starting point for further reflections but it is set up on quite an abstract level. If a more concrete and hands-on "translation" (on what organizational development implies) is needed, a glance at the Framework for teachers in a digitized world by Eickelmann (2020) can be recommended.

The above-mentioned tasks of inclusive digital leadership are already very complex and demanding – even up to this point of the analysis. Despite this, the above-printed visualization (Fig. 1) shall be "cross-checked" against and completed by ideas from the so-called "framework for teachers in a digitized world" by Eickelmann (2020) in the following section of the paper. It goes without saying that teachers and heads of schools do not have same tasks, but nevertheless it makes sense, in our view, to take Eickelmann's (2020) work as a reference for brainstorming because most heads of school simultaneously have teaching functions as well. The framework lists the following five areas: (1) teaching, (2) educating, (3) promoting learning and achievement, (4) advising and (5) developing school. The fifth column falls again into four more subcategories - with regard to media education (not yet focusing on inclusion). In this category, the following four sub-levels are listed: *(1) media related school development, (2) professionalization, (3) innovative processes and (4) organization and administration* (Fig. 2).

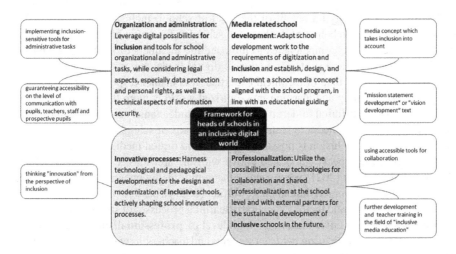

Fig. 2. Framework for heads of school in an inclusive world adapted from Eickelmann (2020).

In the LeadCom project this fifth column, named "developing school" is re-designed here by the authors in the sense that a special focus is laid on inclusion: Referring to *(1) inclusive school development in a digitized world* this means that media concepts and mission statements, websites etc. school take inclusive design principles into account (option for easy language, choice between different languages etc.). Referring to *(2) inclusive professionalization in a digitized world* this means that aspects of inclusive media education, like UDL, assistive technology, etc. should be integrated into the teacher training programs. Referring to an *(3) inclusive innovative processes in a digitized world* this means that all innovative decisions should be checked from the perspective of inclusion to make sure that everybody can participate. Referring to *(4) inclusive organization and administration in a digitized world* it means that everybody should have access to media (e.g. hardware, platforms etc.) – in other words only inclusion-sensitive tools should be implemented.

Comparing the ideas derived from the "framework for teachers in a digitized world" by Eickelmann (2020) to the ideas derived from the "5-level-model" (Eickelmann & Gerick, 2017) presented in the first section it gets clear that several aspects come up in both papers. Yet, both papers have different strengths: The 5-level-model stresses the **technical** aspect (=ICT development) and the **cooperation** aspect (=fostering cooperation), whereas the framework for teachers in a digitized world stresses the **administrational** aspects. Both papers emphasize the idea of HR-**development/**professionalization and the aspect of **organizational development/school development.** In both papers **teaching concepts** play a pivotal role: In the framework a complete column is dedicated to teaching. This column was left out in the analysis at hand to focus on the dimension "school development" but it is worth mentioning that the idea of **"teaching"** is prevalent in both documents (which is not surprising at all because the aim of school development is in fact good education; i.e. good teaching and learning).

A summary at this point – from the perspective of inclusive digital leadership – is that it needs more than just offering apps for individualized learning and furnishing of (assistive) technology on behalf of the head of school. Inclusive digital leadership needs competencies on behalf of the heads of school to find out who the stakeholders in the faculty are and the competencies to motivate the members of staff (e.g. by having created a joint vision and strategy). Inclusive digital leadership is thus perhaps more a question of soft skills than of technical expertise: it is his/her responsibility to create a climate where teaching and learning in a digitized world is more than shifting from an analogous folder to a digital folder; it is a shift of attitude, namely motivating staff to see the potential of digital media to foster inclusion. Heads of schools have to disseminate the knowledge that inclusion is possible *in, at* and *via* digital media (Bosse, 2016).

Comparing the aspects elaborated above with the areas/tasks of heads of schools elaborated by Waffner (2021) when having the aim of media integration in mind it gets clear that there are several redundancies. Waffner (2021) asks for: "the intensification of **student engagement** and thereby successful learning processes of students, creative and **stimulating learning environments,** a high level of **professionalism** among teachers, strengthening **communication** between students and teachers, as well as among teachers, enhancing the **visibility of media use** through the school's public relations initiatives, establishing characteristics or **branding of the school** in relation to media usage and creating diverse **digitally-supported spaces** for learning experiences" (Waffner, 2021; also see Sheninger, 2019).

Intensification of student engagement as well as stimulating learning environments and creating digitally-supported spaces for learning are implied in what Eickelmann & Gerick (2017) call "design of teaching concepts". The equivalent to professionalism is "HR development" in the Eickelmann & Gerick (2017) model. Communication is an essential condition for "collaboration" and could be interpreted as a necessary prerequisite of team processes. The other aspects focused on by Waffner (2021) correspond to "organizational development" in the Eickelmann & Gerick (2017) approach. Vice versa, ICT development in the Eickelmann & Gerick (2017) approach is part of each of the Waffner (2021) dimensions either.

Having identified the leadership tasks the next step beyond this is to delegate responsibility for this process to the staff: "From inclusive digital leadership to distributed inclusive digital leadership". Once again, the competencies which are needed stem from the field of leadership (like: "being able to delegate" etc.) and not so much from the technical field. Nevertheless, this shall not be misunderstood in the sense that technical expertise is not needed. On the contrary, a head of school will not be able to take well-founded decisions if he/she lacks the knowledge on ICT. But this is just a necessary, but not sufficient condition.

3   Leadership Tasks - Identified When Starting from the Perspective of Inclusion

In the summarizing section of the chapter starting from the perspective of digitization it already got clear that leadership needs technical expertise as well as the so-called soft skills or future skills, like communicating, teambuilding etc. Now the findings shall be contextualized from the perspective of an inclusive world. The starting point is quite different for "digitization" on the one hand and "inclusion" on the other hand: For the dimension of ICT and digitization Stalder (2016) pointed out that we live in a digitized world – so the shift from the analogous world to the digital world has already been accomplished. For the dimension of inclusion (cf. UN Convention on the Rights of Persons with Disabilities) a really "inclusive society" or "culture of inclusion" is still a target perspective. Certainly, it is legally anchored that people with all kinds of disabilities can attend a "regular" school in the normal school system. Despite this, people with disabilities of any kind sometimes face discrimination and exclusion (e.g. by classmates). The above-mentioned shift of attitude needs a lot of energy and is far more complex because changing deep-rooted beliefs is far more time consuming than purchasing technology.

Scanning inclusive digital leadership from the starting perspective "inclusion", a point of reference on the international level can be the index of inclusion by Booth & Ainscow (2002). They suggest the following steps to set up a process of inclusive school development: Starting point is the creation of inclusive **cultures,** followed by producing inclusive **policies** and by evolving inclusive **practices.** From the content point of view there are direct links of the index to the "Pedagogy of Diversity" as suggested by Prengel (2006) and the "Diversity Studies" by Krell et al. (2007) (quoted from Kamin et al. (2018)): Diversity is seen as an asset; all pupils shall be seen as ONE inseparable – yet heterogenous – group (Kamin et al. 2018; see Hinz, 2002). The idea is to have a democratic approach - abolishing hierarchic structures. For this idea Prengel (2007) introduces the term "right to diversity".

The first dimension "inclusive cultures" includes a welcoming culture and attitude, helpfulness, collaboration among all involved actors, as well as a connex to everyday life in pedagogical actions. Digital media facilitate collaboration and are thus a catalyst for collaboration. A didactic application for this is the conceptual framework of media projects, which allow pupils to contribute according to their strengths. So, an important leadership task of heads of schools is to minimize discrimination and digital divide and to anchor project work in the didactic set up of the teaching vision.

The second dimension is "inclusive policies" – asking for concrete measures to make barrier-free learning possible. Many mobile devices already allow adjustment settings which make the use of assistive technology in some cases superfluous (Kamin & Hester, 2015; see Kamin et al., 2018.). Inclusive media education has, for example, the potential for individualization. This dimension thus leads back to assistive technology, the UDL-character of mobile devices and barrier-free, individualized learning settings.

The third dimension, called "inclusive practices", means that learning arrangements have to be set up which give respect to inclusion such as gaming or project work (as a high forms of interaction) (see Lütje-Klose & Miller, 2015, Schell, 2003; Kamin et al., 2018.). As mentioned above, project work could be a concept to take this dimension into account. Heads of schools should insist on inclusive practices in the teaching and learning approach of the school.

When reading the index of inclusion from the perspective of digitization, it gets clear that most of the results do have an equivalent match with the points that were listed above when starting out from the perspective of digitization.

Nevertheless, some points shall be highlighted in the index for inclusion, which have a special focus: The first point is that in the index of inclusion the aspect of **culture** is emphasized a lot more. In addition, Booth and Ainscow (2002) stress that inclusion is a time-consuming process which needs several terms and remains an **ongoing process.** The reason for this might be in the fact that an inclusive attitude cannot be raised in a one-day-seminar but needs time to evolve. In order to trigger a real shift of mind in people's heads a shift in culture is needed – which is far more complex than just shifting the communication channel from a letter to an e-mail or a text message. Unlike ordering and setting up ICT in school (which - without considering the further education of the staff - is perhaps just a question of a relatively short time) valuing diversity as a "valuable resource for inspiration" is a question of mind set. This needs a continuous process and at least several school terms. More than in the context of digitization – where the process of digitalization occurs without the active intervention of each individual – the setting up a culture of inclusion needs the individual effort of each person. Therefore, success of establishing an inclusive culture is much more dependent on the individual effort of each school to establish and inclusive school mission statement and to build up a climate of diversity.

A similar and related point is that **values** are given more emphasis. Finally, the **support factor** gets more consideration – in the sense that "support for diversity" is stressed.

To build up an inclusive culture Booth & Ainscow (2002) highlight the factor "support structure" as being significant. Looking back to the digitization model it can be concluded that this item is perhaps implied in the bullet point "organizational development" (by Eickelmann & Gerick, 2017) but in the opinion of the authors it should get further emphasis by being explicitly added to the model. The idea of a support structure is of course also inherent in the approaches starting from digitization, but they are elaborated in less depth – probably because creating a culture of inclusion is more vulnerable and demanding than buying technology. Explicitly stressing the idea of inclusion can create exclusion as well – leading to new forms of stigmatization.

Points that come up both in the digitization approach and also in the index for inclusion approach are building community and collaboration and orchestrating learning processes for a heterogeneous student body.

4 Summary: What Are the Success Factors for Distributed Inclusive Digital Leadership?

Now if we try to sum up the lists of tasks elaborated above, they boil down to the following success factors for schools in the digital age: design of inclusive digital teaching concepts, organizational development with regard to digitally supported inclusion, fostering cooperation and communication, ICT development (with the perspective of digitally supported inclusion) and HR development (with the perspective of digitally supported inclusion) – these points being derived from Eickelmann and Gerick (2017). Merging the ideas from the upper section (model of the 5 levels & framework) the following soft skills leadership points can be added: Provision of financial means and technical infrastructure (including assistive technology), further education and HR development in the area of inclusive media education as well as internal and external communication and collaboration.

From the perspective of schools in an inclusive world (according to Booth & Ainscow, 2002) an **inclusive attitude formation** – seeing diversity and heterogeneity as a value, **on-going efforts to give respect to the participation of all** pupils and the establishment of **maintenance** and **support** structures could be added.

Integrating the above-mentioned findings into the Eickelmann & Gerick (2017) model in the direction of digital inclusive leadership the elaborated points boil down to **three additional items:** one of them being **leaderships soft skills** (like empathy, identifying stakeholders for digital inclusion in the staff, initiating networks among members of staff etc.) and the other one being **"formation of attitude/attitude development with the aim of seeing diversity as an asset /added value"** amongst the staff. These are major milestones for promoting digital, inclusive and professional competencies (see Fig. 3). The last point is the establishment of a **maintenance and support structure.**

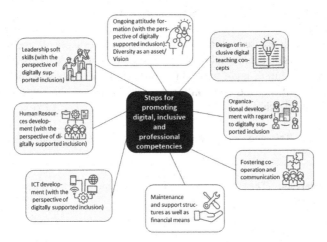

Fig. 3. Steps for promoting digital, inclusive and professional competencies adapted from Eickelmann and Gerick (2017).

Before the application of the tentative and preliminary suggestion of the model (Fig. 3) elaborated by the authors two warnings are to be issued: Up to now the model has neither been piloted in practice nor has it been empirically validated. The merits of the model could be that it might serve as a basis for designing professional development on the state of the art of conceptual scientific findings.

Another limitation is that – except for the index for inclusion - primarily German documents were the basis for elaborating the model. As an alternative approach to the chosen documents the DigCompEdu model or the TPACK model could have been an internationally accepted starting point. However, the decision was taken against the latter two and in favor of the former, as 1) these papers are binding for our project contexts and 2) because these papers focus on school development, whereas the DigCompEdu model or the TPACK model are more generally discussing digitization.

5   Conclusion and Outlook

The tasks mentioned in the model (see Fig. 3) are very challenging and the responsibility should be distributed among several people – which is why, at the very end of the paper, we come back to the point of **distributed** leadership (Bolden, 2004). If there are several stakeholders promoting the idea of inclusive media education, the chances are higher that there will be the needed shift of attitude within the staff. Collaboration helps to share ideas on how to consider the needs of pupils with SEN in brainstorming formats - which will, in the long run, hopefully lead to a more innovative school culture. But what is first and foremost is to spread – via several multipliers - the idea that technical infrastructure is not sufficient on the way to being an inclusive digital school. Inclusive digital leadership goes along with motivating members of staff for the use of ICT to empower pupils (see above). A helpful step in the desired direction might be a triple shift of mind: First of all, to **think digitization and inclusion together in a vision**/a mission statement - for the sake of participation of ALL students. Secondly, it is a leadership task to develop an **open attitude** towards inclusion and digitization, which does not stop on the technical level of infrastructure but likewise **includes didactic concepts** for inclusive media education. This needs **soft skills** on behalf of the leader (in addition to technical expertise). At least, it is a crucial leadership task not to try this alone, but to **identify stakeholders to give responsibilities to these and to collaborate** with them – in the sense of distributed inclusive digital leadership.

Acknowledgments. This study was funded by the BMBF (grant number: 01JA23E01G).

Disclosure of Interests. The authors have no competing interests to declare that are relevant to the content of this article.

References

Agélii Genlott, A., Grönlund, Å., Viberg, O.: Disseminating digital innovation in school – leading second – order educational change. Educ. Inf. Technol. **24**, 3021–3039 (2019). https://doi.org/10.1007/s10639-019-09908-0

Armistead, S.: Digital technologies: from vision to action. Teach. Curriculum **16**(1), 7–15 (2016)

Blau, I., Shamir-Inbal, T.: Digital competences and long-term ICT integration in school culture: the perspective of elementary school leaders. Educ. Inf. Technol. **22**(3), 769–787 (2017). https://doi.org/10.1007/s10639-015-9456-7

Bolden, R.: What is Leadership? 1st edn. University of Exeter, Exeter (2004)

Booth, T., Ainscow, M.: Index for Inclusion: Developing Learning and Participation in Schools. Centre for Studies on Inclusive Education, United Kingdom (2002)

CAST Homepage. https://www.cast.org. Accessed 29 Jan 2024

Cho, V., Allwarden, A., Wayman, J.C.: Shifting the focus to people. Principal **95**(4), 28–31 (2016)

Drossel, K., Oldak, A., Bette, R., Eickelmann, B.: Ergebnisse des UneS-Projektes und mögliche Handlungsempfehlungen für chancengerechte digitalisierungsbezogene Schulentwicklungsprozesse auf Einzelschulebene. Waxmann, Münster (2023a). www.waxmann.com/buch1479. Accessed 29 Jan 2024. https://doi.org/10.31244/9783830914792

Drossel, K., Bette, R., Oldak, A., Eickelmann, B.: Ergebnisse des UneS-Projektes und mögliche Handlungsempfehlungen für die Unterstützung von chancengerechten digitalisierungsbezogenen Schulentwicklungsprozessen durch Schulträger. Waxmann, Münster (2023b), www.waxmann.com/buch1673. Accessed 29 Jan 2024. https://doi.org/10.31244/9783830916734

Endberg, M.: Digitalisierungsbezogene Schulentwicklung: Mehr als die Summe der Einzelteile. Digitales Kolloquium zur Bildungspolitik (2021). https://bildungspolitik.blog.wzb.eu/wp-content/uploads/27/2021/11/Endberg_2021_Digitalisierungsbezogene-Schulentwicklung_mehr-als-Summe-der-Einzelteile.pdf. Accessed 29 Jan 2024

Eickelmann, B.: Lehrkräfte in der digitalisierten Welt. Orientierungsrahmen für die Lehrerausbildung in NRW. Medienberatung NRW, Düsseldorf (2020). https://www.medienberatung.schulministerium.nrw.de/_Medienberatung-NRW/Publikationen/Lehrkraefte_Digitalisierte_Welt_2020.pdf. Accessed 29 Jan 2024

Eickelmann, B.: Förderung von Chancengleichheit im Kontext von Digitalisierung. Bestandsaufnahme und für die schulische Personalentwicklung und unterstützendes Schulleitungshandeln. Paderborn/Essen (2023). https://www.lernen-digital.nrw.de/arbeitshilfen/foerderung-von-chancengerechtigkeit-im-kontext-von-digitalisierung. Accessed 29 Jan 2024

Eickelmann, B., Bos, W., Gerick, J.: Wie geht es weiter? Zentrale Befunde der Studie ICILS 2013 und mögliche Handlungs- und Entwicklungsperspektiven für Einzelschulen. SchulVerwaltung NRW **26**(5), 145–248 (2015)

Eickelmann, B., Gerick, J.: Lehren und Lernen mit digitalen Medien: Zielsetzungen, Rahmenbedingungen und Implikationen für die Schulentwicklung. In: Scheiter, K., Riecke-Baulecke, T. (eds.) Schulmanagement-Handbuch. 164. Lehren und Lernen mit digitalen Medien. Strategien, internationale Trends und pädagogische Orientierungen, pp. 54–81. Cornelsen, München (2017)

Eickelmann, B., Gerick, J.: Herausforderungen und Zielsetzungen im Kontext der Digitalisierung von Schule und Unterricht (III). Neue Aufgaben für die Schulleitung. SchulVerwaltung NRW **29**(5), 136–138 (2018)

Geißler, K.A.: Lernen in Seminargruppen. Studienbrief 3 des Fernstudiums Erziehungswissenschaft. Pädagogisch-psychologische Grundlagen für das Lernen in Gruppen. DIFF, Tübingen (1985)

Gilmore, S., Deos, K.: Integrating technology. A school-wide framework to enhance learning. Heinemann, Portsmouth (2020)

Hakansson Lindqvist, M., Pettersson, F.: Digitalization and school leadership: on the complexity of leading for digitalization in school. Int. J. Inf. Learn. Technol. **36**(3), 218–230 (2019). https://doi.org/10.1108/IJILT-11-2018-0126

Hinz, A.: Von der Integration zur Inklusion. Terminologisches Spiel oder konzeptionelle Weiterentwicklung? Zeitschrift für Heilpädagogik **53**(9), 354–361 (2002)

Holtappels, H.G., Rolff, H.-G.: Einführung: Theorien der Schulentwicklung. In: Bohl, T., Helsper, W., Holtappels, H.G., Schelle, C. (eds.) Handbuch Schulentwicklung. Theorie- Forschungsbefunde -Entwicklungsbefunde -Entwicklungsprozesse -Methodenrepertoire, pp. 73–79. Julius Klinkhardt, Bad Heilbrunn (2010)

Ilomäki, L., Lakkala, M.: Digital technology and practices for school improvement: innovative digital school model. Res. Pract. Technol. Enhanced Learn. **13**(25), (2018). https://doi.org/10.1186/s41039-018-0094-8

Kamin, A.-M., Hester, T.: Medien – Behinderung – Inklusion. Ein Plädoyer für eine inklusive Medienbildung. In: Schiefner-Rohs, M., Gómez Tutor, C., Menzer, C. (eds.) Lehrer.Bildung.Medien – Herausforderungen für die Entwicklung und Gestaltung von Schule, pp. 185–196. Schneider, Baltmannsweiler (2015)

Kamin, A.-M., Schluchter, J.-R., Zaynel, N.: Medienbildung und Inklusion – Perspektiven für Theorie und Praxis. In: Gesellschaft für Medienpädagogik und Kommunikationskultur (GMK), Bundeszentrale für gesundheitliche Aufklärung (BZgA) (eds.) Inklusive Medienbildung. Ein Projektbuch für pädagogische Fachkräfte, pp. 15–43. BZgA, Köln (2018)

Krell, G., Riedmüller, B., Sieben, B., Vinz, D.: Einleitung. Diversity Studies als integrierende Forschungsrichtung. In: Krell, G., Riedmüller, B., Sieben, B., Vinz, D. (eds.) Diversity Studies. Grundlagen und disziplinäre Ansätze, pp. 7–16. Campus, Frankfurt/Main (2007)

Kotter, J.P.: Leadership als Kraft des Wandels. In: Kennedy, C. (ed.) Management Gurus, pp. 124–129. Gabler, Wiesbaden (1998). https://doi.org/10.1007/978-3-322-82771-5_23

Lorenz, R., Yotyodying, S., Eickelmann, B., Endberg, M.: Schule digital – der Länderindikator 2021. Erste Ergebnisse und Analysen im Bundesländervergleich (2021). https://www.telekom-stiftung.de/aktivitaeten/schule-digital-der-laenderindikator. Accessed 29 Jan 2024

Lütje-Klose, B., Miller, S.: Inklusiver Unterricht – Forschungsstand und Desiderata. In: Peter-Koop, A., Rottmann, T., Lükern, M. (eds.) Inklusiver Mathematikunterricht in der Grundschule, pp. 10–32. Mildenberger Verlag, Offenburg (2015)

Mußmann, F., Hardwig, T, Riethmüller, M., Klötzer, S.: Digitalisierung im Schulsystem 2021. Arbeitszeit, Arbeitsbedingungen, Rahmenbedingungen (2021) und Perspektiven von Lehrkräften in Deutschland. Ergebnisbericht. Göttingen (2021). https://publications.goettingen-research-online.de/handle/2/89741. Accessed 29 Jan 2024. https://doi.org/10.3249/ugoe-publ-10

Müller, U.B., Kuhl, P.: Kooperation an inklusiven Schulen: Zur Zusammenarbeit in einer inklusionsbezogenen Fortbildungsreihe und in der schulischen Praxis aus Sicht von Lehrkräften. QfI - Qualifizierung für Inklusion 3(1) (2021). https://doi.org/10.21248/qfi.62

Prengel, A.: Pädagogik der Vielfalt. Verschiedenheit und Gleichberechtigung in Interkultureller, Feministischer und Integrativer Pädagogik. VS, Wiesbaden (2006). https://doi.org/10.1007/978-3-531-90159-6

Prengel, A.: Diversity education. Grundlagen und Probleme der Pädagogik der Vielfalt. In: Krell, G., Riedmüller, B., Sieben, B., Vinz, D. (eds.) Diversity Studies. Grundlagen und disziplinäre Ansätze, pp. 4–67. Campus, Frankfurt/Main (2007)

Razak, N.A., Ab Jalil, H., Krauss, S.E., Ahmad, N.A.: Successful implementation of information and communication technology integration in Malaysian public schools: an activity systems analysis approach. Stud. Educ. Eval.Eval. 58, 17–29 (2018). https://doi.org/10.1016/j.stueduc.2018.05.003

Schiefner-Rohs, M.: Distributed Digital Leadership. Schulleitungshandeln im Wandel. Schulleitung und Schulentwicklung (4), 1–22 (2019)

Schulte, J.: Medienkonzepte zur chancengerechten Schulentwicklung. Fallstudien an Schulen mit besonders herausfordernden Schüler*innenkompositionen. Springer VS, Wiesbaden (2021). https://doi.org/10.1007/978-3-658-34416-0

Stalder, F.: Kultur der Digitalität, 1st edn. Suhrkamp, Berlin (2016)

Toh, Y.: Leading sustainable pedagogical reform with technology for student-centred learning: a complexity perspective. J. Educ. Change 17(2), 145–169 (2016). https://doi.org/10.1007/s10833-016-9273-9

Waffner, B.: Schulentwicklung in der digital geprägten Welt: Strategien, Rahmenbedingungen und Implikationen für Schulleitungshandeln. In: Wilmers, A., Achenbach, M., Keller, C. (eds.) Bildung im digitalen Wandel. Organisationsentwicklung in Bildungseinrichtungen, pp. 67–103. Waxmann, Münster, New York (2021). https://doi.org/10.25656/01:23605

Wagner, A.: Schulentwicklung. Digitalisierungsprozesse im Rahmen der Schulentwicklung erfolgreich gestalten. Zeitschrift des Bundesverbandes der Lehrkräfte für Berufsbildung e.V. **4**(11/12), 373–380 (2021)

Wahl, D.: Lernumgebungen erfolgreich gestalten. Vom trägen Wissen zum kompetenten Handeln. 3rd edn. Julius Klinkhardt, Bad Heilbrunn (2013)

Author Group Educational Reporting (2020). https://www.bildungsbericht.de/de/bildungsberichte-seit-2006/bildungsbericht-2020/pdf-dateien-2020/bildungsbericht-2020-barrierefrei.pdf. Accessed 29 Jan 2024

ICT Usage at the Family-School Interface: A Systematic Review on the Situation of Children with Special Educational Needs

Daniela Nussbaumer⬥ and Chantal Deuss(✉)⬥

Interkantonale Hochschule für Heilpädagogik (HfH), Schaffhauserstrasse 239,
8050 Zürich, Switzerland
{daniela.nussbaumer,chantal.deuss}@hfh.ch

Abstract. Information and Communication Technologies (ICT) present novel avenues for communication, engagement, and education among children and adolescents with Special Educational Needs (SEN). Their utilization of ICT occurs both within the home and school environments, making the interface between family and school a pivotal area for understanding the conditions conducive to effective ICT utilization. Through a systematic review, this study aims to provide an overview of international research on the ICT usage of children with SEN at the family-school interface. A comprehensive search yielded 28 studies. Key findings underscore the importance of consistent device usage between home and school settings, as well as the ongoing social and technical support provided to parents and their children with SEN by trained professionals (educators, therapists, disability support personnel, tutors, and assistive technology specialists). Moreover, the positive attitudes of parents towards their children's ICT usage and the facilitation of communication and interaction within the family are crucial factors. Effective communication with the school and professional staff also emerges as paramount. Mainstream mobile technologies, such as smartphones and tablets, exhibit significant potential for assistive purposes owing to their widespread acceptance and capacity to mitigate stigmatization associated with SEN.

Keywords: Information and Communication Technologies · ICT · Special Educational Needs · SEN · Interface Family-School · Assistive Technologies · AT

1 Introduction

Information and Communication Technologies (ICT) hold promise for enhancing the engagement of children with Special Educational Needs (SEN). Despite ICT's pervasive nature and its significant impact on communication, interaction, and learning, there is a lack of comprehensive understanding regarding its specific utilization at the nexus of family and school, particularly among children and adolescents with SEN. The integration of ICT into learning at school is closely intertwined with the diverse usage patterns within the family environment and the individual significance of ICT for children, adolescents, and their parents. Initial exposure to ICT typically occurs at home, where students across countries tend to use ICT more frequently during their leisure time than at school.

M. Antona and C. Stephanidis (Eds.): HCII 2024, LNCS 14698, pp. 144–158, 2024.
https://doi.org/10.1007/978-3-031-60884-1_10

In accordance with Sustainable Development Goal 4 set forth by UNESCO in 2017, ensuring inclusive and equitable quality education, and promoting lifelong learning opportunities for all is the key for a participatory society. For special education, digitization in schools fundamentally presents the same challenges as in general education: On one hand, there is the task of promoting media literacy. On the other hand, ICT (Information and Communication Technology) tools are essential for media didactics to achieve subject-specific learning objectives. Additionally, there are specific issues for special education such as assistive technologies (AT), accessibility, universal design for learning, and reasonable accommodation. These components are fundamental pillars in fostering an educational environment that caters to the diverse needs of learners, including those with disabilities.

Although access to ICT is often available, there remains unequal distribution in device diversity, which influences learning opportunities and usage behavior. Studies like those conducted in Australia (Harris et al., 2017) have demonstrated the persistence of the "Digital Divide" among schoolchildren, with disparities in ICT usage based on socioeconomic status (SES). Further exploration of SES influences can provide valuable insights into managing the effects of ICT usage on health and development of young people.

Competence in handling ICT is a prerequisite for participating equitably in an increasingly digitized society. Media education from an inclusive perspective addresses the digital divide (Nguyen et al., 2023). From the perspective of media education, inclusivity encompasses addressing the digital divide, as highlighted by Nguyen et al. (2023). This divide refers to the gap between individuals who have access to and benefit from digital technologies and those who do not – often exacerbated by socioeconomic disparities, geographical location, and disability status. Recognizing and bridging this gap is essential for ensuring equal opportunities for learning and participation in the digital age.

The "ICILS - International Computer and Information Literacy Study" (Senkbeil et al., 2019) has highlighted a significant correlation between educational achievement in ICT skills and the socioeconomic background of families, aligning with the "Digital Divide" model. Secondary analyses of ICILS data from 2013 and 2018 further underscore the role of cultural capital, notably home book inventory, as a primary predictor of ICT skills across various countries.

While current media usage studies have not explicitly focused on children with SEN, parental support, alongside adequate device provision and diversity, is crucial for facilitating successful learning with ICT at home, particularly for children facing learning difficulties and behavioral challenges. The overlap between family and school settings in ICT usage is therefor particularly relevant.

This review aims to systematically collect international research on the ICT usage of children with SEN at the family-school interface, addressing key research questions concerning the nature of this interface, the emphasized aspects of ICT usage by children with SEN, and the insights into the interaction between school and home provided by existing studies.

2 Methodological Approach

2.1 Definition of Special Educational Needs

The concept of Special Educational Needs (SEN), as delineated by the British Department for Education and Department for Health (2015) and referenced by Nussbaumer and Hövel (Nussbaumer & Hövel, 2021), serves as the conceptual framework for this discourse. The SEN definition articulated in the "code of practice" is tailored to children and young individuals aged 0–25 in England and holds relevance to the studies under examination owing to its focus on the educational milieu and learning environment. It outlines specific provisions for educational services pertaining to SEN and disabilities, identifying SEN when learning difficulties surpass those typical of most children within the same age cohort. Disability is acknowledged when impairment impedes participation in recreational and scholastic activities. For this discussion, impaired participation in learning and social endeavors is subsumed under SEN (non-specific impairment). The studies scrutinized herein identify various categories, including learning difficulties (LD), physical-motor impairment (PD), autism spectrum disorder (ASD), and intellectual impairment (ID).

The role of parents, as underscored in the code of practice, accentuates a collaborative and supportive partnership between professionals and parents of children with SEN. Upon reaching the age of 16, young individuals, contingent on their abilities, possess the autonomy to make certain educational decisions independently. In instances of disagreement between parents and children, professionals are encouraged to engage impartially with both parties, ensuring that parents have access to pertinent information (Department for Education & Department for Health, 2015). The utilization of the English term SEN throughout this article is deliberate, reflecting an Anglo-Saxon definition, the English-language search methodology, and its relevance across diverse contexts (educational settings, teaching practices, and extracurricular activities), irrespective of country-specific support frameworks.

2.2 Definition of Information and Communication Technologies

In alignment with the methodology employed by Nussbaumer and Hövel (2021), we adopt Ratheeswari's (2018) delineation of Information and Communication Technology (ICT) within the educational sphere. This definition underscores the communication enabled by technology (IT), encompassing a spectrum of (mobile) devices such as computers, tablets, smartphones, etc., equipped with internet connectivity, along with software applications like educational apps tailored for information utilization, manipulation, and dissemination. Within the domain of special education, as articulated by the Swiss Foundation for Special Education and Rehabilitation, ICT embodies several critical dimensions, including its function as a facilitator for learning content with specialized interactive features, the provision of AT, digital accessibility (E-Accessibility), and the cultivation of digital competencies, encompassing both the exploitation of opportunities and the management of associated risks (Schweizer Stiftung für Heil- und Sonderpädagogik, 2023). AT in the domain of special education encompass a diverse range of technological tools, devices, software applications, and systems aimed at mitigating barriers and enhancing the functioning, learning experience, communication, and independence of individuals with disabilities. AT serves to facilitate inclusive and equitable access to educational opportunities, enabling learners with disabilities to participate more fully in academic activities, engage with educational content, communicate effectively, and navigate their learning environments with increased autonomy and efficacy. To adhere to an ICT definition rooted in the Anglo-Saxon tradition and to enhance the discoverability of our article, we employ the commonly used acronym in the English language. Moreover, following the recommendation put forth by Nussbaumer and Hövel (2021), we refrain from utilizing specific device terminology (tablet, PC, smartphone, iPad, etc.) to ensure consistency in searchability. Instead, we prioritize the keyword "ICT," highlighting its pivotal role in facilitating communication through technology (Ratheeswari, 2018), with the specific device playing a secondary role.

AT, often customized to meet the unique needs of learners with disabilities, encompass a wide spectrum of devices, software applications, and adaptive equipment aimed at enhancing accessibility, communication, learning, and participation. These may include screen readers, alternative input devices, communication boards, tactile displays, and specialized software for cognitive support or augmentative and alternative communication (AAC). On the other hand, mainstream technologies, such as computers, tablets, smartphones, and educational software applications, are designed for a broad user base but can also offer significant benefits for learners with disabilities when appropriately adapted or utilized. The seamless integration of mainstream technologies into educational practices provides opportunities for personalized learning experiences, interactive engagement, and access to a vast array of educational resources and digital content. Exploring the intersection between assistive and mainstream technologies in the context of special education entails examining how these technologies complement and reinforce each other to support diverse learners' needs.

2.3 Literature Search

The search methodology follows to the PRISMA (Preferred Reporting Items for Systematic Reviews and Meta-Analyses, see www.prisma-statement.org) guidelines, aiming to ascertain the global research landscape regarding the utilization of ICT by children with SEN. The systematic exploration of the EBSCO-Host databases was conducted by one of the authors in December 2021, with the final search date noted as December 17, 2021. To delineate the search parameters, a multi-step approach was employed to capture terms relevant to "ICT" and "out-of-school" contexts. Initially, several trial searches were conducted within the EBSCO-Host databases to ascertain the most appropriate criteria reflecting the family-school interface. Subsequently, the search strategy underwent refinement: first, by inputting the search terms into the respective databases' thesauri, second, by adopting the most pertinent criteria, and third, by screening and documenting them based on their thematic relevance. In the December 2021 search, a combination of criteria outlined in Table 1 was utilized.

The study has several limitations that warrant acknowledgment: The publication period considered spans from January 2010 to December 2021, encompassing primary studies and reviews written in English or German (with no German studies identified). The age range of the children studied falls between 4 and 18 years, covering school

Table 1. Presents the search criteria categorized into three sections.

Technology	Out of School Setting	Special Need
ICT	Family	Special Educational Need
Digital Media	Parents	Disability
Computer Use	Care Giver	Physical Impairment
Information Literacy	Home	Learning Difficulties
Mobile Devices	Leisure	Behavioural Retardation

levels from kindergarten to secondary education. Employing the search criteria outlined in Table 1, a total of 180 studies were initially identified in the EBSCO-Host databases, following the removal of duplicates through both automatic and manual processes. These 180 hits underwent scrutiny based on the following criteria: (a) Focus on the ICT usage of children with SEN, (b) ICT usage in settings outside of school, (c) thematic relevance to participation and learning, and (d) availability of published articles or studies with accessible full text. Studies were excluded if they centred on (a) ICT usage among adults, (b) ICT usage within school environments, or (c) were anecdotal reports or secondary sources.

Figure 1 provides a visual representation of the inclusion and exclusion process. After screening the abstracts, a random cross-check conducted by an intercoder revealed a 100% agreement on the included studies and a 90% agreement on the excluded ones. Subsequently, the 34 studies deemed eligible following full-text screening by one of the authors underwent review by three intercoder. A random sampling of 14 papers for full-text review resulted in a 100% agreement on the exclusion of papers (n = 5) and a 40% agreement on the inclusion of papers (n = 5). Following the assessment of intercoder reliability, the selection process culminated in a final list of 28 studies.

The delineation between ICT and AT has necessitated a revaluation within the framework of mainstream technologies. While the initial focus was on mainstream technologies, the recognition of ICT serving as AT has redirected our attention. This realization underscores the need for a comprehensive understanding of the interplay between these categories and prompts a deeper exploration into the evolving landscape of technology implementation in educational contexts, particularly within the domain of special education. In the realm of special education, the term "assistive and mainstream technologies" refers to a comprehensive array of technological resources, encompassing both specialized assistive tools designed explicitly for individuals with disabilities and mainstream technologies commonly used by the general population. This inclusive approach acknowledges the fluid interface between assistive and mainstream technologies, highlighting the interconnectedness and potential synergies between these two categories of technology within educational settings.

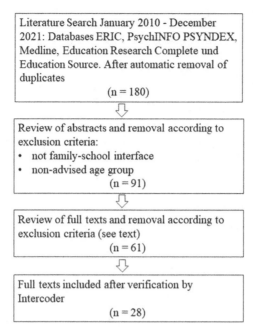

Fig. 1. Shows the inclusion and exclusion process.

3 Results

The identified studies can be classified into four categories based on the purpose of use of the digital device as outlined in Fig. 2, reviews are listed separately. Figure 2 presents a comprehensive overview of the studies, categorizing them by study type, authors, countries of origin, sample sizes, research inquiries, and methodologies employed.

3.1 Reviews

The systematic search yielded two review articles. Hsin et al. (2014) conducted an analysis of 87 empirical studies spanning from 2003 to 2013, exploring the impact of ICT on the learning of children aged zero to eight years. Their findings predominantly suggest a positive influence of ICT on children's performance. Notably, Hsin et al. did not specifically isolate SEN but grouped it with other factors such as migration status and low SES under the "miscellaneous" category. A significant portion of the studies in this category focused on children facing various disadvantages. The authors proposed a model outlining the typology of factors influencing learning with technologies, distinguishing between three main aspects: a) characteristics of children (age, gender, ICT knowledge, and experience), b) attributes of technologies (device design, apps, content, and teaching approaches), and c) influence of adults, who mediate children's learning with ICT through their behaviours, support at home, and instructional design. The attitudes and knowledge of adults, along with their guidance to children, were identified as influential

Author	Title	Country	Sample	Research Question	Method
Review					
Hsin, L. & Tsai (2014)	The influence of young children's use of technology on their learning	Taiwan	SEN / n = 87, studies	ICT learning, influencing factors	Literature Review
Chantry & Dunford (2010)	How do computer assistive technologies enhance participation in childhood occupations for children with multiple and complex disabilities?	International	SEN / n = 27, studies	ICT use, influencing factors, everyday activities, participation	Literature Review
ICT Access and Usage Patterns					
Alfredsson Ågren, Kjellberg & Hemmingsson (2020)	Access to and use of the Internet among adolescents and young adults with intellectual disabilities in everyday settings	Sweden	ID / n = 15, P	ICT access and use	Descriptive: Interview, self-assessment
Soyza & Al Mahmud (2019)	Technology for children with autism spectrum disorder: What do Sri Lankan parents and practitioners want?	Sri Lanka	ASD / n = 50, parents (32), PS (15)	ICT use, comparison with the global North	Descriptive: Interview, external assessment
Raspa, Fitzgerald, Furberg, Wylie, Moultrie, DeRamus, Wheeler & McCormack (2018)	Mobile technology use and skills among individuals with fragile X syndrome: Implications for healthcare decision making	International	SEN / n = 385, parents	ICT use, expertise, communication	Descriptive: Questionnaire
Wu, Chen, Yeh, Wang & Chang (2014)	Is digital divide an issue for students with learning disabilities?	Taiwan	LD / n = 234, P	ICT access and use, competence, skills	Descriptive: Questionnaire, experimental-control group design
Palmer, Wehmeyer, Davies & Stock (2012)	Family members' reports of the technology use of family members with intellectual and developmental disabilities	USA	ID / n = 1617, family	ICT use	Descriptive: Questionnaire, external assessment
AT to enable Communication					
Borgestig, Al Khatib, Masayko & Hemmingsson (2021)	The impact of eye-gaze controlled computer on communication and functional independence in children and young people with complex needs – A multicenter intervention study	International	ID / n = 33, P (17), parents (7), T (9)	ICT use, satisfaction, participation	Intervention: pre-post comparison
Carmo Rodrigues Almeida, Ribeiro & Moreira (2021)	Assistive technologies for children with cognitive and/or motor disabilities: interviews as a means to diagnose the training needs of informal caregivers	Portugal	ID / n = 10, parents, PS	ICT use, training needs of parents	Descriptive: Multi-perspective
Hettiarachchi, Kitnasamy & Gopi (2020)	"Now I am a techie too" – parental perceptions of using mobile technology for communication by children with complex communication needs in the Global South	Sri Lanka	SEN / n = 16, parents	ICT use	Descriptive: Interview, external assessment
Maor & Mitchem (2018)	Hospitalized adolescents' use of mobile technologies for learning, communication, and well-being	Australia	SEN / n = 51, P (18), T (29), parents (4)	ICT use, factors influencing learning, communication, well-being	Descriptive: Interview
Holmqvist, Thunberg & Dahlstrand (2018)	Gaze-controlled communication technology for children with severe multiple disabilities: Parents and professionals' perception of gains, obstacles, and prerequisites	Sweden	SEN / n = 11, parents, PS	ICT use, opportunities and risks	Descriptive: Interview, external assessment
Hynan, Murray & Goldbart (2014)	"Happy and excited": Perceptions of using digital technology and social media by young people who use augmentative and alternative communication	Great Britain	ID / n = 25, P	ICT access and use, participation	Descriptive: Interview, self-assessment
Lidström, Almqvist & Hemmingsson (2012)	Computer-based assistive technology device for use by children with physical disabilities: A cross-sectional study	Sweden	PD / n = 287, P	ICT use, satisfaction	Descriptive: experimental-control group design
Castillo (2017)	Tablet technology and its impact on families with autistic children	USA	ASD / n = 1, family	ICT use, participation	Descriptive: Single case study
ICT use for Learning					
McCorkell & Lobo (2021)	Learning in lockdown: A small-scale qualitative study exploring the experiences of autistic young people in Scotland	Scotland	ASD / n = 7, P	ICT learning, factors influencing engagement	Descriptive: Interview, self-assessment
Grindle, Murray, Hastings & Lovell (2019)	Parent-mediated online reading intervention for children with Down Syndrome	USA	ID / n = 9, P	ICT learning, reading skills/usability	Intervention: pre-post comparison
Parsons, Wilson, Vaz, Lee & Cordier (2019)	Appropriateness of the TOBY Application, an iPad Intervention for Children with Autism Spectrum Disorder: A Thematic Approach	Australia	ASD / n = 24, parents	ICT Learning, appropriateness for users	Intervention: pre-post comparison, interview, external assessment
McDougall, Readman & Wilkinson (2018)	The uses of (digital) literacy	Great Britain	SEN / n = 10, P, parents	ICT competencies, facilitating spatial factors	Action research
Ng, Augustine & Inchley (2018)	Comparisons in Screen-Time Behaviours among Adolescents with and without Long-Term Illnesses or Disabilities: Results from 2013/14 HBSC Study	International	SEN / n = 61329, P	Screen Time Behaviour (STB), comparison	Descriptive: Questionnaire, group comparison
Chuang, Kuo, Fan & Hsu (2017)	A kinect-based motion-sensing game therapy to foster the learning of children with sensory integration dysfunction	China	LD / n = 5, P	ICT use, self-efficacy, participation	Intervention: pre-post comparison
Kirk, Gray, Ellis, Taffe & Cornish (2016)	Computerised attention training for children with intellectual and developmental disabilities: A randomised controlled trial	Australia	LD / n = 75, P	ICT-supported attention training, efficacy	Intervention: Trial-control group design
Curry (2020)	Parents' perceptions of mobile device learning for students in special education	USA	SEN / n = 8, parents	ICT learning, advantages	Descriptive: Interview, external assessment
ICT Use for leisure					
Alfredsson Ågren, Kjellberg & Hemmingsson (2020)	Internet opportunities and risks for adolescents with intellectual disabilities: A comparative study of parents' perceptions	Sweden	ID / n = 94, parents	ICT use, opportunities and risks	Descriptive: Questionnaire, experimental-control group design, external assessment
Newman, Browne-Yung, Raghavendra, Wood & Grace (2017)	Applying a critical approach to investigate barriers to digital inclusion and online social networking among young people with disabilities	Australia	PD / n = 18, P, family	ICT access and use, opportunities and risks, influence of economic, cultural and social capital	Descriptive: Interview
Parker, Summerfeldt, Taylor, Kloosterman & Keefer (2013)	Problem gambling, gaming and internet use in adolescents: Relationships with emotional intelligence in clinical and special needs samples	Canada	SEN / n = 526, P (256), comparison (270)	ICT use, relationship between addictive behaviour and emotional intelligence	Descriptive: Questionnaire, experimental-control group design
Schreuer, Keter & Sachs (2014)	Accessibility to information and communications technology for the social participation of youths with disabilities: A two-way street	Israel	SEN / n = 63, P	ICT use, participation	Intervention: Trial-control group design
Raghavendra, Newman, Grace & Wood (2013)	"I could never do that before": Effectiveness of a tailored Internet support intervention to increase the social participation of youth with disabilities	Australia	SEN / n = 18, P	ICT learning, participation	Intervention: Trial-control group design

Legend: SEN = Special Educational Needs, LD = Learning Difficulties, PD = Physical Motor Disability, ASD = Autism Spectrum Disorder, ID = Intellectual Disability, P = Pupils, T = Teacher, PS = Professional Support

Fig. 2. Presents a comprehensive overview of the studies.

factors. Adults were seen to play a crucial role as mediators in the interaction between children and technologies.

Chantry and Duford (2010) reviewed 27 articles from 1995 to 2010 concerning the impact of computer use, including AT, by children with severe and complex disabilities on their participation in daily activities. Their search focused on databases in paediatrics, occupational therapy, rehabilitation sciences, and related health professions. Through thematic analysis based on an occupational therapy model, they assessed areas of everyday performance including productivity, self-regulation, and leisure. Despite limitations such as small sample sizes and a scarcity of studies with measurable participation indicators, the reviewed literature suggested that ICT use, including from an occupational therapy perspective, could benefit the participation of these children, particularly in education, communication, and play. The authors highlighted the potential of Virtual Reality (VR) as a therapeutic tool, enabling interaction between children with and without SEN, and fostering inclusion. Additionally, VR offers a safe environment for trying out activities that may be risky in real-life settings. Both review articles, although predating our study, provide valuable insights, with one indirectly touching on SEN, laying a foundation for our research.

3.2 ICT Access and Usage Patterns Referencing to the Three Categories

Additionally, significant gender disparities were observed in computer gaming, with boys, particularly those with chronic illnesses, reporting higher usage than girls (Alfredsson Ågren et al., 2020a). Authors recommended enhanced coordination of computer-based AT usage between school and home, stressing the importance of increased communication between parents and professionals on this front. Multiple studies highlighted the significance of comprehensive training for adolescents and the provision of problem-solving strategies for effective ICT utilization, underscoring the necessity for ongoing support (Alfredsson Ågren et al., 2020b). Soysa and Al Mahmud (2019) observe that children with ASD predominantly exhibit passive engagement with ICT, with interactive applications primarily utilized within therapeutic contexts under professional supervision. Raspa et al. (2018) noted a high ownership rate of mobile devices among parents of children with Fragile X syndrome, indicative of a growing trend of ICT utilization during leisure time. Other studies explored the digital gap between children with and without Learning Disabilities (LD) (Wu et al., 2014. Wu et al.'s study (2014) supported the idea that mere access to ICT for children with SEN is inadequate for developing ICT skills; instead, tailored ICT teaching programs are essential. Consistent with pre-pandemic studies, two pivotal factors were identified in fostering engagement in online learning: the presentation of tasks online and supportive adult contact. Palmer et al. (2012) conducted surveys among parents and siblings regarding the ICT utilization of family members with Intellectual Disabilities (ID), revealing a surge in device ownership without a commensurate increase in usage frequency.

3.3 AT to Enable Communication

A total of eight studies examining the utilization of AT by children with Special Educational Needs (SEN) within the family-school interface have been identified. These trials differ in their choice of methods and the demographics surveyed. For instance, one intervention with a pre-post comparison involved interviews with parents, pupils, and teachers (Borgestig et al., 2021), while another study employed a descriptive approach questioning the same group of individuals (Maor & Mitchem, 2018). Furthermore, the remaining studies predominantly adopt a descriptive approach, focusing either on pupils

(Hynan et al., 2014; Lidström et al., 2012) or on the perspectives of parents and families regarding the use of AT by young people (Carmo Rodrigues Almeida et al., 2021; Hettiarachchi et al., 2020; Holmqvist et al., 2018; Cataldo, 2016).

According to the international intervention trial conducted by Borgestig et al. (2021), most children and adolescents with physical-motor impairment (PD) face significant limitations in their use of ICT for communication. In response, 17 participants were provided with eye-gaze controlled computers (EGCC) both at school and at home, along with technical support from an AT-Centre. The results demonstrate an expanded activity repertoire and increased general computer use with the aid of AT, particularly EGCC. The authors assert that ICT use with AT significantly enhances the expressive communication skills and functional independence of children and adolescents with PD, especially with support from professionals at the Centre for AT. Notably, interpersonal communication emerges as a primary motivation for young individuals to utilize EGCC as AT, with parents and teachers expressing high satisfaction levels with the device following a six-month intervention.

In a different vein, Maor and Mitchem (2018) delve into the experiences of adolescents without specific disabilities in a hospital environment, highlighting the pivotal role of mobile technologies in fostering communication, facilitating learning, and nurturing overall well-being. Technology emerges as a potent tool in mitigating isolation, alleviating pain distraction, and fostering motivation in learning and problem-solving tasks, with educators particularly emphasizing its therapeutic benefits.

Turning to the utilization of social media by adolescents with AT, Hynan et al. (2014) explore their ICT behaviour and motivations. Adolescents utilizing AT exhibit strong motivation for internet and social media usage, driven by the opportunities provided for self-expression, self-determination, and maintaining social connections. However, disparities in satisfaction levels are noted between children and adolescents who utilize AT solely in class compared to those who use it in both class and extracurricular activities (Lidström et al., 2012).

In the descriptive study by Carmo Rodrigues Almeida et al. (2021), the dynamics of interactions between parents and adolescents are elucidated, emphasizing the critical role of frequent engagement and the proficiency of all involved parties in effectively utilizing AT. Moreover, tablets and mobile phones are recognized as potential AT tools, particularly in augmenting communication for children with ASD and their parents (Cataldo, 2016). Hettiarachchi et al. (2020) further investigate parents' perspectives on utilizing mobile devices as AT for ASD, ID, and PD, acknowledging the potential of mainstream technologies in facilitating communication and learning.

Moreover, frustration with ICT use is identified as a common occurrence, with factors such as time management, collaborative efforts, engaging content, and specialized knowledge about ICT being identified as indispensable prerequisites and catalysts for successful ICT adoption (Holmqvist et al., 2018). These findings underscore the multifaceted nature of ICT utilization within the context of SEN, highlighting the need for tailored interventions and comprehensive support mechanisms to optimize outcomes.

3.4 ICT Use for Learning Purposes

Moreover, some articles have delved into the learning experiences of children with ASD during the Covid-19 pandemic (McCorkell & Lobo, 2021). Flexibility and control over targeted schedules were also highlighted as crucial components in this context (Mc Corkell and Lobo, 2021).

Grindle et al. (2019) observed that parent-mediated ICT-based interventions, such as the Headsprout® Early Reading Program, could enhance the reading skills of children with Down Syndrome (ID). This underscores the potential of technology-assisted interventions to address specific learning needs within diverse populations. Addressing concerns regarding excessive screen time and increased sedentary behavior among adolescents with chronic illnesses or disabilities, Ng et al. (2018) shed light on the discrepancies between ownership of internet-enabled devices and actual internet access. They highlighted obstacles to internet utilization for young people with ID, including literacy skills and managing technical updates. Notably, adolescents with chronic illnesses reported heightened usage of technical devices such as computers and tablets (Ng et al., 2018).

Chuang et al. (2017) similarly demonstrated a positive effect on self-efficacy and participation in social life through kinesthetic intelligence training. Their study in China showcased the efficacy of an ICT-based therapy utilizing motion-controlled games (Microsoft Kinect Game) for children with learning difficulties (LD), leading to increased learning motivation and functional capacity, outperforming commercial games (Nintendo Wii).

Likewise, Kirk et al. (2016) found that tablet-based attention training tailored to individual characteristics of children with ID resulted in small to moderate improvements in visual search task performance. These findings underscore the potential of personalized interventions to enhance cognitive functioning among children with developmental disabilities.

Inquiries into learning with mobile devices have also been conducted (Conry, 2020). Conry (2020) investigated parents' viewpoints regarding the use of mobile phones and tablets for educational purposes, elucidating the perceived benefits for children's academic and professional prospects. This highlights the evolving landscape of educational technology and its potential to shape learning outcomes positively.

3.5 ICT Use for Leisure Purposes

Alfredsson Ågren and colleagues (2020b) undertook a comparative analysis examining attitudes and perceptions concerning opportunities and risks related to internet usage (Alfredsson Ågren et al., 2020b). Alfredsson Ågren et al. (2020b) compared the perceived opportunities and risks of internet usage between parents of adolescents with ID and a reference group, revealing a greater emphasis among parents of adolescents with ID on the opportunities associated with digital engagement, indicative of a positive attitude toward digital participation.

Further the impact of family resources on ICT usage was examined (Newman et al., 2017). Newman et al. (2017) delved into the influence of economic, cultural, and social capital on ICT access and usage among young people with Physical Disabilities (PD), emphasizing the imperative of intensive and personalized support from families, services, and schools to ensure sustained digital participation. Schreuer et al. (2014) found that equipping adolescents with SEN with computers, internet access, AT, and tutors significantly contributed to their social participation, although concerns about the limitations of digital social interactions were raised. Two articles highlight competence growth through ICT usage. Schreuer et al. (2014) also highlight the potential limitations of digital social interactions for children with SEN. It is evident that digital interventions are most effective when devices and content are tailored to the specific needs of children with SEN and their families. One study specifically focused on addiction-related behaviours like internet gambling (Parker et al., 2013). The study by Raghavendra et al. (2013) found that adolescents with SEN faced challenges in transferring training and workshops conducted in school settings to the home environment, highlighting the need for comprehensive one-on-one support for students and family members to foster a positive attitude towards ICT usage. In summation, the discourse surrounding ICT usage for leisure pursuits intertwines with a nuanced examination of attitudes and perceptions concerning the opportunities and risks associated with internet engagement.

4 Discussion and Conclusion

The comprehensive review of studies (n = 28) spanning from January 2010 to December 2021 sheds light on the utilization of Information and ICT by children and adolescents with Special Educational Needs (SEN) within the familial and educational domains across diverse global regions, encompassing Europe, North America, Australia, Asia, Israel, and Sri Lanka. The findings collectively underscore the pivotal role of access to ICT-equipped devices with internet connectivity in fostering digital inclusivity. However, mere access is insufficient in itself. Embracing a variety of devices, ranging from computers to tablets and smartphones, is perceived positively, fostering adaptability in usage patterns. Yet, ensuring consistent access to identical devices both at school and home is imperative for children with SEN and their families, necessitating regular updates to maintain relevance. It's noteworthy that training initiatives within the school milieu may encounter limitations in their transferability to the home environment, owing to technical disparities or institutional regulations, such as constraints on social media usage.

A noteworthy trend is observed the increasing integration of mainstream mobile devices as AT, offering a departure from conventional AT tools and fostering inclusivity. However, the discourse on ICT usage at the nexus of family and school predominantly leans towards qualitative investigations, primarily focusing on students with SEN, their parents, and, to a lesser extent, other family members. Notably, the involvement of teachers and other professionals remains scant in the literature.

Moreover, a significant proportion of studies concentrate on delineating the prevailing landscape of ICT usage and elucidating parental perceptions and attitudes. Positive aspects of ICT usage, particularly its role in enhancing social participation and facilitating learning, predominate the discourse, with limited attention paid to potential adverse effects. Regarding the typologies of ICT utilization among children with SEN, the spectrum encompasses AT, educational endeavours, therapeutic interventions, and leisure activities. Notably, communication facilitated through AT and the broader promotion of participatory experiences, including social media engagement, emerge as prominent thematic areas.

Parents emerge as central figures in fostering ICT adoption, shouldering the responsibility of administering regular training sessions, albeit encountering inherent challenges. The interplay between the educational and familial realms vis-à-vis ICT utilization emerges as intricate, underscoring the indispensability of seamless coordination between the two spheres for efficacious implementation. Sustained support, encompassing both technical assistance and pedagogical guidance, emerges as imperative for parents to effectively nurture their children's ICT competencies.

Moving forward, there exists a paucity of research concerning the measurement of family characteristics, necessitating standardized approaches for data collection and analysis. Furthermore, there is a pressing need for multiperspective longitudinal studies encapsulating the viewpoints of children with SEN, their parents, and professionals, to comprehensively elucidate the dynamics of ICT utilization. In essence, research at the juncture of family and school holds paramount significance in empowering children with SEN to leverage ICT optimally across diverse contexts. Collaborative efforts among stakeholders, including parents, educators, and professionals, are imperative in surmounting barriers and fostering a conducive environment for ICT integration among children with SEN.

AT encompass a spectrum of devices and technologies, including mainstream devices adapted for AT purposes. AT, in general, contributes to enhanced participation, with mainstream technologies for AT offering significant potential. A crucial aspect for exchange among professionals, parents, and children involves discussing how mainstream technologies can be utilized for AT purposes, emphasizing the practical application of devices as AT. It is paramount to consistently center the perspective of the child in these discussions, fostering mutual understanding between parents and professionals.

Integrating AT into leisure and educational contexts should ideally occur on the same devices to blur distinctions and promote equal opportunities for all users, thus destigmatizing AT usage. While a variety of devices may enhance flexibility, they can also lead to overwhelm, particularly considering the maintenance requirements. This underscores the importance of long-term, continuous, and regular support to ensure effective utilization of AT devices.

In general, the opportunities afforded by Information and Communication Technology (ICT) for AT are substantial. ICT can support and facilitate communication, enabling social interactions both in educational and familial settings. Adaptations and support functions can enhance adaptive learning experiences in schools, while ICT in leisure activities facilitates connectivity and self-expression, thus paving the way for future integration into the workforce.

However, limitations exist within the current body of research. The number of studies included in the review may be insufficient, and the interface between school and home environments is poorly defined. Longitudinal studies and studies from multiple perspectives are desirable. Therefore, it is recommended to consistently prioritize the perspective of the young individual. Furthermore, the findings should inform the development of new technologies, ensuring that considerations of accessibility are integrated from the outset of the development process.

References

Alfredsson Ågren, K., Kjellberg, A., Hemmingsson, H.: Access to and use of the Internet among adolescents and young adults with intellectual disabilities in everyday settings. J. Intell. Dev. Disabil. **45**(1), 89–98 (2020). https://doi.org/10.3109/13668250.2018.1518898

Alfredsson Ågren, K., Kjellberg, A., Hemmingsson, H.: Internet opportunities and risks for adolescents with intellectual disabilities: a comparative study of parents' perceptions. Scand. J. Occup. Ther. **27**(8), 601–613 (2020). https://doi.org/10.1080/11038128.2020.1770330

Borgestig, M., Al Khatib, I., Masayko, S., Hemmingsson, H.: The impact of eye-gaze controlled computer on communication and functional independence in children and young people with complex needs – a multicenter intervention study. Dev. Neurorehabil. **24**(8), 511–524 (2021). https://doi.org/10.1080/17518423.2021.1903603

Carmo Rodrigues Almeida, I., Ribeiro, J., Moreira, A.: Assistive technologies for children with cognitive and/or motor disabilities: interviews as a means to diagnose the training needs of informal caregivers. Disabil. Rehabil. Assist. Technol. **16**(3), 340–349 (2021). https://doi.org/10.1080/17483107.2019.1680750

Cataldo, B.: Tablet Technology and its Impact on Families with Autistic Children. Northeastern University, Boston (2016)

Chantry, J., Duford, C.: How do computer assistive technologies enhance participation in childhood occupations for children with multiple and complex disabilities? A review of the current literature. Br. J. Occup. Ther. **73**(8), 351–365 (2010). https://doi.org/10.4276/030802210X12813483277107

Chuang, T.-Y., Kuo, M.-S., Fan, P.-L., Hsu, Y.-W.: A Kinect-based motion-sensing game therapy to foster the learning of children with sensory integration dysfunction. Educ. Tech. Res. Dev. **65**(3), 699–717 (2017). https://doi.org/10.1007/s11423-016-9505-y

Conry, P.: Parental Perceptions of Mobile Device Learning for Students in Special Need Education. Walden University, New York (2020)

Department for Education & Department for Health: Special educational needs and disability code of practice: 0 to 25 years. Abgerufen von (2015). https://www.gov.uk/government/publications/send-code-of-practice-0-to-25

Grindle, C., Tyler, E., Murray, C., Hastings, R.P., Lovell, M.: Parent-mediated online reading intervention for children with down syndrome. Support Learn. **34**(2), 211–230 (2019). https://doi.org/10.1177/0743558417753953

Harris, C., Straker, L., Pollok, C.: A socioeconomic related divide exists in how, not if, young people use computers. PloS ONE **12**(3) (2017)

Hettiarachchi, S., Kitnasamy, G., Gopi, D.: "Now I am a techie too" - parental perceptions of using mobile technology for communication by children with complex communication needs in the Global South. Disabil. Rehabil. Assist. Technol. **15**(2), 183–194 (2020). https://doi.org/10.1080/17483107.2018.1554713

Holmquvist, E., Thunberg, G., Dahlstrand, M.: Gaze controlled communication technology for children with severe multiple disabilities: parent's and professionals perception of gains, obstacles and prerequisites. Assist. Technol. **30**(4), 201–208 (2018). https://doi.org/10.1080/10400435.2017.1307882

Hsin, C.-T., Li, M.-C., Tsai, C.-C.: The influence of young children's use of technology on their learning: a review. Educ. Technol. Soc. **17**(4), 85–99 (2014)

Hynan, A., Murray, J., Goldbart, J.: Happy and excited. Perceptions of using digital technology and social media by young people who use augmentative and alternative communication. Child Lang. Teach. Ther. **30**(2), 175–186 (2014)

Kirk, H.E., Gray, K.M., Ellis, K., Taffe, J., Cornish, K.M.: Computerized attention training for children with intellectual and developmental disabilities: a randomized controlled trial. J. Child Psychol. Psychiatry **57**(12), 1380–1389 (2016). https://doi.org/10.1111/jcpp.12615

Lidström, H., Hemmingsson, H., Almqvist, L.: Computer-based assistive technology device for use by children with physical disabilities: a cross sectional study. Disabil. Rehabil. Assist. Technol., 287–293 (2012). https://doi.org/10.3109/17483107.2011.635332

Maor, D., Mitchem, K.: Hospitalized adolescents' use of mobile technologies for learning, communication, and well-being. J. Adolesc. Res. 35(2), 225–247 (2018). https://doi.org/10.1177/0743558417753953

Mc Corkell, L., Lobo, L.: Learning in lockdown: a small-scale qualitative study exploring the experiences of autistic young people in Scotland. Educ. Child Psychol. 38(3) (2021)

Mc Dougall, J., Wilkinson, P., Readman, M.: The uses of (digital) literacy, learning, media and technology. Learn. Media Technol. 43(3), 263–279 (2018). https://doi.org/10.1080/17439884.2018.1462206

Newman, L., Browne-Yung, K., Raghavendra, P., Wood, D., Grace, E.: Applying a critical approach to investigate barriers to digital inclusion and online social networking among young people with disabilities. Inf. Syst. J. 27(5), 559–588 (2017). https://doi.org/10.1111/isj.12106

Ng, K., Augustine, L., Inchley, J.: Comparisons in screen-time behaviours among adolescents with and without longterm illnesses or disabilities. Int. J. Environ. Res. Public Health 15(2276) (2018)

Nguyen, T.D, Redding, C., Bettini, E.: No child left behind and the individuals with disabilities education act: examining special educators' outcomes. Remedial Spec. Educ., 1–13 (2023). https://doi.org/10.1177/07419325231193332

Nussbaumer, D., Hövel, D.C.: Nutzung von Informations- und Kommunikationstechnologien (ICT) in der Schulischen Heilpädagogik (IN_USE). (V. S. e.v., Hrsg.) Zeitschrift für Heilpädagogik, S. 628–639 (2021)

Palmer, S., Wehmeyer, M., Davies, D., Stock, S.: Family members' reports of the technology use of family members with intellectual and developmental disabilities. J. Intellect. Disabil. Res. 56(4), 402–414 (2012)

Parker, J., Summerfeldt, L., Taylor, R., Kloosterman, P., Keefer, K.: Problem gambling, gaming and Internet use in adolescents: relationships with emotional intelligence in clinical and special needs samples. Pers. Individ. Differ. 55, 288–293 (2013)

Parsons, D., Wilson, N.J., Vaz, S., Lee, H., Cordier, R.: Appropriateness of the TOBY application, an iPad intervention for children with autism spectrum disorder: a thematic approach. J. Autism Dev. Disord. 49(10), 4053–4066 (2019). https://doi.org/10.1007/s10803-019-04115-9

PRISMA Transparent Reporting of Systematic Reviews and Meta-Analyses (2023). Abgerufen am 03.11.2023 von. www.prisma-statement.org

Raghavendra, P., Newman, L., Grace, E., Wood, D.: 'I could never do that before': effectiveness of a tailored internet support intervention to increase the social participation of youth with disabilities. Child Care Health Dev. 39(4), 552–561 (2013). https://doi.org/10.1111/cch.12048

Raspa, M., Fitzgerald, T., Furberg, R., Wylie, A., et al.: Mobile technology use and skills among individuals with fragile X-Syndrome. J. Intellect. Disabil. Res. 62(10), 821–832 (2018)

Ratheeswari, K.: Information communication technology in education. J. Appl. Adv. Res. 3, 45–47 (2018). https://doi.org/10.21839/jaar.2018.v3S1.169

Schreuer, N., Keter, A., Sachs, D.: Accessibility to information and communications technology for the social participation of youths with disabilities: a two-way street. Behav. Sci. Law 32(1), 76–93 (2014). https://doi.org/10.1002/bsl.2104

Senkbeil, M., Drossel, K., Eickelmann, B., Vennemann, M.: Soziale Herkunft und computer- und informationsbezogene Kompetenzen von Schülerinnen und Schülern im zweiten internationalen Vergleich. In: Eickelmann, B., et al. (eds.) ICILS 2018#Deutschland (S. 301–333). Waxmann, Münster, New York (2019)

Schweizer Stiftung für Heil- und Sonderpädagogik: SZH.ch. Abgerufen am 03.11.2023 von (2023). https://www.szh.ch/themen/ict

158   D. Nussbaumer and C. Deuss

Soysa, A.I., Al Mahmud, A.: Technology for children with autism spectrum disorder: what do Sri Lankan parents and practitioners want? Interact. Comput. **31**(3), 282–302 (2019). https://doi.org/10.1093/iwc/iwz020

Wu, T.-F., Chen, M.-C., Yeh, Y.-M., Wang, H.-P., Chang, S.: Is digital divide an issue for students with learning disabilities? Comput. Hum. Behav. **39**, 112–117 (2014)

Talktile: Accessible Educational Tool to Augment Independent Learning for Students with BVI

Saumik Shashwat[(✉)] [iD], Parth Barthwal[iD], Deep Sharma[iD], Richa Gupta[iD], and Shourya Pathak[iD]

Indraprastha Institute of Information Technology Delhi, New Delhi, India
{saumik20404,parth21341,deep20370,richa.gupta,shourya18311}@iiitd.ac.in

Abstract. Blindness and visual impairment (BVI) are significant barriers to independent learning. While there have been advancements in assistive technologies, a critical need remains for tailored tools that empower individuals with blindness to access and navigate educational materials independently. This gap was particularly amplified during the COVID-19 lockdown when students primarily relied on self-learning with limited interactions with their instructors. This work addresses the issues and proposes solutions for effective, independent, affordable and equitable learning opportunities for students with BVI through technology. We present a multimodal interactive system that makes widely available printed textbooks accessible by superimposing digital layers of audio annotations, which are triggered based on the position of the user's finger on a page. This tool aims to fill the gap created by the lack of affordable, multimodal and accessible educational resources for independent learning by students with BVI, particularly for remote and self-learning scenarios.

Keywords: Accessible Education · Visual Impairment · Inclusive Design · Voice User Interface · Audio-AR · Machine Learning

1 Introduction

Blindness or Visual Impairment (BVI) is a "low incidence" and "high needs" disability, triggering unique challenges pertaining to inclusion [4]. It calls for skilled instructors and specific measures around training and teaching the affected. Today, 18 crore children are taught by almost 57 lakh teachers in more than 12 lakh primary and upper primary schools nationwide [12]. Inclusive education bridges the opportunity gaps between students with and without physical disabilities.

Our primary stakeholders for this study are high school students with blindness and visual impairment (BVI). School teachers are our secondary stakeholders. We found that most institutions were not well equipped with resources to provide quality high school education. Additionally, most accessible educational material is available either as Braille books or audiobooks. Both formats limit the communication of accompanying graphical information, seriously limiting information in graphic-intensive subjects like geography and biology.

M. Antona and C. Stephanidis (Eds.): HCII 2024, LNCS 14698, pp. 159–173, 2024.
https://doi.org/10.1007/978-3-031-60884-1_11

Following the double-diamond model [17], we defined our problem statement, reviewed the literature, and conducted on-site focus group interviews for localised need identification. We integrated the learnings to design and develop the first iteration (proof-of-concept) of Talktile, which we evaluated using blindfolded roleplay testing methodology. All our cumulative learnings were then used to iteratively build the second and latest version of the Talktile system, which we tested with children with BVI on-site.

Our work presents our overall research, design and development journey. We propose a novel approach to make print books and tactile maps more accessible by introducing layers of informational audio tags triggered using gesture and voice-based navigation. This approach adds a multimodal dimension to independent learning from printed books and tactile graphics. Additionally, the contributions of this work include: 1) Describing the critical usability and accessibility issues in currently existing solutions by gathering insights from literature reviews and need identification studies; 2) Describing the design and technology framework of the Talktile system, its evolution over iterations, and presenting the qualitative and quantitative user evaluation insights.

Considering the challenges faced by the BVI population in India, there is a motivation to contribute to improving their quality of life. The project aims to provide an affordable, portable, and easily accessible way to assist students with BVI, aligning with the economic conditions and limited accessibility to study material in the country. This paper aims to strike consequential discussions around creating novel and affordable interactive systems that aid accessible education.

2   Background

We conducted scoping literature reviews on the relevant research, design and technological developments to understand the range of challenges faced by students with BVI. According to a World Health Organisation (WHO) survey, India accounts for approximately 20% of the world's visually impaired population, a significant number considering its vast population. Despite the alarming figures, it is crucial to understand the challenges faced by visually impaired individuals in the context of India's economic conditions and limited accessibility to medical assistance [13].

Students with BVI encounter difficulties in accessing educational materials, particularly in tool subjects like Braille. The apparent attempts to teach Braille and other tools have limitations, with auditory senses having limited value in providing concrete clues about objects [18]. The lack of material for second language acquisition challenges visually impaired learners. However, there is potential for proficiency in acquiring a second language, especially for those who may not read Braille.

Despite challenges, there is a consensus that visually impaired students do not face serious problems with listening skills. Listening is a primary learning method; these students rely on auditory data to process information effectively. Developing speaking skills is essential for visually impaired students to request and transfer information. These skills enable effective communication and participation in academic activities.

Visually impaired students often face limitations in their knowledge regarding various concepts and areas, impacting their academic performance. Addressing this challenge is vital for their active participation in assignments and group discussions.

Emphasising the need for inclusion in the Indian education system, there is a call to enrol children with visual and hearing impairments into mainstream schools. The National Association for the Blind (NAB) in India is crucial in advocating for inclusive education, ensuring that every visually impaired child has access to formal education [20].

Despite efforts like Braille and audio translations, accessing print media remains challenging. Tactile diagrams considered the closest to vision in terms of semantic and cognitive processing, have been explored to communicate graphical information [16]. Tactile diagrams or tactile graphics (TGs) are significant in making graphical information accessible to blind individuals.

An increasingly popular alternative to braille labels is the use of audio labels, which enable audio-haptic exploration of the object, whereby the user explores the surface naturally with the fingers and queries locations of interest; note that blind people typically prefer to explore objects with multiple fingers or hands instead of just one [14], which is compatible with the use of audio labels.

3   Need Validation Study

Through our literature review, we found that the previous works and existing solutions were over budget, sparsely available and required specialised hardware, making them inaccessible in a scenario that calls for a highly accessible, budget-friendly, easy-to-use technological intervention- a gap we aim to fill with Talktile. Our primary objective with the need validation study was understanding the stakeholders' needs, pain points and wants.

3.1   Methodology

We conducted on-site focus group interviews at three blind institutions/ associations to comprehensively understand the challenges faced by students with BVI. We performed the pilot testing of the focus group interviews at NAB India Centre for Blind Women and Disability Studies (NABICBWD), New Delhi [6], which gave us a general overview. We conducted the following interviews at All India Confederation of the Blinds (AICB), New Delhi [1] and Bhartiya Blind School (BBS), New Delhi [2]. We interviewed 52 students and 3 teachers after getting their informed verbal and written consent. We used a mixture of English and Hindi for the interviews, and the transcripts were later translated verbatim into English for analysis.

Each session, consisting of semi-structured interviews, lasted 70–90 min in focus group sets of 12, 14, and 26 students. The questionnaire comprised general queries about the students' backgrounds, school life, classes and subjects and detailed queries about the challenges faced while transitioning between inclusive schools and blind schools. Participants expressed anxiety and sadness while narrating personal experiences and challenges.

Understanding the instructor's point of view was crucial as they are the primary facilitators in their students' learning. The semi-structured one-on-one interviews lasted for around 30–45 min. We gathered insights into their problems while instructing and mentoring students with BVI.

3.2 Demographics

NABICBWD is a women-only association. We interviewed 14 students [14F] aged 15–20 years. Most students completed their schooling during the COVID-19 pandemic and were pursuing their higher education at the institution.

At AICB, we interviewed 12 students [5F, 7M] aged 16–20 years. All students were enrolled in high school (grades 9–12) at the time of the study. Most students were comparatively older than the sighted students enrolled in the same grades, owing to difficulties taking classes due to their disability. We also interviewed one school teacher.

At BBS, we interviewed 26 students aged 16–19 years and two school teachers. This institution was one of the select few schools active in-person during the pandemic (Fig. 1).

Fig. 1. Need identification studies at A) NABICBWD, B) AICB, and C) BBS. Participants' faces are covered to conceal their identities.

3.3 Findings

Our engagement with students with BVI unveiled poignant narratives. The challenges faced by students extended beyond the classroom, encompassing limitations within the educational system and adapting to online education. The impact of curriculum design on practical courses, the struggle with inaccessible websites and materials, and the unique issues encountered in inclusive educational settings came to the forefront. Students expressed a desire for more tailored support, detailing the strain of competing with sighted peers and grappling with inaccessible educational content. These revelations underscore the urgent need for inclusive practices, acknowledging the diversity in learning capacities among visually impaired students.

The insights from interviewing teachers provided a broader canvas, offering perspectives on how they navigate the challenges faced by students with VI and guide them. Four distinct sub-themes emerged, highlighting the limitations of existing resources, issues surrounding accessibility, and the diverse methods employed by teachers to impart knowledge effectively. Teachers illuminated the struggles faced by students with limited resources, emphasising the gap between available tools and the capacity to utilise them. Accessibility challenges were underscored, especially in the realm of graphics and visual content, posing hurdles in comprehension and practical engagement. Teachers used innovative methods, such as visualising concepts, teaching special symbols, and emphasising fundamental building blocks, which emerged as crucial strategies to bridge the learning gap.

4   Proof of Concept Prototype

4.1   Design and Working

Need identification insights set the guiding design principles for developing the proof of concept on Unity utilising Vuforia SDK [5,10]. The first iteration of Talktile, as seen in (Fig. 3), featured a custom-designed, easy-to-assemble MDF stand with adjustable height and a phone mount. A mobile phone device running our AR application sat atop and above the appropriate educational material. The Vuforia SDK uses a computer vision-enabled image-detection algorithm and compares the input image with a database uploaded on its cloud network. Using Unity, we overlaid virtual buttons on top of image targets on a printed science textbook and a political map of India as our sample educational materials. Finger-based interactions triggered the appropriate virtual buttons and played back audio tags relevant to the target beneath.

For independent learning using the first iteration of Talktile, users place the learning material on the base of the assembled stand. Then, they choose the chosen subject by clicking its virtual button on the phone screen. The rest of the interactions are natural, as the user moves their finger across the relevant texts or graphics on the placed material.

4.2   User Evaluation of Prototype and Findings

Our primary objective with the initial evaluation was to gain insights into the system's efficacy in engaging students and usability problems. We conducted blindfolded roleplay tests with 12 participants [8M, 4F] to cover the temporary and situational blindness spectrum and comply with the limitations of the COVID-19 lockdown. During the evaluation, the blindfolded participants adjusted to the new environment with an ice-breaking session, following which

Fig. 2. Design and setup for Talktile PoC (first iteration).

they studied the provided educational resources using our prototype. Each session lasted 10 min, after which we asked them qualitative questions. Insights mainly were in favour of the prototype, with around 70% of participants completing the tasks. Around 50% found the UI buttons small, and 10% found the solution a hassle due to the steep learning curve. Other notable limitations of this iteration were related to the touchscreen GUI nature of the interface (Fig. 2).

Fig. 3. Blindfolded roleplay testing of Talktile PoC (first iteration).

5   Proposed Interactive System - "Talktile"

5.1   Design and Working

Encompassing all previous learnings, we developed the design and framework of the latest and the proposed iteration of the Talktile interface. It features a laser-cut MDF stand with more height and phone position adjustments than the outgoing version. The audio tags augment the supplied NCERT textbook and thermoformed tactile maps (Fig. 4B) we procured from RLF [9]. The student places their smartphone atop the low-cost stand. The smartphone is the hub for processing the gestural and voice-based user inputs and educational material through the camera feed, running our application, and playing back the audio outputs.

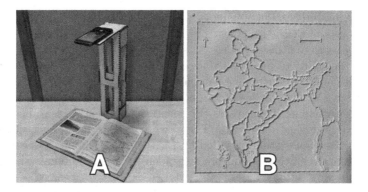

Fig. 4. A) Design and setup for Talktile, the proposed interactive system. B) Thermoformed tactile political map of India.

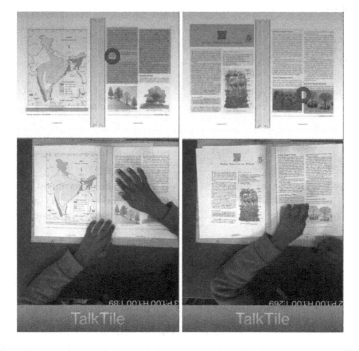

Fig. 5. Sample screenshots during user testing with Talktile. The coloured boxes seen here are the annotation regions to help identify audio interaction to be played within a region.

Our application integrates technologies, including TensorFlow [11] for model training, TFLite for model inference on smartphones, and Android Studio for application logic development. Its capabilities include page identification within a book and precise hand position tracking on a page or a tactile map. These features are instrumental in enhancing the accessibility of user interactions with printed books and tactile graphics.

The application utilises an easy-to-use speech-based interaction method. Users have the ability to speak out voice commands, and in response, the application provides auditory outputs. Examples are provided in (Table 1). The voice-user interface (VUI) provides seamless and organic interactions between the user and the machine. It addresses the constraints and steep learning curve of a gesture-based navigation system. The Voice User Interface (VUI) utilises the wake word detection system provided by PicoVoice Porcupine [8]. This enables the application to efficiently and precisely identify user commands and initiate the corresponding actions.

The machine learning model can be used on a smartphone without being connected to the internet.

Table 1. Sample user interactions on the second iteration of Talktile.

Interaction Type	Command	Response/Action
Open a new page	Automatic (no command)	"Chapter 5. Page 39, 40."
Bring hand over a section	Automatic (no command)	"Paragraph - Government steps to protect flora and fauna..."
Reading out loud	"Read this"	"To protect the flora and fauna of the country, the government has taken many steps. 1. Eighteen biosphere reserves have..."
Summarise text	"Explain"	"Describe the government's steps to protect flora and fauna, including biosphere reserves and conservation projects."
Describe image/figure	"Explain"	"Figure 5 shows a Montane Forest with conical trees..."

5.2 Vision Model Development

Our neural network used an EfficientNetV2 B0 backbone [19] for picture information extraction. It was trained to do three tasks: page identification, hand presence identification, and hand position localization.

The hand-position dataset was created using the FreiHAND dataset, a hand-segmentation task dataset [21]. Multiple hand images were masked and overlaid onto page images. We trained our vision model on this data, and sample screenshots of its working are shown in (Fig. 5).

5.3 User Evaluation and Findings

Our primary objectives were to investigate how students with BVI interacted and what they felt about the iterative version of Talktile, and its efficacy in creating an independent learning experience. We performed the study with ten participants [10M], aged 12–16 years [Mean: 14.3, SD: 1.25], at the National Association for the Blind, New Delhi [7]. Each session was conducted after taking informed verbal and written consent. The study was divided into four major sections: Pre-Test Discussion, Prototype Testing after briefing them about the system, Technology Acceptance Model (TAM) Testing [15], and Post-test Discussion. The open-ended semi-structured discussions covered the methods participants previously used for independent learning scenarios, their experience interacting with the Talktile system, and how they felt about it. The prototype testing measured the user's ability and time taken to perform three tasks: **Onboarding**, where the user had to open the book to a prompted chapter; **Textbook Reading**, where they had to use the Talktile system to read 2 text paragraphs and 1 figure from the chapter; **Map Reading**, where they had to switch from the textbook to the tactile map, use the system to read map data and answer 2 questions we asked them about it (Fig. 6).

Fig. 6. User evaluation of Talktile, our latest iteration. Participants' faces are covered to conceal their identities.

We formulated a Technology Acceptance Model (TAM) questionnaire consisting of 6 prompts about Perceived Usefulness (PU) and another 6 prompts about Perceived Ease-of-Use (PEU), as shown in (Table 2).

Our analysis of the TAM survey data for the Talktile system (Fig. 7) uncovered insightful findings about user perceptions. The data, collected on a Likert scale of 1 to 7, with 1 being the most favourable, indicated mean ratings for all variables ranging from 1.8 to 2.6. This range reflects a generally positive reaction to the system. Notably, the most positive reception was observed for PU1, which relates to the system's ability to enable quick task accomplishment (Mean = 1.8, SD = 0.8), and PU4, which measures the enhancement of effectiveness in independent learning (Mean = 1.8, SD = 1.2). The relatively lower standard deviation for PU1 suggests a more consistent agreement among users regarding this aspect of the system. Conversely, areas for potential improvement

Table 2. Descriptive Statistics for Technology Acceptance Model (TAM)

TAM Variable	TAM Prompt	Mean	SD
PU1	Using the Talktile system in my independent learning would enable me to accomplish tasks more quickly.	1.8	.8
PU2	Using the Talktile system would improve my independent learning performance.	2.3	1.6
PU3	Using the Talktile system in my independent learning would increase my productivity.	2.4	1.5
PU4	Using the Talktile system would enhance my effectiveness in independent learning.	1.8	1.2
PU5	Using the Talktile system would make it easier to do my independent learning.	2.1	1.4
PU6	I would find the Talktile system useful in my independent learning.	2.5	1.6
PEU1	Learning to operate the Talktile system would be easy for me.	2.1	1.7
PEU2	I would find it easy to get the Talktile system to do what I want it to do.	2.6	2.1
PEU3	My interaction with the Talktile system would be clear and understandable.	2.3	1.3
PEU4	I would find the Talktile system would be clear and understandable.	2.2	1.2
PEU5	It would be easy for me to become skilful at using the Talktile system.	2.0	1.9
PEU6	I would find the Talktile system easy to use.	1.9	1.4

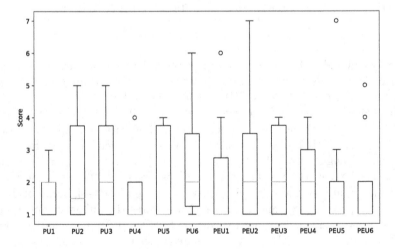

Fig. 7. Box Plot of TAM Survey

were identified, notably in PEU2 (ease of getting the system to do what one wants, Mean = 2.6, SD = 2.1), where the higher standard deviations indicate a wider variability in user experiences and perceptions.

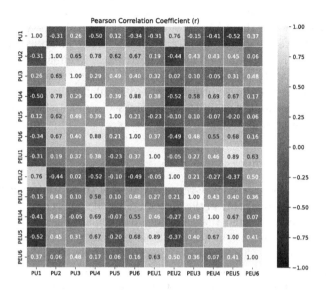

Fig. 8. Pearson Correlation Coefficient (r) matrix of the TAM survey results.

Correlation analysis from data in (Fig. 8) revealed strong positive relationships between several key variables, such as between PEU5 (ease of becoming skillful) and PEU1 (ease of learning to operate) with an r value of 0.886. This suggests a robust link between the ease of learning the system and becoming skilled in its use. However, certain negative correlations emerged, notably between PEU5 (ease of becoming skilful) and PU1 (quick task completion) with an r value of −0.523, and between PEU2 (ease of getting the system to do what one wants) and PU4 (effectiveness) with an r value of −0.516. These negative correlations suggest a possible trade-off between the perceived effectiveness of the system and its ease of use or speed in task completion.

These negative correlations underscore the importance of enhanced user training. Effective training can help users better understand and navigate the system. This approach can mitigate the perception that effectiveness requires a steeper learning curve. By focusing on practical, hands-on training that emphasizes best practices for using the system, users can become more adept at navigating the system effectively.

The overall correlation between the averages of Perceived Usefulness (PUs) and Perceived Ease of Use (PEUs) was found to be moderate, at 0.317. This moderate correlation indicates that while there is some association between the system's perceived usefulness and its ease of use, the relationship is not as strong as might be anticipated. This finding has important implications for system development and user experience design. It suggests that enhancing the system's usefulness might not necessarily lead to proportional improvements in its ease of use, and vice versa. Therefore, further efforts to make the system more useful should not compromise its usability, and improvements in ease of use should not overlook the system's utility.

In conclusion, while the TAM survey data for the Talktile system indicates a generally positive reception, there are specific areas identified for improvement. The system is well-regarded for its effectiveness in enhancing independent learning and facilitating quick task completion. However, the identified trade-offs between effectiveness and ease of use or speed highlight the need for enhanced user training. Such training could lead to increased user satisfaction and a more comprehensive acceptance of the system.

5.4   Notable Challenges

Participants were surprised by the responsiveness of the system, but they noted that it would be beneficial only in the absence of braille books or ebooks (depending on their preference), and that it would not replace their primary method of studying. They agreed that it would be especially beneficial when braille texts become scarce at the start of each academic year. Some demonstrated a greater interest in the application's underlying technology and suggested that the Text-to-Speech narrator be equipped with additional media controls (pause, stop, replay, forward, and rewind) and control over playback speed. Participants tended to utilise both hands when engaging with the Talktile interface, suggesting a requirement for a more intuitive and user-friendly design that assumes two-handed usage. They expressed concern about not knowing if they had covered all the information on a page, raising questions about the effectiveness of the tactile learning experience. Instead of smoothly dragging their finger across the page, some students tended to jump across, potentially leading to a disjointed understanding of the content. Furthermore, they expressed difficulties determining the subsequent paragraph's location upon finishing one, indicating a desire for enhanced navigation indicators. Several participants encountered challenges in comprehending the exact boundaries of geographical elements on tactile maps, highlighting a potential limitation in the Map Reading component of the current iteration of Talktile.

6   Discussion

In this research, we have presented a novel multimodal intervention aimed at improving the independent learning process for students with BVI. We drew insights from the need identification study provided with the breadth of problems and challenges faced by students with BVI and their teachers. We explored the challenges faced by students with BVI in pursuing higher education, particularly in STEM fields. Applying these learnings, we built the first iteration of the Talktile interface as a proof of concept. To address the situationally blind user spectrum and late-blindness to some degree while adhering to COVID-19 lockdown constraints, we conducted blindfold roleplay testing. By integrating all prior knowledge, we iteratively developed the second and proposed version of Talktile and assessed its performance at a facility for visually impaired individuals.

In general, the participants had developed a habitual approach to education in which they had no difficulty self-studying so long as they had access to pertinent material in their preferred formats, such as braille books or laptops with ePub files. The assistance of a sighted individual was only required if they had any uncertainties concerning the material's content. They had all previously utilised a tactile board that their instructor employed to instruct on shapes and diagrams; thus, they had all been acquainted with tactile graphics.

Insights primarily indicated that Talktile addressed the gaps that were present in learning from printed non-Braille textbooks. Students also noted how the interface allowed them to gather more knowledge from tactile graphics, as they could attribute informational data to their respective geographical locations on the tactile map.

However, Talktile still has unexplored potential. The final testing of the interface reveals various future development tangents, including a mature Voice-User Interface capable of effectively communicating with students and providing them with additional information on demand. We learned about navigability challenges students had when studying with our system, such as a lack of knowledge of the layout and boundaries of printed content and using both hands as they normally do when engaging with their surroundings. Enhanced tutorials pertaining to the system's operation will effectively address these challenges.

7   Future Work and Conclusion

Existing large language models (LLMs) such as ChatGPT [3] or a custom model can be fine-tuned to allow students to explore the out-of-book knowledge and ideas, which can take the independent learning experience to a new level. The potential for automating the image labelling and explanation generation process is considerable. Future enhancements can further integrate document extraction models and image caption generators to streamline the content preparation process. These developments would improve the efficiency and expand the application's capabilities and, ultimately, the learning experience.

The proposed multimodal Talktile interface effectively enhances the independent learning experience for students with BVI. We discussed what we learned through the different research and development stages and highlighted user study results. The evolution of the interface is prominent through the two presented iterations. Future explorations into this idea can add many more better-featured functionalities, ultimately making opportunities around education more equitable and accessible. We hope this work sparks consequential ideas and discussions around the specific interaction methods and accessible education in general. We envision a future where all students are afforded equal access to educational opportunities.

Acknowledgments. We want to thank AID Lab, IIIT Delhi, for providing us with the opportunity and resources to perform this long-term study into the challenges faced by students with BVI in independent learning scenarios. This project would not have been possible without our collaborations with the institutions and associations for students with BVI that go well and beyond to provide accessible learning and nurturing environments. We also sincerely thank Dr Richa Gupta for her guidance and unwavering support throughout the different phases of the project.

Disclosure of Interests. The authors have no competing interests to declare that are relevant to the content of this article.

References

1. AICB home. https://www.aicb.org.in/
2. Bhartiya Blind School. https://www.bhartiyablindschool.com/
3. ChatGPT. https://chat.openai.com
4. Education Sciences | Free Full-Text | A Systematic Review on Inclusive Education of Students with Visual Impairment. https://www.mdpi.com/2227-7102/10/11/346
5. Home | Engine Developer Portal. https://developer.vuforia.com/
6. NAB Centre For Women Home Page. https://nabcentreforwomen.org/
7. National Association For The Blind | NAB Delhi. https://www.nabdelhi.in
8. Picovoice - Wake Word Detection & Keyword Spotting. https://picovoice.ai/platform/porcupine/
9. RLF | Home. https://raisedlines.org/
10. Unity Real-Time Development Platform | 3D, 2D, VR & AR Engine. https://unity.com/
11. Abadi, M., et al.: TensorFlow: large-scale machine learning on heterogeneous distributed systems (2016)
12. Bhan, S.: Inclusion of children with visual impairment in India. Eur. J. Soc. Behav. Sci. **Issue 3** (2012). https://doi.org/10.15405/FutureAcademy/ejsbs(2301-2218).2012.3.3. https://www.europeanpublisher.com/article/10.15405/FutureAcademy/ejsbs(2301-2218).2012.3.3
13. Chaturvedi, S., Chechani, M., Gautami, K., Joshi, K.: System to provide reading aid to visually impaired people. Asian J. Converg. Technol. (AJCT) **7**(2), 60–64 (2021). https://doi.org/10.33130/AJCT.2021v07i02.013. https://www.asianssr.org/index.php/ajct/article/view/1134. ISSN -2350-1146
14. Coughlan, J., Miele, J.: AR4VI: AR as an accessibility tool for people with visual impairments, vol. 2017, pp. 288–292, October 2017. https://doi.org/10.1109/ISMAR-Adjunct.2017.89
15. Davis, F.D.: Perceived usefulness, perceived ease of use, and user acceptance of information technology. MIS Q. **13**(3), 319–340 (1989). https://doi.org/10.2307/249008. https://www.jstor.org/stable/249008
16. Gupta, R., Balakrishnan, M., Rao, P.: Tactile diagrams for the visually impaired. IEEE Potentials **36**(1), 14–18 (2017). https://doi.org/10.1109/MPOT.2016.2614754. http://ieeexplore.ieee.org/document/7814367/
17. Gustafsson, D.: Analysing the Double diamond design process through research & implementation (2019)

18. Kapur, D.R.: Challenges experienced by visually impaired students in education, vol. 4 (2017)
19. Tan, M., Le, Q.V.: EfficientNetV2: smaller models and faster training, June 2021. https://doi.org/10.48550/arXiv.2104.00298. http://arxiv.org/abs/2104.00298. arXiv:2104.00298 [cs]
20. Tripathi, D.P.V.: Educating visually impaired in India **5**(3) (2018)
21. Zimmermann, C., Ceylan, D., Yang, J., Russell, B., Argus, M., Brox, T.: FreiHAND dataset - project page. In: International Conference on Computer Vision (ICCV) (2019). https://lmb.informatik.uni-freiburg.de/projects/freihand/

Accessmath: Towards Developing an Accessible Interactive Learning Platform to Overcome the Challenges of Blind and Visually Impaired Students in Learning Mathematics

Muhammad Shoaib[1]([✉]) [iD], Rosane Minghim[1], Donal Fitzpatrick[2], and Ian Pitt[1]

[1] School of Computer Science and Information Technology,
University College Cork, Cork, Ireland
`muhammad.shoaib@cs.ucc.ie`

[2] Centre for Excellence in Universal Design, National Disability Authority, Dublin, Ireland

Abstract. Smartphone-based apps and games can provide an enjoyable and inspiring atmosphere for learning mathematics. They potentially offer an engaging and exciting way to help students utilize their previously acquired abilities. Implementing such platforms has become increasingly significant in the rapidly evolving educational technology landscape. However, the integration of such technologies poses unique challenges and opportunities, particularly when it comes to catering to the needs of blind and visually impaired primary school students. This article is based upon a survey designed to investigate the needs of blind and visually impaired students and identify enablers that improve the effectiveness of interactive learning platforms specifically for learning mathematics. Nineteen people participated in this study: five blind and visually impaired students, nine teachers, and five professional experts. Participants highlighted important functionalities which would help them address their needs in primary education settings. Using the findings from this study, the authors aim to develop an interactive learning game to fulfill the participants' needs. This interactive game focuses on enhancing numbering skills, performing basic mathematics operations, and learning about shapes and digits because most school children struggle to learn these topics. This game can engage blind and visually impaired students and help them quickly understand these topics. The aim has been to introduce educational aspects in a way that does not compromise game enjoyment.

Keywords: Smartphone · Interactive · Learning · Mathematics · Blind and Visually-Impaired

1 Introduction

The popularity of smartphones and other mobile devices in our daily lives keeps increasing. These devices add novel features with each new version, improving ease and affordability. New applications are regularly developed to simplify numerous aspects of our lives. This technological advancement has motivated researchers and developers to take advantage of these devices within the educational sector to move from traditional class-rooms to more dynamic and engaging learning environments [1]. It allows teachers to educate students without being confined by location or time. It also encourages learning inside and outside the classroom, during or after classes [2]. These devices also allow teachers to interact with their students more efficiently and enhance their student's concept-building [3]. Chiong and Shuler analyzed the impact of smart mobile devices and their applications on preschool- and early-elementary-aged children. They found that children can use these devices easily, and the apps can boost their learning skills [4].

Based on these and similar findings, the idea of developing a learning game has emerged. Educational games entertain students and help them learn several subjects, including mathematics. Mathematics is compulsory for primary school students in Ireland and many other countries. This subject is constructive for developing problem-solving skills in students, but sometimes it's very confusing and challenging [5]. Blind and visually impaired students face particular challenges when accessing visual mathematics content, i.e., graphs, formulas, and mathematical notations. The UN Convention on the Rights of Persons with Disabilities states that persons with visual disabilities should not be overlooked or left behind in terms of quality of life [6]. Similarly, the World Health Organization requires that implementation of its Sustainable Development Goals "leaves no one behind", including those with a visual disability [7].

The continual improvement in digital assistive technologies offers novel opportunities to overcome many barriers faced by people with visual disability. Smartphones are one of them, and they include several accessible features and applications for blind and visually impaired students. For example, MathMelodies is an iPad application developed for primary school students, including those with vision difficulties. The developers examined the problems that occur during the design of an accessible learning environment by using a user-centered design. They evaluated the usability of this application with professionals, blind students, and sighted students. They found that inclusion of object-based interactions, audio cues, and text-to-speech enhanced user engagement [9]. AudioMath, introduced by Jaime and Hector, is another example. It supports blind children in learning mathematics using audio-based interactions. The developers focused on improving short-term memory and arithmetic knowledge using an interactive auditory interface. The application was built with input from blind students and was tested for its efficiency in increasing memorization and learning skills. The study reveals that audio can be a powerful aid for boosting memory and learning maths in visually impaired children [10]. Further examples are discussed in Sect. 2.

This article is based upon a study conducted among domain experts, teachers, and blind and visually impaired students in order to identify design guidelines for developing an accessible solution for learning mathematics. This research aims to design and develop a mobile-device-based mathematics learning game called AccesMath. Students can use this learning application from anywhere. Using and playing this game can enhance the children's understanding of mathematics. The remainder of this article is organized as follows: Section 2 explains the related work; Sect. 3 illustrates the study's procedures; Sect. 4 describes the proposed learning game architecture; Sect. 5 provides the participants' comments and information; Sect. 6 concludes this article and provides recommendations for future work.

2 Related Work

Previous research has revealed several software tools available for blind and visually impaired students to access mathematical content. Mejia et al. provided an extensive survey of software tools available for visually impaired persons to access, create, and manipulate mathematical material. They analyzed the issues visually impaired persons faced when accessing mathematical resources. They categorized the tools into two groups: those for accessing mathematical content and those that enable them to execute mathematical operations. The report also examined the advantages and disadvantages of essential technologies for interacting with mathematics material [11]. Audio Games [12] was a novel technique that analyzed the impact of audio games on visually impaired individuals' learning and cognitive skills development. They showed how audio-based teaching aids and combining user-centered design can significantly boost visual representation, memory, and problem-solving skills among blind students. The research evaluated the audio games developed for teaching, focusing on the potential for improving learning skills in blind and visually impaired learners. Shoaib et al. [13] investigated the development of a mobile e-learning application designed to aid visually impaired children in learning basic mathematics. The aim of the research was to enhance smartphone application accessibility through a user-centered design approach. The study focussed on a prototype application that was modified in the light of user feedback. The modified version yielded reduced task completion time and greater user satisfaction. The modifications were designed to simplify navigation, improve color contrast, and provide more rapid feedback, and user testing confirmed the usefulness and reliability of the application for visually impaired students.

Song et al. [14] examined the design and execution of mobile learning games for visually challenged children. They focused on increasing spatial skills using two audio mobile games: "Cardinal Direction and a modified Tower of London". The study comprised both quantitative and qualitative evaluation, with results indicating enhanced enjoyment among participants. The results provided insights into building more efficient and interactive smartphone games for visually impaired users. Sánchez and Sáenz [15] analyzed the usage of "The Natomy's Journey Games" an audio-based video game. It demonstrated the game's design and implementation by emphasizing an interactive environment among blind and sighted students. The study examined the game's accessibility and its influence on integrating blind students into mainstream classrooms, highlighting considerable improvements regarding learning and integration into society. Arlinwibowo et al. [16] focused on constructing an Android application to aid visually impaired students in learning mathematics. The project involved specialists from several sectors to produce a realistic, feasible, and practical app. They highlight the need to establish accessible educational technologies that respond to the special needs of blind and visually impaired students, enhancing their capacity to learn and test skills effectively. Ramos et al. [17] discussed two case studies employing gamification approaches for blind and autistic individuals. The first study offers an application teaching Mexican currency to blind persons using interactive interfaces and gamification. The second study explored an app for autistic children, enabling them to better navigate and engage through a virtual reality game. Both studies indicated the beneficial use of technology and gaming in teaching for those with disabilities.

3   The Procedure of the Study

This research study was carried out with blind and visually impaired students, teachers, and professionals working in accessibility. A group of nineteen users took part in the research, including five blind and visually impaired students, nine teachers, and five domain specialists. The thirteen female and six male participants in this study were 9 to 58 years old. The research was organized in two phases. In the first phase, we conducted a study with students, teachers, and domain experts to explore several themes. In the second phase, we gathered their opinions and suggestions for developing a smartphone-based accessible solution. Table 1 offers comprehensive details about each participant.

Table 1. Demographic information of the Users

User ID	Age	Gender	Type
U1	12	Female	Student
U2	10	Male	Student
U3	11	Female	Student
U4	9	Male	Student
U5	12	Female	Student
U6	52	Female	Teacher
U7	42	Female	Teacher
U8	26	Female	Teacher
U9	29	Female	Teacher
U10	45	Male	Teacher
U11	37	Male	Teacher
U12	43	Female	Teacher
U13	54	Female	Teacher
U14	44	Female	Teacher
U15	43	Female	Professional
U16	58	Male	Professional
U17	40	Male	Professional
U18	57	Female	Professional
U19	41	Female	Professional

3.1   The Interviews for This Study

The study was conducted from August to November 2023, and interviews were conducted via video call (on Teams). The semi-structured interviews were conducted with students, teachers, and domain experts. Most questions were open-ended, allowing participants to explore the topic comprehensively. Towards the end, participants had the chance to express any views they felt were not addressed during the interview.

3.2   The Analysis Process and General Findings

From the collected interview data, we have explored the challenges of blind and visually impaired students and the experiences of teachers and experts. Using thematic analysis, we identified several essential themes, i.e., "Mathematics Topics," "Challenges, Obstacles, and Issues", "Digital and Non-digital Resources", and "Ways to make learning mathematics easy" etc. A full description of the study and the thematic analysis will be published as a separate paper. Moreover, information was gathered from blind and visually impaired students about what kind of applications might help them to learn mathematics. The opinions of teachers and domain experts regarding the design of smartphone-based solutions for these students were also noted. This article focuses on the design guidelines for an accessible solution resulting from the study i.e., independence, font and color contrast, proper labeling, clear navigation, etc. These guidelines were used in the design of a game called "AccessMath".

3.3   Ethical Considerations

Permission was obtained from the University, school management, and the participants for the conduct of this study. All participants were given an information sheet and fully briefed on the study's purposes. All participants signed informed consent forms. They were told that the entire experiment would be recorded for evaluation purposes. The respondents were assured that no harm was involved either before their participation or during the study to extract information. It was emphasized that the participant's involvement in the study was voluntary. Additionally, the participants received assurances about the confidentiality of their identity, with explicit instruction that real names and addresses would not be used in the final report. To uphold ethical standards, we followed the guidelines outlined by Bogdan and Biklen [18], encompassing informed consent and protecting participants from any potential psychological harm or danger.

4   Proposed Learning Game (AccessMath)

This study highlighted essential guidelines and opportunities for developers: independence, font and color contrast, proper labeling and clear navigation, multimodal approach, easy access, and no internet dependency. See below the details about these guidelines:

Independence. Support blind and visually impaired students to work without supervision. Provide them with straightforward game rules and motivate them with the game's entertainment factor that can keep them focused on the task.

Font and Color Contrast: Make it easy for them to adjust font size and color contrast based on their needs.

Proper Labeling and Clear Navigation. Ensure proper labeling of the interface elements, i.e., buttons, etc., and clear navigation between screens to make the app more accessible.

Multimodal Approach. Make appropriate use of text-to-speech, vibro-tactile, and auditory feedback.

Easy Access. Students should be able to access and use the app from anywhere. It also refers to obtaining the app (e.g., free of charge, simple download and installation).

No Internet Dependency: Students should be able to use the app without Internet availability.

Subsequently, we applied these recommendations and guidelines in developing a game named AccessMath to help the blind and visually impaired. This game has three main modules named "Basic Operations", "Shapes and Digits," and "Numbering". There details are mentioned below:

Basic Operations. Through interactive challenges, the game presents addition, subtraction, multiplication, and division concepts to blind and visually impaired students. We have utilized audio narratives, swipe functions, audio, and vibro feedback. Students can solve the questions and learn more about basic operations using them.

Shapes and Digits. Using a multimodal approach, teach geometry shapes, lines, symbols, and digits drawing to blind and visually impaired students. Users can draw the shapes by touching the screen, and audio explanations illustrate them more appropriately for them. It can be useful for designing games where players can recognize and classify shapes using their touch and auditory perception.

Numbering. Start with basic counting activities using auditory cues for numbers where blind and visually impaired users can learn counting skills. Also, introduce a comparison of numbers using sound-based activities that could help them in learning.

Figure 1 presents a detailed overview of our proposed game. All these activities are interactive, engaging, and accessible for blind and visually impaired students. Frequent feedback, encouragement, and progressively challenging levels can enhance their learning experience.

5   Interesting Guidelines/Suggestions/Opportunities Suggested by Participants

As described above, the study comprised two parts. The first part involved a thematic analysis of survey results concerning inclusive learning. The second part focused on the design of an inclusive learning platform, and some of the resulting guidelines and suggestions for researchers and developers are listed below:

"Blind and visually impaired students like games. But for my blind students, unless somebody sits beside them all the time and explains exactly what's happening in the game or helps them manage it. So, I think the independence of students is essential."

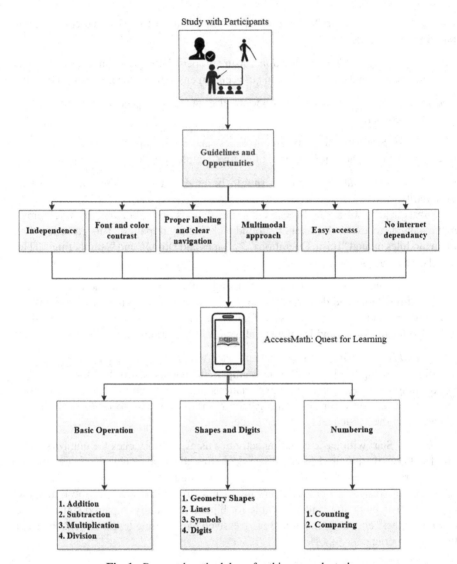

Fig. 1. Proposed methodology for this research study

"Games can be quite useful because using them on the tablet or other mobile device makes students happy. They can use screens if the interface elements and fonts of the apps are big enough to see."

"Measuring skills-based solutions and devices we need. Some of these resources are available in America but not in Ireland. England is also making resources that will make measuring more accessible."

"I think a possible solution might be something like preparation for leaving CERT. Students can prepare math for Leaving Cert with the help of a learning app, which helps them learn different topics like measuring and graphs."

"Anything they will do with speech and students can use from anywhere."

"There were a lot of topics that they could learn through playing games like understanding the numbers and quantity of numbers, graphs, basic math operations etc."

"For a developer developing a tool to support them, I think the first thing is to use co-design, so they have to work with these people to have live experience. For example, if you are working with students, try to recruit one or two nine-year-old students to be a part of your team; I think they'd take great pride and ownership, and they really appreciate being invited onto something like that to be a part of building the solutions to support themselves."

"The best platform all depends on the end users. You know what I mean? And it depends on what's available to them. So a lot of them will have smartphones, but maybe what you're building is not going to necessarily if it's in this classroom environment, you know, smartphones and now being banned everywhere and all this kind of stuff, especially if it's a mainstream classroom and the school of no bond smartphones, it kind of rules out the opportunity of having that tool on the smartphone, which is a bit crazy. I think the smartphone is the most accessible as it's the one the kids will engage in the most, but this is good for their home. If you're actually talking practicality, I'd probably go down the tablet route, as in that's what if you look at the broader scale of things, if you look at how like big screens, how they will work really well and integrate really well with systems, I think a lot of that is built for tablets. If it's something that's actually going to be educational, then a tablet could be a good choice."

"If the audience is primary school kids, then gamification will be really important, and games will be a motivation. Another thing, it's better that the game does not have internet dependency. And if it's an older cohort of students like secondary school students who are just trying to pass the Leaving Cert, they will have a different motivation. And so, in their case, it will be the laptop because when they walk into that leaving CERT exam, it's a laptop they will be in front of."

"If you are designing a solution, you must see the curriculum. Considering the end users like the persons with the disability and their needs, his teachers, and his family members views."

"I think taking a universal approach to learning is really important, and using a multimodal approach to integrate the solution is more beneficial if possible."

"The work we're finding on sites is to do with poorly labeled or unlabeled things. Developers should avoid this; proper labeling, clear navigation, and color contrast matter a lot."

"I've heard about games and even the VR experiences where you can learn about different subjects. VR-based solutions could help people in their learning."

"During the planning stage of an app, you should engage with the audience. Also, it's important to include people with disability in the research."

"I suppose providing audio and vibro feedback to understand the number sequence, numbering lines, 1, 2, 5, getting vibrational feedback on doing something, even moving from one cell to another, anything like that will help them."

"I have never used a screen reader. I like easy things that I can easily access and use from anywhere, for example, a scanning pen; I want to scan text, giving me audio information about this. So, it is something that gives me information in voice, or I can learn it through play again. Something provides me with feedback in speech and vibration, I like it."

6   Conclusion and Future Work

Educational and assistive technology are evolving day by day. Because of this, providing equal opportunity for learning for blind and visually impaired primary school students is very important. We have conducted a study with blind and visually impaired students, their teachers, and domain experts to introduce an inclusive learning solution for them. The results of this study illustrated that providing them with an independent learning environment, proper opportunities for font and color contrast settings, adequate labeling of user interface elements, straightforward navigation between screens, the introduction of a multimodal approach, easy access to the learning platform, and running of the application without internet dependency can make the solution more accessible for them.

We have developed a learning game, "AccesMath", for these students by keeping these guidelines in mind. This math learning game provides inclusive education for blind and visually impaired primary school students. This game involves basic mathematical operations, shapes and digits, and numbering skills. Our game consists of special accessibility features by keeping a range of learning requirements in mind and considering the influence of mobile devices on blind and visually impaired student's educational experience. We have attempted to understand the nature of learning for blind and visually impaired students and to develop an interactive and user-friendly platform. This platform introduced a multimodal approach for feedback and user setting based on their needs that enhance the accessibility nature of this app. In a follow-up study, we plan to investigate the usefulness and effectiveness of this mobile application for the learning enhancement of blind and visually impaired students. We will examine whether blind and visually impaired students use this to improve their learning skills.

Future researchers can introduce machine learning-based algorithms that customize the game to each player's learning preferences and skill level. These customizations could be based on each student's strengths and weaknesses. Furthermore, the game's features could be expanded to include more complex topics appropriate for elementary school grades. This expansion might cover more advanced geometric shapes, fractions, and decimals, offering a more extensive mathematical education. Moreover, we suggest that researchers and developers should work together with experts and organizations that specialize in accessibility to carry out comprehensive studies on the efficacy of the game in various educational settings. Maximizing the game's impact and obtaining insights might involve collaborating with academic institutions, accessibility specialists, and teachers. Finally, we should explore other ways to use the game to involve parents in their children's education and provide them with possibilities to engage in educational opportunities at home with their children.

Acknowledgments. This publication has emanated from research conducted with the financial support of Science Foundation Ireland under Grant number 18/CRT/6222. For the purpose of Open Access, the author has applied a CC BY public copyright licence to any Author Accepted Manuscript version arising from this submission.

Disclosure of Interests. On behalf of all authors, the corresponding author states that there is no conflict of interest.

References

1. Shen, R., Wang, M., Pan, X.: Increasing interactivity in blended classrooms through a cutting-edge mobile learning system. Br. J. Edu. Technol. **39**(6), 1073–1086 (2008)
2. Huang, Y.M., Lin, Y.T., Cheng, S.C.: Effectiveness of a mobile plant learning system in a science curriculum in Taiwanese elementary education. Comput. Educ. **54**(1), 47–58 (2010)
3. Ward, N.D., Finley, R.J., Keil, R.G., Clay, T.G.: Benefits and limitations of iPads in the high school science classroom and a trophic cascade lesson plan. J. Geosci. Educ. **61**(4), 378–384 (2013)
4. Chiong, C., Shuler, C.: Learning: is there an app for that. In: Investigations of Young Children's Usage and Learning with Mobile Devices and Apps, pp. 13–20. The Joan Ganz Cooney Center at Sesame Workshop, New York (2010)
5. Amirali, M.: Students' conceptions of the nature of mathematics and attitudes towards mathematics learning. J. Res. Reflections Educ. **4**(1) (2010)
6. The United Nations Convention on the rights of persons with disabilities. https://www.un.org/development/desa/disabilities/convention-on-the-rights-of-persons-with-disabilities.html. Accessed 30 Jan 2024
7. The United Nation Sustainable Development Goal, leave no one behind. https://unsdg.un.org/2030-agenda/universal-values/leave-no-one-behind. Accessed 30 Jan 2024
8. Phillips, M., Proulx, M.J.: Social interaction without vision: an assessment of assistive technology for the visually impaired. Technol Innov **20**(1–2), 85–93 (2018)
9. Gerino, A., Alabastro, N., Bernareggi, C., Ahmetovic, D., Mascetti, S.: Mathmelodies: inclusive design of a didactic game to practice mathematics. In: Miesenberger, K., Fels, D., Archambault, D., Peňáz, P., Zagler, W. (eds.) Computers Helping People with Special Needs. LNCS, vol. 8547, pp. 564–571. Springer, Cham (2014). https://doi.org/10.1007/978-3-319-08596-8_88
10. Sánchez, J., Flores, H.: AudioMath: blind children learning mathematics through audio. Int. J. Disabil. Hum. Dev. **4**(4), 311–316 (2005)
11. Mejía, P., Martini, L.C., Grijalva, F., Larco, J.C., Rodríguez, J.C.: A survey on mathematical software tools for visually impaired persons: a practical perspective. IEEE Access **9**, 66929–66947 (2021)
12. Balan, O., Moldoveanu, A., Moldoveanu, F., Dascalu, M.I.: Audio games-a novel approach towards effective learning in the case of visually-impaired people. In: ICERI2014 Proceedings, pp. 6542–6548. IATED (2014)
13. Shoaib, M., Khan, S., Fitzpatrick, D., Pitt, I.: A mobile e-learning application for enhancement of basic mathematical skills in visually impaired children. Universal Access Inf. Soc., 1–11 (2023)
14. Song, D., Karimi, A., Kim, P.: Toward designing mobile games for visually challenged children. In: Proceeding of the International Conference on e-Education, Entertainment and e-Management, pp. 234–238. IEEE, December 2011
15. Sánchez, J., Sáenz, M.: Video gaming for blind learners school integration in science classes. In: Gross, T., et al. (eds.) Human-Computer Interaction – INTERACT 2009. LNCS, vol. 5726, pp. 36–49. Springer, Heidelberg (2009). https://doi.org/10.1007/978-3-642-03655-2_5
16. Arlinwibowo, J., Mustaqim, Y., Prihandono, A., Hana, F.M., Ridwan, A., Himayati, A.I.A.: Developing mathematical exercise software for visually impaired students. Psychol. Eval. Technol. Educ. Res. **3**(2), 77–88 (2021)

17. Ramos Aguiar, L.R., et al.: Implementing gamification for blind and autistic people with tangible interfaces, extended reality, and universal design for learning: two case studies. Appl. Sci. **13**(5), 3159 (2023)
18. Bogdan, R.C., Biklen, S.K.: Qualitative Research for Education: An Introduction to Theory and Methods, 3rd edn. Allyn and Bacon, Boston (1998)

Bridging the Digital Divide: Using Free Open-Source Tools to Expand Access to Shared-Use Computers in Schools and Libraries

Gregg Vanderheiden[1]([✉]) [iD], Crystal Marte[2] [iD], and JBern Jordan[1] [iD]

[1] University of Maryland, College Park, MD 20742, USA
GreggVan@umd.edu
[2] Raising the Floor, Washington, DC 20002, USA
crystal@raisingthefloor.org

Abstract. The use of computers in everyday life has moved from hobby and technical professional use to being essential to almost all activities in people's lives. However, not everyone has a computer themselves or access to the internet at home. To address this, society provides computers that people can use at school, in libraries, at job centers, in community centers, and at government service centers. However, these are not accessible to those who need assistive technologies (AT), and they are not allowed to install the AT they need to use the computers. This puts people who need to use AT at a severe disadvantage to their peers at best and, at worst, prevents them from participating at all where computer use is required. This is a problem when a person is required to use a particular computer instead of their own and is a total barrier to computer use for those who do not own their own computer. Proposed is the installation of a free utility on all public or shared use computers that both a) exposes the built-in accessibility features in computers to make them easier to discover and use, and b) allows AT users to have any AT the need automatically installed on any computer they encounter, and then set up just for them. When they are done, the AT disappears.

Keywords: Assistive Technology · Computers · Accessibility · Digital Inclusion

1 Introduction

In the rapidly evolving digital landscape, the ability to access and interact effectively with computers is not just a convenience but a necessity for participation in almost all aspects of society. From education and employment to personal communication and access to services, digital technologies play a central role. However, computers are not accessible to many populations, especially those with disabilities, chronic illnesses, mental health conditions, and older adults.

Despite the existence of tools to enable and simplify computer use, such as built-in accessibility features (zoom, text-to-speech, contrast, keyboard behavior adaptations)

and third-party assistive technologies (AT) (screen readers, writing aids, alternate keyboards, screen readers), these solutions often are not known to or available to those who need them the most. For example, almost all accessibility features are buried in control/settings panels where they remain unknown or are where users are afraid to go. And those for whom the built-in accessibility tools are not sufficient – and who need 3rd party AT – frequently are unable to use the computers at all due to the inability to install their AT on computers that they need to use [1].

These challenges are not merely technical, as they are also rooted in the interface design and accessibility feature discoverability of current operating systems. Users who need built-in features are often unaware of their existence, have difficulty navigating and using them, or are unable to configure them to their needs [2].

To address these multiple challenges to both AT and non-AT populations, a free, open-source tool called Morphic was developed, which provides four key features:

1. Easy discoverability of built-in accessibility features along with simplified, one-click access to key features via a MorphicBar,
2. Access to third-party AT on 'locked down' computers via AT-on-Demand; access to their AT anywhere as long as they have a license personally or from school or the location).
3. The ability to save, access, and apply their personalized (AT or accessibility feature) settings on any computer and
4. The ability to create custom MorphicBars for those who are unable to understand and use files, folders, programs, etc.

These novel capabilities not only bridge the accessibility gap for AT users but also simplify the digital experience for many who do not consider themselves to have a disability, but nonetheless have trouble using the interface on computers – and bring forth a new kind or level of digital equity.

In this paper, we discuss Morphic's development from its initial conception to its current iteration, presenting the early findings that guided our process, and the lessons learned along the way. We also discuss the place of this development in the evolution of accessibility and highlight its potential impact on both existing unsolved problems around AT delivery and availability, particularly to users and communities with fewer resources – including its potential to define a new level or standard for digital equity in places that provide public access or shared-use computers.

2   Background/Related Work

2.1   Assistive Technologies and Computer Access

Assistive technology (AT) encompasses a wide range of devices and software designed to aid individuals with disabilities in using technology. According to the World Health Organization (WHO), AT is a critical element in bridging the gap for people with disabilities, non-communicable diseases, mental health conditions, gradual functional decline, and older adults – and can ensure their participation in an increasingly digital world [3]. Although it is understood that access to AT is a human right, only 1 in 10 people in need of AT have access to it, underscoring the global scale of this issue [3].

Accessibility solutions for computer access have evolved significantly from their early inception. Originally, they were all third-party add-ons and involved the use of physical devices and adapters. This was initially due to the lack of a sophisticated operating system. Keyboards and other input and output devices were "memory mapped," meaning that software would directly read input from keyboards (for example) by reading a location in memory. Computers also didn't multitask the way they do today. As a result, adaptations were often physical (keyguards or levers that held down shift keys) and alternate keyboards or keyboard substitutes (that plugged into the keyboard port and looked like keyboards). One notable adaptation was the Adaptive Firmware Card (byte) developed by Paul Schwejda and Judy McDonald that cleverly stole CPU cycles and used the most ingenious methods to fake input events and allow alternate interface approaches such as morse code and scanning to control Apple II computers.

Over time, as operating systems evolved, it became possible to create completely software-based assistive technologies. These AT were able to both read contents from the screen for presentation in speech or braille, and to 'inject' fake keystrokes and, later, mouse and other input actions into the operating systems such that they appeared to software running on the computer to be standard input from the standard input devices.

In the 1980s, computer companies, starting with Apple, began building accessibility features directly into their products. Taking features developed in universities such as StickyKeys and MouseKeys, as well as working with 3rd-party AT developers, they build accessibility features directly into their operating systems so that they are available to all users of the computers or operating systems.

This was a breakthrough in accessibility and was among the first examples of 'inclusive design' in computers. However, built-in accessibility features were limited, and could not cover the full range of types, degrees, and combinations of disability. This continued to be filled by third-party assistive technology manufacturers. Initially, these companies would attach their assistive technology software by reverse engineering the operating systems and latching onto or injecting information into them. This created problems for both the AT manufacturers and the operating system companies. Since each company was attaching in different places, unknown to the operating system companies, every time, the operating system companies updated their software, they would invariably break one or many different Assistive technologies. Thus, a simple operating system upgrade could disable an AT user for an extended period of time until the company could discover and fix the problem. Sometimes, the place they connected to no longer existed, creating an even more severe problem. Over time, operating system companies worked with AT companies to identify the type of information they needed and the type of control they needed and developed special accessibility APIs that were stable, reducing the effort needed by assistive technology companies and bringing much more stability to third-party AT. Installing multiple ATs on the same computer often created problems with the different AT interfering with each other. This also has been greatly reduced over time but can still exist today if many different assistive technologies are all installed on the same computer at the same time. This can be a problem, for example, for a place wanting to make a wide variety of different assistive technologies available on a single computer at the same time.

2.2   The Gaps Between Availability, Usability, and Use of AT

Although many computer users would benefit from both built-in accessibility features and third-party software, only a fraction use it. This is due to a number of barriers.

Barriers to Use for Built-in Features

- Awareness – many are not aware that the features even exist. A number of studies have been conducted pointing to the disparity between the number of people who could benefit from these features, and the number who are even aware they exist [2, 4].
- Ease of Access – one problem identified in our work was the number of people who found that the features, buried in the control/settings panels, were too difficult and time-consuming to find and turn on each time. Some received negative feedback for using them if they forgot to turn them off afterward (a second tedious task). Some reported getting lost in the settings and finding them very confusing. One honestly said that it just made them feel stupid, so they avoided it.
- Fear – a surprising finding from our work was the number of people who were afraid to go into the control/settings panels. In some cases, they were told to never go into the settings. Others were simply afraid they would "break" the computer. Interestingly, even among people at a library tasked with helping patrons use their computers, some were afraid to go into the control/settings panels and had never done so. For some going into the control/settings panel to make their computer (or the library's computer) work better for them was akin to asking them to go under the hood of their car (or the library's or school's car) and make adjustments to make it work better for them.

Barriers to Use for 3rd Party Assistive Technology

- Availability – For almost all public and shared computers there is no assistive technology installed on them. Sometimes there is a computer or two in some location at the facility with AT on it, but AT users have no ability to use all the computers in all the locations, programs, classrooms, labs, etc., that others do.
- Wrong AT on Computer – When AT is provided on a computer, it is usually just one or two of the 50 to 100 different Assistive technologies that people may use to access computers. Having the wrong assistive technology on the computer is kind of like being given a pair of glasses with the wrong prescription. It might or might not help, but it still leaves you at a distinct disadvantage or completely unable to use the computer.
- Locked Out from Installing AT – The biggest barrier, however, is the fact that AT users are unable to install their assistive technologies on computers they need to use and that do not already have the AT they need on them. This blocks them from using between 98 and 99.9% of all the public and shared-use computers that are available to everyone else. And in many/most locations, it is 100%.
- Cost for AT and Computer to Run it on – Another final barrier is cost [3, 5]. While some assistive technologies are free, many assistive technologies are expensive. But a

big barrier can be the need for AT users to have their own computers, due to the above factors. In many cases, an individual with a disability is qualified through a state or insurance program to be provided with assistive technologies. The same programs, however, will not provide the individual with a computer to run their AT on. Without the ability to install and run these AT on public computers, the AT is of no value to the user. In other cases, students may be able to have assistive technologies provided to them through their school. However, these schools/programs do not usually provide the individual with their own computer as well. As a result, the individual again has no ability to use the AT outside of the school in order to do homework, etc. And they are unable to use it in the school as well except on a particular computer - and not on all of the computers in all of the classrooms, labs, etc. that the other students can. As a result, even if the AT is free or is provided to the individual, without the ability to afford their own computer, their inability to install the AT on other computers prevents them from being able to use any 3rd party AT they may need.

2.3 Research Efforts and Existing Solutions

While there have been numerous AT solutions developed over the years, and some applications such as SA2GO (no longer available) that could run on computers without being installed, there has been no general solution to allow AT, which a user needs, to be installed to work on public and shared use computers. There have also been mainstream programs like AppsAnywhere that can be used to allow apps to be installed or run on demand. They are quite expensive, though, and do not include the ability to set up the programs to match user's needs.

In order to meet the needs of libraries, schools, community centers, government programs, and other places where there are public and shared-use computers, there is a need for an affordable and safe (i.e., no data mining of users) solution that provides better access to a computer's built-in accessibility features and anywhere access to a user's AT. In order to be universally deployed in all schools, libraries, and communities, including small, rural, and low-resource communities (rural and urban), such a utility would need to be free or essentially free.

3 Morphic and AT-on-Demand

3.1 Morphic's Evolution

Initially, the goal of the effort was "auto-personalization," a settings transfer capability for AT users who encountered difficulties using computers that were not their own and needed to have their AT settings applied to other computers. However, over the course of development and working with schools and job centers, two much broader problems were discovered. First, even when accessibility features were already built into the computer, users were unaware of it, or afraid to use it, because it was buried in the control/settings panels. Secondly, the benefit of being able to transfer one's AT settings to a computer is severely limited if their AT is not on that computer – and there is no mechanism for the user to install their AT on that computer. This latter problem is particularly severe since the AT they need is seldom on the computers they need to use, making it impossible for them to use the computers.

3.2   Low Awareness and Use of Built-In Accessibility Features

As noted above, a key finding from our efforts was the discovery that there were large numbers of people who needed, but were not using, the accessibility features that are already built into computers. This, in itself, was not unexpected, as this had been found in numerous other studies. What did surprise us was all the reasons:

- Scale of the Lack of Awareness – We were surprised that not only users and people at libraries whose responsibility was to help people use computers, but we even found people in accessibility programs were not aware of the features built into the operating systems.
- Too Hard or Too Much Effort – Even when people did know of a feature, many found that it was too difficult to find it buried in the control/settings panels. Others said it was too much work to navigate all the way into the panels to find the settings to turn them on – and then again to turn them off.
- Fear of Breaking the Computer – We first heard people in American Job Centers expressing a fear of breaking the computer when they used it, or particularly if they did anything different than they had in the past. We thought this was a problem experienced just by people who weren't used to technology. Then we heard it in a community college with people who are "digital natives." Then, we heard it spontaneously uttered by someone in a major research university. In exploring further, we found that such feelings were widespread and prevented people from using accessibility features even when they were aware of them. Being located in the control/settings panels seemed to contribute to this.

To address these issues, we first tried using NFC cards that could sit next to the computer with signage showing how to use them to adjust one or more features on the computer (Fig. 1). However, even with a demonstration, we did not see usage. One subject who thanked us profusely after we demonstrated a "zoom screen" function was seen using the computer but not the NFC cards a few days later, saying she was afraid to use it.

Our next idea was to create a simple keypad with the name of each function on one of the keys. Our theory was that they might feel more comfortable pressing keys that looked like keyboard keys since they were already pressing keys like this. This idea, however, did not survive our first meeting with the IT staff at a community college. Even if we provided the keypads for free, they said that adding a keypad was a non-starter. Keyboards were one of their largest points of failure and adding one would be a problem. They also cited the speed with which mice disappeared and the lack of space at the workstations.

This led to our third and penultimate approach of putting each of the accessibility features directly on the bottom of the screen in a pop-up bar we called the QuickStrip (Fig. 2). This approach was successful, and users found features they did not previously known were there, and felt comfortable using them since they were right there on screen. This worked, but a person had to first click on a feature, and a pop-up menu appeared. They would then click on a button in the pop-up. This provided more options but added complexity, and for features that needed to be turned on and off, it added extra button

Fig. 1. User holding an NFC card up to the side of a computer screen to activate special accessibility features built into the operating system. Instructions are provided on the stand-up card next to the computer and on the card attached to the side of the computer. A rack of additional NFC cards, each with different accessibility settings, is to the left of the computer.

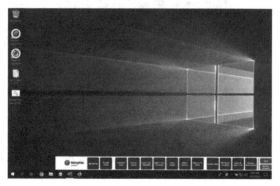

Fig. 2. A Windows 10 computer with the QuickStrip across the bottom. Each of the 13 buttons popped up a menu allowing the user to activate and/or adjust that feature.

clicks. Also, it was less obvious what items did before you clicked to open them. Finally, the number of choices made the bar somewhat intimidating.

The current implementation goes further in simplifying the bar (now called the MorphicBar) (Figs. 3 and 4). First, any settings that are not frequently used (e.g., used once to set up but not again after that) were moved to the MorphicBar menu, where they were still easy to discover but more out of the way. This simplified the look of the MorphicBar, making it more attractive to users. Second, the pop-up menus were eliminated, making all items 1-click items. With the new design and the accompanying explanatory pop-up, it was faster, simpler, clearer, and friendlier. We found that people were using it without any introduction or instruction.

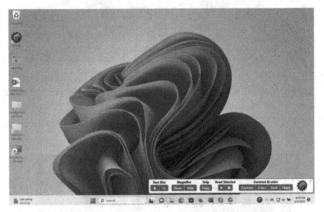

Fig. 3. Closeup of the new (current) MorphicBar.

Fig. 4. New, Current MorphicBar, shown here on Windows 11. The small Morphic icon on the system tray shows and hides the MorphicBar.

3.3 Just Transferring Settings is Not Enough

Although transferring the settings for built-in accessibility settings would be helpful, these features have relatively simple settings, and with the MorphicBar, they were easy to get to and adjust if needed. The larger need for transferring settings was for transferring the settings of assistive technologies, which can be quite a bit more complex and involved. However, in most instances where a person needed to transfer their AT settings to another computer, the other computer would not have the AT they needed, installed on it. Even the few computers that had AT on them, only had one or a few and usually not the AT that a person needed.

This led to a renewed effort to implement an idea long in discussion but not yet implemented: AT-on-Demand. With AT-on-Demand, when a person sat down to a computer with Morphic installed on it, Morphic would determine that the user's AT was not on the computer and use its AT-on-Demand functionality to install a copy of their software and then configure it for them. Although a simple concept, it was difficult to implement reliably on locked-down computers while preserving or improving site security.

4   The Development Process

At the beginning of our study, we collaborated with job centers to identify the challenges their clients faced, which we found revolved around AT. Although job centers had these accommodations for blind users due to support from Division of Vocational Rehabilitation (DVR) agencies, findings revealed a significant knowledge gap among job center staff. Many were unaware of the functionalities of AT at their center or even if it worked. Frequently, the designated computer with AT was older and had remained unused for extended periods. For example, one job center mentioned that they had not powered on this particular computer for approximately five years. If a client arrived at the center and encountered issues with their AT, job center personnel were unable to diagnose the problem or determine if the AT was functional, as they had limited or no expertise with it. Their understanding was limited to the existence of AT and their intended audience.

Subsequently, while engaging with libraries and job centers, we learned that none of the built-in accessibility features within the computer operating system were being used and, most of the time, were not even known about. Therefore, the necessity of exposing the built-in operating system features became evident, and we expanded our focus to include these. In exploring these, the design underwent several iterations, as described above, to determine the most useful and effective approach.

To understand which features might be most useful to patrons, we conducted both interviews and in situ observations. These observations revealed that individuals frequently exhibited behaviors such as squinting or closely approaching computer screens. These behaviors indicated a potential preference for features related to screen enlargement and magnification. Additionally, when developing the tool, we aimed to include features that were obvious and provided immediate feedback, whether through visual or auditory means. Ensuring this immediacy was critical, as it eliminated any ambiguity for users wondering if the feature had been activated successfully.

Various methods were explored to promote awareness and understanding and encourage utilization of these features, including textual descriptions, NFC (Near Field Communication) cards, on-screen toolbars, and finally, on-screen toolbars with pop-up large print help text.

Descriptions of the access features and how to find and access them were initially tried but proved ineffective. Next, we attempted to introduce NFC cards as a means of activating features. With this method, each of the computers was equipped with screens that had NFC readers embedded in their right screen border. The NFC cards were accompanied by signs with instructions such as "Touch your card here." Written on the NFC cards were the feature(s) each card would activate, such as "large print" and "large print with high contrast." The intended user interaction appeared to be simple: pick up the card and touch it to the screen to trigger the corresponding feature. However, this method encountered limited success as well. Exploration identified several reasons.

Primarily, users were unfamiliar with the concept of using cards for this purpose, and the process was not intuitive. An illustrative anecdote involved a woman who was struggling to see items on the computer screen and resorted to squinting. After being guided by a team member to employ the NFC card labeled "large print," she experienced an immediate improvement and expressed appreciation for the assistance, even hunting down the researchers when she was done for the day to say thank you and how much easier and faster it was to use the computer. However, on a subsequent visit, she returned to squinting at the screen from close range rather than touching the "large print" card to the screen as shown before. When asked, she said that she was afraid to use the card for fear of inadvertently causing damage to the equipment, a sentiment shared by multiple users. When the researcher questioned her further, noting how simple it was when they were shown the last time – she replied that we might feel safe doing that, but not her. Despite being aware of the card's functionality and ease of use, users were apprehensive about independently employing something that they were not already used to doing.

As a result, we sought to find a method that would be more like what they were already used to doing. First, we looked at using a keypad with one key per function since pressing keys on the keyboard was already a familiar task – though pushing a key to carry out a function was not quite the same. As noted above, that was nixed by the head of IT over concerns about adding a new piece of (easily removed) hardware to every computer. Next, we turned to an on-screen toolbar with buttons, since pressing buttons onscreen was a common activity. This last approach ultimately proved successful.

In its initial configuration, this toolbar comprised ten settings or functions, each leading to a pop-up menu, enabling users to toggle features on or off and make adjustments. However, this design proved somewhat confusing for users. First, the number of buttons made it look complicated. Second, the number of features was sufficient to be less inviting for people to just try one. The pop-up menu added more complexity and less immediacy and made it harder to turn things on and off in use – or to explore. Also, our attempts to put prompts or descriptive information on the pop-up menus along with the action buttons to make it clear what the buttons were for and how to use them, only made it more complex.

What proved effective in the end was a) prioritizing features that were more commonly used and that provided immediate and obvious results, b) moving features that were set-and-forget (one-time activation) off the bar and into a general menu to simplify the bar, c) making all of the functions single click actions. With this new setup - instead of navigating through multiple steps to activate or deactivate the magnifier, a single click would show the magnifier, and a single click would put it away. Similarly, rather than requiring users to pop up a menu to make the screen a little larger – each single click made everything larger until it reached the level desired by the user. This revised approach improved not only efficiency but also user comprehension, rendering the system more straightforward and user-friendly. It also had a gamification effect in that there was essentially no bar and nothing to learn in order to try just one button to see what it did. The pop-up large print help text also lets them know exactly what would happen, before they press it, reducing their fear of trying something. Once one button was clicked, and users found they could easily change it back with one click, users usually would move down the line with some confidence trying other features.

To further promote social acceptance and alleviate the potential stigma surrounding accessibility or disability-related tools, common usability features such as "snip" (i.e., screenshot) and "dark mode" were added alongside the accessibility features. In this manner, it became more of a utility bar rather than a 'disability bar,' allaying users from feeling like they were identifying as disabled if they used the bar.

5   How Morphic and AT-on-Demand Work in Use

First, a user starts out on a computer that has been set up for them. This could be their personal computer or a computer at a clinic, or school, or AT center. With Morphic installed on the computer, the "Save this Setup" is chosen from the MorphicBar menu. This will cause Morphic to see what AT is installed on the computer and active. It will then note these AT and collect all their settings – as well as accessibility settings on the computer. These are then saved into an encrypted "Vault" in the cloud that only the user has access to and is only used by and for the user.

When the user sits down to any other computer with Morphic installed on it (any computer at the library, school, community center, government program, etc.) and signs in, Morphic will call up the list of their AT and the AT's setting. If the AT is on the computer, it will set it up for the user. If the computer does not have the user's AT on it., Morphic, with its AT-on-Demand, will pull a clean sterile copy of their AT from a special bundle of AT installation packages the Morphic has provided to the institution and that is installed on the institution's own server. Thus, no software is downloaded from outside of the firewall as part of the AT-on-Demand operation. The clean copy of the user's software is installed and configured to fit the person, using the settings they have saved to the cloud. When the user is done, the AT and all the settings disappear from the computer.

Morphic exceeds all user privacy regulations, and all user data is strictly limited to operational needs, secured, and encrypted. To underscore our commitment, an external Privacy and Data Ethics Council has been established that oversees the implementation and privacy measures.

6   Evaluators Tool

The existence of Morphic with AT-on-Demand also opens the possibility of an evaluator tool that would, for the first time, allow people evaluating children or adults for the use of computer assistive technologies to be able to have all of the assistive technologies available at their fingertips. Using the AT-on-Demand's bundle of installation packages, and a special program, they would be able to pick any technology, and have it instantly installed on their computer, ready to try with a client. With Morphic ability to store different configurations, they could also have multiple configurations for each assistive technology. Instead of evaluating a person with only the few assistive technologies they may have on hand, they would be able to evaluate them with the full spectrum of assistive technologies available. All AT companies contacted to explore this concept have said they would be happy to provide the ability for evaluators to use their software free of charge for evaluation purposes. Many also offered to allow users free trial periods. With Morphic, a clinician could also save the configuration they developed for the user for one or more assistive technologies and share them with the user. When the user gets home, they could have Morphic automatically download the software and install it on their personal computer (or install it temporarily while they are using it at the computer at the library, school, or community center) all set up for them, just as the clinician/teacher/AT specialist set it up for them.

7 Problems Addressed by Morphic and AT-on-Demand

Some examples of existing barriers that AT-on-Demand could now address.

7.1 Problem: Schools, Job Centers, and Government Agencies Provide Computers for Shared or Public Use - but not to AT Users.

This is a common problem in places with shared-use or public-access computers. Due to lack of funds or technical problems installing all AT on all computers, they have no AT on all of their computers, and for security reasons, they cannot allow users to install their AT. Even the few places that have AT on 1 or 2 computers – only have 1 or 2 AT.

- Since AT-on-Demand supports a full spectrum of AT, it would allow students, patrons, or the public to use any computer, in any room or program, at any location, and have the particular AT and settings each individual needs.

7.2 Problem: K-12 Students Who Can't Use Their School-Licensed AT at Home, or Anywhere Else Outside of School – so No Homework or Independent Work.

Many K-12 students cannot use school-provided AT at home due to licensing restrictions. Many AT companies are willing to let students use AT outside of school, but the school can't disclose who their students are.

- By providing an anonymous verification method for using school licenses outside of school, AT-on-Demand would enable K-12 schools to offer their students easy access to the school's AT at home, library, community center, etc. – without compromising privacy.

7.3 Problem: Programs (School, State, or Insurance) Will Pay for the AT a Person Needs - but Will Not Pay for a Computer to Use It On. If the Person Has No Computer – They Can't Use the AT.

Generally, when families cannot afford a computer, their children use computers at libraries or community centers for homework, etc. But when those computers don't have the AT that the child needs, they have no place to go.

- With AT-on-Demand, they would be able to use the school/state/insurance-provided AT license on any computer in the community, allowing them, for the first time, to use the same computers as their peers. Essentially, any computer they sit down to would instantly set up to be their "personal, accessible-to-them" computer – and then change back when they are finished. (This also helps those without a home or a safe place to keep a computer.)

7.4 Problem: Small Libraries, Community Centers, Shelters, and Other Places with Public-Use Computers Often Cannot Afford/Manage the Range of AT Needed by Different Patrons, Seniors, Veterans, and Other Users.

Librarians at small, rural libraries with only a couple of computers, struggle to make their libraries as accessible to anyone as large libraries. But they have limited resources, and no staff to think about, much less address, the diverse AT needs of their patrons. And IT support doesn't understand AT at all. Ditto for community centers, homeless shelters, etc.

- With AT-on-Demand, small libraries, senior or community centers, etc., can allow patrons to use any AT the patron has a license for, on any of the computers—with no cost to the library/community center – and all AT management is done by RTF/AT-on-Demand.
- To address the needs of libraries with users who do not have their own AT license, funding for a "small library program" is being explored to allow them to provide AT free, or at a reduced price, for those who do not have their own licenses.

7.5 Problem: Even for Large, Well-Funded Libraries, Full Digital Accessibility Hasn't Been Possible.

While most libraries work to ensure their entire building, including all rooms and programs, are accessible to people using mobility AT, such as walkers and wheelchairs, they have not been able to ensure the computers in all these rooms are accessible to people who need digital AT. The result is the exclusion of these AT users from programs and spaces.

AT-on-Demand revolutionizes digital accessibility both for libraries and schools, closing the gap between physical and digital accessibility by providing a safe, secure solution to providing the wide range of AT that patrons may need, and providing it on any computer, in all locations in the library, school, etc.

7.6 Problem: AT Is Often Not Provided – or Limited to Just a Few AT on a Few Computers, Due to Real IT Dept Constraints.

IT departments are understaffed and unable to understand, install, update, and ensure security for the wide range of AT that users need. And for security reasons, they cannot allow users to install software themselves on computers.

- AT-on-Demand is designed to support the needs and constraints of IT departments:

  - It decreases or eliminates the need for IT staff to learn about all the different AT.
  - IT department staff no longer need to individually install and keep AT updated.
  - AT is only installed if there is a valid AT license (library or user).
  - Security is assured since AT is only installed from IT dept servers using install packages pre-screened (also screened by IT themselves if desired).
  - Compliance with Privacy laws is assured by an international Privacy and Data Ethics Council.

7.7 Firsts

Morphic with AT-on-Demand presents the field with several first capabilities for AT vendors, AT users, and any place wanting to make its computers cross-disability accessible.

For the first time.

- AT users can use *any* computer at school, library, work, a relative's, etc.– even if the AT they need is not on the computer.
- People *who don't have their own computer* can use any computer in their community - just like their peers.
- Interns or new hires can have their company computer set up for them, *the same morning they come onboard*.
- If an AT user's computer fails or is lost, *a new one can be set up* with all their AT and specific settings – *in minutes rather than days*.
- Institutions can have AT available on *all computers* at all their locations, so their users who need AT can use them - on an equal footing with everyone else.
- IT departments can provide any assistive technology on any computer a user needs, anywhere at their location – instantly – *without having to install it on any computer*. They can also *use a single disk image* for all computers rather than having to maintain a special image for special computers with AT on them.

8 Conclusion

The development and implementation of Morphic and AT-on-Demand represent a paradigm shift in the approach to digital accessibility. In the past, a school or library was considered to be providing good, or at least sufficient, accessibility for computers if they had one or two computers with a few AT located somewhere in their library (or even library system). This is quite a different standard than for wheelchair access, where all rooms, programs, labs, etc., would need to be accessible. With AT-on-Demand, computer accessibility can be provided on a similarly equal basis for AT users as for other library patrons. For pure software AT, they would be able to use their AT, which is automatically set up for them, on any of the computers. For AT that has a required hardware component such as a switch or braille display, they would be able to bring that switch or braille display with them and use it on any computer at the library, with Morphic and AT-on-Demand downloading and installing all of the necessary software and drivers. In both cases, any individual with an assistive technology would be able to use it on any computer at the library in the same way that mobility aid users are able to use their assistive technology (their wheelchair or walker, etc.) anywhere in the facility.

If these free, open-source utilities can be deployed universally, this could represent an entirely new level of digital equity for AT users – especially those with fewer resources or from low-resource communities.

Acknowledgments. This work represented here is the result of work funded by grants from the National Institute on Disability, Independent Living and Rehabilitation Research at the Administration for Community Living, U.S. Dept. of Health and Human Services (grant # H133E080022 and 90REGE0008), the Rehabilitation Services Administration, U.S. Dept. of Education (grant H421A150005); the European 7th Framework grants (grant #289016 and 610510), and by the Flora Hewlett Foundation, the Ontario Ministry of Research and Innovation, and the Canadian Foundation for Innovation. The opinions herein are those of the author and not necessarily those of the funding agencies.

Disclosure of Interests.   Both authors are affiliated with both the University of Maryland and the non-profit Raising the Floor. Both the University of Maryland and the non-profit Raising the Floor were integral to the development of the technologies reported, and Raising the Floor is now distributing Morphic and AT-on-Demand as free, open-source software.

References

1. Vanderheiden, G.C.: Ubiquitous accessibility, common technology core, and micro assistive technology: commentary on "computers and people with disabilities". ACM Trans. Accessible Comput. (TACCESS) **1**(2), 1–7 (2008)
2. Stevenson, B., Kolko, J.: Accessible Technology in Computing—Examining Awareness, Use, and Future Potential. Microsoft Corporation (2004)
3. Global report on assistive technology. World Health Organization, Geneva (2022)
4. Wu, J., Reyes, G., White, S.C., Zhang, X., Bigham, J.P.: When Can Accessibility Help?: An Exploration of Accessibility Feature Recommendation on Mobile Devices, 12p. (2021). https://doi.org/10.1145/3430263.3452434
5. Koch, K.: Stay in the Box! Embedded assistive technology improves access for students with disabilities. Educ. Sci. **7**(4), 82 (2017). https://doi.org/10.3390/EDUCSCI7040082

Universal Access to Health
and Wellbeing

Web Diagnosis for COVID-19 and Pneumonia Based on Computed Tomography Scans and X-rays

Carlos Antunes[1]([✉]) [iD], João M. F. Rodrigues[2] [iD], and António Cunha[1,3] [iD]

[1] Universidade de Trás-os-Montes e Alto Douro, Vila Real, Portugal
al75425@alunos.utad.pt
[2] NOVA LINCS & ISE, Universidade do Algarve, Faro, Portugal
[3] Institute for Systems and Computer Engineering, Technology, Porto, Portugal

Abstract. Pneumonia and COVID-19 are respiratory illnesses, the last caused by the severe acute respiratory syndrome virus, coronavirus 2 (SARS-CoV-2). Traditional detection processes can be slow, prone to errors, and laborious, leading to potential human mistakes and a limited ability to keep up with the speed of pathogen development. A web diagnosis application to aid the physician in the diagnosis process is presented, based on a modified deep neural network (AlexNet) to detect COVID-19 on X-rays and computed tomography (CT) scans as well as to detect pneumonia on X-rays. The system reached accuracy results well above 90% in seven well-known and documented datasets regarding the detection of COVID-19 and Pneumonia on X-rays and COVID-19 in CT scans.

Keywords: Web Diagnosis Application · COVID-19 · Pneumonia

1 Introduction

Universal Access in Human-Machine Cooperation is a forward-thinking approach that aims to create an inclusive environment where humans and machines can work together seamlessly. The use of accessible and usable information and communication technologies (ICT) is granted in many countries or regions in the world, nevertheless, this is not true for the entire world. Physicians in some countries and regions with less economic power still have difficulties accessing ICT tools to analyse medical images.

On the other hand, all physicians need tools to help in the diagnosis that should be focused on their needs, and they (physicians) should/must be part of the design teams of any applications, i.e., any application design for physicians should pass through a User-Centered Design (UCD) development, which is an iterative design process in which designers focus on the users and their needs in each phase of the design process.

COVID-19 (SARS-CoV-2) is one of the deadliest diseases on the planet, it has been spreading around the world, causing in some cases severe respiratory problems and death, it has infected at least 542 million humans and killed 6 million. Traditional technologies to detect COVID-19 are very laborious, time-consuming, with high costs, and tend to

M. Antona and C. Stephanidis (Eds.): HCII 2024, LNCS 14698, pp. 203–221, 2024.
https://doi.org/10.1007/978-3-031-60884-1_14

fail sometimes, leading to detection failures at the initial stages of the disease, which can affect future treatment. The detection process of the SARS-CoV-2 can be improved [1].

The World Health Organization (WHO) approximates that more than 4 million premature deaths happen each year due to diseases related to household air pollution, with pneumonia being a significant factor. Annually, over 150 million individuals contract pneumonia, with children under 5 years old being particularly vulnerable [2]. Pneumonia is also a common cause of death among older adults and people with weakened immune systems. It can be caused by bacteria, viruses [3], fungi, or other microorganisms. Risk factors for pneumonia include malnutrition, smoking, air pollution, and other respiratory infections. It is important to seek medical attention if you suspect you may have pneumonia, as early diagnosis and treatment can improve outcomes and reduce the risk of complications.

Both diseases may be detected via the analysis of medical images, like X-rays and Computerized Tomography (CT) scans. Nowadays, deep learning technologies are being more commonly used to detect these diseases because X-rays and CT scans are difficult to analyze by the human eye [4]. Computer vision techniques can make easier the process of detecting diseases, which can save lives.

This paper presents a web diagnosis tool based on UCD principles, for free universal use, that can be used anywhere in the world to assist physicians in medical diagnosis [5]. The physician just needs to have a web browser, and the tool facilitates the process of identifying the disease. The tool is based on a deep learning model, that can cope with different types of images (tested 8 different datasets) and different sources of information (X-ray and CT scans) to identify the existence of COVID-19 and Pneumonia.

The main contribution of the paper is two-fold: (a) a single model that can predict COVID-19 and Pneumonia from two different sources, X-ray and CT scans, integrated with (b) explainable artificial intelligence (XAI) that enables physicians to better explain diagnoses and treatment plans to patients. The last can lead to improved patient-doctor communication and increased confidence in the provided medical care.

Section 2 introduces some background information, examples of existing datasets and a summary of the present state of the art. Section 3 describes briefly the web tool developed as well as a new deep model architecture for the detection of the mentioned diseases. Results and tests are presented in Sect. 4 and the last section (Sect. 5) presents the conclusions and future work.

2   Background and Related Work

As already mentioned, the disease COVID-19 is caused by the mutating virus severe acute respiratory syndrome coronavirus 2 (SARS-CoV-2) which has a spike protein that suffers mutations [6, 7]. The SARS-CoV-2 multiplies easily and has several proteins that can cause damage, in some cases, the virus manages to reach the lungs causing serious symptoms, such as shortness of breath and consequently, less oxygenation of the organs of our body, which can be fatal. Pneumonia is also a lung infection that can be caused by bacteria, viruses, or fungi. It inflames the air sacs in one or both lungs, filling them with fluid or pus, which can cause coughing with phlegm or pus, fever, chills, and difficulty breathing. It is important to stress, that high-quality CT scans provide detailed anatomical information about the lungs, allowing the detection of subtle changes associated with Covid-19. These changes, such as ground-glass opacities, consolidations, and reticulation, are not always easily discernible by human radiologists, but machine learning algorithms can effectively identify these patterns from CT scans. In this section, we will present the existing datasets, models, and methods.

2.1 Datasets

There are several publicly available datasets to detect COVID-19 and Pneumonia. *COVID-19 Radiography Database* [8] released chest X-ray images for COVID-19-positive cases along with normal and viral Pneumonia images, i.e., 3,616 COVID-19, 10,192 normal, 6,012 Lung Opacity (Non-Covid lung infection), and 1,345 viral Pneumonia images and corresponding lung masks.

The extensive COVID-19 X-ray and CT chest images dataset *CoV-Healthy-6k Dataset* [9] contains X-rays and CT scans of healthy individuals and people with the COVID-19 virus, where several X-rays and CT scans can be found with and without the disease. Concerning the CT scans were used 5,427 with Covid-19 and 2,628 without, X-ray 4,044 with Covid and 5,500 nonCovid. *Covid-XRay-5K Dataset* [10] has available 88 X-rays of Covid-19 cases and 2,000 normal. The *COVID-19 lung CT Scans dataset* [11] has more than 8,000 images of CT scans with COVID-19 and without. The images in this dataset were gathered from radiology departments at teaching hospitals in Tehran, Iran. The COVID-19 status of patients in the dataset was verified using reverse transcription-polymerase chain reaction (RT-PCR) tests.

The *SARS-CoV-2 CT-scan dataset* [12] is composed of 2,482 CT scan images, which is divided between 1,252 for patients infected by SARSCoV-2, and 1,230 CT scans for non-infected SARS-CoV-2 patients, but presented other pulmonary diseases. The data was collected from hospitals in São Paulo, Brazil. The (COVID-19 & Pneumonia) *Chest X-ray dataset* [13] has in total 6,432 X-ray images, containing 3,418 X-rays with Pneumonia and 1,266 normal. They also presented 576 X-ray images of COVID-19. The labelled *Optical Coherence Tomography (OCT) and Chest X-Ray Images for Classification dataset* [14] was compiled by the University of California San Diego. The latest version of this dataset is composed of 5,856 X-ray images. It was divided into a training set consisting of 3,883 X-rays corresponding to cases of pneumonia and 1,349 X-rays without detected pathologies, to this they also added a test set with 234 images labelled as pneumonia and 390 without detected pathologies.

The (Pneumonia) *Chest X-Ray Images dataset* [15] comprises three main folders (train, test, validation) with subfolders for each image category (Pneumonia/Normal). These chest X-ray images (anterior-posterior) were sourced from pediatric patients aged one to five at Guangzhou Women and Children's Medical Center as part of routine clinical care. The dataset has 1,341 images for training, and 3,875 X-rays with pneumonia, for tests 234 and 390, and validation, 8 and 8 respectively, including validation and tests there are in total 5,856.

Table 1 summarizes the number of images used for each dataset, X-rays, and CT scans of the datasets mentioned before. It is important to stress that there are more datasets available, e.g. [16–20].

Table 1. Number of images of the nine datasets described.

Dataset	X-Ray		CT		X-ray	
	Covid	Noncovid	Covid	Noncovid	Normal	Pneumonia
[8]	3,616	10,192			10,192	6,012
[9]	4,044	5,500	5,427	2,627		
[10]	88	2,000				
[11]			7,495	944		
[12]			1,252	1,230		
[13]	576	1,266			1,266	3,418
[14]					1,583	4,273
[15]					1,583	4,273

2.2 Models and Methods

In the literature, there are different models and methods to detect both diseases using X-rays and CT scans. Concerning the detection of Pneumonia, certain medical images can be acquired from X-rays [21], CT scans of the thorax, chest ultrasound, or a chest MRI. Nevertheless, it is important to stress that the detection can be inaccurate because the presence of other health complications, like lung cancer, extra blood, overlapping and a variety of other benign anomalies, may cause similar opacification in images [22]. Table 2 summarizes the main datasets and studies used and respective accuracy concerning the detection of COVID-19 on X-rays and CT scans, and the detection of pneumonia on X-rays. The studies will be detailed below.

Hall et al. [23] present a pre-trained deep convolutional neural network, ResNet50, that underwent fine-tuning on a dataset comprising 102 COVID-19 cases and 102 other Pneumonia cases through a 10-fold cross-validation. The process taken by the authors yielded an 89.2% overall accuracy, a COVID-19 true positive rate of 0.8039, and an AUC of 0.95. Following this, both pre-trained ResNet50 and VGG16, alongside the custom small convolutional neural network (CNN) developed by the authors, were fine-tuned or trained on a balanced collection of COVID-19 and Pneumonia chest X-rays. Three CNN classifiers were applied, and the test set consisted of 33 previously unseen COVID-19 cases and 218 pneumonia cases resulting in an overall accuracy of 91.24%. Specifically, for COVID-19, the true positive rate was 0.7879 with 6.88% false positives, leading to a true negative rate of 0.9312 and an AUC of 0.94.

In [24] the authors developed and assessed multiple deep CNNs to distinguish between normal and abnormal frontal chest radiographs. The goal was to aid radiologists and clinicians in flagging potential abnormal findings and facilitating work list prioritization and reporting. One CNN-based model achieved an AUC of 0.9824 ± 0.0043, with an accuracy of $94.64 \pm 0.45\%$, sensitivity of $96.50 \pm 0.36\%$, and specificity of $92.86 \pm 0.48\%$ in classifying normal versus abnormal chest radiographs. The same CNN model yielded an AUC of 0.9804 ± 0.0032, with an accuracy of $94.71 \pm 0.32\%$, sensitivity of $92.20 \pm 0.34\%$, and specificity of $96.34 \pm 0.31\%$ in distinguishing

Table 2. Comparison of accuracy results of different studies.

Dataset	Study	Accuracy
Detection of COVID-19 on X-rays		
Covid-19 image data collection [16]	[23]	89.2%
NIH "ChestX-ray 14" [17]	[24]	94.6%
Chest X-Ray Images (Pneumonia) [15]	[25]	93.9%
Detection of COVID-19 on CT scans		
Private dataset	[27]	91.7%
Covid-19 Radiography Database [8] & Chest CT-Scan images Dataset [18]	[31]	93.0%
SARS-COV-2 Ct-Scan [19]	[30]	92.0%
Detection of Pneumonia on X-rays		
ImageNet [20]	[36]	87.5%
The Chest X-Ray Images (Pneumonia) dataset [15]	[32]	91.0%
Labeled OCT and Chest X-Ray Images for Classification dataset [14]	[33]	90.0%

normal versus lung opacity cases. On an external dataset, the CNN model developed by the authors demonstrated potentially high generalizability, achieving an AUC of 0.9444 ± 0.0029.

Ahsan et al. in [25] identify COVID-19 symptoms employing 8 distinct deep learning methodologies, VGG16, ResNet50, InceptionResNetV2, DenseNet201, VGG19, MobilenetV2, NasNetMobile, and ResNet15V2 utilizing two datasets: one containing 400 CT scans and another comprising 400 chest X-ray images. The authors indicated that NasNetMobile exhibited superior performance, attaining an accuracy of 82.94% in CT scans and 93.94% in chest X-ray datasets. The authors also used Local Interpretable Model-agnostic Explanations (LIME). In the work of [26], they have modified standard architectures and the best classification accuracy was achieved using a modified VGG19 model, reaching 99.84% accuracy in binary classification (COVID-19 versus normal). Additionally, in the triple classification (COVID-19 vs Pneumonia vs Normal), the modified VGG16 model performed exceptionally well, achieving an accuracy of 98.26%.

Concerning the detection of COVID-19 on CT scans, Sun et al. [27] proposed an Adaptive Feature Selection-guided Deep Forest (AFS-DF) model for the classification of COVID-19 based on chest CT images. Initially, was extracted location-specific features from the images. Additionally, the authors introduced a feature selection technique based on a trained deep forest model to diminish feature redundancy, allowing adaptive integration with the COVID-19 classification model. The evaluation performed by the authors of the AFS-DF on a COVID-19 dataset encompassing 1,495 COVID-19 patients and 1,027 patients with community-acquired pneumonia demonstrated promising metrics: an accuracy of 91.79%, sensitivity of 93.05%, specificity of 89.95%, area under the curve of 96.35%, precision of 93.10%, and F1-score of 93.07%.

Akter et al. [28] detect COVID-19 using a deep learning algorithm on chest X-ray images. Dahmane et al. [29] use transfer learning to predict pneumonia using a combination of the VGG 19 with a CNN they developed. Hasan et al. [30] introduced a prospective method for forecasting COVID-19 cases from CT images utilizing convolutional neural networks. The researchers presented an innovative method that relies on the latest adaptation of CNN architecture, specifically DenseNet-121, to anticipate COVID-19. The outcomes demonstrated the work of the researchers with an accuracy surpassing 92%, along with a 95% recall rate, indicating satisfactory predictive performance for COVID-19 diagnosis.

In [31] the authors propose a deep transfer learning approach for the classification of patients infected with COVID-19. A top-2 smooth loss function incorporating cost-sensitive attributes is applied to address issues related to noisy and imbalanced datasets in COVID-19 classification. Experimental findings done by the authors demonstrated that the suggested deep transfer learning-based model for COVID-19 classification yields superior outcomes when compared to other supervised learning models.

Concerning the detection of Pneumonia on X-rays, Szepesi and Szilágyi [32] suggest a method by employing an innovative deep neural network architecture. The novelty of the proposal of the authors lies in integrating dropout within the convolutional segment of the network. The method underwent training and testing using a dataset comprising 5,856 labelled images sourced from a medical imaging challenge hosted on Kaggle. The chest X-ray images (anterior-posterior) were culled from retrospective cohorts of pediatric patients, aged between one and five years, from Guangzhou Women and Children's Medical Center, Guangzhou, China. The results produced by the network of the authors showed the following metrics: 97.2% accuracy, 97.3% recall, and 97.4% precision. In [33] the authors used two deep learning models, DenseNet169 and a pre-activation version of ResNet, which were merged to automatically detect Pneumonia. DenseNet169 extends the ResNet model, the latter is an altered form of ResNet known for its effectiveness in medical imaging. For the problem of imbalanced data, the authors used two methods: class weight manipulation, allowing control over the proportion of original data utilized for each class, and resampling, which generates modified images achieving equal distribution through data augmentation. The performance of the proposed model by the researchers was assessed by using a balanced dataset comprising 5,856 images. The model achieved a precision rate of 98%, an area under the curve of 97%, and a loss value of 0.23.

Hayat et al. [34] present two distinct deformable deep networks derived from the traditional convolutional neural network and the advanced ResNet-50, aiming to identify COVID-19 cases within chest CT images. The impact of integrating the deformable concept was assessed by comparing the performance of the deformable models with standard models. The findings of the authors indicate that the deformable models exhibited superior predictive capabilities compared to their standard counterparts. The researchers used the gradient class activation mapping technique. The evaluation performed by the authors encompassed 2,481 chest CT images, split randomly into training, validation, and testing sets at a ratio of 80:10:10. The proposed deformable ResNet50 model by the researchers achieved a training accuracy of 99.5%, test accuracy of 97.6%, specificity of 98.5%, and sensitivity of 96.5%.

Ali et al. [35] identify pneumonia focusing on addressing the issue of class imbalance. The developed method by the authors involved using a combination of generative adversarial networks, specifically a mix of deep convolutional generative adversarial network and Wasserstein GAN with gradient penalty (WGAN-GP), to augment the underrepresented Pneumonia class. Random under-sampling was employed for the overrepresented *No Findings* class to tackle the imbalance problem. The effectiveness of the framework provided by the researchers was evaluated using the extensive ChestX-Ray8 dataset. The training phase used transfer learning on advanced deep learning models like ResNet50, Xception, and VGG16. The achieved results by the authors were robust. In summary, all recent models are based on deep learning methods.

3   Web Diagnosis for COVID-19 and Pneumonia

Web diagnosis application, designed by **AI Health**, is divided into 3 main blocks, illustrated in Fig. 1: (i) data selection and reading, left block, (ii) disease detection, middle block, and (iii) user interface (UI), right block.

In the next sections, we will go into detail for each of these blocks.

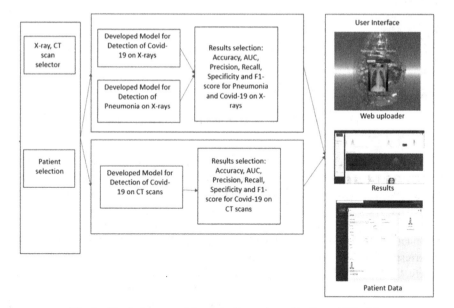

Fig. 1. Block diagram of the web diagnosis application: AI Health.

3.1   Data Selection and Reading

AI Health offers the possibility via UI to choose a patient. After selection, all the data relevant to that person is displayed, along with predictions if the patient has a disease. Figure 2 shows a partial view of a UI from a patient. In the interface (left) the physician has to select if he wants to upload an X-ray or a CT scan to detect Covid-19 or Pneumonia. There is, of course, an option to edit the details of the patient as well as the results obtained.

3.2 Disease Detection

Several standard models were trained and tested, they are shown in Sect. 4 Tests and Results, here, we propose a new model **CPAlexNet** for disease detection, it is focused on a specific deep learning architecture, in the case of AlexNet [37] trained with ImageNet, i.e., AlexNet is the backbone of the present model. The network was fine-tuned by adjusting layers and adding new ones to better capture features relevant to COVID-19 and Pneumonia patterns in X-rays and CT scans.

Fig. 2. Partial view of AI Health UI from a patient file.

As known, AlexNet's network head has three dense layers: The first fully connected layer (FC6) comprises 4,096 neurons and is connected to the flattened output of the last convolutional layer (Conv5). FC6 learns intricate patterns and relationships within the extracted features. The second fully connected layer (FC7) also consists of 4,096 neurons and further refines the learned features from FC6. It continues to abstract higher-level representations from the previous layer's output, and the final (FC8) has 1,000 neurons that correspond to 1,000 outputs (classes).

Here, the top head layer, fully connected layer - FC8, was replaced by a 2D convolutional layer called *Conv_1*, and added, along with a freshly integrated batch normalization layer labelled *BN_1*, with a ReLU activation function, over those, full connected layer with 1,000 neurons with a SoftMax activation function and the final layer with 2 outputs was introduced, the last with also a SoftMax activation function produce class probabilities for the input image: covid, noncovid or pneumonia, nonpneumonia (Fig. 3).

Connecting to the previous model, XAI techniques were employed to facilitate the process of explaining to the physicians how the detection was made. In the present case, it was applied the *Gradient-weighted Class Activation Mapping* (Grad-CAM) and *Local Interpretable Model-agnostic Explanations* to visualize which regions of X-ray images and CT scans are influential in the model's predictions.

Fig. 3. Representation of the modifications done to the FC8 of the standard AlexNet architecture (see text for details).

Figure 4 shows in the top row the application of Grad-CAM on an X-ray highlighting the areas of importance for X-rays. COVID-19 on the left and Pneumonia on the right. The importance map is generated by deriving the reduction layer output concerning a specific class's convolutional feature map. In classification tasks, the Grad-CAM function autonomously identifies the appropriate layers for computing this importance map. In the same figure in the bottom row the results applying LIME in two COVID-19 (left) and Pneumonia (right). Test and results of the proposed model and comparison with other models will be presented in Sect. 4.

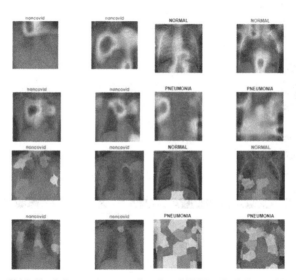

Fig. 4. Top row, XAI Grad-Cam representation for COVID-19 (left) and Pneumonia (right), bottom row, the same for LIME.

3.3 Web Diagnosis Interface

The web application, see Fig. 5, was developed in PHP, paired with a MySQL server database, and serves as a versatile platform for medical imaging analysis. The application features a user-friendly web uploader specifically designed for X-ray and CT scan uploads. Once uploaded, the system employs the deep learning model (see Sects. 3.2 and 4) developed in Python Flask to assess the presence of COVID-19 in X-rays and CT scans, alongside pneumonia detection for X-ray images. Figure 5 shows two partial views of the AI Health UI. The top image represents information about the patient and the bottom image the dashboard.

The application architecture follows the model view controller (MVC) design pattern, separating components into three distinct layers: The model handles data-related operations, and manages data interactions with the database. In this context, it manages interactions with the MySQL database, storing and retrieving uploaded images and associated information. The view layer deals with the user interface, providing an interactive

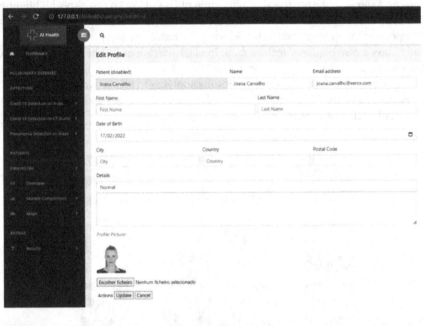

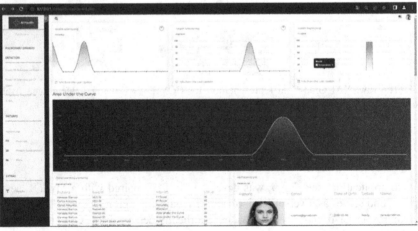

Fig. 5. Partial views of the UI from the AI Health application. At the top is information about the patient, and at the bottom is the dashboard of the patient. No patient or data is real; all information and images are purely illustrative.

platform for users to upload X-ray and CT scan images. It presents the results of the analysis performed by the deep learning models.

The controller serves as an intermediary, managing user inputs and orchestrating the interaction between the model and the view. It triggers the execution of deep learning models to analyze uploaded images and fetches results to display them in the user interface.

Several APIs were implemented within the controller layer to facilitate communication between different parts of the application. These APIs are responsible for tasks such as handling image uploads, triggering the deep learning analysis, and retrieving and displaying the analysis results within the web interface.

4   Tests and Results

The development was done using several technologies like MatLab, and Python and the libraries Keras and TensorFlow. For training and testing, it was used a desktop with CPU Intel i7 – 1165G7 2.8 GHz, RAM 8Gb GPU Intel UHD Graphics. As usual, traditional metrics such as accuracy, precision, recall, and F1-score were calculated to measure how well the model classifies Pneumonia and COVID-19.

Figure 6 illustrates some of the images available in the datasets for COVID-19.

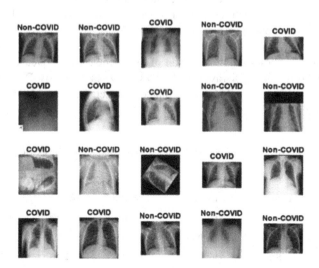

Fig. 6. Examples of COVID or non-COVID X-ray images.

Normalization techniques were applied to standardize the images and ensure consistent interpretation. The lungs were segmented from the CT scan images to isolate the region of interest for analysis. This step involved identifying and separating the lung parenchyma from other structures such as bones, heart, and mediastinum. CT scans can contain noise due to various factors, including scanning parameters and patient movement. Noise reduction techniques were employed to minimize noise artefacts and improve the quality of the images.

For the tests done with the standard architectures, VGG-16, VGG-19, ResNet-50 and AlexNet, the datasets were balanced, and properly annotated. It was used 80% of the samples for training these architectures and 20% for testing and validation. All the hyperparameters remained at the same standard (no changes were made). All these pre-trained model weights were leveraged from ImageNet and fine-tuned with the datasets to expedite learning. The output layer was modified to match the number of classes needed for COVID-19 and Pneumonia detection. Data preprocessing was performed by standardizing, cleaning, and augmenting the images to ensure consistency and quality.

The CPAlexNet was trained on the nine datasets, which were divided into sets for training, validation, and testing sets (80:10:10), except for the datasets where that division was already done. The hyperparameters used were: a learning rate of 0.01 (1e−2), the Adam optimization algorithm, for 100 epochs. When needed the datasets were balanced before the training using data augmentation like rotation, flipping and contrast adjustments.

4.1 Tests

The first test, **Test 1**, consists of comparing our model against traditional architectures. For the case of COVID-19 detection on X-rays, the architectures tested were VGG-16, VGG-19, ResNet-50 and AlexNet. Table 3 shows a comparison of the results obtained using those different architectures and our proposed model CPAlexNet. The tests were done using the *Covid-19 Radiography Database* [8].

The second test, **Test 2**, consists of testing our model against several state-of-the-art models. Table 4 shows the comparison of our model, CPAlexNet, concerning the detection of COVID-19 on X-rays for the Covid-19 Radiography Database [8], the extensive Covid-19 X-Ray and CT chest images dataset, CoV-Healthy-6k Dataset [9] and the Covid-XRay-5K Dataset [10].

Table 3. Comparison of the results obtained using different models on the Covid-19 Radiography Database [8].

Model	Accuracy	Precision	Recall	AUC	F1-score
VGG-16	92.4%	86.9%	84.9%	91.0%	85.9%
VGG-19	93.5%	90.9%	85.6%	93.0%	88.2%
ResNet-50	**97.8%**	**99.8%**	95.7%	94.2%	95.6%
AlexNet	96.2%	95.1%	**97.4%**	**99.4%**	96.2%
CPAlexNet	97.6%	98.3%	97.0%	**99.4%**	**97.6%**

The third test, **Test 3**, consists of the detection of Covid-19 in CT scans, against traditional architectures VGG-16, VGG-19, ResNet-50 and AlexNet. It used Covid-19 lung CT Scans dataset [11], Table 5 shows the results. **Test 4** consists of comparing the results of our models against state-of-the-art models for CT scans. Results for datasets [9, 11, 12] are shown in Table 6. **Test 5** consists of the detection of Pneumonia on X-rays,

Table 4. Comparison of the results for COVID-19 X-ray images with state-of-the-art models.

Model	Architectures (summarized)	Accuracy
Covid-19 Radiography Database [8]		
[38]	Fine-tuned AlexNet	99.0%
[26]	Modified VGG-19 [39]	**99.8%**
CPAlexNet *(AUC = 99.4%)*		97.6%
CoV-Healthy-6k Dataset [9]		
[40]	CB-STM-RENet	**98.5%**
[41]	Proposed model	97.1%
CPAlexNet *(AUC = 97.8%)*		95.1%
Covid-XRay-5K Dataset [10]		
[42]	Proposed SqueezeNet	92.2%
[43]	Genetic Deep Learning Convolutional Neural Network	**98.8%**
CPAlexNet *(AUC = 88.6%)*		85.1%

against traditional models, it used Chest X-ray dataset [13]. Results are shown in Table 7. The last test, **Test 6**, consists of detecting Pneumonia on X-ray datasets and comparing them with state-of-the-art models. Tests were done in datasets [13–15], results shown in Table 8.

Table 5. Results obtained concerning the Covid-19 lung CT Scans dataset [11].

Model	Accuracy	Precision	Recall	AUC	F1-score
VGG-16	85.3%	96.4%	72.0%	88.0%	82.4%
VGG-19	88.7%	93.3%	79.1%	90.0%	85.6%
ResNet-50	95.9%	96.8%	98.6%	94.6%	95.6%
AlexNet	92.4%	92.1%	**100.0%**	89.8%	92.2%
CPAlexNet	**98.9%**	**98.9%**	99.9%	**99.8%**	**99.3%**

Table 6. Comparison of the results with state-of-the art models for the Covid-19 lung CT Scans.

Model	Architectures (summarized)	Accuracy
Covid-19 lung CT Scans dataset [11]		
[44]	Proposed method	**99.9%**
[45]	NASNet	99.4%
CPAlexNet (AUC = 99.8%)		98.9%

(continued)

Table 6. (*continued*)

Model	Architectures (summarized)	Accuracy
CoV-Healthy-6k Dataset [9]		
[46]	CNN-based diagnostic model	96.0%
[34]	SCovNet	**98.7%**
CPAlexNet (AUC = 99.4%)		93.9%
SARS-CoV-2 CT-scan dataset [12]		
[47]	(BO)-based MobilNetv2, ResNet-50 models, SVM and kNN	**99.4%**
[48]	EfficientNet-B3-GAP-Ensemble	88.2%
CPAlexNet (AUC = 99.3%)		94.4%

Table 7. Results obtained concerning Pneumonia in Chest X-ray dataset [13].

Model	Accuracy	Precision	Recall	AUC	F1-score
VGG-16	85.3%	96.4%	72.0%	88.0%	82.4%
VGG-19	88.7%	93.3%	79.1%	90.0%	85.6%
ResNet-50	95.9%	96.8%	98.6%	94.6%	95.6%
AlexNet	92.4%	92.1%	**100.0%**	89.8%	92.2%
CPAlexNet	**98.9%**	**98.9%**	99.9%	**99.8%**	**99.3%**

Table 8. Comparison of the results with state-of-the-art models for Pneumonia Chest X-ray.

Model	Architectures (summarized)	Accuracy
Chest X-ray dataset [13]		
[49]	LWSNet	97.4%
[50]	Xception	**97.9%**
CPAlexNet (AUC = 99.2%)		92.7%
Chest X-Ray Images for Classification dataset [14]		
[51]	VGG-16	87.5%
[52]	Custom sequential CNN arch	90.2%
[53]	Generated models	83.3%
CPAlexNet (AUC = 99.3%)		**95.6%**
Chest X-Ray Images (Pneumonia) dataset [15]		
[54]	EL approach	93.9%
[3]	Proposed method	**98.8%**
CPAlexNet (AUC = 99.3%)		96.8%

4.2   Discussion

When comparing the different metrics, CPAlexNet presents in almost any case results above the traditional architectures (VGG-16, VGG-19, ResNet-50 and AlexNet) as well as present state-of-the-art results when comparing with the state-of-the-art models. Nevertheless, our model (CPAlexNet) is not the best in all tests presented, but as always an accuracy above 90% except in one situation.

In the case of Test 1, detecting COVID-19 in X-ray, we achieved the best result when the metrics were AUC and F1-score, in accuracy, recall and precision we were the second-best model. In Test 2 X-ray for the detection COVID-19 against state-of-the-art models we did not achieve such good results, being this our poor performance.

In Test 3 detecting COVID in CT scans, we achieved the best results in all metrics except recall, where we were the second-best model. Test 4 detecting COVID in CT scans against state-of-the-art models, again we did not achieve as good results as the present state-of-the-art models, but we achieved results always above 93.9% in the three datasets used. In the case of Test 5, consisting the detecting Pneumonia in X-ray, and comparing it against traditional architectures, again we had always the best results except in the metric recall. The final test, Test 6, detecting Pneumonia in X-ray and comparing it with the state-of-the-art models, once again we did not achieve state-of-the-art results, except when using Chest X-ray images for the dataset [12]. In this case, our model had the best results.

Our model, the same model, can be used in all three situations, X-ray for the detection of Covid and Pneumonia, and detection of Covid in CT scans, as well as present state-of-the-art or near state-of-the-art results in any of the 8 datasets tested [8–15]. In conclusion, we can not say that CPAlexNet is the state-of-the-art model at present, but it is a model that can fit any dataset or disease detection (COVID Pneumonia) or source of data available (X-ray, CT-scan).

5   Conclusions and Future Research

The integration of deep learning models for COVID-19 detection from X-rays and CT scans, alongside pneumonia detection from X-rays, marks a significant advancement in medical diagnostics. This research took into consideration the development of a new model, that can still be improved, to detect COVID-19 from X-rays and CT scans and also Pneumonia from X-rays. XAI was used to facilitate the interpretation of the results.

The use of deep learning algorithms has shown promising results in accurately identifying patterns and anomalies associated with these conditions, aiding in timely and efficient diagnosis.

Universal Access in Human-Machine Cooperation refers in general to the idea that every person should have equal access to technology, such as computers, software, and machines, and should be able to use them to their advantage regardless of their physical capabilities. This covers the ability to use the data, services, and activities that these technologies make available. In the present case, we present the prototype version of a web application - AI Health - to place the detection online of the mentioned diseases and to provide a way to analyse data by physicians anywhere in the world, allowing them to compare the results of different sources and provide a patient clinical record mentioning the possibilities of the existence of COVID-19 or Pneumonia.

AI-generated patient files may raise ethical and legal concerns regarding the responsibility for clinical decisions made based on AI predictions, this includes issues related to liability, accountability, and the ethical implications of AI's role in healthcare decision-making. Addressing these limitations necessitates a multidisciplinary approach involving collaboration between AI researchers, healthcare professionals, ethicists, and policymakers. Further advancements in AI interpretability, model explainability, robustness testing, continuous model updates, and ensuring ethical and legal compliance are imperative to overcome these challenges in integrating AI into healthcare systems responsibly and effectively.

The application of deep learning models in detecting COVID-19 and Pneumonia from medical imaging provides a non-invasive and potentially rapid method for screening and diagnosing these conditions. The ability to distinguish between different lung conditions from imaging data is crucial, especially in the context of COVID-19, where early detection can greatly impact patient outcomes and disease management.

Overall, this comprehensive approach, combining deep learning-based diagnostic models with web applications for image uploading, patient records, and result comparisons, demonstrates a significant stride forward in leveraging technology to enhance medical diagnostics and patient care in the realm of respiratory conditions.

Future work consists of (a) improving the proposed model, i.e., developing CPAlexNet2.0, so it can be the state-of-the-art model in the present; (b) exploring more deepness XAI models, aiming to create a model that can explain the choices in detail to help the physicians to trust the results presented; (c) train the model with all available data to create a universal model, where any image from any source can enter, and the model returns one of three outputs: COVID, Pneumonia, Normal. Last but not least, (d) improve the web application, so it can be even more intuitive and practical for the physicians.

Acknowledgments. This work was supported by the Portuguese Foundation for Science and Technology (FCT) project LA/P/0063/2020, and by NOVA LINCS (UIDB/04516/2020) with the financial support of FCT.IP.

References

1. Echtioui, A., Zouch, W., Ghorbel, M., Mhiri, C., Hamam, H.: Detection methods of Covid-19. SLAS Technol. **25**(6), 566–572 (2020). https://doi.org/10.1177/2472630320962002
2. Stephen, O., Sain, M., Maduh, U.J., Jeong, D.-U.: An efficient deep learning approach to pneumonia classification in healthcare. J. Healthcare Eng. **2019**, 1–7 (2019). https://doi.org/10.1155/2019/4180949
3. Kundu, R., Das, R., Geem, Z.W., Han, G.-T., Sarkar, R.: Pneumonia detection in chest X-ray images using an ensemble of deep learning models. PLOS ONE **16**(9), e0256630 (2021). https://doi.org/10.1371/journal.pone.0256630
4. Moreira, C., Nobre, I.B., Sousa, S.C., Pereira, J.M., Jorge, J.: Improving X-ray diagnostics through eye-tracking and XR. In: 2022 IEEE Conference on Virtual Reality and 3D User Interfaces Abstracts and Workshops (VRW). IEEE, March 2022. https://doi.org/10.1109/vrw55335.2022.00099

5. Antunes, C., Coutinho, C.: Employment of artificial intelligence mechanisms for e-health systems in order to obtain vital signs improving the processes of online consultations and diagnosis. In: 2022 International Symposium on Sensing and Instrumentation in 5G and IoT Era (ISSI). IEEE, 17 November 2022. https://doi.org/10.1109/issi55442.2022.9963223

6. Villalá, G., Rico, S.D., Quiroga, C., Calvo, G.-R.J.L., Guadalquivir, A.: COVID 19. Pathophysiology and prospects for early detection in patients with mild symptoms of the controversial virus in underdeveloped countries: an update on the state (2020, Unpublished). https://doi.org/10.13140/RG.2.2.29110.24647

7. Jamison, D.A. Jr., et al.: A comprehensive SARS-CoV-2 and COVID-19 review, Part 1: intracellular overdrive for SARS-CoV-2 infection. Eur. J. Hum. Genet. **30**(8), 889–898 (2022). https://doi.org/10.1038/s41431-022-01108-8

8. Rahman, T.: Covid-19 radiography database, Kaggle. https://www.kaggle.com/datasets/tawsifurrahman/Covid19-radiography-database. Accessed 24 Nov 2023

9. El-Shafai, W.: Extensive Covid-19 X-ray and CT chest images dataset. Mendeley, 12 June 2020. https://doi.org/10.17632/8H65YWD2JR.3

10. Minaee, S.: Shervinmin/deepcovid, GitHub. https://github.com/shervinmin/DeepCovid. Accessed 2 Dec 2023

11. Aria, M.: Covid-19 lung CT scans. Kaggle. https://www.kaggle.com/datasets/mehradaria/Covid19-lung-ct-scans. Accessed 24 Nov 2023

12. Angelov, P., Soares, E.: Explainable-by-design approach for Covid-19 classification via CT-scan. Cold Spring Harbor Laboratory, 29 April 2020. https://doi.org/10.1101/2020.04.24.20078584

13. Patel, P.: Chest X-ray (Covid-19 & pneumonia). Kaggle. https://www.kaggle.com/datasets/prashant268/chest-xray-Covid19-pneumonia. Accessed 24 Nov 2023

14. Kermany, D.: Labeled optical coherence tomography (OCT) and chest X-Ray images for classification. Mendeley, 6 January 2018. https://doi.org/10.17632/RSCBJBR9SJ.2

15. Mooney, P.: Chest X-ray images (pneumonia). Kaggle. https://www.kaggle.com/datasets/paultimothymooney/chest-xray-pneumonia. Accessed 24 Nov 2023

16. Cohen, J.P.: Covid chest xray dataset. GitHub. https://github.com/ieee8023/covid-chestxray-dataset. Accessed 26 Nov 2023

17. Wang, X., Peng, Y., Lu, L., Lu, Z., Summers, R.M.: TieNet: text-image embedding network for common thorax disease classification and reporting in chest X-rays. arXiv (2018). https://doi.org/10.48550/ARXIV.1801.04334

18. Singh, D., Kumar, V., Vaishali, Kaur, M.: Classification of COVID-19 patients from chest CT images using multi-objective differential evolution–based convolutional neural networks. Eur. J. Clin. Microbiol. Infect. Dis. **39**(7), 1379–1389 (2020). https://doi.org/10.1007/s10096-020-03901-z

19. Angelov: SARS-COV-2 CT-scan dataset, Kaggle. https://www.kaggle.com/datasets/plameneduardo/sarscov2-ctscan-dataset. Accessed 26 Nov 2023

20. Deng, J., Dong, W., Socher, R., Li, L.-J., Li, K., Fei-Fei, L.: ImageNet: a large-scale hierarchical image database. In: 2009 IEEE Conference on Computer Vision and Pattern Recognition. IEEE, June 2009. https://doi.org/10.1109/cvpr.2009.5206848

21. Zein, O., et al.: Transfer learning based model for pneumonia detection in chest X-ray images. Int. J. Intell. Eng. Syst. **14**(5), 56–66 (2021). https://doi.org/10.22266/ijies2021.1031.06

22. Ranjan, A., Kumar, C., Gupta, R.K., Misra, R.: Transfer learning based approach for pneumonia detection using customized VGG16 deep learning model. In: Misra, R., Kesswani, N., Rajarajan, M., Veeravalli, B., Patel, A. (eds.) Internet of Things and Connected Technologies. LNNS, vol. 340, pp. 17–28. Springer, Cham (2022). https://doi.org/10.1007/978-3-030-94507-7_2

23. Hall, L.O., Paul, R., Goldgof, D.B., Goldgof, G.M.: Finding Covid-19 from chest X-rays using deep learning on a small dataset. arXiv (2020). https://doi.org/10.48550/ARXIV.2004.02060

24. Tang, Y.-X., et al.: Automated abnormality classification of chest radiographs using deep convolutional neural networks. npj Digit. Med. **3**(1) (2020). https://doi.org/10.1038/s41746-020-0273-z

25. Ahsan, M.M., Gupta, K.D., Islam, M.M., Sen, S., Rahman, Md.L., Shakhawat Hossain, M.: Covid-19 symptoms detection based on NasNetMobile with explainable AI using various imaging modalities. Mach. Learn. Knowl. Extr. **2**(4), 490–504 (2020). https://doi.org/10.3390/make2040027

26. Karac, A.: Predicting COVID-19 cases on a large chest X-ray dataset using modified pre-trained CNN architectures. Appl. Comput. Syst. **28**(1), 44–57 (2023). https://doi.org/10.2478/acss-2023-0005

27. Sun, L., et al.: Adaptive feature selection guided deep forest for Covid-19 classification with chest CT. IEEE J. Biomed. Health Inf. **24**(10), 2798–2805 (2020). https://doi.org/10.1109/jbhi.2020.3019505

28. Akter, S., Shamrat, F.M.J.M., Chakraborty, S., Karim, A., Azam, S.: Covid-19 detection using deep learning algorithm on chest X-ray images. Biology **10**(11), 1174 (2021). https://doi.org/10.3390/biology10111174

29. Dahmane, O., Khelifi, M., Beladgham, M., Kadri, I.: Pneumonia detection based on transfer learning and a combination of VGG19 and a CNN built from scratch. Indonesian J. Electric. Eng. Comput. Sci. **24**(3), 1469 (2021). https://doi.org/10.11591/ijeecs.v24.i3.pp1469-1480

30. Hasan, N., Bao, Y., Shawon, A., Huang, Y.: DenseNet convolutional neural networks application for predicting Covid-19 using CT image. SN Comput. Sci. **2**(5) (2021). https://doi.org/10.1007/s42979-021-00782-7

31. Pathak, Y., Shukla, P.K., Tiwari, A., Stalin, S., Singh, S., Shukla, P.K.: Deep transfer learning based classification model for Covid-19 disease. IRBM **43**(2), 87–92 (2022). https://doi.org/10.1016/j.irbm.2020.05.003

32. Szepesi, P., Szilágyi, L.: Detection of pneumonia using convolutional neural networks and deep learning. Biocybernetics Biomed. Eng. **42**(3), 1012–1022 (2022). https://doi.org/10.1016/j.bbe.2022.08.001

33. Al-Taani, A.T., Al-Dagamseh, I.T.: Automatic detection of pneumonia using concatenated convolutional neural network (2022). https://doi.org/10.21203/rs.3.rs-2220817/v1

34. Hayat, A., Baglat, P., Mendonça, F., Mostafa, S.S., Morgado-Dias, F.: Novel comparative study for the detection of Covid-19 using CT scan and chest X-ray images. Int. J. Environ. Res. Public Health **20**(2), 1268 (2023). https://doi.org/10.3390/ijerph20021268

35. Ali, W., Qureshi, E., Farooqi, O.A., Khan, R.A.: Pneumonia detection in chest X-ray images: handling class imbalance. arXiv (2023). https://doi.org/10.48550/ARXIV.2301.08479

36. Sitaula, C., Hossain, M.B.: Attention-based VGG-16 model for Covid-19 chest X-ray image classification. Appl. Intell. **51**(5), 2850–2863 (2020). https://doi.org/10.1007/s10489-020-02055-x

37. Krizhevsky, A., Sutskever, I., Hinton, G.E.: ImageNet classification with deep convolutional neural networks. Commun. ACM **60**(6), 84–90 (2017). https://doi.org/10.1145/3065386

38. Pham, T.D.: Classification of Covid-19 chest X-rays with deep learning: new models or fine tuning? Health Inf. Sci. Syst. **9**(1) (2020). https://doi.org/10.1007/s13755-020-00135-3

39. Simonyan, K., Zisserman, A.: Very deep convolutional networks for large-scale image recognition. arXiv (2014). https://doi.org/10.48550/ARXIV.1409.1556

40. Khan, S.H., Sohail, A., Khan, A., Lee, Y.-S.: Covid-19 detection in chest X-ray images using a new channel boosted CNN. Diagnostics **12**(2), 267 (2022). https://doi.org/10.3390/diagnostics12020267

41. Elpeltagy, M., Sallam, H.: Automatic prediction of Covid−19 from chest images using modified ResNet50. Multimedia Tools Appl. **80**(17), 26451–26463 (2021). https://doi.org/10.1007/s11042-021-10783-6

42. Minaee, S., Kafieh, R., Sonka, M., Yazdani, S., Jamalipour Soufi, G.: Deep-Covid: predicting Covid-19 from chest X-ray images using deep transfer learning. Med. Image Anal. **65**, 101794 (2020). https://doi.org/10.1016/j.media.2020.101794

43. Babukarthik, R.G., Adiga, V.A.K., Sambasivam, G., Chandramohan, D., Amudhavel, J.: Prediction of Covid-19 using genetic deep learning convolutional neural network (GDCNN). IEEE Access **8**, 177647–177666 (2020). https://doi.org/10.1109/access.2020.3025164

44. Ghose, P., et al.: Detecting Covid-19 infection status from chest X-ray and CT scan via single transfer learning-driven approach. Front. Genet. **13** (2022). https://doi.org/10.3389/fgene.2022.980338

45. Ghaderzadeh, M., Asadi, F., Jafari, R., Bashash, D., Abolghasemi, H., Aria, M.: Deep convolutional neural network–based computer-aided detection system for Covid-19 using multiple lung scans: design and implementation study. J. Med. Internet Res. **23**(4), e27468 (2021). https://doi.org/10.2196/27468

46. Masud, M., Dahman Alshehri, M., Alroobaea, R., Shorfuzzaman, M.: Leveraging convolutional neural network for Covid-19 disease detection using CT scan images. Intell. Autom. Soft Comput. **29**(1), 1–13 (2021). https://doi.org/10.32604/iasc.2021.016800

47. Canayaz, M., Şehribanoğlu, S., Özdağ, R., Demir, M.: Covid-19 diagnosis on CT images with Bayes optimization-based deep neural networks and machine learning algorithms. Neural Comput. Appl. **34**(7), 5349–5365 (2022). https://doi.org/10.1007/s00521-022-07052-4

48. Alhichri, H.: CNN ensemble approach to detect Covid-19 from computed tomography chest images. Comput. Mater. Continua **67**(3), 3581–3599 (2021). https://doi.org/10.32604/cmc.2021.015399

49. Lasker, A., Ghosh, M., Obaidullah, S.M., Chakraborty, C., Roy, K.: LWSNet - a novel deep-learning architecture to segregate Covid-19 and pneumonia from x-ray imagery. Multimedia Tools Appl. **82**(14), 21801–21823 (2022). https://doi.org/10.1007/s11042-022-14247-3

50. Jain, R., Gupta, M., Taneja, S., Hemanth, D.J.: Deep learning based detection and analysis of Covid-19 on chest X-ray images. Appl. Intell. **51**(3), 1690–1700 (2020). https://doi.org/10.1007/s10489-020-01902-1

51. Saboo, Y.S., Kapse, S., Prasanna, P.: Convolutional neural networks (CNNs) for pneumonia classification on pediatric chest radiographs (2023). https://doi.org/10.7759/cureus.44130

52. Kusk, M.W., Lysdahlgaard, S.: The effect of Gaussian noise on pneumonia detection on chest radiographs, using convolutional neural networks. Radiography **29**(1), 38–43 (2023). https://doi.org/10.1016/j.radi.2022.09.011

53. Ortiz-Toro, C., García-Pedrero, A., Lillo-Saavedra, M., Gonzalo-Martín, C.: Automatic detection of pneumonia in chest X-ray images using textural features. Comput. Biol. Med. **145**, 105466 (2022). https://doi.org/10.1016/j.compbiomed.2022.105466

54. Mabrouk, A., Díaz Redondo, R.P., Dahou, A., Abd Elaziz, M., Kayed, M.: Pneumonia detection on chest X-ray images using ensemble of deep convolutional neural networks. Appl. Sci. **12**(13), 6448 (2022). https://doi.org/10.3390/app12136448

Designing More Accessible Health Services

Pamela Baker and Simeon Keates[✉] [iD]

University of Chichester, Chichester PO19 6PE, West Sussex, UK
{p.baker,s.keates}@chi.ac.uk

Abstract. The University of Chichester opened a new School of Nursing and Allied Health three years ago and is working closely with the Sussex Integrated Care Board (ICB – the local health authority) and designing a new approach to delivering health services across East and West Sussex. The University's engagement in this process is on multiple levels, including:

- creation of a new Community Diagnostics Centre on its Bognor Regis campus;
- further expansion of the Nursing and Allied Health programmes;
- training and retention of members of the workforce, including equality of opportunity;
- development of simulation facilities for improving pedagogical approaches and flexibility of delivery;
- exploration of a new type of social and healthcare worker in a more community-based role; and,
- helping to shape the research and development agenda of the ICB, through co-operative working with the Brighton and Sussex Medical School.

This paper will explore the underlying rationale for these developments, provide further detail on each of these initiatives and the importance of ensuring universal access to the systems and processes that underpin each of these activities. Central to all of the above is the role of information technology, which is pivotal in the design and delivery of new services as well as facilitating seamless transfer of information across the numerous disparate stakeholders, bodies and agencies that are inevitably involved in the effective operation of an integrated care system.

Keywords: Health service · independent living · virtual wards · simulation · VR

1 Introduction

The COVID pandemic presented many health services with a challenge that was unique in modern times. As the immediate threat to health of that disease has receded, legacy issues have arisen in many countries around backlogs of patients with other conditions, such as cardiovascular disease and cancer.

Many of those health services are still periodically affected by local resurgences of new COVID variants or with other viruses that went into temporary abeyance during the

M. Antona and C. Stephanidis (Eds.): HCII 2024, LNCS 14698, pp. 222–233, 2024.
https://doi.org/10.1007/978-3-031-60884-1_15

periods of lockdown and may have spikes in infections that are coincident with those of other such diseases. This appears to be a particular problem in those countries that locked down for longer periods.

In the UK, the Government's response has been to begin reconsidering how the National Health Service (NHS) delivers healthcare to the wider population, including how to lessen pressures on acute settings (e.g., hospitals), especially during infection peaks, while also addressing the backlog of cases from the COVID pandemic years.

Some of these changes are internal structure changes. For example, the past two years have seen the creation of c. 42 Integrated Care Boards (ICBs) covering England and Wales. The focus of these ICBs is to understand better how to create a coherent, connected healthcare service, creating better interfacing with social care provision (e.g., retirement homes, hospices and the like). The ICBs need to not only consider how to make the existing provision and services work together more effectively, but also more fundamental revision to the design and structure of those. One of the principal reasons for the backlog in treatment in the NHS is the severe pressure on acute settings, which is often exacerbated through hospitals becoming the option of last resort for people (service users) in need of medical attention who have not been able to access primary services, such as their local general practitioner (GP). In those circumstances, those service users either put off seeking medical attention, which has the potential to make their condition very much worse and thus require more significant medical intervention at a later point, or they turn up at their local accident and emergency unit (A&E), where they can find themselves waiting many hours to be seen, sometimes in very difficult circumstances if the A&E department is full at that time.

The solution is thus to begin to consider how to make services easier to access and at an earlier stage to avoid service users feeling that their best, or often only, option is a trip to the A&E department. Central to achieving this goal is a shift in perception from the NHS being a national (anti)*sickness* service, focused on the treatment of disease and trauma, to a genuine national *health* service, where the focus is on prevention, swift treatment where necessary and enabling maintenance of quality independent living. It is recognised that the best way to keep demand for social care to a minimum is to facilitate people living in their own accommodation for as long as possible supported, where necessary, by the use of carefully chosen assistive technologies. The technologies that became ubiquitous through the COVID period, such as videoconferencing being available in almost all households, can be repurposed to support innovations such as virtual wards, where patients can be monitored in their own homes remotely, allowing them to return home earlier in their recovery period and freeing up valuable hospital beds to allow new patients to be admitted for medical care and treatment.

Historically, health care in the UK was delivered by the NHS through local health authorities. Their remit was exclusive health/sickness focused. Social care is overseen by county councils rather than the health service, so creating a seamless interface between the two involves navigating two large and often incompatible bureaucratic systems.

The ICBs are newly created powerful entities overseeing all aspects of the health provision across large geographical regions. Their remit includes not only acute settings (hospitals), but co-ordination with primary care practitioners (general practitioners and family doctors) and specialist services as well as supporting research, workforce development and education/training. Their budgets are typically in the £5+ billion (US$6+ billion) range. As such, they are well positioned to deliver on this new model of support and delivery of a truly integrated approach.

1.1 The UK Context

The UK has not been alone in searching for better health and social care solutions with accessibility, availability, cost and quality being the key driving issues. COVID pushed the need for the use of digital platforms to address healthcare issues and they are increasingly being applied in non-COVID related settings.

Globally, the drive is to provide accessible cost-effective healthcare to low and medium resourced geographies. In countries with better resources the challenge is the ever-increasing life expectancy and cost of evermore advanced available treatments driving a demand that UK healthcare, like many other similar countries, is finding difficult to keep pace with.

Thus, in the UK as in many others geographies, digitisation of healthcare systems is being seen as the answer to solve basic assignments and needs through the increased use of digital aids and tools, capitalising on the efficiencies and functionality offered by information and communication technologies, including electronic health records, health analytics and data visualisation; wearables and mobile health; telemedicine and remote care; and through the rise in the application of AI and predictive analytics providing greater efficiency in diagnostics; all of which have the potential to deliver a revolutionary transformation in the health and social care systems. However, the full benefits of that revolution will only be realised if the resultant systems are sufficiently usable and accessible by the widest possible population of users.

The role for higher education is not only to develop the digital future through research and partnership with healthcare innovators and patients, but also to ensure that health and social care students are prepared for the future demands and needs of the patients, both for existing technologies and for those that may not yet exist. There is an equally important need to understand the challenges and issues that are arising and how these may be addressed.

This paper will explore the rationale for the University initiatives set within the context of the NHS drive for digitalisation of health and social care to achieve better solutions for patients (service users) and providers.

1.2 "A Plan for Digital Health and Social Care"

In June 2022, NHS England (the body that oversees all health provision in England) published the policy paper "A plan for digital health and social care" [1] aimed at putting the health and social care system in a position to deliver the 4 goals of reform identified by the Government, i.e., to equip the system to:

- prevent people's health and social care needs from escalating;
- personalise health and social care and reduce health disparities;
- improve the experience and impact of people providing services; and,

- transform performance.

In his forward to the report, Dr Timothy Ferris NHS National Director of Transformation emphasised the role that digital had played and would need to play in the future of the health and social care system:

"If it wasn't the case before, COVID-19 has shown us that having the right digital and data tools at the NHS' disposal can be as important as having the right medicines in our formularies. Whether through underpinning the initial operational planning, clinical research into treatments, and then the rapid, highly targeted NHS COVID vaccine roll-out, data and digital technology has played a central, but largely hidden, role in how the health service has responded to the biggest public health threat in a century.

The same must also now be true of how we tackle the wider challenges of the coming years: recovering our services, reducing health inequalities and building resilience for the future." [1].

As with an any ambitious and transformative plan, many challenges will need to be addressed. The service must be designed to be:

- Easy to use – service providers (clinicians, nurses, etc.) must be able to access the relevant information needed in a timely manner while service users (patients) must understand what is happening and feel reassured and safe throughout the process.
- Secure – the information being used must be reliable and trustworthy to ensure that correct clinical decisions are reached. The data must also be simultaneously portable and secure, which are often conflicting requirements.
- Adaptable – the needs of the patients will change over time and the data records used will need to be able to evolve with those needs. Similarly new treatment options will also become available and existing records need to be checked to see whether any patients might benefit from the new treatments or advice. This checking ought to be proactive (i.e. actively seek out patients who may benefit from the treatment/advice) rather than reactive (i.e. only done when the patient has encountered a problem).
- Usable and accessible – as with all human-computer systems, these are only truly beneficial to users if those systems are both usable (i.e. provide straightforward access to the functionality) and accessible (i.e. able to meet different user functional capabilities).
- Safe – while the new systems will not provide treatments directly, if clinicians act upon incorrect information, they can end up doing significant harm to patients. Traditional databases can be scrutinised and audited, but AI systems are often harder to interrogate directly to ensure the correctness of the data stored and the recommendations made. It is thus essential that standards for verifying and validating the AI systems are established and complied with.

The NHS goals form an ambitious technological plan, but there are always significant challenges rolling out solutions on this scale, especially through the public sector. Additionally, the delivery of health and social care to the wider population cannot rest on technology alone. It requires the workforce to develop skills and capability in and understanding of how to deploy technology and to work through patient access in the digital and physical space. Key areas will be in the use of electronic health records, wearables for both healthcare workers and patients, data analytics and accessibility with patient engagement in directing and managing their own care [2].

If fully embraced, this introduction of new technology will lead to new ways of working both for health and social care staff and for patients in interacting with the services they use.

Thus, with the regional NHS team (Sussex Health & Care ICB) the University is participating in the design of a new approach to delivering health and social care services through developing our educational and place- based delivery.

The University's engagement in this process is on multiple levels, including:

- creation of a new Community Diagnostics Centre on its Bognor Regis campus;
- further expansion of the Nursing and Allied Health programmes;
- training and retention of members of the workforce, including equality of opportunity;
- development of simulation facilities for improving pedagogical approaches and flexibility of delivery;
- exploration of a new type of social and healthcare worker in a more community-based role; and,
- helping to shape the research and development agenda of the ICB, through co-operative working with the Brighton and Sussex Medical School.

2 The Workforce and the Digital Future

In the UK, nearly every health and social care organisation holds its own records, sometimes digitally but some still on paper. In trying to provide a service to patients, health and social care staff often work on fragmented and incomplete information. It is a common frustration for patients – "*you give the same information over and over*" being a common complaint – and opens the potential of sub optimal diagnosis. Frequent questions occur when there is a need to rely on the service user for inflation about their case, such as:

- Did the patient reveal all the relevant information?
- Do they know what is relevant?
- Did the staff member have the time to even ask?

To avoid these challenges, the aspiration in the UK for shared health and social care patient records opens the opportunity to integrate information about patients across the system that will not only allow personalised and connected care, but will open up a new realm of possibilities on offering predictive care and, in the short term, deliver a significantly more efficient and effective service.

Thus, starting from the basic premise of the need to develop joined up records, the challenge for the University is to establish the relevance of this development for its research and teaching activities, and also how to ensure that activities at the University support and align with the ICB/NHS requirements. This is an interesting question, especially as those requirements are continually emerging and evolving.

Regardless of their job level, health and social care staff will need to be capable, comfortable and confident to work digitally for this transformation to be a success. When the current general environment is so digitally enabled – Facebook, Instagram,

TikTok, numerous apps, etc. – it is tempting to imagine that there is little need for any training and yet 18–21 year-old undergraduates, and mature students, often display a surprising lack of capability to handle the digital world outside of social media usage. Thus, building digital skills into the curriculum to provide basic IT literacy and also show how digital implementation makes work more manageable and efficient and can improve the patient experience and patient outcomes is key.

Beyond being able to access and input to shared patients records they will also need to develop an enquiring mind set that understands what the record says about the patient, their story and their health and social care journey. The technology enables compassionate and informed healthcare and, if the workforce is guided and trained in how to approach and use the patient record, can be utilised in a way that is more than a set of facts and medications for staff engaged in face-to-face contact.

The increased digitization and development in the eHealth area enables new ways of creating knowledge and conducting care, but information about people's health is very sensitive, and incorrect handling of data can lead to serious consequences for the individual person and also for the organisation that fails to protect any personal data properly. In the UK, data protection is overseen by the Information Commissioner's Office, which has the power to levy very substantial fines of up to 10% of an organisation's turnover if it is found to be in breach of its duty to protect sensitive personal data. Thus, ensuring all such data is adequately protected and respected at all stages of its handling is important for all parties.

The available digital information about patients can be aggregated and processed to support better understanding of identification of diseases and, subsequently, their pathological development and progression. This is not a quick process and takes both time and resource. However, as a consequence of this better understanding and knowledge, diseases will become more preventable; medical quality and patient safety can be raised; and healthcare can be more efficient, effective, coordinated, accessible, and transparent. To meet future demands, nursing, medical and allied health professional students need to have knowledge about new technologies and eHealth [3].

However, the volume of data that will be increasingly available to practitioners will mean that the use of dashboard systems will be needed to access data quickly. The skills required will go beyond the ability to operate IT systems and tools as passive recipients, and they should be involved in the process of participatory design as an advocate for user needs.

This involvement will become even more pertinent as the system begins to explore a new type of social and healthcare worker that is place-based, i.e. out in the community, and visits the care facility where the patient is or the patient's home if still living independently, thus shifting the emphasis to preventative and/or early intervention and diagnosis rather than waiting until an emergency response is required, often necessitating an acute hospital stay and the subsequent challenges of discharge. The need for "digital" competency across a range of situations and technology becomes even more vital in supporting the short-term aspirations of the NHS for home-based patients. Targets for the NHS to support this agenda include:

- increase the availability of digital monitoring of vital signs for people in care homes and at home, with the aim of a further 500,000 people being supported by this technology;
- scale hospital at home and tech-enabled virtual ward services – these will be used as step-down pathways for frailty and respiratory care to reduce length of stay and the ambition is to have 40 to 50 virtual ward 'beds' per 100,000 of the population;
- develop a tech-enabled annual physical check for people with severe mental illness, with roll-out taking place in a selection of ICBs; and,
- define clinical pathways where people are supported to self-monitor and self-manage.

Effectively, the NHS is looking for a more extensive deployment of what is often defined as telemedicine, i.e. the use home care technology to monitor patients remotely using various Internet of Things-based medical devices, using approaches such as monitoring vital signs and blood pressure through the use of wearable technology to improve the management of chronic diseases such as heart, diabetes and respiratory disease.

Supporting deployment and use of devices to enable patients to become and remain comfortable with the use of technology and for the health and social care worker to understand what, when and how the digitally enabled solution should be used will need to be a new part of the curriculum and skill set as will development of interpretive skills. Typical questions will include:

- What is the data saying to me?
- What actions need to be taken?
- Do I need to refer this patient?
- Can I advise?
- What are the applicable boundaries and protocols?
- What are the decision support tools embedded within the records advising?

These are difficult enough questions to answer when the healthcare professional and the patient are in the same room and the healthcare worker has the full range of sensory perception available to help guide the judgement. Telemedicine necessarily reduces the number of information channels available to the healthcare worker, so it is important that the availability of the most pertinent information is prioritised at all times. The challenge, as with all human-computer interface design, is knowing what the most relevant and pertinent information actually is. Given the sheer variety of possible medical situations that the technology may need to be used to support, the task of identifying the most relevant information requires significant data processing and intelligence.

The new nursing and allied health graduate will need to understand the future environment of a range of support tools and understand their deployment, both within and outside the acute hospital setting; but the question is then how do educators prepare their students to become effective in the digital future. Furthermore, the existing workforce will also need continuing professional development (i.e. training) to also gain this knowledge.

A report by the World Health Organisation [4] about eHealth and how it can be beneficial for supporting universal health coverage (UHC) emphasised the different areas in eHealth that were rapidly expanding not only in high income countries. 80% of low-income countries had at least one mobile health (mHealth) programme in their country and for high-income countries, the percentage was 91%. Thus, "training of students as professionals in eHealth and electronic learning" is much needed to support the goal of UHC. A way to progress this is via the adoption of a framework that can be integrated to the curriculum and used as a basis for CPD for existing staff.

The 2018 study *"Technology Informatics Guiding Education Reform – TIGER An International Recommendation Framework of Core Competencies in Health Informatics for Nurses"* [5] developed a recommendation framework of 24 core competency areas in health informatics defined for five major nursing roles. These areas were clustered in the following domains:

- data, information, knowledge;
- information exchange and information sharing;
- ethical and legal issues;
- systems life cycle management;
- management; and,
- biostatistics and medical technology.

The Canadian Entry to Practice Competencies similarly delineates the list of nursing informatics competencies that all registered nurses should possess upon graduating from an undergraduate nursing program in Canada [6]. Ensuring these are imbedded in the curriculum in a way that is received as pedagogically relevant will be important to how these competencies are understood and accepted by learners.

An approach that the University of Chichester will be developing is through simulation, which will allow students to interact in a more realistic way with technology. This is an already well-developed area for clinical training, but putting these core competencies and technologies into an interactive situation is a comparatively new feature in the direction of much of simulation training and a shift from much of the classroom-based lectures that are often utilised now. Traditional lectures will most likely continue to cover the fundamental principles of areas such as ethical and legal issues around personal data, but the immersive simulation suites that are becoming increasingly commonplace will allow a more complete range of pedagogical experience. Through careful use of the principles of scaffolded learning (i.e. carefully building layers of knowledge on existing layers to create a more solid structured knowledge base), it is anticipated that the learner will retain more knowledge about how to use the technology and data correctly than through more traditional educational approaches.

To build these scenarios effectively will require those with the requisite knowledge, which as technology moves quickly will require a wider range of technical competencies tin addition to clinical expertise. Where and how universities access and "train the trainer" may be the pre-requisite to successfully undertaking simulation with these learning outcomes in mind alongside access to necessary equipment and data sets.

3 Place Based and the Digital Future

The digital future envisaged by the NHS is built around a further realisation of a placed based approach of locating healthcare service in patients' homes and to locate planned services closer to "visited" places – shopping centres or accessible areas – easy parking and public transport. The Community Diagnostic Centres (CDC) funded in a new initiative by Government were to be set up be 'one-stop shops for checks, scans and tests', designed to achieve early diagnoses for patients and timely treatment and intervention, and as a way of tackling health inequalities by moving the available of diagnostics closer to patients' homes.

The Bognor Regis campus of the University of Chichester is in an area of the southern coastal strip of the UK that is characterised by localised significant levels of deprivation and health inequalities in areas in contrast with the population that is encountered 10 miles further inland. In the Bognor region of the coastal strip life expectancy is c. 14 years lower than in nearby Chichester (7 miles inland), rates of cancer, respiratory, heart disease and diabetes are significantly higher, and the levels of patients presenting themselves for routine screening are commensurately lower. Taken together these contributory factors result in inequality throughout the care pathway from early identification of symptoms to diagnosis and effective treatment.

There was thus an opportunity to work with the ICB to locate a CDC in an area that needed such a facility and to support the current and future diagnostics workforce. The co-location of an academic facility for both training and research would enable the furtherance of the NHS drive for digitally-enabled diagnostic methods and processes delivered through new diagnostics capacity being developed to enable image-sharing and clinical decision support based on artificial intelligence (AI).

At the most basic level, sharing diagnostic images and pathology records will support streamlining of pathways, triaging of waiting lists, faster diagnoses and levelling up under-served areas and risk-based screening. The University will support this by undertaking work on improving the efficiency of diagnostic pathways and understanding how best to enable patients to use the services.

However, a developing interest for the University and the NHS is the potential to develop and deploy AI technology. The NHS AI Lab imaging team is "*working to develop and support the systems that will enable AI to achieve its potential by creating a user-friendly route to getting the best AI into use in the NHS*" [7]. Their goal is to improve the access to high-quality imaging data for developers to ensure the most beneficial solutions for patients, "*creating an environment where the most successful AI technologies can be easily procured and used by hospitals and increase the development and deployment of AI innovations*" [7].

The algorithms already developed can analyse images with greater speed and accuracy than human radiologists and work through and learn from large data sets. However, there will be a continuing need for work to be done on validating AI systems and fine-tuning them for continually improving results. For example, MRI scanners have difficulty analsying the liver because the natural concentration of iron in that organ leads to distortion of the image. To compensate for that, the MRI scanners need to be recalibrated to compensate for this distortion, which requires careful data collection and analysis.

The algorithms learn from historic data and when discussing health inequalities in terms of patient access it is possible that the objectivity of the data sets could be compromised by the comparative omission of under-represented groups leading to potential errors that could lead to patient harm, bias risk and further exacerbating the health inequalities that may already exist for those communities.

From the patient perspective, obtaining broad patient engagement, ensuring data is obtained for under-represented groups and establishing how this can be achieved will be important for long term success and confidence by clinicians and patient alike. As with many new adoptions of technology, early promise and significant benefit can be comprised by a "bad" incident or a failure to consider all service user needs.

4 The Patient and the Digital Future

While the digital future holds out much promise for healthcare systems and patients, it is not only health and social care staff and technology innovators who need to be engaged throughout the design, delivery and education process; there is a danger that too many of the patient population are left behind and health inequalities that are currently manifest in the system are exacerbated. Across the range of digitalisation what becomes evident from the research is the need for development of a strong evidential base of benefit across all parties and aspects.

For instance, electronic patient records belong to patients, should be available to them and should be portable (with the patients' consent) between care providers. Those records can improve patient engagement, care quality, and, consequently, health outcomes. Even given in a structured electronic form, medical records still have a complex narrative that lower literate and ethnically diverse population may find especially difficult to navigate. Service providers need to decide how to support the ability to physically access these records electronically, for example whether portal needs to be made available for accessing and viewing such records in healthcare settings at the point of user. Similarly, those service providers will need to ask what "training" populations of service users will need for them to fully realise the benefits of these electronic data records. An evaluation of 20 years of published evidence of the impact of shared patient records delivered inconsistent results for patient-centredness outcomes (including satisfaction, activation, self-efficacy, empowerment, and health literacy [8]), but beneficial effects were observed in various outcomes, regarding general adherence and medication safety. However, the review found no studies focussed specifically on the impact of these records on timeliness or equity [8].

While the electronic patient record offers significant improvements in how patients are diagnosed and treated and given that they are utilised anonymously in medical research, concerns remain around data leaks and malicious access that can impact patient response and trust adversely. Service provider staff also express concerns of who has data access. This concern extends further than the data record itself and into areas such as wearable technologies. Often these devices are provided by private companies with their own networks and systems that then need to interface with the health service systems, introducing new layers of data vulnerabilities as new electronic systems are introduced into the wider health data ecosystem.

Ways to explore enhancing privacy and simultaneously provide patient and doctor reassurance will be a fruitful area of research for higher education and innovators across a variety of disciplines ranging through public and private key encryption, role-based authentication and blockchain technology alongside the highly complex area issue of ownership, which has significant implications for privacy and ethics.

These areas are of fundamental interest to all parties and policy makers and are ethically and multi-layered in their complexity; the trade-off is the substantive area of benefit against the damaging and ethical consequences of leaks and misuse.

Wearables can provide the capability for patients to monitor their health status in real-time, potentially avoiding in-person visits to clinicians and providing evidence of when intervention is required. However, a review of randomised and observational studies published between January 1, 2016, and July 1, 2021 [9] noted that their influence on healthcare outcomes is not yet fully understood with a key finding being the lack of a *"clear association between the use of a particular wearable and its acceptability within a chronic disease population"* [9]. Although wearables may provide clinically useful information, it was not clear that patients used such information to self-manage their condition or found it useful.

While evidence shows that wearables can reduce the cost of care, the review concluded that *"Supporting mobile apps should be designed using a patient-centred approach, incorporating personalized advice and recommendations from the health data provided by the accompanying wearable. This may unlock the potential of wearables in chronic diseases"* [10].

AI offers significant potential to be of benefit here, but is not without its associated challenges. AI can be viewed as an entirely objective technology, but one that still needs the developers to assess the potential impacts of their system through its lifecycle to mitigate against possible risks and legal liabilities while also establishing how it can actually be best deployed by clinicians. This is beginning to be addressed through interest by Governments in "Algorithmic Impact Assessments" [11] and future deployment in healthcare to also ensure that the left behind do not become left out.

5   Conclusion

While the digital future holds exceptional promise, involving the patient in design of any service is critical to early adoption and effective use.

The examples provided in this paper highlight the need to work with higher end clinical research institutions to address patient-centred design across a wide range of settings from shared patient records to wearables and telemedicine to deployment of AI technology.

The University's co-operative working with the local ICB research agenda and the Brighton and Sussex Medical School will further this agenda. For example, while high end research is being undertaken on medical imaging, research to understand and reduce patient "did not attends" (DNAs), which average 7% of all appointments nationally, will be not only key to running a cost-effective and efficient service, but will also ensure that health inequalities and accessibility of services are addressed while providing expedited patient diagnosis and improved outcomes. To achieve this goal fully will require the engagement of interdisciplinary teams, including clinicians, nursing and allied health staff, data scientists, experts in artificial intelligence and patient advocates; all will need to play a part in creating the new digital future.

Acknowledgments. This work is conducted with the support and co-operation of University Hospitals Sussex Foundation Trust, the Sussex Integrated Care Board (Sussex Health and Care) and the Brighton and Sussex Medical School Health Research Partnership.

Disclosure of Interests. The authors have no competing interests to declare that are relevant to the content of this article.

References

1. Department for Health and Social Care/NHS England. A plan for digital health and social care. https://www.gov.uk/government/publications/a-plan-for-digital-health-and-social-care. Accessed 23 Jan 2024
2. Risling, T.: Educating the nurses of 2025: technology trends of the next decade. Nurse Educ. Pract. **22**, 89–92 (2017)
3. Anderberg, P., Björling, G., Stjernberg, L., Bohman, D.: Analysing nursing students' relation to electronic health and technology as individuals and students and in their future career (the eNursEd Study): protocol for a longitudinal study. JMIR Res. Protoc. **8**(10), e14643 (2019). https://doi.org/10.2196/14643
4. World Health Organization: Global Diffusion of eHealth - Making Universal Health Coverage Achievable: Report of the Third Global Survey on eHealth. Geneva, Switzerland: World Health Organization (2017)
5. Hübner, U., et al.: Technology informatics guiding education reform - TIGER. Methods Inf. Med. **57**(S1), e30–e42 (2018). https://doi.org/10.3414/ME17-01-0155
6. Canada Health Infoway: Nursing Informatics Entry to Practice Competencies for Registered Nurses. https://www.casn.ca/wp-content/uploads/2014/12/Nursing-Informatics-Entry-to-Practice-Competencies-for-RNs_updated-June-4-2015.pdf. Accessed 24 Jan 2024
7. NHS England: AI Imaging. What we do. https://transform.england.nhs.uk/ai-lab/ai-lab-programmes/ai-in-imaging/ai-imaging-what-we-do/. Accessed 24 Jan 2024
8. Neves, A.L., Freise, L., Laranjo, L., et al.: Impact of providing patients access to electronic health records on quality and safety of health: a systematic review and meta-analysis. BMJ Qual. Saf. **29**(12), 1019–1032 (2020)
9. Mattison, G., et al.: The influence of wearables on health care outcomes in chronic disease: systematic review. J. Med. Internet Res. **24**(7), e36690 (2022). https://doi.org/10.2196/36690
10. Steel, N., Hardcastle, A.C., Bachmann, M.O., et al.: Economic inequalities in burden of illness, diagnosis and treatment of five long term conditions in England: panel study. BMJ Open **4**, e005530 (2014). https://doi.org/10.1136/bmjopen-2014-00553
11. Ada Lovelace Institute: Algorithmic impact assessment: a case study in healthcare. February 2022. https://www.adalovelaceinstitute.org/project/algorithmic-impact-assessment-healthcare/. Accessed 24 Jan 2024

Empowering Mobility: Brain-Computer Interface for Enhancing Wheelchair Control for Individuals with Physical Disabilities

Shiva Ghasemi[1]([✉]) [ID], Denis Gračanin[1] [ID], and Mohammad Azab[2] [ID]

[1] Virginia Tech, Blacksburg, VA 24060, USA
{shivagh,gracanin}@vt.edu
[2] Virginia Military Institute, Lexington, VA 24459, USA
azabmm@vmi.edu

Abstract. The integration of brain-computer interfaces (BCIs) into the realm of smart wheelchair (SW) technology signifies a notable leap forward in enhancing the mobility and autonomy of individuals with physical disabilities. BCIs are a technology that enables direct communication between the brain and external devices. While BCIs systems offer remarkable opportunities for enhancing human-computer interaction and providing mobility solutions for individuals with disabilities, they also raise significant concerns regarding security, safety, and privacy that have not been thoroughly addressed by researchers on a large scale. Our research aims to enhance wheelchair control for individuals with physical disabilities by leveraging electroencephalography (EEG) signals for BCIs. We introduce a non-invasive BCI system that utilizes a neuro-signal acquisition headset to capture EEG signals. These signals are obtained from specific brain activities that individuals have been trained to produce, allowing for precise control of the wheelchair. EEG-based BCIs are instrumental in capturing the brain's electrical activity and translating these signals into actionable commands. The primary objective of our study is to demonstrate the system's capability to interpret EEG signals and decode specific thought patterns or mental commands issued by the user. By doing so, it aims to convert these into accurate control commands for the wheelchair. This process includes the recognition of navigational intentions, such as moving forward, backward, or executing turns, specifically tailored for wheelchair operation. Through this innovative approach, we aim to create a seamless interface between the user's cognitive intentions and the wheelchair's movements, enhancing autonomy and mobility for individuals with physical disabilities.

Keywords: Accessibility · BCI · EEG · Smart wheelchair

1 Introduction

According to the Americans with Disabilities Act (ADA) [32], a physical impairment encompasses any physiological disorder or condition, disfigurement, or

M. Antona and C. Stephanidis (Eds.): HCII 2024, LNCS 14698, pp. 234–245, 2024.
https://doi.org/10.1007/978-3-031-60884-1_16

anatomical loss impacting one or more of the body's systems. This includes, but is not limited to, systems such as neurological, musculoskeletal, respiratory, reproductive, cardiovascular, or endocrine systems. World Health Organization (WHO) states, approximately 15% of the global populace experiences some form of disability [17,33]. Individuals with physical impairments may experience congenital disabilities or acquire such impairments later in life due to various etiologies, including accidents, diseases, the aging process, or military service. These impairments, manifesting in forms such as limb loss, paralysis, or reduced mobility, can profoundly impact one's capacity to execute activities of daily living (ADLs) and instrumental activities of daily living (IADLs) - both of which are pivotal for autonomous living. Extensive research, such as the studies by McGrath et al. [18] and Lee et al. [15], have delved into the impact of physical impairment on ADLs and IADLs. These studies highlight the complex interplay between these functional domains and their consequential effects on an individual's overall functionality and well-being.

Aging often brings about various physical impairments. Common age-related impairments include reduced mobility, muscle weakness, joint pain, and bone fragility. Additionally, a decrease in spatial cognitive abilities has been associated with advancing age [13]. There exists a link between physical and cognitive impairments. Studies have demonstrated that greater physical activity is associated with lower incidence of cognitive impairment in later life. For instance, research has indicated that individuals with physical disabilities, such as stroke survivors, may experience cognitive deficits, including memory impairment and executive dysfunction [15]. In addition to mobility constraints, cognitive aging impacts the ability of older adults to find their way, affecting both their sense of direction and navigation skills [21].

The integration of EEG-based BCIs technology into the control of mobile robots, has led to a multidisciplinary approach which encompasses several fields, including neuroscience, computing, signal processing, and pattern recognition. EEG signals are created by the activity of neurons in the brain [24]. The pattern of the EEG signals, correspond to the thoughts, emotions and behavior of an individual [14,24]. This technique is used to gauge variations in voltage attributable to the ionic current conduction within the neural networks of the cerebral cortex [20]. Human brain can produced five major brain waves classified by frequency as illustrated in Sect. 2, Fig. 1.

The remainder of the paper is organized as follows: Sect. 2 discusses related works and summarizes relevant research in EEG technology and signal pattern recognition. The needs for universal accessibility, ethical considerations for physical impairment individuals are described in Sect. 3. Our design approach for physical impairments is introduced in Sect. 4 and Sect. 5 concludes the paper.

2   Related Works

Recent studies have been undertaken by researchers in the realm of BCIs, focusing especially on its usage in controlling wheelchairs [1,2,12,20,28]. These studies have demonstrated the feasibility and potential of using EEG- based BCIs to control wheelchairs, offering new possibilities for individuals with limited mobility.

2.1 Wheelchair-BCI Control Systems

Research in BCIs has opened up new possibilities for creating interactive systems that can translate human brainwaves into control signals for computer application devices [16]. This study [20] introduced a groundbreaking approach to mobility for individuals with disabilities by developing a mind-controlled wheelchair. By harnessing the power of an EEG headset coupled with an Arduino microcontroller, the system captures brain and eye signals. These signals are then translated into precise movement commands that the Arduino microcontroller executes, propelling the wheelchair. Another study involved a double-blind randomized controlled trial where subjects use an EMOTIV Insight EEG headset to control a cursor on a computer screen. The results indicate that allowing users to select their mental commands and training strategies enhances their control accuracy [30]. In [7] EEG used to record brain activity, focusing on its application in motor imagery - the mental simulation of movement. Nisar et al. reported that their system, which captures EEG signals using a 14-sensor headset and then transmits them to a robot through a computer interface, could control the robot's movements in real-time with a sensitivity and specificity exceeding 90% [24].

2.2 EEG Signal Recognition

Human brain can produce five major brain waves, classified by their frequency ranges, known as Brain Rhythms. These major waves range from low frequency (0.5 Hz) to high frequency (100 Hz). These are known as delta (0–4 Hz), theta (4–8 Hz), alpha (8–13 Hz), beta (13–30 Hz), and gamma (30–100 Hz) waves [10]. Alpha waves are indicative of a relaxed, idle state of the brain. Beta waves are observed when the brain is actively engaged in cognitive tasks such as thinking or problem-solving. Theta waves are associated with stress, emotional tension, disappointment, deep meditation, or unconscious states. Gamma waves are linked to consciousness and higher mental activity. Lastly, Mu waves are typically observed in response to spontaneous motor activities [34]. These various brain wave patterns have significant implications in the development of brain-computer interfaces, particularly in applications such as controlling wheelchairs, where different states or intentions like moving forward, turning, or stopping are crucial.

The EEG may show unusual electrical discharge when some abnormality occurs in the brain. The measurement of placing the electrodes in the brain area, namely, frontal pole (Fp), frontal (F), parietal (P), temporal (T), and occipital (O), provides meaningful communication. Even numbers and odd numbers as subscript have been decided to differentiate the brain's hemisphere. The position of Fp2, F4, F8, C4, T4, T6, P4, and O2 electrodes indicates right hemisphere and Fp1, F3, F7, C3, T3, T5, P3, and O1 electrodes indicates left hemisphere, respectively. The position of FZ, CZ, and PZ electrodes indicates the midline in frontal, central, and parietal regions [23].

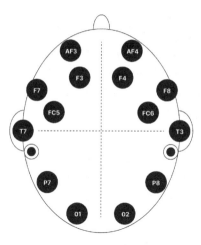

Fig. 1. EEG electrodes placement on head [10].

2.3 Machine Learning Algorithms

Advanced algorithms in signal processing and pattern recognition are used to interpret these brain signals accurately. Machine learning algorithms, including supervised learning techniques such as Support Vector Machines (SVMs), neural networks, and deep learning models [6], are increasingly pivotal in the analysis of brain signals. In supervised learning, algorithms are trained on labeled datasets to perform tasks like classifying mental states or detecting abnormalities in brain signals. SVMs excel in classification tasks [9], effectively differentiating between various mental states or identifying abnormal brain patterns, particularly in EEG signal analysis. Neural networks, mimicking the human brain's structure, adapt flexibly for both classification and regression tasks in brain signal interpretation, such as predicting neurological disorder progression from brain imaging. Deep learning models, especially Convolutional Neural Networks (CNNs), are adept at processing grid-like data, like MRI or fMRI scans, to recognize patterns indicative of brain conditions. Recurrent Neural Networks (RNNs) and Long Short-Term Memory (LSTM) networks are suitable for sequential data, like time-series EEG or MEG signals, capturing the temporal dynamics of brain activity. Additionally, autoencoders in unsupervised learning paradigms facilitate dimensionality reduction, crucial for visualizing high-dimensional brain data. These algorithms' capability to process large datasets and discern intricate patterns significantly enhances our understanding of neural processes and augments the diagnosis and treatment of neurological disorders. Limited studies have explored the combination of EEG-BCI data with the RF algorithm [2]. In study [2] the experimental findings demonstrated that the RF algorithm surpassed other methods, achieving a high accuracy rate of 85.39% in a 6-class classification scenario due to relatively fast training time, a small number of user-defined parameters and superior performance compared to the other five widely used classification algorithms.

Another research [3] focused on enhancing smart wheelchair control through EEG and machine learning. It proposed an attention meditation cost-benefit analysis (AMCBA) model, aiming to improve performance and decision-making in BCI systems [3].

3 Discussion

Mobility constraints significantly impede the autonomy and overall well-being of individuals with physical disabilities. The capacity for autonomous mobility is imperative for one's self-esteem and constitutes a pivotal component in the paradigm of aging in place [29]. Wheelchairs emerge as indispensable aids for mobility [26]. However, manual wheelchair users still face challenges like limited mobility due to difficulty navigating uneven terrain, leading to restricted access to essential places and reliance on caregivers, which increases social isolation. These issues, combined with physical demands and environmental barriers, underscore the need for improved infrastructure and supportive systems for better quality of life. This limitation has given rise to the innovation of smart wheelchairs, equipped with robotics and human-computer interaction (HCI) capabilities, offering enhanced navigation for those with physical impairments [29].

Our system is meticulously designed to pioneer an innovative paradigm in wheelchair mobility within the realm of digital twin environments, affording users the unprecedented ability to exert control through cognitive processes. We conducted a thorough evaluation of the system's precision and responsiveness, employing EEG-based control mechanisms juxtaposed against conventional wheelchair navigation methods. This comparison not only accentuates the system's enhancements in fostering user autonomy but also delineates its potential constraints.

Table 1. Comparison of EEG-Based control and conventional wheelchair navigation.

Aspect	EEG-Based Control	Conventional Navigation
Precision	High precision in capturing brain signals	Limited by manual control
Responsiveness	Immediate response to user intent	Delayed mechanical response
User Autonomy	Enhanced by intuitive control	Restricted to physical ability
Constraints	Requires calibration and learning curve	Limited by physical constraints

In our exploration, we confront and dissect technical hurdles, including signal interference, and the pivotal role of machine learning algorithms in deciphering neural signals. The incorporation of user feedback stands as a cornerstone of our research, offering invaluable insights into the system's practicality and ergonomic considerations, thereby paving the way for design optimizations. Moreover, we engage in a critical discourse on ethical implications, with a special focus on privacy and data security concerns, underscoring the imperative to protect sensitive user information. This ethical scrutiny extends to ensuring the responsible deployment and usage of this technology. Looking ahead, we outline prospective research avenues aimed at refining the system's accuracy, enhancing its user interface, and ensuring its adaptability to accommodate a broad spectrum of disabilities. We also ponder the broader societal ramifications of our work, advocating for the democratization of access to this cutting-edge technology. Our discourse culminates in a contemplation of the transformative potential of such innovations, highlighting the necessity to bridge the gap between technological advancement and its equitable distribution among diverse user demographics, thereby magnifying its beneficial impact on society (Table 1).

3.1   Ethical Considerations

The advancement of assistive technology brings with it a range of challenges and ethical dilemmas that must be carefully navigated. A key ethical issue is finding the right balance between fostering independence and creating dependency in users of technology-assisted mobility devices. The transition towards inclusive security should be comprehended as part of the wider evolution of security and privacy technology that is accessible to all [11].

To effectively address the safety, privacy, and integrity concerns associated with BCIs in wheelchair technology, a comprehensive strategy is essential. The risk of malicious interference with BCIs signals is significant, posing a threat to user safety. It is crucial to ensure that BCIs not only accurately interpret user intentions but also reliably respond in complex environments. The open transmission and processing of brain signals introduce vulnerabilities to unauthorized access and manipulation. Safeguarding the integrity and confidentiality of these signals is critical to prevent harm. This is particularly vital as inaccuracies or misinterpretations in signal processing could lead to dangerous situations, compromising the wheelchair's role as a safe mobility tool.

Moreover, the deeply personal nature of brain signals raises significant privacy issues. It is imperative to protect these data from unauthorized access and ensure their use is strictly confined to intended mobility functions. Addressing these multifaceted challenges demands robust encryption, strict safety protocols, and comprehensive privacy policies. A collaborative approach involving researchers, technologists, and regulatory bodies is needed to develop standards and guidelines for the safe and ethical application of BCIs in wheelchair technology.

3.2   Universal Accessibility

Universal accessibility for individuals with physical impairments is a critical aspect of societal inclusion and well-being. The concept of universal design, which aims to create environments and products that are accessible to all individuals, including those with disabilities, has gained significant attention in research and policy [8]. This approach emphasizes the importance of integrating older and disabled individuals into mainstream society, highlighting the need for inclusive design strategies [5] as well as human-centered design approach [22]. Furthermore, the significance of universal design in addressing the needs of individuals with physical impairments is underscored by the increasing recognition of the impacts of mobility impairments on transportation systems and the importance of designing inclusive transport networks [27]. The need for standardized and readily accessible datasets to facilitate the management and comparison of global studies is emphasized in the context of metadata and taxonomic identification, reflecting the broader importance of standardized approaches in promoting universal accessibility [31].

Given the importance of universal accessibility, it is notable to consider that people with physical impairments may also experience other conditions concurrently, such as visual, auditory, and cognitive impairments. Recognizing and considering this intersectionality of disabilities is crucial for developers and researchers to offer the required assistance to individuals facing such conditions is essential. It enables them to adopt a more inclusive and comprehensive approach in their work, thereby ensuring that the solutions and technologies they develop cater effectively to a broader spectrum of needs and challenges faced by individuals with disabilities. In this context, the importance of developers' roles in advancing universal accessibility has gained increased prominence.

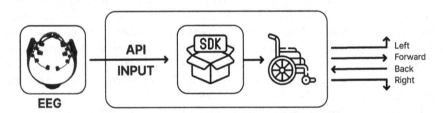

Fig. 2. A pipeline of the proposed design system.

4   Design

We have developed a design system that illustrates the feasibility of controlling wheelchair navigation via neural input, specifically harnessing the user's brain activity. Our approach facilitates a direct communication pathway between the brain and the wheelchair, bypassing the need for physical movement, which can be a significant advancement for those with severe mobility challenges. In addition, our research incorporates a digital twin approach using the Unity Engine to simulate a 3D wheelchair. This simulation can execute commands in real-time, such as moving forward or backward, directed by cognitive actions like "Push" and "Pull" that are identified from the user's brain activity.

This methodology is systematically delineated in Fig. 2, which provides a visual representation of the entire pipeline. The process is executed through the following sequential stages:

1. The initial stage involves capturing brain activity through an EEG headset, specifically the Emotiv EPOC+. This device is equipped with 14 electrodes that are strategically placed on the user's scalp. These electrodes detect electrical signals generated by brain activity, which are crucial for interpreting the user's intent regarding wheelchair navigation.
2. Once the EEG signals are acquired, they are processed using EmotivPro and EmotivPro Analyzer, cloud-based platforms designed for analyzing brainwaves. This step is vital for filtering out noise and extracting meaningful data from the raw EEG signals. The platforms provide tools for visualizing and understanding the brain's activity patterns, which are instrumental in developing algorithms for interpreting navigational commands.
3. The processed signals are then manipulated using the Cortex software development (SDK) provided by Emotiv. This SDK is a cornerstone for integrating mental commands into the system. It allows developers to access both raw and processed EEG data, facilitating the translation of brain activity into specific commands for wheelchair navigation. The SDK's ability to handle real-time data processing is key to creating responsive applications that adapt to the user's mental commands instantly.
4. The final step involves the Emotiv Unity Plugin, which is used to control a three-dimensional simulation of a wheelchair within the Unity environment. This plugin acts as a bridge between the EEG data processing software and the Unity engine, enabling the real-time control of virtual objects—or, by extension, a physical wheelchair—through brain activity.

4.1 Pilot Study and Training Session

Within the Emotive BCI visualizer, a 3D cube animation appears on the control panel. Initially, training with neutral session which ensures readiness for

Table 2. Mental commands in a training session.

Command's Name	3D Cube Movements
Push	Move Forward
Pull	Move Backward
Right	Turn Right 90°
Left	Turn Left −90°

the first command. This phase is crucial for calibrating the system to recognize unique brain patterns associated with each command. Successful training guarantees accurate control of the cube (or simulated wheelchair) per user intentions. Then, four movements are programmed: pull (to move forward), push (to move backward), left (to turn left), and right (to turn right), as depicted in Table 2.

4.2 Digital Twins in Unity Game Engine

Digital twins are virtual representations of physical objects or systems, and they have gained significant attention in various fields such as robotics, urban planning, manufacturing, and smart cities [4]. These digital replicas are created using advanced technologies such as Unity, a popular game engine, which allows for the development of virtual environments and simulations [19]. The use of Unity in digital twin development enables the training and visualization of trajectories for robots, the creation of virtual replicas of manufacturing cells, and the modeling of smart cities for urban planning and decision support [19]. Furthermore, digital twins are not limited to static representations but have evolved to become actionable and experimentable, allowing for dynamic interactions and simulations [25].

Fig. 3. A digital twin of Wheelchair 3D prototype in Unity engine.

Based on the digital twin concept, we developed a 3D wheelchair simulation in Unity, which its built-in physics engine is employed to simulate real-world physics, thereby ensuring realistic interaction of the digital twin with its virtual environment (Fig. 3). Additionally, custom C# scripts are developed within Unity to replicate the operational behaviors of the entity, including movements, and interactions with environmental factors. Inside the script, we initialized the Emotiv API and set up a connection to the headset. We implemented functionality to process real-time data from the headset, focusing on mental commands that we want to use for controlling the wheelchair (e.g., move forward, turn).

Finally, we translated recognized mental commands into movements of the 3D wheelchair model. This could involve changing the position and rotation of the model based on the commands detected. Beyond real-time interaction, we can link Unity with the BCI Visualizer for training purposes and facilitate offline control by assigning mental commands from the cube to a 3D model of a wheelchair.

5   Conclusion and Future Works

We proposed an innovative approach to wheelchair navigation by leveraging neural input from EEG signals. This method represents a significant advancement in assistive technology, particularly for individuals with mobility impairments. It showcases a promising step towards more independent and adaptable mobility solutions. The research highlights the effectiveness of EEG-based systems in real-time control and underscores the importance of user-centred design in assistive technology. While challenges remain, such as improving system responsiveness and broadening accessibility, this work lays a foundation for future innovations in the field, ultimately contributing to enhanced quality of life for those with physical disabilities. The application of BCIs technology in this context holds the promise of revolutionizing standard wheelchair models, transforming them into more intuitive and responsive tools that are in sync with the cognitive commands of the user.

Future work for the EEG-Cortex SDK wheelchair control study should focus on enhancing EEG signal interpretation using advanced machine learning algorithms, improving user training for better system adaptability, and expanding the system's applicability to a broader range of physical disabilities. Additionally, conducting long-term real-world evaluations to assess effectiveness and user satisfaction, and addressing scalability and cost concerns to increase accessibility, are crucial steps forward.

Acknowledgments. The authors express their sincere appreciation for the significant contribution made by Conor McGovern and Caroline Marie Lassalle to the development of the prototype.

Disclosure of Interests. The authors declare that they have no competing interests relevant to the content of this article.

References

1. Al-Qaysi, Z., Zaidan, B., Zaidan, A., Suzani, M.: A review of disability EEG based wheelchair control system: coherent taxonomy, open challenges and recommendations. Comput. Methods Programs Biomed. **164**, 221–237 (2018)
2. Antoniou, E., et al.: EEG-based eye movement recognition using brain–computer interface and random forests. Sensors **21**(7), 2339 (2021)
3. Badajena, J.C., Sethi, S., Sahoo, R.K.: Data-driven approach to designing a BCI-integrated smart wheelchair through cost-benefit analysis. High-Confid. Comput. **3**(2), 100118 (2023)
4. Dembski, F., Wössner, U., Letzgus, M., Ruddat, M., Yamu, C.: Urban digital twins for smart cities and citizens: the case study of Herrenberg, Germany. Sustainability **12**(6), 2307 (2020)
5. Dianat, I., Molenbroek, J., Castellucci, H.I.: A review of the methodology and applications of anthropometry in ergonomics and product design. Ergonomics **61**(12), 1696–1720 (2018)
6. Essa, A., Kotte, H.: Brain signals analysis based deep learning methods: recent advances in the study of non-invasive brain signals. arXiv preprint arXiv:2201.04229 (2021)
7. Fakhruzzaman, M.N., Riksakomara, E., Suryotrisongko, H.: EEG wave identification in human brain with emotiv EPOC for motor imagery. Procedia Comput. Sci. **72**, 269–276 (2015)
8. Iwarsson, S., Ståhl, A.: Accessibility, usability and universal design—positioning and definition of concepts describing person-environment relationships. Disabil. Rehabil. **25**(2), 57–66 (2003)
9. Iyortsuun, N.K., Kim, S.H., Jhon, M., Yang, H.J., Pant, S.: A review of machine learning and deep learning approaches on mental health diagnosis. Healthcare **11**(3), 285 (2023)
10. Jayarathne, I., Cohen, M., Amarakeerthi, S.: Person identification from EEG using various machine learning techniques with inter-hemispheric amplitude ratio. PLoS ONE **15**(9), e0238872 (2020)
11. Jones, D., Ghasemi, S., Gračanin, D., Azab, M.: Privacy, safety, and security in extended reality: user experience challenges for neurodiverse users. In: Moallem, A. (ed.) HCII 2023. LNCS, pp. 511–528. Springer, Cham (2023). https://doi.org/10.1007/978-3-031-35822-7_33
12. Kim, Y., et al.: A literature review on the smart wheelchair systems. arXiv preprint arXiv:2312.01285 (2023)
13. Klencklen, G., Després, O., Dufour, A.: What do we know about aging and spatial cognition? Reviews and perspectives. Ageing Res. Rev. **11**(1), 123–135 (2012)
14. Lam, L., Suen, S.: Application of majority voting to pattern recognition: an analysis of its behavior and performance. IEEE Trans. Syst. Man Cybernet. A Syst. Hum. **27**(5), 553–568 (1997)
15. Lee, P.H., Yeh, T.T., Yen, H.Y., Hsu, W.L., Chiu, V.J.Y., Lee, S.C.: Impacts of stroke and cognitive impairment on activities of daily living in the Taiwan longitudinal study on aging. Sci. Rep. **11**(1), 12199 (2021)
16. Lin, J.S., Chen, K.C., Yang, W.C.: EEG and eye-blinking signals through a brain-computer interface based control for electric wheelchairs with wireless scheme. In: Proceedings of the 4th International Conference on New Trends in Information Science and Service Science, pp. 731–734 (2010). https://api.semanticscholar.org/CorpusID:17541177

17. Maksud, A., Chowdhury, R.I., Chowdhury, T.T., Fattah, S.A., Shahanaz, C., Chowdhury, S.S.: Low-cost EEG based electric wheelchair with advanced control features. In: Proceedings of the TENCON 2017 — 2017 IEEE Region 10 Conference, pp. 2648–2653 (2017). https://api.semanticscholar.org/CorpusID:28261455
18. McGrath, R.P., et al.: Impairments in individual autonomous living tasks and time to self-care disability in middle-aged and older adults. J. Am. Med. Dir. Assoc. **20**(6), 730–735 (2019)
19. Mignan, A.: A digital template for the generic multi-risk (GenMR) framework: a virtual natural environment. Int. J. Environ. Res. Public Health **19**(23), 16097 (2022)
20. Mirza, I.A., et al.: Mind-controlled wheelchair using an EEG headset and Arduino microcontroller. In: 2015 International Conference on Technologies for Sustainable Development (ICTSD), pp. 1–5. IEEE (2015)
21. Moffat, S.D., Zonderman, A.B., Resnick, S.M.: Age differences in spatial memory in a virtual environment navigation task. Neurobiol. Aging **22**(5), 787–796 (2001)
22. Morshedzadeh, E., Dunkenberger, M.B., Nagle, L., Ghasemi, S., York, L., Horn, K.: Tapping into community expertise: stakeholder engagement in the design process. Policy Des. Pract. **5**(4), 529–549 (2022)
23. Nanthini, B.S., Santhi, B.: Electroencephalogram signal classification for automated epileptic seizure detection using genetic algorithm. J. Nat. Sci. Biol. Med. **8**(2), 159 (2017)
24. Nisar, H., Balasubramaniam, H.C., Malik, A.S.: Brain computer interface for operating a robot. In: Sun, C., Bednarz, T., Pham, T.D., Vallotton, P., Wang, D. (eds.) 2013 International Symposium on Computational Models for Life Sciences. American Institute of Physics Conference Series, vol. 1559, pp. 37–46, October 2013. https://doi.org/10.1063/1.4824994
25. Pérez, L., Rodríguez-Jiménez, S., Rodríguez, N., Usamentiaga, R., García, D.F.: Digital twin and virtual reality based methodology for multi-robot manufacturing cell commissioning. Appl. Sci. **10**(10), 3633 (2020)
26. Rushton, P.W., Labbé, D., Demers, L., Miller, W.C., Mortenson, W.B., Kirby, R.L.: Understanding the burden experienced by caregivers of older adults who use a powered wheelchair: a cross-sectional study. Gerontol. Geriatr. Med. **3** (2017)
27. Schmöcker, J.D.: Access, aging, and impairments part a: impairments and behavioral responses. J. Transp. Land Use **2**(1), 1–2 (2009)
28. Shahin, M.K., Tharwat, A., Gaber, T., Hassanien, A.E.: A wheelchair control system using human-machine interaction: single-modal and multimodal approaches. J. Intell. Syst. **28**(1), 115–132 (2019)
29. Simpson, R.C.: Smart wheelchairs: a literature review. J. Rehabil. Res. Dev. **42**(4) (2005)
30. Siow, E.K.S., Chew, W.J., Mun, H.K.: Human computer interface (HCI) using EEG signals. J. Phys. Conf. Ser. **2523**(1), 012012 (2023)
31. Tedersoo, L., Ramirez, K.S., Nilsson, R.H., Kaljuvee, A., Kõljalg, U., Abarenkov, K.: Standardizing metadata and taxonomic identification in metabarcoding studies. GigaScience **4**(1), s13742-015 (2015)
32. U.S. Department of Justice: ADA standards for accessible design. https://www.ada.gov/law-and-regs/design-standards/. Accessed 16 Feb 2024
33. World Health Organization: Disability. https://www.who.int/news-room/fact-sheets/detail/disability-and-health. Accessed 16 Feb 2024
34. Xavier, G., Su Ting, A., Fauzan, N.: Exploratory study of brain waves and corresponding brain regions of fatigue on-call doctors using quantitative electroencephalogram. J. Occup. Health **62**(1), e12121 (2020)

Guttastemning in a Box - Fostering Emotional Connections Beyond the Screen

Kasper Iversen[1], Knut Ole Kvilhaug Magnussen[1], Paolo Cerutti[1],
and Juan C. Torrado[1,2(✉)]

[1] Østfold University College, Halden, Norway
jctorrado@nr.no
[2] Norwegian Computing Center, Oslo, Norway

Abstract. This study explores the Norwegian gendered term of guttastemning through the design and creation of a digital box (the "Guttastemning Box") that captures moments of lively and cheerful atmosphere when a group of people is having a great time together. The paper recognizes the importance of capturing and reliving such moments, emphasizing the challenges posed by the digital era, such as fluctuations in emotions, digital overload, and the lack of emotional resonance in digital photos. We carried out a Research through Design (RtD) process to assess the effectiveness of the Guttastemning Box in capturing and preserving these moments while fostering emotional connections. We evaluated this artifact through a pilot study in a natural setting in addition to a pre- and post-questionnaire. The results shed light on the Guttastemning Box's ability to capture and preserve guttastemning moments, as well as foster connections. The box has shown promising results, with high overall impressions, positive usability feedback, and intention to use among participants.

Keywords: Guttastemning · Emotional connection · Human-Computer Interaction · Digital overload

1 Introduction

In today's fast-paced digital landscape the volatility of emotional moments and the challenges associated with preserving them have become prominent. The absence of a tangible method for capturing and reliving emotions, in particular *guttastemning* moments presents significant challenges, including digital overload and no emotional resonance.

Guttastemning is a Norwegian term directly translated to "Boys mood". It is commonly used in a setting when a group of boys are together, having a good time. According to the Norwegian dictionary [4], the word is defined as "bawdy, loud, vulgar atmosphere that can be felt in gatherings of boys". However, the term is ambiguous and is in the context of this paper more correctly defined as "A feeling of pure joy and excitement experienced in a group of people.". This redefinition emphasizes that *guttastemning* transcends gender and should not be confined to a specific demographic. With this clarified definition, *guttastemning* becomes an emotion universally accessible to everyone. While recognizing the broader human experience, we embark on a journey to create a tangible means of capturing and preserving these moments. The Guttastemning Box seeks to transcend gender stereotypes and become a vessel for encapsulating and cherishing moments of *guttastemning*, regardless of the participants' gender. In peoples pursuit of control and precision in the digital age, the importance of embracing spontaneity and the beauty found in not having complete control is often overlooked. Therefore a element of the Guttastemning Box is deliberately random. Much like the feeling of *guttastemning* appearing randomly, the moments to be captured also should be displayed and printed randomly. As we explore the design and implementation of the box, we also aim to break down barriers associated with traditional gender norms and demonstrate that moments of *guttastemning* are shared human experiences. Through this paper we introduce an approach to preserving emotions in a rapidly evolving digital age. Following this aim, the following research question is explored in this paper:

"How can the Guttastemning Box effectively capture and preserve guttastemning moments while fostering emotional connections, regardless of gender?"

In our pursuit of researching this and encapsulating the essence of *guttastemning*, we present in this paper the creation of the box. Throughout the development phases, we crafted both low-fidelity and high-fidelity prototypes, alongside a prototype for an accompanying app. As a part of our research, we conducted an evaluation, utilizing an experiment designed to gauge the effectiveness of our creation. The results of this experiment is presented in subsequent sections, offering insights into the impact of our box on the capture and reliving of *guttastemning* moments. Through this approach, we aim to introduce an analysis of the project's design, functionality and user experience for researchers to build further on.

1.1   Related Work

BeReal is a photo-sharing application similar to Instagram. However, it distinguishes itself by allowing users to upload just one photo each day, selecting random times throughout the day for these uploads. The intention behind this approach is to provide followers with a glimpse into the user's daily activities, thereby fostering a representation of their life compared to the edited and curated photos found on social media [1]. Snapchat is a multimedia messaging app that enables users to send photos, videos, and messages to their contacts. What sets Snapchat apart from other messaging platforms is its ephemeral nature. When you send a photo or video, the recipient can view it for a limited amount of time, typically a few seconds, before it disappears. This feature encourages spontaneous and candid sharing, as content shared on Snapchat is meant to be temporary [5].

The Guttastemning Box shares some similarities to the features of a digital frame [2]. The idea to have looping images on a screen was built on the basis of a digital frame. However, in addition to displaying images we also wanted to add some other functions. To make the feeling more tangible, it was thought of also making the images tangible. The printed images were then combined with the element of randomness from the BeReal app. Together with a time constraint for unlocking, to not make it just an image printer, the box became a product of its own.

2   Method

We used the Research through Design (RtD) methodology for this study. RtD is a methodology used primarily in the field of design research where the act of designing itself constitutes a method of knowledge production [6]. It means that researchers can understand and answer complex problems by making and creating things. It involves the process of iteratively designing, prototyping, and testing to both understand a problem in depth and propose potential solutions. The outcomes of this approach are both the understanding gained during the process and the designed artifact. The key principle of research through design is that we can understand more about the world by trying to build things and seeing how these things affect the world.

2.1   Prototypes

The primary aim of the following prototypes is to provide users with an understanding that captures the essence of the Guttastemning Box. Through its design and features, the prototype seeks to communicate the concept of preserving and reliving *guttastemning* moments, fostering a connection with personal memories and emotions.

To materialize our vision, we started by crafting a low-fidelity prototype using Fusion 360 Fig. 1. Fusion 360 is a design program that allows users to visualise ideas. The low-fidelity prototype shows the product design in images, but not its functionalities. The high-fidelity prototype was created by hand and with the low-fidelity prototype as inspiration. It is constructed using sheets of 4mm thickness MDF, assembled to form a box. It has 3D printed components and an iPad to show images uploaded to the box. This prototype has a different placement for the phone stand, as we found it better to have a defined front-part of the box, where you can both place the phone and see the uploaded images. Another change is that a NFC tag was added as an easier way to connect to the box and upload images.

Image Descriptions

- **External Appereance:** On top of the box there is placed a phone-stand, to help users capture *guttastemning* moments.
- **Embedded Screen:** We have embedded a display within the box showcasing random images that has been uploaded to it.

- **Time Lock:** The box will not be able to be opened until a specified duration has elapsed.
- **Random Printing Function:** Our design incorporates random printing function, a feature that will print physical copies of the images uploaded to the box. The pictures will be stored inside the box, awaiting the time lock.

Below is visual representation of the prototype:

Fig. 1. The box designed in Fusion 360

Incorporated Components

- **Screen Integration:** One side of the box features a cut aperture, tailored to accommodate an iPad. This embedded iPad simulates the photo display function, offering users a visual experience.
- **Time Lock:** As mentioned in the description above we integrated a solution for the time lock feature. By threading the straps of the smartwatch through the loops, it simulated a locked box until the specified time elapsed. This approach serves to simulate the experience of an authentic time lock, adding a tangible and interactive element to the prototype's functionality.
- **Random Printing Function:** To simulate the effect of random printing, we placed a collection of pre-printed photos inside the box. This approach allowed us to replicate the sensation of random photo selection without the need for actual printing within the prototype.
- **Honourable Mentions:** A phone-stand was mounted onto the top of the box. It was also added a Near-field communication (NFC) tag to connect to the box.

Web Application. To upload images to the box we created a web application for users to connect to. The app has the following functions:

- **Function 1:** As displayed in Fig. 3 the user can either connect through a code on the box or tap the NFC tag.
- **Function 2:** The same Figure shows what the user see once connected to the box. The only option is to take a picture. If pressed they start a session where they can upload images.

Fig. 2. The boxes front with the display, and its side with the time lock

- **Function 3:** Once the user chooses to take a picture, they will be redirected to a camera-page as displayed in the same Figure.
- **Function 4:** If the user is not happy with the picture they can choose to retake. If they are satisfied they can upload as shown in Fig. 4.
- **Function 5:** After the upload of a image the user get the option to either take another image or end the session. Ending the session results in the time lock starting its countdown. It will then no longer be possible to upload images.
- **Function 6:** When pressing "End Session" the user is redirected to the end-page where the countdown is displayed. The user can either check the page or wait for a notification stating that the countdown is finished.

Fig. 3. The first pictures show connect screen, connected screen and camera screen

Fig. 4. The offer to retake or upload image is given. After upload the option to end session starts the timer.

2.2   Evaluation

As the purpose of this project is to evoke a feeling in people it is hard to generate measurable data. Therefore the evaluating techniques for the Guttastemning Box will be mainly qualitative. In the pursuit of understanding user interactions and evaluating the effectiveness of the Guttastemning Box, we conducted a user experiment. Our approach combined some principles of discount usability testing in a controlled environment. Our methodology integrates the "thinking-aloud" method, which encourages participants to verbalize their thoughts and experiences as they engage with the product. The user study was designed to provide insights into how the participants perceive and interact with the Guttastemning Box in a controlled environment. The primary goal is not only to assess the Guttastemning Box's usability but also to gauge user satisfaction, overall impressions and its potential for capture of *guttastemning* moments. By employing the "thinking-aloud" method, we aimed to capture real-time feedback and gain an understanding of participants' experiences. In this study, we have involved 3 groups of 3 participants each. Through a series of operations we observed participants as they navigated the Guttastemning Box and respond to inquiries. This approach allowed us to draw conclusions about functionality, usability, and its resonance with users. Throughout this section we will provide an explanation of the experimental procedures and operations including time lock engaging and image uploading. The data from the experiment was collected through notes and analysed afterwards. We also discuss limitations and variables that may have affected the results. Our methodology seeks to offer a complete view of the Guttastemning Box's performance, thereby contributing to an understanding of its usability and user experience.

Pre-experiment

Participant Recruitment. For the selection of participants, we have adhered to the theory outlined in the work by [3], who argues how small designs can be studied in terms of usability and user experiences with no more than 5 users in each session. Additionally, in line with our commitment to inclusiveness, each group was composed of individuals of diverse genders, allowing us to account for potential variations in emotional responses.

Briefing. Before the start of the experiment, the participants received a briefing. During this session, the conductors provided an explanation of the Guttastemning Box, its purpose, and its intended function. In addition to the explanation of the box, we performed a two-question questionnaire of the participants' mood. This is important data as negative mood can potentially prevent evoking the feeling of *guttastemning*. The questionnaire results were used in the analysis along with the results of the session. The anonymous questionnaire was composed of the following questions:

1. On a scale from 1 to 10 how was your mood in the last month? (1 Being depressed, 10 being looking back at the month with a huge smile)
2. On a scale from 1 to 10 how is your mood today? (1 Being depressed, 10 being filled with joy and happiness)

Furthermore, the participants were informed about the nature of their involvement in the study, the operations they were to undertake and the subsequent use of the results. Additionally, the conductors addressed any privacy concerns and ensured compliance with local regulations.

Experiment Environment. The experiment took place in the Common room of student residence in Halden. The room facilitate a range of activities such as board games, video games, and videos. The participants had between 30 to 45 min to engage with the room and interact with the Guttastemning Box. During this time, participants were given a set of structured operations to perform. To ensure thorough data collection, participants interacted with the box at least once during their time in the environment.

Execution. The participants had the opportunity to interact with the Guttastemning Box, allowing them to perform the first-time setup and familiarize themselves with the product. Furthermore, the participants engaged in a session of board games or videos at their disposal, with the option to use the Guttastemning Box during this time. When the participants utilized the Guttastemning Box, they completed the following operations:

1. **Start the session & Image Upload:** The participants begun the session and uploaded an image of their choice to be displayed on the screen.
2. **View images:** The participants verified that the images they uploaded were correctly displayed on the screen.
3. **End the session & Start Time Lock:** The participants concluded the session and activated the time lock.

4. **Wait for the Time Lock to Open:** The participants continued with their activities, observing the screen and waiting for the time lock to open as scheduled.

5. **View printed pictures:** Once the time lock opens, the participants retrieved and examined the printed pictures produced by the Guttastemning Box.

As mentioned, the participants were encouraged to think aloud and articulate their thoughts and experiences during the operations. This enabled the conductors to understand the smoothness and effectiveness of the operations. At the end of the session, the conductors asked the participants to answer a five questions Google form. The form used a scale from 1 to 5 and provided space for non-mandatory open-ended answers:

1. What are your overall impressions of the Guttastemning Box? (1 being very bad and 5 being very good)
2. Did you find the box easy to use? (1 being very difficult and 5 being very easy)
3. Do you feel like the box captured your moments of *guttastemning*? If so, why? (1 being "No, not at all" and 5 being "Yes, totally!". Please explain why.)
4. Is there a difference for you between the printed images and digital images in terms of evoking the feeling? (1 being "No difference" and 5 being "Yes, totally". Please tell us why.)
5. Can you envision yourself using the Guttastemning Box in the future? (1 being "No, not at all" and 5 being "Yes, totally!")

The participants also had the opportunity to share any additional feedback, thoughts, or suggestions regarding the Guttastemning Box and its usability. To mitigate potential uncontrollable variables, we opted for a controlled environment. However, certain constraints remained unavoidable. In particular participants' varying emotional states, diverse backgrounds, and experiences may have influenced their ability to experience *guttastemning* hence potentially affect the authenticity and depth of their responses. Additionally, the presence of a conductor in the room to take notes could impact the participants' experiences. Ideally, the participants should have had privacy during their interactions, but that would have required the use of microphones and cameras, which would have introduced additional privacy concerns and bureaucratic obligations.

3   Results

In this section we first highlight the participants' mood before the evaluation of the Guttastemning Box. Then we present the analysis of their feedback and questionnaire responses to answer our research question.

3.1   Pre-experiment Questionnaire

We established that a score of 6 out of 10, with 10 representing the best mood of the month or day and 1 being the worst, is the minimum threshold for participants to consider themselves feeling well. According to the results from the two-question questionnaire, it was evident that all participants were in a positive mood over the last month as shown in Fig. 5. The majority, six out of nine, provided scores ranging between 8 and 9 out of 10, while the remaining three participants reported scores of 6, 7, and 10. However, the answers from the daily mood assessment, visible in Fig. 6, revealed some variation, with two people scoring 4 and 5, falling below the established minimum threshold. The other participants distributed themselves in the range of 6 to 9, with none reporting a perfect score.

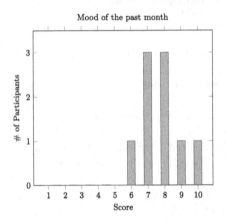

Fig. 5. Comparison of monthly mood

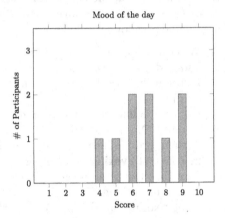

Fig. 6. Comparison of daily mood

3.2 Experiment

During the experiment we took notes on what the participants said while interacting with the Guttastemning Box and performing the operations. Each group encountered a common challenge in locating the code printed on the side of the box. For 2 out of the 3 groups, this difficulty led to the decision to abandon the code search and resort to connecting through the NFC tag. The third group misunderstood the symbol on the box and on the app as a Wi-Fi signal rather than a NFC tag. As they eventually found the code, they opted to ignore the NFC feature. Subsequently, every group successfully completed Operation 1. During Operation 2, as photos appeared on the display, certain images prompted groups to react with laughter or expressions of surprise and delight. Operation 3 and 4 were executed seamlessly by each group. Notably, during Operation 5, when photos were retrieved from the box, an additional appreciation for the captured moments was expressed by the participants.

3.3 Post-experiment Questionnaire

The participants provided their feedback through the post-experiment questionnaire, and the results indicate that each participant expressed favorable impressions of the Guttastemning Box. Specifically, seven participants gave it a score of 4 out of 5, while two participants rated it 5 out of 5. Moreover, 80% of the participants found the box easy to use, while the remaining 20% deemed it acceptable but not particularly easy. When inquired about the *guttastemning* feeling, half of the participants responded affirmatively, stating that the box effectively captured the essence of *guttastemning*. 30% percent expressed neutrality on the matter, while the remaining 20% believed that the feeling could not be adequately captured by the box. In providing responses to this question, the participants were given the opportunity to elaborate. This lead to comments such as: *"Because it prints random pictures, and at the end, what you remember of a good night are random moments, not every single moment"* or *"Because it is authentic, but it would be more authentic if we didn't choose the moment of the picture"* or *"To me, the feeling of guttastemning can't be captured due to its nature."* Regarding the question of whether the participants perceived any difference between the photo displayed on the screen and the printed version, the results revealed that 100% believed that a printed photo holds a distinct significance. The comments provided included:

– *"Having a material memory means for me that the time was more extraordinary than other times. It deserves more attention for me. It was worth taking pictures there."*
– *"A printed picture it's like a never ending memory. On your phone you can edit it while on the printed one you can't and you must keep it forever like that."*
– *"Because you see them constantly if you put the picture in a frame. Moreover, printed pictures are real memories while digital pictures aren't."*
– *"There's no comparison between having an album with all the pictures printed and having them in your phone."*

In response of whether the participants would use the box again, 80% indicated they would, while 20% expressed they would not. Additionally, when asked for general feedback, almost everyone highlighted certain aspects they did not find enjoyable. Notably, some participants raised concerns about the size of the box, suggesting the creation of a portable version. There were also comments about the inability to retrieve non-printed photos from the app.

4 Discussion

The results of the pre-experiment questionnaire provide insights into the baseline mood of participants before their interaction with the Guttastemning Box. The majority of participants reported a positive mood over the past month, with scores averaging at 7,77 out of 10. This indicates that participants were generally in good spirits before engaging with the Guttastemning Box. However, the daily mood assessments (Fig. 6) revealed some variance, with two participants scoring below the established threshold of 6. This discrepancy suggests that individuals experienced fluctuations in their daily mood, emphasizing the importance of assessing both short-term and long-term emotional states. The post-experiment questionnaire provided insights into participants' impressions and usability perceptions of the Guttastemning Box. The reported high impressions, indicates a positive overall experience with the box; this satisfaction level could be attributed to the design and functionality of the box. The reported ease of use was positive; this suggests that the Guttastemning Box has the potential for widespread acceptance, given its user-friendly design. The 20% who considered it okay have provided valuable feedback on areas for improvement or customization. This includes the box size and not being able to retrieve non-printed photos from the web application.

When assessing the Guttastemning Box's effectiveness in capturing the targeted emotional moments, 50% of participants felt that it effectively captured the *guttastemning* feeling. This indicates a promising outcome, with half of the participants recognizing the box's ability to preserve meaningful emotional experiences. The 30% expressing neutrality could be influenced by individual differences in how participants define and perceive *guttastemning* moments. The 20% disagreeing matches the participants reporting a "Mood of the day" under the threshold of 6. This means that the data could be unrelated to the box, and instead related to the participants not being able to experience *guttastemning* that day. Due to the sample size there should be conducted a post-hoc analysis to determine whether this is the case, or if its unrelated. The participants' intentions to use the Guttastemning Box post-experiment are indicators of its potential adoption. With 80% expressing a willingness to use the box, demonstrate a high level of acceptance. However, the 20% stating they would not use it, indicates that there are factors or features that need attention to address the concerns of this subgroup.

In addressing the research question, the findings suggest a meaningful impact on the tangible representation of emotions through printed pictures. The act of printing photos provides a concrete manifestation of moments, contributing to the preservation of emotional experiences. However, it is noteworthy that this aspect may not be exclusively tied to the essence of *guttastemning*, but extends to emotions in general. The feedback regarding the desire for a smaller, more portable box that allows spontaneous capture of moments, suggests a practical improvement to enhance the box's usability and convenience. While the study indicates that the Guttastemning Box aids in capturing and preserving moments, it also highlights the need for further research to delve into exactly how it achieves this goal. Another important aspect from the research question is the "regardless of gender" part. As the experiment was conducted with a diverse group of people, gender wise, it is possible to state that the feeling can be achieved by everyone. However, in terms of gender it is not possible to draw a conclusion. While feedback may provide a sense that the box contributes, it cannot be concluded whether it had any influence on individuals experiencing the feeling without research involving different gender groups.

Future research should explore gender-specific experiences and perceptions to enhance the Guttastemning Box's gender neutrality. Additionally, qualitative methods, such as in-depth interviews and user feedback sessions, could provide richer insights into participants' emotional experiences and expectations.

There are some limitations to be acknowledged. The reliance on self-reported data, introduces the potential for response bias and subjective interpretation. The brief duration of the experiment may also not fully capture the sustained impact of the box. Future research with larger and more diverse samples and control groups could address these limitations and provide a more robust understanding of the Guttastemning Box's effectiveness. To ensure a better understanding of gender-related nuances, we sought the expertise of "Lin Prøiz", a researcher in the field of gender studies. We formally requested her insights via email regarding the conceptualization of *guttastemning* and its implications for gender. However, due to time constraints she could not give an opinion.

5 Conclusion

In conclusion, our research has produced a prototype for the Guttastemning Box, a tangible box designed to address challenges in capturing and reliving shared *guttastemning* moments. The Guttastemning Box prototype captures the essence of *guttastemning* moments by providing a tangible memory through printed photos. The random selection process of which photo to print and share, maintains the uniqueness of each captured moment. The simulated functionalities within the prototype contribute to enhancing emotional resonance and preserving the authenticity of shared experiences. In summary, our study indicates positive perceptions of the Guttastemning Box's ability to capture and preserve *guttastemning* moments, as well as foster connections. The box has shown promising results, with high overall impressions, positive usability feedback, and intention to use among participants. However, the study also highlights the need for further experimenting to address the "how" aspect of the research question.

References

1. Cheong, C.: I tried bereal, the buzzy photo-sharing app trying to stop people using filters, and after 7 days i was hooked (2022). https://www.insider.com/what-is-bereal-app-how-does-it-work-2022-4
2. Hope, C.: Digital photo frame (2022). https://www.computerhope.com/jargon/d/digital-photo-frame.htm
3. Nielsen, J., Landauer, T.K.: A mathematical model of the finding of usability problems. In: Proceedings of ACM INTERCHI'93 Conference, pp. 206–213. ACM, Amsterdam (1993)
4. Ordbok, D.N.A.: guttastemning, November 2023. https://naob.no/ordbok/guttastemning

5. Vaterlaus, J.M., Barnett, K., Roche, C., Young, J.A.: Snapchat is more personal: an exploratory study on snapchat behaviors and young adult interpersonal relationships. Comput. Hum. Behav. **62**, 594–601 (2016). https://doi.org/10.1016/j.chb.2016.04.029. https://www.sciencedirect.com/science/article/pii/S0747563216303041

6. Zimmerman, J., Forlizzi, J., Evenson, S.: Research through design as a method for interaction design research in HCI. In: Proceedings of the SIGCHI Conference on Human Factors in Computing Systems, pp. 493–502 (2007)

Striking the Privacy-Model Training Balance: A Case Study Using PERACTIV Device

Vishnu Kakaraparthi$^{(\boxtimes)}$ ⬤ and Troy McDaniel ⬤

Arizona State University, Tempe, USA
{vkakarap,troy.mcdaniel}@asu.edu

Abstract. In recent years, the healthcare industry has witnessed a surge in the adoption of wearable devices, transforming how individuals manage their well-being. This paper explores the intersection of healthcare technology, data protection, and the evolving regulatory landscape. It emphasizes the critical importance of preserving user data privacy and introduces different privacy-preserving solutions. The paper delves into various Federated Learning techniques, focusing on Federated Transfer Learning (FTL), and presents a practical application for medication adherence using the PERACTIV wrist-worn device. The proposed framework safeguards sensitive information, enabling a personalized and effective healthcare experience while addressing the challenges of medication non-adherence.

Keywords: Wrist-centric view · Wrist-worn Camera · Wearables · Data Privacy · Federated Learning · Federated Transfer Learning

1 Introduction

In recent years, the healthcare industry has undergone a revolutionary transformation driven by an unprecedented surge in the adoption of wearable and healthcare-related devices. This transformative shift has redefined how individuals monitor and manage their well-being, providing real-time health insights and fostering a proactive approach to personal healthcare [1]. These advancements, propelled by innovations in sensor technology and data analytics, have empowered users to take an active role in their health management.

However, a critical imperative has emerged amidst this technological wave - preserving user data in an era where these devices collect and process sensitive health information. The need to ensure the security and privacy of user data has become paramount, considering the potential consequences of unauthorized access or misuse of health-related information [1].

Adding complexity to this landscape, the Biden administration's release of the Executive Order has established new AI safety and security standards [2].

Supported by National Science Foundation under Grant No. 2142774 and Arizona State University.

This development underscores the necessity to explore technologies that preserve user information privacy and facilitate the responsible training of neural network models, especially in healthcare.

This paper addresses the intersection of healthcare technology, data protection, and the evolving regulatory landscape. It aims to navigate the delicate balance between leveraging cutting-edge technologies for healthcare innovation and maintaining the highest standards of security and privacy. The focus extends beyond theoretical considerations to practical applications, specifically delving into the critical challenge of medication non-adherence.

Medication non-adherence is a multifaceted challenge affecting individuals, healthcare providers, and the healthcare system. Its prevalence leads to dire consequences, including worsened health outcomes, increased healthcare costs, and a diminished quality of life for patients [3]. Leveraging the capabilities of the PERACTIV wrist-worn device (as seen in Fig. 1), this paper explores the application of Federated Transfer Learning (FTL) to enhance medication adherence while addressing significant privacy concerns associated with such technology.

Fig. 1. PERACTIV Device.

The synthesis of cutting-edge technologies, ethical considerations, and privacy preservation outlined in this paper signifies a promising direction for future healthcare systems. By combining technological advancements with responsible deployment practices, the proposed framework aims to revolutionize healthcare, providing a personalized and effective experience while mitigating the social consequences of non-adherence.

2   Background

In the era of pervasive digital connectivity, major players such as Google and Apple have assumed prominent roles in collecting and analyzing sensitive health and location data through their respective ecosystems [4]. While these technological giants contribute significantly to the advancement of healthcare technology, the sheer volume and sensitivity of the data they handle raise paramount security and privacy concerns.

The collection of health-related data, including vital signs, physical activity, and even medical histories, has become commonplace in today's digital health landscape [4]. Simultaneously, integrating location-based services further amplifies the information available, presenting a comprehensive profile of an individual's daily life. While these data-driven insights hold immense potential for personalized healthcare, the potential misuse or unauthorized access to such information poses substantial risks [4].

Security breaches and data leaks have become prevalent in recent years, underscoring the vulnerabilities inherent in handling vast amounts of sensitive health data [5]. The mishandling of this information could not only compromise individual privacy but also result in significant legal and ethical ramifications. The need for robust security measures, encryption protocols, and stringent access controls is evident to mitigate these risks.

Moreover, the ethical dimension of data ownership and consent becomes increasingly complex in the context of healthcare-related data. It is a delicate challenge to balance leveraging data for the greater good and respecting individuals' rights to control their personal information. Policies and regulations must evolve to keep pace with technological advancements, ensuring individuals have transparency, control, and autonomy over their health data.

As we navigate this landscape, the subsequent sections will delve into the Biden administration's Executive Order, which underscores the importance of AI safety and security standards, and explore methodologies such as Federated Transfer Learning (FTL) as potential solutions to enhance privacy while harnessing the benefits of advanced healthcare technologies.

3   Technological Wave in Healthcare

The contemporary healthcare landscape is characterized by a remarkable technological wave, propelled by innovations in sensor technology, data analytics, and the widespread adoption of wearable and healthcare-related devices. This section delves into the pivotal role played by these technological advancements, reshaping how individuals engage with their health and well-being.

3.1   Wearable and Healthcare Devices

Wearable devices have become integral to the modern healthcare ecosystem, fostering a paradigm shift from reactive to proactive health management. These devices encompass various form factors, including smartwatches, fitness trackers, and specialized healthcare wearables. They are equipped with sensors to monitor various physiological parameters, providing real-time data on vital signs, physical activity, and sleep patterns.

Integrating healthcare-related devices extends beyond consumer wearables to encompass a broader spectrum of medical devices. These may include smart inhalers, continuous glucose monitors, and portable ECG monitors. The collective impact of these devices is transformative, enabling individuals to participate actively in monitoring and managing their health conditions.

This technological convergence has empowered users with unprecedented access to personalized health insights. Individuals can track their fitness goals, receive timely reminders for medication adherence, and even monitor specific health metrics indicative of chronic conditions. The ubiquity of these devices has catalyzed a cultural shift towards preventive healthcare, with users taking proactive measures to maintain and enhance their well-being.

However, the proliferation of wearable and healthcare devices raises critical considerations regarding the security and privacy of sensitive health information. As these devices collect and process personal data, safeguarding user information has become paramount. The subsequent sections will explore the intricate balance required to harness the potential of these technologies while ensuring robust security and privacy measures are in place.

3.2   Biden Administration's Executive Order

In response to the escalating influence of artificial intelligence (AI) on various sectors, including healthcare, President Biden has issued a landmark Executive Order [2] to establish new standards for AI safety, security, and trustworthiness. This pivotal directive is not only a strategic move to ensure that America leads in harnessing the benefits of AI but also addresses the potential risks and challenges associated with its widespread adoption.

New Standards for AI Safety and Security. As the capabilities of AI systems grow, so do the implications for Americans' safety and security. The Executive Order mandates the implementation of sweeping actions to protect citizens from the potential risks associated with powerful AI systems. Specifically, it requires developers of such systems to share safety test results and critical information with the U.S. government. This transparency ensures that AI systems undergo rigorous safety testing before being made public, particularly if they pose serious risks to national security, economic security, or public health and safety.

The Executive Order leverages the Defense Production Act to enforce these measures, compelling companies to notify the federal government when training high-risk AI models. Additionally, it calls for developing standards, tools, and tests by the National Institute of Standards and Technology, ensuring extensive red-team testing before the public release of AI systems. Collectively, these actions represent a comprehensive approach by any government to advance the field of AI safety.

Furthermore, the Executive Order addresses the risks associated with AI-engineered biological materials by establishing strong new standards for biological synthesis screening. This includes incentivizing appropriate screening and risk management for life-science projects funded by federal agencies.

Protecting Americans' Privacy. If not safeguarded, AI can pose significant risks to Americans' privacy. Recognizing this, the President calls on Congress to pass bipartisan data privacy legislation. In healthcare wearables, where sensitive health data is increasingly collected, the emphasis on protecting individuals' privacy is crucial.

The Executive Order prioritizes federal support for developing and using privacy-preserving techniques. This includes cutting-edge AI techniques that allow AI systems to be trained while preserving the privacy of the training data. It also supports strengthening privacy-preserving research and technologies through funding initiatives, promoting rapid breakthroughs and development in cryptographic tools that preserve individuals' privacy.

Moreover, the order evaluates how agencies collect and use commercially available information, particularly from data brokers, and seeks to strengthen privacy guidance for federal agencies to account for AI-related risks. This is particularly relevant to healthcare wearables as agencies must manage commercially available information containing personally identifiable data, ensuring privacy safeguards are in place.

Advancing Equity and Civil Rights. Recognizing the potential for irresponsible AI use to deepen discrimination, bias, and other abuses, the Executive Order directs actions to ensure that AI advances equity and civil rights. In healthcare wearables, preventing discrimination and ensuring fair practices become critical considerations.

The order provides guidance to prevent AI algorithms from exacerbating discrimination. It addresses algorithmic discrimination through training, technical assistance, and coordination between the Department of Justice and Federal civil rights offices. In healthcare, this involves ensuring fairness throughout the criminal justice system, specifically in sentencing, parole, probation, risk assessments, and predictive policing.

Standing Up for Consumers, Patients, and Students. AI can benefit consumers, patients, and students, but it also raises concerns about potential harms. In healthcare wearables, where AI can influence healthcare practices, the Executive Order takes measures to protect consumers.

It directs actions to advance the responsible use of AI in healthcare and the development of affordable and life-saving drugs. This includes establishing a safety program within the Department of Health and Human Services to receive and address reports of harm or unsafe healthcare practices involving AI. Additionally, the order shapes AI's potential to transform education, supporting educators in deploying AI-enabled educational tools such as personalized tutoring in schools.

Supporting Workers. Recognizing the impact of AI on jobs and workplaces, the Executive Order seeks to support workers' ability to bargain collectively and invest in workforce training and development. This addresses the potential risks of increased workplace surveillance, bias, and job displacement in the healthcare sector.

The order develops principles and best practices to mitigate the harms and maximize the benefits of AI for workers, providing guidance to prevent unfair employment practices and evaluating job applications. It also produces a report on AI's potential labor-market impacts and explores options for strengthening federal support for workers facing labor disruptions, including from AI.

Promoting Innovation and Competition. In acknowledging America's leadership in AI innovation, the Executive Order takes action to promote a fair, open, and competitive AI ecosystem. This is particularly relevant to the healthcare wearables industry, where innovation can significantly impact patient care and outcomes.

The order catalyzes AI research across the United States through the National AI Research Resource pilot, providing researchers and students access to key AI resources and data. It also promotes a competitive AI ecosystem by providing small developers and entrepreneurs access to technical assistance and resources.

Advancing American Leadership Abroad. Recognizing the global nature of AI challenges and opportunities, the Executive Order emphasizes collaboration with other nations. This collaboration aims to support the safe, secure, and trustworthy deployment and use of AI worldwide, aligning with international frameworks and standards. This approach facilitates responsible AI use globally in the healthcare sector, where cross-border data exchange is crucial.

Ensuring Responsible and Effective Government Use of AI. The Executive Order recognizes the transformative potential of AI in government operations while acknowledging the associated risks. Responsible AI deployment becomes imperative in healthcare, where government agencies play a significant role.

The order issues guidance for agencies' use of AI, setting clear standards to protect rights and safety, improve AI procurement, and strengthen AI deployment. It helps agencies acquire specified AI products and services more efficiently and accelerates hiring AI professionals to ensure a government-wide AI talent surge. Collectively, these measures aim to modernize federal AI infrastructure while ensuring ethical and responsible government use of AI.

In conclusion, the Biden Administration's Executive Order on AI encompasses a comprehensive strategy that aligns with safety, security, privacy, equity, and innovation principles. The order's emphasis on privacy protection, responsible innovation, and fair practices holds significant implications in healthcare wearables. It sets a trajectory for integrating AI into healthcare practices, ensuring that advancements prioritize patient well-being, data security, and ethical considerations.

4   Privacy-Preserving Methodologies

The issue of preserving privacy while training machine learning models, especially when dealing with sensitive and private data, has become increasingly significant. Traditional anonymization methods, such as removing personal identifiers, have proven insufficient, as demonstrated by cases like Netflix's recommender challenge [6] and Strava's location data release [7]. Even aggregate data without explicit personal identifiers can inadvertently disclose sensitive information when analyzed or queried.

Anonymizing data, a commonly suggested solution for privacy and security concerns in deep learning, encounters challenges during the model inference phase, as noted in recent research [8]. This emphasizes the need for robust, lightweight methods that balance data utility and privacy preservation [9]. Integrating deep learning with advanced privacy-preserving techniques like differential privacy, secure multiparty computing, and homomorphic encryption adds another layer of complexity to achieving privacy in deep learning [11].

The realm of cloud computing introduces the concept of privacy-preserving deep computation models to enhance the efficiency of big data feature learning [12]. Similarly, exploring privacy-preserving deep learning schemes over aggregated encrypted data underscores the critical importance of securing deep learning processes [13]. Despite these advancements, safeguarding sensitive data in machine learning and deep learning remains a paramount concern, demanding comprehensive solutions for security and privacy [14].

Federated learning, emerging as a promising approach, addresses privacy concerns by building shared models from multicenter data while keeping training data local [15]. This aligns with the growing interest in leveraging federated learning across various domains, including healthcare and IoT, to mitigate privacy and security challenges [16,17]. However, the limitations of existing privacy protection methods, such as incomplete image watermark removal, must be acknowledged, as they impact image information security and privacy in IoT applications based on federated learning [18].

While anonymizing data has been considered a potential approach for privacy and security in deep learning, recent research has highlighted its limitations, particularly during the model inference phase. Integrating deep learning with privacy-preserving techniques such as differential privacy, secure multiparty computing, and homomorphic encryption has posed challenges, emphasizing the complexity of achieving privacy in deep learning. Additionally, federated learning has shown promise in addressing privacy concerns, particularly in scenarios involving sensitive data from multiple sources. However, it is crucial to address the limitations of existing privacy protection methods to ensure comprehensive security and privacy in deep learning applications [10]. The growing significance of preserving privacy, especially with sensitive data, is evident, and traditional anonymization methods must evolve to meet the demands of an increasingly interconnected and data-driven world.

4.1   Deep Learning with Differential Privacy

Differential privacy [11] emerges as a solution to this privacy challenge. It introduces a quantitative measure, privacy budget (epsilon), to limit the privacy loss incurred by any mechanism accessing the data and producing an output. The core idea is to enable learning from general trends in the data set without revealing specific individuals' private information. The formal definition of differential privacy involves comparing probabilities before and after adding or removing a particular data record and bounding the log probability ratio by epsilon [19].

Differential privacy can be achieved by adding noise to the outputs, making the model less prone to memorizing specific data points. Techniques such as noise addition and sampling are employed to limit privacy loss. The privacy amplification theorem allows for adjusting the privacy level by tuning parameters like epsilon and delta, where epsilon represents privacy loss, and delta is the failure probability.

The paper on differential privacy for deep learning [11] introduces the concept of differentially private stochastic gradient descent (DP-SGD). DP-SGD modifies the standard stochastic gradient descent algorithm by clipping gradients and adding noise during updates to limit the privacy loss per iteration or minibatch. The privacy budget is tracked using the moments accountant technique, which provides a more accurate estimation of the overall privacy loss compared to traditional methods [11]. The moments accountant technique leverages probability distributions and concentration inequalities to monitor the privacy loss over time, allowing for a tighter upper bound on the overall privacy budget [11]. This refined tracking mechanism significantly improves the accuracy of privacy loss estimation during the training process.

While DP-SGD provides a robust method for training deep neural networks with privacy guarantees, it has limitations. It is most effective for large datasets where privacy loss per individual example is minimized. The noise introduced during training can disproportionately affect minority subgroups, impacting fairness.

4.2   Private Aggregation of Teacher Ensembles (PATE)

Privacy-preserving machine learning has become increasingly vital in today's data-driven world, and among the key algorithms addressing this concern is

Private Aggregation of Teacher Ensembles (PATE) [20]. The essence of differential privacy (DP-SGD) lies in minimizing the risk of divulging sensitive information about individual data points by introducing controlled noise into the machine-learning process. In DP-SGD, the noise is added during the training process so that the model itself is differentially private, and we are free to query its outputs however we like, but we trade off accuracy for privacy as the gradient updates to our model are a bit noisier.

PATE adds noise at different stages of the process, introducing noise solely to the outcomes during model training; unfortunately, the noise needed for privacy would overpower the output and drastically reduce our accuracy. Thus, PATE operates on the premise of training an ensemble of models, each independently trained on disjoint datasets, ensuring that individual models do not memorize specific examples but instead learn general trends within the data. The noisy max operation, a pivotal component of PATE, aggregates the predictions of the ensemble models while introducing noise to conceal the identity of the specific model contributing to each prediction [20]. This mechanism allows for differential privacy, where the privacy budget is managed by adjusting the amount of noise added to the aggregated predictions.

However, deploying the model ensemble as is presents challenges. Every query to the ensemble leaks a small amount of information about the data, and this privacy loss accumulates over time. Additionally, the model's weights encode information about the data they were trained on, posing a risk if made public. A solution is proposed based on the concept in DP-SGD, where noise is added during the training process to prevent encoding private information in the model and weights. The ensemble is used to train a separate model that is deployed noisily, ensuring differential privacy. In this setup, unlabeled public data is employed to train the deployed model, with the ensemble serving as teacher models and the deployed model as the student. The noisy max operation used to predict labels adds the necessary noise in the training process to ensure differential privacy. Once training is complete, the privacy loss is capped, as in deployment, queries are made to the student model, not the teacher models [20]. PATE thus emerges as a nuanced approach, extending differential privacy principles to the practical realm of machine learning, with the ensemble serving as teachers and a subsequent differentially private model serving as the student in the learning process [20]. Advanced techniques like PATE-G or Scalable private learning with PATE can be utilized to enhance the robustness and scalability of the privacy-preserving machine learning framework.

4.3 Federated Learning (FL)

In federated learning, researchers explore innovative methodologies to harness the collaborative potential of distributed datasets. This paper delves into three paradigms within the federated learning framework: Horizontal Federated Learning, Vertical Federated Learning, and Federated Transfer Learning [21].

Horizontal Federated Learning [21] is characterized by datasets that share a uniform feature space across participating clients, ensuring consistency in the types of information processed by each device. This approach fosters collaborative model training while maintaining common features across all contributing clients.

On the other hand, Vertical Federated Learning [21] takes a different approach, leveraging disparate datasets with distinct feature spaces from different domains. Combining information from diverse sources, such as movie purchases on Amazon and movie reviews on IMDB, this variant of federated learning aims to enhance customer services, providing more informed recommendations by tapping into a broader spectrum of user-related data.

Furthermore, Federated Transfer Learning [21] emerges as an intriguing extension of Vertical Federated Learning, introducing the concept of pre-trained models. In this scenario, a model initially trained on a similar dataset for a distinct problem is adapted to a new task. A practical example of Federated Transfer Learning is developing personalized models, such as movie recommendation systems tailored to users' historical browsing behavior.

Various techniques, including FedAvg, FedProx, q-FedAvg, per-FedAvg, and Federated Multi-Task Learning, are explored to facilitate the realization of these federated learning paradigms.

FedAvg (Federated Averaging). FedAvg [22] is a seminal federated learning algorithm introduced in the field. It aims to train a shared model across multiple clients by minimizing a global loss that is a weighted average of individual client losses. The algorithm operates in rounds, where a fraction of clients is sampled in each round, and their local models are updated through stochastic gradient descent. The server aggregates these updates, computing a weighted average to update the global model. While FedAvg works well in practice, it has some simplifying assumptions. For instance, it assumes all devices complete the same number of local epochs, potentially facing challenges with stragglers. Additionally, it may not guarantee convergence in highly heterogeneous data scenarios.

FedProx (Federated Proximal). FedProx [23] is an improvement over FedAvg by introducing a regularization term to penalize large changes in weights during model updates. This addresses convergence challenges, especially when dealing with highly heterogeneous data. The regularization term controls the extent of penalization, offering better adaptability to varying device capabilities and diverse data distributions.

q-FedAvg. q-FedAvg [24] is another enhancement that aims to enhance fairness in federated learning by penalizing worse-performing devices more. The introduced parameter 'q' allows tuning the balance between fairness and overall model performance, enabling customization based on specific use cases and data characteristics.

per-FedAvg (Personalized Federated Averaging). per-FedAvg [25] takes a personalized approach, allowing devices to train a model that can be personalized after a few steps of local gradient descent. It formulates federated learning as a multi-task problem, treating each client's distribution as a separate task. This approach contrasts with FedAvg, providing a more tailored and adaptive model for individual devices.

Federated Multi-task Learning. Federated Multi-Task Learning [26] is a broader approach that extends the federated learning framework by treating each client's data distribution as a separate task. This approach, reminiscent of meta-learning, enables the model to adapt to diverse data sources and varying device capabilities. It introduces a more versatile strategy for handling non-IID data distributions across devices.

The advantages of these approaches include addressing issues related to stragglers, improving fairness, enabling personalization, and accommodating diverse data distributions. However, potential disadvantages may include the need for careful parameter tuning, increased computational complexity, and challenges in achieving convergence under certain circumstances. These algorithms represent a spectrum of solutions for different aspects of federated learning, catering to the evolving landscape of privacy-preserving machine learning.

4.4   Gossip Learning

In recent years, distributed machine learning has witnessed significant advancements, with various approaches emerging to address the challenges of large-scale, decentralized systems. One such technique, known as gossip learning [27], draws inspiration from how information spreads organically through a group of individuals, mimicking a decentralized exchange of knowledge among nodes in a network. Gossip learning is a distributed machine learning paradigm where each node updates its model parameters by exchanging information with other nodes, promoting convergence to a global optimum. Unlike traditional distributed learning methods, which rely on a central authority for model aggregation, gossip learning offers a decentralized alternative, particularly advantageous when communication between nodes is expensive or unreliable.

The decentralized nature of gossip learning introduces a variety of algorithms, each tailored to specific aspects of distributed machine learning. From the Push-Sum Algorithm facilitating distributed averaging to Gossip-based Coordinate Descent Algorithm addressing optimization problems, these algorithms collectively enable nodes in a network to share information and make decisions collaboratively. As the field continues to evolve, researchers have identified privacy preservation, robustness, bandwidth utilization, latency, cost-effectiveness, computational load distribution, and adaptability to dynamic environments as key differentiators between gossip learning and traditional learning. This subsection explores the foundations, algorithms, and distinctions of gossip learning, setting the stage for a detailed examination of its empirical performance compared to the widely employed federated learning approach.

5   Federated Transfer Learning (FTL)

5.1   FTL Framework Overview

Federated Transfer Learning (FTL) [28] represents an evolution of FL, focusing on recent research trends that underscore knowledge transfer from decentralized nodes to new nodes with distinct data domains. The FTL framework enhances statistical models within a data alliance, facilitating knowledge sharing without compromising user privacy.

FedHealth [29] addresses two critical challenges in the context of smart healthcare - the fragmented nature of user data and the lack of personalization in models trained on the cloud. To overcome these challenges, FedHealth leverages federated learning for data aggregation and employs transfer learning to construct relatively personalized models.

Building upon the success of FedHealth, an extension called FedHealth 2 [30] was proposed. It aims to enhance the capabilities of its predecessor by addressing issues related to domain shifts and placing a greater emphasis on achieving personalized models for local clients. The extension employs a weighted federated transfer learning approach, where client similarities are determined using a pre-trained model. The weighted models are then averaged while preserving local batch normalization. The experiments conducted with wearable activity recognition demonstrate that FedHealth 2 achieves better accuracy, with a notable improvement of over 10% in activity recognition. FedHealth and FedHealth 2 prioritize privacy and security in healthcare using federated learning techniques.

5.2   Use Case with PERACTIV Employing FTL

In this use case, we explore the application of PERACTIV [3], with its wrist-centric data [31] and Federated Transfer Learning (FTL), to enhance medication adherence while extending its impact to object detection, micro-action recognition, and broader Activities of Daily Living (ADLs).

Consider an individual using PERACTIV's wrist-centric data for medication adherence. The focus extends beyond the act of taking pills to encompass the nuanced details such as pill detection, hand movements, and micro-actions like ingesting the pill. Traditional models often struggle with these granular aspects, necessitating a more specialized and personalized approach.

FTL plays a central role in prioritizing privacy. Each PERACTIV device, with wrist-centric data, serves as a rich-featured node and contributes to the FTL framework by sharing insights into object detection, hand gestures, and micro-actions. The decentralized learning process retains sensitive information on individual devices, safeguarding user privacy while facilitating collaborative model improvement.

FTL's unique feature lies in its adaptability and personalization. As PERACTIV, with its wrist-centric data, refines the model for medication adherence, this use case extends its capabilities to encompass other ADLs. The system learns to detect and recognize objects beyond pills, adapting to diverse user behaviors and preferences in daily activities.

Through the personalized models empowered by FTL as seen in Fig. 2, PER-ACTIV, with its wrist-centric data, significantly improves object detection capabilities. The device becomes adept at identifying pills and other relevant objects in the user's environment. Utilizing wrist-centric data, this expanded functionality enhances the overall user experience and opens avenues for broader applications.

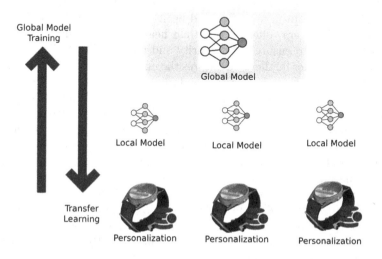

Fig. 2. Federated Transfer Learning model.

Micro-action detection gains precision through this use case. PERACTIV, with the support of FTL and its wrist-centric data, refines its ability to recognize intricate hand movements and gestures associated with medication adherence. Moreover, leveraging wrist-centric data, this proficiency extends to other micro-actions within different ADLs, providing a comprehensive understanding of user behaviors.

Let's consider an example. A user of PERACTIV relies on the device with its wrist-centric data for his medication adherence. As they approach the scheduled pill-taking moment, PERACTIV detects the pill container in hand, recognizing the specific pill through advanced object detection. Simultaneously, it captures the nuanced hand movements, utilizing wrist-centric data, as they grasp the pill, accurately identifying the entire micro-action. Federated Transfer Learning, operating in the background and leveraging wrist-centric data, utilizes this information to enhance the overall model, providing a personalized [32] and efficient solution for their unique medication adherence needs.

The amalgamation of PERACTIV, with its wrist-centric data and FTL, transcends medication adherence, offering a versatile and user-centric technology solution. The enhanced object detection and micro-action recognition, utilizing wrist-centric data, benefit medication management and pave the way for applications in broader healthcare contexts and ADLs. This paradigm shift, utilizing wrist-centric data, marks the evolution of PERACTIV into a comprehensive tool for understanding and improving various aspects of daily life.

6   Conclusion

In conclusion, this research paper navigates the evolving landscape of healthcare technology, emphasizing the critical need for user-centric, secure, and ethically-driven practices. Adopting wearable and healthcare-related devices has ushered in a transformative era, offering real-time health insights while necessitating stringent measures to ensure data security and privacy. The Biden administration's Executive Order further underscores the imperative to explore technologies aligning with AI safety and security standards.

The paper addresses the multifaceted challenge of medication non-adherence, highlighting its profound impact on individuals, healthcare providers, and the broader healthcare infrastructure. The study acknowledges the privacy concerns associated with such innovations by introducing the PERACTIV wrist-worn device and leveraging computer vision technology for enhanced medication adherence insights.

The paper delves into privacy-preserving methodologies to tackle emerging privacy challenges, specifically focusing on Federated Learning (FL). The exploration extends to Federated Transfer Learning (FTL), emphasizing its evolution and application in the context of medication adherence. By detailing various FL methods and the practical application of FTL with the PERACTIV device, the paper presents a privacy-preserving solution that tailors medication adherence strategies while respecting individual privacy.

In summary, this research paper discusses a comprehensive approach, synthesizing human-centered technology, privacy, and healthcare to address medication non-adherence. The proposed framework, combining innovative devices and privacy-preserving methodologies, signals a promising direction for future healthcare systems. This synthesis aims to revolutionize healthcare by enhancing medication adherence, improving health outcomes, and mitigating the social consequences of non-adherence, all within the framework of responsible and ethical technological deployment.

References

1. Guk, K., et al.: Evolution of wearable devices with real-time disease monitoring for personalized healthcare. Nanomaterials **9**(6), 813 (2019). https://doi.org/10.3390/nano9060813
2. Executive order on the safe, secure, and trustworthy development and use of artificial intelligence (2023) The White House. https://www.whitehouse.gov/briefing-room/presidential-actions/2023/10/30/executive-order-on-the-safe-secure-and-trustworthy-development-and-use-of-artificial-intelligence/. Accessed 06 Dec 2023

3. Kakaraparthi, V., McDaniel, T., Venkateswara, H., Goldberg, M.: PERACTIV: Personalized Activity Monitoring - Ask My Hands (2022). https://doi.org/10.1007/978-3-031-05431-0_18

4. Filkins, B.L., et al.: Privacy and security in the era of digital health: what should translational researchers know and do about it? Am. J. Transl. Res. **8**(3), 1560–1580 (2016)

5. Seh, A.H., et al.: Healthcare data breaches: insights and implications. Healthcare **8**(2), 133 (2020). https://doi.org/10.3390/healthcare8020133

6. Narayanan, A., Shmatikov, V.: Robust de-anonymization of large sparse datasets. In: 2008 IEEE Symposium on Security and Privacy (SP 2008) [Preprint] (2008). https://doi.org/10.1109/sp.2008.33

7. Fitness tracking app Strava gives away location of secret US Army Bases: The Guardian (2018). https://www.theguardian.com/world/2018/jan/28/fitness-tracking-app-gives-away-location-of-secret-us-army-bases. Accessed 02 Feb 2024

8. Chi, Y.: Privacy partitioning: protecting user data during the deep learning inference phase. arXiv preprint arXiv:1812.02863 (2018)

9. Majeed, A., Lee, S.: Anonymization techniques for privacy preserving data publishing: a comprehensive survey. IEEE Access **9**, 8512–8545 (2021). https://doi.org/10.1109/access.2020.3045700

10. Xue, Y., et al.: Machine learning security: threats, countermeasures, and evaluations. IEEE Access **8**, 82811–82831 (2020). https://doi.org/10.1109/access.2020

11. Abadi, M., et al.: Deep learning with differential privacy. In: Proceedings of the 2016 ACM SIGSAC Conference on Computer and Communications Security (CCS 2016), pp. 308–318. Association for Computing Machinery, New York (2016). https://doi.org/10.1145/2976749.2978318

12. Zhang, W., et al.: Privacy preserving deep computation model on cloud for big data feature learning. IEEE Trans. Comput. **66**(12), 2092–2105 (2016). https://doi.org/10.1109/tc.2015.2470255

13. Owusu-Agyemang, M., et al.: MSCryptoNet: multi-scheme privacy-preserving deep learning in cloud computing. IEEE Access **7**, 74898–74908 (2019). https://doi.org/10.1109/access.2019.2901219

14. Hameed, I.A., et al.: A taxonomy study on securing blockchain-based industrial applications: an overview, application perspectives, requirements, attacks, countermeasures, and open issues. arXiv preprint arXiv:2105.11665 (2021)

15. Ślazyk, J.: A secure federated transfer learning framework. IEEE Intell. Syst. **35**(4), 70–82 (2022). https://doi.org/10.1109/mis.2020.2988525

16. Wang, C., et al.: The applications of blockchain in artificial intelligence. Secur. Commun. Netw. **2021**, 6126247 (2023). https://doi.org/10.1155/2021/6126247

17. Wang, L., Yang, L.: CXR-FL: deep learning-based chest X-ray image analysis using federated learning. arXiv preprint arXiv:2204.05203 (2022)

18. Li, Y., et al.: An image watermark removal method for secure Internet of Things applications based on federated learning. Expert Syst., e13036 (2022). https://doi.org/10.1111/exsy.13036.

19. Bun, M., Steinke, T.: Concentrated differential privacy: simplifications, extensions, and lower bounds. Theory Cryptogr. 635–658 (2016). https://doi.org/10.1007/978-3-662-53641-4_24

20. Papernot, N., Abadi, M., Erlingsson, Ú., Goodfellow, I., Talwar, K.: Semi-supervised knowledge transfer for deep learning from private training data (2016). ArXiv. /abs/1610.05755

21. Yang, Q., Liu, Y., Chen, T., Tong, Y.: Federated machine learning: concept and applications. ACM Trans. Intell. Syst. Technol. (TIST) **10**(2), 1–19 (2019)

22. McMahan, H.B., et al.: Communication-efficient learning of deep networks from decentralized data. ArXiv, 2016, /abs/1602.05629. Accessed 7 Dec 2023
23. Li, T., et al.: Federated optimization in heterogeneous networks. ArXiv, 2018, /abs/1812.06127. Accessed 7 Dec 2023
24. Li, T., et al.: Fair resource allocation in federated learning. ArXiv, 2019, /abs/1905.10497. Accessed 7 Dec 2023
25. Fallah, A., Mokhtari, A., Ozdaglar, A.: Personalized federated learning with theoretical guarantees: a model-agnostic meta-learning approach. Adv. Neural. Inf. Process. Syst. **33**, 3557–3568 (2020)
26. Smith, V., et al.: Federated multi-task learning. ArXiv, 2017, /abs/1705.10467. Accessed 7 Dec 2023
27. Hegedűs, I., Danner, G., Jelasity, M.: Gossip learning as a decentralized alternative to federated learning. In: Pereira, J., Ricci, L. (eds.) DAIS 2019. LNCS, vol. 11534, pp. 74–90. Springer, Cham (2019). https://doi.org/10.1007/978-3-030-22496-7_5
28. Liu, Y., et al.: A secure federated transfer learning framework. IEEE Intell. Syst. **35**(4), 70–82 (2020). https://doi.org/10.1109/mis.2020.2988525
29. Chen, Y., Wang, J., Yu, C., Gao, W., Qin, X.: FedHealth: a federated transfer learning framework for wearable healthcare. IEEE Intell. Syst. **35**, 83–93 (2019)
30. Chen, Y., Lu, W., Wang, J., Qin, X.: FedHealth 2: weighted federated transfer learning via batch normalization for personalized healthcare. ArXiv, abs/2106.01009 (2021)
31. Kakaraparthi, V., Goldberg, M., McDaniel, T.: Wrist view: understanding human activity through the hand. In: Antona, M., Stephanidis, C. (eds) HCII 2023, vol. 14021, pp. 581–595. Springer, Cham (2023). https://doi.org/10.1007/978-3-031-35897-5_41
32. McDaniel, T., Goldberg, M., Venkateswara, H.K.D., Panchanathan, S., Kakaraparthi, V.P.: U.S. Patent Application No. 18/296,908 (2023)

Exergames for Children with Special Needs

Christian Scherer[1]([✉]) [iD], Sacha Guyser[1] [iD], Thomas Keller[1] [iD],
and Andreas Illenberger[2]

[1] Institute of Business Information Technology, ZHAW, 8400 Winterthur, Switzerland
shhc@zhaw.ch
[2] Vivala, Mühlenbachstrasse 1, 8570 Weinfelden, Switzerland

Abstract. In a world of decreasing physical activity, games in immersive Virtual Reality (VR) that playfully engage in exercises bear a lot of attraction. This paper explores the application of these so called "exergames" in an inclusive educational setting. Children with special needs normally require a large amount of care and attention. Self-directed exergames reduce the load on support staff while offering playful exercise and training to this group of children. Through a suite of three exergames developed for the Oculus Quest 2, we investigate the suitability of this technology as well as the impact on children's motivation and attention span. Our observational field study, conducted over two months with six children aged seven to nine, demonstrates a high acceptance of immersive VR and a positive short-term effect on the attention span of the children as well as heightened motivation. We show that this technology is a valuable tool due to its accessibility and new forms of interaction as well as easy creation of controllable content. However, we conclude that for a persistent effect more diverse, customisable and challenging exergames are needed. Our observations heavily imply that design patterns of exergames in VR can be extended to children with special needs at a very young age. Although conducted with a small sample size, this study contributes to the expanding body of research on the utilisation of VR in inclusive education and provides valuable insights for educators and developers in this domain alike.

Keywords: Exergames · Accessible Virtual Reality · Design for Children with special needs

1 Introduction

Virtual Reality (VR) exhibits great potential to extend our digital experiences and facilitate processes in various fields and industries by presenting unique opportunities for engagement and interaction, which traditional methods cannot. One such area of application this technology greatly enhances is the gamification of exercise. Lack of physical activity, increasingly observed in young people, is a threat to personal health and wellbeing. Video games that encourage physical exercise, or exergames in short, offer a fun and engaging way to stay active.

With the rapid advancement and growing accessibility, including declining hardware costs, VR technologies captivate an ever-growing audience. For instance, its utilisation is also gaining momentum in schools. Studies by Berger et al. (2022), Curcio (2022) and Keller et al. (2018, 2022) present a selection of individual use cases in education. Despite this, the adoption of VR in the specific domain of school-based special and inclusive education remains limited. However, it is becoming increasingly important, including to the group of students with autism spectrum disorders (Bradley & Newbutt 2018; Schulz & Skeide Fuglerud 2022) and with intellectual impairments (Bjelic & Keller 2021; Ip et al. 2018).

Like Keller et al. (2023) and the "Virtual Reality for Children with Special Needs" project by Bosse et al. (2022), this paper addresses students on the autistic spectrum as well as students with other diagnoses in the special focus of mental development. It focuses specifically on the aspect of physical education for young students. We examine their reaction to being exposed to VR in form of three newly developed exergames as well as potential positive effects on the students' everyday life. For this we work with a remedial teacher and children of the Vivala school[1]. A positive outcome would mean that the children can get accustomed to the technology of VR at an early age. This opens doors to versatile educational tools for different fields, as virtual experiences enable new teaching and learning concepts as part of contemporary media education (Buchner 2021).

The paper is structured as follows: Section 2 describes the situation in the application domain of inclusive, physical education as well as the objectives for this project. Section 3 describes the methodology and Sect. 4 the design of a prototype consisting of the three exergames. Section 5 introduces our observational field study to evaluate the prototype and presents our findings. Finally, the paper is concluded with Sect. 6.

2   Initial Situation and Objective

AR and VR have garnered significant attention in educational research over recent years. The utilisation of these technologies enhances cognitive, affective, and psychomotor learning objectives, as demonstrated by various systematic reviews and meta-analyses. Among these, Chang et al. (2022) as well as Garzón and Acevedo (2019) specifically investigate the impact of AR on education, while Howard et al. (2021) examines the effectiveness of (non-)immersive VR training programs. Wu et al. (2020) explicitly focus on the impact of immersive VR using Head Mounted Displays (HMDs) compared to non-immersive VR. They conclude that immersive VR using HMDs is generally more effective, but that learning implementation and research design pose a critical factor in this assessment and HMDs work best as a complement in certain areas. Ultimately, these meta-analyses consistently demonstrate a consensus stating a positive impact of AR and VR on learning attitudes and perception. However, for the biggest impact it is crucial for specific domain-knowledge to inform the choice which form of AR or VR to use and to guide the learning design.

A relevant domain for this paper is exercising and physical education. Surveys such as Lamprecht et al. (2020) indicate a decrease in young people engaging in sport due to stress, lack of time and long working hours. Yet, sport remains important to prevent illnesses caused by a lack of exercise and to compensate for insufficient physical

---

[1] https://www.vivala.ch/.

activity as well as one-sided physical strain (Staatssekretariat für Bildung, Forschung und Innovation SBFI, 2014). In short, sport and exercise are essential components of health and wellbeing. Innovative solutions are required to tackle the lack of exercise in individuals. Several approaches incorporate new technologies including AR and VR. Mouatt et al. (2020) summarise and evaluate existing literature to demonstrate the influence of VR on motivation, affect, enjoyment, and engagement during exercise. They conclude that highly immersive VR has more beneficial effects than exercise without VR or even low immersive VR. Sauchelli and Brunstrom (2022) highlight the specific benefit that incorporating VR into exercise routines enhances the emotional experience of physical activity among inactive adults and even diminishes their subsequent food intake. VR technology holds promise in encouraging adults, especially those prone to overeating after exercise, to become more physically active. Lin et al. (2019) provide evidence supporting the use of VR treatment in relieving pain, increasing joint mobility, and improving motor function in patients with chronic musculoskeletal disorders. In their systematic review, Moeinzadeh et al. (2023) present statistically significant effects of VR-exergaming in aiding the recovery of physical and cognitive abilities and maintaining quality of life, reducing fatigue, and enhancing psychological well-being among Multiple Sclerosis (MS) patients.

Such new approaches are especially important to the group of students with special needs. Doing sports and exercise has a particular relevance to their health and wellbeing because the promotion of physical and motoric development as well as the encouragement of physical activity are central aspects of the support and teaching of this group (Jennessen & Lelgemann, 2016). At the same time, digitally assisted teaching concepts can significantly expand the educational opportunities for physically impaired students by significantly expanding the didactic options for teachers, even if adaptations and the use of assistive technologies are often required (Bergeest & Boenisch, 2019).

There are several approaches of applying exergames of various degrees of immersion to improve skills of students with intellectual and developmental disabilities. An AR system developed by Lin and Chang (2015) motivates and assists students to perform physical activities like stepping. Both, the system's guidance and feedback, affected the students' bodily engagement and motivation. The study also finds that the interface interaction in AR is significant for people with disabilities. While Lin and Chang only use a webcam and an interface designed in Scratch 2.0, Gatica-Rojas et al. (2017a) investigate the effectiveness of the Wii Balance Board. They show that training sessions incorporating the device can improve standing balance of children with cerebral palsy type spastic hemiplegia. In the space of immersive VR, McMahon et al. (2020) used a VR exergame to increase physical activity in individuals. Schmidt and Glaser (2021) applied a design research approach to develop an inclusive VR system for persons with autism spectrum disorder (ASD). Their paper seeks to address gaps in research on the use of VR for individuals with ASD and the lack of design precedent as well as theoretical guidance. The multi-phase study shows that the participants enjoy the VR experience and successfully practice learning objectives relevant in ASD training programs. Children with ASD are more prone to develop social phobia. This anxiety problem is likely to guide their behaviour in social interaction (Deckers et al., 2014). It appears likely, that the experience of stress and fear in social interaction, which children have already had in their life, now works as a trigger: All the stressful emotions are reactivated, when the situation is similar to the situation where they have felt stress and anxiety. In a study about the perception of fear and stress symptoms, Hoffarth et al. (2023) measured a reduction of stress symptoms and perception of users with ASD when they could practice in a virtual environment. They seemed to find the virtual situation helpful. Ke et al. (2022) also report positive results of VR training systems when used with persons with ASD on the facilitation of social skills.

In summary, AR and VR are promising technologies in the field of intellectual and physical education. Existing studies and analyses show persistently positive effects on learning to various degrees depending heavily on the interface design. Results of studies including students with ASD are favourable as well. Nevertheless, experiences and knowledge in this domain remain sparse. This paper seeks to further study the potential of immersive VR with focus on children with special needs. The objective is to investigate their reaction to VR as well as the acceptance of HMDs and to find which factors keep the children engaged. This works towards the aim of promoting sustainable health by integrating AR and VR deeper into children's education and in turn, playfully build the students' health-related competencies to do sports and exercise. Our hypothesis is that the nature of exergames in VR adds fun to exercises and therefore motivates the player to physical activity without being fully aware of exercising due to the immersion. We argue that with this approach the children are engaged for a longer period of time compared to classical methods and their attention span is extended. Additionally, we observe the children's attraction to VR over time.

3 Methodology

From a computer science perspective, our approach is based on a combination of evolutionary prototyping (Sherrell 2013) and iterative design to develop a final prototype consisting of three exergames. We adapt these principles by integrating the methodological insights of the SELFMADE project by Bosse and Pelka (2020). This allows the participation and self-determination of students with special needs.

The development process commences with the input and initial requirements gleaned from a needs analysis conducted with a professional remedial teacher from the Vivala school. In the initial stage, a rudimentary prototype is refined based on feedback received on two occasions from two children with special needs aged 12 and 13, as well as the remedial teacher. During this co-creation process we follow the six principles of design thinking (Plattner et al., 2012):

1. Understanding: Initially, one needs to comprehend and define the problem as well as the desired outcome.
2. Observation: The second step helps to refine the understanding of the problem through user observation. This provides insights into their needs, priorities and processes that could be improved.
3. Point of view: The insights gathered in the first two steps are amalgamated to define the point of view.
4. Brainstorming: Various ideas are developed and analysed.
5. Prototype: A potential solution is further developed in the form of a prototype.

6. Testing: Feedback for the prototype is collected and incorporated into further development to deliver an optimised and user-centric solution.

The resulting intermediate prototype is then used in a field study (further described in Sect. 5), which is conducted weekly over a two-month period with six children aged seven to nine from a different class at the Vivala school. After each session, the children are asked simple questions regarding their perception and whether they would like to alter the procedure. Iterative changes are made to the prototype based on their feedback and our observations to investigate the question what keeps the children engaged. In addition, the staff of the Vivala school is asked to note any perceived changes regarding the behaviour of the participants.

4   Design of the Prototype

4.1   Hardware and Software

A primary concern about the prototype is its accessibility as it is aimed at children, especially those with special needs, such as children with cerebral palsy. Controllers of conventional HMDs are often too large for children's hands and difficult or even impossible to hold for people with physical impairments. Additionally, due to the nature of exergames a lot of movement is involved, which expresses the need for a standalone solution. A wired connection to a computer is too limiting and distracting, as also confirmed by feedback during the development of the initial prototype. As a lower priority, there is also an economic aspect if this technology is to be widely adopted by schools. Considering these points, the prototype is developed for the Oculus Quest 2[2]. It eliminates the need for controllers in our prototype completely by natively supporting hand tracking and it is an HMD that can be used without a connection to a computer. The prototype also works on the more advanced (but also more expensive) Quest Pro and the Quest 3, which was released towards the end of this project.

On the software side, the prototype is implemented using **Unity**[3] version 2022.3.7 (LTS) with C#. The hand tracking is done with the **XR Hands** package (1.3.0) while interactions are based on the **XR Interaction Toolkit** (2.5.1). As a backbone, the **OpenXR Plugin** (1.7.0) is used. This would allow for the prototype to be ported to a different platform supported by OpenXR, needing a relatively low effort as long as the new platform supports hand tracking, of course. Lastly, various assets from the unity assetstore[4] are used for 3D models as well as a Mixamo[5] character as a player avatar, which then uses a standard animation rig. The hands of the model are removed and replaced by the XR Hands models, which carry the pose of the player's real hands. An attempt to apply the hand pose received by the hand tracking to the model hands visually failed due to the two different hand models having different amount of differently placed bones. Our approach can lead to gaps between the hands and arms, especially when stretching.

---

[2] https://www.meta.com/ch/en/quest/products/quest-2/.

[3] https://unity.com/.

[4] https://assetstore.unity.com/.

[5] https://www.mixamo.com/.

Nevertheless, to keep the prototype accessible and simple to use, a manual setup phase of the avatar, during which the player has to adopt a pose, is omitted. However, there is an initial scaling applied to it automatically. For this, the height above the floor of the HMD is the determining factor. The character model is scaled in such a way that the eyes of the model align with the HMD when the feet are placed on the ground. While this does assume the player is standing upright at the beginning, we find this a good trade-off between simplicity/accessibility and visual appearance.

4.2   Content

For the prototype there are four scenes created in Unity. These consist of one lobby scene and three different exergames. In each, the player performs movements to interact with a type of object in a specific way.

Lobby. Upon start-up, the player is placed in the lobby (Fig. 1). There are four main components present besides the player avatar:

- Static environment: Besides a skybox, there is a very simple play area consisting of textured planes. Children with ASD (like children with ADHD) often show highly sensitive perceptual processing of light and sound stimuli. They quickly become overwhelmed by incoming perceptions. This would cause a stress reaction in the brain's limbic system (Rollet and Kastner-Koller, 2001). The environment therefore remains the same in each game. It is deliberately kept simple to avoid overwhelming the children. It is important that they feel comfortable in their own world and that they are not overloaded with stimuli.
- Animals and progress bar: In the final prototype, there are three different animals and a progress bar in front of the player. While the player is in the lobby, the animals have a static size. When starting a game, the animals shrink to their minimum size, configurable in the Unity editor before compiling. Each time the player executes a successful interaction one of the animals gets some food and starts to eat and grow a step until they reach their maximum size. If an interaction is unsuccessful, one of the animals shrinks again. The number of growing steps can also be easily configured before compilation.

  Commercial games often use reward systems that have the purpose to get the brain to eject dopamine. This hormone stimulates the concentration and zeal on the game. But dopamine is highly addictive, too (Weinstein et al., 2017). A high concentration of dopamine in a child's brain can have negative influence on the social behaviour of children (Vinopal, 2024). With the animals we deliberately want to avoid an unhealthy rewards system. The intent behind the animals is to give the children some playful motivation and an intuitive sense of progress independent of the progress bar. Once all animals reach their maximum size and the progress bar is full, the player reaches the next level.

- Game selection buttons: There are three big buttons with an object hovering above each, which symbolises each game. The buttons can easily be pushed with the index finger of either hand to start a game.

- Menu table: Lastly, there is a menu table located behind the player. In the lobby it is empty besides a button, which ends the app.

Fig. 1. Lobby Scene (without player avatar)

Buttons. In the first level, the player has a wall of nine buttons in front of them (Fig. 2). Level 2 adds more rows and columns of buttons and level 3 places them further apart from each other to increase the necessary movement. Whenever a button lights up yellow, the player has to push it with one of their index fingers. A successful interaction is whenever they achieve to do so. An unsuccessful interaction is only possible if the timed mode is activated, in which buttons only stay active for a limited duration. The duration is decreased and increased on every successful and unsuccessful interaction.

Another mode, which can be separately activated, needs the player to push the button with the correct hand. For this, the hand models are coloured in red (left) and blue (right) (Fig. 3). The buttons light up in either of these colours or yellow, in which case either hand can be used. The button to (de-)activate these modes are located on the menu table (Fig. 4). The menu table also allows the player to choose an order of activation. One can choose from either *random*, *in order* or *shuffled*, which means every object is randomly

Fig. 2. Buttons scene with the top left button active

activated once before the next iteration starts. There exists also the possibility to create custom patterns for this game, which might be useful for a physical therapist or remedial teacher.

In contrast to the buttons in the lobby, these buttons are smaller and hence, more difficult to push. Making them bigger or allowing pushing with the whole hand is deliberately avoided to train **coordination**. The coloured mode requires the use of both hands alternatingly. Most children have a dominant hand, which they prefer to use. The other hand is used less, so there is less training effect on the brain side that coordinates this hand. The coloured mode gives training opportunities for a wide range of movements to be coordinated by motor neurons, which are normally less active.

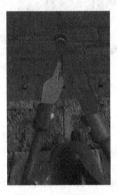

Fig. 3. Button scene player perspective: Avatar with coloured hands

Fig. 4. Menu table in the button scene

Catch the Ball. The second game is conceptually rather simple. The player faces several basketballs, which start flying towards them one after another (Fig. 5). Again, there are the three patterns *random*, *ordered* and *shuffle*. For a successful interaction the player simply touches the basketball. This increases the speed of the next ball. Missing the basketball is an unsuccessful interaction and the speed is decreased. To stimulate **movement** in the player, the target the ball moves towards deviates randomly from a central point.

Adaptable parameters to fine-tune the difficulty in this game are the minimum and maximum speeds and the deviation distance from the centre.

Level 2 adds three more basketballs to either side of the player, such that they need to be more aware of their surroundings. In level 3, up to two basketballs can fly towards the player at the same time, which requires the player to plan their movement and sometime engage in decision making, which ball they want to catch.

Fig. 5. Catch the ball scene with a flying basketball (left)

Throw the Ball. In this last game, the player has to throw a small basketball through some circular targets (Fig. 6). It can be picked up with either hand by a pinch of the thumb and index finger (Fig. 7). The player then must do a throwing movement and release the ball at the right moment. A limitation of the hand tracking is that during the throw, the hand needs to be always visible to the camera. Otherwise, the ball is dropped. While the player basically can stand at the same place the whole time and does not need to move much, the throwing demands coordination and **concentration**. For this game we decided again not to have unsuccessful interactions as a standard due to the difficulty, increased at times by imprecisions of the tracking during the throwing movement. However, there

Fig. 6. Throw the ball scene

is a timed mode again, which can be activated the same way as in the buttons game. A successful interaction is to throw the ball through the target.

There are five different levels for this game. In the first level, all targets are stationary at the same height. Level 2 starts to move the targets up and down. Level 3 makes the targets smaller, while level 4 places them a little bit further away from the player. Lastly, in level 5 there is a moving wall, which poses as an obstacle.

Fig. 7. Throw the ball player perspective: grab the ball with a pinch

5 The Field Study

5.1 Setup

The field study starting with the intermediate prototype had been conducted on-site at the Vivala school. Six children participated in seven sessions each over the span of two months. The group consisted of two girls and four boys aged from seven to nine with ADHD, ADD or Cerebral Palsy and one child currently undergoing assessment for ASD. They each were allotted time slots of half an hour to play the three games.

During the first session the prototype was quickly explained. After that the children were given the freedom to decide for themselves how to spend their time. Other than helping whenever problems occurred, the only intervention was to encourage the children to play all three games. Naturally, they were allowed to not play or stop playing earlier e.g. if they were tired.

Our findings are based on observations during these sessions and interviews directly after. The children were asked how they liked each game and what they would like to have changed or added. We started to implement feedback with some specific changes after the third session, because we observed a declining interest.

5.2 Session Observations

Weeks 1–3. The initial reaction to immersive VR was largely positive. Most children were excited to step into the virtual worlds and showed no problems like motion sickness or stimulus overload. However, even though the children will be immersed in a completely different world, we think that the well-known surrounding and support are important for the children. One child only wanted to put on the headset after some positive encouragement by the known support staff. Once playing, all children were heavily engaged in exploring the prototype and playing the games. For all children we even observed a higher attention span to the games than they show during classic educational sessions.

Unfortunately, by week 3 the novelty aspect had worn off. Even though the children still enjoyed spending time in VR, over the span of the three weeks the initial excitement decreased. Similarly, we observed the attention span to converge towards the same as experienced in school. For some children, the time spent in VR went from almost the whole half hour to their usual five to ten minutes.

By far the most popular game was catching the ball. Interestingly, despite coordinative difficulties, the child with cerebral palsy often played the buttons game and activated the hand mode himself. His "weak" hand, the side that is more affected by the cerebral palsy, came into the focus of his attention. He appeared eager to improve the coordination of that hand in the game.

Weeks 4–7. For the following sessions we adapted the prototype to see if the changes would motivate the children again. In the first weeks, we observed little effect of the animals as a motivation. To counter that, we increased the maximum size and reduced the number of growing steps, which makes a successful interaction more impactful. We also introduced a mechanic which makes the food not simply appear in front of the animal but flying from the player to it. This indeed made the children focus on the animals while the bigger size impressed them. Some children noticed the growing animals for a first time at this point, which had a motivating impact.

Since we observed that some children had stopped playing before reaching higher levels, we not only reduced the number of growing steps but also the number of animals. This leads to the player progressing more quickly. We generally observed the difficulty to be an important factor. Most children reacted positively to a challenge at first but gave up quickly when it became too inconvenient or hard. The addition of a progress bar somewhat counteracted this effect up to a point by giving a clearer goal.

Lastly, we introduced an additional reward. After completing the exergames session the children were allowed to paint (also in VR). Sometimes, this motivated the children to perform well in the games while at other times it made them focus on the reward. Overall, the popularity of catching the ball shifted towards throwing the ball.

5.3 Findings

In addition to our observations being based on a small number of participants, the reactions of the children to the exergames were highly heterogeneous. Not only were there big differences between children but also between the same child's responses across different sessions. Hence, it is difficult to form universal statements and to prove them. Nevertheless, we conclude that the children generally react immensely positive to immersive VR and that they have no problem in adopting this technology. Due to the hand tracking, the prototype was usable and accessible by every child of the Vivala class.

Like the consensus of papers mentioned in Sect. 2, our observations show similarly positive results for the early ages of seven to nine years. The children can be motivated to engage in exercises or training motor activity. According to the school staff, the attention spans of the participants were noticeably longer at the beginning than the attention spans in everyday school lessons. This effect wore off over time and the attention spans decreased. However, they did never fall under the spans the participants showed in class. Following this observation, several changes were made in the game design. The attention span increased again. The most when something new was added. This means once the novelty factor of the specific game fades, some thoughtful considerations on how to keep up the engagement are needed.

Due to the heterogeneous responses, the measures and additions should be adapted to the player. An important and easily adaptable factor is the difficulty. Some children already choose their own challenge by selecting a specific game, such as the button game or changing from catching the ball to throwing the ball, which seems to be more difficult. Other children are quickly frustrated. Ideally, difficulty is changed automatically more heavily during playing or between the games by a teacher or the player themself. There is also the possibility to introduce a competitive component in which the challenge would be to reach a high score. However, at this point we consciously avoided any kind of scoring because we did not want to introduce competition among the children. Since we did not know how the children would react, our main priority was not to overwhelm them or induce potentially bad emotions. As mentioned earlier, none of the children showed any problem being overstrained. In fact, as seen by the increasing of the maximum animal size, the children reacted even positively to bigger changes.

In the end, the class teacher could not observe a long-lasting impact of the games on the behaviour of the participants in other school lessons. However, he described, how high the motivation of the children before every project lesson was. They were looking forward to that sequence. All in all, he confirmed the observation that the attention span and the motivation during the game was above the normal level.

6   Conclusion

The field study with our prototype shows a very high acceptance of VR with HMDs and effectiveness in motivating the children at a young age. For this group, our concern in overwhelming the children with audiovisual inputs were not met. In fact, the lack of stimuli led to a fast decrease in engagement once the novelty factor wore off. While we ultimately also did not observe a lasting increase in attention span, immersive VR is still a great tool. Besides the possibility to create virtual games, which would not be easily realisable physically, the additional value is a general fascination of the technology by the children, its accessibility as well as many possibilities to fine tune and customise the experience to each child.

Going forward we can see VR exergames being used in two different ways. One possibility would be to treat them more like exercises, which the children have to do like tasks in school. The sessions would need to be more guided by a teacher who might also work with external rewards. From our point of view, the more desirable possibility would be to further develop more diverse, complex and challenging exergames to avoid the games becoming repetitive and motivate the children on their own. The participation of experienced professionals such as remedial teachers or physical therapists in this process is also highly desirable to ensure educationally meaningful games. Since the heterogeneity of the children is high, adaptability (e.g. in difficulty) is crucial. A side effect of this heterogeneity as well as the small number of subjects is that the universal statements are difficult to prove. More work is needed in this field to gain an extensive insight about immersive VR used in the diverse field of special education. However, our observations strongly imply that findings regarding design of exergames in VR can be extended to children with special needs at a young age.

References

Bergeest, H., Boenisch, J.: Körperbehindertenpädagogik: Grundlagen - Förderung – Inklusion, 6th edn. Verlag Julius Klinkhardt, Bad Heilbrunn (2019)

Berger, M., Kraus, K., Keller, T., Brucker-Kley, E., Knaack, R.: Virtuelle Lernumgebungen in der betrieblichen Ausbildung – eine Analyse am Beispiel der Elektrobranche in der Schweiz — Bwp@ Berufs- und Wirtschaftspädagogik — Online (2022). https://www.bwpat.de/ausgabe/43/berger-etal

Bjelic, D., Keller, T.: Preliminary findings of a virtual reality app for children with special needs, pp. 350–354 (2021). https://digitalcollection.zhaw.ch/handle/11475/23504

Bosse, I., Pelka, B.: Selbstbestimmte und individualisierte Fertigung von Alltagshilfen per 3D-Druck für Menschen mit Behinderungen. Orthopädie Technik **71**(2), 42–48 (2020)

Bosse, I.K., Haffner, M., Keller, T.: Virtual reality for children with special needs. In: ICCHP-AAATE 2022 Open Access Compendium "Assistive Technology, Accessibility and Inclusion" Part I (2022). https://doi.org/10.35011/icchp-aaate22-p1-09

Bradley, R., Newbutt, N.: Autism and virtual reality head-mounted displays: a state of the art systematic review. J. Enabling Technol. (2018)

Buchner, J.: Generative learning strategies do not diminish primary students' attitudes towards augmented reality. Educ. Inf. Technol. **27**(1), 701–717 (2021). https://doi.org/10.1007/s10639-021-10445-y

Chang, H.-Y., et al.: Ten years of augmented reality in education: a meta-analysis of (quasi-) experimental studies to investigate the impact. Comput. Educ. **191**, 104641 (2022). https://doi.org/10.1016/j.compedu.2022.104641

Curcio, R.: Router Learning Unit (2022). https://osf.io/tvd86/

Deckers, A., Roelofs, J., Muris, P., Rinck, M.: Desire for social interaction in children with autism spectrum disorders. Res. Autism Spectr. Disord. Spectr. Disord. **8**(4), 449–453 (2014)

Garzón, J., Acevedo, J.: Meta-analysis of the impact of augmented reality on students' learning gains. Educ. Res. Rev. **27**, 244–260 (2019). https://doi.org/10.1016/j.edurev.2019.04.001

Gatica-Rojas, V., et al.: Effectiveness of a Nintendo Wii balance board exercise programme on standing balance of children with cerebral palsy: a randomised clinical trial protocol. Contemp. Clin. Trials Commun. **6**, 17–21 (2017). https://doi.org/10.1016/j.conctc.2017.02.008

Gatica-Rojas, V., Méndez-Rebolledo, G., Guzman-Muñoz, E., Soto-Poblete, A., Cartes-Velásquez, R., Elgueta-Cancino E.: Does Nintendo Wii balance board improve standing balance? A randomized controlled trial in children with cerebral palsy. Eur. J. Phys. Rehabil. Med. **53**, 535–5344 (2017). https://doi.org/10.23736/S1973-9087.16.04447-6

Hoffarth, E., Zinn, B.: Entwicklung der Anwendung der virtuellen Realität eines Arztbesuches. In: Workshops der 21. Fachtagung Bildungstechnologien, pp. 1–216, Gesellschaft für Informatik, Bonn (2023). https://doi.org/10.18420/wsdelfi2023-26

Howard, M.C., Gutworth, M.B., Jacobs, R.R.: A meta-analysis of virtual reality training programs. Comput. Hum. Behav. **121**, 106808 (2021). https://doi.org/10.1016/j.chb.2021.106808

Ip, H.H., et al.: Enhance emotional and social adaptation skills for children with autism spectrum disorder: a virtual reality enabled approach. Comput. Educ. **117**, 1–15 (2018)

Jennessen, S., Lelgemann, R.: Körper—Behinderung—Pädagogik, 1st edn. Kohlhammer, Stuttgart (2016)

Ke, F., Moon, J., Sokolikj, Z.: Virtual reality-based social skills training for children with autism spectrum disorder. J. Spec. Educ. Technol. **37**(1), 49–62 (2022). https://doi.org/10.1177/016 2643420945603

Keller, T., Glauser, P., Ebert, N., Brucker-Kley, E: Virtual reality at secondary school–first results. In: Proceedings of the 15th International Conference on Cognition and Exploratory Learning in the Digital Age (CELDA 2018), pp. 53–60 (2018)

Keller, T., Botchkovoi, S., Brucker-Kley, E.: Findings from a field experiment with a VR learning unit. In: International Conference on Educational Technologies 2022 (2022)

Keller, T., Guyer, S., Manoharan, V., Bosse, I.: Preliminary Findings About an Office Chair as a Low-Threshold Treadmill Substitute. In: Antona, M., Stephanidis, C. (eds.) Universal Access in Human-Computer Interaction. HCII 2023. LNCS, vol. 14021, pp. 17–28. Springer, Cham. (2023) https://doi.org/10.1007/978-3-031-35897-5_2

Lamprecht, M., Bürgi, R., Gebert, A., Stamm, H.: Sport Schweiz 2020. Kinder- und Jugendbericht. Bundesamt für Sport BASPO (2021)

Lin, C.-Y., Chang, Y.-M.: Interactive augmented reality using Scratch 2.0 to improve physical activities for children with developmental disabilities. Res. Dev. Disabil. **37**, 1–8. (2015) https://doi.org/10.1016/j.ridd.2014.10.016

Lin, H., Yen-I, L., Wen-Pin, H., Chun-Cheng H., Yi-Chun, D.: A scoping review of the efficacy of virtual reality and exergaming on patients of musculoskeletal system disorder. J. Clin. Med. **8**(6), 791 (2019). https://doi.org/10.3390/jcm8060791

McMahon, D.D., Barrio, B., McMahon, A.K., Tutt, K., Firestone, J.: Virtual reality exercise games for high school students with intellectual and developmental disabilities. J. Spec. Educ. Technol. **35**(2), 87–96 (2020). https://doi.org/10.1177/0162643419836416

Moeinzadeh, A.M., Calder, A., Petersen, C., Hoermann, S., Daneshfar, A.: Comparing virtual reality exergaming with conventional exercise in rehabilitation of people with multiple sclerosis: a systematic review. Neuropsychol. Rehabil. **33**(8), 1430–1455 (2023) https://doi.org/10.1080/09602011.2022.2107021

Mouatt, B., Smith, A., Mellow, M., Parfitt, G., Smith, R., Stanton, T.: The use of virtual reality to influence motivation, affect, enjoyment, and engagement during exercise: a scoping review. Front. Virtual Reality **1** (2020). https://doi.org/10.3389/frvir.2020.564664

Plattner, H., Christoph, M., Larry, L.: Design Thinking Research: Studying Co-Creation in Practice, 1st edn. Springer, Heidelberg (2012). https://doi.org/10.1007/978-3-642-21643-5_1

Rollett, B., Kastner-Koller, U.: Autismus – Ein Leitfaden für Eltern, Erzieher, Lehrer und Therapeuten., Jena: Urban und Fischer, München (2001)

Sauchelli, S., Brunstrom, J.: Virtual reality exergaming improves affect during physical activity and reduces subsequent food consumption in inactive adults. Appetite **175**, 106058 (2022). https://doi.org/10.1016/j.appet.2022.106058

Schmidt, M., Glaser, N.: Investigating the usability and learner experience of a virtual reality adaptive skills intervention for adults with autism spectrum disorder. Educ. Tech. Res. Dev. **69**(3), 1665–1699 (2021). https://doi.org/10.1007/s11423-021-10005-8

Schulz, T., Skeide Fuglerud, K.: Creating a robot-supported education solution for children with autism spectrum disorder. In: Miesenberger, K., Kouroupetroglou, G., Mavrou, K., Manduchi, R., Covarrubias Rodriguez, M., Penáz, P. (eds.) ICCHP-AAATE 2022. LNCS, vol. 13342, pp. 211–218. Springer, Cham (2022). https://doi.org/10.1007/978-3-031-08645-8_25

Sherrell, L.: Evolutionary prototyping. In: Runehov, A.L.C., Oviedo, L. (eds.) Encyclopedia of Sciences and Religions, p. 803. Springer, Netherlands (2013) https://doi.org/10.1007/978-1-4020-8265-8_201039

Staatssekretariat für Bildung, Forschung und Innovation SBFI: Rahmenlehrplan für Sport in der beruflichen Grundbildung (2014)

Vinopal, L.: How screen time creates kid dopamine addicts with bad habits. https://www.fatherly.com/health/screen-time-hurts-kids-dopamine-addiction. Accessed 19 Jan 2024

Weinstein, A., Livnz, A., Weizman, A.: New developments in brain research of internet and gaming disorder. Neurosci. Biobehav. Rev. **75**, 314–330 (2017). https://doi.org/10.1016/j.neubiorev.2017.01.040

Wu, B., Yu, X., Gu, X.: Effectiveness of immersive virtual reality using head-mounted displays on learning performance: a meta-analysis. Br. J. Edu. Technol. **51**(6), 1991–2005 (2020). https://doi.org/10.1111/bjet.13023

An Evaluation of Portuguese to Libras Translator Apps Applied to the Medical Context

Julia Manuela G. Soares[iD], Isabel F. de Carvalho[iD], Elidéa L. A. Bernardino[iD], Milena Soriano Marcolino[iD], and Raquel Oliveira Prates[(✉)][iD]

Federal University of Minas Gerais, Belo Horizonte, Minas Gerais 31270-901, Brazil
{juliamanu,elidea,milenamarc}@ufmg.br, rprates@dcc.ufmg.br

Abstract. With over 2.4 million Brazilians experiencing hearing loss, effective communication between deaf individuals and healthcare professionals is crucial but still faces various barriers. Existing studies highlight shortcomings in the availability of interpreters and in the proficiency in Brazilian Sign Language (Libras) by healthcare professionals, leading to a dependency on imperfect methods of communication and compromising patient autonomy and care quality. Although the technological advancements are promising, including automatic translation tools, they still have limitations, particularly in the context of medical communication. This paper evaluates three popular Brazilian applications - HandTalk®, Rybená®, and VLibras®- aimed at translating Brazilian Portuguese to Libras, employing both Semiotic Inspection Method (SIM) analysis and evaluation of translation quality in medical contexts. Overall, SIM analysis revealed good communicability, albeit, with occasional breakdowns, while translation evaluations uncovered numerous issues ranging from minor to critical, potentially impacting patient understanding and health. Our findings point to critical deficits in existing translation apps, emphasizing the urgent need for improvements adapted to medical settings and bidirectional translation capabilities. By shedding light on these challenges, our study contributes to the advancement of accessible healthcare for deaf individuals and the development of more effective translation technologies.

Keywords: Deaf · Sign language · Libras · Translator app · Health · Medical context · Deaf patient · Health professional

1 Introduction

In Brazil there are over 2.4 million Brazilians with hearing loss [1], which raises concerns about communication barriers between deaf and hearing people, especially in critical situations, such as the health context. Some studies carried out in recent years have reported on the difficulties of deaf patients in hospital settings [6,10,17,22,24,26]. Among the problems described are the lack of interpreters and the health professionals' lack of knowledge of the Brazilian Sign Language

M. Antona and C. Stephanidis (Eds.): HCII 2024, LNCS 14698, pp. 290–304, 2024.
https://doi.org/10.1007/978-3-031-60884-1_20

(Libras). The absence of interpreters forces patients to rely on family members or acquaintances to serve as translators, compromising their autonomy, independence, and privacy. Additionally, the lack of training of health professionals in Libras affects the healthcare experience of deaf patients, with many expressing frustration due to ineffective communication with these professionals. Although techniques such as lip-reading, written communication or the help of third parties may allow for some interaction, they have limitations that range from a lack of emotional connection to the omission of important information about their state of health, potentially leading to misdiagnosis and impacting patients' treatments outcomes, prognosis, and quality of life.

On the other hand, technological advances have brought new tools to make life easier for users, including automatic translators from Brazilian Portuguese to Libras. However, despite these tools having many advantages, there are some inherent limitations, mainly in the sense of the translations themselves - considering that they translate in only one direction (Brazilian Portuguese to Libras) and that the translation is between two languages with significantly different bases, oral and signs. As a result, there have been studies that have addressed the quality of automatic Portuguese to Libras translations [15,16] and others that have focused on identifying *mHealth* apps that could support the communication between health professionals and deaf patients [3]. However, to the best of our knowledge, there have been no studies that present a systematic analysis of the Portuguese-to-Libras applications in the context of medical care.

Considering machine translation technologies and communication barriers in the medical context between deaf people and health professionals, the goal of this paper is to describe the evaluation of three popular Brazilian applications: HandTalk®[1], Rybená®[2] and VLibras®[3], which aim to translate written/oral content in Brazilian Portuguese into Libras. The evaluation is divided into two phases: (i) Analysis of the systems using the Semiotic Inspection Method (SIM) [20,21]; (ii) Evaluation of the quality of the applications' translations in a medical context.

SIM is an inspection method [20,21], which focuses on examining the system's communicability [19], that is, how well the system conveys to users its design intention and principles. To evaluate the quality of the translations in a medical context, a corpus created by health professionals to represent the main sentences (questions and answers) in a medical appointment was used. In our evaluation, we focused on a set of 48 questions relevant in medical anamnesis and translated them using each application. Two specialists fluent in both Brazilian Portuguese and Libras analyzed the translation taking into consideration a set of linguistic criteria, and classified the problems found according to their severity as minor, major or critical, or as understandable - when no translation problem was identified.

---

[1] https://www.handtalk.me/en/.
[2] https://rybena.com.br/.
[3] https://www.vlibras.com.br/.

Our results show that in general the communicability of the systems was good, and users could interact easily. Nonetheless, for one of the apps the avatar's behavior indicated some sociability issues that could impact users' experience negatively. With regard to the quality of the translation, our analyses identified several problems, including critical problems that could cause users to misunderstand the intended sentence or not understand it all. Thus, significant translation problems were identified, which means that the use of these systems in medical contexts could impact deaf patients' health and even generate life-threatening situations.

Our findings contribute to the accessibility challenges faced by deaf people in medical contexts, and to the research and development of automatic Portuguese-Libras systems that could support their communication with hearing health professionals. Regarding Brazilian Portuguese to Libras translation apps, the problems identified could be used to improve existing apps or guide new ones that take into account the medical context. Furthermore, it points to the need for technology that could provide a bidirectional translation (not only Brazilian Portuguese to Libras), to allow for actual communication between deaf patients and hearing doctors.

This paper is organized into 6 sections. Section 2 presents related works on the challenges faced by the deaf in medical care and evaluations of automatic translation systems for Brazilian Sign Language (Libras). In Sect. 3, the methodologies adopted for the analysis of the communicability of applications and the quality of the translations are described. The results are presented in Sect. 4 and discussed in Sect. 5. Finally, Sect. 6 provides the conclusions of this study.

2   Related Work

In this section, we present the related work organized into two main topics, addressing key aspects of our investigation. Firstly, we delve into the challenges faced by deaf patients in medical contexts (Sect. 2.1). Subsequently, we turn our attention to the evaluation of sign language translation apps (Sect. 2.2), exploring the technological landscape that seeks to facilitate communication for the deaf community and its limitations.

2.1   Challenges for Deaf Patients in Medical Context

Emergency situations are always challenging for both patients and health professionals. However, for deaf patients challenges are even greater due to communication barriers. Normally, hearing medical staff do not know sign language, which is a problem for deaf patients and generates dissatisfaction [22]. In the work of Vieira, Caniato, and Yonemotu [26], a questionnaire was administered, utilizing closed-ended questions to gather information about the perception of deaf patients regarding their healthcare experiences. The results revealed that the majority of respondents encounter difficulties in understanding and being understood by physicians. A significant number, 76.5%, reported not having their doubts clarified, reinforcing the existence of communicative barriers.

Furthermore, sometimes they have to reveal their very private and sensitive information to unknown people (such as professional interpreters) or even to family members. The situation is worsened by the fact that there is a scarcity of sign language interpreters dedicated to attending to deaf people in health services. This is reflected in the work of Rezende, Guerra, and Carvalho [17], who conducted a study with 124 deaf individuals to answer the open-ended question: "Do you have any suggestions to improve healthcare services for the deaf?". The results indicated that the fact that 39% of the respondents communicate solely through Brazilian Sign Language (Libras) is reflected in the suggestion for the presence of interpreters and healthcare professionals fluent in Libras. However, regarding the presence of an interpreter, many deaf individuals indicated feeling uncomfortable and embarrassed.

Another worthy-of-notice challenge is the fact that deaf people prefer to use sign language instead of reading/writing due to their poor written language skills [13]. This preference is reinforced by findings from [10], where a qualitative field research study revealed that only 27% of the surveyed deaf individuals had previous exposure to sign language during medical care. Notably, the majority of them emphasized the crucial importance of sign language, especially considering that merely 30% of them could comprehend writing and lip reading without significant difficulties. These insights collectively underscore the pivotal role of sign language in addressing the communication challenges faced by the deaf community in medical settings.

Although we have focused on studies that report on challenges faced the Brazilian deaf community, the communication barriers between deaf patients and medical professionals are experienced in other countries as well (e.g. [2,9,13,23]).

2.2 Evaluation of Sign Language Translation Apps

Currently, the ubiquitous presence of technology directs our focus to its assistive potential in enhancing communication for individuals who are deaf during medical consultations. In 2021, Ossada et al. [18] presented a systematic literature review reporting on the communication problems deaf individuals experience in medical contexts. The authors argued that the use of assistive technology could be helpful in this context, potentially addressing dissatisfaction reported by deaf individuals regarding communication in hospital settings and the discomfort caused by the presence of third parties to mediate this interaction. They identified 20 assistive technologies aimed at the deaf community that could potentially be used in this context to alleviate the listed problems. However, they merely indicate the technologies' potential for use in the medical context. They did not analyze them, nor did they identify other works reporting their use in medical contexts.

According to Naranjo-Zeledón et al. [11], the landscape of technologies facilitating sign language (SL) machine translation is complex, revealing key techniques, trends, and challenges. This highlights the need for regular updates to grammar bases and software systems underscoring the importance of continuous improvement and user-centered design in the development of translator apps tailored for medical communication in Portuguese to Libras context.

Focusing on evaluations of translation systems, some studies have been published in recent years. Considering the usability aspect of these applications, the work of Godoi et al. [8] addresses the interaction of deaf users with assistive technologies in mobile devices. They highlight the need for technologies that offer good interaction and make daily tasks easier to do. Their conclusions show that it is important to improve usability, user experience, and accessibility to minimize obstacles in the interaction with assistive technologies, providing an overall view to help in the development of future tech solutions for the deaf community. However, different from the present work, there is no focus on the specific context of healthcare.

In terms of translation evaluation, in [3], a cross-sectional and descriptive analysis of applications addressing Brazilian Sign Language, both in the Play Store and Apple Store, was conducted. The study aimed to identify possible systems that could be used as communication mediators in medical contexts. Their analyses focused on criteria based on educational health content for Libras. They concluded that apps were easy to use and, although not developed exclusively for the healthcare context, they could be an interesting alternative to aid in the communication process.

Finally, in the work of Reis et al. [15], three automatic translation applications were analyzed: HandTalk®, Rybená®, and VLibras®. The analysis focused on evaluating the translation of content from Brazilian Portuguese to Brazilian Sign Language. In the experiment, 30 interpreters analyzed and assessed how the systems addressed and treated 7 grammatical aspects in translations - a complex process, considering that if specific aspects are not treated correctly, they can greatly impact content comprehension and communication quality. As a result, they observed that the applications have limitations in terms of homonyms, adverbs (negation, mode, and intensity), directional verbs, and phrases (interrogative and exclamatory) and require future improvements. Different from this work, their study did not take into account the medical context.

3   Methodology

The methodology used in this study was divided into three stages: (i) the selection of the apps; (ii) the generation of the material for the evaluation; and (iii) the application of the evaluation methods.

The selection of the applications was based on the review of the literature to identify the existing systems that could translate Brazilian Portuguese into Libras, and the ones that were most commonly used in Brazil[4]. As a result, 3 applications were chosen: HandTalk®, Rybená®, and VLibras®. Figure 1

---

[4] Notice that different countries have different sign languages, even if they speak the same oral language [5]. For instance, Libras and other sign languages of Portuguese-speaking countries, e.g. *Língua Gestual Portuguesa - LGP* are very different.

depicts the interface of each of the three apps selected. We chose to analyze only Android versions of the applications, as 80.65% of the mobile devices in Brazil use Android operational system[5].

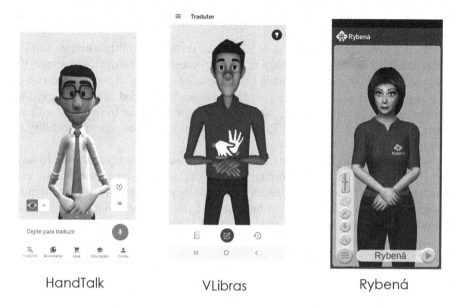

Fig. 1. Screenshot for HandTalk®, VLibras®, and Rybená®.

To evaluate the apps, a corpus consisting of a set of 48 medical sentences, formulated by medical specialists, was created. These sentences consisted of 48 questions that would commonly be asked in a medical consultation, such as: *"What are you feeling that made you come to the hospital?"*. The corpus was initially created by the medical experts in our research team and consolidated through a survey with other health professionals. This corpus enabled a more accurate investigation of the linguistic and terminological nuances present in the translation of medical phrases, contributing to the improvement of communication in this context.

Finally, two different analyses were conducted as an evaluation. In the first, we applied the Semiotic Inspection Method [20] in the selected apps, aiming to evaluate the communicability of the systems and to identify possible interaction issues. The second analysis consisted of evaluating the translations produced by the applications. Next, we describe how each analysis was conducted.

---

[5] See https://gs.statcounter.com/os-market-share/mobile/brazil (Last access January 2024).

3.1   Semiotic Inspection Method

The Semiotic Inspection Method (SIM) is based on the Semiotic Engineering Theory [19]. Its purpose consists of evaluating through inspection the communicability of a system, i.e. the system's property to convey to its users the decisions of the designer about who the system is intended for, what it can be used for, and how to interact with it [19].

Figure 2 presents an overview of SIM. The communicability analysis in SIM is composed of 5 steps: (1) analysis of the system's metalinguistic signs; (2) analysis of the system's static signs; (3) analysis of dynamic signs; (4) contrast of the reconstructed metamessages (i.e. the designer's intended message regarding who the system is intended for, what it serves for and how to interact with it) generated in steps (1), (2) and (3); (5) appreciation of the communicability of the system.

Note that signs may be defined as "anything that represents anything to anyone" [12]. The Semiotic Engineering Theory defines metalinguistic, static, and dynamic signs as being signs present in an interactive system [21]. Metalinguistic signs are signs that explain other signs of the interface (e.g. tooltips, help systems); static signs are those that represent the system's state (e.g. buttons); and dynamic signs represent the behavior of the system (e.g. the translation presented by an avatar if the button "play" is pressed in a translation app).

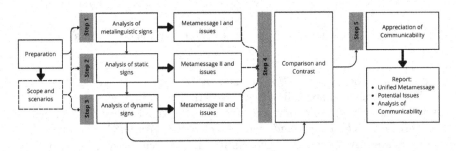

Fig. 2. Steps of the Semiotic Inspection Method.

3.2   Analysis of Translation Quality

To assess the quality of the translations in a medical context, a corpus of the main sentences (questions and answers) used in a medical consultation was created. The corpus contained 48 relevant questions, such as *"Where is the pain? What is the pain like?"*. These questions were translated using the applications.

For the analysis, two specialists, fluent in Brazilian Portuguese and Libras, analyzed the translations for each of these sentences by each of the three apps: HandTalk®, VLibras®, and Rybená®. Four linguistic criteria were assessed: a) use of non-explicit verb tense, (b) expression of question marker, (c) word order, and (d) choice of lexical items. The analysis of the translation of the medical corpus was conducted individually by each specialist on each of the translation apps. Based on the problems identified in each translation, each specialist categorized errors as **minor, major,** or **critical** (based on the TAUS model of evaluation [25]). **Minor errors** are perceived by the users but do not generate meaning loss; **major errors** generate (partial) meaning loss and could either confuse the users or hinder their understanding; finally, **critical errors** are those that prevent users from making sense of the sentence and could impose a risk to their health and well-being. When there were no problems found, the translation was categorized as **understandable.** Afterward, the results were discussed and consolidated by the specialists.

4   Results

In this section we present the results of our analyses: first the communicability issues generated by the analysis conducted with SIM, and then the translation issues identified.

4.1   Communicability Issues

As a result of our inspection with SIM, it was observed that all three applications adopted similar design and communication strategies. In each case, there is a noticeable emphasis on the use of dynamic signs, that is, signs that are related to the system's behavior. This emphasis encourages users to learn the system by exploring and interacting with it. In essence, designers seem to suggest that by exploring the system, users could comprehend the available functionalities and tools, as well as how to use them.

Beyond the dynamic signs, in HandTalk®️ and VLibras®️ applications, designers chose to clarify the most important functions using metalinguistic signs. HandTalk®️ features a tutorial that provides more detailed explanations of functions directly related to translation, while other possibilities are less explored in the tutorial, implying that designers consider that users are already familiar with them (e.g. downloading, logging in, etc.). In summary, the designers of HandTalk®️ and VLibras®️ focused on informing users about what they can do in the system rather than how to do it. An example of this is the speed icon in HandTalk that shows a metalinguistic sign explaining that users can "Increase or decrease the speed of the translation", but does not explain how to do it, leaving it to users to discover how it works.

For both of them, the meta-message conveyed was considered sufficient for the targeted users to understand what the system is for and how to use it. Overall their interface is simple and intuitive. Designers often chose to use static signs common in other systems, and that would already be known by users, making it easier for users to understand the intended meaning. In cases where there were static signs that might not be known, they opted to include a meta-linguistic sign that would explain the static sign.

Different from the other two, Rybená® does not include metalinguistic signs within the app itself. Meta-linguistic signs are mainly available on its download page from the app store. Furthermore, Rybená® presents less static signs in its interface, presenting a "cleaner" interface that focuses on the main translation functions of the system.

Although VLibras®, is considered easy to use, some of the design decisions regarding the avatar's behavior can be problematic and impact its sociability. For instance, when users did not activate it for some time, the avatar took on a bored expression, which could impact users' experience negatively.

4.2 Translation Issues

Although the applications are easy to access, we found a large number of problems in the translations generated by each of the apps. Figure 3 presents the overall results of the translation, indicating the category of the translation problems found for the medical corpus in each app. In our analysis, HandTalk® had the best performance, with the largest set of translated sentences considered understandable, and had fewer translation problems in the categories depicting errors. On the other hand, VLibras® and Rybená® had a similar performance, considering the classification of the translations, with Rybená® performing slightly better than VLibras®.

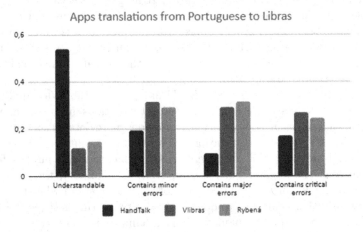

Fig. 3. Quality of apps translations from Portuguese to Libras

Although HandTalk® had the best performance, it still has many limitations. From all the sentences translated, half of them were understandable, the other half had some problems, and almost 20% presented critical errors. Thus, its use in the medical context could have negative impacts on patient-doctor communication and, as a result, generate damage to the deaf patients' health.

Due to space limitations, we will not present all the problems identified, but will illustrate some of the problems identified, and discuss their impact for users.

First, when the sentence in oral language presented non-explicit verb tense, HandTalk and Rybená inconsistently presented the sentence in the past tense by presenting a sign which means *"past"* in Libras. In other cases, the past tense was not translated, and the sentence was presented in the present tense in Libras. None of the apps showed an adequate non-explicit verb tense translation. Even though the verb tense was not correct, it was considered that deaf patients could understand the sentence's meaning, and the error was classified as a minor error.

Another problem frequently observed was the absence or inadequacy of facial expressions (such as the grammatical ones that are used for questions), which makes some of the translations difficult to understand. According to Quadros [14] and Figueiredo and Lourenço [7] *'wh'* questions (e.g. *who, when, what*, etc.) in Libras are made using a slight elevation of the head accompanied by a frown or lowering of the eyebrow. In yes/no type questions, there is a slight lowering of the head, accompanied by a raising of the eyebrows. These grammatical head movements in Libras spread over the sentence. One cannot do these only at the end of the sentence, as if it were a written question mark.

One app (VLibras®) opted to use a head elevation and protuberant lips to indicate the question mark, which seemed like that the avatar was sending a kiss, at the end of question sentences. After using the app for a while, it is possible that users could understand the "kiss" as a question. However, it is not an adequate sign for questions and it would not be guaranteed that users would reach its intended meaning. Therefore, this error was considered a major one, for confusing the users as to whether it was a question or an affirmative, and whether the marker done at the end was a kiss or not.

HandTalk® does a better job in translating *'wh'* questions. To do so, it changes the word order in the question, moving pronouns to the end of the sentences, as it is used in Libras, and thus, making it easier for a deaf person to understand. When translating a question, the avatar also made the gesture of a question mark in the air, at the end of the sentences, which facilitates understanding (this strategy is often used by deaf people, especially when communicating with hearing people). Thus, for HandTalk® posing a question was considered understandable.

Different from HandTalk®, VLibras® and Rybená® maintain the same word order of Portuguese in their translation, often generating a very odd sentence in Libras. Nonetheless, this problem alone was considered a minor problem, as deaf users would still be able to make sense of the translation.

Most critical errors observed were due to an inadequate choice of lexical items. The use of dactylology was observed, even when there are adequate signs for the translation; and mistaken translation due to the existence of two or more identical words in Portuguese, called cognates, are two types of critical errors of this nature. An example of problems with cognates was in the translation of the sentence *"Qual o tempo de duração da dor?"* or *"What is the duration time of the pain?"*. In Portuguese the word *'tempo'* can mean both *'weather'* or *'time'*.

In VLibras® it was translated as *'weather'* (which is a completely different sign in Libras), which would not make sense to the deaf user.

Problems with cognates were observed in several cases (e.g. the word *'sente'* in Portuguese can mean the present tense of the verb *'feel'* or the imperative for the verb *'sit'*, which caused many medical questions about how the user was feeling to be wrongly translated using the sign for *sit*, instead of *feel*, which was considered a critical error. In another example the word in Portuguese *'plano'* that is the same for *'plan'* or *'flat (ground)'*, was wrongly translated.

There are also situations in which there exists more than one word in Portuguese (i.e. synonyms), but only one sign in Libras. For instance, when translating *"Sente ardor ao urinar?"* (*"Do you feel burning pain when urinating?"*). In Portuguese *'urinate'* and *'pee'* can be considered synonyms, but both of them translate to the same sign in Libras. However, as the word *'urinate'* is probably less commonly used in Portuguese, not all apps were able to translate it. VLibras® presented the dactylology for *'urinating'* instead of the commonly used sign for *'pee'*. Such inadequate choice of lexical item could make the sentence incomprehensive if the user does not know the Portuguese written word. HandTalk® did not present any translation for the word. Therefore, this was considered a critical error both in VLibras® and HandTalk®. In this case, only Rybená® provided the commonly used sign for *'pee'*.

Furthermore, there were other situations in which the translation would not make sense, and generate a critical error for the user. For instance, when translating *"Does the pain get worse when pressure is applied?"* Rybená® translated the word *'pressure'* as *'crowded'*, instead of translating *'pressure'* to Libras as a movement of seizing and pressuring a part of the body. This could cause a misunderstanding that the question was *"Does it hurt when you are in a crowded room?"*, completely altering its original meaning.

Another problem that was noticed was that in our medical corpus, some questions were related to each other, as is common in medical anamnesis. For instance, *"Do you feel anything else along with this symptom? Are there any worsening factors? Are there any improving factors?"*. However, the apps did not allow long texts to be input into their translation field. Thus when the questions were translated independently, the context of the translation often was lost. For instance, when translating the word *'factors'*, VLibras®'s choice was to use the sign with a math meaning; Rybená® used dactylology, and HandTalk® used the sign for *'influence'*, instead of *'factor'*.

Regarding the use of dactylology in their translations, it was observed that all three apps used it even when there existed an adequate sign in Libras for the Portuguese word. The reason was probably because the app did not have a sign associated with the word in Portuguese in their database. When dactylology is used, the word is not really being translated, but the Portuguese word is spelled out. Thus, it requires the deaf user to know the Portuguese written word in order to understand it. However, most deaf users in Brazil are not fluent in Portuguese, and would not be able to understand words presented in dactylology [4].

It is worth noting that one of the apps (HandTalk®) presented a disclaimer saying that it *"uses AI to translate from Portuguese to Libras. This means that characters learn and improve translations with phrases, contexts, and feedback sent. Therefore, sometimes translations may not be perfect."*. Although the disclaimer can warn users, it does help in any way users to know if a given translation is trustworthy or not.

5 Discussion

In this section, we discuss the main results of our study and their implications in the context of our research. Firstly, our results showed that the three applications analyzed have simple and intuitive interfaces, contributing to user interaction. In all three cases, there was a predominance of static signs (e.g. icons) common to other systems, building upon users' (expected) previous knowledge, and when this was not the case, the use of meta-linguistic or dynamic signs was used to clarify them.

Furthermore, through the application of the Semiotic Inspection Method, it was possible to conclude that the designers of the systems adopted an approach that favors the exploration of applications to communicate with the user. In other words, as users interact with the system it "reveals" itself. This could be a challenge if users are not digitally literate or have difficulties with technology in general.

Even though the system's communicability was considered good, and the problems identified were classified as temporary breakdowns, it is important to mention some of its limitations in the context of medical care. First of all, although they translate content from Brazilian Portuguese to Libras, the systems evaluated do not perform the reverse translation, that is, from Libras to Brazilian Portuguese. Thus, it could only solve part of the communicative problems between hearing health professionals and deaf patients.

Regarding the quality of the translation generated from Brazilian Portuguese to Libras, a significant number (around 20%) of critical errors were identified, that is errors that would prevent deaf users from understanding the intended meaning. In some cases, the user would clearly notice that the sentence did not make sense. However, in some situations, the translation would make sense in Libras but would convey a meaning completely different from the original question. We could argue, that this situation would be even more problematic, as the communicative breakdown might go unnoticed and generate misunderstandings in the conversation.

The use of dactylology was also a strategy used by all three apps. For users who do not know written Portuguese (which is usually the case [4]), this strategy would generate major (if only one word was not understood) or critical errors (if the word impacted the understanding of the whole sentence) for users. As the medical interview has utmost importance for the correct diagnosis, these problems could lead to misdiagnosis, delayed diagnosis, and wrong treatment, which may expose patients to unnecessary side effects and impair prognosis, and could put the deaf patient's health in danger.

It is important to mention that the analysis of translations involves many aspects and nuances, and because it is a complex topic, various approaches can be used. In this study, we had the participation of a linguist specialized in sign languages, as well as a Libras interpreter to evaluate the translations, and although there was no deaf person included in the process, our results bring interesting points that can be applied in the future to the improvement of these systems.

6   Conclusion

Nowadays, deaf people face various communicative barriers in the healthcare context. The use of existing automatic translation systems between Brazilian Portuguese and Libras could potentially mitigate the problem. In this paper, we analyzed three Brazilian Portuguese to Libras translation apps to investigate their potential use in a medical context. Although the systems have good communicability and are easy to use, the limitations identified in the translation indicate that they are not enough to support communication. Furthermore, considering some of the misunderstandings that could take place, one could argue that they should not be considered in situations that could even lead to serious health issues or even death.

This study contributes to the raising awareness of the challenges faced by the deaf community in the healthcare context and the limitations of the existing technology. It highlights the importance of accessible and effective solutions to ensure the equality of access to medical services. Thus, it is expected that the findings of this study could lead to future research and initiatives to improve communication and promote the inclusion of the deaf in the healthcare field. Possible future directions include the development and evaluation of new technologies that could overcome the limitations identified. The next steps in our research, include investigating the use of photo-realistic representations in translation systems, and the inclusion of bidirectional translation - from Brazilian Portuguese to Libras and from Libras to Brazilian Portuguese.

Acknowledgments. This study was funded in part by Financiadora de Estudos e Projetos (FINEP, grant 01.21.0097.00, reference number 2797/20) and SignumWeb Comunicação Inclusiva Ltda, as part of the Project *"Captar-Libras: Sistema de Comunicação por vídeos para surdos aplicado ao pré-atendimento médico"*. MSM was supported in part by the National Council for Scientific and Technological Development (Conselho Nacional de Desenvolvimento Científico e Tecnológico - CNPq) [grant number 310561/2021-3].

Disclosure of Interests. The authors have no competing interests to declare that are relevant to the content of this article.

References

1. Agência de Notícias IBGE: Pessoas com deficiência têm menor acesso à educação, ao trabalho e à renda (2019). https://agenciadenoticias.ibge.gov.br/agencia-noticias/2012-agencia-de-noticias/noticias/37317-pessoas-com-deficiencia-tem-menor-acesso-a-educacao-ao-trabalho-e-a-renda
2. Areeb, Q.M., Nadeem, M., Alrobaea, R., Anwer, F.: Helping hearing-impaired in emergency situations: a deep learning-based approach. IEEE Access **10**, 8502–8517 (2022). https://doi.org/10.1109/ACCESS.2022.3226696
3. Batista, J.D., et al.: Língua brasileira de sinais: análise das tecnologias mhealth. Revista de Saúde Digital e Tecnologias Educacionais (2022)
4. Bernardino, E.L.A., da Cunha Pereira, M.C.: Desafios no ensino-aprendizagem da segunda língua numa proposta bilíngue de educação para surdos. Línguas & Letras (2020)
5. Farooq, U., Shafry, M., Rahim, M., Khan, N., Hussain, Abid, A.: Advances in machine translation for sign language: approaches, limitations, and challenges. Neural Computing and Applications (2021). https://doi.org/10.1007/s00521-021-06079-3
6. Ferreira, N.L.M., Brayner, I.C.D.S.: O acesso da comunidade surda aos serviços de saúde: mãos que falam. Temas em Educação e Saúde **17**(00), e021016 (ago 2021). https://doi.org/10.26673/tes.v17i00.15169, https://periodicos.fclar.unesp.br/tes/article/view/15169
7. Figueiredo, L., Lourenço, G.: O movimento de sobrancelhas como marcador de domínios sintáticos na língua brasileira de sinais. Revista da Anpoll **1**(48), 78–102 (2019). https://doi.org/10.18309/anp.vli48.1235
8. de Godoi, T.X., da Silva Junior, D.P., Costa Valentim, N.M.: A case study about usability, user experience and accessibility problems of deaf users with assistive technologies. In: Antona, M., Stephanidis, C. (eds.) HCII 2020. LNCS, vol. 12189, pp. 73–91. Springer, Cham (2020). https://doi.org/10.1007/978-3-030-49108-6_6
9. Ko, S.K., Kim, C.J., Jung, H., Cho, C.: Neural sign language translation based on human keypoint estimation. Appl. Sci. **9**, 2683 (2019). https://doi.org/10.3390/app9132683
10. Lessa, R.T.C., Andrade, E.G.S.: Libras e o atendimento ao cliente surdo no âmbito da saúde (translation to English: Libras and deaf customer service in the health sector). Rev. Cient. Sena Aires **5**(2), 95–104 (2016)
11. Naranjo-Zeledón, L., Peral, J., Ferrández, A., Chacón-Rivas, M.: A systematic mapping of translation-enabling technologies for sign languages. Electronics **8**(9) (2019). https://doi.org/10.3390/electronics8091047, https://www.mdpi.com/2079-9292/8/9/1047
12. Peirce, C.S.P., Peirce, C.S.: The essential Peirce, volume 1: Selected philosophical writings?(1867–1893), vol. 1. Indiana University Press (1992)
13. Pikoulis, E.V., Bifis, A., Trigka, M., Constantinopoulos, C., Kosmopoulos, D.: Context-aware automatic sign language video transcription in psychiatric interviews. Sensors **22**, 2656 (2022). https://doi.org/10.3390/s22072656
14. Quadros, R.M.D.: Gramática das Línguas Gestuais. Universidade Católica Editora, Lisboa (2011)
15. Reis, L.S., de Araújo, T.M.U., Aguiar, Y.P.C., Lima, M.A.C.B.A.: Evaluating machine translation systems for Brazilian sign language in the treatment of critical grammatical aspects. In: Proceedings of the 19th Brazilian Symposium on Human Factors in Computing Systems. IHC '20, New York, NY, USA. Association for Computing Machinery (2020). https://doi.org/10.1145/3424953.3426536

16. Reis, L.S., de Araújo, T.M.U., Aguiar, Y.P.C., Lima, M.A.C., da Silva Sales, A.S.: Assessment of the treatment of grammatical aspects of machine translators to libras. In: Anais Estendidos do XXIV Simpósio Brasileiro de Sistemas Multimídia e Web. SBC, Porto Alegre, RS, Brasil, pp. 73–76 (2018). https://doi.org/10.5753/webmedia.2018.4570

17. Rezende, R.F., Guerra, L.B., Carvalho, S.A.D.S.: The perspective of deaf patients on health care. Revista CEFAC 23(2), e0620 (2021). https://doi.org/10.1590/1982-0216/20212320620

18. Ribeiro Ossada, S.A., Ossada, K.T., Ossada Junior, J.C., Issa, B.: A colaboração de software para auxiliar na comunicação de surdos em hospitais. Revista Brasileira em Tecnologia da Informação 3(1), 2–13 (2021). https://www.fateccampinas.com.br/rbti/index.php/fatec/article/view/56

19. de Souza, C.S.: The Semiotic Engineering of Human-Computer Interaction. MIT Press, Cambridge (2005)

20. de Souza, C.S., Leitão, C.F., Prates, R.O., da Silva, E.J.: The semiotic inspection method. In: Proceedings of VII Brazilian Symposium on Human Factors in Computing Systems. IHC '06, New York, NY, USA, pp. 148–157. Association for Computing Machinery (2006). https://doi.org/10.1145/1298023.1298044

21. de Souza, C.S., Leitão, C.F.: Semiotic engineering methods for scientific research in HCI. Syn. Lect. Human-Centered Inform. 2(1), 1–122 (2009)

22. Souza, V.D.D., Hoeckele, A.G., Borim, M.L.C., Christinelli, H.C.B., Costa, M.A.R.: Percepção de surdos sobre o atendimento nos serviços de saúde / perception of the deaf on the service in health services. Brazilian J. Dev. 6(8), 55347–55356 (2020). https://doi.org/10.34117/bjdv6n8-091, https://ojs.brazilianjournals.com.br/ojs/index.php/BRJD/article/view/14576

23. Soza-Jimenez, C.O., Rios-Figueroa, H.V., Solis-Gonzalez-Cosio, A.L.: A prototype for Mexican sign language recognition and synthesis in support of a primary care physician. IEEE Access 10, 127620–127635 (2022). https://doi.org/10.1109/ACCESS.2022.3142918

24. Steinberg, A.G., Barnett, S., Meador, H.E., Wiggins, E.A., Zazove, P.: Health care system accessibility: experiences and perceptions of deaf people. J. Gen. Intern. Med. 21, 260–266 (2006). https://doi.org/10.1111/j.1525-1497.2006.00340.x

25. Teixeira, M.d.S.: O jogo da avaliação: Um estudo prático sobre tradução automática (2018). https://doi.org/10.17771/PUCRIO.ACAD.41711

26. Vieira, C.M., Caniato, D.G., Yonemotu, B.P.R.: Comunicação e acessibilidade: percepções de pessoas com deficiência auditiva sobre seu atendimento nos serviços de saúde (translation to English: communication and accessibility: perceptions of people with hearing impairment about their care in health services). Revista Eletrônica de Comunicação, Informação & Inovação em Saúde 11(2) (2017). https://doi.org/10.29397/reciis.v11i2.1139, https://www.reciis.icict.fiocruz.br/index.php/reciis/article/view/1139

Development of a System to Support Exercises for Successful Aging Using Smartphones and Verification of Its Effectiveness

Yuma Takeda[1] , Kazuhiko Hirata[2], Masaomi Kurokawa[3], Ariaki Higashi[1], and Yuichi Kurita[1(✉)]

[1] Hiroshima University, 1-4-1 Kagamiyama, Higashi-hiroshima, Hiroshima 739-8527, Japan
`ykurita@hiroshima-u.ac.jp`
[2] Hiroshima University Hospital, Kasumi 1-2-3 Minami-ku, Hiroshima 734-8551, Japan
[3] Kotobuki Solution Co., Ltd., Breezy FLAG 2F 6-10-3 Saijoshitami, Higashi-hiroshima, Hiroshima 739-0047, Japan

Abstract. In this study, we developed a system that enables people to voluntarily perform exercises for successful aging while maintaining their motivation. The system evaluates exercises based on camera images from a smartphone. The system uses posture estimation AI to estimate posture and evaluates exercises by comparing them with scoring criteria created based on a model posture. The evaluation results are fed back to the user in real time as audiovisual effects on the screen, allowing the user to enjoy the exercises as if they were a game. Based on the evaluation results, the system creates an appropriate exercise menu from the viewpoint of improving motivation. To verify the effectiveness of the application, we asked healthy elderly people to continue the exercises for two months and compared their motivation to exercise and their physical performance before and after the intervention. The results showed that the exercise motivation of the app group was higher than that of the video group using the conventional method, and that the shoulder joint range of motion increased in both groups.

Keywords: Motion recognition and analysis · Exercise game

1 Introduction

The number of people requiring nursing care in Japan's aging society continues to increase, increasing the burden on medical and nursing care facilities. In recent years, efforts to promote "Successful Aging" have been promoted. According to the "Prevention of functional disabilities (leading to long-term care needs) manual" [1] published by Japan's Ministry of Health, Labour and Welfare, Successful Aging means "to prevent the occurrence of conditions requiring long-term care

M. Antona and C. Stephanidis (Eds.): HCII 2024, LNCS 14698, pp. 305–316, 2024.
https://doi.org/10.1007/978-3-031-60884-1_21

as much as possible. Successful aging is defined as "preventing (delaying) the onset of long-term care needs as much as possible" and "preventing the worsening of long-term care needs as much as possible, and even aiming to alleviate them. One of the measures for Successful Aging is the implementation of exercise. Exercise is an integral part of Successful Aging because the deterioration of musculoskeletal function is a direct cause of the need for support and care. Exercise for Successful Aging is generally performed at nursing homes and hospitals under the guidance of specialists. However, there is also a method in which people can exercise voluntarily by viewing pictures, illustrations, and videos. This method is accessible because it does not require professional guidance and can be performed alone, regardless of time and place.

Matsuguma et al. [3] researched and developed a serious rehabilitation game for training standing up and sitting down. The game recognizes posture with an RGBD camera and presents animations and sound effects of a tree growing by standing and sitting. The effectiveness of this system was verified by introducing it to a geriatric healthcare facility, and it was reported that the system improved the positive attitude and persistence of the users. Sakoda et al. [4] developed a squat training system that adjusts the load based on the estimation of the locomotive risk level. They developed a VR squat game that estimates physical capacity from squatting movements acquired by an RGBD camera and adjusts the load based on the results. These systems require an RGBD camera. The RGBD camera can recognize depth information in addition to the color information obtained with the RGB camera and can, therefore, acquire the human posture in three dimensions. However, since only some have these devices, systems using them cannot be easily implemented. Tanaka et al. [7] evaluated the validity of a motion measurement platform, AKIRA. This system enables simple motion measurement using non-contact sensors and is intended to maintain and improve patient motivation in medical and nursing care settings. SapplyM, Inc. [5] also provided "Rehakatsu," a home rehabilitation support service. Rehakatsu is a service that allows patients to perform rehabilitation at home alone with support from specialists. Rehakatsu uses a smartphone camera and artificial intelligence to evaluate rehabilitation exercise movements and suggest rehabilitation menus tailored to the user's daily condition. In the previous studies described above, "movement evaluation," "game elements" to encourage exercise and appropriate "menu suggestions" have been considered (Table 1), but no system that considers all three has yet been developed.

This study aims to develop an exercise support system equipped with a comprehensive support function for exercise and verify its effectiveness. We will investigate whether exercises using the proposed system help improve the motivation to exercise and physical ability. An overview of the objectives is shown in Fig. 1. In the development of the system, we created a system that incorporates a "movement evaluation" function, a "game" function, and a "menu suggestion" function to maintain and improve motivation to exercise. The system can be efficiently executed with a smartphone. The system's effectiveness was verified by having older adults perform exercises using the system, examining their moti-

Table 1. Conventional System

	Evaluation	Game	Suggestion
AKIRA [7]	○		
VR Squat Training [4]	○	○	
REHABILIUM [3]		○	
Rehakatsu [5]	○		○

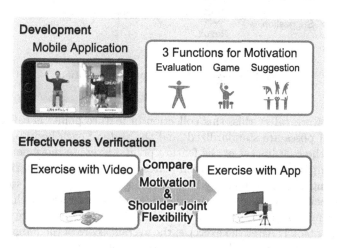

Fig. 1. Purpose

vation to exercise and the flexibility of their shoulder joints, and comparing the results with those of a conventional method that uses a video exercise model.

2 Developed System

2.1 Overview

An overview of the application functions is shown in Fig. 2. This application is an exercise game. The screen transitions in the following order: exercise menu, demonstration video, exercise execution, and evaluation results. The motion evaluation function evaluates the user's ability to perform the exercise by converting the exercise video into a numerical value. The evaluation results are presented on the screen as audiovisual effects. The evaluation results are used to propose the subsequent menus.

2.2 Exercise Movement Evaluation

From the user's exercise posture video (size 640[px]×480[px]) acquired with an RGB camera, 14 feature points of the human body are estimated using Apple's

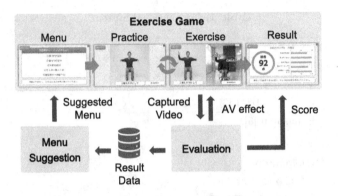

Fig. 2. Application Function Configuration

Vision framework (after this, this collection of feature points is called a pose). The acquired poses are standardized, and the state of each body part is determined from the coordinates of the feature points. Exercise movements are evaluated by comparing the discriminated states with the scoring criteria described below. Scoring criteria are created by defining the position of a specific body part at a specific time based on a model video of the exercise. Each item of the created scoring criteria is compared with the user's exercise posture in real-time and judged as 0 or 1. After the exercise, the average score of the judgment results of all items is calculated, and the total score is obtained.

2.3 Game

This system incorporates audiovisual effects based on the evaluation results of the exercise movements as a game element. Sound and visual effects are superimposed on the exercise postures and presented in real time to make it easy to understand when and which postures are good or bad (Fig. 4). The following factors determine the presence, type of visual effects, and display position. The scoring criteria and judgment results of the movement evaluation are used to determine whether or not to present visual effects, the type of visual effects, and the display positions. The procedure is described below. First, the judgment results are organized as shown in the table in Fig. 3. The table's columns represent the "time" of the scoring criteria, the rows represent the Body Part of the scoring criteria, and the table elements are the judgment results assigned to the scoring criteria.

Next, the elements in the table are grouped by time and body part. In Fig. 3, a group is a collection of elements surrounded by a rectangular box. The group indicated by the orange frame contains all the elements of the table and is used to calculate the total score of the exercise. As explained in the previous section, the average score of all the elements in the table is the total score of the exercise. The group indicated by the green frame is a group of elements of the same "time" and is used to assign the auditory effect. Depending on the

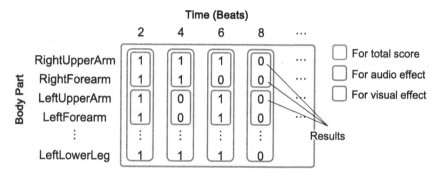

Fig. 3. Grouping Of Results

Great Effect   Bad Effect

Fig. 4. Audio Visual Effect

average score of this group, either "GREAT," "GOOD," or "BAD" sounds are played. The group indicated by the purple frame is a group of elements of the same "Time" and the same "Body Part" and is used for visual effects. Depending on the average score of this group, either "GREAT," "GOOD," or "BAD" text and effects are displayed. The correspondence between the average score of the group and the type of audiovisual effect is as follows: the audiovisual effect of GREAT is presented when the average score of the group is 1, the audiovisual effect of BAD when the average score of the group is 0, and the audiovisual effect of GOOD when the average score of the group is greater than 0 and less than 1. The "Body Part" value determines the position of the visual effect. The above is the method of presenting audiovisual effects. Figure 4 shows how this method presents visual effects on the screen.

2.4   Exercise Suggestion

This system targeted 54 kinds of exercises that are effective in preventing care-giving, which physical therapists created. These exercises involve various body parts such as the neck, shoulders, shoulder blades, elbows, chest, back, trunk, pelvis, hips, and knees. For safety reasons, all exercises can be performed sitting on a chair. Table 2 and Fig. 5, 6, 7, 8, 9 and 10 show examples of typical exercises.

Table 2. Exercise Examples

Name	Purpose
Shoulder Abduction	Improving shoulder joint flexibility
Punch	Improving shoulder joint flexibility
Elbow Bending	Improving elbow joint flexibility
Trunk Bending	Improving trunk flexibility
Thigh Raise	Improving hip flexibility
Knee Extension	Improving knee joint flexibility

This system proposes menus based on the policy of prioritizing exercises that improve the user's motivation to exercise. Bandura et al. [2] showed that self-efficacy (confidence in one's abilities) is related to maintaining and improving motivation and that accumulating successful experiences effectively enhances self-efficacy. Therefore, this system increases the probability of selecting exercises likely to improve scores and provide successful experiences. The priority P_i of the gymnastics with moderate evaluation results, which are considered to have room for improvement and are likely to be effective, is set by (1). Each exercise is selected for the menu with a probability proportional to P_i. Where i is the type of exercise, and $\overline{S_i}$ is the average score of the exercise i performed in the past.

$$P_i = exp(-\frac{(\overline{S_i} - \mu)^2}{2\sigma^2}) \qquad (\mu = 0.5,\ \sigma = 0.2) \tag{1}$$

3   Experiment

3.1   Method

Outline. The experiment was conducted on 20 healthy subjects (7 males and 13 females) aged 60–79 years. The experimental period was two months, from November 2022 to January 2023. Subjects were asked to perform the exercises at home for about 10 min a day, at least three times a week (intervention), and to answer a questionnaire about their motivation to exercise after performing the exercises. This experiment was conducted with the approval of the Research

Fig. 5. Shoulder Abduction

Fig. 6. Punch

Fig. 7. Elbow Bending

Fig. 8. Trunk Bending

Fig. 9. Thigh Raise

Fig. 10. Knee Extension

Ethics Review Committee of the Graduate School of Advanced Science and Engineering, Hiroshima University (approval number: ASE-2022-7). The experiment is shown in Fig. 11. The subject's exercise movements were acquired with a smartphone camera, and the corresponding audiovisual effects were displayed on the screen. Since the smartphone screen is small, the smartphone screen is mirrored on the monitor screen. The subjects perform the exercises while looking at the monitor screen.

Fig. 11. Photograph of the Experiment

Subjects were divided into two groups: a video group (conventional method) and an app group (proposed method), performing the exercises differently. The video group performed the exercises by watching only the model videos. On the other hand, the application group performed the exercises while receiving audiovisual effects from the movement evaluation and the model videos. The method of proposing a menu of exercises was also different. The video group selected exercises randomly, while the app group selected exercises with medium scores, as described in Sect. 2.4.

Assessment of Motivation to Exercise. A questionnaire was administered to evaluate exercise motivation. Subjects were asked to rate each item on a 7-point scale for the following questions, which were used by Matsukuma et al. [3] to assess their motivation to exercise. Students' t-tests were conducted on the samples of the video group and app groups' samples, with the average value of the whole period for each subject as the sample.

Q. Do you want to do again?

Q. Are you exhausted?

Measurement of Shoulder Joint Range of Motion. The shoulder joint range of motion was measured before and after the intervention to examine the effects on physical performance. The specific measurement items and their descriptions are listed in Table 3. CAT (Combined Abduction Test), HFT (Horizontal Flexion Test), SMT (Shoulder Mobility Test), and Internal and External rotation were all used to evaluate shoulder joint flexibility. Angle measurements were taken on both sides, with the subject lying on their back on the bed using a brass angle meter. The SMT was measured with tape on both sides while the subject stood. Paired-sample t-tests were performed on the samples before and after the intervention in the video and app groups, respectively, using the average of the left and right values for each subject as the sample.

Table 3. Evaluation Items for Shoulder Joint ROM

Item	Description
CAT	Fix the scapula and abduct the upper arm in the direction of the head and measure the angle.
HFT	Fix the scapula and flex the upper arm inward and measure the angle.
Internal	Fix the upper arm horizontally, rotate the forearm in the direction of the foot with respect to the vertical, and measure the angle.
External	Fix the upper arm horizontally and rotate the forearm in the direction of the head with respect to the vertical and measure the angle.
SMT	Place one arm above the shoulder and the other arm at the waist, bring the hands close together behind the back, and measure the distance between them.

3.2 Result

Motivation to Exercise Figure 12 shows the results of the motivation questionnaire as a box-and-whisker diagram. To compare the conventional method using video and the proposed method using the application in terms of motivation to exercise, a Student's t-test was conducted on the samples of the Video viewing group and the Proposed method group, and the results were as follows: "Q Would you like to do it again?" was significantly higher in the Proposed method group ($t(18) = 2.2717, p < 0.05$).

On the other hand, no significant difference was found in the score for the question "Q. Are you exhausted?" while the median and mean scores were lower for the proposed method group. The video-viewing group had a median of 1.75 and a mean of 1.90, while the Proposed method group had a median of 1.15 and a mean of 1.26.

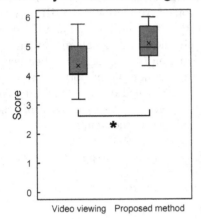
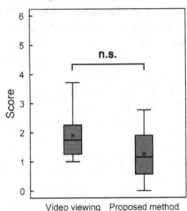

Fig. 12. Motivation Survey Results

Shoulder Joint Range of Motion. Figure 13 shows box-and-whisker plots of the CAT results before and after the intervention, divided into a video-viewing group and a proposed method group. A paired-sample t-test was performed on the pre- and post-intervention samples to determine whether the exercises helped improve shoulder joint flexibility. For CAT, the range of motion after the intervention was significantly greater than before the intervention in both groups (Video viewing: $t(9) = 5.8789, p < 0.01$, Proposed method: $t(9) = 4.092, p < 0.01$).

The mean increase after the intervention relative to the pre-intervention baseline was +10.1% for Video viewing and +6.8% for the Proposed method.

4   Consideration

In the experiment, to verify the effectiveness of the developed gymnastics support application, we examined changes in exercise motivation and shoulder joint flexibility before and after the intervention after the implementation of the exercises. Regarding the exercise motivation questionnaire results, the score for the question "Would you like to do it again? was significantly higher in the application group. Therefore, the application developed in this study may increase users' desire to continue exercising and make it easier to do so for an extended period. Both groups found Significant improvements in the shoulder joint range of motion measurement results. Therefore, it was found that the exercises using the application in this study had the same effects as those using the conventional method. From the above, it was found that the gymnastics using the proposed system helps improve the motivation to exercise and physical ability. In this

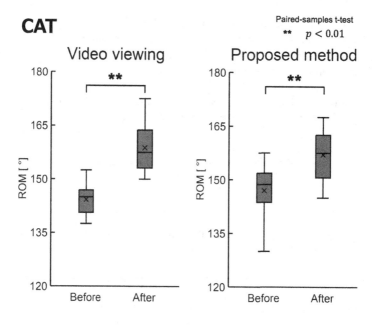

Fig. 13. CAT Results

study, we proposed a system that provides comprehensive support for exercise as a method for voluntary exercise to prevent nursing care. The app-based exercises can be performed easily by individuals. They may be a new option for the elderly who cannot go to facilities due to concerns about infectious diseases. Another advantage of this method over conventional video-based methods is that it is interactive and provides feedback to the user according to their exercise movements. Suzuki et al. [6] found that a human, friendly, loud, radiant, and simple impression in the user interface is important to keep the recipient highly motivated. The system's voice guidance made the system's behavior more human-like, and the flashy audiovisual effect of praise may have contributed to the motivation to exercise.

5   Conclusion

In this study, a smartphone application was developed to improve the motivation to exercise, and three functions were incorporated: "movement evaluation," "game elements," and "exercise menu suggestions" to increase the motivation of the users. In an experiment to verify the effectiveness of the application, older people were asked to use the application for two months, and their motivation to exercise was compared with that of conventional methods using a questionnaire. The results of the questionnaire showed that the app was more effective than the conventional method of using exercise videos in increasing the desire to continue exercising and improving motivation. In addition, the measurement results of the shoulder joint range of motion showed that the proposed method was as effective as the conventional method in improving shoulder joint flexibility. Future research will include more detailed movement evaluation and audiovisual feedback of different magnitudes and intensities.

Acknowledgments. This paper is based on results obtained from a project commissioned by the New Energy and Industrial Technology Development Organization (NEDO).

Disclosure of Interests. There are no conflicts of interest to disclose.

References

1. Arai, H.: [Prevention of functional disabilities (leading to long-term care needs) manual] Kaigo yobo manual, 4th edn. Nomura Research Institute, Ltd. (2022). (in Japanese)
2. Bandura, A.: Self-efficacy: toward a unifying theory of behavioral change. Psychol. Rev. **84**(2), 191–215 (1977)
3. Matsuguma, H., et al.: Research and development of serious games to support stand-up rehabilitation exercises. J. Inf. Process. **53**(3), 1041–1049 (2012)
4. Sakoda, W., Tadayon, R., Kishishita, Y., Yamamoto, M., Kurita, Y.: Ski exergame for squat training to change load based on predicted locomotive risk level. In: 2020 IEEE/SICE International Symposium on System Integration (SII), pp. 289–294. IEEE (2020)
5. SapplyM, Inc.: Mainichi undo rehakatsu (2022). https://prtimes.jp/main/html/rd/p/000000002.000099528.html
6. Suzuki, T., Jose, Y., Nakauchi, Y.: Impression difference between intelligent medicine case and small service robot in self-medication support situations. J. Robot. Mechatron. **25**(5), 855–862 (2013)
7. Tanaka, R., Takimoto, H., Yamasaki, T., Higashi, A.: Validity of time series kinematical data as measured by a markerless motion capture system on a flatland for gait assessment. J. Biomech. **71**, 281–285 (2018)

Radiological Medical Imaging Annotation and Visualization Tool

Inês Teiga[1,2], Joana Vale Sousa[1,2] (iD), Francisco Silva[1,3] (iD), Tania Pereira[1,4] (iD), and Hélder P. Oliveira[1,3(✉)] (iD)

[1] INESC TEC, Instituto de Engenharia de Sistemas e Computadores, Tecnologia e Ciência, Porto, Portugal
helder.f.oliveira@inesctec.pt
[2] FEUP, Faculdade de Engenharia da Universidade do Porto, Porto, Portugal
[3] FCUP, Faculdade de Ciências da Universidade do Porto, Departamento de Ciência de Computadores, Porto, Portugal
[4] FCTUC, Faculdade de Ciências e Tecnologia da Universidade de Coimbra, Coimbra, Portugal

Abstract. Significant medical image visualization and annotation tools, tailored for clinical users, play a crucial role in disease diagnosis and treatment. Developing algorithms for annotation assistance, particularly machine learning (ML)-based ones, can be intricate, emphasizing the need for a user-friendly graphical interface for developers. Many software tools are available to meet these requirements, but there is still room for improvement, making the research for new tools highly compelling.

The envisioned tool focuses on navigating sequences of DICOM images from diverse modalities, including Magnetic Resonance Imaging (MRI), Computed Tomography (CT) scans, Ultrasound (US), and X-rays. Specific requirements involve implementing manual annotation features such as freehand drawing, copying, pasting, and modifying annotations. A scripting plugin interface is essential for running Artificial Intelligence (AI)-based models and adjusting results. Additionally, adaptable surveys complement graphical annotations with textual notes, enhancing information provision.

The user evaluation results pinpointed areas for improvement, including incorporating some useful functionalities, as well as enhancements to the user interface for a more intuitive and convenient experience. Despite these suggestions, participants praised the application's simplicity and consistency, highlighting its suitability for the proposed tasks. The ability to revisit annotations ensures flexibility and ease of use in this context.

Keywords: Medical Image Visualization · Annotation Tool · Clinical Users

1 Introduction

A software tool for medical imaging visualization and analysis is essential to assist medical evaluation and care, as it grants the visual assessment and annotation of various types of clinical examinations, in a quick and trustworthy

M. Antona and C. Stephanidis (Eds.): HCII 2024, LNCS 14698, pp. 317–333, 2024.
https://doi.org/10.1007/978-3-031-60884-1_22

way. Ideally, the application to be developed should be able to open, display, annotate, and save images as Digital Imaging and Communications in Medicine (DICOM) formatted images, as it is the most used format in the clinical environment [5]. The medical images encompass various modalities, including Computerized Tomography (CT), Magnetic Resonance Imaging (MRI), Ultrasound (US), and X-rays.

In the context of medical imaging, image annotation refers to the process of labelling or classifying an image using text, graphical tools, or a combination of both. This labelling approach generates a set of corresponding labels for each image, which is often used to train machine learning (ML) and deep learning (DL) models. Medical image annotation specifically involves labelling medical images obtained from various imaging modalities. These annotations play a pivotal role in the healthcare sector by aiding in disease diagnosis, organ segmentation for radiation therapy planning, and facilitating robotic surgery procedures [1]. Manual annotation can be noticeably useful for generating a high-quality dataset; however, it is often toilsome, exhausting, and time-consuming. Both algorithm developers and health professionals are interested in simple, flexible, and time-sparing tools, so the need for automatic and semi-automatic functionalities increased. Medical image analysis and processing steadily benefit from the extensive recent research on artificial intelligence (AI), ML and especially DL. However, to effectively and expertly incorporate several image data is necessary to recognize complex health conditions, so that doctors are capable of providing the finest prescription to patients [7]. The integration of a scripting plugin comes out as remarkably convenient, as it allows developers and users to write a customized script to operate in the program order during a simulation.

Visualization and annotation tools adapted for the clinical user are tremendously significant for disease diagnosis and treatment, contributing to the well-being of the patient [16]. Furthermore, the development of the algorithms to assist the annotation, especially the ones based on machine learning, can be quite convoluted, which makes a simple and convenient graphical user interface (GUI) particularly interesting for developers. Addressing this subject, many software tools are endeavouring to satisfy these requirements [17], yet there is still a lot of room for improvement, which makes the research for new tools essential.

The main objective of this research project is to plan and develop an interface that allows user visualization, annotation, and navigation through medical images, in particular DICOM files, in a clinical environment. Surveys are commonly useful for receiving feedback from possible users. They should be accessible throughout this project to verify if the tool is appealing and fulfils the requirements presented in Table 1.

During the elaboration of this project the following contributions in the engineering and medical departments were produced:

- Construction of an accessible and clean graphical user interface (GUI) that supports human-computer interaction, appropriate for clinicians;
- Implementation of advantageous functionalities for manual annotation;
- Run developed algorithms and be able to adjust the results afterwards;

Table 1. Parameters to evaluate clinical visualization and annotation tools.

Requirements	Definition
3D Visualization	Ability of displaying 3D images
Re-annotation	Possibility of re-opening a mask to change the annotation
Script Incorporation	Capacity of running user-developed scripts
Configurable GUI	Capability of adapting the GUI and open-source code
Manual Annotation	Possibility of performing graphical and semantic annotations

– Incorporation of surveys to assist the annotations with linguistic notes.

1.1 Related Tools

Nowadays, various clinical tools stand out for offering different annotation functionalities, that can be manual, semi-automatic, and automatic [16]. Testing and analyzing them was important to understand the possible functionalities that can be executed and evaluate their utility.

Itk-snap. A free 3D medical image segmentation software that employs active contour mechanisms, along with manual delineation[1]. Key features include:

– Simultaneous manual segmentation in three orthogonal planes.
– Support for manipulation of multiple images in the same workplace.
– Agile post-processing through a 3D cut-plane tool.

Itk-snap offers advantages such as a user-friendly GUI and compatibility with various image formats. However, the tool lacks flexibility in adopting new techniques when provided options prove inadequate and scripting is limited to a specific algorithm syntax.

Seg3D. A cross-platform semi-automatic segmentation tool that is both free and open-source, offering robust image processing algorithms[2]. Key features include:

– A 3D interface managing multiple volumes concurrently as layers.
– Integration of algorithms from the Insight Toolkit (ITK).
– Real-time demonstration of ITK filtering output.

Seg3D supports any image file format recognized by ITK, with an adaptable GUI permitting 3D annotation and Python scripting. It excels in annotation through semi-automatic and automatic methods via Python scripts. Despite these strengths, Seg3D lacks of basic image visualization features like zooming, has issues with file importation and lacks tutorials and examples.

---

[1] Itk-snap retrieved from http://www.itksnap.org.
[2] Seg3D retrieved from https://www.sci.utah.edu/download/seg3d.

MeVisLab. A robust medical image processing tool[3] that offers:

- 6D image processing: x, y, z, colour, time, and user dimensions.
- Scripting support in Python and Micro Development Language (MDL).
- Comprehensive error handling with configurable exception usage, diagnosis modules, and automatic module tester.

While MeVisLab stands out for its completeness and sophistication in functionalities and guides, supporting 4D efficient annotation saved in DICOM and Tagged Image File Format (TIFF) formats, it is unsuitable for manual annotation and the non-trial version is not free.

Fiji. Distribution of the software ImageJ that enhances its functionality with various plugins contributed by specialists[4]. Key features include:

- Automated and reproducible workflows facilitated by scripting.
- A vibrant and supportive user community.

Despite these strengths, Fiji is inadequate for 3D annotation and the GUI, lacks support for visualization and manipulation of images, restricting it to managing images mainly in TIFF format.

On the positive side, Fiji supports some DICOM file types, offers a configurable GUI, and allows scripting in various languages, with a primary focus on Python. However, its interface is relatively modest, permitting only one image to be opened at a time, relying on extensibility to maintain relevance.

1.2   Evaluation of the Related Tools

The analyses after testing each of the tools considering the proposed requirements pinpoint specific gaps in each tool, indicating opportunities for improvement and emphasizing the ongoing need for development and innovation in this domain. The summary of the evaluation is presented in Table 2.

Table 2. Summary of the evaluation of the related tools.

Requirements	Itk-Snap	Seg3D	MeVisLab	Fiji
3D Images	●	●	●	○
Re-annotation	◑	●	●	◑
Script Incorporation	○	●	●	●
Configurable GUI	●	●	○	●
Manual Annotation	●	○	●	●

● Implemented	◑ Half Implemented	○ Inutile	○ Missing

---

[3] MeVisLab retrieved from https://www.mevislab.de/download.
[4] Fiji retrieved from https://imagej.net/software/fiji/downloads.

2   Developed Tool

As the developed application depends on the interaction with a graphical user interface, it is crucial to have a well-defined design and user workflows. The user interactions are thoughtfully considered to guarantee that the application is appealing and enables smooth navigation and task execution.

First, it was necessary to define the programming language to be used. Since the application to be developed is a desktop application, the following high-level languages stand out: JAVA, C++, C#, and Python. After taking a look into them, it was possible to choose the one that better suits the need for a clear and intuitive GUI and the demand for computer vision incorporation. Python is highly convenient for medical image processing, as it has Pydicom, an open-source library that facilitates DICOM file management and metadata extraction. Pydicom clears the way for reading DICOM files into natural Pythonic structures for easy manipulation. Moreover, modified datasets can be written again to DICOM format files, which is ideal as the goal was to save annotations made in the image by the user.

2.1   Graphical User Interface Design

The application's user interface contains various groups of controls and significant areas, depicted in Fig. 1.

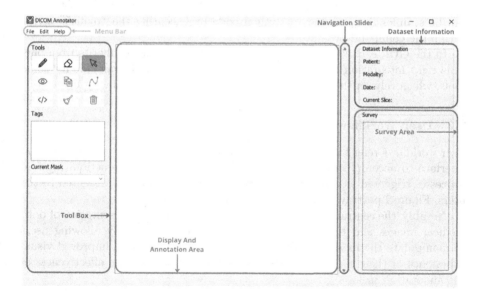

Fig. 1. Graphical User Interface (GUI) application components highlighted in boxes. (Color figure online)

The primary and largest area is denoted as the *Display and Annotation Area* or *GraphicsView* (in green, see Fig. 1). Within this area, medical images are presented individually, allowing users to perform manual annotations using mouse interactions. Adjacent to the view, positioned on the right side, is the *Navigation Slider* (in pink), which permits the navigation through the image slices, imparting a sense of depth or spatial dimension to the displayed two-dimensional images. The *Tool Box* (in red) provides options and tools related to manual and automatic annotation. The *Menu Bar* (in yellow), offers a comprehensive range of file management functionalities, including importing DICOM sets, loading or creating new masks, importing surveys, and saving both masks and surveys, options to process the medical images and getting assistance through a starting guide or support requests. The *Dataset Information* section (in purple), consists of labels that convey specific details associated with the displayed medical image. Lastly, the *Survey Area* (in blue), serves as a designated space for users to take notes. It comprises a group of labels and buttons, imported from a JavaScript Object Notation (JSON) file.

The PyQt5 library, a Python binding for the widely-used Qt framework, serves as another pivotal component within the application. By harnessing the comprehensive collection of PyQt5's classes and widgets, developers can create robust, intuitive, and visually appealing GUIs. Besides these useful and customizable User Interface (UI) components, PyQt5 is associated with highly regarded applications such as Qt Creator and Qt Designer, which exemplify a "what you see is what you get" approach. These applications allow developers to easily design interfaces through a drag-and-drop interface, resulting in UI designs that can be seamlessly converted to Python code by executing the "pyuic5" script within the command prompt.

In the GUI, each element corresponds to a Qt element or inherits from one. This tight integration with the Qt framework is particularly valuable for some tools, which rely on the rich assortment of functions provided by Qt elements.

2.2 User Workflows

User workflows refer to the sequential routes that users traverse within a digital interface to accomplish specific tasks, encompassing their interactions, system processes triggered as a result, and the corresponding outputs presented to the users. Figure 2 portrays the user workflows of the tool.

Notably, the central focus of the tool revolves around the presentation of both medical images and the accompanying annotation overlay. By allowing users to manipulate the masks independently, the tool facilitates an improved visual experience of their contents, thereby potentially enhancing the effectiveness of the annotation task.

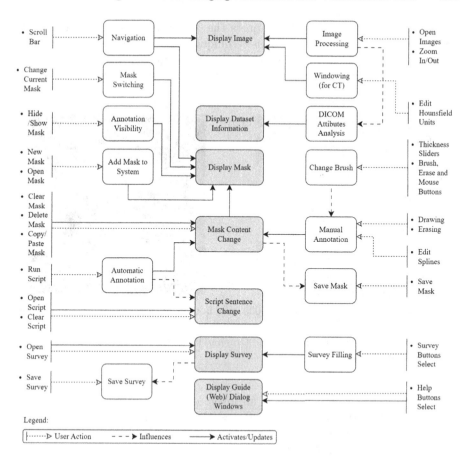

Fig. 2. User workflows of the developed application.

2.3   Visualization

The central component of the application is the *Display and Annotation Area*, which is coded as an instance of the *GraphicsView* class. This class is based on the highly versatile UI element known as *QGraphicsView*. In the application's framework, this widget is responsible for displaying and presenting images (as a background pixmap) and masks (as items), facilitating their visualization. In the case of CT modality, the image can undergo a process known as windowing.

Hounsfield Units (Windowing). In a CT scan, Hounsfield Units (HU) refer to the composition and properties of tissues or materials. These units are calculated by comparing the density of water, which is considered zero. If tissue or material has a higher density than water, it will have positive CT numbers, while those with a lower density will have negative CT numbers [4].

Windowing is a process that adjusts the grayscale representation of a CT image based on the CT number. This technique can highlight specific structures in the image according to the user's preferences, emphasizing desired aspects visually [2]. This feature can be used in the application, as shown in Fig. 3.

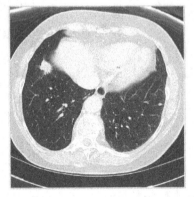 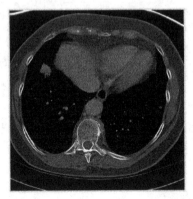

(a) Lung window (level -600, window 1500).   (b) Bone window (level 300, window 1000).

Fig. 3. CT Windowing presented in the *Graphics View* with different level and window (brightness and contrast) values.

The brightness and contrast of an image can be adjusted separately using the level (center) and window (width), respectively (Fig. 4).

Fig. 4. Windowing settings in the *Tool Box*, when selecting *Edit-Hounsfield Units*.

2.4   Annotation

The application is designed to accommodate three complementary types of annotation: manual, automatic, and semantic annotations. The manual and automatic annotation methods work together to improve the quality of annotations. Manual annotation is great at identifying intricate details but requires a lot of time and effort. Conversely, automatic annotation is swift and user-friendly but may lack precision, given the absence of a perfect script, even with the application of ML and DL techniques.

Recognizing the need for a comprehensive approach, both manual and automatic annotations are integrated into the application to harness the strengths of each and achieve optimal graphical annotation (Fig. 5). The final piece of the puzzle involved incorporating linguistic notes to facilitate mask interpretation, leading to the emergence of semantic annotation as the solution.

Fig. 5. Tools available in the *Tool Box*, highlighted in groups: brush, erase and mouse tools for manual annotation (red); hide/show, copy/paste, spline edit, clean and delete tools (yellow); and script for automatic annotation (blue). (Color figure online)

Manual Annotation. There are two groups of buttons for manual annotation. The first group changes brush mode between drawing, erasing, and clicking (red box in Fig. 5). The second group assists with annotation, offering functions like hide/show and delete masks, and edit, copy/paste and clean annotations (yellow box). The edit option with splines is presented in Fig. 6.

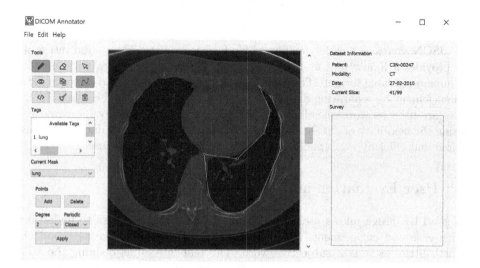

Fig. 6. Spline edition tool to unify, update and modify annotations.

Automatic Annotation. The button highlighted in blue in Fig. 5 is related to the automatic annotation. It runs external scripts that return the new masks [12, 13]. After being displayed, they can be adjusted with the available tools.

Semantic Annotation. The survey is a JSON file displayed in the *Survey Area* (Fig. 7) after being selected and loaded, allowing the user to interact with it and save it back to a JSON file.

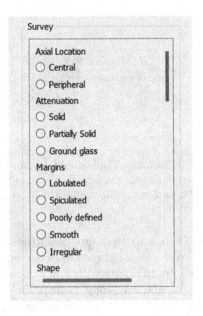

Fig. 7. *Survey Area* with an example of notes the user can take.

JSON serves as a widely employed file format for data storage and retrieval. It provides a lightweight and flexible means of representing data structures in a human-readable format. This approach ensures modularity and effective data management by separating data from the application's logic and control. JSON files are used to store questions and answers in surveys as key-value pairs. By using the flexibility of JSON, the application can manage survey data in a structured and efficient way, enabling dynamic interactions with the user.

3   User Evaluation and Discussion

A good UI design allows users to perform all the tasks they wish to undertake with ease and engagement. However, describing a user interface as "good" is worth little, as it is a subjective word. The real interest is defining the UI's usability [15]. Usability is defined in ISO 9241 standard [14] as the "extent to which a product can be used by specified users to achieve specified goals with effectiveness, efficiency and satisfaction in a specified context of use".

Measurement of the usability is essential to answer questions related to software processes. It helps in project planning, identifying the areas of improvement, and assessing the quality of processes and products. The selected model for measuring usability in this project is the Goals Questions Metrics (GQM) approach, based on the idea that an organization must first specify its projects' goals (Conceptual level). Then, it should trace those goals to the data intended (Operational level) and provide a framework for interpreting the data concerning the stated goals (Quantitative level) [3].

3.1 Conceptual Level

Usability criteria are recognized dimensions in human factors that enhance user interface behaviour. However, their definitions lack consistency in literature, with different authors proposing various dimensions. After a review and comparison, nine criteria have been identified: suitability for the task, self-descriptiveness [9], flexibility [10], user control [6], error management, user workload, consistency [11], time behaviour and attractiveness [8].

Table 3. Synthesized guidelines for user interface design of a clinical tool for annotation and visualization of medical images.

Usability Criteria	Sub Criteria	Guidelines
Suitability for Tasks (ST)	Needs/Requirements	Meet the needs and requirements of users when performing tasks
	Easy to accomplish	Help accomplish specific tasks
Flexibility (F)	-	Allow customization to suit the needs of different users
User Control (UC)	-	Provide appropriate controls (save, reset, exit, etc)
Self-descriptiveness (SD)	Feedback/Tutorials	Provide sufficient feedback, guidance, and support to help users
	Hints/Clues	Provide task-related hints and clues
Error Management (EM)	-	Provide mechanisms for error prevention and correction
User Workload (UW)	Concept	Familiar concepts
	Intuitive	Ease to learn and intuitive to use
Time Behavior (TB)	Tasks	Time to complete tasks
	Loading	Time to respond to actions
	Learning	Learning time
Consistency (C)	-	Appearance and behavior should remain consistent
Attractiveness (A)	User experience	Satisfaction with overall user experience
	Starting guide	Satisfaction with the user starting guide
	Motivation	Motivation to use the system on a daily routine

While these usability characteristics and criteria are important, their relative importance needs to be weighted, as depicted in Fig. 8.

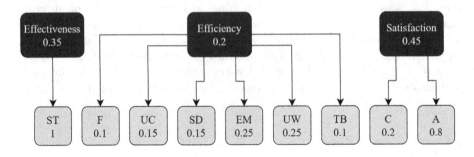

Fig. 8. Weights of Usability Characteristics and Criteria.

3.2   Operational Level

To assess the achievement of a specific goal, a set of questions is used based on a characterizing model. From the specification of each goal, we can derive meaningful questions that quantify the progress toward achieving that goal. The goals and guidelines are used to formulate a list of questions that assess each goal, making sure the questions can be answered.

3.3   Quantitative Level

Each question relates to objective or subjective data that can be used to answer it quantitatively. Objective data only depends on the object being measured and not on the viewpoint from which it is being observed. In contrast, subjective data depends on both the object and the viewpoint. This association considers:

- The amount and quality of the existing data: try to maximize the use of existing data sources, if they are available and reliable;
- Maturity of the objects of measurement: objective measures to more mature measurement objects, and we will use more subjective evaluations when dealing with informal or unstable objects;
- Learning process: GQM models always need refinement and adaptation. The measures defined must help the developer in evaluating not only the object of measurement but also the reliability of the model used to evaluate it.

The resulting goals, questions, and objective and subjective metrics for usability evaluation of the developed clinical visualization and annotation tool are shown in Table 4. These objective and subjective metrics are used in the next phase to develop evaluation instruments that are a user-starting guide with tasks and a survey, respectively.

Table 4. Usability characteristics, goals, questions, and metrics. Objective metrics are highlighted in bold, while the remaining are subjective metrics.

Usability Characteristics	Goals	Questions	Metrics
Effectiveness	Suitability for the task	How well does the system meet your needs and requirements when performing the proposed task?	Rating scale for user needs and requirements met in each task
			Rating scale for support in accomplishing each task
		How would you rate the system's support in helping you accomplish the proposed task?	**Percentage of users completing each task**
			Ratio of successful interactions to errors in tasks
			Number of tasks completed in a given time
Efficiency	Flexibility	How would you rate the system's flexibility and customization options?	Rating scale for flexibility and customization
	User Control	To what extent do you feel in control of the interface?	Rating scale for user control
	Self-descriptiveness	How well does the system provide clear feedback, guidance, and support?	Rating scale for feedback, guidance and support
		How would you rate the system's ability to help you understand and effectively use its features?	Rating scale for support in understanding and effectively using the system features
	Error Management	How effectively does the system prevent errors?	Rating scale of error prevention
	User Workload	How efficient is the system in preventing the cognitive overload?	Rating scale of cognitive overload prevention
		How would you rate the system's alignment with your existing conventions and expectations?	Rating scale of alignment with user conventions and expectations
	Time Behavior		**Number of references to help**
			Time spent loading masks
			Learning time
Satisfaction	Consistency	How would you rate the system's consistency throughout your interaction?	Rating scale of interface consistency
	Attractiveness	Did you have any complaints about the system when performing this task? If yes, please rate their severity.	Rating scale of frequency of complaints in each task
		How satisfied are you with the overall user experience?	Rating scale of user satisfaction in using the application
		How satisfied are you with the user starting guide?	Rating scale of user satisfaction regards the user starting guide
		Would you consider using the system?	Proportion of users who say they would use the system
			Number of suggestions to improve the system

3.4   Results and Discussion

The chosen methodology involved observing user interactions with the system and distributing surveys to gather feedback from potential users. The collected data was subsequently converted into a quantitative scale of 1 to 5, as specified in Table 5. This conversion was done to eliminate ambiguity and facilitate comparison, with a rating of 5 representing the ideal interface.

Table 5. Usability Characteristics and Criteria to evaluate the usability of the application with respective weights and measures on a scale of 1 to 5.

Usability Characteristics and Criteria	Normalized Weight	Actual Measure
Effectiveness	0.35	4.60
Suitability for the task (ST)	1 [0.35]	4.60
Efficiency	0.20	3.92
Flexibility (F)	0.10 [0.02]	4.10
User Control (UC)	0.15 [0.03]	4.00
Self-descriptiveness (SD)	0.15 [0.03]	3.70
Error Management (EM)	0.25 [0.05]	3.80
User Workload (UW)	0.25 [0.05]	4.20
Time Behavior (TB)	0.10 [0.02]	3.52
Satisfaction	0.45	4.3
Consistency (C)	0.20 [0.09]	4.40
Attractiveness (A)	0.80 [0.36]	4.36
Rating	1.00	4.36

There were ten participants in the user evaluation phase. Eight of them were engineers, five specialize in biomedical engineering, while the other three specialize in a different engineering area. The remaining two participants were radiologists with eleven and thirteen years of experience.

The user began the test by carefully reading the starting guide and then performed nine well-defined tasks aimed at testing all the available tools:

- Task 1: image loading, navigation, and windowing;
- Task 2: manually annotate using the brush tool;
- Task 3: test the copy-and-paste function;
- Task 4: use the erase, clear, and delete tools;
- Task 5: open and run an external script for automatic annotation;
- Task 6: open a previously annotated mask and experiment the visibility tool;
- Task 7: test spline edition, by moving, adding and deleting control points;
- Test 8: survey opening and filling for semantic annotation;
- Task 9: save both the mask and the survey.

Figure 9 shows the average time spent on each task by the users, along with the time taken by the developer to complete each task. The developer's time represents the duration required to complete the task when the user is aware of the functionality. By subtracting the developer's time from the mean user time for each task, it is possible to arrive at the learning time.

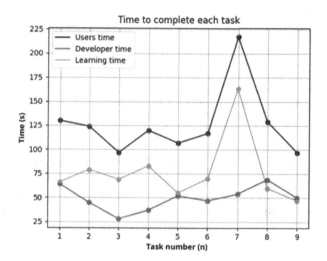

Fig. 9. Mean time spent on each task by the users (blue) and by the developer (orange) and learning time (green). (Color figure online)

Based on the data gathered, it was found that the seventh task, which involved spline editing, was the most difficult for users to learn. Further analysis revealed that the task had a high error rate and a significant number of user assistance requests, as shown in Fig. 10.

These findings reinforce the idea that users faced difficulties when working with spline-based annotations, suggesting that the spline functionality is relatively challenging compared to other tasks and should be revised later on.

An analysis of correlation was conducted utilizing the coefficient of determination among the variables academic background, user errors, references to help, and time to complete all proposed tasks. The findings indicate that no statistically significant correlation was observed.

After analyzing the results obtained from the usability evaluations, it was possible to identify the strengths of the application and the necessary improvements. Receiving feedback from the questionnaire's open-ended question, which asked for additional feedback and suggestions, was especially helpful. Most of the responses suggested simple improvements that were already implemented, such as enhancing the user interface for a more pleasing and user-friendly experience, adding a *Help* button for more guidance and support, a *Zoom* function to assist the annotation and loading screens, as it takes a while opening and

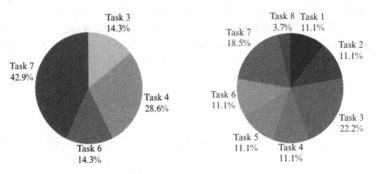

Fig. 10. Graphs showing the percentage of help references and errors per task. Tasks with zero values are not displayed.

saving big datasets. However, some major functions like *Undo* and *Redo* options were also requested and are addressed as future work. It was also mentioned that the simplicity of the application was a clear advantage since, compared to other applications previously used by the participants, it was much easier to use.

4   Conclusions

Communication among medical teams is fundamental to achieving positive influence in the lives of patients. They must deal with a considerable amount of information in the minimum amount of time. It is then fundamental for software design engineering to develop simple modules for visualization, annotation, detection, segmentation and classification of medical images to guide them to the best decision. As a result, a variety of applications that attempt to answer all the clinical user's needs have been implemented.

The PL chosen to implement the tool was Python, as it has an immeasurable amount of libraries that help the developer create GUIs, such as the employed PyQt5, work with DICOM files, such as PyDicom, and integrate scripting plugins and external storage of information, for example in JSON format. The development process prioritized creating a clear and user-friendly GUI design and intuitive user workflows to ensure a positive experience for the end user.

The analysis of the user evaluation's results underscored numerous areas for improvement. Nonetheless, participants acknowledged the application's simplicity, favourably contrasting it with previous tools, and recognized its suitability for completing the tasks, consistency and attractiveness.

Acknowledgment. This work is financed by National Funds through the FCT - Fundação para a Ciência e a Tecnologia, I.P. (Portuguese Foundation for Science and Technology) within the project LUCCA, with reference 2022.03488.PTDC and the PhD Grant Numbers: 2021.05767.BD (Francisco Silva) and 2023.03408.BD (Joana Sousa).

The collaboration with Dr Silvia Dias and Dr Miguel Castro, radiologists from Centro Hospitalar Universitário de São João, as well as Tânia Mendes, Tomé Albuquerque, Margarida Gouveia, Eduardo Rodrigues, Luís Pereira, João Nunes and Isabel Rio-Torto, members from the INESC TEC VCMI team, also contributed greatly to the success of this work through usability evaluation.

References

1. Aljabri, M., AlAmir, M., AlGhamdi, M., Abdel-Mottaleb, M., Collado-Mesa, F.: Towards a better understanding of annotation tools for medical imaging: a survey. Multimedia Tools Appl. **81**(18), 25877–25911 (2022)
2. Berland, L.L.: Practical CT technology and techniques (1987)
3. Caldiera, V.R.B.G., Rombach, H.D.: The goal question metric approach. Encycl. Softw. Eng. **1**, 528–532 (1994)
4. DenOtter, T.D., Schubert, J.: Hounsfield Unit (2019)
5. Dong, Q., et al.: DicomAnnotator: a configurable open-source software program for efficient DICOM image annotation. J. Digit. Imag. **33**(6), 1514–1526 (2020). Cited by: 3; All Open Access, Green Open Access
6. Holcomb, R., Tharp, A.L.: What users say about software usability. Int. J. Hum. Comput. Interact. **3**(1), 49–78 (1991)
7. Holzinger, A., Haibe-Kains, B., Jurisica, I.: Why imaging data alone is not enough: AI-based integration of imaging, omics, and clinical data. Eur. J. Nucl. Med. Mol. Imag. **46**(13), 2722–2730 (2019)
8. ISO/IEC 9126-1:2001: Software engineering-product quality-part 1: quality model. International Organization for Standardization, Geneva, Switzerland **21** (2001)
9. Prümper, J.: Software-evaluation based upon ISO 9241 part 10. In: Grechenig, T., Tscheligi, M. (eds.) VCHCI 1993. LNCS, vol. 733, pp. 255–265. Springer, Heidelberg (1993). https://doi.org/10.1007/3-540-57312-7_74
10. Ravden, S., Johnson, G.: Evaluating Usability of Human-Computer Interfaces: A Practical Method. Halsted Press (1989)
11. Scapin, D.L.: Organizing human factors knowledge for the evaluation and design of interfaces. Int. J. Hum. Comput. Interact. **2**(3), 203–229 (1990)
12. Silva, F., Pereira, T., Morgado, J., Cunha, A., Oliveira, H.P.: The impact of interstitial diseases patterns on lung CT segmentation. In: 2021 43rd Annual International Conference of the IEEE Engineering in Medicine & Biology Society (EMBC), pp. 2856–2859 (2021)
13. Sousa, J., Pereira, T., Neves, I., Silva, F., Oliveira, H.P.: The influence of a coherent annotation and synthetic addition of lung nodules for lung segmentation in CT scans. Sensors **22**(9), 3443 (2022). https://www.mdpi.com/1424-8220/22/9/3443
14. ISO 9241-11: Ergonomic requirements for office work with visual display terminals (VDTs)-part 11: guidance on usability. ISO Standard 9241-11: 1998. International Organization for Standardization **55** (1998)
15. Stone, D., Jarrett, C., Woodroffe, M., Minocha, S.: User Interface Design and Evaluation. Elsevier (2005)
16. Teixeira, J.P.F.: An anatomical breast atlas: automatic segmentation of key points in multiple radiological modalities. Ph.D. thesis, University of Porto (2022). https://hdl.handle.net/10216/141586
17. Zhuang, M., et al.: AnatomySketch: an extensible open-source software platform for medical image analysis algorithm development. J. Digit. Imaging **35**, 1623–1633 (2022). Cited by: 0; All Open Access, Green Open Access, Hybrid Gold Open Access

Technological Empowerment for Aging Workforce in Elderly Care Programs: Service Model Design and Development of an Elderly Care Shared Service Platform

Tsai-Hsuan Tsai[1,2,3]([✉]), Hsin-Yu Lo[1], Shih-Lin Wu[4], Yueh-Peng Chen[2,5,6], and Chien-Lung Hsu[7]

[1] Department of Industrial Design, Chang Gung University, Taoyuan, Taiwan
ttsai@gap.cgu.edu.tw

[2] Master of Science Degree Program in Innovation for Smart Medicine, Chang Gung University, Taoyuan, Taiwan

[3] Department of Physical Medicine and Rehabilitation, Linkou Chang Gung Memorial Hospital, Taoyuan, Taiwan

[4] Department of Computer Science and Information Engineering, Chang Gung University, Taoyuan, Taiwan

[5] Center for Artificial Intelligence in Medicine, Chang Gung Memorial Hospital at Linkou, Taoyuan, Taiwan

[6] Division of Rheumatology, Allergy and Immunology, Chang Gung Memorial Hospital at Linkou, Taoyuan, Taiwan

[7] Department of Information Management, Chang Gung University, Taoyuan, Taiwan

Abstract. This study introduces a platform designed to address the challenges of global aging by implementing an "elderly assist for elderly" concept. It aims to alleviate the long-term care service manpower shortage by integrating elderly individuals into the market for in-home elderly care. Utilizing the Person-Job Fit model, the platform adopts a personalized approach to match task assignments with the elderly's changing values, needs, and competencies. Intelligent scheduling and automatic service provider recommendations are employed to enhance the user experience by ensuring optimal matches between providers and services. The platform's performance analysis is grounded in the Job Demands-Resources theory, ensuring its stability and reliability. Additionally, a point system inspired by time banking encourages user participation and sustains service value. Comprehensive internal testing was conducted to identify and address potential issues before formal testing, improving the prototype's usability. Overall, this study proposes a novel solution to the challenges of global aging by integrating time banking, personalized design, and technological innovation, promoting a healthier and more sustainable elderly lifestyle.

Keywords: Aging workforce · Technological empowerment · Silver economy

M. Antona and C. Stephanidis (Eds.): HCII 2024, LNCS 14698, pp. 334–344, 2024.
https://doi.org/10.1007/978-3-031-60884-1_23

1   Introduction

The evolution toward a super-aged society is a significant global demographic trend, with the population aged 65 and above reaching approximately 727 million in 2022, up from 258 million in 1980. This demographic transformation was highlighted in 2018 when, for the first time, the number of older individuals surpassed the number of children under five. Projected to reach 1.6 billion by 2050, this segment will constitute 16% of the global population, effectively doubling the number of children under five and approaching the population of children under 12 [1]. This shift, driven by declining fertility rates and reduced mortality rates, amplifies the need for comprehensive long-term care services for the elderly, placing significant financial pressure on national care systems [2].

In response, international policy initiatives are accelerating. The World Health Organization (WHO) in 2019 updated the Integrated Care for Older People (ICOPE) guidelines to support healthy aging through community health and care worker initiatives [3]. Concurrently, the United Nations advocates for pension system reforms, including raising the retirement age and expanding benefits, to address the economic challenges of an aging workforce. The WHO and UN member states further cemented their commitment with the launch of the UN Decade of Healthy Ageing: Plan of Action in 2020, aiming to enhance the quality of life for older individuals on personal, family, and community levels. This initiative reflects a collective effort to develop professional medical talent, enhance social awareness, and innovate financial and social frameworks in support of the aging populace [4–6].

Yet, the growing demand for elderly life services and a dwindling workforce remain daunting challenges. Time banking has surfaced as an innovative solution, promoting a "helping people help themselves" philosophy by enabling the exchange of labour or knowledge for necessary services. This approach suggests that the active engagement of healthy seniors could fortify the well-being of those aged 55 and above [7–9]. Moreover, the advent of the sharing economy, marked by its emphasis on the sustainable use of underutilized resources, along with technological advancements, has spotlighted the potential of sharing platforms to mediate between services and demands. There is a notable increase in senior engagement with technology, not only to alleviate physical burdens but also to enhance their overall work and life quality [10–12].

This study aims to capitalize on these developments by designing a platform that empowers seniors, facilitating their contribution to the silver economy through mutual assistance in "elderly assist elderly." By exploring the platform's development and its effectiveness through prototype testing, this research seeks to offer insights into leveraging technology to address the challenges and opportunities presented by global aging, thereby contributing to the discourse on aging and technological solutions.

2   Design and Development Aligned with the Needs of the Elderly

Our study presents a holistic strategy to integrate elderly individuals into the workforce, employing the Person-Job Fit (P-J Fit) model as a foundational framework for a personalized methodology [13]. This approach, illustrated in Fig. 1, recognizes the evolving nature of an individual's values, needs, and skills with age, emphasizing the necessity to assess compatibility between job requirements and personal capabilities. By integrating personal interests, talents, and job characteristics through the P-J Fit model, we expand its application to our system's architecture [14]. A comprehensive user questionnaire enables the collection and analysis of retirees' interests, talents, and capabilities, culminating in a personalized database. This process ensures task assignments are precisely aligned with daily life's intricacies, customizing workforce integration to individualized profiles.

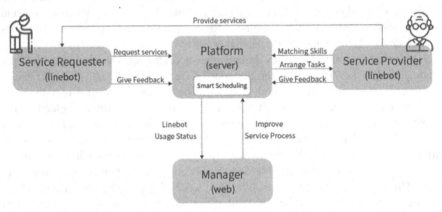

Fig. 1. Conceptual Model Illustrating Interactions among Service Providers, Service Requesters, Managers, and the Platform Server.

The platform is designed with an acute focus on user traits, incorporating intelligent scheduling to automatically recommend service providers based on the alignment of talents and interests. It further meets the needs of service requesters by providing personalized services, thus fostering a harmonious ecosystem. The Order Creation and Management section reveals how the platform enhances service times and user satisfaction through customized service recommendations. Anchored in the Job Demands-Resources (J D-R) theory, our Performance Analysis section emphasizes the balance between job demands and resources, integrating feedback from service requester satisfaction and service provider self-assessments to systematically evaluate preferences and suitability. This establishes a feedback loop that boosts job satisfaction and streamlines service delivery.

Addressing the manpower shortage in elderly care, the Rewards section introduces an innovative point system inspired by time banking, designed to motivate active participation, enhance service value, and improve the user experience. Moreover, embracing technology suitable for the elderly demographic, our research utilizes LINE, Taiwan's foremost Conversational User Interface (CUI) application, as the foundational platform. A Linebot ensures effective connections between service providers and requesters, facilitating an optimal match of abilities and needs. As depicted in Fig. 2, this mechanism visually distinguishes the functionalities available to service providers and requesters, highlighting the streamlined process for connecting users through the platform. This feature is crucial in enhancing matchmaking efficiency and operational effectiveness in elderly care services, showcasing our strategy's capacity to tackle the challenges of an aging workforce and underscore the vital role of technology in enriching the elderly care ecosystem.

Fig. 2. Linebot Integration for Service Coordination via the LINE App.

2.1 Skill and Interest Matching

As individuals age, their values, needs, physical conditions, cognitive abilities, and skills experience significant transformations, necessitating the reevaluation of job goals and development strategies [14]. Acknowledging that previous occupations may no longer align with the capabilities of older workers, our study utilizes the Person-Job Fit (P-J Fit) model to examine the compatibility between job requirements and an individual's abilities [15]. This model amalgamates personal interests, talents, and job characteristics across nine evaluative dimensions to ascertain job suitability. Extending the P-J Fit model's application to the architecture of our system underscores the critical role of understanding user traits. Upon account registration, users are prompted to complete a questionnaire that probes their talents, interests, and job capabilities. The responses contribute to a personalized database, directing task assignments towards "daily life" activities. This ensures that service providers are positioned to effectively leverage their abilities, aligning with the preferences of retirees. Figure 3 depicts this initial phase, highlighting the prerequisite of filling out a comprehensive form detailing personal characteristics prior to accessing the system's features.

Fig. 3. Initial Setup: Completing the Personal Characteristics Information Form.

2.2 Order Creation and Management

The system meticulously analyzes questionnaire results to independently recommend service providers whose talents, interests, and job characteristics align with the demands of the service, thereby ensuring an efficient deployment of skills and superior task management. It utilizes intelligent scheduling to refine service times, alongside offering services precisely tailored to the specific requirements of service requesters. This approach not only boosts user satisfaction but also fosters a harmonious ecosystem. By harnessing data on the capabilities of service providers, the system proactively customizes services to meet the unique needs of service requesters. This personalized strategy significantly enhances user satisfaction and develops a dynamic and unified ecosystem, facilitating seamless interactions based on individual preferences and requirements. The aim is to enrich the overall user experience and encourage mutually beneficial interactions.

As illustrated in Fig. 4, the system's proficiency in employing intelligent scheduling to cater to the distinctive needs of service requesters is showcased. The figure demonstrates how inputs from the Personal Characteristics section guide the system's service recommendations, with the interfaces for service providers and requesters depicted on the left and right, respectively. This visualization highlights the system's capability to tailor services, ensuring a personalized and efficient service delivery process.

Fig. 4. Intelligent Scheduling for Tailored Services.

2.3 Performance Analysis

The reliance on the Person-Job Fit model for assessing work motivation is deemed insufficient as it does not fully capture the array of daily work experiences, including both positive achievements and potential challenges that may contribute to worker fatigue [15]. The Job Demands-Resources (J D-R) theory, introduced by Bakker, A. B., Demerouti, E., & Sanz-Vergel, highlights the essential requirement for a balance between job demands and resources. This balance is crucial for cultivating a sense of achievement and enhancing well-being among employees [16].

In our study, we extend the J D-R framework by including assessments of service requester satisfaction and service provider self-reflection. This comprehensive approach allows for an in-depth analysis of service providers' preferences and their suitability for specific tasks, thereby fostering a work environment that supports both personal satisfaction and professional growth. The establishment of a continuous feedback loop is central to our methodology, with the objective of significantly improving job satisfaction and the quality of service delivery.

Figure 5 provides a detailed view of the feedback mechanism between service providers and requesters. It demonstrates how evaluations and self-reflections contribute to ongoing improvements and satisfaction in the service exchange process. The diagram is divided, with the left side focused on service providers and the right on service requesters. This division effectively illustrates the system's capacity to adapt and refine service offerings based on direct feedback, thereby operationalizing the J D-R theory's principles in a practical setting.

Fig. 5. Dynamic Feedback Loop in Service Provision

2.4 Rewards

In response to the critical manpower shortage in care services, this study innovatively incorporates the concept of "saving" from time banks into a point system on our platform, calibrated according to the complexity of services offered. This pioneering approach is designed to stimulate active participation and extend the service's intrinsic value. By amalgamating the principles of time banking with a points-based system, we infuse the platform with diverse and engaging features, enabling users to accrue more substantial rewards as they contribute their services. This enhances user engagement and maintains the service's value in the face of demographic shifts and other prevailing challenges.

To further bolster the sustainability of service value, our study employs a nuanced integration of time banking "savings" into a platform-centric point system. Points are allocated based on the difficulty level of services provided by users, with a carefully designed mechanism for the accumulation and redemption of these points. This strategy not only encourages users to participate more fervently but also promotes the longevity of the service's value. The fusion of time banking with a point system introduces a spectrum of enticing features to the platform, augmenting the rewards available to users for their service contributions. This strategic integration is aimed at enhancing user participation and ensuring the continuous allure and efficacy of the service offered.

Figure 6 illustrates the platform's feedback-driven rewards system, designed to enhance user participation and satisfaction. It details the process through which feedback and performance are transformed into tangible rewards, highlighting the innovative approach the system employs to acknowledge and reward user contributions and achievements. This visualization emphasizes the system's ability to promote a positive and engaging user experience by directly associating service quality and user feedback with the rewards mechanism.

Fig. 6. Reward System to Enhance User Engagement.

3 Prototype Testing

Drawing from prior research, paper prototypes are frequently utilized in the initial phases of user-centered design to enhance communication among designers, developers, users, and stakeholders [17–21]. These prototypes are not only crucial for validating design concepts and gathering user feedback but also offer several benefits over digital prototypes, including lower costs, quicker development, easier modifications, and the facilitation of participatory design approaches [22]. Although testing with the study's target group—older adults—has not been conducted, such an evaluation is planned as the next phase. At this juncture, internal testing is imperative to assess the prototype's performance and quality through detailed functional, user experience, and usability evaluations. Consequently, this study employed paper prototyping for in-depth internal testing. The findings from the usability assessment, conducted through paper prototype evaluations, are summarized below:

1. Concepts and Terms: The assessment verified that target users could understand the chosen terminology and that no key concepts were overlooked or misunderstood, ensuring intuitive system interaction.
2. Navigation/Workflows: The evaluation confirmed that the designed processes or steps met user expectations, eliminating the need for frequent screen switching and ensuring users were not required to input non-existent or undesired information, streamlining the user experience.
3. Content: The system was found to provide essential information without overwhelming users with unnecessary or extraneous details, maintaining user engagement and satisfaction through a careful balance of content.

4. Page Layout: Testing ensured that users could easily locate the required information, with fields organized as anticipated. The amount of information was deemed optimal, avoiding both excess and scarcity to optimize the user interface for efficiency and ease of use.
5. Functionality: The evaluation affirmed that all essential functions were included in the prototype, excluding features considered irrelevant by target users, thereby focusing on functionality that enhances the user experience.

These findings highlight the importance of a user-centered design approach in developing systems that are both functional and user-friendly. This assessment identified and resolved potential usability issues, paving the way for further development and refinement of the prototype.

4 Conclusion

This study addresses the critical global challenge of an aging population by proposing an innovative platform that leverages the concept of time banking to alleviate manpower shortages in long-term care services. Integrating elderly individuals into the labor market, our approach employs the Person-Job Fit (P-J Fit) model to tailor opportunities in line with the dynamic changes in values, needs, and skills of this demographic. The platform is distinguished by its intelligent scheduling and automatic service provider recommendations, ensuring a seamless match between service providers and required services, significantly enhancing the user experience.

Furthermore, the research introduces a novel point system inspired by time banking principles, designed to motivate active participation and maintain the value of offered services. This system, correlating the complexity of services with point allocation, aims to foster a dynamic and engaging platform environment, thereby increasing user satisfaction and the benefits of service provision.

While the prototype awaits evaluation by the intended elderly user group, comprehensive internal testing across eight crucial dimensions has identified and addressed potential issues, improving the prototype's usability and effectiveness in anticipation of future testing.

In summary, our study presents a forward-looking solution to the complexities of global aging, integrating time banking concepts, personalized design, and technological innovation. It endeavors to establish a robust and sustainable long-term care service system, promoting healthier and more sustainable living conditions for the elderly. This research not only fills a significant gap in the existing literature but also lays the groundwork for future innovations in elderly care services.

Acknowledgments. We express our profound gratitude to Chang Gung Health and Culture Village for their invaluable contributions. Their willingness to share extensive experiences in elderly care, along with providing robust support, advice, and suggestions, has significantly facilitated the smooth conduct of this project. We also acknowledge the financial support received from the National Science and Technology Council (Taiwan), under Grants NSTC 111-2221-E-182-035 and NSTC 112-2410-H-182-014-MY2, which has been instrumental in advancing this study. It is crucial to note that the funders had no role in the study design, data collection and analysis, decision to publish, or preparation of the manuscript, ensuring the integrity and independence of our research.

Disclosure of Interests. The authors declare no conflict of interest related to this study. Research activities, including study design, data collection, analysis, decision to publish, and manuscript preparation, were conducted independently of the funding sources. The financial support from the National Science and Technology Council (Taiwan) and the non-financial contributions from Chang Gung Health and Culture Village did not influ-ence the content of the research or the findings reported in this manuscript.

References

1. United Nations Department of Economic and Social Affairs, P.D., World Population Prospects 2022: Summary of Results, in UN DESA/POP/2022/NO.3. United Nations Department of Economic and Social Affairs, Population Division (2022)
2. Ariaans, M., Linden, P., Wendt, C.: Worlds of long-term care: a typology of OECD countries. Health Policy **125**(5), 609–617 (2021)
3. World Health Organization, Integrated care for older people (ICOPE): guidance for person-centred assessment and pathways in primary care. World Health Organization: Geneva (2019)
4. Amuthavalli Thiyagarajan, J., et al.: The UN Decade of healthy ageing: strengthening measurement for monitoring health and wellbeing of older people. Age Ageing **51**(7) (2022)
5. Song, P., Tang, W.: The community-based integrated care system in Japan: health care and nursing care challenges posed by super-aged society. Biosci. Trends **13**(3), 279–281 (2019)
6. Fang, E.F., et al.: A research agenda for ageing in China in the 21st century (2nd edition): focusing on basic and translational research, long-term care, policy and social networks. Ageing Res. Rev. **64**, 101–174 (2020)
7. David Boyle, N.W.I.: The potential of time banks to support social inclusion and employa-bility: an investigation into the use of reciprocal volunteering and complementary currencies for social impact, I.f.P. James Stewart and T.S. (JRC-IPTS), Editors. Institute for Prospective Technological Studies: Spain, p. 92 (2014)
8. Chou, W.H., Lee, L.H.: Investigating the preferences for time banking for senior citizens: local needs and constraints in the context of Taiwanese culture. デザイン学研究**61**(5), 5_97–5_106 (2015)
9. Collom, E.: Engagement of the elderly in time banking: the potential for social capital generation in an aging society. J. Aging Soc. Policy **20**(4), 414–436 (2008)
10. Hossain, M.: Sharing economy: a comprehensive literature review. Int. J. Hosp. Manag. **87**, 102470 (2020)
11. Puschmann, T., Alt, R.: Sharing economy. Bus. Inf. Syst. Eng. **58**(1), 93–99 (2016)
12. Pang, C., et al.: Technology adoption and learning preferences for older adults. In: Proceedings of the 2021 CHI Conference on Human Factors in Computing Systems, pp. 1–13 (2021)
13. Wong, C.M., Tetrick, L.E.: Job crafting: older workers' mechanism for maintaining person-job fit. Front. Psychol. **8**, 1548 (2017)
14. Brkich, M., Jeffs, D., Carless, S.A.: A global self-report measure of person-job fit. Eur. J. Psychol. Assess. **18**(1), 43–51 (2002)
15. Gurbuz, S., et al.: Measuring sustainable employability: psychometric properties of the capability set for work questionnaire. BMC Public Health **22**(1), 1184 (2022)
16. Bakker, A.B., Demerouti, E., Sanz-Vergel, A.: Job demands-resources theory: ten years later. Annu. Rev. Organ. Psych. Organ. Behav. **10**(1), 25–53 (2023)

17. Walker, M., et al.: High-fidelity or low-fidelity, paper or computer choosing attributes when testing web prototypes. Proc. Hum. Factors Ergon. Soc. Annu. Meet. **46** (2002)
18. Sefelin, R., Tscheligi, M., Giller, V.: Paper prototyping - what is it good for? A comparison of paper- and computer-based low-fidelity prototyping. In: CHI 2003 Extended Abstracts on Human Factors in Computing Systems. Association for Computing Machinery, Ft. Lauderdale, Florida, USA, pp. 778–779 (2003)
19. Snyder, C.: Paper Prototyping: The Fast and Easy Way to Design and Refine User Interfaces (2003)
20. Arnowitz, J., Arent, M., Berger, N.: Effective Prototyping for Software Makers (Interactive Technologies) (2006)
21. Miller, D.: The best practice of teach computer science students to use paper prototyping. Int. J. Technol. Innov. Manag. (IJTIM) **1**(2), 42–63 (2021)
22. Snyder, C.: Paper prototyping: Sure, it's low-tech, but this usability testing method can help you sidestep problems before you write your code (2001). https://redirect.cs.umbc.edu/courses/undergraduate/345/spring11/mitchell/Assignments/CSnyderPaperPrototyping.pdf. Accessed 21 Feb 2024

Effectiveness of Technology-Assisted Medication Reminder Systems in Neurodegenerative Diseases: Systematic Review and Meta-analysis

Kevin C. Tseng[1,2,3](✉) [iD] and Yi-Han Wang[2,3](✉)

[1] Department of Industrial Design, National Taipei University of Technology, Taipei, Taiwan
ktseng@pddlab.org
[2] College of Design, National Taipei University of Technology, Taipei, Taiwan
yihanwang0210@gmail.com
[3] Product Design and Development Laboratory, Taoyuan, Taiwan

Abstract. Neurodegenerative diseases are currently irreversible conditions. As these diseases often occur in older people, the patients often have other chronic diseases, leading to the possibility of multiple medications and associated problems such as drug interactions, nonadherence, and adverse reactions. This study aims to evaluate the effectiveness of technology-assisted medication reminder systems in patients with neurodegenerative or chronic diseases. Additionally, it explores the architecture and design of technology-assisted medication reminder systems alongside their functional modules. A systematic search was conducted through December 2023 across various databases, including PubMed, ScienceDirect, Scopus, Web of Science, and IEEE, for clinical studies on the effectiveness of technology-assisted medication reminders. The preferred reporting items for systematic reviews and meta-analyses (PRISMA) guidelines were followed. The Cochrane risk of bias (RoB) assessment tool was used to assess bias at each stage of each selected study. Statistical analysis was performed with Stata SE 15©. Due to the limited research on this topic, only two articles were included in the study, comprising a total of 240 patients in clinical studies. The results indicated that technology-assisted reminders significantly improved medication adherence. Particularly, the use of mobile apps for medication reminders was more accurate with respect to time and frequency. Our study highlights the importance of feedback and gamification to increase patient engagement with the application. The results emphasise the integration of multifunctional systems to provide relevant information to physicians and caregivers to monitor patient health conditions in real time.

Keywords: Application software · dementia · medication reminder · neurodegenerative diseases · Parkinson's disease

1 Introduction

Among neurodegenerative diseases, Parkinson's disease (PD) has a complicated treatment approach because patients often experience mood disorders and cognitive impairment, which lead to low medication adherence [1]. As a result, treatment efficacy is poor,

© The Author(s), under exclusive license to Springer Nature Switzerland AG 2024
M. Antona and C. Stephanidis (Eds.): HCII 2024, LNCS 14698, pp. 345–360, 2024.
https://doi.org/10.1007/978-3-031-60884-1_24

so deterioration occurs. Adherence to treatment can improve the effect of medication and quality of life in patients with PD [2]. As early as 2017, Choudhry et al. [3] discussed the use of the medicine bottle itself as a design strategy for improving medication adherence, and they calculated the adherence and correctness of medication use at the time when the patient took the medication.

In recent years, with the popularisation of smartphones and advancements in software technology, many studies have begun to use smartphones as platforms to design and develop medication reminder systems. He et al. [4] found that a medication reminder app was effective and made the patients feel connected with their family members, improving their quality of life. Li et al. [5] provided more concrete evidence for this phenomenon. Their research team developed a smartphone app named Perx, which is specially designed for patients receiving multiple drug treatments, helping them obtain better clinical results throughout the treatment process. Through its user-friendly interface and functions, the Perx app helps patients manage their drug treatment plans more effectively. This includes not only medication reminders but also the ability to track the medication history and determine the effect of treatment. Li et al. [5] found that the Perx app can significantly improve patient medication adherence, which is critical for maintaining the continuity and effectiveness of drug treatment. Compared with traditional medication methods, the main advantage of medication reminder apps is that they can provide a multifunctional interactive feedback mode, thereby improving patients' active treatment and medication adherence.

For the treatment of PD, taking medication on time and seeing the doctor on time are the main ways to stabilise the condition. Due to the complexity of taking PD medications and the limited time available for face-to-face consultation between clinicians and PD patients, it is difficult to comprehensively address the issue of patients' noncompliance with medication. Therefore, self-management of PD patients through smartphone apps can improve self-reported medication adherence and the quality of clinical treatment [6].

PD patients are usually elderly people, who often have multiple diseases as well as frailty. This makes them prone to multiple diseases and increases the likelihood of drug-induced adverse reactions, interactions between the disease and drugs, and interactions between drugs [7]. Many recent studies focused on the side effects of polypharmacy, whereas few studies have focused on the efficacy of technology-assisted medication reminders and the architecture and design of technology-assisted medication reminder systems [8, 9]. This study is the first meta-analysis of the effectiveness of a technology-assisted medication reminder for improving medication adherence and the first study to test whether this method is superior to traditional medication. This paper also summarizes the systematic design of the technology-assisted medication reminder system and the technology-assisted medication reminder mode through a systematic literature review.

2   Methods

This study was performed in accordance with the preferred reporting items for systematic reviews and meta-analysis (PRISMA) guidelines.

2.1 Database Search and Search Strategy Use

The research questions were transformed into the PICOS (P, participation/population; I, intervention; C, comparison; O, outcomes; S, study) model (Table 1). We searched the PubMed, ScienceDirect, Scopus, Web of Science, and IEEE databases for relevant papers. The search covered 2013 through 2023 (Table 2).

Table 1. The specified population, intervention, comparison, outcomes, and study items

Items	Details
P	Neurodegenerative diseases, Parkinson's disease, and chronic patients with medication
I	Technology-assisted medication reminder system
C	The control group (traditional intervention or no intervention) and the intervention group (medication system) were compared to examine the intervention effect
O	Medication adherence
S	Randomised controlled trial

Table 2. Search strategy

Database	Search strategy
PubMed	"neurodegenerative diseases" OR "Parkinson's disease" OR chronic AND "Medication" OR ("medication reminder" OR "reminder devices") AND Application OR ("App")
Science Direct	"neurodegenerative diseases" OR "Parkinson's disease" OR chronic AND "Medication" OR ("medication reminder" OR "reminder devices") AND Application OR ("App")
Scopus	"neurodegenerative diseases" OR "Parkinson's disease" OR chronic AND "Medication" OR ("medication reminder" OR "reminder devices") AND Application OR ("App")
Web of Science	"neurodegenerative diseases" OR "Parkinson's disease" OR chronic AND "Medication" OR ("medication reminder" OR "reminder devices") AND Application OR ("App")
IEEE	("All Metadata": "neurodegenerative diseases") OR "("All Metadata": "Parkinson's disease") OR ("All Metadata": "chronic" AND ("All Metadata": "Medication") OR ("All Metadata": "Medication") ": "medication reminder") OR ("All Metadata": "reminder devices") AND ("All Metadata": Application) OR ("All Metadata": "App")

2.2 Inclusion and Exclusion Criteria

The inclusion criteria of this study were as follows: (1) articles published in English; (2) patients with neurodegenerative diseases, PD, or chronic diseases who required long-term medication control as the main research subjects; and (3) Randomised controlled trials (RCTs) using a medication-assist system. The exclusion criteria were as follows: (1) studies that did not have the full text, (2) studies that did not use systems or equipment for assistance, (3) no medication needs, (4) review articles, and (5) case reports.

2.3 Data Extraction

We searched different databases through keyword searches, identified relevant articles after reading the titles and abstracts, excluded duplicate articles, and checked their inclusion criteria one by one. The screen was conducted by two independent researchers. When opinions differed, a third researcher reviewed the article to make sure each article met the inclusion criteria.

2.4 Quality Assessment

This study used the Cochrane risk of bias (RoB) assessment tool. A staged review of the selected research articles was also conducted, covering seven stages: random sequence generation (selection bias), allocation concealment (selection bias), blinding of participants and personnel (performance bias), blinding of outcome assessment (detection bias), incomplete outcome data (attrition bias), selective reporting (reporting bias), and other bias. Each stage was classified as having low risk of bias, unclear risk of bias, and high risk of bias for error assessment.

2.5 Statistical Analysis

Statistical analysis was performed using the statistical software Stata SE 15 ©. Meta-analysis was used to compare medication adherence outcomes between the experimental group (EG), which used technology-assisted medication reminders as a treatment method, and the control group (CG), which used traditional medication methods before and after technology-assisted medication reminders. The number of samples and the mean ± standard deviation were calculated for the present study and were used as effect indicators. The data of continuous variables in the meta-analysis submitted to statistical analysis. The point estimates for each effect amount were given with the 95% confidence interval (CI), which we used as a reference for subsequent analysis. The study used a random-effects model. For all analyses, the statistical significance level was set to $P < 0.05$, and the statistical results are displayed in the form of a forest plot.

3   Results

3.1 Study Screening

As shown in Fig. 1, with the set search strategy, a total of 31,450 articles were retrieved, and after 378 duplicate articles were deleted, five important studies were ultimately screened. In all five studies, informed consent was obtained before any treatment.

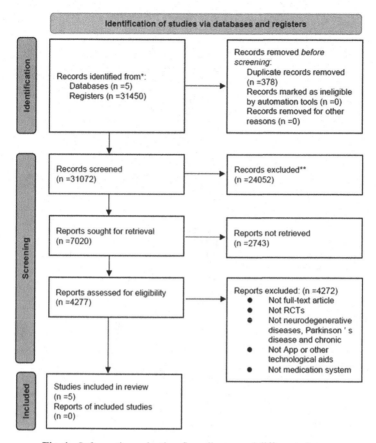

Fig. 1. Information selection flow diagram of different phases.

3.2 Quality of the Included Studies

Among the five included studies, three studies used tables to present the data and clearly described the data extraction methods, so they had low detection bias. The other two studies were assessed as having unclear biases because the screening methods were not fully explained (Fig. 2).

3.3 Data Extraction

The data extracted for this study are shown in Table 1. In the end, only two studies used the same scale and provided comparable data, which reduced the number of experimental participants to 240 in the final analysis (experimental group, n = 109; control group, n = 131). Although the sample was small, these results were screened from patients with neurodegenerative diseases, including PD, cancer, chronic diseases, and type 2 diabetes. These patients had usually been dependent on drug treatment for a long time, and their PD was often accompanied by other diseases. Therefore, we did not exclude other diseases from screening. Our analysis showed that at least 12 weeks of a

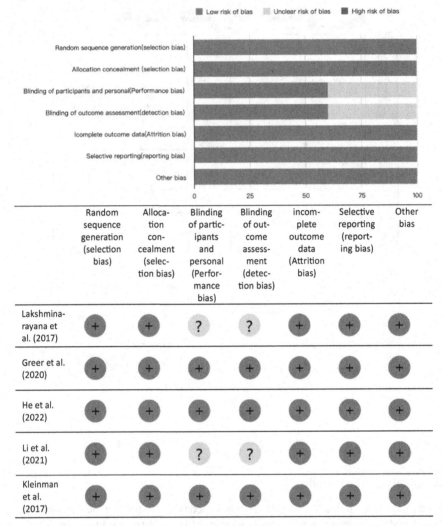

Fig. 2. Percentage of each Cochrane risk of bias (RoB) level and list of all RoB assessments of the included papers

technology-assisted medication reminder intervention significantly improved patients' self-management ability and adherence to medications, thereby helping them control their condition and reducing their anxiety. From the perspective of nurses or caregivers, the overall quality of life of families significantly improved after the use of technology-assisted medication reminder tools. In Table 3, we compile and analyse the findings of these previous studies.

Table 3. Basic information about the included studies

Author (year)	Inclusion Criteria	Numbers (EG/CG)	Intervention characteristics	Intervention setting			Measuring Instrument	Results
				Intervention duration	Data collection time points			
Lakshminarayana et al. (2017)	PD	EG:68 CG:90	EG: 1. Self-monitoring: sleep, exercise, mood, movement, flexibility, energy; 2. Drug reminder system; 3. My body reports; 4. Finger tapping and cognitions; 5. Information on the treatment of PD in the UK	16 weeks	16 weeks 16 weeks		1.Self-reported score of adherences to treatment (MMAS-8); 2. Quality of Life (PDQ-39); 3. PCQ-PD; 4. Impact on non-motor symptoms (NMSQ); 5. Depression and anxiety (HADS); 6. Beliefs about medication (BMQ) at 16 weeks	Self-management of PD through smartphones to improve medication adherence
Greer et al. (2020)	cancer	EG:91 CG:90	EG: 1. Medication plan with reminders; 2. Symptom reporting module; 3. Patient education	12 weeks	12weeks		1. Per electronic pill caps; 2. Symptom burden (per MDASI); 3. Quality of life (per FACT-G); 4. Medication adherence (MMAS-4) anxiety and depression symptoms; 5. Social support; 6. Quality of care; 7. Healthcare utilisation	For oral drug therapy for cancer, the application is predisposed to patients with difficulty with medication adherence or anxiety

(continued)

Table 3. (*continued*)

Author (year)	Inclusion Criteria	Numbers (EG/CG)	Intervention characteristics	Intervention setting		Measuring Instrument	Results
				Intervention duration	Data collection time points		
He et al. (2022)	chronic	EG:41 CG:41	EG: Manage with a smart medication management system with family involvement CG: Chronic disease is managed by routine medication management	24 weeks	24 weeks	1. MMAS-8; 2. SEAMS; 3. Medication knowledge assessment questionnaire; 4. The family support scale	The intelligent medication management system with family participation can effectively improve medication compliance, self-efficacy of rational drug use, medication knowledge assessment scores, and family support for middle aged and elderly patients with chronic diseases in rural areas

(*continued*)

Table 3. (*continued*)

Author (year)	Inclusion Criteria	Numbers (EG/CG)	Intervention characteristics	Intervention setting		Measuring Instrument	Results
				Intervention duration	Data collection time points		
Li et al. (2021)	chronic	EG:62 CG:62	EG: Perx APP (Reminder + Game) 1. Drug schedule (drug name, drug appearance, dose, unit, frequency). Verification method: take a photo; 2. Every time the subject takes the medicine, the subject must take a photo and upload it. After uploading, the subject can participate in the game to exchange gifts	12 months	12 months	-	Mobile device application can improve medication adherence in adults

(*continued*)

Table 3. (*continued*)

Author (year)	Inclusion Criteria	Numbers (EG/CG)	Intervention characteristics	Intervention setting		Measuring Instrument	Results
				Intervention duration	Data collection time points		
Kleinman et al. (2017)	Type 2 Diabetes	EG:44 CG:46	EG: APP 1. Medication reminders keep a record of the medications taken; 2. Blood sugar test reminders review the subject's own reports; 3. Chat with the subject's care team; 4. Time spent on the app	6 months	6 months	1. Assessed the impact of an mHealth diabetes platform on clinical outcomes; 2. Patient reported outcomes; 3. Patient and provider satisfaction; 4. App usage	This app provides chronic disease care and improves treatment outcomes

Note: -, not available,

Abbreviations: BMQ, beliefs about medicines questionnaire; FACT-G, functional assessment of cancer therapy – general; HADS, hospital anxiety and depression scale; MDASI, MD Anderson symptom inventory; MMAS-8, Morisky medication adherence scale - 8; NMSQ, non-motor symptoms questionnaire; PCQ-PD, patient-centred questionnaire for Parkinson's disease; PD, Parkinson's disease; PDQ-39, Parkinson's disease questionnaire – 39; SEAMS, self-efficacy for the appropriate medication use scale

3.4 Meta-analysis

We tested medication adherence with the 8-item Morisky medication adherence scale (MMAS-8). Among the five studies that were screened, a special focus was placed on the studies of Lakshminarayana et al. [6] and He et al. [4]. In the study of Lakshminarayana et al. [6], the patient population was PD patients, while the He et al. [4] study focused on patients with chronic diseases. Both study populations needed long-term dependence on medication to control their conditions. Both studies used the MMAS-8 scale to measure whether medication adherence improved after the use of technology-assisted reminders.

Next, we performed a meta-analysis of the MMAS-8 score and present the results in a forest plot. Figure 3 (upper) shows the statistical results of the MMAS-8 score in the control group and the experimental group before the use of technology assistance (SMD = 0.01; 95% CI: -0.39 to 0.4; P = 0.183). Figure 3 (lower) showed the statistical analysis of the effect of the MMAS-8 score on the control group and the experimental group after technology assistance (standardised mean difference, SMD) = 1.43; 95% CI: -0.27 to 3.14; P < 0.05). These results indicate that after the use of technology assistance, medication adherence improved significantly, as did the treatment effect.

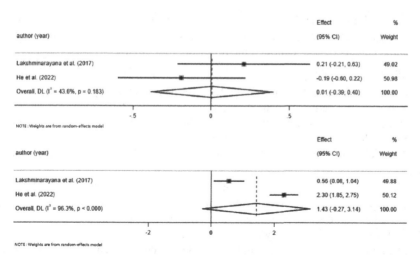

Fig. 3. Forest plot of medication adherence without (upper) and after use (lower) of technology assistance

4 Discussion

4.1 Effect of Technology-Assisted Medication Reminder System

The meta-analysis in this study found that the use of a technology-assisted medication reminder system is an effective method for significantly improving medication adherence, especially in terms of medication duration and frequency. This technology-assisted approach has shown clear advantages over traditional medication methods. It is worth mentioning that all the patients included in this study used the software app. In the early stage of screening, we found that there were fewer cases in which the app was used for neurodegenerative diseases. Therefore, the user group that was eventually included was not limited to patients with neurodegenerative diseases but also included patients with chronic diseases, type 2 diabetes, and cancer. All of these patients depended on drug treatment.

In the smartphone era, sleek and easy-to-use apps have become indispensable parts of life. However, the apps used for technology-assisted medication reminders still require the patient to actively input the times and types of medications as well as their personal information. No clinical studies have indicated whether medical staff can actively input relevant information. This means that if patients are not clear about their medication information, they may make errors when inputting them into the system, resulting in medication errors. For example, Tripathi et al. [10] noted this problem in 2017. Therefore, when designing this type of system, the active and passive nature of the information input should be considered to ensure the actual effectiveness and security of the system.

4.2 Four Medication Reminder Modes

As mentioned above, the devices used in the included studies were all smartphones. We reviewed the smartphone application systems currently on the market to improve medication adherence and identified the following four modes:

1. Medication reminder + health education information + physical report record: This app provides basic medication reminder information, similarly to an alarm clock, and requires the patient to actively input the medication time. Once the set time is reached, the app reminds the patient through vibration or sound. In addition, the patient can input disease-related health education information and physical condition report records, such as sleep and exercise records and blood glucose and blood pressure data.
2. Medication reminder + health education information + physical report record + finger tapping cognitive game: In addition to providing the above functions, this app also includes a finger tapping cognitive game specially designed for PD patients to help stimulate hand sensitivity and responsiveness.
3. Medication reminder + photo upload for gift exchange: This mode encourages patients to take their medications on time to improve adherence. Patients are required to take photos to record the process of taking the medication and upload them to the platform to collect points in exchange for gifts. This incentive method can significantly increase the use of the app.
4. Medication reminder + physical report record + chat with nursing staff: This app can also let the patient communicate with nursing staff when their bodies have abnormalities. Due to the many patients who need to be cared for, nursing staff may not be able to respond to the information in real time.

In summary, the ease of use and the interactivity of smartphone apps can significantly improve patients' medication adherence, especially those patients who have difficulty with medication adherence, feel anxious, or require multidrug therapy. In recent years, technology-assisted therapy has gradually become a popular research direction, and multifunctional systems can meet the needs of different user groups. For patients with complex medications such as PD, in addition to basic medication reminders, adding elements such as interactive games and point redemption for gifts can improve their motivation to use the programs for a long time. Family caregivers can also remind patients to take medications by sharing these apps.

4.3   Use of a Reminder Device for Smartphone Apps

Because of their small size and high convenience, smartphones have gradually become an important tool for supporting health care. Through mobile applications, smartphones can support internet-based connections between multiple devices to provide more personalized and convenient medical and health services. According to Choudhry et al. (2017) [3], the use of smartphone apps in medical research was still relatively rare. In contrast, several earlier studies tended to use sensors as auxiliary functions for medicine bottles. With the rapid development of technology, smartphones and their applications have matured, providing more convenience to patients and caregivers. This technological progress has been especially beneficial for PD patients and their family caregivers. Lennaerts et al. (2017) [11] noted that PD poses many challenges to patients and their family caregivers. Prizer et al. (2020) [12] found that even with poorer cognitive and motor function, patients with family caregivers still had a greater quality of life and less mental distress. Additionally, Sturkenboom et al. (2014) [13] that family-based personalized occupational therapy could improve the self-cognitive performance of daily activities of PD patients. These studies show that the intervention by family caregivers plays an important role in improving the quality of life of patients.

Against this background, smartphone application developers should consider integrating the functions of family care terminals into their application design to better serve this specific patient population. These apps not only help patients better manage their condition but also provide necessary support and resources to family caregivers, thereby jointly improving the overall treatment efficacy and quality of life of patients.

4.4   Function and Efficacy of the App Medication Reminder

Recent studies have pointed out several challenges in the use of smartphone applications in medication management, especially for PD patients. For example, Mill et al. (2020) [14] discovered delays in dosing, incorrect doses, and formulation errors through the use of a reporting system and medical records. Richard et al. (2022) [15] also found that among PD patients, incorrect medication timing (such as delayed medication) and imprecise prescription are common problems, particularly prominent in female patients. Viudez-Martínez et al. (2023) [16] showed that for prescriptions of anti-PD drugs, the prevalence of medication errors reached 59.8%. Among them, entrustment errors (91.62%) were more common than missing drugs (8.38%). The most common medication errors were time-, frequency-, and dose-related. Frahm et al. (2021) [17] that polypharmacy was associated with polytherapy, and elderly people had a high risk of comorbidities, which led to an increased risk of polypharmacy and drug side effects, making medical assistance and care particularly important.

In summary, technology-assisted drug reminders work well at improving the accuracy, frequency, and dosing of drugs taken by patients. This approach is more effective and accurate than traditional medication. Notably, these apps not only have a reminder function but also are designed to record body functions, health education information, and game feedback for specific groups of people, increasing the positive reinforcing effect of their use.

5 Conclusion

Based on the relevant literature published in recent years, this study found that there are relatively few studies on the use of technology-assisted intervention to improve patients' medication adherence. We found five relevant studies covering PD, chronic diseases, diabetes, and cancer. These studies highlighted the importance and potential for future development in this field. Especially for PD patients, due to the complexity of medication and the fact that patients often have other diseases, it is particularly urgent to develop a medication system targeting this disease. Future research can focus on the development and improvement of PD medication systems, especially technology-assisted intervention methods, to improve the structure and effectiveness of medication reminders.

The five selected publications focused on smartphone app–based interventions. Through the strengthening of medication reminder functions and the combination of health education information, physical health monitoring, game rewards, and other elements, the usage rate of apps and medication adherence significantly increased. These studies showed that such apps can significantly improve medication adherence, stabilize conditions, and reduce the burden of care.

These studies also had several limitations and challenges. For example, research subjects are usually from specific institutions, which limits the broad applicability of research results. In addition, the medication timing for each patient is different, so a customized solution is needed, which may incur additional manpower and information costs. After long-term use, patients may become bored with the medication reminders. Therefore, how to make the system attractive and interesting to keep patients actively involved has become another important consideration.

Acknowledgements. The author(s) disclosed receipt of the following financial support for the research, authorship, and/or publication of this article: This work was supported in part by the National Science and Technology Council under grant number NSTC 112-2410-H-027-017-MY2 and NSTC 111-2410-H-027-021-MY3, by the Ministry of Science and Technology under grant numbers MOST 109-2410-H-027-003-MY2, MOST 108-2410-H-027-024-MY3, and by Chang Gung Memorial Hospital and the National Taipei University of Technology joint research programme under grant number NTUT-CGMH-110-05, NTUT-CGMH-112-02 and CORPG3L0141. The funders had no role in the study design, data collection and analysis, decision to publish, or the preparation of the manuscript.

Disclosure of Interests. The authors have no competing interests to declare that are relevant to the content of this article.

References

1. Hannink, K., et al.: A randomized controlled efficacy study of the Medido medication dispenser in Parkinson's disease. BMC Geriatr. **19**(1), 273 (2019). https://doi.org/10.1186/s12877-019-1292-y

2. Daley, D.J., et al.: Adherence therapy improves medication adherence and quality of life in people with Parkinson's disease: a randomised controlled trial. Int. J. Clin. Pract. **68**(8), 963–971 (2014). https://doi.org/10.1111/ijcp.12439

3. Choudhry, N.K., et al.: Effect of reminder devices on medication adherence: the REMIND randomized clinical trial. JAMA Intern. Med. **177**(5), 624–631 (2017). https://doi.org/10.1001/jamainternmed.2016.9627

4. He, J., et al.: Application of family-involved smart medication management system in rural-dwelling middle-aged and older adult participants with chronic diseases: management of chronic diseases in rural areas. Medicine **101**(45), e31662 (2022). https://doi.org/10.1097/md.0000000000031662

5. Li, A., et al.: Effect of a smartphone application (Perx) on medication adherence and clinical outcomes: a 12-month randomised controlled trial. BMJ Open **11**(8), e047041 (2021). https://doi.org/10.1136/bmjopen-2020-047041

6. Lakshminarayana, R., et al.: Using a smartphone-based self-management platform to support medication adherence and clinical consultation in Parkinson's disease. NPJ Parkinson's Dis. **3**, 2 (2017). https://doi.org/10.1038/s41531-016-0003-z

7. Tenison, E., Henderson, E.J.: Multimorbidity and frailty: tackling complexity in Parkinson's disease. J. Parkinsons Dis. **10**(s1), S85–S91 (2020). https://doi.org/10.3233/jpd-202105

8. Kleinman, N.J., Shah, A., Shah, S., Phatak, S., Viswanathan, V.: Improved medication adherence and frequency of blood glucose self-testing using an m-health platform versus usual care in a multisite randomized clinical trial among people with type 2 diabetes in India. Telemed. J. E Health **23**(9), 733–740 (2017). https://doi.org/10.1089/tmj.2016.0265

9. Greer, J.A., et al.: Randomized trial of a smartphone mobile app to improve symptoms and adherence to oral therapy for cancer. J. Natl. Compr. Canc. Netw. **18**(2), 133–141 (2020). https://doi.org/10.6004/jnccn.2019.7354

10. Tripathi, R.K., Kapse, S.V., Potey, A.V.: Prescription pattern and awareness of disease and treatment in patients of Parkinson's disease. Neurodegener. Dis. Manag. **7**(5), 299–306 (2017). https://doi.org/10.2217/nmt-2017-0020

11. Lennaerts, H., et al.: Palliative care for patients with Parkinson's disease: study protocol for a mixed methods study. BMC Palliat. Care **16**(1), 61 (2017). https://doi.org/10.1186/s12904-017-0248-2

12. Prizer, L.P., Kluger, B.M., Sillau, S., Katz, M., Galifianakis, N.B., Miyasaki, J.M.: The presence of a caregiver is associated with patient outcomes in patients with Parkinson's disease and atypical parkinsonisms. Parkinsonism Relat. Disord. **78**, 61–65 (2020). https://doi.org/10.1016/j.parkreldis.2020.07.003

13. Sturkenboom, I.H., et al.: Efficacy of occupational therapy for patients with Parkinson's disease: a randomised controlled trial. Lancet Neurol. **13**(6), 557–566 (2014). https://doi.org/10.1016/s1474-4422(14)70055-9

14. Mill, D., Bakker, M., Corre, L., Page, A., Johnson, J.: A comparison between Parkinson's medication errors identified through retrospective case note review versus via an incident reporting system during hospital admission. Int. J. Pharm. Pract. **28**(6), 663–666 (2020). https://doi.org/10.1111/ijpp.12668

15. Richard, G., Redmond, A., Penugonda, M., Bradley, D.: Parkinson's disease medication prescribing and administration during unplanned hospital admissions. Mov. Disord. Clin. Pract. **9**(3), 334–339 (2022). https://doi.org/10.1002/mdc3.13408

16. Viudez-Martínez, A., Ramírez-López, A., López-Nieto, J., Climent-Grana, E., Riera, G.: Antiparkinsonian medication reconciliation as a strategy to improve safety by preventing medication errors. Mov. Disord. Clin. Pract. **10**(7), 1090–1098 (2023). https://doi.org/10.1002/mdc3.13789

17. Frahm, N., Hecker, M., Zettl, U.K.: Polypharmacy in chronic neurological diseases: multiple sclerosis, dementia and Parkinson's disease. Curr. Pharm. Des. **27**(38), 4008–4016 (2021). https://doi.org/10.2174/1381612827666210728102832

Universal Access to Information
and Media

Understanding the Effects of Visual Impairment on Visual Search

Dalal Aljasem[1]([✉]) and Andrew Howes[1,2]

[1] School of Computer Science, University of Birmingham, Birmingham, UK
dka813@bham.ac.uk
[2] University of Exeter, Exeter, UK
andrew.howes@exeter.ac.uk

Abstract. The effect of vision loss on visual search has been extensively studied in psychology, but little is known about the relevance of these insights to human-computer interaction (HCI). This paper takes a first step towards a user model of visual impairments. Variants of the model are used to explain how people with Age-related Macular Degeneration (AMD), glaucoma or cataracts search for visual information on a computer display. The model formulates the visual search problem as a reinforcement learning (RL) problem. It is tested on its ability to predict the effects of visual impairments on how people search for objects in a crowded display or within a wide visual field. We discuss how the model might help the design of more accessible user interfaces and enhance user experience for those with vision impairments.

Keywords: Reinforcement learning · Visual search · Computational rationality

1 Introduction

The process of designing a new computer interface requires many decisions to consider. For example, during the initial stages of the design, the designers should consider how users are supposed to interact with the given interface and what the best representation of the elements appearing on the computer screen is [9]. Visual communication is the main element when it comes to building computer interfaces; this, in turn, negatively reduces the impact and uptake of Human-Computer Interaction (HCI) techniques for people with vision impairment [10]. There are an estimated 2.2 billion people who are either blind or visually impaired (BVI) worldwide based on the World Health Organisation (WHO) [31]. Many diseases cause vision impairment, such as uncorrected refractive errors, cataract, diabetic retinopathy, age-related macular degeneration, and glaucoma, where the causes vary between countries, based on their average income [31]. The WHO also stated that most people with vision impairment are above the age of 50, and as the population grows, the number of older people will increase, which in turn impacts the number of visually impaired people. People who are BVI interact with technology and use computer devices on

M. Antona and C. Stephanidis (Eds.): HCII 2024, LNCS 14698, pp. 363–381, 2024.
https://doi.org/10.1007/978-3-031-60884-1_25

a daily basis, and despite the significant effort at designing accessibility, interaction for the visually impaired remains challenging [12,23]. One response, amongst many, to this problem must be a deeper understanding of how people with specific impairments interact with computers. Effective redesign may be urgent, but in order for it to be successful, it has to be informed by a deep scientific understanding of impaired vision in interactive contexts. In this paper, we propose a computational model that is built based on the theoretical framework, *computational rationality* [17] assuming that human behaviours are the results of the adaptation to the bounds of the human brain as well as the structure of the environment. The theoretical framework that informed building the proposed model uses cognitive science and rationality as an empirical tool to explain *why* people adapt to their environment. In contrast, the implementation of decision theory (i.e. Partially Observable Markov Decision Processes, or POMDPs) and policy optimisation in RL methods explains *how* people with vision impairment would interact with their environment. Even though Machine Learning (ML) methods have been widely used to make predictions, our aim is to model HCI. This approach has been discussed in a review by [22]. Several authors have considered the importance of building computational models using both cognitive science and ML where they also discussed its potential to help to understand the human perceptual strategies to support HCI [5–8,18]. However, the majority of those studies have only focused on normal vision and did not consider those models' importance in supporting people with vision impairment in HCI.

In this paper, we make the following contributions:

1. The paper represents a computational model that explains the behaviours of different types of vision impairment (i.e. glaucoma, age-related macular degeneration (AMD) and cataract) by implementing the cognitive bounds into the ML model.
2. The model finds visual search strategies through the implementation of probabilistic environments, information processing and utility maximisation.
3. The model presented supports HCI where it would help the design of a more accessible user interfaces.

2   Background

2.1   Computational Models in HCI

Researchers have explored the use of computational models in HCI and proposed recommendations to designers to deliver better user interface (UI). In a recent work by Leiva et al. [16], they trained a deep learning model to predict users' preferences in website aesthetics. The model had high accuracy and could predict the suitability of an interface design for different age groups. HCI scientists also used POMDP and ML methods to model human interactions behaviours by understanding and implementing cognitive strategies, which in return can support the design of UI with a better understanding of people's psychology and with less need for experiments including human participants. For example, Chen et al. [7] demonstrated that human decision-making is an emergent consequence of the chosen environment and the relevant psychological limitations. Furthermore, Chen et al. [6], proposed a computational model which can predict selection times and the average number of saccades given target size and eccentricity. In a more recent work, Li et al. [18] implemented a computational model that behaves similarly to blind users in a menu selection task. Different interaction methods were simulated in the model, including swiping, gliding, and direct touch. It was built based on the assumption that users' selection behaviours result from adaption to the user's memory of where the items are located, which is gained through experience and feedback. A menu selection task was formulated as POMDP, and then the model was trained using Deep Q-Network (DQN). Their results showed that the model could learn the strategies of those with vision impairment by predicting the effect of menu length and object locations on selection time. The latter model has similarities to the model we are proposing in this paper. However, the scientists in the latter research did not focus on a specific type of vision impairment, but their model is more general for people with different levels of vision impairments

2.2 Eye Movements in Vision Impairment

Eye Movements in Glaucoma. Glaucoma is a result of neuropathy, which leads to progressive loss of ganglion cells and visual field loss, as was stated by The National Eye Institute [20]. Studies showed that patients with glaucoma tend to make fewer saccades, and those with severe visual field defects can make less eye movements during visual search [25]. Additionally, in tasks like target finding or reading, glaucoma patients may show slower saccade latency and a phenomenon called *text saturation*, where a person fixates on every letter when trying to read the text [4]. In a task involving finding a target located within a wide visual fiel [1], patients with glaucoma showed low accuracy and slower saccade latency, especially at higher eccentricities beyond 40°.

Eye Movements in AMD. AMD is an eye condition that causes blurriness in the central visual field. It is considered one of the main reasons for blindness that mainly affects older people globally [19,31]. The effect of AMD on the visual field and eye movements has been studied by different experiments using eye-tracking tools. Van der Stigchel et al. [26] reported longer search times and smaller saccades in AMD patients, especially in pop-out conditions. A study done by Thibaut et al. [28] reported lower accuracy, increased saccades, and longer scan paths in AMD patients during object recognition tasks. In a different study by Thibaut et al. [27], they found that AMD patients are less accurate and need longer search time with an increased number of fixations, particularly in crowded conditions.

Eye Movements in Cataract. Cataract is a condition that causes cloudiness in the visual field, causing the patients to experience blurred vision, light sensitivity and difficulty seeing at night. Cataract symptoms can be improved by cataract extraction surgery [21]. An experiment presented by Wan et al. [29] showed that visual search behaviours improved after participants underwent cataract surgery with decreased search time, increased fixations on the target, and better accuracy in object search and face recognition tasks. The findings also showed that reading speed significantly improved post-operation, and regressive saccades (i.e. when the eyes move to parts of the text that was read previously) notably decreased.

3   Theory and Model of Vision Impairment

3.1   Theory

The model is built based on the theoretical assumptions that human visual behaviours and decision strategies result from adaptation to the statistical environment (e.g. the distance between the target and the fixation or the spatial distance between objects), the constraints imposed by the human visual system (e.g. spatial uncertainty and the partial vision of the visually impaired) and the reward associated with actions and decisions. We formulate the tasks as Partially Observable Markov Decision Processes (POMDP), which is a model for deciding how to act in "an accessible, stochastic environment with a known transition model" [24], and solve them using RL methods to find optimal search and decision strategies. For a more in-depth background on the strategy used in this paper, see [6,13]

3.2   Model

An overview of the framework is presented in Fig. 1. The model consists of a learning agent with internal processes representing the cognitive theory and an external environment representing the task the agent interacts with. The external display includes the objects on the screen which remain unchanged. The agent should have an initial probabilistic belief about the environment. Then, it interacts with the environment through action and starts collecting information about the environment, using both the fovea (fixating on the centre of an object) and peripheral vision. The agent's input is a noisy observation of the environment. Our theory suggests that more noise in the observation would cause partial vision in the model, which can represent vision impairment. The reward function determines the agent's best policy or strategy. The model utilises Reinforcement and Deep Reinforcement Learning techniques to find an optimal strategy. The strategies found by the model are bounded-optimal, meaning that the learning agent finds the optimal policy by adapting to the architecture of the task, the perceptual processes and the reward function. Figure 2 illustrate the workflow of our experiments.

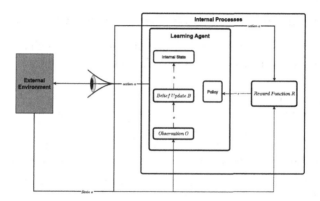

Fig. 1. Overview of the model's structure. The agent starts by taking an action a in the given environment based on its belief state $b(s)$. It receives observation o based on the state s and updates the belief state b accordingly. It also receives a reward r based on the state s and action a, which updates the policy. The eye icon is only a representation of the agent-environment interaction as the model is a visual search model.

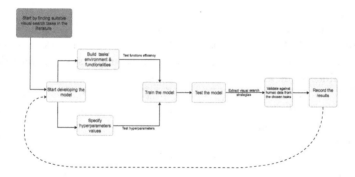

Fig. 2. This figure shows a simplified illustration of the iterative process of developing the model. First, we collected suitable research papers that conducted visual search experiments on people with vision impairment. Second, we developed the model by generating the environment and all the relevant functionalities. In parallel, we implemented a grid search to find the best noise level that fits the human data. Third, we train and test the ML model given the POMDP and the hyper-parameters. Lastly, we validate our results against the human data and record the results.

4   Tasks Formulation as POMDP

In this paper we use three visual search experiments from the literature that were implemented to simulate the visual search behaviours in people with vision impairment. The tasks are as follows: (1) a accadic choice task with glaucoma [1], (2) object search task with AMD testing the crowding effect [27] and (3) a visual search in cataract [29].

4.1   Experiment 1: A Model of Saccadic Choice Task with Glaucoma

This section explains how the task by Boucart et al. [1] is formulated as POMDP. Please refer to [1] for more details about the human experiment.

POMDP Formulation

- **State S:** A state in this task represents the possibility of the target being on the left or on the right (i.e. $s_t = (s_{\text{left}}, s_{\text{right}}) \in S$). Each state s_t is a tuple of 1 and 0 indicating the presence of the target, where 1 is a target and 0 is a distractor (i.e. (0,1) and (1,0)). A state is picked randomly at every trial, and it remains the same until the trial ends.
- **Action A:** At each time step t, the agent takes action a_t to either fixate and receive an observation or decides that the target is on the left or right.
- **Reward function $R(S, A)$:** A reward $r(s_t, a_t)$ is a cost of -3 (empirically found) for fixation actions, 0 for correctly identifying the target's location, and -100 for uncorrectly identifying the target's location.
- **Transition function $T(S_{t+1}|S_t, A_t)$:** As the state remains unchanged in each trial, hence $T(S_{t+1}|S_t, A_t) = 1$ only when $S_{t+1} = S_t.T(S_{t+1}|S_t, A_t)$, or 0 otherwise.
- **Observation O and observation function $O = f(S, A)$:** The observation is a function of state and action, $o_t = f(s_t, a_t)$. The target location has a spatial uncertainty of peripheral vision, represented as a standard deviation which is linearly dependent on the eccentricity. Therefore, $o_t = (o_{t_{\text{left}}}, o_{t_{\text{right}}})$, where $o_{t_{\text{left}}} \sim \mathcal{N}(s_{\text{left}}, \sigma_o)$, $o_{t_{\text{right}}} \sim \mathcal{N}(s_{\text{right}}, \sigma_o)$, and σ_o is the variance of the observation which does not depend on time and is linear to the eccentricity. Meaning that $\sigma_o = noise\,level \times eccentricity$, where $noise\,level$ is a hyperparameter that we use in the observation to represent the different levels of uncertainty and find the best fit to the human data.
- **Discount rate $\gamma \in [0, 1]$:** Determines the future reward. The agent should learn an optimal strategy that maximises the long-term expected reward of $R = E\left[\sum \gamma^t r(s_t, a_t) \right]$.

Belief Update: As the state is not fully observable, the model maintains a belief state $b(s)$ of the current state. The initial belief is assumed to be a uniform distribution representing the unknown target location. In this task, the belief is the pair consisting of the Gaussian distribution of the left value and that of the right value, stored as the mean μ and the variance σ^2 for each (four values in total: $\mu_{\text{left}}, \mu_{\text{right}}, \sigma^2_{\text{left}}, \sigma^2_{\text{right}}$). The initial belief is chosen as (0.5, 0.5, 100, 100). We choose the initial belief with the correct means and very large variances to reflect the very high uncertainty of this initial value (i.e. 0.5). After taking action a, the model will receive a noisy observation o, about the value of the left and the value of the right, which are represented as a Gaussian distribution with mean μ_o and variance σ^2_o, where μ_o and σ^2_o are the mean and variance of the received observation respectively. Then, the estimate of the belief for each left and right pair of mean and variance will be updated independently using the Kalman filter formula [11] as follows:

$$k = \frac{\sigma^2}{\sigma^2 + \sigma_0^2}$$

$$\acute{\mu} = \mu + k(\mu_0 - \mu) \tag{1}$$

$$\acute{\sigma}^2 = \sigma^2 - k\sigma^2 \tag{2}$$

where k is the *Kalman gain*, representing a weight parameter used in the recursively updated process in the equations. It is used to give a weight that indicates the importance of the current observation to be used to estimate the current state.

After creating the environment and formulating the tasks as POMDP, we input the environment into the RL agent.

Implementation. We implemented Q-learning method [30] for this task and our choice of hyper-parameters are:(1) $\gamma = 1$ for the discount rate and (2) $\epsilon = 0.9$, for ϵ-*greedy*. There is a starting learning rate, $\alpha = 1$, which decreases by 0.99 at every episode. The model was trained with a random set of eccentricities that varies between 10 and 80. Then, it was evaluated against each eccentricity from the human experiment (i.e. [10, 20, 40, 60, 80]). To find the best *noise level* for the observations, we conducted a grid search with different noise levels (see Fig. 3). Additionally, we added a constant value to the noise in the observation to prevent the model from over-performing the human data. An example of the noise would be, $noise_{\text{left}} = constant + \sim \mathcal{N}(s_{\text{left}}, \sigma_o)$. The constant value was found empirically as 0.25. We then calculated the Euclidean Distance between our results and the human data to find a local minimum that represents the best fit.

4.2 Experiment 2: A Model of the Crowding Effect with Age-Related Macular Degeneration

In the second experiment we simulate the visual search behaviours in Age-Related Macular Degeneration (AMD) from [27], which tested the impact of the crowding effect on visual search strategies in those with AMD. It required participants from three categories (i.e. young, age-matched controls, and AMD) to find a target surrounded by distractors within different crowding settings (i.e. crowded and uncrowded). Please refer to the original paper [27] for more details about the human experiment.

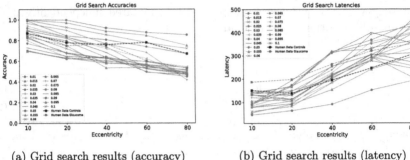

<table>
<tr><td>(a) Grid search results (accuracy)</td><td>(b) Grid search results (latency)</td></tr>
</table>

Fig. 3. The Figs. (a) and (b) show the grid search results when tested against five different eccentricities, compared with the human data provided by Boucart et al. [1]. It can be seen that there is some decrease in accuracy and an increase in saccade latency as the eccentricity increases.

POMDP Formulation

- **State S:** A state s_t is a vector of $(x, y, targetedness) \times number\ of\ objects$, which represents the objects' locations. The $targetedness = 1$ if an object is a target, or -1 if it is a distractor. The locations of the objects are randomly distributed in each trial and bounded by the size of the screen ($31.6°$ horizontally $\times 25.4°$ vertically) as given in the human experiment, and the object's width ($object\ width = 5$). The state remains unchanged in each trial until a final action is taken.
- **Action A:** The action space consists of fixation to get observations or to press the space bar to confirm the final decision. At each time step, the agent takes an action a_t where the fixation action $a = [x, y]$ is bounded by the number of objects and the screen size. The press space bar action $= [0, 1]$, where 1 means press the space bar and end the trial, and 0 means do not press the space bar and continue collecting information about the environment.
- **Reward function $R(S, A)$:** After taking action a_t, the agent should receive a reward that depends on the state and the action taken in that state, $r(s_t, a_t)$. For the given problem, a cost of -1 was empirically chosen for fixation actions. As for the decision action (i.e. when the space bar is pressed), $reward = 100$, for correctly identifying the target location (when the fixation location is within the object, which is a circle of radius 5 around its centre). When the agent does not correctly identify the target, then $reward = -5 \times distance$, where $distance$ is the distance between the fixation location and the centre of the target.
- **Transition function $T(S_{t+1}|S_t, A_t)$:** As explained in Experiment 1 in Sect. 4.1.
- **Observation O and observation function $O = f(S, A)$:** In this task, the observation is a tuple of the observation $o_{t,obj}$ for each object obj, and it depends on the action the agent takes, the true target location in the state s_t, and the spatial distance between objects (flanker distance). Meaning that

the distance noise $(d_{t,obj})$ and the crowding noise $(c_{t,obj})$ were added to the actual value(s) in the observation $o_{t,obj}$. The distance noise $d_{t,obj}$ is a Gaussian distribution, $d_{t,obj} \sim \mathcal{N}(\mu = 0, \sigma_{o,d})$, where $\sigma_{o,d}(t, obj) = distance\ factor \times eccentricity(t)$ which explains the spatial uncertainty. The distance factor is, $distance\ factor = 0.9 \times Noise\ Level$, in our experiment, the hyper-parameter 0.9 is referred to as *base distance factor*, as this value showed a better fit to the human data. On the other hand, for the crowding noise $c_{t,obj}$, we experimented with two types of noises explained as follows:

1. Gaussian noise $c_{t,obj}^{(G)} \sim \mathcal{N}(\mu = 0, \sigma_{o,c}^{(G)})$: Gaussian noise $(c_{t,obj}^{(G)})$ represents the noise with a mean of 0 and standard deviation $\sigma_{o,c}^{(G)} = crowding\ factor \times crowding\ probability$, where $crowding\ factor = 10 \times Noise\ Level$, and 10 is the *base crowding factor* that was found to be best at producing the crowding effect in the results. It is important to note that the crowding noise considers the spatial distance between the fixation point and all the objects in the state. The *crowding probability* is computed from the literature and based on Bouma's law (see [2] for more in-depth explanation). The function of crowding probability c used in our model is as follows:

$$c = 1 - \lambda - \Phi(flanker\_distance - \beta \times eccentricity) \qquad (3)$$

For this problem, lapse rate, λ is considered 0, Φ is used for the proportional correct flanker distance vs. the eccentricity, and β is a scaling factor around 0.5 as given in the original equation. Then, from the crowding probability c, we compute the observation noise.

2. Blending noise: $c_{t,obj}^{(B)} \sim \mathcal{N}(\mu = average\ crowding, \sigma_{o,c}^{(B)})$: The mean *average crowding* is a representation of how close an object is to its flanker. For example, if the flanker distance is 0 (two objects very close together), the average of the observed value will be the average between the object value and the flanker value. The observed value is a weighted average between the observed object feature value and the flanker feature value using a blending crowding factor of 0.5. The blending crowding factor accounts for the balance between these feature values. It is then multiplied by the proximity, which measures the spatial relationship between the objects, indicating how close one object is to its flanker [15]). This proximity is computed as shown in Eq. 4:

$$proximity = 1/(1 + flanker\ distance) \qquad (4)$$

Consequently, the calculation of the average crowding is as follows:

$$average\ crowding = \quad (flanker\ features - object\ feature) \qquad (5)$$
$$\times\ blending\ crowding\ factor \times proximity \qquad (6)$$

The standard deviation $\sigma_{o,c}^{(G)}$ is computed in the same way as $\sigma_{o,c}^{(G)}$.

The observation o_t is a list of pairs. Each pair includes the noisy value of the feature ($targetedness$) and its confidence for each element in the object observed (i.e. $(x, y, targetedness)$). The observation is calculated as follows:

$$targetedness = f_{obj} + d_{t,obj} + c_{t,obj} \qquad (7)$$

Where f_{obj} is the true feature value for the object, and the feature confidence is computed as follows:

$$feature\,confidence = \sqrt{\sigma_{o,c}^2 + \sigma_{o,d}^2} \qquad (8)$$

Therefore, the observation is a tuple of the ($targetedness, feature\,con-fidence$) for each objects.

After computing the observation, the agent updates the belief state. This will be explained in more detail as part of this section.
- **Discount rate** γ: As explained in Experiment 1 in Sect. 4.1. The discount rate for this study was left unchanged as a parameter in the implemented library which will be explain in the implementation section.

Belief Update: The belief in this study is a vector of tuples, where each tuple represents one object with two values (*targetedness* and *confidence*). The initial belief consists of the initial targetedness value (unknown value = 0), and initial confidence, representing the very high uncertainty (i.e. 1000000). At every fixation action, the agent gets a new noisy observation (including both distance and crowding noise), and then updates its belief state using the Kalman filter formula as explained in Experiment 1 in Sect. 4.1.

Implementation. In this experiment, we used OpenAI Gym [3] and built a suitable environment to train the model and make use of the built-in libraries of deep reinforcement, PPO algorithm provided by Stable Baselines[1]. All the default hyper-parameters for PPO remained the same except for the learning rate, which we updated to 1×10^{-4}. In order to choose the values of the hyper-parameters that we introduced in the model, we conducted an iterative process of experiments to examine the performance of the model with different *Noise Level* values. Our final choices of hyper-parameters, based on empirical observations, are $[0.1, 0.15, \ldots, 0.9]$ for the *Noise Level*. As mentioned previously the *Noise Level* is multiplied by the base crowding factor 10, and the base distance factor 0.9. Therefore to clarify the actual values for the *Crowding Factor* and the *Distance Factor*, we created Table 1.

We only considered four and six objects in the model due to the high complexity of the problem. The model was trained through a grid search for each noise level on a random set of spacing S, where $S = [1.5, 6.5]$ (see Fig. 5 in Sect. 5). Then, in the testing stage, the model was given the same spacing values

---

[1] https://github.com/DLR-RM/stable-baselines3.

Table 1. Actual values for *Crowding Factor* and *Distance Factor* as implemented in the observation

Noise Level	Crowding Factor	Distance Factor
0.1	1	0.09
0.15	1.5	0.14
0.2	2	0.18
0.25	2.5	0.23
0.3	3	0.27
0.35	3.5	0.32
0.4	4	0.36
0.45	4.5	0.41
0.5	5	0.45
0.55	5.5	0.49
0.6	6	0.54
0.65	6.5	0.58
0.7	7	0.63
0.75	7.5	0.67
0.8	5	0.72
0.85	8.5	0.76
0.9	9	0.81

as those used in the human experiment (i.e. 6 for the uncrowded condition and 1.5 for the crowded condition). After testing the model, the results were evaluated against the human data provided by Thibaut et al. [27]. The human data provided to us only included the accuracy and search time (in seconds), which allowed us to compare the model's accuracy and search time against the data. We also measured the number of fixations and scan path ratio in the model as these measures were considered secondary outcomes for the human experiment. Lastly, to find the best noise level that fits the data, we computed the difference between the model's results and the data to find a local minimum that best fits the human data.

4.3   Experiment 3: A Model of Visual Search with Cataract

Lastly, in the third experiment we implemented the model to a visual search task that is specified for cataract patients [29]. The task aim was to test eye movements in people with cataract before and after surgery, when they interact with three visual search tasks (i.e. object search, face recognition, and reading) (see [29] for more details about the human experiment). Only the object search task is presented in this paper.

POMDP Formulation

- **State S:** The state in this experiment is similar to experiment 2 in Sect. 4.2 with the objects being distributed within the screen size ($40°\,horizontally \times 23.5°\,vertically$), and the object's width ($object\,width = 4$). The distractor value in this experiment is the average between a $minmum\,distractor\,value = 0$, and $maximum\,distractor\,value = -1$, which is -0.5, while the target value is 1. The reason for creating this distractor value rather than -1 is to create similarities between the target and the distractor features.
- **Action A:** The action space is the same as in the experiment 2 in Sect. 4.2, except that in this experiment, there is no action to confirm the decision. Therefore, the agent would remain fixated on the target (once it finds it) until the time cap ends (6 s).
- **Reward function $R(S, A)$:** The reward function is the same as in Experiment 2 in Sect. 4.2
- **Transition function $T(S_{t+1}|S_t, A_t)$:** As explained in Experiment 1 in Sect. 4.1.
- **Observation O and observation function $O = f(S, A)$:** The observation is the same as in Experiment 2 in Sect. 4.2. Although we do take the crowding noise into consideration, we reduced the $base\,crowding\,factor$ to 5. The reason for this choice is that there are more objects in this experiment, and having a high crowding noise can increase the complexity of the observations. We add the crowding noise in the observations to produce the crowding effect, but we do not test with different spacing.
- **Discount rate γ:** As explained in Experiment 2 4.2

Belief update The belief in this task is the same as the belief in the crowding task in Sect. 4.2. The difference is in the unknown value, which is considered 0.25 in this experiment.

Implementation. The implementation of this task is very similar to the crowding task in Sect. 4.2. However, ijn this task, we considered a different set of noise levels. It is also important to note that in this experiment, the spacing between objects ($S = 1.5$) remains the same during all the trials, to match the human experiment. We considered both Gaussian and Blending noise (the two types of noise explained in section 4.2). Due to the high accuracy of the humans, we expect that the best fit would be within the low noise levels. Therefore, for the grid search, we chose the noise levels $[0.1, 0.2, \ldots, 1]$. The base crowding factor is 5 in this experiment, while the base distance factor remains the same as reported in Experiment 2 (0.9). Table 2 illustrates the actual noise values for this experiment.

The number of objects in our model is 12, which is half the number of objects in the human experiments. Although our model was able to learn with more objects (up to 18 objects), the experiment would potentially be time-consuming due to the nature of the workflow (Fig. 2).

Table 2. Actual values for *Crowding Factor* and *Distance Factor* implemented in the observation

Noise Level	Crowding Factor	Distance Factor
0.1	0.5	0.09
0.2	1	0.18
0.3	1.5	0.27
0.4	2	0.36
0.5	2.5	0.45
0.6	3	0.54
0.7	3.5	0.63
0.8	4	0.72
0.9	4.5	0.81
1	5	0.9

5 Results

As explained in the experiments implementations in Sect. 4 that grid search was implemented in the three experiments and the best noise level that fits the human data was found by calculating the difference between our results and the human data (using the Euclidean Distance for experiment 1 4.1).

5.1 Experiment 1 Results

As can be seen in Fig. 4 that the model was able to learn the visual behaviours of normally sighted people and those with glaucoma, given the methods used and parameters tuning. It showed increased saccade latency at higher eccentricities and simultaneously decreased accuracies. The model predicted that less noise is needed to match the normal vision's accuracy, and a higher noise level is needed to match the glaucoma vision. Furthermore, the drastic drop in accuracy after eccentricity 40° was also noticeable in our model which shows similarities to the human experiment results.

5.2 Experiment 2 Results

The results for experiment 2 (see Fig. 5) show clear bounded-optimal adaptation performance in response to the constraints introduced to the stochastic environment and the parameters that were introduced in the model to give some representation of the human vision limitations. It also showed that the model can give an estimation of the visual behaviours of those with AMD when interacting with a task involving crowded conditions, specifically with accuracy and number of fixations. Although the accuracy remained high for all the uncrowded conditions, it can be observed that the model is still learning the optimal strategies through the number of fixations, search time and scan path ratio. The high

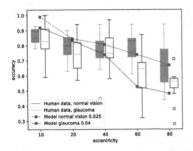
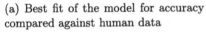
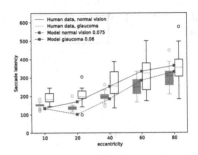

(a) Best fit of the model for accuracy compared against human data

(b) Best fit of the model for latency compared against human data

Fig. 4. In Figs. (a) and (b), the model was compared to the human accuracy and latency. It demonstrated the linear relationship between the accuracy of correctly locating a target in the peripheral vision and the eccentricity when a suitable proportion of noise is chosen. It also shows the increase in latency as the eccentricity increases with the right proportion of noise levels and sufficient training.

accuracy only indicates that the model learned the best policy which always produces high accuracy despite the noise levels in the observations. Despite the model failing to learn in some noise levels, especially for the six objects experiment, the noise levels with which it did manage to optimise behaviours still showed good strategies and were similar to the human data. Although there were no data provided by Thibaut et al. [27] for the number of fixations and scan path ratio, it stated in the paper that participants with AMD did more fixations and that the number of fixations increased with adding more distractors in the display. The paper also stated that increasing the number of distractors caused a less efficient scan ratio which is an observation matching our findings.

5.3 Experiment 3 Results

Figure 6 show that the model's results met our hypothesis as higher noise levels matched the accuracy of people with cataract before the operation. Although the human data was from a visual search task with 24 objects, we believe that these results can indicate the outcome of the model if it was set to be trained with 24 objects. The only difference would be finding a suitable set of noise levels to experiment with, possibly smaller values. The difference between using the Gaussian noise and the Blending noise can also be observed, as the Blending noise showed less accuracy at lower noise levels (e.g. if we compare the accuracy at noise level 0.4 with Blending noise, it is lower than the accuracy at noise level 0.4 with Gaussian noise). Hence, the best-fit values were at 0.5 for pre-operation rather than 0.7 (see Figs. 6a and 6b). This clearly indicates that the crowding effect is more apparent in the Blending noise.

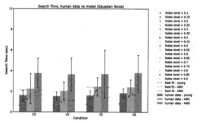

(a) Accuracies, using Gaussian noise. The effect of increasing the number of objects on accuracy is noticeable in this figure.

(b) Accuracies, using Blending noise. The results show a better fit to the human data, especially in the case of C5.

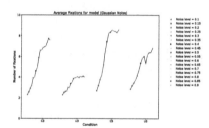

(c) Search time with Gaussian noise.

(d) The search time is shorter in all four cases with Blending noise compared to Gaussian noise.

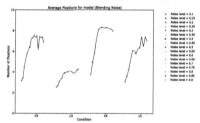

(e) Fixation with Gaussian noise. Model requires more fixations in crowded conditions, with noticeable effect of increasing object numbers.

(f) Fixation with Blending noise. Similar to Figure 5e. Clear effect of noise type at higher levels, impacting model realism.

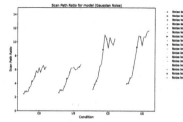

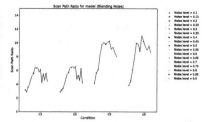

(g) Scan path ratio with Gaussian noise. Crowded effect has minimal impact, but increasing object numbers is significant.

(h) Scan path ratio with Blending noise. Less consistent results, especially at higher noise levels.

Fig. 5. The figures illustrates the impact of increasing the number of objects, and the effects of using different noise types on the accuracy, search time, the number of fixations and the scan path. C3 refers to (Crowded 3 distractors), U3 (Uncrowded 3 distractors), C5 (Crowded 5 distractors), and U5 (Uncrowded 5 distractors

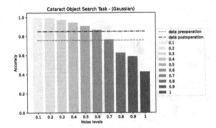
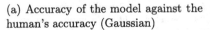
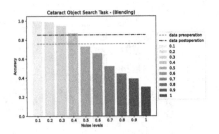

(a) Accuracy of the model against the human's accuracy (Gaussian)

(b) Accuracy of the model against the human's accuracy (Blending)

Fig. 6. Figure (a) represent the accuracy during testing (Gaussian noise). The noise level of 0.7 fits the human data pre-operation, and the noise level of 0.6 fits the post-operation data from [29]. Whereas the Fig. (b) shows the accuracy during testing with the Blending noise, and it can be observed that the best fit is at smaller noise levels (0.5 for pre-operations and 0.4 for post-operation).

6 Discussion

The results of the experiments simulate the cognitive processes that lead to visual behaviour. It can provide valuable insights into computational modelling of vision impairment in HCI. Our search suggests that if interaction for people with visual impairment is to be improved, then HCI research must understand the nature of the problems faced by visually impaired users. Our model explains visual search under impairment due to glaucoma, AMD and cataract as a policy that is optimally adapted to the selective deficits imposed by the conditions. As a consequence of this adaptation, the model offers quantitative predictions of why people with glaucoma have higher saccade latency with higher eccentricities, why people with AMD require more fixations to find a target, why this number increased when the crowding effect was introduced to those with AMD and why people with cataract, before surgery, were less accurate in finding a target. Our research aim to lay the groundwork for future research into providing better design for UI in computers, phones and tablets. Using ML methods showed its reliability in producing simulations of eye movements through the understanding and implementing the mechanism of the mind rather than training them based on big set of data. The results of this research support the idea that future interactive systems will more actively engage with users, anticipating their needs and adjusting accordingly. For example, an interactive system might automatically adjust the display layout, including button sizes, eccentricities and latencies, to an individual's visual impairment. Nevertheless, if such systems are to be successful, then they must do more than merely classify users into normal versus visually impaired. They must also be able to explain why users behave as they do. In summary, the explanation of those three experiments suggests that people with glaucoma, AMD and cataracts adapt to their condition by searching differently, and while their performance is still impaired, it is not as bad as it would have been had no adaptation occurred.

It is important to note that the model reported in this paper is very much an initial exploration, and it has a big room for exploration and further development. One limitation is the number of tasks used in the study. Implementing the model using more tasks and measuring different visual search behaviours can provide better support to the results the model produced. Another important limitation is that we only implemented one feature to the objects in the visual search tasks (i.e. the *targetedness*). Future work needs to consider other features such as shape, colour and size, which can give better insight into how people with vision impairments perceive the differences in these features. Another major limitation of this study is the inability of the model to learn with some of the high noise levels in the observation in the experiment in AMD experiment. Although this limitation did not affect the overall outcome of the results, as the model predicted human behaviours with different noise levels, this problem could be improved by further experiments. We believe further investigating the reward function and the environment dynamic can improve the outcome. We also believe that it is worth experimenting with different RL methods. Additionally, using grid search to find the best-fit hyper-parameters can be time-consuming and computationally expensive. We believe the first step to improve this limitation is to estimate the parameters using the Approximate Bayesian Computation (ABC) inference model which showed that it can obtain fixation duration from human experiments, predict the model's parameters and find the best fit for individuals [14].

7 Conclusion

In conclusion, the paper reported a computational model that learns to perform visual search given bounds that model visual limits imposed by glaucoma, AMD and cataracts. The model behaviour corresponds well to previously reported human behaviour in three tasks. The experiments demonstrate that computational rationality can predict the visual search behaviours in those with vision impairments.

Acknowledgments. I would like to acknowledge that the work presented in this paper is a publication of my PhD thesis project supervised by Professor Andrew Howes. I would like to thank the researchers eBoucart Muriel, Miguel Thibaut and Yu Wan, for providing the data from their experiments. I appreciated their collaboration in this project. Lastly, I would like to acknowledge that the results of experiment 2 and 3 were produced using a combination of BluBear HPC service (http://www.birmingham.ac.uk/bea) at the University of Birmingham, which gives access to High-Performance Computing service, and Baskerville Tier 2 HPC service (https://www.baskerville.ac.uk) which is funded by the EPSRC and UKRI under the World Class Labs scheme (EP/T022221/1) and the Digital Research Infrastructure program (EP/W032244/1). It is operated by the Advanced Research Computing team at the University of Birmingham.

Disclosure of Interests. The authors declare that they have no competing interests relevant to the content of this article.

References

1. Boucart, M., Bachet, V., Corveleyn, X., Bacchetti, P., Rouland, J.F.: A saccadic choice task for target face detection at large visual eccentricities in patients with glaucoma. Optom. Vis. Sci. **97**(10), 871–878 (2020)
2. Bouma, H.: Interaction effects in parafoveal letter recognition. Nature **226**(5241), 177–178 (1970)
3. Brockman, G., et al.: Openai gym. arXiv preprint arXiv:1606.01540 (2016)
4. Burton, R., Smith, N.D., Crabb, D.P.: Eye movements and reading in glaucoma: observations on patients with advanced visual field loss. Graefes Arch. Clin. Exp. Ophthalmol. **252**(10), 1621–1630 (2014)
5. Chen, X.: An optimal control approach to testing theories of human information processing constraints. Ph.D. thesis, University of Birmingham (2015)
6. Chen, X., Acharya, A., Oulasvirta, A.: An adaptive model of gaze-based selection. In: CHI Conference on Human Factors in Computing Systems (CHI'21). Association for Computing Machinery (2021)
7. Chen, X., Bailly, G., Brumby, D.P., Oulasvirta, A., Howes, A.: The emergence of interactive behavior: a model of rational menu search. In: Proceedings of the 33rd Annual ACM Conference on Human Factors in Computing Systems, pp. 4217–4226. ACM (2015)
8. Chen, X., Starke, S.D., Baber, C., Howes, A.: A cognitive model of how people make decisions through interaction with visual displays. In: Proceedings of the 2017 CHI Conference on Human Factors in Computing Systems, pp. 1205–1216. ACM (2017)
9. Dudley, J., Kristensson, P.O.: Bayesian optimisation of interface features. In: Bayesian Methods for Interaction and Design, p. 259 (2022)
10. Edwards, A., et al.: Extraordinary Human-Computer Interaction: Interfaces for Users with Disabilities, vol. 7. CUP Archive (1995)
11. Faragher, R.: Understanding the basis of the Kalman filter via a simple and intuitive derivation [lecture notes]. IEEE Signal Process. Mag. **29**(5), 128–132 (2012). https://doi.org/10.1109/MSP.2012.2203621
12. Griffin-Shirley, N., et al.: A survey on the use of mobile applications for people who are visually impaired. J. Vis. Impairment Blindness **111**(4), 307–323 (2017)
13. Howes, A., Chen, X., Acharya, A., Lewis, R.L.: Interaction as an emergent property of a partially observable markov decision process. Comput. Interact., 287–310 (2018)
14. Kangasrääsiö, A., Athukorala, K., Howes, A., Corander, J., Kaski, S., Oulasvirta, A.: Inferring cognitive models from data using approximate Bayesian computation. In: Proceedings of the 2017 CHI Conference on Human Factors in Computing Systems, pp. 1295–1306. ACM (2017)
15. Kennedy, G.J., Whitaker, D.: The chromatic selectivity of visual crowding. J. Vis. **10**(6), 15–15 (2010)
16. Leiva, L.A., Shiripour, M., Oulasvirta, A.: Modeling how different user groups perceive webpage aesthetics. Univers. Access Inf. Soc. **22**, 1–8 (2022). https://doi.org/10.1007/s10209-022-00910-x

17. Lewis, R.L., Howes, A., Singh, S.: Computational rationality: linking mechanism and behavior through bounded utility maximization. Top. Cogn. Sci. **6**(2), 279–311 (2014)
18. Li, Z., et al.: Modeling touch-based menu selection performance of blind users via reinforcement learning. In: Proceedings of the 2023 CHI Conference on Human Factors in Computing Systems, pp. 1–18 (2023)
19. Lim, L.S., Mitchell, P., Seddon, J.M., Holz, F.G., Wong, T.Y.: Age-related macular degeneration. The Lancet **379**(9827), 1728–1738 (2012). https://doi.org/10. 1016/S0140-6736(12)60282-7, https://www.sciencedirect.com/science/article/pii/ S0140673612602827
20. National Eye Institute: at a glance: Glaucoma (2022). https://www.nei.nih.gov/ learn-about-eye-health/eye-conditions-and-diseases/glaucoma
21. National Eye Institute: at a glance: cataracts (2023). https://www.nei.nih.gov/ learn-about-eye-health/eye-conditions-and-diseases/cataracts
22. Oulasvirta, A., Jokinen, J.P., Howes, A.: Computational rationality as a theory of interaction. In: Proceedings of the 2022 CHI Conference on Human Factors in Computing Systems, pp. 1–14 (2022)
23. Pal, J., et al.: Agency in assistive technology adoption: visual impairment and smartphone use in Bangalore. In: Proceedings of the 2017 CHI Conference on Human Factors in Computing Systems, pp. 5929–5940 (2017)
24. Russell, S.J., Norvig, P.: Artificial Intelligence: A Modern Approach. Pearson Education Limited, Malaysia (2016)
25. Smith, N.D., Glen, F.C., Crabb, D.P.: Eye movements during visual search in patients with glaucoma. BMC Ophthalmol. **12**(1), 45 (2012)
26. Van der Stigchel, S., Bethlehem, R.A., Klein, B.P., Berendschot, T.T., Nijboer, T., Dumoulin, S.O.: Macular degeneration affects eye movement behavior during visual search. Front. Psychol. **4**, 579 (2013)
27. Thibaut, M., Boucart, M., Tran, T.H.C.: Object search in neovascular age-related macular degeneration: the crowding effect. Clin. Exp. Optom. **103**(5), 648–655 (2020)
28. Thibaut, M., Delerue, C., Boucart, M., Tran, T.H.C.: Visual exploration of objects and scenes in patients with age-related macular degeneration. J. Fr. Ophtalmol. **39**(1), 82–89 (2016)
29. Wan, Y., Yang, J., Ren, X., Yu, Z., Zhang, R., Li, X.: Evaluation of eye movements and visual performance in patients with cataract. Sci. Rep. **10**(1), 9875 (2020)
30. Watkins, C.J.C.H.: Learning from delayed rewards (1989)
31. World Health Organisation: blindness and vision impairment (2023). https://www. who.int/en/news-room/fact-sheets/detail/blindness-and-visual-impairment

Evaluating Signage Accessibility for Individuals with Visual Impairments: A Case Study in Ecuador

Hugo Arias-Flores[1(✉)] ⓘ, Kevin Valencia-Aragón[1] ⓘ, Sandra Sanchez-Gordon[2] ⓘ, and Tania Calle-Jimenez[2] ⓘ

[1] Centro de Investigación en Mecatrónica y Sistemas Interactivos - MIST, Universidad Indoamérica, 170103 Quito, Ecuador
hugoarias@uti.edu.ec
[2] Department of Informatics and Computer Science, Escuela Politécnica Nacional, 170525 Quito, Ecuador

Abstract. A signage system is a visual design consisting of identification, guidance, explanation, warning, and other functions through a combination of text, graphics, and color that facilitates the orientation and movement of occupants in buildings by representing explicit information about the configuration and overall structure of the building. In this sense, well-placed signage provides information and significantly influences the search for paths in public spaces, but not all of these spaces meet the conditions of accessibility and inclusion. From this perspective, the general objective of this research is to identify, analyze, and evaluate the shortcomings of signage for individuals with visual impairments based on the requirements and legal regulations in Ecuador. The methodology was based on collecting photographs of signage located in a higher education institution. These photographs were selected in a way that they encompass the most important characteristics of informative signage. The results show that 44.44% comply with the current regulations in Ecuador, and 66.66% comply with the regulations for the inclusion of individuals with low vision. In the future, it is considered to propose a signage system that incorporates technology.

Keywords: signage system · public spaces · accessibility · visual impairments · regulations for the inclusion

1 Introduction

Signage systems enhance the orientation and navigation of building occupants by providing explicit information about the building's layout and general structure [1]. The perceived complexity of environments by occupants is reduced when a well-designed signage system is in place, thus improving their ability to find their way from an origin to a destination [2]. Signage plays a vital role in the orientation process [3] and is predominantly sought after by individuals who are unfamiliar with the surroundings [4].

© The Author(s), under exclusive license to Springer Nature Switzerland AG 2024
M. Antona and C. Stephanidis (Eds.): HCII 2024, LNCS 14698, pp. 382–392, 2024.
https://doi.org/10.1007/978-3-031-60884-1_26

In this manner, a signage system is a visual design encompassing identification, guidance, explanation, warnings, and various other functions through a combination of text, graphics, and color [5]. The design of signage is of paramount importance, as it assists individuals from diverse backgrounds in accessing information easily, breaking down language barriers, and providing comprehensive information about their surroundings [6].

Furthermore, the strategic placement of signage not only provides vital information but also significantly influences the quest for pathways in public spaces [7]. However, it's important to acknowledge that these spaces do not always meet the criteria for accessibility and inclusion. Clear visibility, easy comprehension, and efficient placement are crucial for successful signage, but addressing deficiencies in the space from a Design perspective is essential to ensure inclusivity [8].

In addition, aligning with global inclusion policies presents a significant challenge for institutions, especially higher education institutions. They must create spaces that not only validate, integrate, and recognize the diversity of the university population and its visitors but also meet the requirements of a broad spectrum of abilities and needs. This includes individuals with visual impairments who rely heavily on clear and accessible signage.

To enhance the efficiency and effectiveness of signage design, involving users in the solution creation process becomes a powerful strategy to promote intelligent and accessible environments. This approach takes into consideration elements of communication, visual perception, semiotics, color psychology, typographic organization, and more, ultimately enabling the development of a universal signage system that provides the necessary accessibility conditions for everyone [9].

The International Classification of Functioning, Disability, and Health, approved in 2001 by the World Health Organization, considers disability as an overarching term encompassing impairments, activity limitations, or participation restrictions, particularly those arising during the interaction of a person with a limitation and the context in which they operate [10]. According to this classification, individuals with visual disabilities include those who are blind or have total vision loss, as well as those with low vision. In Ecuador, as of August 2022, the Ministry of Public Health has registered 619,135 people with disabilities, of which 73,771 are individuals with visual disabilities [11].

In this perspective, the general objective of this research is to identify, analyze, and evaluate the deficiencies present in signage for individuals with visual disabilities, based on the requirements and legal regulations in Ecuador. This undertaking not only promotes accessibility but also aligns with the global shift toward greater inclusivity, ensuring that individuals of all abilities can navigate their surroundings with confidence and independence.

1.1 Related Works

Locating a destination within a building is akin to achieving a goal. Challenges in orientation can lead to a host of negative emotions, including confusion, frustration, anger, and stress. To tackle this issue, an experimental approach involving a virtual environment was employed to explore navigation solutions within the building. The study involved a total of 64 participants, divided into two groups. Each group was tasked with completing a set of 12 tasks within two different scenarios. The initial round of testing highlighted issues with the existing signage system, subsequently necessitating a comprehensive redesign of the system. In the follow-up testing phase, the effectiveness of the newly designed signage system was evaluated. This research underscores the importance of an improved signage layout that enhances legibility and information coherence, rooted in the principles of Gestalt, as a driver of positive changes in the orientation behavior of visitors [12].

When evaluating the orientation skills and visual signal preferences of adults concerning color and placement, a survey conducted among 375 visitors to healthcare centers yielded valuable insights. The findings revealed that young adults displayed a preference for visual signals characterized by "mixed colors positioned in the center of the floor." On the other hand, early middle-aged adults leaned towards "visual signals featuring warm colors placed in the middle of the wall," while late middle-aged adults exhibited a preference for "visual signals with warm colors positioned at the bottom of the wall." Additionally, the study shed light on the impact of aging on orientation skills, suggesting that as individuals grow older, their orientation abilities tend to decline, often accompanied by heightened spatial anxiety [13].

It's important to note that the integration of color into signage can present challenges for individuals with color vision deficiencies, as they may struggle to effectively comprehend the conveyed information. Consequently, the role of color in signage is pivotal in ensuring effective communication through signage and information systems. A study by Lee and colleagues [14] harnessed a simulation-based approach to investigate how individuals with color vision deficiencies perceive eight distinct shades, encompassing red, green, blue, yellow, orange, purple, cyan, and chartreuse. The study's outcomes not only proposed discernible and aesthetically pleasing color combinations for orientation signage within public spaces but also considered the needs of individuals with color vision deficiencies. Leveraging color theories and harmonies, this research contributes to the development of more inclusive orientation signage [14].

In this context, the design of signs should prioritize the presentation of essential information in a format that ensures easy readability for visitors. This is especially relevant when considering the reading performance of individuals with visual degeneration, as it is significantly influenced by the specific characteristics of the printed signage. An experimental study conducted with participants suffering from macular degeneration (comprising 24 individuals) measured reading performance using four versions of MNRead charts. These charts featured different fonts, namely Times New Roman, Arial, Courier, and Andale Mono. The results clearly demonstrated that reading acuity significantly improved with the Courier font, while it deteriorated with the Arial font. Notably, a significant 71% of patients were able to read at least one additional sentence with the Courier font in comparison to the Times New Roman and Arial fonts. Furthermore, the study revealed that reading speed dropped below the threshold for fluent reading first with the Arial font. In conclusion, font choice plays a substantial role in shaping the reading performance of individuals with macular degeneration, with the Courier font emerging as the most advantageous option for reading smaller letters, and Arial as the least suitable [15].

2 Method

Methodologically, this research was based on a case study conducted at a higher education institution located in South America, in the city of Quito, Ecuador. Approximately 95 photographs of the signage within the administrative and classroom areas of this institution were analyzed, and these areas are depicted in Fig. 1.

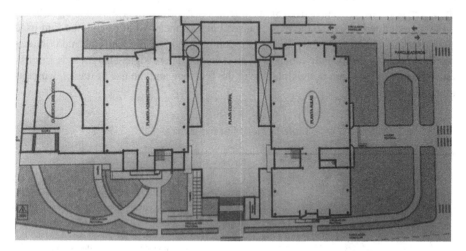

Fig. 1. Institution map

Initially, a review was conducted of the various types of signage located in the administrative area, which serves as the main entrance to the institution. This study placed a particular emphasis on analyzing informational and identification signage within the institution, while disregarding safety, evacuation, and prohibition signage. Data regarding the characteristics of each sign were recorded, specifically its positioning height, type (whether embedded or hanging), and inclusivity. During the assessment, considerable attention was also given to Braille code plates associated with specific signs. In some instances, it was evident that these plates were placed in areas unsuitable for individuals with visual impairments, as they were located near stairs or mezzanines, posing potential safety risks. In such cases, photographic documentation of the entire area along with the deficiency was carried out.

In the classroom area, similar data related to classroom and restroom signage were recorded. In this zone, inconsistencies were noted, primarily concerning improper placement and inappropriate color usage in the signage.

Finally, an analysis was performed on nine photographs that are considered to encompass the characteristics of informational and identification signage within this institution, in accordance with the Ecuadorian Technical Standard NTE INEN 2850 [16]. This standard addresses accessibility requirements for signage and is equivalent to the Spanish Standard UNE 170002:2009.

3   Results

In Ecuador, the INEN 2850 standard [16] establishes certain criteria that must be met for signage to be considered inclusive. In Table 1 and Table 2, the most relevant signs obtained during the assessment have been documented. The displayed images feature both embedded and hanging signs, sharing specific characteristics such as the chromatic contrast between blue and white on the plates, as well as the typography that includes text. The letter sizes, in all cases where Spanish text is present, comply with the regulations, as they are defined based on the expected reading distance. Additionally, the font used is appropriate, characterized by low stroke contrast and large, round internal contours to prevent confusion for individuals with low vision. These signs also include English translations, but these are not visible due to the font size and the use of italics, which is not recommended.

Table 1. Non-inclusive signage

#	Image	Height	Observation
1		1.70 m	It's non-inclusive embedded wall signage. It's positioned at a recommended height, and the letters can be clearly seen from a distance of 4 meters. However, the English letters cannot be seen clearly due to the use of italics, which is not recommended for individuals with visual impairments.
2		2.15 m	It's non-inclusive hanging signage. The letter size is visible from a distance of 4 meters.
3		1.80 m	It's non-inclusive embedded wall signage. It's placed at a height higher than recommended, and some letters are not very visible.
4		2.1 m	It's non-inclusive embedded signage placed above the elevator entrance door. It's positioned in a very high location and does not provide an option for users with visual impairments as there is no Braille code.
5		2.1 m	It's non-inclusive hanging signage. The letter size in Spanish is visible from a distance of 4 meters, but the English letters should be larger and not in italics.

Regarding the contrast between the signs and the surfaces they are placed on, it can be stated that, in most cases, it is correct. However, there is an exception with Sign 3 in Table 2, where the color of the Braille code plate is white against a wall with light colors.

Table 2. Inclusive signage

#	Image	Height	Observation
1		1.30 m	This pertains to a type of inclusive signage embedded on a glass door. The width of the band is visible.
2		1.65 m (signage) 1.40 m (Braille)	These are inclusive signs embedded on the wall. The height of the Braille code is appropriate, but the arrangement concerning the signage should be improved.
3		1.65 m (signage) 1.40 m (Braille)	These are inclusive signs embedded on the wall. The position of the Braille code is poorly located, and the color of the plate is not suitable.
4		1.70 m (signage) 1.40 m (Braille)	These are inclusive signs embedded on a wooden door and wall. The height of the signage above the door is too high. The Braille code is located in a hard-to-access area, but its height is appropriate.

For the proper placement of signs, it should be ensured that they are situated in areas where lighting does not create shadows or reflections that might hinder visibility. Furthermore, the lighting should be consistent throughout the entire building. Given that the institution's facilities are primarily intended for use by adults, the placement height should be defined based on the comfort of this user group. That said, concerning non-inclusive embedded signage in Table 1, it can be observed that the placement height is not uniform. However, the majority are appropriately located, considering that the average height of an Ecuadorian is 1.67 m.

In the case of the haptic signage in Table 2, which is associated with Braille code plates (Signs 2, 3, and 4), it is evident that the arrangement of the signs with the Braille plates is disorganized. The bathroom sign shown in Sign 4 does not seem to be placed at an appropriate height for people with disabilities. Such signage should preferably be positioned to the right of the door, and in the case of signage with Braille or high relief, it should be placed in the ergonomic sweep area. This is the zone where arm movement and the information presented on the signage interact, with a minimum height of 90 cm up to 175 cm from the floor and a maximum width of 60 cm (see Fig. 2).

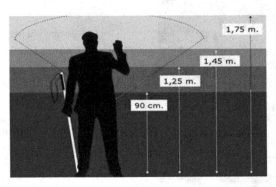

Fig. 2. Area for positioning adequate signage [16]

3.1 Dangerous and Irrelevant Signage

Figure 3 presents two examples in which the Braille code plates are placed in hazardous positions for individuals with visual impairments as they are situated very close to stairs (Fig. 3(a)) and mezzanines (Fig. 3(b)). Additionally, in Fig. 3(b), it's evident that the arrangement of the Braille code sign is poorly positioned, located at the opposite end of the informational signage.

Furthermore, there are cases in which signage is easily overlooked, rendering it irrelevant. In Fig. 4, an example is illustrated where the entrance door to a building, which includes a Braille code plate, is inconspicuous and challenging to access for users with visual impairments. Such instances highlight the critical need for signage that not only complies with inclusive standards but is also thoughtfully positioned to ensure safety and accessibility.

(a)   (b)

Fig. 3. Hazardous Braille code plate placement

Fig. 4. Irrelevant signage in entrance door with Braille code plate

4 Discussion and Conclusions

Educational institutions must wholeheartedly embrace policies aimed at ensuring the social inclusion of all individuals without any form of discrimination, as emphasized by [17]. In this context, the significance of a comprehensive signage system cannot be overstated, as it plays a pivotal role in providing vital information to every member of the institution's community.

In the specific research under consideration, the researchers meticulously analyzed a selection of nine informational and identification signs. These signs were chosen to reflect the unique characteristics of the institution being studied. The outcomes of this investigation underscore a critical aspect of inclusion – that only 44.44% of the signage met the criteria outlined in the INEN 2850 standard [16].

On a related note, the research highlights the crucial issue of haptic signage, which presents several challenges related to positioning, height, and color contrast, as evident in Figs. 3 and 4. These issues directly impact the experience of individuals with visual disabilities, especially those with low vision who encounter difficulties with reading. Furthermore, the International Classification of Functioning provides a categorization framework for individuals with visual disabilities, encompassing those with low vision who face reading challenges. As such, the design of signage must consider factors such as visual acuity, with the parameter of 20/200 equating to 40 cm or 16 inches, as [18] aptly suggests. This standardized measurement is instrumental in ensuring the legibility of signage content, ultimately enabling individuals to access the information contained in embedded signage. Encouragingly, 66.66% of the studied signage was found to be accessible to individuals with low vision.

It's crucial to acknowledge that inclusivity extends beyond visual disabilities. The use of italics for English text, although prevalent, has been shown to hinder the reading performance of individuals with dyslexia, further emphasizing the need for careful consideration in design choices.

However, it is essential to recognize that this research is not without its limitations. The study's scope was confined to the signage of a single institution, making it difficult to generalize the findings to other educational contexts. Moreover, there is a noticeable scarcity of research in the realm of inclusive signage within higher education institutions, underlining the necessity for further exploration in this field.

Looking ahead, it is advisable to establish parameters for designing signage that incorporates technology, thereby enhancing accessibility through the use of mobile devices. This technological advancement holds the potential to revolutionize the way individuals interact with and access educational signage, fostering inclusivity in innovative and transformative ways.

References

1. Jin, W., Yao, Y., Ren, G., Zhao, X.: Evaluation of integration information signage in transport hubs based on building information modeling and virtual reality technologies. Sustainability **14**(16), 9811 (2022)
2. Yenumula, K., Kolmer, C., Pan, J., Su, X.: BIM-controlled signage system for building evacuation. Procedia Eng. 118, 284–289 (2015)

3. Motamedi, A., Wang, Z., Yabuki, N., Fukuda, T., Michikawa, T.: Signage visibility analysis and optimization system using BIM-enabled virtual reality (VR) environments. Adv. Eng. Inform. **32**, 248–262 (2017)
4. Smitshuijzen, E.: Signage Design Manual, Lars Muller, Baden (2007)
5. Calori, C., Vanden-Einden, D.: Signage and Wayfinding Design: A Complete Guide to Creating Environmental Graphic Design Systems. John Wiley & Sons, Inc., Hoboken (2015)
6. Deng, L., Romainoor, N., Zhang, B.: Evaluation of the usage requirements of hospital signage systems based on the kano model. Sustainability **15**(6), 4972 (2023)
7. Dubey, R.K., Khoo, W.P., Morad, M.G., Hölscher, C., Kapadia, M.: AUTOSIGN: a multi-criteria optimization approach to computer aided design of signage layouts in complex buildings. Comput. Graph. **88**, 13–23 (2020)
8. Campos, L., Maia, I., Rocha, L., Rosa, L.: Redesign and improvement of the system of signaling and visual communication for the rectory of the federal institute of maranhão that meets the needs of visually impaired people. In: Advances in Ergonomics in Design, pp. 387–397. Springer, Cham (2019)
9. Rocha, L., Lima, T., Brito, L.: Universal signaling based on the articulation between the ergonomic practices and the perception of the visually impaired. In: Advances in Design for Inclusion, pp. 35–43. Springer, Cham (2020)
10. Servicio de Información sobre Discapacidad. Accessed 14 Sept 2023. https://sid-inico.usal. es/clasificacion-internacional-del-funcionamiento-de-la-discapacidad-y-de-la-salud-cif/
11. Ministerio de Salud Pública. Ecuador avanza hacia un proceso inclusivo y de reducción de las desigualdades para personas con discapacidad. Accessed 3 Dec 2022. https://www.salud. gob.ec/ecuador-avanza-hacia-un-proceso-inclusivo-y-de-reduccion-de-las-desigualdades-para-personas-con-discapacidad/
12. Wang, C.-Y., Chen, C.-I., Zheng, M.-C.: Exploring sign system design for a medical facility: a virtual environment study on wayfinding behaviors. Buildings **13**(6), 1366 (2023)
13. Asli, A., Moshfeghifar, S., Mousighichi, P., Samimi, P.: Adults' visual cue preferences and wayfinding abilities in healthcare centers. HERD: Health Environ. Res. Des. J. **16**(3), 104–118 (2023)
14. Lee, H., Lee, E., Choi, G.: Wayfinding signage for people with color blindness. J. Interior Des. **45**(2), 35–54 (2020)
15. Tarita-Nistor, L., Lam, D., Brent, M., Steinbach, M., González, E.: Courier: a better font for reading with age-related macular degeneration. Can. J. Ophthalmol. **48**(1), 56–62 (2013)
16. INEN. NTE INEN 2850 - Requisitos de accesibilidad para rotulación. Servicio Ecuatoriano de Normalización (2014)
17. Luna-Rodríguez, S., Rojas-Rodríguez, C.: Ergonomic considerations for the inclusive communication of low vision people academic spaces. Legado De Arquitectura Y DiseñO **17**(31), 85–92 (2022)
18. Arditi, A.: Rethinking ADA signage standards for low-vision accessibility. J. Vision **17**(5), 8 (2017)
19. Carvalho, D., Queiroz, Í., Araújo, B., Barbosa, S., Carvalho, V., Carvalho, S.: Augmentative and alternative communication with adults and elderly in the hospital environment: an integrative literature review. Rev. CEFAC **22**(5), e16019 (2020)
20. Moreschi, C., Almeida, M.: A comunicação alternativa como procedimento de desenvolvimento de habilidades comunicativas. Rev. Bras. Educ. Espec. **18**(4), 661–676 (2012)
21. Hervás, R., Bautista, S., Méndez, G., Galván, P., Gervás, P.: Predictive composition of pictogram messages for users with autism. J. Ambient Intell. Human. Comput. **11**(11), 5649–5664 (2020)
22. MedlinePlus. Deterioro del lenguaje en adultos (2023). https://medlineplus.gov/spanish/ency/article/003204.htm

23. BBVA. La brecha digital que desconecta a nuestros mayores en la crisis del coronavirus (2020). https://www.bbva.com/es/es/la-brecha-digital-que-desconecta-a-nuestros-mayores-en-la-crisis-del-coronavirus/. Último acceso 15 Dec 2022

24. Callari, T.C., Ciairano, S., Re, A.: Elderly-technology interaction: accessibility and acceptability of technological devices promoting motor and cognitive training. Work **41**(Supplement 1), 362–369 (2012)

25. Light, J., et al.: Challenges and opportunities in augmentative and alternative communication: Research and technology development to enhance communication and participation for individuals with complex communication needs. Augment. Alternat. Commun. **35**(1), 1–12 (2019)

26. Fager, S.K., Fried-Oken, M., Jakobs, T., Beukelman, D.R.: New and emerging technologies for adults with complex communication needs and severe motor impairments: State of the science [Special Issue]. Augment. Alternat. Commun. **35**(1) (2019)

27. Morin, K.L., et al.: A systematic quality review of high-tech AAC interventions as an evidence-based practice. In: Baltimore, M. (ed.) Augmentative and Alternative Communication, vol. 34, no. 2, pp. 104–117 (2018)

28. Rodríguez-Fórtiz, M., et al.: Sc@ut: developing adapted communicators for special education. Procedia Social Behav. Sci. **1**(1), 1348–1352 (2009)

29. Mendes, K., Silveira, R., Galvão, C.: Revisão integrativa: método de pesquisa para a incorporação de evidências na saúde e na enfermagem. Texto contexto enferm **17**(4), pp. 758–764, 2008

30. Cave, R., Bloch, S.: Voice banking for people living with motor neurone disease: views and expectations. Int. J. Lang. Commun. Disord. **56**(1), 116–129 (2021)

31. Hawley, M.S., et al.: A voice-input voice-output communication aid for people with severe speech impairment. IEEE Trans. Neural Syst. Rehabil. Eng. **21**(1), 23–31 (2013)

32. Beringer, A., Tonsing, K., Bornman, J.: The self-determined and partner-predicted topic preferences of adults with aphasia. Aphasiology **27**(2), 227–251 (2013)

33. Dada, S., Tonsing, K., Goldbart, J.: Friendship experiences of young adults who use augmentative and alternative communication. Int. J. Disabil. Dev. Educ. **69**(3), 951–975 (2022)

34. Halder, S., Takano, K., Kansaku, K.: Comparison of four control methods for a five-choice assistive technology. Front. Human Neurosci. **12** (2018)

35. Iacono, T., Bould, E., Beadle-Brown, J., Bigby, C.: An exploration of communication within active support for adults with high and low support needs. J. Appl. Res. Intellect. Disabil. **32**(1), 61–70 (2019)

36. Kim, M., Shin, S.: The effect of AAC display types on message production and its relationship with reading ability in patients with cognitive-communication disorders. Commun. Sci. Disord. **27**(1), 107–118 (2022)

37. Caligari, M., Giardini, M., Arcolin, I., Godi, M., Corna, S., Colombo, R.: Writing with the eyes: the effect of age on eye-tracking performance in non-disabled adults and a comparison with bimanual typing. Comput. Intell. Neurosci. (2021)

38. von Tetzchner, S., Øvreeide, K., Jørgensen, K., Ormhaug, B., Oxholm, B., Warme, R.: Acquisition of graphic communication by a young girl without comprehension of spoken language. Disabil. Rehabil. **26**(21), 1335–1346 (2004)

ExcelViz: Automated Generation of High-Level, Adaptable Scatterplot Descriptions Based on a User Study

Christin Engel[(✉)] and Jan Schmalfuß-Schwarz

TUD Dresden University of Technology, Dresden, Germany
christin.engel@tu-dresden.de

Abstract. Digital charts enable quick and effective analysis of complex data, while they pose a barrier for people with visual impairments. Image descriptions are intended to provide equivalent access to the chart's content, which is challenging and requires interpretations of the data, especially for complex data sets. Therefore, this paper investigates which key messages and categories sighted students perceive in scatterplots based on two user studies. First, we discussed five exemplary scatterplots with a group of sixteen students, who are familiar with digital accessibility and scatterplots in the academic context. We further analyzed this sample of scatterplots through an online survey with 222 participants, primarily students. We also compared the statistical correlations with the correlations reported by the participants, finding a high degree of agreement on outliers and trends. The results highlight the potential of image descriptions for accessible data analysis and form the basis for their automated generation.

Keywords: Accessible Charts · Image Descriptions · User Study · Scatterplots

1 Introduction

Charts serve a crucial role in daily life and profession to gain insights from the data. They are tailored to the visual sense and make use of domain-specific skills to enable quick recognition of patterns, outliers, and distributions. People with blindness or visual impairment have no access to visual charts and their content. Textual descriptions are therefore a suitable way to provide access to the meaning of charts. Which are mandatory according to legal standards (e.g., Germany: Barrier-free Information Technology Ordinance (BITV); International: Web Content Accessibility Guidelines (WCAG)). Chart descriptions should describe the structure of the chart and the data in a neutral manner without interpretations [3,15], e.g. by presenting data in a table. However, data tables are unsuitable for effective data analysis and independent access to the

---

C. Engel and J. Schmalfuß-Schwarz—The authors contributed equally to this research.

insights of the data. Established guidelines do not offer useful alternatives for ensuring equal access for people with and without sight to the message of visual charts, especially for large data sets. The key messages conveyed by a chart and the information required for an equal description are still unclear, due to the relative nature of visual perception. Moreover, both the creation of complex verbal descriptions and the understanding are very time-consuming and require a high effort. Due to a lack of standards for the specification and description of key messages of charts, the description often depends strongly on the individual author, so that it is still unclear how the relationships between the data can be described to provide equal access.

This paper investigates generating high-level descriptions capturing perceived messages in scatterplots. We analyze message categories through two user studies: one with 16 computer science students and another with 222 participants in an online survey. Results were compared, identifying consistent message categories. Additionally, we compare perceived visual features with computed statistics to identify suitable categories for automated descriptions. Scatterplots, representing large datasets and relationships, are ideal for this investigation due to their widespread use and underrepresentation in existing research.

2   State of the Art

Charts are lively tools for visual data analysis, offering various types such as bar charts, line charts, and scatterplots, each suited to different data types and analysis tasks. Shneiderman's [16] Information Seeking Mantra outlines a process for gaining insights from interactive visualizations: providing an overview, zooming and filtering, and enabling detailed analysis. Tactile charts offer non-visual access to data for people with blindness or visual impairments but have limitations in resolution and availability. [7,8,18] Automating effective descriptions for scatterplots is beneficial due to existing challenges in accessibility standards. Guidelines (e.g. WCAG, BITV) and template-based approaches aid in creating consistent descriptions, though challenges persist in reflecting key messages, particularly for scatterplots. Automated analysis and description tools aim to provide independent access to charts, especially for individuals with visual impairments. However, current research predominantly focuses on bar charts and line graphs, leaving scatterplots underrepresented. Addressing this gap is crucial for enhancing accessibility to visual data representations.

Supported Creation of Chart Descriptions. Guidelines aid in crafting consistent descriptions [3], yet challenges persist in conveying key messages, especially for scatterplots. For example, Ault et al. [1] and De Oliveira et al. [17] offer strategies to enhance comprehension and accessibility. However, both works don't describe the handling of large amounts of data, which can be represented in scatterplots.

Various approaches automate chart description generation, such as Ferres et al.'s [10] "iGraph Lite" system and Murilloales and Miesenberger's [13] "AUDiaL". Semantic-preserving methods like GraSSML [11] and Engel et al.'s [6] Excel plugin enable independent creation and access to chart descriptions. Despite advancements, challenges remain in describing visual features effectively, particularly for scatterplots, highlighting the importance of capturing perceived messages for meaningful chart access.

Automated Analysis and Description of Charts. Various approaches automate description creation, enabling independent chart access for people with visual impairments [4,5,12,14,19]. While research primarily focuses on bar charts and line graphs, scatterplots are often overlooked. Bajic and Job's [2] review underscores this disparity, noting a scarcity of studies on scatterplots in chart data extraction and description generation. They emphasize the importance of bridging this research gap to enhance chart accessibility.

3   User Study on the Intended Messages of Scatterplots

Research has shown various approaches to analyze charts automatically. Our goal is to provide meaningful access to the content of scatterplots by identifying the intended messages. The key messages depend not only on the represented data but also on the visual characteristics. Both must therefore be taken into account. To ensure equivalent access, it is necessary to capture the perceived content.

Therefore, we investigated two user studies with sighted people related to the following research questions:

– What key messages are conveyed by visual characteristics of scatterplots?
– Which visual characteristics influence the key messages and should therefore be included in the description?
– Do different people perceive the same or similar key messages in scatterplots?
– Does a small group of students agree on the key messages in the same way as a larger group?
– Can we identify message categories and their relevance for scatterplots based on the identified messages?
– To what extent do the perceived key messages correspond to those resulting from a statistical analysis?

To answer these questions, we conducted two separate studies with students - one with a small group of 16 students of an accessibility seminar on-site and an online study with 222 students.

3.1   Materials of the Studies

Both studies were based on scatterplots created using MS Excel, which represent various correlations of real data sets.[1] The visual language of Excel-based charts

---

[1] Data sources: https://OurWorldInData.org, https://population.un.org/wpp/BY-SA, https://data.worldbank.org/indicator/SP.DYN.TFRT.IN (received on Mai 2019), Hans Rosling et al.: Factfulness. Ullstein Buchverlage, 2018.

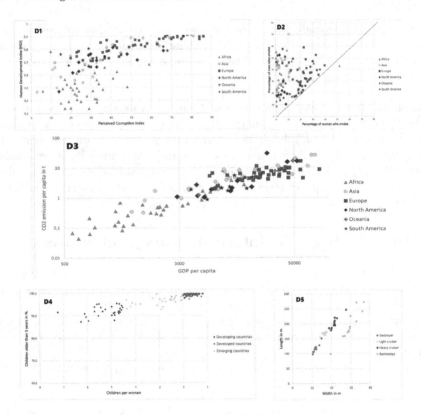

Fig. 1. Overview of the five scatterplots D1 to D5 used in the studies.

is familiar to both students and many people with blindness. [8]. The scatterplots differ in the represented number of categories (3 to 6 different per chart) and the applied symbols, the colors, formats, subjects, and the number of data points. This is intended to minimize biases due thus visual attribution, which is only relevant for distinguishing the data. The generated scatterplots represent common correlational relationships, i.e., linear correlation, clusters, outliers, or gaps (see Fig. 1). The following relations were shown:

1. D1: Perceived corruption index in different countries in relation to the level of human development on the y-axis (134 points).
2. D2: Relationship between men and women smokers in different countries (151 data points).
3. D3: CO2 emissions per head in relation to gross domestic product per head (122 points)
4. D4: Children per woman related to a state of development of a country (180 data points).
5. D5: The ratio of length and width of warships (51 data points)

In the following, we will present the procedure and results of the studies separately, followed by a comparison of the outcomes.

4   Small Group: Panel Discussion on Perceived Messages

The panel was conducted with 16 students of a course on accessibility, lasting 1.5 h. Three study investigators participated in the discussion.

4.1   Methodology

First, the students were introduced to message categories in charts illustrated by pie charts as well as the requirements and creation of chart descriptions. The participants were then asked to note the perceived main and secondary messages as well as visual highlights about the five scatterplots individually on a worksheet handed out in about 35 min.

This was followed by a 40-min panel discussion about the results moderated by the study directors. Each participant presented the perceived messages for each scatterplot, followed by a brief discussion. All participants were then asked to indicate their agreement for each message by hand voting. Due to time constraints, not all messages could be discussed in detail, so the written answers on the worksheets were also taken into account.

4.2   Participants

16 students of computer science as part of a course on digital accessibility participated voluntarily in the study. Non-participation had no consequences, and participation had no influence on the course grade. All participants were familiar with scatterplots and basics of statistical characteristics and data analysis. No participant stated to have visual impairments or color vision deficits. Data protection aspects were explained and confirmed by all participants.

4.3   Results

As a result, main and secondary messages were identified for each of the five scatterplots and further qualitative feedback was recorded. Messages mentioned by the majority of the students ($>=50\%$) were taken into account and assumed to be relevant.

Chart D1. The linear relationship between the variables was most frequently perceived as the main message (11 votes): The higher the HDI, the lower the perceived corruption. Furthermore, three secondary messages were rated by the majority of the participants to be relevant:

- No country is perceived to be free of corruption (81%).
- The development of European countries is very high, while the perceived corruption varies greatly (81%).
- Africa is the only continent with a development index smaller than 0.45 (63%).

Europe and Africa were rated as visual highlights (each by 5 participants).

Chart D2. All participants consider the ratio of men smoking compared to women smoking, with men being much more likely to smoke, as the main message. 38% also vote for the only country with a different ratio (more women smoke than men) should be named in the main message. Three secondary messages were rated by the majority:

– Proportion of men and women smoking in Europe is nearly equal. (68.8%)
– Less than 10% of women smoke in North America. (56.3%)
– Only one country has more women than men smokers. (56.3%)

The similarity in the distribution of the data points of Africa and Asia located close to the y-axis was mentioned most frequently (69%) as a visual highlight.

Chart D3. All students agreed that the linear relationship between the two variables is the main message of the scatterplot: The higher the GDP in a country, the higher the CO2 emissions. Furthermore, two secondary messages were rated by the majority:

– Europe, parts of Asia, North America, Oceania, and South America have both high CO2 emissions and a high GDP. (68.8%)
– Africa has the lowest GDP and lowest CO2 emissions. (68.8%)

Finally, 63% of the students emphasized the logarithmic scale.

Chart D4. Two main messages were rated by the majority to be relevant: (1) Developing countries have higher infant mortality than other countries (81.3%). (2) The less developed a country is, the higher the infant mortality rate (62.5%). While the first message highlights the category with maximum values, second message relates to the linear correlation. Overall, secondary messages secondary messages achieve high consensus:

– Most children across all countries reach the age of five (100%).
– The points of the three groups are clearly separated from each other (100%).
– The number of children is significantly higher in developing countries compared to the others (75%).

In addition, 56% of the students identified two empty areas on the x-axis, ranging from 3.25 to 3.75 and from 6.25 to 7.25 children per woman.

Chart D5. Half of the participants indicated the linear correlation between length and width of the ships as main message. Besides, four further relevant secondary messages were voted:

– No ship is wider than long (75%).
– The size of battleships is more spread out than the other groups (75%).
– Ship types can be divided into two groups based on its ratio, with battleships forming a separate group (62.5%).
– The length-to-width ratio is about 1:10 for most points, except for the battleships (56.3%).

Furthermore, no further visual highlight, which was not named as main or secondary message, was indicated by the majority of students.

Overall, a consensus was reached for each scatterplot covering main and secondary messages. The relationship between the two variables was named as the main statement by the majority in all charts. The secondary messages often relate to between-group or within-group comparisons. Furthermore, students conclude similarities of all data or relate to outliers. Specific data values were rarely provided.

5   Online Survey

Parallel to the panel discussion, an online survey was conducted with a larger group of students using the same questions and materials in order to compare the results. We also aim to determine whether a smaller group reaches similar results as a larger sample of participants.

5.1   Methodology

The online survey targets people without vision impairments. Participants were invited to take part in the questionnaire via the mailing list of our university, which is why mainly students took part. The survey could be completed within one month. At the beginning of the survey, participants had to confirm that they had not previously taken part and that they agreed to the data protection declaration. The data was collected anonymously. The survey consists of four parts: First, the participants' experiences with diagrams were recorded. Afterward, few demographic data were collected. In the third part, basic terms, characteristics of scatterplots, and message categories, such as outlier, cluster, point, group, and image descriptions were explained textually and visually. The last part relates to the main and secondary messages, as well as visual highlights of the five scatterplots already used in the discussion study. The order of the charts was randomized for each participant to avoid a learning effect. For each chart, three blocks of questions were asked. The first part involved rating messages about the perception of the chart elements on a 5-point-Likert scale. The second set of questions points to visual highlights, in particular clusters, free spaces, outliers, and trends. Some questions of this part requested participants to select elements (e.g., outliers) directly on the chart, while numerical answers were also requested. The third part relates to the main and secondary messages. In contrast to the discussion study, several possible main messages were suggested to the participants, of which the most important could be selected, or an alternative message could be given. The same predefined messages could also be rated as relevant for secondary messages on a 5-Point-Likert scale (agreement very strong to very weak). They were also able to indicate for each message that it was not included or that they could not estimate it. Alternatively, participants could provide further secondary messages within a text field.

5.2   Participants

Below we will present both demographic data of the participants and some questions about their experiences with charts. A total of 222 people participated in the study, with 116 females, 103 males, and 3 non-binary persons. Most of the participants are between 15 and 34 years old (96%) with a total of almost half of the people being between 20 and 24 years old. It is clear that all participants have at least completed high school or already have a university degree since the survey invitation was sent only to students. 43% have no visual impairment at all, while 56% stated to have farsightedness or nearsightedness, and 2 persons indicated to have a red-green deficiency. The majority of respondents (79%) deal with charts at least one time a week or daily, 16% at least once a month. Accordingly, almost all respondents are familiar with analyzing charts. Participants were also asked about their experience in creating charts. Nearly half of the participants reported creating charts at least once a week or once a day, while the majority created charts less frequently than once a month. Almost all participants (93%. multiple answers possible) use charts to illustrate data, while 61% do so for data analysis. More than half also use them to illustrate scientific texts. We also asked for the context of use. Most respondents use charts in courses (76%. multiple answers possible), at home (59%), or at work (45%). Charts are most frequently accessed on the internet (83%), which highlights the relevance of accessible digital charts. However, print media often also include charts, which was mentioned by 64% as well.

Simple bar charts (100%) and pie charts (99.6%) are the most common, known by all participants. However, line charts (90.1%), scatter plots (86.5%), stacked bar charts (78.4%), histograms (68.9%), and area plots (60.8%) are also familiar to the majority of participants. Less of the participants are familiar with starplots (49.1%), bubble charts (38.3%) as well as box-whisker-plots (31.1%). At the same time, more than half of the respondents indicated high or very high experience with simple bar charts, pie charts, and line charts, while 45% also had high or very high experience with scatterplots (see Fig. 2). Finally, participants were asked about their experiences with chart descriptions. Again, the overall level of experience is very high, with 60% having already created chart descriptions and 50% having used them on their own.

5.3   Results of the Online Survey

The responses were analyzed descriptively, with those messages considered as main messages that were selected or mentioned by at least 50% of the respondents. If there is no majority for an answer, then a message is still categorized as a main message if the value is at least twice the standard deviation. This allows a main message to be identified and clearly distinguished even with a wide spread of votes. No clear main message can be determined otherwise. Secondary messages were considered relevant if at least 50% strongly or very strongly agreed with them.

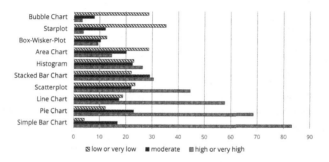

Fig. 2. Bar chart showing level of experience with various chart types in percentages (very high and high as well as low and very low were summarized).

The results regarding the visual features in the charts were examined to discover whether the perceived visual features correspond to those statistically determined. The results regarding the visual features in the charts were examined to investigate whether the subjectively perceived visual features correspond to the statistical calculations. This forms the basis to better compute perceived features in scatterplots. For this purpose, we compare the outliers selected by the participants with the results of the nearest neighbor algorithm. In addition, the mean distance between the outliers and their 5 nearest neighbors is determined, which is compared across all five charts. The goal is to find out the existence of a consistent threshold above which points are visually classified as outliers across all charts. We also performed a K-Means cluster analysis and a DB scan algorithm to analyze the graphs statistically for clusters, all calculations were performed in R.

Chart D1. In order to avoid problems with recognition, questions were initially asked about perception. The vast majority, approximately 80%. Stated being able to distinguish the data points by color or shape, well or very well. The spatial dimension of the groups could be perceived very well or well by 66%.

Main Message: Overall, the respondents were presented six possible main messages for D1. 90% of all respondents selected one of the messages presented as the main message, while the minority considered another message (6%) or no main message in the chart. The most frequently selected message relates to the linear correlation between both represented variables, rated by 41% (91 rates) of all participants (SD = 33.5). The second most frequently selected message (25%) described the correlation of the overall data (tendency toward high corruption perception and high HDI).

Secondary Messages: On average, 5% in each case indicated that the respective message was not included. However, 5 of the 6 messages presented were rated as relevant or very relevant by a total of more than 50%. Since one of the messages has already been rated as the main message with a significantly higher number of votes, since is excluded from consideration as a secondary message. The following 3 messages are included (decreased order):

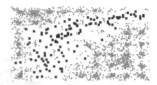

Scatterplot representing the outliers
indicated by participants (blue) and
the original data of the chart (black).
The five points most frequently
identified are outlined in red.

Scatterplot representing the empty
spaces indicated by participants (blue)
and the original data of the chart
(black rectangles).

Fig. 3. Indicated outliers (left) and empty spaces (right). (D1) (Color figure online)

- The level of development in Africa is the lowest (83%).
- Countries in Europe are more developed than those in Africa (80%).
- The countries in Europe have a higher level of development (62%).

About one-third of responses indicated no identifiable clusters, consistent with statistical calculations. Moreover, the responses varied widely regarding the number of empty spaces, with the majority identifying at least one. Figure 3 illustrates these spaces, predominantly outside the perimeter of all points. On average, three outliers were noted, with most respondents identifying at least one. Notably, the most frequently mentioned outliers corresponded strongly to the calculated ones, having the greatest mathematical distance to the nearest neighbor. Furthermore, most respondents (72.0%) observed a curved trend among data points, with some noting gaps in the curve. In summary, the majority of respondents described the course of the data points as curved, perceived at least one empty space, and at least one outlier in chart D1. Almost all the most frequent outliers mentioned by the participants have the greatest mathematical distance to the nearest neighbor so the perceived outliers strongly correspond to the calculated ones.

Chart D2. More than 70% of respondents were able to assign the points to a group well or very well based on their color and to identify trends in the data. For about three-quarters of the respondents, the diagonal line shown supports the perception.

Main Message: Six different messages were presented to the participants, where 97% selected one of the suggested messages. The following message was selected as the main message by the vast majority (87.5%): In most countries, more men smoke than women.

Secondary Messages: Overall, the majority of respondents strongly or very strongly agreed with 4 out of 6 secondary messages, with the message rated as the main message before achieved the highest score (95%). Moreover, the following 3 secondary messages were identified:

- The proportion of men smoking is significantly greater than the proportion of women smoking in Africa and Asia. (82%)

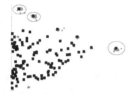 

Scatterplot representing the outliers indicated by participants (blue) and the original data of the chart (black). The three points most frequently identified are outlined in red.

Visualization of the distance matrix of the points in D2. The points with ID 46, 53 and 74 were also selected as outliers by the participants.

Fig. 4. Indicated outliers (left) and empty spaces (right). (D2) (Color figure online)

- In one country more women smoke than men. (76%)
- Some countries in Africa and Asia are outliers. (65%)

On average, participants identified 2 clusters, with three-quarters determining at least one. The calculated values align with the majority's perceptions. In addition, over 90% identified at least one empty space, averaging 10 points per respondent. Moreover, Participants noted 3 outliers (see Fig. 4), with almost all recognizing at least one. These outliers were consistently identified by other methods, exhibiting significantly greater distances from their nearest neighbors. More than 90% of respondents perceived neither a curvilinear nor a linear trend in the data. The majority stated no clear trend, while some provided descriptions such as "point cluster" or "triangle". In summary, participants generally identified clusters and outliers, with consistent findings across different methods. Most perceived no clear trend in the data.

Chart D3. With almost 80%, the vast majority could assign the points to a group well or very well based on their color, 67.9% were also able to perceive the spatial extent of the different groups well or very well, while 57.7% were able to detect an overall maximum limit in terms of CO_2 emissions (y-axis).

Main Message: All respondents selected one of the 5 messages presented, with one message being chosen as the main message by most respondents (83.8%): The higher the GDP per capita, the higher the CO_2 emission per capita. This message represents the perceived relationship between the two variables represented across all data.

Secondary Messages: The majority selected 3 messages, whereby the one with the highest values (95%) has already been declared as the main message and is therefore not listed here:

- Europe has both a high GDP and a high CO_2 emission per capita. (84%)
- Europe, North America, South America and Oceania have both high 'GDP per capita and high CO_2 emissions per capita. (58%)

On average, respondents perceived 2 clusters, with 22% not identifying any. The screeplot, dendrogram, and DB scan analysis also suggest 2 to 3 clusters.

Empty spaces indicated by the
participants (blue circles) and data
points of chart D3 (black rectangles).

Outlier selected by the participants
(blue circle) and original data points
of chart D3 (black rectangles).

Fig. 5. Indicated empty spaces (left) and outliers (right). (D3) (Color figure online)

Additionally, 87% of respondents indicated at least one empty space, with most selecting 2 (see Fig. 5). On average, 5 empty spaces were identified, mostly outside the value range, with two gaps noted on the left half of the x-axis. Furthermore, one outlier was identified, with over half of respondents indicating one. However, results from the db scan and nearest neighbor methods did not match with participants' choices, likely due to the logarithmic scaling of the chart's axis (see Fig. 5). Finally, the majority (96%) perceive a trend in the data, with over half indicating a linear progression and 44% considering it curved. Summarizing, participants generally perceived 2 clusters and noted empty spaces and outliers. However, discrepancies were observed in outlier identification due to the chart's logarithmic scaling.

Chart D4. In each case. More than 90% were able to assign all points to a group well or very well based on their color, to recognize the spatial extent of the points, and to identify a trend in the data. In contrast, about half of the respondents were able to identify clusters across groups.

Main Message: One of the four messages shown was identified as the main message by a slight majority (49.7%) of the respondents: The more children a woman has in a country, the higher the mortality rate of children up to 5 years of age. This message aims to summarize the general relationship over all data points.

Secondary Messages: 3 of the 4 messages presented were received by the majority, with one being the main message. The two secondary messages identified are:

– Fewer children in developing countries reach the age of 5 years than in developed countries. (90%)
– The majority of children worldwide reach the age of 5 years. (66%)

The respondents indicated 2 clusters (see Fig. 6), with about three-quarters recognizing at least 2. The dendrogram and scree test also support 2 clusters. Regarding empty spaces, 7 points were specified, with some respondents indicating none (15.7%). Empty spaces were mainly marked below the data and in the upper left corner, as well as between the gray dots in the upper right area. In addition, the majority also indicated one outlier (69.8%) (see Fig. 6). This outlier had the largest average distance to its 5 nearest neighbors and was identified by

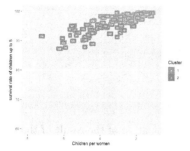

Results of k-means clustering analysis
in R with two clusters (k=2).

Outlier selected by the participants
(blue circle) and original data points
of chart D4 (black rectangles).

Fig. 6. Indicated Clusters (left) and outliers (right). (D4) (Color figure online)

the DB scan algorithm. Its mean distance to its 5 nearest neighbors was almost 3.8 times the standard deviation above the mean of all values. Finally, only 3.1% of respondents perceived no trend in the data, with the vast majority observing a linear trend. In the end, participants generally identified 2 clusters and noted empty spaces and one outlier. Most observed a linear trend in the data.

Chart D5. More than 90% of the participants were able to assign the points to the groups based on their color, to perceive the spatial extent very well or well of each group, and to recognize a progression within the groups. 77% also perceived a progression in the overall data.

Main Message: A total of 6 messages or the submission of a further message were available for selection. One was chosen as the main message by more than half of the respondents: The longer a warship is, the wider it is. This message aims to clearly illustrate a correlation between the variables presented.

Secondary Messages: 5 out of 6 messages were chosen by at least half of the respondents, with one of them already being the main message. The following 4 secondary messages were indicated:

- The length-to-width ratio of battleships differs from other ships. (83%)
- The points of the battleship group are more spread out. (81%)
- The group destroyers, light cruisers, and heavy cruisers can be distinguished by their length and width. (62%)
- There is one outlier in the battleship group. (61%)

On average, respondents selected two clusters, with a small percentage indicating no cluster (7.7%). The dendrogram and scree test also suggest two clusters, while DB scan results in one. Furthermore, seven points were marked for empty spaces. The area around data points and between different groups was frequently marked. Regarding outliers, respondents marked one outlier (34%), with nearly 40% indicating none (see Fig. 7). Although points 38, 43, and 44 had the greatest average distance, the outlier selected by participants (ID 50) was closer to a group of blue dots, possibly due to perception influenced by dot color. Additionally,

Outlier selected by the participants
(blue circle) and original data points
of chart D5 (black rectangles).

Visualization of the result of the db
scan of D5.

Fig. 7. Three outliers (left) marked by the majority of participants, and visualization
of the DB scan (right). (D5) (Color figure online)

more than three-quarters recognized a linear progression, while a minority could
not identify a clear trend (7.7%). Summarizing, respondents generally selected
two clusters, noted empty spaces, and identified an outlier. Most observed a
linear trend in the data.

In this section, the results regarding the main and secondary messages as well
as the visual characteristics of the 5 scatterplots were presented and partially
compared with statistical calculations. The next section summarizes the results
of both studies and the outcomes.

6   Outcomes of Investigations

We conducted two studies to find out how scatterplots with different characteristics were perceived by sighted people. The goal is to generate equivalent
descriptions of scatterplots that contain the main messages as well as visual
highlights. In the following, the findings of both studies will be summarized and
discussed in a structured way. We first briefly discuss the current relevance of
charts. We then present the message categories for scatterplots identified based
on both studies. In conclusion, we discuss our results in terms of how they reflect
the statistical characteristics of scatterplots. Finally, we draw a clear contribution by means of significant findings.

6.1   Use of Visual Charts

Charts are very well known among the respondents and are frequently used in
both the private and professional fields. They are consumed in printed as well
as digital form. The creation of charts is also frequently carried out in the university context. According to this, charts play an important role, at least in the
university context, with the majority of respondents using them to analyze data
or illustrate scientific texts. Almost half of the respondents further have high or
very high experience with scatterplots. In contrast, Engel et al. [9] demonstrate
that scatterplots are known to few people with blindness or visual impairment,

and charts are used less frequently for data analysis. Charts are of great importance and frequently used, at least in the context of education, which is why further efforts must be made to make charts accessible. The automated creation of chart descriptions can contribute to this. In addition, More than half of the respondents in our online study reported to have generated or consumed chart descriptions on their own. This suggests that the descriptions can be useful for all people to analyze data.

6.2 Message Categories

Overall, it was possible to find a majority for at least one main and one secondary message in both the discussion study and the online study. The main messages D1 to D4 were each selected by more than 80% in the discussion study, while there was an average of 85% agreement with the main messages across all 5 charts (SD = 0.19, V = 0,22). Essentially the same main messages were identified in both studies, although responses in the online survey were more scattered, with an average agreement of 62.7%. Only the main messages of D4 are somewhat different. In both studies, the second messages were selected on average by around three-quarters of the respondents in each case.

We also categorized the messages into the following identified categories:

- **Comparison:** This category contains messages that compare multiple values of data points, reflecting the similarities and differences between data.
- **Correlation:** The message category refers to relationships in the data, e.g., whether the values have linear relationships.
- **Outlier/extreme:** Outliers indicate one or more values with extreme values that are either particularly high or low or visually far away.
- **Cluster/distribution:** Clusters refer to groups of points that have similar properties or are located close to each other.

These 4 message categories can apply to three contexts relating to the data:

- **Global:** The message relates to all data in general, not considering the categories.
- **Within-Group:** The message only considers the data within a group or category.
- **Between-Group:** The message refers to several groups or categories.

We used the results of both studies to determine the relevance of the different message categories Overall charts, 11 main messages, and 28 secondary messages were selected by the majority of participants as relevant for the respective chart, all the main messages selected relate to correlations in terms of the overall data (9 out of 11). Two main messages provided a global comparison. Here, both studies come to similar results.

In both studies, comparisons between groups were most frequently identified as a secondary message. Overall, 60% of all secondary messages comprised between-group comparisons. About a quarter of all secondary messages described outliers, with all three contexts being present here. Clusters were described only between groups (10%) and correlations between groups were reported once in each study.

6.3   Perceived Visual Characteristics

We examined the results of the online survey concerning information on clusters, outliers, empty spaces, and trends. In addition, the results were compared with the statistically determined values to find out to what extent the answers of the participants reflect the statistical relationships. We also compared the standard deviation and coefficient of variance (relative standard deviation) of the responses in each case in order to conclude the level of agreement among the participants (see Table 1).

Almost all calculated variance coefficients are greater than 1, which means that the standard deviation is greater than the mean value. This indicates a relatively large dispersion of the answers given in relation to the mean value, which means here that a particularly large number voted for one answer. Nevertheless, in most cases, at least a majority could be found for the presence of a feature, for example at least one empty space. The greatest scattering of answers relates to the trends presented and the empty spaces over all answers. The number of clusters and empty spaces achieved a relatively low agreement rate across all charts and participants. This is partly due to the study design, as empty spaces were marked as points and not as areas. Furthermore, it was not clearly defined what an empty space is, to measure the different views of it. Just the clusters have a variance coefficient smaller than 1, although the agreement rate is relatively low. Nevertheless, the average number of clusters indicated generally corresponds to the number of clusters calculated. Although the answers are relatively scattered, a majority (over 50% of the answers) could be found for trends in each chart, which leads to a high rate of agreement for trend detection. However, the question regarding trends was also the only one with predefined answers.

On average, almost half of the respondents also agreed on the number of outliers. The outliers identified by the respondents mostly corresponded to the points that have the greatest calculated distance to their neighbors. One exception is D3, where the logarithmic scale does not allow a comparison in this manner. It is also noticeable that most respondents chose an outlier in D5 that is relatively close to other points. This discrepancy can be explained by the characteristics of visual perception, where the contrast between the colors of points from different groups has a great influence in this example. The outliers that were correctly identified as such differ from the mean in a range of 2 to 4 times the standard deviation. Overall, the majority of respondents indicated an average of two outliers, which essentially correspond to the calculated outliers. It can be concluded from the results that, in particular, trends and outliers indicated by the respondents often match the statistical results.

Table 1. Comparison of answers relating to visual highlights with the respective standard deviation and variance coefficient of the given answers.

Chart	Result	Cluster	Empty Spaces	Outlier	Trend	Average
D1 - Corruption	Average	2	9	3	Curve	
	Agreement	36.50%	27.50%	28.80%	71.60%	41.10%
	SD	1.56	12.46	2.75	3	4.94
	Variance	0.75	1.37	0.92	1.5	1.14
D2 - Smoke	Average	2	10	3	No trend	
	Agreement	33.33%	22.90%	49.01%	70.27%	43.88%
	SD	1.4	14.42	1.67	26.95	11.11
	Variance	0.77	1.44	0.55	1.08	0.96
D3 - CO2	Average	2	2	1	Linear	
	Agreement	35.58%	45.95%	53.15%	51.80%	46.62%
	SD	1.32	7	2.2	27.31	9.46
	Variance	0.86	1.4	1.5	1.09	1.21
D4 - Children	Average	2	7	1	Linear	
	Agreement	41.44%	19.37%	69.82%	72.27%	50.73%
	SD	0.98	8	1.72	27.8	9.625
	Variance	0.49	1.23	1.27	1.11	1.03
D5 - Ships	Average	2	7	1	Linear	
	Agreement	32.43%	25.67%	39.19%	76.58%	43.47%
	SD	1.3	7.5	1.7	29.80	10.08
	Variance	0.55	1.1	1.3	1.92	1.22
Average	SD avg	2.31	9.88	2.01	22.97	
	Agreement avg	35.68%	28.28%	47.99%	68.50%	
	Variance avg	0.68	1.31	1.11	1.34	

6.4 Summarizing Outcomes

Overall, the following main conclusions can be drawn from the results:

- Scatterplots play an important role in the academic field, so methods need to be established to provide access to the content of printed and digital charts.
- The main message of a scatterplot is evaluated similarly by several people.
- The main messages provided by a small group of students and a larger sample of people regarding the charts are comparable.
- The main message of scatterplots usually refers to the depicted relationship across all data points, if available. Otherwise, conspicuous relating to global comparisons or between-group comparisons are summarized.
- The secondary messages in scatterplots should primarily provide information about similarities and differences between the groups, as well as highlight distinctive outliers.

- Messages categories for scatterplots are: Correlation, Trend, Outlier/Extrema, Cluster/Distribution and could relate to global, within-group, or between-group context.
- The majority of subjective perceptions of outliers and trends usually correspond to the statistical correlations.
- Outliers are perceived as such if they are at least 2.5 times the standard deviation above the mean of all values.
- Empty spaces are primarily considered to be areas that lie outside the perimeter surrounding the data points and do not contain any points.

7   Limitations

Both studies come with some limitations. While the discussion study took place in the context of a discussion, the second study was conducted online, so less is known about the reasons for the responses. This is particularly noticeable in the fact that the free responses in the online survey are more widely distributed than those obtained from the discussion study. Thus, no response was selected from all participants in the online study. The selection of the sample, primarily based on students, is a limitation of both studies. It is therefore unclear whether the results can be generalized to the whole population. However, it was ensured that the respondents were very familiar with charts and data analysis. In addition, the evaluation did not take any cultural differences into account, for example, the interpretation of colors. It also cannot be excluded that the content of the data has influenced the perception, e.g., in the identification of outliers. Following user studies should consider these aspects to prove the results. The studies aimed to find out which message categories are relevant for scatterplots for main and secondary messages. On the other hand, no language analysis was carried out, and it was not the aim to find out how the messages should be worded. With regard to the visual characteristics, the analysis of the open spaces and the clusters was severely limited due to the study format. For example, neither points were assigned to specific clusters nor their meaning in the context of the data was determined in more detail. Furthermore, empty spaces in the online survey were marked with points rather than areas, which is unsuitable for detailed evaluation. Here, a flexible input option (e.g., coloring) with additional qualitative feedback from the respondents should be collected and compared with the proportion of empty spaces calculated. Finally, only 5 different scatterplots were considered in our study, so only some variations were investigated. The generalizability of the results needs to be investigated with a larger number of scatterplots with different visual characteristics.

8   Conclusion and Future Work

We conducted two studies to examine the perceived content of scatterplots in detail. The results form the basis for creating equivalent chart descriptions for people with blindness or visual impairments that reflect the perceived content of the chart as sighted people have. For this purpose, we identified different message categories and their relevance for scatterplots as a result. In addition, we compared a small and larger sample of people in regard to the main messages they identified for scatterplots. It turns out that a small group of students is sufficient to determine the main messages. Furthermore, we examined the extent to which the subjectively perceived messages about the data correspond to the statistical calculations. The results show that the perception of participants often corresponds to the statistical calculation, under certain conditions. Following, an automated interpretation of scatterplots could generate meaningful, accessible descriptions. Following studies should take a more heterogeneous group of users into account and provide ways to adapt the descriptions based on specific needs. Furthermore, more chart types and the influence of visual characteristics should be explored in detail to be able to identify a suitable calculation to automate the creation of accessible high-level chart descriptions. The results should also be evaluated in a next step by implementing a prototype that aims to generate chart descriptions automatically. To prove our concept, we developed a basic Excel plugin that allows the accessible creation of adaptable, accessible chart descriptions. The descriptions are presented as accessible HTML files. So far, simple statistical calculations, such as finding outliers, or correlations, have already been implemented, with no special visual features being taken into account. While we are implementing a rule-based approach, a comparison with AI-based creation of descriptions would be very meaningful. The prototype forms the basis for further evaluation and development of high-level descriptions for various types of charts that can enable their accessible creation by people with blindness or visual impairments.

References

1. Ault, H.K., Deloge, J.W., Lapp, R.W., Morgan, M.J., Barnett, J.R.: Evaluation of long descriptions of statistical graphics for blind and low vision web users. In: Miesenberger, K., Klaus, J., Zagler, W. (eds.) ICCHP 2002. LNCS, vol. 2398, pp. 517–526. Springer, Heidelberg (2002). https://doi.org/10.1007/3-540-45491-8_99
2. Bajić, F., Job, J.: Review of chart image detection and classification. Int. J. Doc. Anal. Recogn. (2023). https://doi.org/10.1007/s10032-022-00424-5
3. Carl and Ruth Shapiro Family National Center for Accessible Media at WGBH (NCAM) in conjunction with the DIAGRAM Center (Digital Image And Graphic Resources for Accessible Materials): Image Description Guidelines (2015)
4. Demir, S., Carberry, S., McCoy, K.F.: Summarizing information graphics textually. Comput. Linguist. **38**(3), 527–574 (2012)
5. Elzer, S., Schwartz, E., Carberry, S., Chester, D., Demir, S., Wu, P.: A browser extension for providing visually impaired users access to the content of bar charts on the web. In: WEBIST (2), pp. 59–66 (2007)
6. Engel, C., Gollasch, D., Branig, M., Weber, G.: Towards accessible charts for blind and partially sighted people. In: Burghardt, M., Wimmer, R., Wolff, C., Womser-Hacker, C. (eds.) Mensch und Computer 2017 - Tagungsband, pp. 415–418. Gesellschaft für Informatik e.V., Regensburg (2017). https://doi.org/10.18420/muc2017-mci-0338

7. Engel, C., Müller, E.F., Weber, G.: Svgplott: an accessible tool to generate highly adaptable, accessible audio-tactile charts for and from blind and visually impaired people. In: Proceedings of the 12th ACM International Conference on PErvasive Technologies Related to Assistive Environments, pp. 186–195 (2019)

8. Engel, C., Weber, G.: Improve the accessibility of tactile charts. In: Bernhaupt, R., Dalvi, G., Joshi, A., Balkrishan, D.K., O'Neill, J., Winckler, M. (eds.) INTERACT 2017. LNCS, vol. 10513, pp. 187–195. Springer, Cham (2017). https://doi.org/10.1007/978-3-319-67744-6_12

9. Engel, C., Weber, G.: User study: a detailed view on the effectiveness and design of tactile charts. In: Lamas, D., Loizides, F., Nacke, L., Petrie, H., Winckler, M., Zaphiris, P. (eds.) INTERACT 2019. LNCS, vol. 11746, pp. 63–82. Springer, Cham (2019). https://doi.org/10.1007/978-3-030-29381-9_5

10. Ferres, L., Verkhogliad, P., Lindgaard, G., Boucher, L., Chretien, A., Lachance, M.: Improving accessibility to statistical graphs: the igraph-lite system. In: Proceedings of the 9th International ACM SIGACCESS Conference on Computers and Accessibility, pp. 67–74 (2007)

11. Fredj, Z.B., Duce, D.A.: Grassml: accessible smart schematic diagrams for all. In: Proceedings of the 2006 International Cross-Disciplinary Workshop on Web Accessibility (W4A): Building the Mobile Web: Rediscovering Accessibility? pp. 57–60 (2006)

12. McCoy, K.F., Carberry, S., Roper, T., Green, N.L.: Towards generating textual summaries of graphs. In: HCI, pp. 695–699 (2001)

13. Murillo-Morales, T., Miesenberger, K.: AUDiaL: a natural language interface to make statistical charts accessible to blind persons. In: Miesenberger, K., Manduchi, R., Covarrubias Rodriguez, M., Peňáz, P. (eds.) ICCHP 2020. LNCS, vol. 12376, pp. 373–384. Springer, Cham (2020). https://doi.org/10.1007/978-3-030-58796-3_44

14. Nazemi, A.: A method to provide accessibility for visual components to vision impaired. Int. J. Recent Trends Hum. Comput. Inter. 4(1), 54–69 (2013)

15. Round Table on Information Access for People with Print Disabilities, I.: Guidelines for producing accessible graphics (2002). https://printdisability.org/guidelines/graphics-2022/

16. Shneiderman, B.: The eyes have it: a task by data type taxonomy for information visualizations. In: Proceedings 1996 IEEE Symposium on Visual Languages, pp. 336–343. IEEE (1996)

17. Teles De Oliveira, C.L., et al.: Proposal and evaluation of textual description templates for bar charts vocalization. In: 2019 23rd International Conference Information Visualisation (IV), pp. 163–169 (2019).https://doi.org/10.1109/IV.2019.00036

18. Tomashek, D.B., Edyburn, K.D., Baumann, R., Smith, R.: The case for next generation text description solutions for visual information accessibility. In: RESNA Annual Conference (2013)

19. Wu, P., Carberry, S., Elzer, S., Chester, D.: Recognizing the intended message of line graphs. In: Goel, A.K., Jamnik, M., Narayanan, N.H. (eds.) Diagrams 2010. LNCS (LNAI), vol. 6170, pp. 220–234. Springer, Heidelberg (2010). https://doi.org/10.1007/978-3-642-14600-8_21

Exploring the Effectiveness of Electrotactile Feedback for Data Visualization for Blind and Visually Impaired Users

Rezylle Milallos, Tae Oh, and Roshan L. Peiris[✉]

School of Information, Rochester Institute of Technology, Rochester, NY 14623, USA
{rm7312,thoics,roshan.peiris}@rit.edu

Abstract. Blind and visually impaired individuals use tactile graphics to interpret any type of image, figure, or graph. However, the production of these materials is resource exhaustive—taking a lot of time, quality assurance, and money. This research project uses recent advancements in electrotactile feedback to provide an accurate and timely approach to data visualizations of users who are blind or visually impaired. For this, we developed Electromouse, a mouse-based prototype where users can navigate the screen and feel an electrotactile sensation every time the cursor hits a significant line on the graphic presented on the screen. We performed an early exploration study with five blind adults to evaluate the effectiveness and safety of the prototype. Overall, participants were excited for this new method, but had suggestions for improvement related to the form factor, additional graphical information, and multimodal notification.

Keywords: Accessibility · Assistive Technologies · Electrotactile Feedback · Haptics · blind · low vision

1 Introduction

Many printed materials are now more accessible with the emergence of eBooks and eReaders. However, the graphics and pictures included in those books and articles are not easily visualized by someone who is blind or visually impaired (BVI) [8,19,32,33]. While text and scene descriptions are often used to aid in data visualization of graphical materials, the explanation is often not enough especially when comprehension of the material relies partly on understanding the figures included in the text such as maps for geography and navigation and graphs for math and science. As of 2018, according to data from the American Community Survey, there are approximately 547,803 BVI students (i.e., 17 years old or younger) in the U.S [3]. These students rely on tactile data visualizations (e.g., tactile graphics), to help them get a better understanding of concepts and

© The Author(s), under exclusive license to Springer Nature Switzerland AG 2024
M. Antona and C. Stephanidis (Eds.): HCII 2024, LNCS 14698, pp. 413–428, 2024.
https://doi.org/10.1007/978-3-031-60884-1_28

other educational materials [2, 26]. Tactile data visualizations convey information through different materials, textures, and embossed plates [8]. While tactile graphics is the preferred modality for data visualization within the BVI population, production of tactile materials for data visualization can be a laborious process [27]. Because of this, the translated tactile data visualizations in textbooks do not represent visual data accurately [34] or materials are delayed [28] and often not available to students at all.

Researchers and organizations have been working to find new ways to provide timely and more accurate tactile data visualizations. They proposed a solution to improve the efficiency of tactile data visualizations production through automation [22] and collaboration between sighted and BVI individuals [4, 5]. More recently, researchers have investigated using modern technology such as 3D printing for create 3D tactile maps [12], small mobile robots with accompanying tactile overlays [11], and guidelines for rendering haptically perceivable graphical elemants on touch screen devices. However, these solutions still require time to process, translate, and print visual information. Furthermore, novel haptic methods [10, 37, 41] and sonic and tonal methods [9, 24, 43] have been researched for data visualization.

Inspired by these previous works, in this work, we present the early exploration of using electrotactile feedback method for presenting data visualizations for BVI individuals. Electrotactile feedback method electrically stimulates the nerves in the skin through electrodes placed directly on the skin of the target feedback area. Since the electrodes can be flexibly designed and placed with high spatial density on the skin, electrotactile feedback can produce stimuli of relatively high spatial resolution [15]. As such, in addition to many other haptic applications, electrotactile feedback has been examined with BVI users for applications such as providing images through electrotactile displays placed on foreheard [17] and providing braille through a display placed on the fingertips [29]. Based on these approaches and taking advantage of the high spatial resolution of electrotactile stimuli, this research examines the ability of electrotactile feedback to provide data visualization information (specifically, visual information of line graphs) through a mouse-like prototype interface-"Electromouse". In this case study, we present the insights and lessons learnt from a preliminary study conducted with 5 blind participants.

2   Method

The objective of this case study was to get preliminary insights into the feasibility of using electrotactile feedback as a potential method for data visualization for the BVI users. The study procedure was approved by the institute's IRB office.

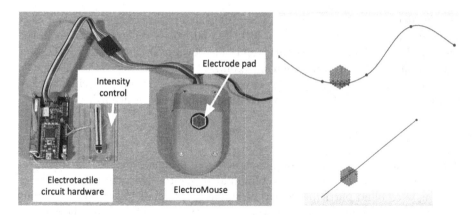

Fig. 1. Left: Electromouse system that consists of the electromouse with the electrode pad and the hardware circuit. Right: On-screen cursor showing a representation of the electrotactile surface on the mouse. When the node is in contact with the data visualization, the nodes are activated and are displayed as red on the screen. (Color figure online)

2.1   Prototype Development and Setup

We utilized a circuit toolkit introduced in a previous research as our main electrotactile feedback hardware [15,16]. After multiple iterations on the design, we developed a 3D-printed interface in the form factor of a computer mouse to house the electrode feedback pad. The 3D-printed mouse proves to be a cost-effective and portable form factor. In addition, previous researchers have looked into the use of tactile mouse interfaces for haptic feedback [1], perceptualization [13], generation of unique velvet-like sensations for users [30], and its direct application as a low-cost alternative for the BVI population [25]. We took advantage of the hardware component of a Microsoft Basic Optical Mouse as the base of the prototype so that all movements of the prototype are captured similar to the movement of a mouse. Multiple iterations of the 3D casing were made to measure the correct sizing and proper ergonomic placement of the user's hand against the electrotactile component. Four screws in each corner were added to lock the electrotactile component in place, ensuring that the all of the actuator nodes can be felt from the hole on top of the mouse. The final prototype is shown in Fig. 1(left). Participants used the mouse in such a way that the index finger is placed on the electrotactile electrode pad (Fig. 2(right)), which is located on top of the mouse.

The software interface presented visual representation of the electrotactile surface can be seen on the screen as shown in Fig. 1. This helped the sighted researcher place the cursor in the correct position and assist the participant whenever necessary. The electrotactile nodes are activated whenever any electrode touches a relevant area of data visualization on the screen (i.e., every time the cursor hits part of the graphic displayed on the screen, the mouse will output an equivalent sensation against the user's finger). The size of the equivalent electrotactile cursor was chosen to help identify and isolate different nuances in the graph such as a diagonal or a curvy end. The level of intensity felt by the user can be adjusted at any time using the control in the hardware (Figure 1(left)). For safety purposes and to reduce any potential distraction, participants were encouraged to adjust the intensity before starting a task if needed.

2.2   Usability Study

Participants. A two-hour usability study was designed to test the effectiveness of the 3D-printed mouse. One blindfolded, sighted user who has experience working with blind participants was recruited as the pilot tester. Five BVI participants were recruited through word-of-mouth. P1 and P2 lost their vision during their teenage years while the others were either born blind (P3) or lost their vision very early in life (P4 and P5). One participant (P4) did not complete the study because he was not confident in his ability to visualize the data after the training session. P4 instead offered feedback through the semi-structured interview. The test was conducted either at a coffee shop (P1 and P3) or at the participants' homes (P2, P4, and P5) based on the participant's preferences. The participants signed a consent form and were asked questions about demographic information, visual impairment, and background experience with data visualization tools.

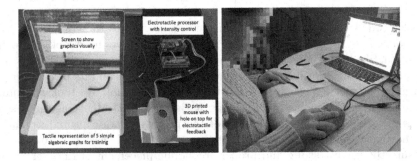

Fig. 2. Setup used for the usability study included a laptop which displayed the data to be identified, an electrotactile processor which controls the nodes depending on the on-screen data, and the ElectroMouse, a 3D-printed mouse with a hole on top to house the electrotactile component.

Training. Participants were allowed a training period where they can adjust the electrotactile feedback based on their comfort level. During this time, they were also shown different shapes (square, circle, triangle) and basic algebraic graphs—linear, absolute value (V-shaped), square root, exponential, and square function (parabola or U-shaped). A tactile data visualization of the five basic graphs was presented to help them picture the graph during the training period (see Fig. 2). The graphs were chosen because they are some of the most common types of graphs and shapes that are learned in school. Previous research have also used some of these to test the usability of audio presentation for data visualization [21]. Each participant was given ample time (an average of one hour for training) to explore each shape/graph using both the electrotactile device as well as the tactile data visualizations. They were asked to move to next shape only when they felt confident about identifying the current data on the screen.

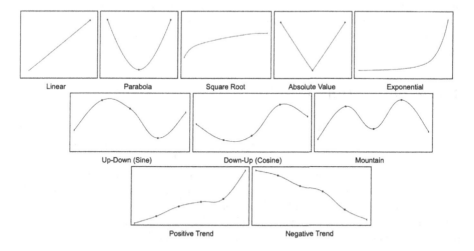

Fig. 3. Algebraic and trending graphs used for the study.

Testing. After the training, participants were asked to identify a total of 12 graphs. The first seven consisted of a random selection of the five basic algebraic graphs presented during the training section, with a chance of repeating. The repetition was suggested by the pilot tester to prevent participants from guessing the remaining graphs through the process of elimination. The last five graphs were more complex, trending graphs (i.e., up-down or sine wave, down-up or cosine wave, mountain, positive, and negative) that participants have not encountered before in the usability study. These were added to gauge the participant's ability to trace and identify a newly-introduced graph. All the graphs used in the testing can be seen in Fig. 3. To sum up the experience in the usability study, a semi-structured interview was conducted to review overall experience, any feedback regarding the form factor, and additional suggestions for future features, applications, and/or design changes.

Data Measurements. For all 12 tasks in the usability study, the researchers compiled three data points: identification rate, time on task (ToT), and satisfaction rate. The identification rate shows how many times the graph was identified correctly given x number of trials. Because of the random nature of the tasks involving the five algebraic graphs, some had more trials than others. ToT is measured based on how long it took for the participants to identify the graph, whether the answer was right or wrong. The timer started as soon as the cursor was placed at the starting point and ended when participants gave their final answer. During this timer, the researchers also recorded the participants' cursor movement to get an idea on how the graph was traced and how close it resembled the original graph. After each task, participants were asked to give a rating between 1 to 7 based on how easy or hard it was to visualize the on-screen graph, with 1 being *Very Hard to Understand* and 7 being *Very Easy to Understand*. Participants were also encouraged to make comments regarding the graph as they deemed necessary.

3   Usability Study Results

A total of 10 graphs were used in the study (5 algebraic, 5 trends). Algebraic graphs had a random chance of repeating per participant. Participants had all previously seen (tactile graph on paper) and interacted with the algebraic graphs during the training session. However, the trending graphs were only introduced during the evaluation and served as a short test on how well participants would recognize graphs given no additional information on what is on the screen. A summary of the results is provided in Table 1. On each type of graph, one participant had a much higher ToT than others and is deemed an outlier. An additional column for the average ToT without the outlier has been added to Table 1.

Table 1. A summary of all the measured data points for each type of graph.

Type of Graph	Identification Rate	Avg. Time on Task (ToT)	Avg. ToT without outlier	Satisfaction Rate (out of 7)
Linear	4 of 6 or 66.67%	216.93 s	41.8 s	4.83
Parabola (U-shaped)	2 of 5 or 40%	187.55 s	71.64 s	3.2
Absolute Value (V-shaped)	4 of 4 or 100%	127.97 s	74.96 s	4.5
Square Root	2 of 6 or 33.33%	490.66 s	99.24 s	2.83
Exponential	3 of 6 or 50%	261.39 s	157.07 s	3.67
Up-Down Curve (Sine Wave)	3 of 4 or 75%	212.50 s	74.71 s	5
Down-Up Curve (Cosine Wave)	3 of 4 or 75%	232.49 s	140.17 s	4.25
Mountain Curve	1 of 4 or 25%	295.84 s	123.21 s	5.25
Positive Trend	3 of 4 or 75%	268.67 s	71.26 s	4.75
Negative Trend	2 of 4 or 50%	155.15 s	40.83	4.75

3.1   Five Basic Algebraic Graphs

The *linear graph* proved to have the fastest average ToT (without the outlier). Participants noted that it is the most recognizable and easy to understand graph, even for those that were born blind (or were blinded at a young age). While the linear graph's identification rate is average at 60%, it is good to note that participants still traced the graphs accurately even if they gave the wrong description. The *absolute value graph or V-shaped graph* had the best identification rate out of all algebraic graphs. Participants noted that it was easier to follow a steeper, straighter line compared to curvy lines (e.g., the parabola or U-shaped graph). Some participants even identified the graph without finishing the entire piece because they easily recognized the first half of the graph as shown in P5's performance in Fig. 4. On the other hand, participants found the *parabola or U-shaped graph* tricky because of its similarity to the V-shaped graph. Most of them took their time feeling the "tip" of the graph to help determine if it is more rounded (U-shaped) or sharper (V-shaped). As such, participants spent more time trying to decide which of the two is the correct answer. P1 specifically noted that the space represented on the ElectroMouse helped identify the feeling of the "tip" of the graph. As an example, P2 correctly identified the parabola (see Fig. 4) because of the curved point. Participants shared that while the electrotactile feedback is harder to use that traditional tactile graph, this difference may be improved by having more trials or more time to learn the electrotactile sensations.

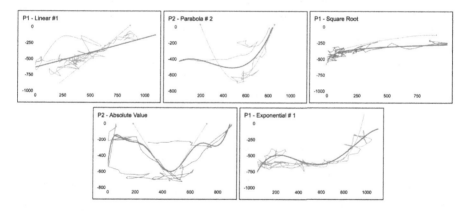

Fig. 4. Best performing algebraic graphs with the fastest, correct identification. The green lines on each graph represent the on-screen graph that was displayed for participants to identify. Organge color graph shows the average movement by the participants. (Color figure online)

The *exponential and square root graph* were often confused with the linear graph because they were both trending upward. Participants also often expected movement (i.e., moving up or down) early in the graph so it was easier for them to get lost in the process as shown in P5's trace of the exponential graph in Fig. 4. When tracing graphs similar to the exponential and square root graphs, participants mentioned that it is hard for a blind person to determine if they are going straight or not. In other words, it is difficult to compare between a horizontal line or a line that is slowly sloping upwards. Additionally, most participants mentioned that the hardest graph to identify is the square root graph because it has the most unfamiliar pattern among all the graphs in the study. For P1 who has had a lot of experience with mathematical concepts and data visualization of graphs through multiple mediums (e.g., visual, tactile, sound), the square root graph did not pose an issue (see P1's square root trace in Fig. 4). On multiple occasions, participants moved the cursor away from the graph which caused confusion with data visualization (see P5's square root trace in Fig. 4). They were often guided back to the start of the graph—participants recommended a quick recall feature in the mouse so that they can retrace and correct their errors independently.

3.2 Trending Graphs

The second half of the evaluation was focused on trending graphs. *Up-Down curves* are trends that show one peak first (curve going up) and then one trough (curve going down)—these are most commonly seen or represented in sine waves. While all participants correctly described the parts of the graph that they explored, two of them, P3 and P5, did not completely finish viewing the graph as shown in Fig. 5. The moderator later explained that the participants did not finish tracing the graphs. Both participants said that the ElectroMouse should have some additional feedback that tells the user if they are at the end of the graph or not. *Down-Up curves* are graphs that presents a trough first, then a peak—these are most commonly seen in cosine waves. Some participants

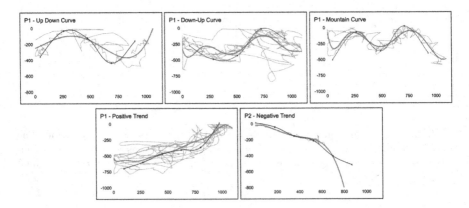

Fig. 5. Best performing trending graphs with the fastest, correct identification. The blue lines on each graph represent the on-screen graph that was displayed for participants to identify (orange shows the average). (Color figure online)

struggled to stay on the curve and went side-to-side to try and get an overall idea of the graph as seen in P5's trace in Fig. 5. *Mountain curves* are graphs with two peaks and one trough. Most participants had a hard time following and identifying this curve. Although some of them traced the graph correctly, they were not able to give a correct description of the graph afterwards (see P3's performance in Fig. 5). Those who moved the mouse faster needed help starting back at the original position. The *positive trend* graph mimics an upward trend that is commonly seen in some news sources or other statistics. Participants mentioned that tracing the graph was harder because of all the small curves along the graph as it trended upward as shown in Fig. 5. The last example task was a *negative trend* graph. Participants were apprehensive when asked to describe the negative slope because they were not confident in the amount of information that was presented on the screen.

4 Participant Feedback on the ElectroMouse

A semi-structured interview was conducted at the end of the usability study to gather participants' thoughts and opinions on the ElectroMouse. They were asked about the form factor, the electrotactile feedback, potential future applications, suggestions, and overall experience with the prototype.

4.1 User Background and Experience

Visual Impairment. P1 shared that users who have seen or closely interacted with specific shapes beforehand may be better at mentally visualizing them. He also spoke about a condition called aphantasia where people are unable to create a mental picture of objects, images, or people [20]. P4 and P5 agreed that it can be difficult for them to visualize shapes and graphs when only little information is provided at a time. Consequently, P4 was not confident enough to try out the usability study because he struggled to identify and follow the shapes and graphs that were presented during training. He mentioned that *"blind people have a hard time following straight line"* and that expectations should be different when one has to move an object to follow shapes. He and other participants suggested adding a path that the mouse can follow, similar to tactile overlays used to enhance maps and mobile interface accessibility [35,42]. While overlays prevent real-time data visualization, they may help beginners train themselves to follow the electrotactile sensations.

Access and Technology Background. All of the participants in the study were professionals and had easy access to tactile data visualization materials. P1 had a lot of experience with other technologies designed for data visualization and is also proficient in mathematical concepts. As such, he did not have a hard time identifying basic algebraic graphs. P2 (Braille Transcriber), P3 (Communication Accessibility Editor), and P5 (Quality Assurance Tester for BVI Technologies) all work closely with traditional tactile data visualization and have access to braille printers. Participant performance and feedback may skew more towards *"advanced"* users because of their experience. During the post interview, they all mentioned that the ElectroMouse would not be their first choice for data visualization. However, they also mentioned that it is not fair to compare this new option to traditional tactile materials or other options that have been in use by the BVI community for the past years. New methods always require initial training and familiarization before it can be adopted by most users. With this consideration, all participants said that the ElectroMouse is a great, low-cost alternative for those who do not have easy access to other materials. They are also open to further exploration of this new feedback, but admit that it may require multiple training sessions.

4.2 Electrotactile Feedback and Form Factor

All participants were new to the electrotactile sensation but were excited and curious about the process. They found the feedback easy to feel with an average of 5 out of 7 in the Likert scale. However, participants noted that the electrotactile feedback hurts after a while and can either make the finger numb or leave a tingling sensation which, eventually, makes it more difficult to recognize the sensation. P5 added that the sensation should be *"a constant line instead of a pulse because the pulse makes it feel like the graph is also moving"*. P1 suggested that a bigger space may allow the finger to rest and instead place the electrotactile on another part of the hand. This would also allow the users to feel a bigger picture at a time and in return, may help with better visualization. P3 expands on this when they said, *"There are so much more stuff to convey than you have room to feel on the mouse. You need to have as much explorability as possible"*.

While the ElectroMouse prevented problems related to delay and accuracy by providing real-time electrotactile response on the 3D printed mouse as soon as the on-screen cursor hits the line [31], issues regarding the unfamiliarity with the form factor arose during the usability study. BVI users do not regularly use mice to interact with their computers and instead mostly rely on keyboard navigation. As such, participants had to adjust and learn how to control the mouse during the training session. Some moved the mouse too fast causing them to lose their position easily while others moved the mouse too slow and therefore had a false impression on the scale of the graph. On average, participants found the mouse ergonomic (5 out of 7) and eventually easy to handle after some experience. They suggested increasing the diameter of the electrotactile opening such that it is easier to place a finger on top.

4.3 Additional Graph Information

To help guide users with their starting point, the researchers placed a tactile corner on the table. However, this proved more confusing to the participants because there is no guarantee that the cursor will revert back to the original starting position if the mouse is dragged to that tactile corner. It further impeded the participants capability to explore the screen. All participants suggested adding a button that would automatically move the cursor to the starting, middle, and end position of the graph. A built-in voice assistant may also prove helpful in helping users get back on track whenever they accidentally move the mouse too far away from the on-screen data. Additionally, adding a border indicator (i.e., different kind of pulsing or voice notification) which informs the user that they are at the edge of the screen may help.

Other components of graphs such as the X and Y axes, legends, title, and description will help eliminate some of the guesswork that is present when the user is simply trying to feel a new graph. The usability study did not add any titles or descriptions because it may influence the participants' answers when identifying the graph. P1 mentioned that the axes may provide a better idea on which part of the graph the cursor is at a certain point in time. They suggested adding different line thickness to differentiate between the two. From this, we also suggest adding different intensities to symbolize line thickness or depth. Different textures may be used for other graphics such as terrains in maps. P5 appreciated having the tactile version of the graph accessible to them—this helped them remember the direction and curvature of the sample graphs. P2 suggested a more mathematical approach where the system can automatically *"estimate the diagram on the screen and give some details regarding the diameter, area, or length. It would help provide an idea on how you should move your mouse"*.

5 Discussion, Limitations, and Future Work

This study explored the effectiveness of an electrotactile sensation in data visualization of the blind and visually impaired. While the study had an in-depth and detailed look into the experiences of BVI users with the ElectroMouse, only a small number of participants were recruited for the study. These participants also worked in a similar field or all had easy access to braille materials that is typically not available for the average BVI user. Future studies may look into recruiting more participants with a wider set of skills and experience with tactile data visualization. Since this option encourages exploration of different types of data visualizations, it may be best to conduct future usability studies in an educational setting. P4, a Braille teacher, mentioned that while they do not use printed graphical materials, they do take advantage of tactile materials to mimic objects for their students. They also said that children may be more excited and may find more use for the ElectroMouse because it will help with their curiosity and education, especially when data visualization materials are late or unavailable. Future research and usability studies may focus on students and may do a comparative study based on those with a lot of math experience versus those who do not.

Form Factor. A 3D-printed mouse form factor was used to case the electrotactile component. However, the BVI participants mentioned that BVI users typically do not have any experience with handling a mouse because they all use the keyboard for navigation. As such, there may have been a larger learning curve with the prototype because participants had to get accustomed to handling a mouse. In the future, researchers may look into an alternate form factor that is more prominently used by BVI participants or provide a tactile overlay such that BVI users have a guide when handling the mouse.

To accommodate changes to the larger electrotactile panel mentioned previously, participants suggested changing the form factor to the size of a tablet or a phone for more portability. P3 suggested that the panel could be attached behind a smartphone so that the user can place their whole palm on the panel and visualize real-time data from the smartphone screen. Inversely, P1 raised the possibility of making the form factor smaller such as a thimble or finger glove similar to the prototype by Tirado *et.al.* [36]. P1 shared that this option will be the most familiar to BVI users because they usually move their fingers around an area at a time instead of having to move an entire mouse. During the later part of the usability study, P1 began moving the mouse by placing their finger on top instead of holding it like a traditional mouse. P3 suggested having a smart form factor that will automatically move and follow the graph on-screen such that users only need to put their hand on the device and not have the need to maneuver the device themselves.

Feedback Methods. Participants all agree that the prototype will perform best by utilizing multiple feedback methods instead of just the electrotactile sensation. Audio descriptions can be added from the basic implementation such as simply reading titles or captions on the screen to smarter alternatives like voice assistants. Vibrations can add more complexity to the device by adding information through different patterns. If the mouse form factor is to be kept, participants suggested adding more buttons and sensations around the mouse (e.g., left and right side). For example, vibrations present on the left side of the mouse may suggest moving the mouse more to the left as the cursor has deviated to the right side of the graph. Such can also be presented through modified wearable devices that can provide a seamless experience to the users [23]. Patterns can also indicate what type of graphic is on the screen—shapes, graph, images, etc. P1 shared that different vibration patterns (e.g. using morse code, etc. [18,39] or audio-haptic [40]) can also represent colors for graphs where color information is crucial. Additionally, other haptic modalities such as thermal feedback [6] can present non-urgent information such as proximity to the edges as a user uses a device.

Applications. Future work may use electrotactile stimulation to explore further applications beyond basic shapes and graphs. Mathematical symbols and Nemeth code—a tool used by teachers where math-related shapes and symbols are represented in braille—can be recognized by the ElectroMouse since the area is large enough to convey at least one character. This way, users can better associate the Nemeth code with the a real-time data visualization [38]. If the field is increased by changing the size of the form factor, mathematical notations and formulas can be added since they have been shown to be some of the most challenging concepts to visualize [38]. More complex geometric figures can be added to explore lessons related to angles and other geometric formulas. Data visualizations representations will help students understand mathematical problems and formulas [7] and encourage understanding and memory [14]. This also opens the possibility for 3D shapes. Textures used in 3D representation can also be used in different kinds of maps, from basic road maps to terrain-based maps. P3 explored the idea of weather mapping as well because there is no dynamic and real-time option for BVI users to read weather maps.

6   Conclusion

Electrotactile feedback is effective for data visualization of the blind and visually impaired. This study presents the ElectroMouse, a 3D-printed mouse prototype with an electrotactile pad on top, as a low-cost alternative for real-time visualization of graphics (e.g., graphs and shapes). A 2-hour usability study was conducted with five BVI users resulting in an average graph identification rate of 59.33% for all 10 graphs–five algebraic and five trending. Participants noted that this method may perform better with additional training and time with the software. They also shared that this would be helpful for data visualization exploration by students and those with limited access to tactile materials. Future versions of the ElectroMouse can be supplemented with other feedback methods such as audio and vibration to relay additional information to the user.

References

1. Akamatsu, M., Sato, S., MacKenzie, I.S.: Multimodal mouse: a mouse-type device with tactile and force display. Presence: Teleoperators Virtual Environ. **3**(1), 73–80 (1994)
2. Beck-Winchatz, B., Riccobono, M.A.: Advancing participation of blind students in science, technology, engineering, and math. Adv. Space Res. **42**(11), 1855–1858 (2008). Publisher: Elsevier
3. For the Blind, A.F.: Statistics about children and youth with vision loss. https://www.afb.org/research-and-initiatives/statistics/statistics-blind-children#population18
4. Bornschein, J., Prescher, D., Weber, G.: Collaborative creation of digital tactile graphics. In: Proceedings of the 17th International ACM SIGACCESS Conference on Computers & Accessibility, pp. 117–126. ASSETS '15, Association for Computing Machinery, New York, NY, USA (2015). https://doi.org/10.1145/2700648.2809869, event-place: Lisbon, Portugal
5. Bornschein, J., Prescher, D., Weber, G.: Inclusive production of tactile graphics. In: Abascal, J., Barbosa, S., Fetter, M., Gross, T., Palanque, P., Winckler, M. (eds.) INTERACT 2015. LNCS, vol. 9296, pp. 80–88. Springer, Cham (2015). https://doi.org/10.1007/978-3-319-22701-6_7
6. Chen, Z., Peng, W., Peiris, R., Minamizawa, K.: Thermoreality: thermally enriched head mounted displays for virtual reality. In: ACM SIGGRAPH 2017 Posters. SIGGRAPH '17, Association for Computing Machinery, New York, NY, USA (2017). https://doi.org/10.1145/3102163.3102222

7. Edens, K., Potter, E.: How students "unpack" the structure of a word problem: graphic representations and problem solving. School Sci. Math. **108**(5), 184–196 (2008)

8. Gardner, J.A.: Tactile graphics: an overview and resource guide. Inf. Technol. Disabil. **3**(4) (1996). Publisher: EASI: Equal Access to Software and Information

9. Gardner, J.A.: Access by blind students and professionals to mainstream math and science. In: Miesenberger, K., Klaus, J., Zagler, W. (eds.) ICCHP 2002. LNCS, vol. 2398, pp. 502–507. Springer, Heidelberg (2002). https://doi.org/10.1007/3-540-45491-8_94

10. Grabowski, N.A., Barner, K.E.: Data visualization methods for the blind using force feedback and sonification. In: Telemanipulator and Telepresence Technologies V, vol. 3524, pp. 131–139. International Society for Optics and Photonics (1998)

11. Guinness, D., Muehlbradt, A., Szafir, D., Kane, S.K.: RoboGraphics: dynamic tactile graphics powered by mobile robots. In: The 21st International ACM SIGACCESS Conference on Computers and Accessibility, pp. 318–328 (2019)

12. Holloway, L., Marriott, K., Butler, M.: Accessible maps for the blind: comparing 3D printed models with tactile graphics. In: Proceedings of the 2018 CHI Conference on Human Factors in Computing Systems, pp. 1–13 (2018)

13. Hughes, R.G., Forrest, A.R.: Perceptualisation using a tactile mouse. In: Proceedings of Seventh Annual IEEE Visualization'96, pp. 181–188. IEEE (1996)

14. Jitendra, A.: Teaching students math problem-solving through graphic representations. Teach. Except. Child. **34**(4), 34–38 (2002)

15. Kajimoto, H.: Electrotactile display with real-time impedance feedback using pulse width modulation. IEEE Trans. Haptics **5**(2), 184–188 (2012). https://doi.org/10.1109/TOH.2011.39

16. Kajimoto, H.: Electro-tactile display kit for fingertip. In: 2021 IEEE World Haptics Conference (WHC), pp. 587–587 (2021). https://doi.org/10.1109/WHC49131.2021.9517192

17. Kajimoto, H., Kanno, Y., Tachi, S.: Forehead electro-tactile display for vision substitution. In: Proceedings of EuroHaptics, p. 11. Citeseer (2006)

18. Kamarushi, M.V., Watson, S.L., Tigwell, G.W., Peiris, R.L.: OneButtonPIN: a single button authentication method for blind or low vision users to improve accessibility and prevent eavesdropping. Proc. ACM Hum.-Comput. Interact. **6**(MHCI) (2022). https://doi.org/10.1145/3546747

19. Keilers, C., Tigwell, G.W., Peiris, R.L.: Data visualization accessibility for blind and low vision audiences. In: Antona, M., Stephanidis, C. (eds.) Universal Access in Human-Computer Interaction, pp. 399–413. Springer Nature Switzerland, Cham (2023)

20. Keogh, R., Pearson, J.: The blind mind: no sensory visual imagery in aphantasia. Cortex **105**, 53–60 (2018)

21. Kim, J., Lee, Y., Seo, I.: Math graphs for the visually impaired: audio presentation of elements of mathematical graphs. In: Extended Abstracts of the 2019 CHI Conference on Human Factors in Computing Systems, pp. 1–6 (2019)

22. Ladner, R.E., et al.: Automating tactile graphics translation. In: Proceedings of the 7th International ACM SIGACCESS Conference on Computers and Accessibility, pp. 150–157. Assets '05, Association for Computing Machinery, New York, NY, USA (2005). https://doi.org/10.1145/1090785.1090814, event-place: Baltimore, MD, USA

23. Maeda, T., Peiris, R., Nakatani, M., Tanaka, Y., Minamizawa, K.: Wearable haptic augmentation system using skin vibration sensor. In: Proceedings of the 2016

Virtual Reality International Conference. VRIC '16, Association for Computing Machinery, New York, NY, USA (2016). https://doi.org/10.1145/2927929.2927946

24. McGookin, D.K., Brewster, S.A.: SoundBar: Exploiting multiple views in multimodal graph browsing. In: Proceedings of the 4th Nordic Conference on Human-Computer Interaction: Changing Roles, pp. 145–154. NordiCHI '06, Association for Computing Machinery, New York, NY, USA (2006). https://doi.org/10.1145/1182475.1182491

25. Owen, J.M., Petro, J.A., D'Souza, S.M., Rastogi, R., Pawluk, D.T.: An improved, low-cost tactile 'mouse' for use by individuals who are blind and visually impaired. In: Proceedings of the 11th international ACM SIGACCESS Conference on Computers and Accessibility, pp. 223–224 (2009)

26. Petit, G., Dufresne, A., Levesque, V., Hayward, V., Trudeau, N.: Refreshable tactile graphics applied to schoolbook illustrations for students with visual impairment. In: Proceedings of the 10th International ACM SIGACCESS Conference on Computers and Accessibility, pp. 89–96 (2008)

27. Prescher, D., Bornschein, J., Weber, G.: Production of accessible tactile graphics. In: Computers Helping People with Special Needs, pp. 26–33. Springer International Publishing, Cham. https://doi.org/10.1007/978-3-319-08599-9_5, https://go.exlibris.link/vvHqcF10

28. Race, L., Kearney-Volpe, C., Fleet, C., Miele, J.A., Igoe, T., Hurst, A.: Designing educational materials for a blind Arduino workshop. In: Extended Abstracts of the 2020 CHI Conference on Human Factors in Computing Systems, pp. 1–7 (2020)

29. Rahimi, S.M.: FingerEye: an Electrotactile-mechanism enabled adaptive sensory-substitution aid for the blind and visually impaired. Ph.D. thesis (2019)

30. Rajaei, N., Ohka, M., Nomura, H., Komura, H., Matsushita, S., Miyaoka, T.: Tactile mouse generating velvet hand illusion on human palm. Int. J. Adv. Rob. Syst. **13**(5), 1729881416658170 (2016)

31. Rastogi, R., Pawluk, D.T., Ketchum, J.M.: Issues of using tactile mice by individuals who are blind and visually impaired. IEEE Trans. Neural Syst. Rehabil. Eng. **18**(3), 311–318 (2010)

32. Rosenblum, L.P., Herzberg, T.S.: Braille and tactile graphics: youths with visual impairments share their experiences. J. Vis. Impairment Blindness **109**(3), 173–184 (2015), publisher: SAGE Publications Sage CA: Los Angeles, CA

33. Sharif, A., Chintalapati, S.S., Wobbrock, J.O., Reinecke, K.: Understanding screen-reader users' experiences with online data visualizations. In: The 23rd International ACM SIGACCESS Conference on Computers and Accessibility. ASSETS '21, Association for Computing Machinery, New York, NY, USA (2021). https://doi.org/10.1145/3441852.3471202

34. Smith, D.W., Smothers, S.M.: The role and characteristics of tactile graphics in secondary mathematics and science textbooks in braille. J. Vis. Impairment Blindness **106**(9), 543–554 (2012), publisher: SAGE Publications Sage CA: Los Angeles, CA

35. Taylor, B., Dey, A., Siewiorek, D., Smailagic, A.: Customizable 3D printed tactile maps as interactive overlays. In: Proceedings of the 18th International ACM SIGACCESS Conference on Computers and Accessibility, pp. 71–79 (2016)

36. Tirado, J., Panov, V., Yem, V., Tsetserukou, D., Kajimoto, H.: ElectroAR: distributed electro-tactile stimulation for tactile transfer. In: Nisky, I., Hartcher-O'Brien, J., Wiertlewski, M., Smeets, J. (eds.) EuroHaptics 2020. LNCS, vol. 12272, pp. 442–450. Springer, Cham (2020). https://doi.org/10.1007/978-3-030-58147-3_49

37. Van Scoy, F., McLaughlin, D., Fullmer, A.: Auditory augmentation of haptic graphs: developing a graphic tool for teaching precalculus skill to blind students. In: Proceedings of the 11th Meeting of the International Conference on Auditory Display, vol. 5. Citeseer (2005)
38. Vandana, A.S.: Trends and challenges in the world of the blind for education in mathematics. J. Positive School Psychol., 1213–1229 (2022)
39. Varma, M., Watson, S., Chan, L., Peiris, R.: Vibroauth: Authentication with haptics based non-visual, rearranged keypads to mitigate shoulder surfing attacks. In: Moallem, A. (ed.) HCI for Cybersecurity, Privacy and Trust, pp. 280–303. Springer International Publishing, Cham (2022). https://doi.org/10.1007/978-3-031-05563-8_19
40. Wang, Y., Li, Z., Chelladurai, P.K., Dannels, W., Oh, T., Peiris, R.L.: Haptic-captioning: using audio-haptic interfaces to enhance speaker indication in real-time captions for deaf and hard-of-hearing viewers. In: Proceedings of the 2023 CHI Conference on Human Factors in Computing Systems. CHI '23, Association for Computing Machinery, New York, NY, USA (2023). https://doi.org/10.1145/3544548.3581076
41. Yu, W., Ramloll, R., Brewster, S.: Haptic graphs for blind computer users. In: Brewster, S., Murray-Smith, R. (eds.) Haptic HCI 2000. LNCS, vol. 2058, pp. 41–51. Springer, Heidelberg (2001). https://doi.org/10.1007/3-540-44589-7_5
42. Zhang, X., et al.: Interactiles: 3D printed tactile interfaces to enhance mobile touch-screen accessibility. In: Proceedings of the 20th International ACM SIGACCESS Conference on Computers and Accessibility, pp. 131–142 (2018)
43. Zhao, H., Plaisant, C., Shneiderman, B., Lazar, J.: Data sonification for users with visual impairment: a case study with georeferenced data. ACM Trans. Comput.-Hum. Interact. 15(1) (2008). https://doi.org/10.1145/1352782.1352786

Designing Refreshable Tactile Graphics for Accessing Visual Imagery for the Blind and People with Visual Impairments

Amaan Zubairi[1,2], Dalal Aldossary[1,2], Aliaa Maar[3], and Areej Al-Wabil[1,2(✉)]

[1] Software Engineering Department, Alfaisal University, Riyadh, Saudi Arabia
{azubairi,daldossary,awabil}@alfaisal.edu
[2] Human-Computer Interaction (HCI) Lab, Alfaisal University, Riyadh, Saudi Arabia
[3] Penn State University, Pennsylvania, USA
amaar@psu.edu

Abstract. The accessibility of digital content is an important aspect in the lives of individuals who are blind, as the visualization of graphs and symbolic images in software user interfaces creates an informational barrier between a person with a visual impairment and digital content. Technology solutions have shown promise for individuals with partial or total visual impairment in augmenting human abilities to access visual imagery via sound or tactile alternatives. In this project, we outline the design methodology for creating assistive technologies that translate visual imagery into tangible forms. The feasibility of this approach relies on successful mapping of pixelated images to tangible interfaces. One of the main challenges with existing tactile technologies is the high cost, which makes them inaccessible to a significant percentage of people with visual impairments. Our design aims to develop a tactile tablet at a reduced cost by co-creating the solution with people who have the lived experience of having a visual impairment and via utilizing localized supply chains and production facilities. Additionally, our team adopted a co-design methodology, wherein the designer works closely with the potential user through a feedback loop to refine the design to meet the user's requirements iteratively. Co-design was chosen primarily due to the unique experiences of people with visual impairments and the reported gap in user engagement in the context of designing and developing assistive technology.

Keywords: Assistive technology · Co-design · Prototyping · Tactile Graphics · Engineering · Design methodology · Mechatronics

1 Introduction

Historically, persons with visual impairment have faced significant challenges accessing information conveyed in graphical forms, such as charts and graphs, due to limited access to assistive technology. The traditional technologies used in educational institutes, such as text summaries and sonification, are straightforward and cost-effective, but engineering fails in many aspects. They do not allow self-exploration of the learner

© The Author(s), under exclusive license to Springer Nature Switzerland AG 2024
M. Antona and C. Stephanidis (Eds.): HCII 2024, LNCS 14698, pp. 429–443, 2024.
https://doi.org/10.1007/978-3-031-60884-1_29

space and fail to convey complex visual 2D relationships and 3D topographies. Understanding spatial analysis is crucial, particularly in STEM fields. This leaves individuals with visual impairment to navigate a narrower set of educational options and distances them from engaging in science and engineering education and practice. The problem of technology inadequacy to meet unique requirements is not limited to higher education but originates in primary school arithmetic mathematics education, particularly in developing nations. This contributes to a cycle that perpetuates the gap in technological design. More alignment is needed in the context of assistive technology design and development. In designing for individuals with visual impairments, a participatory design approach contributes towards alignment in understanding the requirements and context of use.

This paper describes the design process of an assistive technology in the form of a refreshable tactile graphics display for accessing visual imagery. The product was co-designed with people who have the lived experience of being blind or with visual impairment. Through a co-creation effort and a common interest to innovate, a team of engineers worked together with users with the intent of making a difference for all persons with visual impairments in our communities and society. In this article, we describe a series of design iterations and several user studies aimed at understanding (1) how blind users engage with tactile graphic displays and (2) the usability and accessibility issues encountered by blind users of tactile graphics displays.

2 Background

Disabilities affect a significant portion of the global population. According to the World Health Organization (WHO), approximately 15% of the world's population, or roughly 1 billion people, experience some form of disability [1]. This number is expected to rise due to an aging population and increasing chronic diseases [1]. The economic burden of a disability (physical, sensory, cognitive) is well established. A 2011 World Bank study estimated the global cost of disabilities at US$8 trillion annually, with healthcare and social services accounting for a significant portion of this expense [1]. Individuals with disabilities often face challenges maintaining their independence and well-being, leading to diminished quality of life. Studies have shown a higher prevalence of depression, anxiety, and social isolation among this population compared to individuals without disabilities. The prevalence of visual impairments is relatively higher than other sensory disabilities, as noted in recent statistics from the World Health Organization (WHO), which estimated that more than 2.2 billion people have a visual impairment or blindness [1].

Understanding the existing landscape of visual information access methods is important. Options for individuals with visual impairments include alternative text descriptions, screen readers, refreshable braille displays, sonification, and printed tactile graphics. Each method offers specific advantages and limitations, setting the backdrop for the innovation introduced by the refreshable tactile graphics display [12]. Refreshable braille displays, an established technology since 1975, have provided an effective reading experience but at a high production cost. This project recognizes the need for cost-effective solutions and undergoes three major underlying changes in structural and software architecture, design, and implementation [22].

These changes, guided by design signatures, aim to enhance usability, accessibility, and cost-effectiveness. There are three main options for people with severe visual impairments to access visual information, alternative text descriptions, sonification or tactile interfaces.

1. **Alternative text descriptions** via screen readers or refreshable braille displays. These provide a limited sense of spatial awareness and restrict the user to linear exploration [20, 21].
2. **Sonification** represents visual information through auditory rhythm, harmony, or melody. This method works well with patterns but is limited to linear datasets with two variables and requires extra work to implement properly.
3. **Printed tactile graphics** offer the best sense of spatial awareness and can be freely explored. However, they are expensive to produce in high quantities. Refreshable braille displays, first created in 1975, use small, powered actuators in every cell, providing a good reading experience but at a high production cost. A 40-cell, single-line display costs nearly $3000 today [10], with future models expected to cut this cost to $1400 [11]. Other companies have attempted to replace this mechanism with different ones, but the refusal to compromise on refresh speed means they still use multiple actuators per cell, maintaining a high cost [13, 25].

The refreshable Taction Tablet aims to bridge the gap in visual information access, offering a compelling alternative to existing methods and addressing their limitations. Though refreshable braille displays offer text information, they lack spatial awareness and restrict users to linear exploration [13]. This limitation hinders understanding complex visuals like charts, diagrams, and maps. While sonification is effective for pattern recognition, it struggles with complex datasets beyond two variables [9]. Additionally, implementing sonification effectively requires extra effort and resources. While printed tactile graphics provide the best spatial awareness and freedom of exploration, they are relatively costly to mass produce, limiting accessibility for many users [10].

Unique Advantages of the Refreshable Tactile Tablet

- **Cost-Effectiveness:** Compared to traditional refreshable braille displays that use multiple actuators per cell, the Taction Tablet seeks to utilize a more cost-effective approach, potentially bringing the price down significantly [8, 10, 11].
- **Spatial Awareness and Exploration:** Similar to printed tactile graphics, the tablet aims to provide a clear sense of spatial relationships between elements, allowing users to explore information freely and efficiently.
- **Dynamic Representation:** Unlike static printed graphics, the refreshable tablet offers the ability to display and manipulate various visuals on-demand, overcoming the limitations of pre-produced materials.

The design process for the Taction Tablet aims to bridge the gap between existing visual information access methods and the limitations they pose for individuals with visual impairment. By co-designing a refreshable tactile graphics display with direct input from users in mind, we were able to address the challenges faced by individuals with visual impairments in accessing complex visual 2D relationships and 3D topographies.

This device aims to provide a cost-effective and user-friendly solution that enhances spatial awareness and allows for self-exploration. By involving users directly in the design process, we were able to tailor the refreshable tactile tablet to enhance spatial awareness, encourage self-exploration, and provide a cost-effective solution. This inclusive approach allows us to address the challenges faced by blind users when accessing complex visual information [18].

The prevalence of visual impairment and blindness, affecting over 2.2 billion individuals worldwide [1], necessitates innovative technological solutions. Traditional software user interfaces, heavily reliant on visual elements, pose a significant barrier to accessing information for people with visual impairments. This section explores the design process of a refreshable tactile graphics display—a form of assistive technology—co-created with individuals who have the lived-experience of visual impairment [19]. The design process is embedded within the Humanistic Co-Design of Assistive Technology program, leveraging a Design Innovation (DI) process to address challenges and enhance usability [26]. The project kept track of all design modules through the design signatures method, as noted in [26]. The advantages of employing design signatures in co-creating the refreshable tactile graphics display are multifaceted. The iterative nature of the DI process ensures continuous integration of user insights, aligning the development with real-world needs. Co-design not only enhances the functionality of the tactile graphics display but also fosters inclusivity and empowerment among end-users [3, 5, 19].

Results from user studies served as the litmus test for the success of the design signatures employed. Usability and accessibility issues are systematically addressed, providing a roadmap for future iterations and improvements. The narrative presented in this section underscores the strategic application of design signatures in the pursuit of creating impactful assistive devices for the blind and visually impaired. By significantly reducing the production cost of the refreshable tactile tablet, the aim is to expand its accessibility to a larger population of individuals with visual impairment. This reduction in cost could potentially enable more people to benefit from the device's innovative features, enhancing spatial awareness and promoting self-exploration.

3   Methodology

Our team adopted the design innovation (DI) modules in the Taction Tablet's product development cycles. The DI process is an iterative process that holistically provides an order of action in design projects. DI comprises four phases: Discover, Define, Develop, and Deliver [4]. The co-designer in the context of this project refers to the individual with visual impairment who works closely with the design team to provide feedback related to usability, viability, and effectiveness.

3.1   The Design Process

The Taction Tablet initiative is a project led by Dr. Kyle Keane developed further through the Humanistic Co-design for Assistive Technology initiative. The Humanistic Co-design emphasizes a deeply collaborative product development process, connecting designers directly with the individuals with impairments for whom the technology is intended (co-designers) such as the products described in [6] and [7]. Doing so ensures that the resulting designs are both innovative and responsive to end-users needs as noted in [5]. Figure 1 shows Co-Create fellows ideating and interacting in co-design sessions as part of the design innovation modules that are considered in the iterative development process. The Co-Create program is a 12-month fellowship program that launched in January 2020 and has been in operation for four years 2020–2024 with four cohorts of Co-Create Fellows.

Co-Design Workshops for Assistive Technolo-gy

Humanistic Co-Design Modules

Fig. 1. Fellows in the Co-Create program

An early version of the Taction Tablet provided the foundation and design inspiration for the prototypes that followed [8]. The DI process unfolds through iterative cycles,

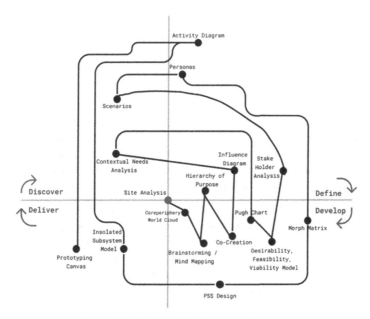

Fig. 2. The Taction Tablet's Design Signature

involving discovery, definition, development, and delivery phases. The insights gained from the Taction Tablet's design innovation modules contribute towards understanding the nuanced needs of blind users and people with visual impairments. The co-creation effort facilitates a holistic approach to product development with a focus on inclusivity [3, 19] (Fig. 2).

3.2 Scenario-Based Personas

Scenario-based personas were considered throughout the project to reflect on the target user population of individuals with visual impairment. The scenario-based personas are fictional characters that emerge from User-Centered Design research such as [6, 18]. The personas for people with visual impairment were made up of archetypes that express the behaviors, goals, and difficulties of a particular user group that vary in demographics, socio-economic backgrounds, and proficiency with assistive technologies (Fig. 3).

Fig. 3. Depictions of Scenario-based personas for users of the Taction Tablet

4   Prototyping

This section describes the Taction Tablet's iterative design process by showcasing the device's previous iterations up until the current version. The first functioning prototype was developed by a team from MIT, while all the successive iterations were developed by an interdisciplinary team from Alfaisal University. The teams collaborated under the umbrella of the Co-Create fellowship program.

How Does it Work? The Taction Tablet contains major features that are common between alliterations: a planar frame, two independent actuators for the x and y directions, pins, a pin-pushing mechanism, a grid surface, a pin retracting mechanism, and a digital control system. Each iteration uniquely incorporated different mechanisms, materials, and manufacturing techniques to produce prototypes.

The Taction Tablet controller processes the G-code of a pixelated image, directing this information to each actuator one by one. This G-code includes details about which pins need to rise. The actuators, equipped with mechanisms to push the pins, move to the specified location and activate to push the pins upward. They then proceed to the next designated pin location, repeating this process. This sequence continues until the entire image or path is recreated with pins that can be felt on the tactile grid, allowing graphics to be understood through touch. The manufacturing processes were slightly different between iterations; however, they all encompassed laser-cutting, 3D printing, and assembling. In the tactile tablet design, the manufacturing process is chosen to be one of the design constraints to allow reproducibility and ease of assembly.

4.1 Prototype 1

The first functioning prototype was developed by a team from MIT [8]. The prototype was made mostly by a laser cutting chipboard. The actuating system consists of DC motors connected to a pulley system; one side has the driver pulley and a driven pulley on the other. The pin-popping mechanism consists of one actuator coupled with the grid display; a key advantage over the existing designs that employ numerous actuators for each single pin. The prototype is connected to an Arduino with a test code to control the actuators directly. The total cost of the prototype was less than $30. Although a grid of 28×29 pins is not regarded as a Braille resolution, this prototype is considered a leap in cutting the cost of refreshable tactile graphical tablets such as the Taction Tablet, offering a functioning prototype that exhibits the main concept. Figure 4 shows the components of the prototype.

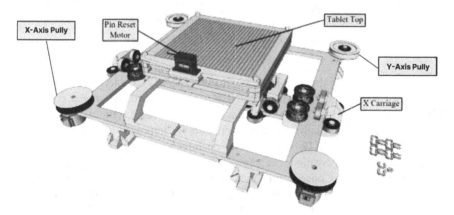

Fig. 4. Illustration of the Taction Tablet's 1st Prototype - adapted from [8].

The team reported issues with malfunctioning pulleys and positioning inaccuracies throughout the design and testing processes. Besides, the overall concern is with the user's safety utilizing an open system with a set of pulleys. This first iteration laid the groundwork for subsequent refinements for enhanced accuracy, incorporating some safety features and utilizing more durable material.

4.2   Prototype 2

The second prototype was developed by a team from MIT, building upon the lessons learned from the first iteration. Prototype two marked a significant leap forward regarding stability, functionality, and durability. The design team focused on creating a more robust platform and refined user experience. This prototype was generated in two major stages; one focused on the structure; and another focused on the electronics and mechanics integration. Before finalizing the frame and the material, several concepts were modeled.

Firstly, the device's frame was upgraded from simple bars to sturdy aluminum, providing a rigid foundation for precise actuator movement and improved overall durability, as shown in Fig. 5. Aluminum is a durable, light, and cost-effective option. The aluminum tubes used are a standard size of 4cm and are commonly used in plotter and 3D printer frames.

Fig. 5. The Taction Tablet's 2nd Prototype

Furthermore, two dual-axis control actuators (NEMA 17) replaced the direct current (DC) motors used in prototype one. The NEMA actuators provide greater control and a longer lifetime. The use of aluminum frame bars to enhance stability and durability, and utilizing NEMA 17 dual-axis control actuators for improved precision and overall lifespan [24]. The NEMA 17 Stepper motor operates with a step angle of 1.8°, which equates to 200 steps or rotations per angle. When active, each phase of this motor can pull a voltage of 12 V. Consequently, the current is able to sustain a holding torque of 3.2 kg-cm. Wires [23]. In addition, the top surface of the device now sported a two-layer design. The bottom layer, made of aluminum, housed the pin bases, while the top rubber sheet layer provided traction and prevented pins from falling through. Each layer had strategically sized square holes of 2.5 mm in the aluminum and 1.9 mm in the rubber. This differential in hole size between aluminum and rubber created a tight fit that securely held the pins in place when raised. The display grid size is 500 × 500 mm which accommodates 300 holes. This configuration allowed the display of more detailed graphics compared to the previous prototype. The grid sizing and spacing was based on matching the Braille standard dot size and spacing as closely as possible, while maintaining the structural integrity of the grid and the pin [25] (Fig. 6).

The pins are pushed through a stepper motor and a cam mechanism mounted on a bracket on the Y-axis actuator. The pin pusher mechanism traversed, lifting each pin

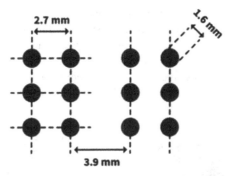

Fig. 6. Braille dots standard dimensions [28]

to the desired height based on the image data. This mechanism eliminated the need for individual actuators for each pin, significantly reducing cost and complexity by trading off the speed of the tactile graphics generation. Arduino Uno microcontroller was used to control the actuators through individual L298N motor controllers. The controller's housing is placed in the center of the structure. By incorporating lessons learned from the initial iteration, prototype two achieved a more stable platform with precise actuator movements, paving the way for further enhancements in subsequent iterations. We envision this prototype to be used in classrooms and not carried along. In the subsequent iterations, the team focused on making the prototype lighter in weight and more portable.

Fig. 7. The Taction Tablet's 3rd Prototype's 3D Rendering

4.3 Prototype 3

Prototype three was a conceptual prototype to test different mechanisms and concepts and aimed to localize the manufacturing in Saudi Arabia. The model, shown in Fig. 7 was developed in the SolidWorks CAD platform. The model incorporated a reset panel to refresh the displayed graphics after each display. We aimed to replace the actuators from pulleys and belt mechanics with threaded rod and nut mechanics to enhance durability without compromising precision. This mechanism is used in the z-axis control in the 3D printers to provide precise layer levels. Various pin designs were generated according to the hole size, as shown in Fig. 8. The pin was conceptualized to provide a smooth tangible end; the pin stem was tapered to provide more traction to the rubber sheet as it is pushed; the pin end was designed to be adaptive to the pushing mechanism.

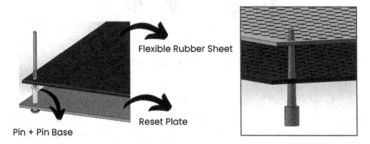

Fig. 8. Previous Pin Design Iterations (Left: Old Design, Right: New Design)

The design team checked the manufacturability of the items locally and through the facilities at CamX (Center of Advanced Manufacturing) at Alfaisal University. The rubber grid was tested in the laser cutter to produce and gird with the required resolution. A successful cut was obtained on a rubber sheet with 1 mm thickness. The tested grid was 1.5 mm in diameter and 3 mm in center distance. Furthermore, the brackets were 3D printed using Ultimaker 3D printer, as shown in Fig. 9.

Fig. 9. 3D Printed stepper motor brackets

Figure 10 shows the base mechanism assembled together. In this iteration, the team considered linear bearing as a carrying mechanism to provide smoother travel with less number of components. In addition, they continued experimenting with the same actuators and driving mechanism, and used the rubber sheet concept for traction, which can be reinforced or replaced with a thin acrylic sheet.

Fig. 10. The Taction Tablet's 3rd Prototype's Mechanical Base Assembly

4.4 Prototype 4

Building upon the recommendations from the previous prototypes, this iteration focused on refining the Taction Tablet for usability, safety, and improved performance. The third prototype adopted a protective wooden box to house the entire device and shield users and components from potential harm. Additionally, the aluminum bars, now arranged in a "#" pattern, maintained stability while reducing overall weight and size. To address vibration concerns and ensure movement precision, two NEMA 17 stepper motors were employed on the X-axis, paired with one on the Y-axis. This was because the load is balanced between two actuators instead of one, which might create a load imbalance during operation (Fig. 11).

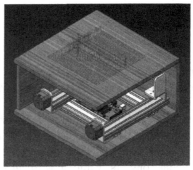

Fig. 11. The Taction Tablet's 4th Prototype (Left: Internal Mechanism, Right: 3D Rendering of the 4th Prototype)

The display surface evolved into a three-layer configuration. The bottom acrylic layer housed the pins, while the middle rubber sheet provided friction and pin retention. The top wooden layer completed the box and stabilized the rubber sheet. Individual motor controllers were replaced with a G-Shield attached to the Arduino Uno, which controlled all three stepper motors via the GRBL software, to provide more consistent and accurate movement. An Arduino MEGA handled additional elements like buttons and a servo motor, while the Arduino Uno focused on motor control, fostering modularity and easier maintenance. Furthermore, micro limit switches at both ends of each axis signaled their position to the software, enabling automatic recalibration and eliminating the need for frequent manual adjustments.

This prototype utilized readily available commercial off-the-shelf (COTS) components for the structure, except for the custom-designed pins which simplified sourcing and repairs. The most advanced software among the prototypes, featuring multi-processing, extensive feedback electronics, and fail-safes, ensured smooth, reliable, and robust operation, which is further explained in the image mapping section. This prototype refined the Taction Tablet's design for usability, safety, and performance. The emphasis on COTS components, advanced software, and modular design laid the groundwork for further development and potential real-world application.

4.5 Image Mapping

The Taction Tablet's ability to translate visual information into a tactile experience hinges on accurate image processing, a series of algorithmic steps performed on a connected laptop before commanding the device's pin movements. This section delves into the technical underpinnings of these steps, highlighting their functional purpose and underlying algorithms.

1. Background **Removal:** Isolating the Subject of Interest
   Background removal employs techniques like K-means clustering or GrabCut, as discussed in [14], to segment the desired image elements from extraneous background noise. This preprocessing stage ensures the subsequent steps focus solely on the relevant information, improving accuracy and reducing computational load.
2. **Rescaling:** Adapting to the Pin Canvas
   Bilinear or Lanczos resampling algorithms, detailed in [15], downscale the image to fit the Taction Tablet's 30 × 30 pixel grid while preserving critical details. This process balances information fidelity with resource efficiency, ensuring an accurate representation for the device's motor control system.
3. **Otsu Thresholding and High-Pass Filtering:** Extracting Edges for Tactile Interpretation
   Otsu's thresholding algorithm, as described in [16], automatically determines an optimal threshold to binarize the grayscale image, converting each pixel into either "on" (high value) or "off" (low value). This binary representation captures the image's essential contours, while subsequent high-pass filtering, often implemented using frequency domain techniques like Fourier transforms [15], further sharpens these edges for accurate pin positioning.
4. **Tactification:** Translating Pixels into Pin Commands
   Each "on" pixel in the binarized image corresponds to a raised pin in the final tactile representation. This straightforward mapping, akin to Braille's raised dots, creates a 25 × 25 grid of pixel activation commands for the device's motors as shown in Fig. 12.
5. **G-code Generation:** Orchestrating Pin Movement
   Based on the tactification map, a sequence of G-code commands is generated using tools like GRBL [17]. This code precisely dictates the movement of each stepper

motor, specifying individual pin heights and travel times. Precise timing and coordinated movements ensure smooth and accurate rendering of the image on the pin canvas.

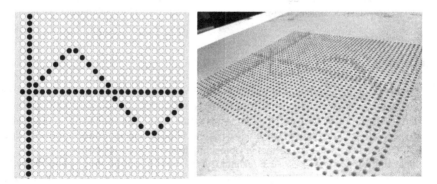

Fig. 12. The Taction Tablet's 25 × 25 Pin Canvas Depicting a Sine wave

These five steps form the backbone of the Taction Tablet's image processing pipeline. By leveraging established algorithms and tailoring them to the device's unique capabilities, the system unlocks a new avenue for visually impaired individuals to experience and interact with visual information through the power of touch.

Future Research Directions to Explore
For the Taction Tablet, advanced image segmentation techniques can enhance complex scene interpretation. Also, Optimizing rescaling algorithms for various image types and user preferences will prove to be crucial. Another suggestion is exploring alternative thresholding and filtering techniques which could improve tactile representation. Lastly, developing adaptive G-code generation algorithms for different pin configurations and rendering fidelity can ease computation and enhance efficiency. The Taction Tablet's image processing pipeline opens avenues for innovation in accessible tactile graphics. It promotes inclusivity, empowering individuals with visual impairments to navigate the visual world through touch.

5 Conclusion

By enhancing the utilization of advanced image processing algorithms, the potential for the Taction Tablet to deliver a rich and detailed tactile experience continues to expand. Further enhancements in image segmentation, rescaling techniques, and G-code generation can unlock new possibilities for rendering complex visual information into tactile graphics. These advancements hold promise for improving the accessibility of graphical content for individuals with visual impairments, fostering inclusivity, and enabling a more interactive engagement with visual data through tactile feedback.

Acknowledgment. The authors acknowledge the support of Alfaisal University College of Engineering and the AI Research Center. Additionally, we extend our sincere thanks to Dr. Kyle Kean (MIT) for his insightful guidance and expertise, which significantly contributed to the project's success Mark Vrablic, whose first prototype of the Taction Tablet helped us evolve and make it better from the lessons learned during his build. Moreover, we would like to thank the Raghad al Sagga and Mohannad Shamsan, for their contribution to this project's development cycles.

References

1. World Health Organization. Vision Impairment and blindness. World Health Organization (2023). https://www.who.int/news-room/fact-sheets/detail/blindness-and-visual-impairment
2. Herskovitz, J., Xu, A., Alharbi, R., Guo, A.: Hacking, switching, combining: understanding and supporting DIY assistive technology design by blind people. In: Proceedings of the 2023 CHI Conference on Human Factors in Computing Systems, pp. 1–17 (2023
3. Shinohara, K.: Designing assistive technology for Blind Users. In: Proceedings of the 8th International ACM SIGACCESS Conference on Computers and Accessibility (2006a). https://doi.org/10.1145/1168987.1169062
4. Lauff, C., Menold, J., Wood, K.L.: Prototyping canvas: design tool for planning purposeful prototypes. In: Proceedings of the Design Society: International Conference on Engineering Design, vol. 1, no. 1, pp. 1563–1572 (2019). https://doi.org/10.1017/dsi.2019.162
5. Almoaiqel, S., Al-Megren, S., Oleksak, M., Alfajhan, G., Al-Wabil, A.: Empowering assistive technology communities to make strategic use of intellectual property: three case studies from the Cocreate Program. In: HCI International 2020 – Late Breaking Papers: Universal Access and Inclusive Design, pp. 14–23 (2020). https://doi.org/10.1007/978-3-030-60149-2_2
6. AlSabban, M., Karim, A., Sun, V. H., Hashim, J., AlSayed, O.: Co-design of color identification applications using scenario-based personas for people with impaired color vision. In: HCI International 2020 – Late Breaking Papers: Universal Access and Inclusive Design, pp. 171–183 (2020). https://doi.org/10.1007/978-3-030-60149-2_14
7. Al-Nafjan, A., Al-Abdullatef, L., Al-Ghamdi, M., Al-Khalaf, N., Al-Zahrani, W.: Designing signspeak, an arabic sign language recognition system. In: HCI International 2020 – Late Breaking Papers: Universal Access and Inclusive Design, pp. 161–170 (2020a). https://doi.org/10.1007/978-3-030-60149-2_13
8. Vrablic, M.E.: TactionTablet : affordable tactile graphics display Author(s). Massachusetts Institute of Technology (2020)
9. Brewster, S.A., Brown, L.M., Ramloll, S.A., Burton, R., Riedel, B.: Design Guidelines for Audio Presentation of Graphs and Tables. Research Gate, Glasgow (2006
10. Braille display focus 40 5G. New England Low Vision (2024). https://nelowvision.com/product/braille-display-focus-40-5g/
11. Orbit reader 40 – braille display, book reader and note-taker. Orbit Research. https://www.orbitresearch.com/product/orbit-reader-40/
12. Wu, X., Zhu, H., Kim, S.-H., Allen, M.G.: A portable pneumatically-actuated refreshable Braille cell. In: TRANSDUCERS 2007 - 2007 International Solid-State Sensors, Actuators and Microsystems Conference (2007). https://doi.org/10.1109/sensor.2007.4300407
13. SBIR Phase I: Full-page electronic braille display. SBIR Phase I: Full-Page Electronic Braille Display | SBIR.gov. https://www.sbir.gov/sbirsearch/detail/392063
14. Huang, X., et al.: An H-grabcut image segmentation algorithm for indoor pedestrian background removal. Sensors **23**(18), 7937 (2023). https://doi.org/10.3390/s23187937
15. Gonzalez, R.C., Woods, R.E.: Digital Image Processing, 3rd edn. Pearson Education, Boston (2008)

16. Otsu, N.: A threshold selection method from gray-level histogram. IEEE Trans. Syst. Man Cybern. **9**(9), 62–66 (1979)
17. Grbl. GRBL/GRBL: An open source, embedded, high performance G-code-parser and CNC milling controller written in optimized C that will run on a straight Arduino. GitHub. https://github.com/grbl/grbl
18. Santos, A.V.F., Silveira, Z.C.: Design for assistive technology oriented to design methodology: a systematic review on user-centered design and 3D printing approaches (2021)
19. Florian, M.C.: What is co-creation in architecture and urban planning? (2023)
20. Holloway, L., et al.: Animations at your fingertips: using a refreshable tactile display to convey motion graphics for people who are blind (2022)
21. Holloway, L., Cracknell, P., Stephens, K., Marriott, K.: Refreshable tactile displays for accessible data visualisation (2023)
22. Choi, C.Y., Rosen, D.: Exploring generative design for assistive devices (2023)
23. Putri, A.Z., Susanti, H., Barri, M.H., Haq, A.I., Fillah, D.F.F.: Implementation of nema-17 stepper motor and SG-90 servo motor as mechanical drivers on spinal needle positioning test equipment. In: 2023 IEEE International Biomedical Instrumentation and Technology Conference (IBITeC), Yogyakarta, Indonesia, pp. 52–57 (2023). https://doi.org/10.1109/IBITeC59006.2023.10390937
24. Robocraze. NEMA 17 - The High Torque Stepper Motor Working Principle. Robocraze (2022). https://robocraze.com/blogs/post/nema-17-the-high-torque-stepper-motor-working-principle
25. Yerknapeshyan, L., Anbarson, V.: Braille Tablet. American University of Armenia, Yerevan (2023)
26. Seow, O., et al.: Design signatures: mapping design innovation processes. In: International Design Engineering Technical Conferences and Computers and Information in Engineering Conference, vol. 51845, p. V007T06A046. American Society of Mechanical Engineers (2018)

Author Index